Hands-On Virtual Computing

Hands-On Virtual Computing

Second Edition

Ted Simpson

Jason Novak

Cengage

Australia • Brazil • Canada • Mexico • Singapore • United Kingdom • United States

Hands-On Virtual Computing,
Second Edition
Ted Simpson and Jason Novak

SVP, GM Science, Technology & Math:
Balraj Kalsi

Senior Product Director: Kathleen
McMahon

Product Team Manager: Kristin McNary

Associate Product Manager: Amy
Savino

Senior Director, Development: Julia
Caballero

Senior Content Development Manager:
Leigh Hefferon

Associate Content Developer: Maria
Garguilo

Product Assistant: Jake Toth

VP, Marketing for Science,
Technology, & Math: Jason Sakos

Marketing Director: Michele McTighe

Marketing Manager: Stephanie Albright

Marketing Coordinator: Cassie Cloutier

Production Director: Patty Stephan

Senior Content Project Manager:
Brooke Greenhouse

Senior Designer: Diana Graham

Cover Image: © iStock.com/robertiez

For product information and technology assistance, contact us at
**Cengage Customer & Sales Support, 1-800-354-9706
or support.cengage.com.**

For permission to use material from this text or product, submit all
requests online at **www.copyright.com.**

Library of Congress Control Number: 2017930061

ISBN: 978-1-337-10193-6

Cengage
200 Pier 4 Boulevard
Boston, MA 02210
USA

Cengage is a leading provider of customized learning solutions with employees residing in nearly 40 different countries and sales in more than 125 countries around the world. Find your local representative at: **www.cengage.com.**

To learn more about Cengage platforms and services, register or access your online learning solution, or purchase materials for your course, visit **www.cengage.com.**

Notice to the Reader
Publisher does not warrant or guarantee any of the products described herein or perform any independent analysis in connection with any of the product information contained herein. Publisher does not assume, and expressly disclaims, any obligation to obtain and include information other than that provided to it by the manufacturer. The reader is expressly warned to consider and adopt all safety precautions that might be indicated by the activities described herein and to avoid all potential hazards. By following the instructions contained herein, the reader willingly assumes all risks in connection with such instructions. The publisher makes no representations or warranties of any kind, including but not limited to, the warranties of fitness for particular purpose or merchantability, nor are any such representations implied with respect to the material set forth herein, and the publisher takes no responsibility with respect to such material. The publisher shall not be liable for any special, consequential, or exemplary damages resulting, in whole or part, from the readers' use of, or reliance upon, this material.

Printed in the United States of America
10 11 12 13 14   26 25 24 23 22

Brief Table of Contents

Table of Contents

Introduction

The IT field is experiencing a dramatic change in computing models, moving from proprietary hardware-based infrastructures to software-defined data centers and cloud computing. The driving force behind this change is virtualization. To be in a position to take advantage of the new opportunities these changes will bring, you need to understand how virtualization of computer resources can be used to create IT environments that are flexible, scalable, and affordable. This book is the best way to start learning about virtualization as it combines theories and concepts with practical hands-on activities and projects that allow you to apply the concepts you are learning to real world scenarios. Currently there are two major commercial leaders in the virtualization products, VMware and Microsoft. This book is unique in that it presents products from both of these leaders so you can learn about and gain comparative experience with them.

This book will provide you with a working knowledge of the leading virtualization products, including Oracle VirtualBox, VMware Workstation, Microsoft Hyper-V, and VMware vSphere. In addition to learning how to install and use the products, you learn how to apply virtualization technology to create virtual data centers that use clusters for high availability, use management software to administer multiple host systems, implement a virtual desktop environment, and leverage cloud computing to build or extend the data center and provide disaster recovery services. By the time you finish reading this book and performing the activities you will have a solid base in virtualization concepts and products that you can use to build your IT career.

Intended Audience

Hands-On Virtual Computing, 2e, is intended for people who want to increase their employment opportunities in the IT field by learning how to configure and use virtualization software to meet a variety of computing needs. This book can be used in a college computer lab environment or with computer equipment you have in your home or office. The activities in this book have been planned and written carefully to allow you to use open-source and trial versions of virtualization and Windows software.

This Book Includes:

- Complete coverage of virtualization concepts, including abundant screen captures and diagrams to visually reinforce the text and hands-on activities

- Coverage of the features each major virtualization package offers

- Instructions on how to download free and trial versions of virtualization products, including Oracle VirtualBox, VMware Workstation, and Microsoft Hyper-V

- Step-by-step hands-on activities that walk you through installing, configuring, and using virtualization products for a variety of real-world tasks

- Extensive review and end-of-chapter materials that reinforce what you've learned

- Challenging activities and case projects that build on one another and require you to apply the concepts and technologies learned throughout the book

- Appendixes that expand on virtualization concepts and products, including the technology behind virtualization, using VMware Player and Hyper-V Server, disaster recovery, and high availability

Chapter Descriptions

The book starts with an overview of virtualization technology in Chapter 1 and then proceeds with chapters dedicated to the latest virtualization products including Oracle VirtualBox, VMware Workstation, Microsoft Hyper-V, and VMware vSphere. Chapters 2 and 3 cover workstation virtualization products and techniques that may be used by developers, students, and home users to run multiple operating systems on a single computer. Chapter 4 moves the reader from using virtualization in a workstation environment to the virtual data centers. The chapter includes a discussion of topics related to using virtualization in software defined data center environments including building virtual networks, implementing high-availability clusters, enhancing performance and security, and managing the virtual data center. Chapters 5–8 provide you with concepts and experience building virtual data centers using Microsoft Hyper-V and VMware vSphere. Chapters 9 and 10 focus on some of the newest IT challenges. Chapter 9 introduces you to implementing virtual desktop infrastructures using both VMware Horizon and Microsoft VDI. Chapter 10 provides a background in utilizing cloud computing environments with VMware vCloud and Microsoft Azure. The following list provides more detailed information on each of this book's chapters:

- **Chapter 1,** "Introduction to Virtual Computing," gives you an overview of how virtualization works and describes the different types of virtualization products as well as cloud computing models. This chapter introduces the virtualization products covered in this book, compares product features, and gives you instructions on downloading free versions of the software you use for subsequent chapter activities.

- **Chapter 2**, "Working with Oracle VM VirtualBox 5," provides detailed information and hands-on activities installing and working with the freely available Oracle VirtualBox. Topics include creating and configuring virtual machine environments, installing Windows Server 2016 as a guest OS, working with virtual hard disks, using the administrative console, and working with features such as snapshots.

- **Chapter 3**, "Working with VMware Workstation 12 Pro," provides detailed information and hands-on activities installing and working with VMware Workstation 12 Pro. Topics include creating and configuring virtual machine environments, installing Windows Server 2016 and Ubuntu Linux as guest OSs, working with virtual hard disks, using the administrative console, and working with VMware Workstation 12 Pro features, such as cloning virtual machines, using Snapshot Manager, file sharing, and enabling Unity view.

- **Chapter 4**, "Data Center Virtualization and Cloud Computing," is an overview of virtualization software and technologies that are used in data center and cloud-based environments. The chapter compares data center virtualization features available in both VMware and Hyper-V. The chapter builds a base of terminology and concepts that you will use in the remaining chapters.

- **Chapter 5**, "Working with Microsoft Hyper-V," covers Microsoft's virtualization product, Hyper-V, which is included with Windows Server 2016. You learn how to add the Hyper-V role to a host and how to use Hyper-V Manager to create and interact with virtual machines running Windows Server 2016, create checkpoints, manage virtual disks, and configure the virtual switches.

- **Chapter 6**, "Working with Virtual Machine Manager," covers using Microsoft System Center Virtual Machine Manager (VMM) 2016, which has advanced features for managing multiple Hyper-V and hosts. In this chapter you install VMM and its prerequisites. You then learn how to use VMM Administrator Console to create and deploy virtual machines across multiple hosts and manage a library of shared resources for generating new virtual machines easily.

- **Chapter 7**, "Working with VMware vSphere," introduces you to using VMware's data center virtualization product. The activities in this chapter focus on the freely available ESXi hypervisor and vSphere Windows client. Using these tools you will learn how to install ESXi hypervisors along with the Windows-based vSphere client, and then use these products to build a simple virtual data center environment for a fictitious company consisting of two ESXi hosts, shared storage, and virtual machines connected to the physical network using virtual network switches.

- **Chapter 8**, "Working with VMware vCenter Server," introduces using the licensed version of vSphere to manage a data center consisting of multiple ESXi hosts. In this chapter you will learn how to install vCenter server as a virtual machine as well as use the Web-based vCenter client to create objects and centrally manage the entire virtual data center. Topics include licensing, creating distributed switches, implementing iSCSI shared storage, cloning virtual machines, creating clusters, and moving virtual machines between hosts.

- **Chapter 9**, "Implementing a Virtual Desktop Infrastructure," provides students with a hands-on introduction to setting up a virtual desktop infrastructure. Virtual desktop infrastructure or VDI is one of the fastest growing applications of virtualization technology as it can reduce IT support costs and provide a solution that allows users to work from a variety of different devices and physical locations. This chapter covers the concepts and challenges of VDI architectures and provides the student with hands-on experience implementing a simple Virtual Desktop Infrastructure using both VMware Horizon 7 and Microsoft VDI products.

- **Chapter 10**, "Introduction to Cloud Computing," introduces you to the way in which the cloud can be used to build and extend the virtual data center. Cloud-based services are becoming a major part of the IT environment and virtualization is the backbone supporting cloud computing, allowing resources and services to be provisioned as neededsaving time and costs. In this chapter we focus on the services offered through VMware vCloud Air and Microsoft Azure, as well as introduce the student to cloud environments based on OpenStack architecture. Hands-on activities in this chapter will allow you to experience vCloud Air by using VMware's lab environment as well as working directly with Microsoft Azure to build a cloud-based data center for a simulated application.

- **Appendix A**, "The Technology Behind Virtualization," explains how virtualization products use hardware and software to work behind the scenes, including how virtual machines emulate physical hardware. You learn about early virtualization methods as well as how virtualization works on today's x86 processors. You will also learn how hardware virtualization, which uses features built into modern processors, is improving virtualization performance.

- **Appendix B**, "Using VMware Workstation Player and Hyper-V Server 2016 Virtualization Products," explains installing and using the free VMware Player to run virtual machines and applications (called virtual appliances). Topics include installing VMware Player, running virtual machines and appliances, and performing basic configuration tasks, such as accessing CDs with ISO images. This appendix also includes a section that covers using Hyper-V Server 2016. Based on Server Core, this free, UI-less operating system can run virtual machines without a full version of Windows Server 2016. In this section you will learn how to install and configure Hyper-V Server using the command line and a simple text-based menu system.

- **Appendix C**, "Disaster Recovery and High Availability," provides an overview of disaster recovery services and high availability in virtualized data centers. This appendix also gives you an introduction to backup systems, including Microsoft Volume Shadow Copy Service (VSS), which allows backing up data while applications and files are open, and VMware's Virtual Data Protection (VDP) server. You also learn about using high-availability techniques used by VMware and Microsoft to keep virtual servers available continuously using host clusters.

Features

This book is unique in that it incorporates real world scenarios into hands-on activities using trial versions of the latest products. Combining hands-on activities with easy to read text allows students to build the skills necessary for a successful career in a computer industry that is increasingly focused around virtualization and the software defined data center. This book includes the following features to help you learn about the latest virtualization products and how to use them in a variety of IT settings:

- *Hands-on* activities—Nearly 100 hands-on activities and case projects give you practice in installing, configuring, managing, and operating virtualization software in a simulated organization. In addition, in the hands-on activities in Chapters 5–8, you use data center virtualization products for common IT tasks, such as networking, clustering, enhancing performance, and improving security. These activities give you a strong foundation for carrying out server virtualization tasks in the real world. In Chapter 9 you will perform activities that allow you to experience using both VMware's Horizon and Microsoft VDI products to implement a simple virtual desktop infrastructure. Cloud-based, on-demand services have become a major player in the IT infrastructure. In the activities in Chapter 10 you work with VMware vCloud labs and Microsoft Azure to learn how to create and manage virtual machines in the cloud.

- *Software*—The activities in each chapter are written to use free downloads or trial versions of virtualization software and include instructions on obtaining software from the VMware or Microsoft Web sites. Chapter activities are designed with a common theme of using Windows Server 2016 and Windows 10 in evaluation mode as the guest OS.

- *Product focus*—This book is designed to maximize your learning options and can be used in multiple courses. By showcasing both VMware and Microsoft virtualization and cloud services, students can compare the benefits and limitations of both environments.

- *Certifications*—This book provides you with the knowledge you need to pass the VMware Certified Associate 6–Data Center Virtualization Exam (VCA exam).

- *Class curriculum*—This textbook is designed to be used in a single Introduction to Virtualization class or may be applied to multiple classes that have a specific product focus. For example, if you want to learn only about VMware products, you can do the activities in Chapters 1–4, and then skip to Chapters 7–10. If you're working with only Microsoft products, you can do the activities in Chapters 1–6 before moving on to Chapters 9 and 10.

- *Chapter objectives*—Each chapter begins with a list of the concepts to be mastered. This list is a quick reference to the chapter's contents and a useful study aid.

- *Screen captures, illustrations, and tables*—Numerous screen captures and illustrations aid you in visualizing theories and concepts and seeing how to use tools and desktop features. In addition, tables are used often to provide details and comparisons of virtualization products and features.

- *Chapter summary*—Each chapter ends with a summary of the concepts introduced in the chapter. These summaries are a helpful way to recap and revisit the material covered in the chapter.

- *Key terms*—All terms in the chapter introduced with bold text are gathered together in the Key Terms list at the end of the chapter. This list gives you a way to check your understanding of all new terms.

- *Review questions*—The end-of-chapter assessment begins with review questions that reinforce the concepts and techniques covered in each chapter. Answering these questions helps ensure that you have mastered important topics.

- *Case projects*—Each chapter closes with one or more case projects designed to develop your critical and analytical skills in applying the virtualization concepts covered in that chapter.

- *Instructional flexibility*—This book has been written to meet a variety of instructional needs. The first chapters give students an overview of several virtualization products so that they can make better decisions about selecting a product. This book can also be used for a course on using a specific product, such as Microsoft Hyper-V or VMware ESXi, for a variety of server IT tasks, including networking, clustering, enhancing performance and security, and managing servers. For more information on instructional options, download the instructor's guide and materials.

Text and Graphics Conventions

Additional information has been added to this book to help you better understand what's being discussed in the chapter. Icons throughout the text alert you to these additional materials:

Tips offer extra information on resources, problem-solving techniques, and time-saving shortcuts.

Notes present additional helpful materials related to the subject being discussed.

Each hands-on activity in this book is preceded by the Activity icon.

Case Project icons mark the end-of-chapter case projects, which are scenario-based assignments that ask you to apply what you've learned in the chapter.

Instructor's Resources

The following supplemental materials are available when this book is used in a classroom setting. All the supplements available with this book are provided to instructors for downloading at www .cengage.com/sso.

- *Instructor's manual*—The instructor's manual that accompanies this book includes additional material to assist in class preparation, including suggestions for classroom activities, discussion topics, and additional activities.

- *Solutions*—The instructor's resources include solutions to all end-of-chapter materials, including review questions, hands-on activities, and case projects.

- *PowerPoint presentations*—This book comes with Microsoft PowerPoint slides for each chapter. They're included as a teaching aid for classroom presentation, to make available to students on the network for chapter review, or to be printed for classroom distribution. Instructors, please feel free to add your own slides for additional topics you introduce to the class.

System Requirements

Hardware:

One computer per student to act as the host machine that meets the following minimum requirements:

- Windows 10 (VMware) or Windows Server 2016 (Hyper-V) installed
- 2.4 GHz or faster CPU with hardware virtualization
- 4 GB RAM (8 GB or more recommended to do VMware activities)
- 120 GB disk minimum (more disk space is recommended for VMware activities)
- DVD-ROM drive or bootable USB
- Network interface card connected to the classroom, lab, or school network

Software:

- Windows Server 2016 Standard or Enterprise Edition (students can download an evaluation copy through Microsoft's DreamSpark program at *www.dreamspark.com*; see Chapter 1 for more details)
- Windows 10: Any edition except Home Edition (you can download an evaluation virtual machine from the Microsoft Web site)

Acknowledgments

We would like to thank Cengage Associate Product Manager, Amy Savino, for her vision in supporting this challenging book project. In addition, our thanks go to Maria Garguilo who was able to kindly and professionally deal with many technical and scheduling issues. Credit for helping us identify technical problems and find solutions to our questions goes to the technical editor, John Freitas, whose technical knowledge and meticulous testing has validated the accuracy of technical material in the chapters and ensured that activities work as they were intended. We also feel fortunate to have had such a good group of peer reviewers: Joanne Ballato, Lonestar College; Steve Ebben, Fox Valley Technical College; Bob Silbaugh, Riverland Community College; and Brenda Wamsley, Southeastern Community College. Their thoughtful advice and constructive criticism have contributed to this book's content and organization. In addition, no book can be completed without all the work required to get it ready for printing. We're grateful to have Harold Johnson, who provided careful copyediting.

Ted Simpson: While they are no longer with us, I want to thank my parents, William and Rosemary Simpson, for all the sacrifices they have made over the years to provide a foundation for my life. I also owe a deep debt of thanks and gratitude to my co-author, Jason Novak, who has steered a steady course in providing support, material, and vision to this book. Finally, I want to dedicate my writing efforts in this book to my wife, Mary, who is a great partner in sharing life and helping to support and accommodate my many endeavors, which range from teaching and writing books to making maple syrup. She has also helped keep me sane through the sometimes daunting challenges of meeting the ever-changing schedules and requirements that go with writing projects.

Jason Novak: I want to thank my co-author, Ted Simpson, for giving me the opportunity to work with him on this book once again. We have worked together on previous books, and he has provided invaluable insight for a beginning author. I also want to thank Tom for some much needed distraction with our weekly gaming sessions. I would like to dedicate my writing in this book to my family: my parents, John and Lynn, and sisters Jamie, Janna, and Hope.

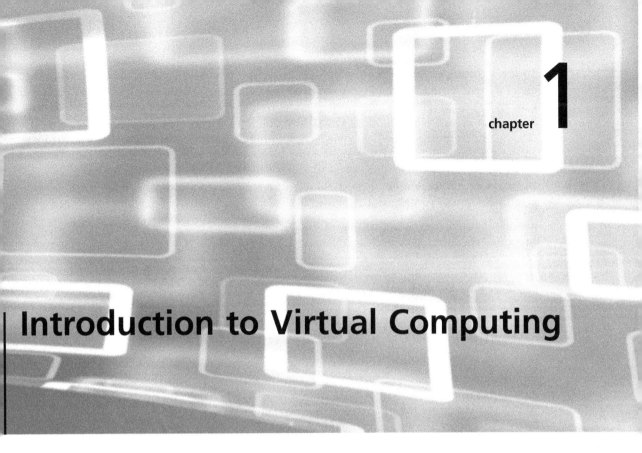

Introduction to Virtual Computing

After reading this chapter and completing the exercises, you will be able to:

- Understand the advantages of virtualization
- Describe how virtual machines work
- Give an overview of features in virtualization software
- Identify the categories of virtualization software products and how they are used in today's IT environment
- Summarize features of virtualization products from Microsoft and VMware
- Describe Virtual Desktop Infrastructure (VDI) and application virtualization, and identify the products used in supporting VDI environments
- Describe cloud services and identify features in Microsoft Azure and VMware vCloud

Today's high-powered multi-core CPUs with gigabytes of memory are often underutilized. Virtual Computing is the process of empowering these high-powered computer systems to run multiple operating systems, reducing the number of physical computers needed in the data center. Not only does virtual computing save hardware and energy costs, it also offers other features for the data center such as rapid provisioning of new systems, load balancing, high availability, backup, and disaster recovery. These capabilities, along with the ability to adapt computing resources quickly to a variety of customer requirements, have made virtualization the backbone of most cloud computing services, affecting most if not all computer users and IT professionals.

In addition to its use in data centers, virtualization offers a number of benefits for workstation environments. Developers may use virtual machines to develop and test their applications on a variety of platforms. IT professionals often use virtual machines to pre-configure servers as well as deploy desktop environments quickly to many users. Users benefit from virtual machines by using them to run other operating systems and applications side by side that normally couldn't be installed on a single system. Additional features available through virtualization include suspending the system to continue work later or taking a snapshot so that you can return to a specific system point if you make a mistake.

In this book you will learn about the many capabilities of virtual computing, how it differs from traditional computing environments, and how to implement this technology using the most popular virtualization products from VMware, Microsoft, and Oracle. In this chapter, you're introduced to these virtualization software packages, how virtualization works, and how virtualization features can be applied in the IT world to enhance existing data center services and enable new cloud-based services.

Overview of Virtual Machines and Virtualization Software

In traditional computing, a physical computer supports a single operating system.

The operating system provides an environment for applications and manages the physical computer's hardware resources including the CPU, memory, disk, and I/O devices. During installation, the operating system is configured to the physical computer's hardware environment using a specialized kernel along with a variety of device drivers. This hardware dependency makes it very difficult to move an operating system from one computer to another without re-installing the operating system or using nearly identical hardware.

Virtual computing frees the operating system from its hardware dependency and provides hardware resource sharing that allows a physical computer to simultaneously run multiple operating system environments. Each of these virtualized computer environments is called a **virtual machine** or VM and can run its own operating system as though it were running on a dedicated computer.

Virtual computing technology shares hardware resources by placing a piece of software called the **hypervisor** (see Figure 1-1) between the physical computer hardware and the operating system environments. The hypervisor allows you to create an environment for each virtual machine containing its own virtual CPU, memory, hard disk, and network interface card. These virtual devices appear to the virtual machine's operating system like physical devices.

By sharing hardware resources, the hypervisor makes it possible to run multiple computer environments on a single computer. As illustrated in Figure 1-1, hypervisors can be classified as type-1 or type-2. **Type-1 hypervisors** are called **bare metal hypervisors** because they run directly on the hardware without the need of a host operating system. **Type-2 hypervisors** require a host operating system and are often used to run other operating system environments on desktop computers.

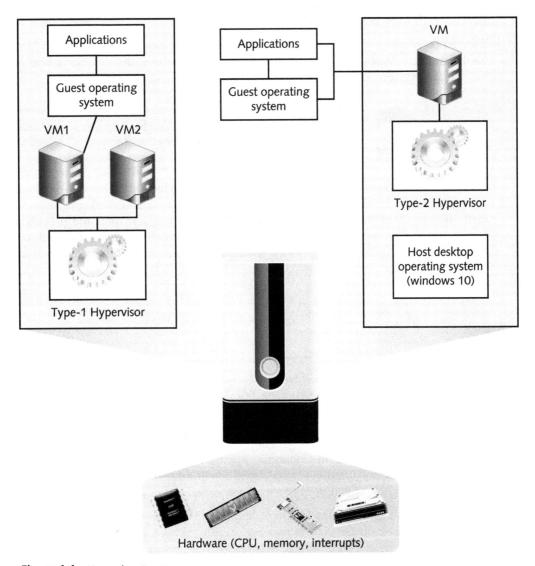

Figure 1-1   Hypervisor types

Running directly on the hardware without the overhead of a host operating system allows bare metal hypervisors to provide better performance and security, making them the choice of data centers to run virtual machines containing server operating systems. Bare metal hypervisors include products such as VMware vSphere, Microsoft's Hyper-V, and Xen hypervisor. You will work with VMware and Microsoft products in the later chapters.

Type-2 hypervisors require an operating system such as Windows, Linux, or Macintosh to manage the computer environment and are intended for use on personal workstations. The advantages of type-2 hypervisors are that they are easy to install and use, are not as hardware-specific as type-1 hypervisors, and allow you to use your normal desktop applications while still running virtual machines. Type-2 hypervisors include such products as VMware Workstation, VMware Workstation Player, and Oracle VirtualBox. You will learn how to work with these products in Chapters 2 and 3.

The computer running the hypervisor is referred to as the **host computer** since it hosts virtualized computers. When an OS is installed on a virtual machine, the virtual machine is referred to as a **guest system**, and the OS running on it is called a "guest OS."

A number of terms are used for a physical computer running a virtual machine, including "host computer," "desktop computer," and "local computer." For the purposes of this book, "host computer" is used to refer to the physical computer that is running the virtual machines.

Many of the concepts used in today's virtualization products date back to IBM mainframe computers of the 1970s. In 1998, VMware began developing and marketing commercial virtualization products for Intel x86 computers. Being first to the market and providing a number of advanced features allowed VMware to get the lion's share of the virtualization market. Today VMware still holds a large share of the virtualization market, but Microsoft and others are gaining ground.

According to a Nasdaq poll conducted in 2014, VMware held 21% of the market, but was declining due to competition from Microsoft and others.

Connectix, another company involved in early virtualization products for PCs, developed a type-2 virtualization product for running Windows applications on the Macintosh platform. Connectix ported its virtualization technology to the Windows platform in 2001 to create Virtual PC. In 2003, Microsoft purchased Virtual PC from Connectix and released it as Microsoft Virtual PC 2004. Windows 7 includes Microsoft Virtual PC 2007, an enhanced version of the original Virtual PC from Connectix. Microsoft's latest hypervisor, Hyper-V, ships with Professional versions of Windows 8 and later. If you want to run VMs on a home version of Windows 8 or later, you will need to install the virtualization software from another source.

A few companies including Oracle, Citrix, and Red Hat currently offer open source virtualization solutions based on the Xen hypervisor. Xen hypervisor is a bare metal hypervisor that began at the University of Cambridge as a research project in the late 1990s. The goal of the project was to create an efficient distributed computing platform. In 2002 the Xen hypervisor code was made open source, allowing anyone to use it and contribute to improving its features and capabilities. The XenSource organization was formed in 2004 to package and market the Xen hypervisor for commercial and educational use. A year later, Novell, Red Hat, and Sun Microsystems added the Xen hypervisor to their product offerings. In 2007, Citrix, a provider of cloud and virtual terminal services, acquired XenSource to complement their application delivery. In 2010, Oracle acquired Sun Microsystems and added a Xen hypervisor product they call Oracle VM Server to their product line. Another popular Xen-based hypervisor called KVM (Kernel-based Virtual Machine) is available through Red Hat, IBM, and other Linux distributions.

While a number of companies offer virtualization software packages, the products we cover in this book from VMware, Microsoft, and Oracle are the leading providers of commercial and open source virtualization products. The commercial products often require purchasing a license and have more advanced features, including technical support, than the free downloadable products. The free type-2 products such as VMware Workstation Player and Oracle's VirtualBox are suitable for home, small office, and school use and give users in these environments a way to enjoy the benefits of virtualization without a high cost. Most companies, including VMware, now offer their hypervisor as a free download. A license is required for technical support and advanced features or management consoles. For example, with VMware's vSphere 6, the vSphere Hypervisor (also referred to as ESXi server or host) is free, but you need to buy a license to obtain the vCenter Server used for employing advanced features and managing multiple hosts. In this chapter you will learn more about how virtualization software works, its features, and its hardware, software, and licensing requirements. In addition, you will learn about the categories of virtualization applications as well as what products are available to meet these types of applications.

How Virtualization Software Works with Virtual Machines

In traditional computer architectures, the operating system interacts directly with the installed hardware. It schedules processes to run on the CPU, allocates memory to applications, sends and receives data on network interfaces, and reads from and writes to attached storage devices. In comparison, an operating system installed in a guest virtual machine interacts with installed hardware through a thin layer of software called the virtualization layer or hypervisor. To support the operation of the guest virtual machines, the hypervisor must provide hardware resources dynamically to each virtual machine as needed. As illustrated in Figure 1-2, using the hypervisor, each virtual machine environment shares the computer's hardware resources, such as CPU, memory, disk, keyboard, video, and I/O ports, with the host computer and other virtual machines.

The hypervisor intercepts and processes requests coming from the guest operating systems and then returns the results back to the virtual machine. For example, the hypervisor uses one or more disk files on the host computer to emulate a hard drive for each virtual machine. When a guest OS requests a disk read, the hypervisor intercepts the request, accesses the data from the file representing that virtual machine's hard disk, and then returns the data to the virtual machine. The virtual machine is never aware of the actual hardware being used to store the data, as it appears to the guest OS that it is working with an actual hard drive. Sharing hardware resources allows virtual machines to operate with a high degree of

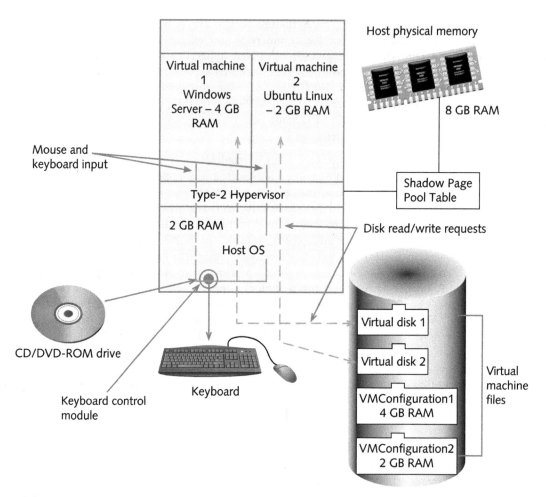

Figure 1-2 Virtualization software operation

independence from the underlying physical hardware, providing the ability for a virtual machine or its data to be moved from one physical host to another.

Type-1, or bare metal, hypervisors are more efficient than type-2 hypervisors because they access the hardware directly rather than going through the desktop operating system as shown in Figure 1-2.

When accessing the hardware, there is a slight difference between VMware hypervisors and Xen-based hypervisors such as Citrix Xen, Oracle VM Server, or KVM. Xen-based hypervisors use a special guest called Domain 0 that loads along with the hypervisor and is used to directly access the hardware. When a Xen-based guest makes a request for a hardware resource, such as doing a disk read, the Xen hypervisor sends the request to the Domain 0 guest. The Domain 0 guest then processes the request by directly accessing the disk system and returns the results to the Xen hypervisor. The hypervisor then sends the data to the guest operating system through its virtualized adapter. The downside to this process is that the Domain 0 guest may compete for resources with the other guest machines, slowing down performance. VMware on the other hand does all the hardware access inside the vSphere Hypervisor (or ESXi host), improving performance. Hyper-V works similarly to the Xen-based hypervisors in that it uses a special guest, called the parent partition, to manage hardware access. You will learn more working with Hyper-V in Chapters 5 and 6.

In addition to the hypervisor, Figure 1-2 illustrates each virtual machine having two main files on the host computer: a configuration file and a virtual disk file. The **configuration file** contains settings for virtual hardware, including the amount of physical RAM the virtual machine uses; the number of CPUs; the name, size, and location of the virtual disk file; CD/DVD-ROM settings; network configuration; port settings; and other configuration options. The hypervisor uses this information to configure the virtual machine when it is loaded. As with a physical hard drive, the **virtual disk file** contains a boot loader along with OS files and applications and data used with the virtual machine. This file will appear to the guest operating system as an entire disk drive or volume.

As shown in Figure 1-2, a virtual machine's disk system may be stored on the host computer as one or more separate files on the host computer's hard drive. Using a file to emulate a virtual machine's hard disk enables you to install and run multiple OS environments on a single host computer without creating multiple disk partitions on the physical hard drive. Virtual machine files can also be stored on shared storage or SAN drives allowing a virtual machine to be quickly moved from one host to another.

When you're running virtual machines, a section of the host computer's memory is reserved for each virtual machine, so the amount of physical memory the host computer has is a critical factor in how many virtual machines you can run simultaneously.

Peripheral devices, such as NICs and USB ports, can be shared by virtual machines and host computers. However, certain peripherals, including USB ports, the keyboard, and mouse, can be used by only one system at a time. With virtualization software, however, you can pass control of these peripherals to a virtual machine by using a menu or keystroke combination. The virtualization software covered in this book also includes optional tools that make transferring keyboard and mouse control as easy as clicking a virtual machine window or desktop. In later chapters, you learn how to install these tools for each virtualization product.

 See Appendix A for a technical description of methods used by hypervisors to perform the virtualization process.

Hardware and Software Requirements for Virtualization

Host computer requirements depend on the type of virtualization software you are installing along with the memory requirements for the guest VMs you will be running. Type-1, or bare metal, hypervisors are installed directly on the host computer's hardware, which must match the hypervisor's requirements. Type-2 hypervisors install in the host computer's operating system requiring you to obtain a version of the virtualization software that is compatible with the operating system and version your computer is running. For example, VMware provides versions of its Workstation 12 package for the Windows, Macintosh, and Linux platforms. As shown in Table 1-1, over the years, Microsoft has offered a variety of type-2 hypervisors that ship with different versions of Windows.

Table 1-1 shown later in this chapter provides a list of type-2 hypervisors and what operating system they are available for.

Processor Requirements

Processor Requirements All modern computer systems since 2003 typically have 64-bit, multi-core processors that are required by most virtualization software. A multi-core processor is a single CPU chip that contains two or more actual processing units called cores. Each core is capable of independently processing instructions, enabling the CPU to run multiple programs at the same time. Multi-core CPUs are a great asset to virtual computing as the multiple cores allow the hypervisor to more efficiently share the CPU across a number of virtual machines. Many Intel processors have a feature called **hyperthreading**, which is used to create additional virtual cores that can be used by the hypervisor to improve the performance of virtual machines. In addition to multiple cores, most CPUs today have a number of features that support hardware virtualization.

Earlier hypervisors relied on software to share hardware resources among virtual machines. Both Intel and AMD now have built-in support for virtualization in their processors, improving the performance of virtualization software designed to work with these enhancements. **Hardware virtualization** helps solve performance issues by performing part of the virtualization process inside the processor chip. AMD calls this feature AMD Virtualization (AMD-V) and started including virtualization support with its Athlon 64 processors. Intel's version is called Intel Virtualization Technology (Intel VT). Depending on your computer, you may need to enable the AMD-V or VT-x support in the Host system's BIOS in order to install the hypervisor.

In addition to having a processor that supports hardware virtualization, your computer's BIOS must be able to enable virtualization. Before purchasing a computer, check to be sure the motherboard supports hardware virtualization.

Another concern when running multiple VMs on a single computer is the potential for malicious software running in one guest environment to access data or modify software running in another virtual machine. The NX/XD CPU feature, also referred to as **Data Execution Prevention**, helps isolate virtual machines by enabling the hypervisor to use a special flag (or bit) to mark certain areas of memory as non-executable. When this happens the processor will refuse to modify or execute any code that resides in the protected areas of memory. Any attempt to execute code from a page that is marked as "no execute" will result in a memory access violation. This feature adds a layer of security to virtual machines by preventing software in one VM from running or accessing information in another VM running on the same host. AMD first added the NX bit feature to their AMD64 processor line starting with the Opteron processor in 2003. Intel followed suit shortly thereafter by introducing the XD (eXecute Disable) bit with their Pentium 4 Prescott processor in 2004. Both the NX bit and the XD bit have the exact same functionality, just different names, so you will often see this CPU technology referred to as NX/XD. The NX/XD technology is standard on most processors, so almost every server built since 2006 should support it. Support for NX/XD is usually enabled or disabled in the server BIOS and is typically found under Processor options, labeled something like "Execute Disable Bit," "NX Technology," or "XD Support."

Memory Requirements The memory requirement of the host is based on the combined memory requirements of the guest systems that you plan to run concurrently. The host system must have enough memory to run the host operating system (if using a Type-2 hypervisor), the guest operating systems that run inside the virtual machines on the host system, and the applications that run on the host and in the guest operating systems. As shown previously in Figure 1-2, the hypervisor assigns physical memory (RAM) from the host computer to each virtual environment that's currently running. The amount of memory assigned to each VM is based on the amount specified in that VM's configuration file.

You can change the amount of RAM a virtual machine uses in the administrative console.

When determining how much RAM is needed on the host running a type-2 hypervisor, you should start by allowing at least 1 to 2 GB of RAM for the host operating system and hypervisor and then add the memory requirements for each virtual machine environment that will be running concurrently.

You can use memory overcommitment, also called overbooking as described below to assign virtual machines more memory than is available in the host computer, however, this can reduce performance.

For example, Figure 1-2 shows the amount of memory used to run two virtual machines on a Windows 10 host computer with 8 GB RAM. In this case we have allowed 2 GB of RAM for the Windows 10 host computer and hypervisor, the Windows Server guest is given 4 GB RAM, and Ubuntu Linux guest is given 2 GB RAM, for a total of 8 GB physical RAM required on the host computer. To determine the guest virtual machine requirements, you will need to check the guest operating system and application documentation for information on memory requirements for each of the virtual machines and then configure the virtual machine for the amount of memory needed. For example, to support Windows Aero graphics in a virtual machine, at least 3.25 GB of host system memory is required (2 GB of memory for the host computer, 1 GB for the Windows guest operating system, and 256 MB to the guest's graphics memory). Computer operating systems manage memory through the use of page tables. The hypervisor manages the real hardware page table for the entire host computer, but each guest operating system keeps its own page table of the memory it has allocated to its applications and services. To do this, the hypervisor places the guest's page mapping in the hardware table only when that guest is running. The hypervisor uses what is called a **shadow page table** to keep track of the memory pages allocated by each guest VM. Whenever a guest OS allocates a page of memory to its VM, that allocation is tracked by the hypervisor in the shadow page table. Often guest VMs do not need all the memory that is allocated to them. Because the hypervisor controls all the physical memory, it has the ability to make any unused memory pages in each guest available for other virtual machines or the host computer. A guest operating system that has been allocated extra memory may hold infrequently used pages of memory in its page table, making that memory inaccessible to other virtual machines. Hypervisors can use a technique called **ballooning** to cause the guest VM to release infrequently used memory pages. To implement ballooning, each VM has a special driver called a balloon driver inserted into its guest OS. When the hypervisor senses that a VM has allocated extra memory that is not used, the balloon driver for that VM is activated and it "inflates," taking up memory on that VM. This inflation process causes the guest OS running on that VM to release memory pages back to the disk pool. After the excessive memory pages are released, the hypervisor de-activates the balloon driver freeing up the extra memory pages. A byproduct of having the hypervisor's management of the physical is called **memory overcommitment** or over-booking. With memory overcommitment you can load more VMs on the host computer than the amount of physical memory. The downside to overcommitment is that it can hurt virtual machine performance when it becomes necessary to swap memory pages to the hard disk due to memory contention. To improve virtual machine performance or run more virtual machines concurrently, you can usually add RAM to the host computer to reduce memory contention.

As described earlier, the hypervisor uses a shadow page table to keep track of which memory pages are in use by each of the guest VMs. Managing this shadow page table requires software overhead and can slow down the virtual machines. Another way to improve virtual machine guest performance is by using a CPU that supports **Second Level Address Translation** (**SLAT**). SLAT, also known as nested paging, is a hardware-assisted virtualization technology that makes it possible to avoid the overhead associated with software-managed shadow page tables, improving virtual machine performance. Newer versions of data center virtualization products such as Hyper-V and VMware vSphere require CPUs that support SLAT. In Chapter 4 you will learn more about memory management and performance issues for data center environments.

Storage Requirements To determine the host computer's disk storage requirement, you need to add up the disk storage needed to install the virtualization software along with the storage needed for each virtual machine, plus any storage requirements needed to support the host computer's operating system and its applications. While memory requirements are based on the number of virtual machines that will be running concurrently, the disk storage requirements will need to include all virtual machines that may be loaded by the host computer. There are a number of storage options available depending on the virtualization software and host computer. Local disk storage includes all disk drives that are attached to the host computer using direct attachment interfaces such as PATA, SATA, and SCSI disk drives. Local disk storage is typically used for workstation virtualization products such as VMware Workstation and Oracle VirtualBox as well as environments where a virtual machine will always run on a certain host. In addition to local storage, data center virtualization products such as vSphere and Microsoft Hyper-V support shared network disk storage.

There are two major types of shared network storage: Network Attached Storage (NAS), and Storage Area Network (SAN). These storage systems will be covered in Chapter 4.

Networking and Peripherals Requirements If the virtual machines will need to access an outside network or the Internet, they can be configured to use the host computer's network interface(s). In data center applications the host computer may require multiple network interfaces to provide higher network speeds and to support more advanced virtualization features such as clustering and load balancing. The hypervisor can also share peripheral devices such as the keyboard, display, USB ports, and optical drives with the virtual machines. Only one VM can be using a specific peripheral device at one time. You will learn more about how the virtualization software shares peripheral devices and networking in later chapters.

Licensing Requirements

Virtualization software packages can either be open or licensed. Examples of open virtualization products that do not require licensing include Oracle VirtualBox, Windows Virtual PC (ships with certain version of Windows 7), Hyper-V with Windows 8 and Windows 10, and VMware Workstation Player. Data center virtualization products such as vSphere and Windows Hyper-V Server provide a free hypervisor, but require licensing for advanced features and management tools.

When you're using virtual machines, keeping licensing requirements in mind is important. From a licensing perspective, installing an OS or application on a virtual machine is usually the same as installing the product on a physical computer. For example, installing Windows 10 on a virtual machine requires activation within 30 days. If your Windows product key is already in use on another physical computer or virtual machine, you get an error message when you attempt to activate it and must purchase an additional license. Be aware that running multiple copies of the same virtual machine might violate the license agreement for software installed on the virtual system.

To make virtualization more economically feasible, Microsoft includes Hyper-V with Server 2008 or later, and has developed a new licensing system that allows network administrators to install multiple Windows Server virtual servers on a computer with a single license.

Virtualization Software Categories and Products

With the rapid increase in the use of virtual machines, hardware and software vendors are designing products to enhance virtual machine performance and capabilities. Based on their area of specialization, today's virtualization products can be classified as workstation, data center, or cloud based. In the following sections, you learn more about these types of virtualization as well as the virtualization products that support each type of virtualization.

Workstation Virtualization Products

Workstation virtualization products use type-2 hypervisors designed for creating virtual machines that run on top of an existing operating system such as Windows, Macintosh, or Linux. Workstation virtualization products have many benefits for use in home, office, education, software development, server administration, and help desk environments. Now that Apple is using the Intel processors in its Macintosh line of computers, it is possible to run Windows guest environments on the Apple Mac platform. The VMware Fusion product is an example of a virtualization package available for the Mac platform. The benefits of using virtual machines with workstation environments include the following:

- *Running user desktop environments*—Virtual machines can be used to provide the user desktop environment instead of relying on the host computer OS. In this model, virtualization software is used to run a virtual machine containing the user's OS and desktop environment settings. Because each user's virtual machine consists of just a few files, the IT Department can roll out new OS releases quickly and restore user environments by simply copying the necessary files to users' computers. In addition, a single computer can run more than one OS easily, allowing it to better meet the user's needs. Home users can also benefit from using virtual machines because each family member can have his or her own OS environment. In Chapters 2 and 3, you use Oracle VirtualBox and VMware Workstation to create and manage user desktops.

- *Running applications*—A **virtual appliance** is a software package that includes a virtual machine containing a preinstalled and configured application that's ready to use. Virtual appliances free you from installing specialized applications on your desktop computer's OS. In addition to keeping your desktop computer less cluttered, using virtual appliances makes it easier for you to move an application to another computer or run the application from different locations. Examples of virtual appliances include Web development systems, security analyzers, and database applications. You can learn more about virtual appliances by visiting *www.vmware.com/appliances.*

- *Software development*—Software developers can use virtual machines to test software by running the programs in different OS environments. Instead of needing multiple computers or having to restart a computer in a different OS, software developers can simply open a virtual machine running the OS they want and test their programs. In addition, some virtualization software can be linked to the developer's programming environment for easy debugging.

- *Configuration Workbench*—Workstation-based hypervisors can be used as a workbench to allow network administrators to install, configure, and test servers and applications prior to deploying them in the production environment.

- *Help desk support*—Virtual machines make supporting users easier for help desk personnel. A help desk agent can bring up the same OS a user is having trouble with to walk him or her through a problem. For example, a help desk agent running Windows 10 can open a Windows XP virtual machine to help a user running that OS.

- *Classroom training*—Training classes often involve using different OS environments. For example, the same classroom might be used for both Windows and Linux classes. By using virtual machines, students in a Windows 10 class can install and work with that OS without interfering with the next class that needs to install and manage a Linux server.

Workstation virtualization software is designed to have more end-user features than data center virtualization products do, such as virtual USB ports, advanced snapshot management, and more user-friendly interfaces. As summarized in the preceding list, these features help support software development, testing, and user training. You will learn more about workstation virtualization features and benefits in "Comparing and Downloading Virtualization Products" later in this chapter.

You have a variety of workstation virtualization products to choose from, including free products from Microsoft and VMware. The products listed in Table 1-1 are designed to run on desktop OSs.

Table 1-1   Workstation virtualization products and requirements

Product Vendor	Product	Supported Host OS	Description
VMware (www.vmware.com)	VMware Workstation	Windows 7 and later Linux	Free download Requires license within 30 days Contains advanced features not available in other free products
	VMware Workstation Player	Windows XP and later Linux	Free and Paid versions available Runs existing VMs Limited features Often used to run virtual appliances
	VMware Fusion 7	Mac OS X 10.8 or later	Free download Requires license within 30 days
Microsoft	Hyper-V (client)	Windows 8 Professional or later	Ships with Windows, but needs to be activated using Control Panel
Oracle	VirtualBox	Windows 7 or later	Free products with good features and support

Although workstation virtualization products can be used to run server OSs, they don't have the performance or management features organizations need to host multiple virtual servers on a single computer. For these reasons, if you're planning to virtualize a server environment, you should consider one of the data center virtualization products described in the following section.

Virtualization in the Data Center

Like workstation virtualization products, server virtualization products emulate a physical computer's hardware. The major difference between data center and workstation virtualization is in the product's specialization. Data center virtualization products are specialized to improve performance, management, and reliability so that several servers can run on a single system. The major benefits of virtual servers are reduced hardware and power costs, server clustering, load balancing, and improved fault tolerance. You learn more about server clusters, load balancing, and fault tolerance in Chapter 4.

As servers have become more economical, many departments have become accustomed to having their own servers to run applications, which increases hardware and operating costs. In addition to separate departmental servers, today it is a recommended practice to dedicate servers to applications rather than running multiple applications on a single server. For example, a separate server is used for email, another for database, and another for file and print sharing. The accumulation of many specialized and departmental servers creates what's called **server sprawl** (see Figure 1-3).

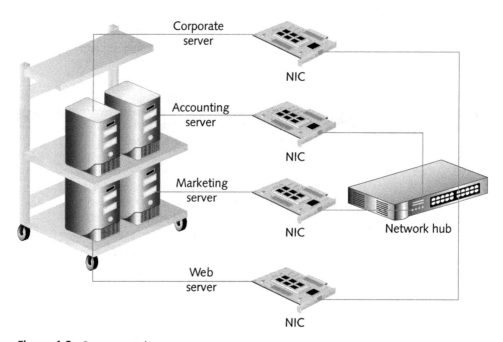

Figure 1-3   Server sprawl

Because of the speed and capacity of today's computers, using servers in this specialized fashion means they're running at only 5% to 40% utilization. Server sprawl increases costs of computer hardware and maintenance and increases power consumption. With current increases in energy costs, power consumption has become an important budgeting consideration. To help reduce hardware and power costs, almost 60% of IT organizations now use server virtualization products to consolidate multiple servers into a single high-performance system, as shown in Figure 1-4.

As mentioned earlier, a benefit of server virtualization is being able to create specialized servers to run different services, such as domain controllers, email servers, and database servers. Before virtualization, dedicating a server to each specialized service wasn't economical because it increased server sprawl and licensing costs. Virtual servers solve this problem because you can run multiple specialized virtual servers on a single computer. In addition, if a physical computer fails or gets bogged down, the virtual servers running on it can be started on another physical computer to ensure continued access during system recovery.

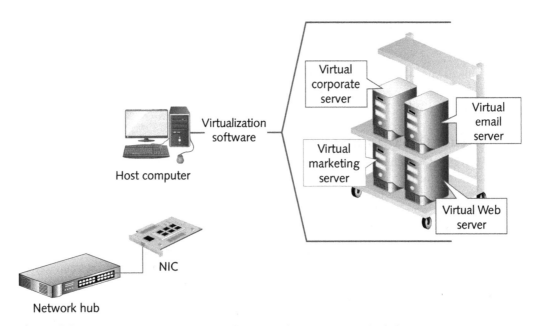

Figure 1-4 Using virtualization to consolidate several servers onto a single host

Being able to move virtual servers between physical computers helps balance server load and improve performance. In addition, reducing the number of services running on a physical server by moving each one to a separate virtual machine simplifies server configuration, improves performance, and enhances security. Keep in mind that you might need to distribute virtual servers over several physical machines to avoid overtaxing a single system when your servers are working at full load.

In addition to using a type-1 bare metal hypervisor, server virtualization products gain performance advantages over workstation virtualization products by eliminating certain features, such as advanced snapshot management, and some workstation device support. Server virtualization products also include administrative consoles for managing and configuring virtual servers remotely across networks, including the Internet. Table 1-2 lists the most common server virtualization products at the time of this book's writing.

Table 1-2 **Data center virtualization products and requirements**

Product	CPU Requirement	Memory Requirement	Disk
VMware vSphere	2 GHz Dual-core CPU that supports Data Execution Prevention and Hardware Virtualization	4 GB RAM	4 GB
Microsoft Hyper-V	1.5 GHz 64-bit processor that supports Data Execution Prevention and Hardware Virtualization	1 GB RAM	32 GB

Microsoft's newest product, Hyper-V, is built into all 64-bit versions of Windows Server 2008 and later. With 64-bit OSs, you can have more than 4 GB of RAM, which is useful for running multiple virtual machines simultaneously. As of this writing, Hyper-V is the only product to require a 64-bit processor with hardware virtualization support. Although including parts of the virtualization process in the processor chip can improve performance, it requires support from the host OS and the virtualization software. Current server products, such as Windows Server 2016, work directly with processor-based virtualization, which reduces software overhead.

Virtual Desktop Infrastructure

As computer technology and user needs have changed, new processing methods have been developed to better facilitate these capabilities. Early computer systems used batch processing to process a single batch of data (often contained on punch cards or magnetic tape), producing a report and updating files. Users submitted data to the data center and then waited until the next day to get their results on printed reports.

With the advent of more powerful computers and data terminals, time sharing allowed many users to share the processing power of one mainframe computer and interactively enter data, make requests, and get instant results on their terminal screens. Microcomputers allowed users to run programs on their own personal computers, accessing shared data from a file server. Personal computers that run their own operating system and applications are known as **thick clients**. The problem with thick clients is the amount of time and support that is required to update the client hardware and software, fix software problems, and ensure security and accessibility. In addition, thick clients limit the number and type of devices and locations available to the user.

Today mobility and support costs are becoming major issues in supporting user applications on thick clients. Virtual Desktop Infrastructure (VDI) helps solve this problem by running user desktops on virtual machines in the data center as shown in Figure 1-5.

A **virtual desktop** is a virtual machine that is running a desktop operating system such as Windows or Linux. In order to host the virtual desktops, the VDI infrastructure shown in Figure 1-5 requires several hardware and software components.

1. First you need host computers that have sufficient memory and storage space to support the number of virtual machines that will be running at any one time.

2. Second, you need a data center virtualization package that includes a bare metal hypervisor for each server and a management console such as the VMware vSphere and vCenter server.

3. Third, you need to create a virtual machine, called a VM image, for each user's desktop. VMware Horizon includes a software component called VMware Composer that can be used to simplify the process of creating and provisioning virtual machines for each desktop. To save disk space, virtual desktops that share a similar environment can be **linked clones**. The parent VM contains the desktop OS and all shared storage, whereas the linked clones contain only the changes that are unique for the user's desktop. You will learn more about the linked clone feature in the next section.

4. Fourth, users need a way to connect their client device to the virtual desktop. This is accomplished by having a small software package called a **thin client** on the user's device. The thin client connects to the user's virtual desktop through a connection broker. Connections can be made on the local network or across the Internet. The

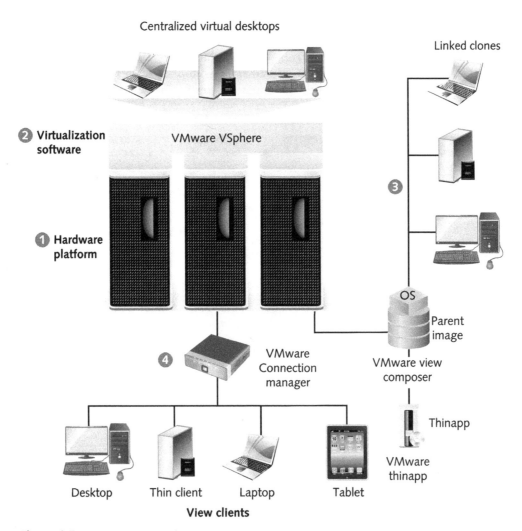

Figure 1-5 Virtual desktop infrastructure

connection broker requires the user's name and password to verify access to a virtual machine. Thin clients can run on a number of devices including desktop computers, notebooks, and tablets providing users with a variety of mobility options. The VMware Horizon product includes both a thin client and connection broker called the Connection Server.

Today, VDI has become a major player in IT data centers with a number of major companies offering VDI products (see Table 1-3). VDI allows the IT staff to host all user desktop environments on virtual machines running on powerful data center hosts or servers. IT staff can quickly deploy new virtual desktop environments or update existing environments at the data center using administrative software tools as compared to going out to the user's office or having the user bring their computer into the data center for maintenance.

In Chapter 9 you will learn more about VMware and Microsoft virtualization products that are used to support the VDI infrastructure. While there are a number of other desktop infrastructure products identified in Table 1-3, in this book we will focus on working with VMware Horizon View and Microsoft Virtual Desktop Infrastructure products and comparing their features to the other products from Microsoft, Oracle, and Citrix.

Table 1-3   Virtual Desktop Infrastructure products

Company/Product	Description	Requirements
VMware/Horizon and View	VMware View provides remote desktop capabilities to users using VMware's virtualization technology. A client desktop operating system and applications run within a virtual environment on a host using the vSphere Hypervisor (ESXi).	VMware Horizon software components (see above)
Microsoft Enterprise Desktop Virtualization (MED-V)	Enables the deployment and management of Windows Virtual PC images throughout an enterprise using Hyper-V.	Windows Server 2012 or later with R2 VDI RDS Cal License required for each user or client
Oracle/Virtual Desktop Infrastructure	Provides access to virtualized desktop environments hosted in the data center using the Oracle Virtual Desktop Infrastructure.	8 GB RAM to run 6 virtual desktops Linux or Solaris OS for the host computer and VirtualBox for the hypervisor Oracle Virtual Desktop Infrastructure
Citrix/XenDesktop and FlexCast	XenDesktop uses the FlexCast system to build a Virtual Desktop Infrastructure that can deliver desktop environments to users across a variety of devices.	XenServer Hyper-V vSphere

Application Virtualization

Application virtualization is a desktop virtualization technology that is used to run applications without affecting the desktop operating system environment. Application virtualization is different from workstation or server virtualization in that it doesn't create a separate virtual hardware environment. Instead, it abstracts the file system and Registry for the virtualized application. Allowing each application to have its own Registry and file system means you can run multiple versions of the same software on the desktop system. For example, you could install the latest version of Microsoft Office but still keep your original version active to maintain productivity while you're learning the new version.

Application virtualization products enable you to run virtual applications the same way you run standard applications on your desktop. The difference is that virtual applications leave no footprint in the host computer's Registry or file system. You can install and run these applications without causing conflicts with other applications or worrying that a new beta application might corrupt the Registry, making it difficult to remove.

Application virtualization has become an important part of VDI environments because it provides an efficient method to deliver and manage applications to a variety of user and desktops. Application virtualization products include VMware ThinApp, Microsoft App-V, and Altiris Software Virtualization Solution (SVS). These products isolate applications from their underlying operating system to eliminate application conflicts and streamline application deployment and mobility. ThinApp is a key component of VMware's Horizon line of virtual desktop products. App-V virtualizes all aspects of an application and offers advanced features, such as streaming application deployment and prepackaged virtualized applications. However, it requires Microsoft Active Directory, limiting its use to large Windows networks. SVS doesn't include all the network features of App-V but has the advantage of being more suitable to stand-alone desktop environments. The disadvantage is that it doesn't virtualize application functions, such as system and COM calls. However, it's adequate for most end-user application needs because it virtualizes the most important application objects, including the Registry and file system. With the success of these products, you can expect to see application virtualization play a bigger role in the future.

Activity 1-1: Creating a VMware Account and View Product Categories

Time Required: 10 minutes

Objective: Create a VMware account you can use for later activities and Case Projects.

Description: In this activity you will create a VMware account that you can use to obtain trial copies of products as well as free educational classes.

1. If necessary, log on to your host computer.

2. Open a Web browser and go to http://www.vmware.com.

3. Point to Login, click **My VMware,** and then click the **Register** link in the Log In frame.

4. Enter your email address and a password in the Login Information section.

5. Enter your name and business information in the Tell Us About Yourself frame.

6. Fill in the Language and Company information frames.

7. Click to put a check in the "I agree to the terms and conditions outlined in the My VMware Terms of Use Agreement" check box.

8. If you do not want to receive email, click to remove the check from the Yes check box.

9. Click the **Continue** button. After correctly entering the data, you should receive a confirmation that asks you to check your email for your registration.

10. After a few minutes check your email for a message from The VMware Team. Open the message and record your Customer Number below:

_____

11. Click the **Activate Now** link in the email, then enter your password and click **Continue** to activate your account.

12. You should now see a window showing any current evaluations you have selected. Click the **Start New Eval** button to view the Evaluate VMware Products page.

13. Notice the various categories of virtualization products available for evaluation. You will be working with some of these products in later chapters.

14. Point to Login, then click **My VMware** to return to your account page.

15. Point to your name located in the upper right section of the page and notice your customer number is displayed. Click the **Logout** link from the pull down menu to log off.

16. Close your browser and log off the computer.

Cloud Environments

In the 1960s the cloud symbol started to be used on network diagrams to represent the complex telephone switching network used to connect devices across a long distance. Since that time, the cloud has become synonymous with data and network services hosted by servers connected through the Internet as illustrated in Figure 1-6.

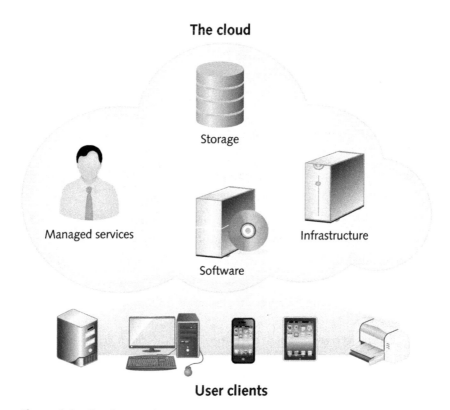

Figure 1-6   Cloud computing

Cloud services are classified depending upon the type of service as shown in Figure 1-7.

At the bottom of the stack, Infrastructure as a Service (IaaS) is the most basic cloud service offering computers and servers (typically virtual machines) along with other resources such as virtual switches, storage, firewalls, and other virtualized devices. IaaS allows a company to configure their own network operating environment using their software licenses and applications without the need to purchase and maintain all the hardware in their data center.

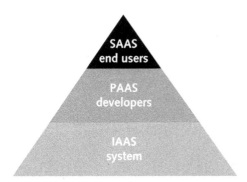

Figure 1-7   Cloud computing services

This is a very attractive option to small firms that cannot afford to invest in an expensive data center and staff. IaaS cloud services allow a company to grow by only paying for the hardware services they need.

Platform as a Service (PaaS) provides the hardware infrastructure along with the operating system software needed to run or develop the client's applications. For example, a small software development company can rent a PaaS cloud environment that includes software development tools and operating system software needed to develop and test their applications without the high cost of a software license. Like with IaaS, the client only pays for what they are using.

Software as a Service (SaaS) is perhaps the most common cloud service as it allows users to run software packages without the cost and hassle of installing the software on a device. SaaS not only saves cost and support time, it also allows users to access the applications and data they need using different devices. You may be able to do your word processing tasks from your desktop computer in the office, or use your tablet to access the software and data while on the road. In Chapter 10 you will learn how to use virtual machines to create a SaaS environment.

Virtualization technology is the backbone of cloud services. For example, when setting up a cloud service, you specify the amount of resources such as memory, CPU, and storage space needed. Rather than provision actual hardware for your account, the cloud provider will create a virtual machine that meets the requirements of your service. The cloud provider can then use load balancing and high availability to ensure that the service meets the required user access needs. As the organization's needs grow, the virtual server's storage space and processing power can be scaled to meet the new requirements. Without virtualization, cloud services have to be tied to physical equipment, making them very expensive and inflexible.

As shown in Figure 1-8, clouds can be classified as Public, Private, or Hybrid.

Public clouds can be configured to offer the services described previously to anyone connected to the Internet with a valid account. There are a number of major public cloud providers including Amazon Web Services, VMware vCloud, and Microsoft Azure. You will learn more about what services these companies provide in Chapter 10. Private clouds are hosted by the company that provides the private cloud service using virtual machines and

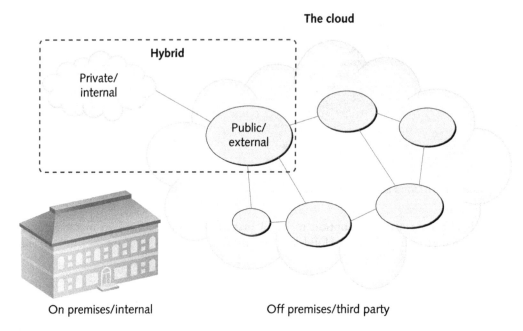

Figure 1-8   Cloud computing types

applications they maintain in their own data centers. Companies such as VMware and Microsoft offer services that can help you build private cloud services. In addition to proprietary solutions from VMware and Microsoft, OpenStack offers an open source solution that is becoming a standard for implementing private clouds. NASA worked with the Rackspace company to develop the OpenStack cloud standard and open source software in 2010. Since that time Rackspace has been a major champion of the OpenStack and provides both public cloud services along with a suite of OpenStack software companies can install to host their own private clouds. In Chapter 10, you will learn how to use these products to set up a simple private cloud environment to create and extend virtual data centers. One possible problem with hosting private cloud services is load balancing. During certain busy times the company's data center can get overloaded, slowing down the service. For example, if a company hosts an online shopping service, the data center servers could get bogged down during Black Friday. This is where a hybrid cloud service provider becomes important. Using a hybrid cloud service along with load balancing allows an organization to configure their data center so that it can off-load certain cloud services to a public cloud server during busy times. Renting the public cloud service for these exceptions is much less expensive than purchasing the additional hardware for the data center. In the following activities you will learn more about Microsoft Azure, and VMware vCloud by setting up accounts and viewing information.

Activity 1-2: Creating a Microsoft Live Account and Viewing Microsoft Azure Product Features

Time Required: 10 minutes

Objective: Create a Microsoft Live account that you can use for later activities and then view Microsoft Azure product features.

Description: In this activity you will create or access your Windows Live account and then view and record information about Microsoft Azure features. You may then use your Windows Live account to obtain a trial subscription to the Microsoft Azure service and use it to work with virtual machines and virtual networks. If necessary, log on to your host computer, open a Web browser.

1. If you already have a Microsoft Live account that you will be using for this class, go to http://live.com, enter your email address and password, and click the **Sign in** button. You may now skip to step 6.

2. If you do not have a Microsoft Live account, go to http://signup.live.com to display the Create an account page.

3. Enter the requested information and click the **Create account** button.

4. You will need to respond to an email message sent to the address you specified in step 4 to activate your account.

5. Enter the URL: http://azure.microsoft.com/en-us/pricing/free-trial/.

6. Click the **Products** link and record the popular solutions listed.

7. Click the **Virtual Machines** solution and record the features listed.

8. Log off of your Windows Live account and close the browser window.

Virtualization Features to Look for in Products

In addition to supporting multiple OSs on a single computer, virtualization software packages include many features for sharing hardware and managing virtual computer environments. You can choose from a variety of virtualization software products that offer many benefits to IT Departments, computer users, and educational environments. The following sections give you an overview of the features and capabilities found in many virtualization packages. You will get a chance to experience these features by working with various virtualization packages throughout this book.

Hardware Virtualization Features

As mentioned earlier, the hypervisor provides guest virtual machines with access to hardware devices on your computer by capturing requests for hardware devices that the virtual machine issues and redirecting them to the physical hardware. Because of this, an OS running on a virtual machine sees devices as though they were physical hardware. The system configuration information that defines memory, I/O ports, and storage devices for a virtual machine is kept in a configuration file, as shown previously in Figure 1-2, and you can view or change this information in the management consoles. The following sections describe the hardware configuration options and features that are available with the virtualization software covered in this book. You learn more details about these hardware features and how they relate to specific products in later chapters.

Motherboard and Processor Support Features The hypervisor software provides a virtual motherboard and chipset along with one or more virtual processors (vCPUs) based on the same processor model on the host computer. The hypervisor also provides emulated firmware and a CMOS for each virtual machine. You can use virtual firmware to change the virtual machine's CMOS settings, including the boot device selection. The latest hypervisors such as VMware Workstation 12, vSphere 6, and Hyper-V provide support for either the traditional BIOS or the new UEFI firmware.

In the mid-1990s, Intel developed the Extensible Firmware Interface (EFI) as an improvement to the original Basic Input Output System (BIOS) used in earlier systems. In 2005, Intel contributed the EFI standard to the Unified EFI Forum, which now manages this new standard known as UEFI.

If you are working with a recent release of the guest OS such as Windows 10 or Windows Server 2016, you may wish to use the virtual UEFI firmware as it provides more flexibility, security, and support. You will learn how to select and use both BIOS and EFI firmware in later chapters.

The CPU is the heart of any computer or virtual machine. As described earlier in this chapter, today most CPUs are designed to support virtualization. When selecting a virtualization package you need to consider how it supports virtualization. Most hypervisors support multiple virtual CPUs (vCPUs) for the guest virtual machines. Configuring multiple processors in a guest VM can help increase speed for certain VMs provided the host computer has multiple CPU cores available. However, if the host is running multiple VMs and applications, assigning extra vCPUs to guest VMs can actually decrease the guest VM performance. For example, if a guest VM has been configured with two vCPUs, the hypervisor will need to have two physical CPU cores available in order to perform the work. Waiting for the two physical CPU cores to be available at the same time can actually slow up the guest VM on a host that has limited number of physical cores. The general rule is to start with your VM using less hardware resources and then increase the number as needed. In addition to the number of vCPUs, you should check to see if the hypervisor supports both Intel and AMD hardware virtualization and Data Execution Prevention features as described earlier in the Processor Requirements section of this chapter.

Host computers that have CPUs with more cores are often preferred for running virtual machines.

Memory Support Features In addition to the CPU, memory plays a major role in virtual machine performance. In a simple world, the amount of memory in the host computer should equal the memory assigned to each concurrently running VM plus the amount needed for the host computer and hypervisor. However, there are a number of other memory management features that affect virtual machine performance. In this chapter you learned about several features including Second Level Address Translation (SLAT), ballooning, and overcommitment. When comparing virtualization products, be sure you are aware of what memory technologies they support. In addition to supporting SLAT, ballooning, and overcommitment technologies, data center virtualization products may also include support for page sharing and page compression. You will learn more about these advanced memory support features in Chapter 4.

Administrative and User Consoles

Virtualization packages include management software that you can use to create and remove virtual machines, configure virtual machine settings, manage virtual storage and network devices, start and stop virtual machines, and many other tasks, such as using templates to easily deploy multiple virtual machines rather than installing software on each virtual machine separately. Management software typically includes both administrative and user consoles. User consoles provide a window to the desktop of the OS running on the virtual machine so that users can interact with the OS and applications.

The administrative console provides an interface for creating, configuring, and managing virtual machine environments. While GUI consoles are typically the preferred environment for administrative consoles, many virtualization products use a combination of GUI and Web-based consoles for both user and administrative purposes. The advantage of Web-based consoles is that they make it easier to manage multiple virtual machines across a network or the Internet without additional software. The disadvantage of Web-based consoles is that they are slower, have lower resolution than GUI consoles, and are more cumbersome for testing systems and switching between virtual machines rapidly. The Microsoft Hyper-V GUI console uses a Microsoft Management Console (MMC) window for interacting with and managing virtual machines. Figure 1-9 shows an example of the Hyper-V MMC running on a host computer to provide user and administrative consoles.

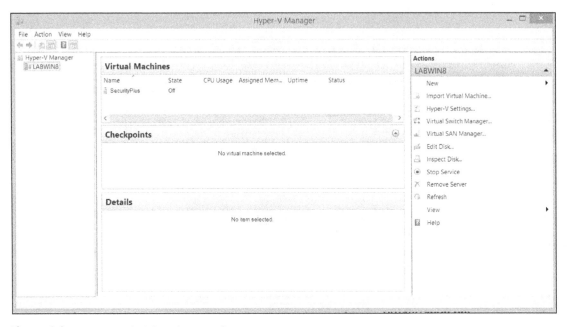

Figure 1-9 Hyper-V administrative console

Source: VMware

You will learn more about working with Hyper-V Manager in Chapter 5. In addition to a Web-based console, VMware vSphere uses the vCenter Server GUI console to manage multiple vSphere hosts or the vSphere Client GUI to work with individual vSphere Hypervisors (also called ESXi hosts). You will work with vSphere and vCenter consoles in Chapters 7 and 8.

COM and LPT Ports You can use the administrative console to configure a virtual machine to use standard COM and LPT ports by bridging them to the host computer's ports or routing their output to a file on the host computer. For example, if you're developing an application that sends output to a COM port, you can capture the virtual COM port's output to a file on the host computer. You could open that file with an editor program later and analyze the contents to make sure the application is working correctly.

USB Ports Universal Serial Bus (USB) has become the standard interface for many peripheral devices, including printers and removable storage media. Connecting a guest VM to the host computer's USB port often requires a few extra steps to enable and then capture the USB device. As of this writing, Hyper-V does not include native support for USB devices, but requires the addition of a product such as USB Redirector to connect a Hyper-V VM to a host computer's USB port. You will learn how to connect USB devices to specific virtualization products in later chapters.

USB support isn't considered as important with server virtualization because most USB devices are designed for use on desktop OSs.

CD/DVD Devices on a Virtual Machine A virtual machine can be configured to have virtual CD/DVD devices that can be linked to the host computer's physical CD/DVD-ROM drive, allowing the virtual machine's OS to use this type of media in the host computer's drive. In addition, a virtual machine's CD/DVD device can be redirected to an ISO image file. **ISO image files** use the ISO 9660 CD format to store a disc's contents in a single file on the host computer's hard drive or a network share. You can create ISO image files with a third-party tool, such as WinISO (www.winiso.com) or MagicISO (www.magiciso .com).

After creating an ISO image file, you can use the administrative console to point a virtual machine's CD/DVD device to the ISO image file rather than the physical CD/DVD-ROM drive, as shown with VMware Workstation in Figure 1-10. Using an ISO image file offers many advantages in both business and classroom settings. For example, an instructor can place an ISO image file on the classroom server for students instead of making copies of a CD/DVD for every student.

Figure 1-10 Setting a virtual optical drive to point to an ISO image file

Source: VMware

Disk Support Features

With virtualization software, a virtual machine typically uses a specially formatted file, called a disk image file, on the host computer as though it were an entire drive. As illustrated in Figure 1-11, using the hypervisor, the guest operating system will see the disk image file (VM2.VMDK) through Windows Server 2016 SCSI controller as though it was a standard SCSI disk drive.

There are a variety of disk image file formats in use by virtualization packages. Table 1-4 contains a list of the disk image file formats used by the virtualization products covered in this book.

Table 1-4 Disk image file formats

Disk File Format	Virtualization Platforms
Virtual Disk Image (VDI)	Native to Oracle VirtualBox
Virtual Machine Disk (VMDK)	Native to VMware
Virtual Hard Disk (VHD)	Native to Microsoft Virtual PC
Virtual Hard Disk Extended (VHDX) (Enhanced version of VHD to support advanced features of data center virtualization)	Native to Hyper-V running on Server 2008 and later

In addition to the primary disk drive, you can use the administrative console to create additional virtual disks for a virtual machine. As when adding drives to a physical system, the virtual machine must be shut down to add a virtual disk. Because the virtual disk file format

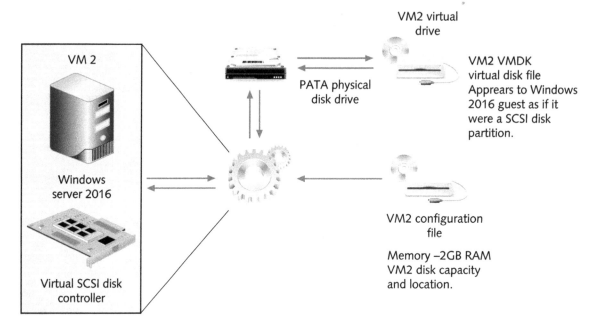

Figure 1-11   Virtual disk configuration

depends on the product used to create it, moving a virtual disk between different brands of virtual machines can be difficult. For example, a virtual machine in Microsoft Hyper-V cannot directly access a virtual disk file created by VMware. To help solve this problem, most virtualization products include an option for importing a virtual disk file from another virtual machine format.

When using workstation virtualization products, the disk image file is usually stored on a local IDE disk drive such as SATA or PATA. Data center virtualization products, such as VMware vSphere and Microsoft Hyper-V, also support storing virtual machine files on shared network drives such as a **Storage Area Network (SAN)** or **Network Attached Storage (NAS)**. In NAS, the storage device acts as a file server, allowing access to files and folders on the network based on name. The problem with NAS devices is they typically have slower access times than local hard drives and are designed to run on slower Ethernet networks. In a SAN, the storage devices are attached to a dedicated high speed network and accessed by blocks in much the same way that disks are accessed on a local file system. The most common form of SAN is an iSCSI network in which SCSI commands are transmitted across a standard TCP/IP network environment. The iSCSI SAN looks up the data by data cluster by block or cluster number and then returns the data across the network to the iSCSI controller running on the host computer. SAN systems can run at speeds similar to local hard drives, operate across high-speed networks, and often provide a more fault-tolerant storage system than NAS systems.

Using NAS or SAN shared storage allows the virtual machine to be moved quickly between host computers for high availability and load balancing. Figure 1-12 shows an example of NAS storage providing shared folders to two different host computers. In this example the virtual server VM2 is currently running on host computer 1 and accessing its virtual hard

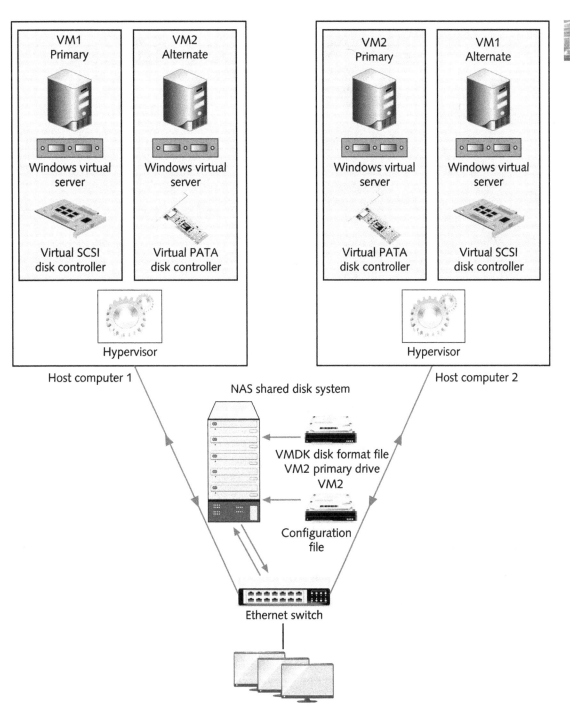

Figure 1-12   NAS system

disk storage, located on the NAS shared disk system, using a virtual SCSI disk controller. If host computer 1 fails, host computer 2 can also run the VM2 virtual machine by using the shared VM2 configuration file to load the VM2 guest. Once loaded, the VM2 guest can continue operations using its SCSI controller to access the primary drive located on the shared disk file just like it did when running on host computer 1. You will learn more about how NAS and SAN systems are used with data center virtualization systems in later chapters.

Virtual Disk Types When you create a virtual machine, you specify the type of virtual disk and the amount of disk space (fixed or dynamic) to reserve for it on the host computer. When you specify a **fixed-size virtual disk** type, the virtualization software creates a file on the host computer that takes up exactly the amount of disk space required for the virtual disk. For example, if you specify a 4 GB fixed-size virtual disk, the virtualization software creates a 4 GB file on the host computer to store the virtual disk data.

When you're using **dynamic virtual disk** types, the virtual disk file on the host computer takes up only the space the virtual disk is actually using. For example, if you select a 4 GB dynamic virtual disk and the virtual disk uses only 1.5 GB, the virtual disk file on the host computer occupies only 1.5 GB. As the amount of virtual disk space used increases, more space is allocated on the host computer's hard drive. Although fixed-size virtual disks provide better performance, they use more of the host computer's hard drive than a dynamic disk does. Because fixed-size disks provide better performance, they are often the default in server virtualization products; dynamic disks are more appropriate for workstation virtualization.

In addition to specifying the virtual disk's type and size, most virtualization products allow you to select either a SCSI or an IDE controller for the guest OS to use when accessing the virtual disk. IDE is the most common disk controller for workstation environments, whereas SCSI controllers are popular with virtual servers because they support a wider range of devices and can provide increased performance.

Saving the Virtual Machine State

An important feature in virtualization software is being able to save a virtual machine's current settings and disk contents so that you can return to this saved state later. Restoring a virtual machine to a saved state is useful in development and education environments because you can experiment with software options by performing a process several times from the same starting point. The virtualization products covered in this book include options for saving a virtual machine's state, although the methods vary depending on the vendor.

Virtualization products often offer two ways to save a virtual machine state: non-persistent disks and snapshots (also known as checkpoints in Hyper-V). With nonpersistent disks, changes made to a virtual machine are used only in the current session. When you power off the virtual machine, the disk is returned to its initial state. Nonpersistent disks are useful when you don't want your virtual machine to be affected by an activity such as testing new software or when you want to protect your system while browsing the Internet. With snapshots, you can return a virtual machine to a specific point if you have problems. For example, if you're installing new software or making a change to the system configuration, take a snapshot first. If something goes wrong, you can return your virtual machine to that point and try again. VMware Workstation includes a Snapshot Manager feature for keeping track of snapshots in a tree structure. You will get a chance to work with VMware Snapshot Manager in Chapter 3.

Early Microsoft virtualization products use undo disks to save machine states. When using an undo disk, all changes are kept in a separate file on the host computer until you shut down the virtual machine, at which time you're given a choice to apply the changes, continue to keep the changes separate, or delete all changes. Deleting all changes effectively returns the virtual machine to its original state. Hyper-V uses a snapshot management system similar to VMware Workstation called checkpoints. Checkpoints enable you to keep multiple states of a virtual machine and then return to any saved state when necessary.

Parenting and Cloning

Virtual machine parenting, which enables you to have a master (parent) copy of a virtual machine that can be distributed to other users, is closely related to snapshots and undo disks. In VMware, the virtual machine created from the parent is called a linked clone. Users don't change the parent virtual machine's settings because all changes are written to a separate virtual disk file for the clone. Parenting can be useful in educational settings. For example, an instructor can create a parent machine for each chapter of a course. Students can then create a virtual machine clone for a chapter's Case Projectsby using the parent virtual machine as the source (see Figure 1-13). Using linked clones to share a standard VM environment is also very important to implementing a VDI environment. Without linked clones, storing virtual machines for 100s of users could take a tremendous amount of disk space. Using linked clones, only a limited number of parent VMs can be shared by many users while keeping the changes and settings that are unique for each user in the small linked clone files. You will learn how to work with linked clones to support VDI in later chapters.

Similar to clones, templates are an important virtualization feature to rapidly deploy fully configured virtual machines. The main difference between a template and a clone is that the clone is a running VM and the template is not. Templates are molds that contain a preconfigured, preloaded VM that can be used to "stamp" out copies of a commonly used server or virtual desktop. Virtualization software that support templates have a check box filter on a virtual machine that allows the administrator flag the VM as a template. Virtual machines that are flagged as templates cannot be run, but they can be used to create new VMs with all the features included in the template. If you need to change the template's configuration you first remove the template flag, launch the virtual machine, make any changes to the software or hardware configuration, and then reflag the machine as a template. You will learn how to work with templates to create virtual machines in later chapters.

Moving Virtual Machines

An important advantage of using virtual machines is the ability to move a virtual machine to another host, even if that host is using a different hardware and a different operating system.

If using the same hypervisor, moving a virtual machine can be as simple as copying the virtual machine files from one host computer to the other. Moving VMs between different hypervisor brands requires using a compatible file format. If you plan to move virtual

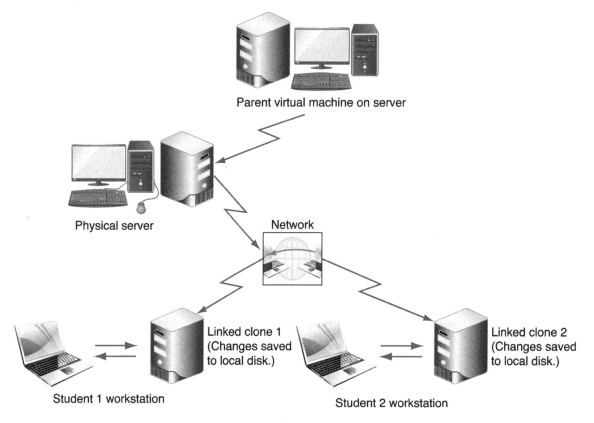

Figure 1-13 Linking clones of virtual machines with VMware

machines between hosts you should be sure the virtualization software you choose supports exporting and importing VMs by using the **Open Virtualization Format (OVF)**. OVF is a standard created by industry-wide vendors in various areas of virtualization for the purpose of copying or moving virtual machines between different platforms. For example, you could install, configure, and test a Windows mail server on a workbench using Oracle VM Virtual-Box. After developing your Windows mail server using VirtualBox, you can use the export function to create a set of OVF files. You next use vSphere's option to import OVF files to place the virtual machine on your vSphere Hypervisor (ESXi). The OVF format is also often used to distribute virtual appliances. After developing the virtual appliance you can export the corresponding VM to a set of OVF files. The files can then be encapsulated into an archive and distributed with an OVF extension. Once the mail server is properly configured, you could use the export and import features to move the virtual machine containing the server, and any application software, to a host running VMware vSphere. Once running on the vSphere hypervisor (ESXi) you could assign additional hardware resources to the virtual machine such as more memory, storage, and even an additional vCPU.

The ability to move virtual machines between hosts can also be a major factor in providing high availability. VMware was the first virtualization company to support live migration of a running VM from one host to another using a process they called vMotion. Live migration of a VM requires that both hosts have the same CPU and hypervisor version. Another high availability process pioneered by VMware allows a VM to be automatically restarted on another host in the event the primary host crashes or is brought down for maintenance. High availability and live migration are now features that are available on both Xen and Hyper-V platforms. When selecting a server virtualization platform it is important to assess your high availability needs and select a virtualization platform that best supports them. You will learn more about implementing high availability and live migration in later chapters.

Network Support

With virtualization software, a virtual machine can have one or more simulated network adapters (NICs), depending on the virtualization product. As shown in Figure 1-14, a virtual network adapter can be configured in a number of ways, including bridged, local, or shared (NAT). You can think of each network mode as being a separate switch (or hub) to which you can connect the virtual machine's NIC.

When a virtual machine is in **local mode** (called **"host-only mode"** in VMware), its emulated NIC is plugged into a virtual switch that includes the host computer and other virtual machines running in local mode on the host computer. For example, in Figure 1-14, virtual machine VM2 and the host computer communicate by using a common IP address scheme on the local switch. If another virtual machine, such as VM1 or VM3, is configured to use the local switch, it can also communicate with VM2 and the host computer.

In Figure 1-14, VM1 uses **bridged mode** through its attachment to the bridged switch. Because the bridged switch includes the host computer's physical NIC, VM1 can use the network's IP address scheme to communicate with all devices on the local network and access other networks, including the Internet, as though it were a separate computer attached to the local network. You can use the administrative console to change a virtual network adapter's connection to any switch, even while the virtual machine is running.

Because communicating directly on the virtual network can cause network problems when you're running test servers or if virtual machines are configured incorrectly, bridged mode is often discouraged in testing environments. In addition, local mode doesn't allow connections to outside networks, such as the Internet. **Shared (NAT) mode**, however, allows access to outside networks yet isolates the virtual machine, preventing it from sending and receiving packets across the physical network. This mode uses a virtual switch running **Network Address Translation (NAT)** to convert packets coming from the virtual machine to use the host computer's IP address. The result is that all network traffic coming from the virtual machine seems as though it's originating from the host computer. The virtualization software on the host computer acts like a router, taking requests from outside networks and passing them to the virtual network, using the IP address assigned to the physical NIC. When a virtual machine is connected to a shared (NAT) switch, the Dynamic Host Configuration Protocol (DHCP) service running on the host computer automatically assigns the virtual machine a private IP address and gateway configuration to send packets to the host computer.

Data center virtualization products such as vSphere and Hyper-V Server allow you to create virtual switches for a variety of purposes. A virtual switch works like a physical switch except that it can have an almost limitless number of ports. You will learn more

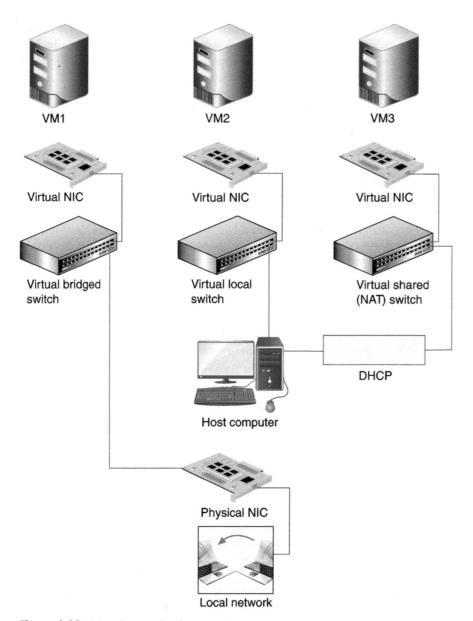

Figure 1-14 Virtual network adapter options

about creating and managing virtual adapters and switches for data center virtualization in Chapter 4.

Migration Tools

Most virtualization packages offer migration tools for importing virtual machine files from other sources and creating a virtual machine environment based on a physical computer. Being able to create virtual machines from physical computers has many benefits, including saving time when converting users to virtual machines and creating backups of existing systems before an upgrade. After the upgrade, users can still access applications, and you can save time because you don't have to build a virtual machine from scratch and set up all the user applications.

VMware Converter, available as a free download, runs on a wide variety of hardware and software platforms. The free version is limited to single machine conversions, but an enterprise version is also available. VMware Converter Enterprise requires purchasing a license, but it's useful for managing and automating large-scale conversions. With the free version, you can do the following:

- Convert local and remote physical computers into virtual machines without any disruption or downtime.
- Perform multiple conversions simultaneously with a centralized management console and an easy-to-use wizard.
- Convert other virtual machine formats or backup images of physical machines (such as Symantec Backup Exec LiveState Recovery or Ghost 9) to VMware virtual machines.
- Clone and back up physical machines to virtual machines as part of your disaster recovery plan.

In the past, Microsoft offered free downloads of its Disk2VHD and Virtual Machine Converter (MVMC) tools to convert a physical server to a VM or to simplify migrating other virtual machine types to Hyper-V. Today Microsoft offers similar services through its Azure Web site.

Additional Options for Virtual Machines

Virtualization software often has options for installing additional tools on a virtual machine. VMware calls these optional additions VMware Tools, and Microsoft Hyper-V refers to them as Integration Services. Table 1-5 lists features in both products.

Table 1-5   Additional virtual machine options

Feature	Description	Product
Shared folders	Makes folders on the host computer available to a virtual machine	VMware Workstation, Oracle VirtualBox, Hyper-V
Mouse and keyboard integration	Allows moving the mouse between a virtual machine and the host computer without using a key combination	VMware Workstation, Oracle VirtualBox, Hyper-V
Time synchronization	Synchronizes the virtual machine's time with the host computer's clock	VMware Workstation, Hyper-V
Optimized video drivers	Increases video resolution on the virtual machine	VMware Workstation, Hyper-V, VirtualBox
Drag and drop	Used to copy files between the virtual machine and host computer	VMware Workstation, Oracle VirtualBox, Hyper-V
Enhanced performance	Adds features that improve the virtual machine's performance—for example, drivers that provide faster access to system resources, such as the video display	VMware Workstation, Oracle VirtualBox, Hyper-V

(continues)

Table 1-5   Additional virtual machine options (*continued*)

Feature	Description	Product
Linked clones	Allows a parent VM to be shared by multiple users; each user's changes are kept separate in the clone file	VMware Workstation, Hyper-V, VMware vSphere
Snapshots	Allows a virtual machine to be saved and then restored to the saved state at a future time	VMware Workstation, Oracle VirtualBox, Hyper-V

Because these optional tools run on the virtual machine's OS, they are operating system-specific. Microsoft and VMware include tools for both Windows and Linux systems (although installation on Linux systems can be trickier).

Comparing and Downloading Virtualization Products

With the variety of virtualization products and features available, selecting the best virtualization solution can be a challenge. In addition to choosing the features you want, other factors include costs, system requirements, level of support, and familiarity with the software. Table 1-6 shows the system requirements for VMware and Microsoft virtualization products.

Table 1-6   Personal workstation virtualization product system requirements

Product	Software	CPU	Memory	Disk
VMware Workstation 12 Player	Windows 7 and later Linux	64-bit Host OS Standard Intel or AMD processors Recommended: 64-bit x86 Intel Core Solo Processor or equivalent or AMD Athlon 64 FX Dual Core Processor or equivalent 1.3GHz speed or faster.	2 GB RAM minimum / 4 GB RAM and above recommended 3 GB RAM for Windows Aero Graphics	1.2 GB for installation plus disk space for each guest VM
VMware Workstation 12 Player	Windows XP and later Linux	Intel Dual Core 2.2GHz or later CPU or AMD Athlon 4200+ or later CPU	2 GB RAM minimum	1 GB for installation plus space needed to store all VMs
VMware Fusion	Macintosh	64-bit Intel Mac with minimum of Core 2 Duo or Xeon I3 or higher processor recommended	4 GB RAM	750 MB free disk to install

Table 1-6 **Personal workstation virtualization product system requirements (*continued*)**

Product	Software	CPU	Memory	Disk
Hyper-V	Windows 8 Professional or later	64-bit Host OS Standard Intel or AMD processors	2 GB RAM	2 GB for installation plus space needed to store all VMs
Oracle VirtualBox	Windows 7 or later	64-bit Host OS Standard Intel or AMD processors.	1 GB RAM	

A major requirement for running virtualization software is having a lot of RAM and disk space on the host computer. The minimum amount of RAM for installing virtualization software is shown in Table 1-6. In addition, you need at least 1 GB RAM to run a Windows 10 virtual machine, 512 MB RAM for SUSE Linux, and 2 GB RAM for Windows Server, for example. The more memory you have, the better your virtual machines will perform.

If you are using a spinning hard drive you can sometimes increase speed by defragmenting the host computer's hard drive. Defragmenting improves performance by placing all disk sectors belonging to the virtual disk file in one area of the physical hard drive. You learn more about improving virtual machine performance in later chapters.

The following sections give you a brief overview of the virtualization software covered in this book. You also download files to use when installing these products in later chapters. Before you begin, create a folder called Downloads (or another similar name) on your C drive to store virtualization software, if you haven't done so already. As noted in the activities, you should also create separate subfolders for each virtualization product you download.

 The steps in this chapter's activities are based on the software vendors' Web sites at the time of this writing. Selections and options will vary if these sites change. If necessary, you can search for the **NOTE** product name, and then follow the prompts to download the software. In addition, to save download times, your instructor might have already downloaded these installation files to your classroom network. Check with your instructor before starting these activities.

Downloading VMware Products

VMware offers both VMware Workstation 12 and VMware Workstation 12 Player as type-2 hypervisor products. VMware Workstation 12 Player comes in both free and paid versions. The free version works well for creating and working with basic virtual machines and running virtual appliances, but has more limited configuration options. You can learn more about setting up and using VMware Workstation 12 Player in Appendix B. VMware Workstation 12 offers improved performance and new features not available in the VMware Workstation Player virtualization products, such as the capability to run a variety of guest Oss, advanced snapshot capability, teaming, and advanced network options. It's intended for software developers, testers, and students to run multiple OSs simultaneously on a single computer. VMware Workstation features include the following:

- Built-in support for most guest OSs, including Linux, Novell NetWare, and 64-bit OSs

- Snapshot Manager for taking and managing snapshots so that you can return to a saved state at any time
- Being able to capture screens from virtual machines or creating a movie consisting of multiple screenshots
- Unity view for separating applications from a virtual machine so that they run in the host OS without the VMware interface being apparent
- Teams of virtual machines connected across a LAN
- The capability to create a virtual machine from a physical computer
- Being able to map drive letters from the host computer to a virtual hard disk for disk and file access while the virtual machine is shut down
- Support for multiple monitors
- Designed to integrate with Visual Studio to develop, test, and debug applications

If you're a professional developer or run a help desk and need a full-featured workstation virtualization product that supports Linux and Novell NetWare, the latest version of VMware Workstation might be your best option. At the time of this writing, you can get a 30-day trial copy.

In the following activities you will log on to your VMware customer account and then download the VMware Workstation installation file. Your customer account will allow you to do the following:

- Manage license keys
- Download products
- Manage Subscription Services
- Manage My VMware Users & Permissions
- Evaluate products
- Interact with VMware experts in Communities
- Contact VMware Support
- Search the Knowledge Base
- Purchase products and services from our online store

Activity 1-3: Downloading VMware Workstation 12

Time Required: 15 minutes

Objective: Download VMware Workstation 12.

Description: In this activity, you download VMware Workstation 12 for Windows and get a 30-day trial serial number.

1. If necessary, log on to your host computer.

2. Start File Explorer, navigate to your Downloads folder, and click **New Folder** to create a folder named "**VMware Products.**"

3. Start your Web browser, go to www.vmware.com, and Point to Login, then click **MyVMware.** Enter your email address and password and click the **Log In** button.

4. Click the **Start New Eval** button to view the Evaluate VMware Products page and notice the various categories of virtualization products available for evaluation. You will be working with some of these products in later chapters.

 Your instructor may supply you with the VMware Workstation files on shared or removable media. If this is the case, you may skip steps 5–10.

5. Under the Personal Desktop heading, click the **VMware Workstation Pro** link to display the Download VMware Workstation Pro Trial page.

6. Click the **Download Now** button located near the VMware Workstation # Pro (where # represents the version number) for Windows 64-bit heading.

7. If requested to do so, click the pull down arrow on the **Save** button and then click **Save as**. Navigate to the VMware Products folder and click the **Save** button to download the file.

8. When the download is complete, return to the Evaluate VMware Products page.

9. When you've finished downloading the files, Point to Login, then click **My VMware** in the upper right of the page.

10. Point to your name located in the upper right section of the page and notice your customer number is displayed. Click the **Logout** link from the pull down menu to log off.

11. You can leave your browser open for the next activity.

Downloading Oracle VirtualBox

Oracle is best known for its database software, but the software giant also provides a number of other software solutions including virtualization products. The free Oracle VirtualBox workstation virtualization software has become quite popular due to its complete line of features and the variety of host platforms it supports. Although it's not as full featured as VMware Workstation, Oracle VirtualBox contains many important features and is free and easy to use. For example, VirtualBox includes a number of disk and network options similar to VMware snapshots and cloning. In this activity you will download a copy of VirtualBox along with the corresponding documentation. You learn more about VirtualBox and other Oracle product features in Chapter 2.

Activity 1-4: Downloading Oracle VirtualBox Files

Time Required: 15 minutes

Objective: Download Oracle VirtualBox and documentation file.

Description: Follow these steps to download the installation file for the Oracle VirtualBox software.

1. If necessary, start your Web browser, and then go to **http://www.oracle.com**.

2. Point to the **Products** link and then click the **Virtualization** option to display the Oracle Virtualization page.

3. Click the **Products** tab.

4. Click the Products heading to the right of the Overview heading. Under Desktop Virtualization Products heading, click the **Oracle VM VirtualBox** link to display the Oracle VM VirtualBox page.

5. Click the **Data Sheet (PDF)** link and read the product features. Click the browser's **Save As** link. Navigate to your Downloads folder and click **New folder** to create a folder named "**Oracle Products.**"

6. Click the **Save** button to save the Data Sheet page. After the save is complete, close the Data Sheet page and return to the Oracle VM VirtualBox page.

 Your instructor may supply you with the Oracle VirtualBox files on shared or removable media. If this is the case, you may skip steps 7–10.

7. Click the **Download** button and then click the **Oracle VM VirtualBox** link to display the Platform list.

8. Click the **Windows Installer** link to the right of the Windows (32-bit/64-bit) platform. From the Save drop down menu, select the **Save As** option.

9. If necessary, navigate to the Oracle Products folder you created in step 5 and click the **Save** button to download the file. Depending on the browser you are using, the download may be placed in the Downloads folder by default. If this is the case, you can later move the file to the Oracle Products folder you created in step 5.

10. When the download is complete, return to your browser home page.

11. Enter the URL **www.virtualbox.org** to display the Oracle VirtualBox welcome window.

12. Click the **End-user docs** link under the Documentation heading and then click the **User Manual** link located under the User manual heading to display a download page. You can use this page to download the product or documentation manual.

13. Under the User Manual heading click the **User Manual** link (not the (HTML version) to download an English copy in PDF format.

14. Click the Browser's **Save as** option. If necessary navigate to your Oracle Products folder and then click the **Save** button to download the PDF manual.

15. Close the User Manual page and any other windows to then return your browser to your home page.

16. You have now completed all the activities in this chapter and may now close your browser and log out of your Windows 10 workstation.

Microsoft Hyper-V

Hyper-V is Microsoft's latest virtualization product and comes in both client and server versions. Hyper-V is a type-1 hypervisor because it runs directly on the hardware. When you install Hyper-V on either a Windows workstation or server, the setup program converts the original OS into a partition something like a VM and puts the hypervisor below it at the hardware layer. Because of this you experience the same speed in the "real machine" and the virtual machines. Hyper-V is available with Professional versions of Windows 8 and later as well as all 64-bit versions of Windows Server 2012 and later. In addition, Microsoft has a stand-alone version requiring no host OS (see Appendix B). Hyper-V runs as a service that can be managed through standard Microsoft Management Consoles (MMCs) for both user and administrative consoles. You will learn more about working with Hyper-V in Chapters 5 and 6.

Acquiring Windows Server 2016 To do the activities in this book, you need both virtualization software and Windows Server 2016 to use as both a Hyper-V host and as a guest OS. Server software tends to be expensive, and although some schools and businesses can get unlimited free licenses for Windows Server through a subscription to Microsoft's MSDN or DreamSpark program, there are legitimate ways to acquire Windows Server 2016 at no cost. You can download a free trial version from the Microsoft Web site that runs for 60 days before requiring activation.

Microsoft also documents a method for pushing the activation time beyond 60 days, which gives you more time to complete the activities in this book. If you're a student with a valid school email address, you can get a free license for Windows Server 2016 through the Microsoft DreamSpark program at *https://www.dreamspark.com*, which is enough for most activities in this book. Keep in mind that this version is limited to a single license for installing a virtual machine.

Chapter Summary

- Virtualization software provides a separate emulated hardware environment on a host computer. It runs in the host computer's OS to create emulated computer environments called virtual machines, also referred to as guest systems.

- A special software layer called the hypervisor allows guest virtual machines to share the hardware environment of the host computer.

- Hypervisors can be classified as either type-1 or type-2. Type-1 hypervisors run directly on the computer hardware without the need for a general purpose operating system. Type-2 hypervisors run on top of another operating system such as Windows or Linux. Type-2 hypervisors are not as fast as type-1, but provide more flexibility for developers.

- With hardware virtualization, virtualization is built into processors, which improves the performance of virtualization software designed to work with these enhancements.

- Virtualization software can be classified as workstation, data center, Virtual Desktop Infrastructure (VDI), or cloud based.

- Workstation virtualization software is intended to support desktop OSs and includes products such as VMware Workstation, VMware vSphere, Microsoft Hyper-V, and Oracle VirtualBox. You can run multiple OSs on a single machine without dual-booting, and workstation virtualization software is also useful for help desk support, classroom training, and software development.

- Data center software reduces server sprawl by consolidating several specialized servers into one physical computer. Other benefits include reduced hardware costs, server clustering, and improved disaster recovery. Current server virtualization products include VMware vSphere and Microsoft Hyper-V.

- Application virtualization enables you to run different software versions on the same host computer. Current products include VMware ThinApp, and Altiris Software Virtualization Solution (SVS).

- Virtual Desktop Infrastructure (VDI) uses virtual machines to provide users with a remote desktop environment that can be available from many devices and locations, yet can be centrally maintained and managed.

- The cloud has come to represent services that are available across the Internet using either public or private data centers. Common cloud services can be classified as Infrastructure as a Service (IaaS), Platform as a Service (PaaS), or Software as a Service (SaaS) depending on the level of service provided.

- Virtualization software has both user and administrative consoles. The user console displays the guest OS interface, and the administrative console is used for configuring virtual machine settings and managing operations.

- Hypervisors use a number of sophisticated technologies to manage the memory of the host computer. Common technologies for most of today's hypervisors include SLAT, shadow page tables, ballooning, and overcommitment.

- Contention for physical memory can slow virtual machine performance. The best way to enhance virtual machine performance is to increase the amount of RAM on the host computer.

- Virtual disk options include the type of hard drive emulation (SCSI or IDE), hard drive size, and whether the disk file is fixed or dynamic. Fixed-size disks provide faster performance, but dynamic disks can grow as needed and use less disk space on the host computer.

- Special features in most virtualization software include saving a virtual machine state for returning it to a specific point in time, parenting/cloning for basing a new virtual machine on a "parent," networking, and additional tools for virtual machines.

- Virtualization software allows you to emulate network adapters for virtual machines. Configuration options include local (host-only), shared (NAT), or bridged.

- Additional tools can be installed on a guest OS to add capabilities such as mouse and keyboard integration and shared folders.

- VMware Workstation is a workstation virtualization product with features for running and managing virtual workstation environments, including snapshots and cloning.

- vSphere is a data center virtualization product that optimizes virtual server performance. VMware's vSphere Hypervisor, also known as ESXi, contains its own Linux kernel for improved performance and is available in free and licensed versions.

- Hyper-V is Microsoft's latest server virtualization software that ships with Windows Server 2008 and later (although a stand-alone version is available, too, if you're not running Server). Hyper-V is designed to take advantage of new processors with built-in virtualization and is efficient when used to virtualize Server environments.

Key Terms

ballooning	linked clones	shadow page table
bare metal hypervisor	local mode/host-only mode	shared (NAT) mode
bridged mode	memory overcommitment	Storage Area Network (SAN)
configuration file	Network Address Translation (NAT)	thick client
Data Execution Prevention		thin client
dynamic virtual disk	Network Attached Storage (NAS)	type-1 hypervisor
fixed-size virtual disk		type-2 hypervisor
hardware virtualization	Open Virtualization Format (OVF)	virtual appliance
host computer		virtual desktop
hyperthreading	Second Level Address Translation (SLAT)	virtual disk file
hypervisor		virtual machine
ISO image file	server sprawl	

Review Questions

1. When using virtualization software to run a virtual machine, the virtual machine's hard disk is which of the following?

   a. A separate partition of the host computer's hard drive

   b. A folder on the host OS

   c. A specially formatted file on the host computer's hard drive

   d. Stored in the virtualization software in a hidden directory

2. Virtualization software runs within the OS of a physical computer that's referred to as which of the following?

   a. Guest computer

   b. Host computer

   c. Type-1 hypervisor

   d. Type-2 hypervisor

3. Which of the following is the most important limit on the number of virtual machines you can run at once on a physical computer?

   a. Amount of RAM

   b. Amount of hard drive space

   c. Speed of the host computer's processor

   d. Version of Windows you're using

4. Virtual machines are managed by using which of the following?

   a. Control Panel on the host computer

   b. Control Panel on the guest system

   c. An administrative console provided by the virtualization software package

   d. A configuration file

5. Which of the following virtualization products requires purchasing a license?

   a. Oracle VirtualBox

   b. Hyper-V

   c. VMware Workstation

   d. VMware Workstation Player

6. Accumulating many specialized servers in an organization is often referred to as which of the following?

   a. Server virtualization

   b. Server sprawl

   c. Server deployment

   d. Server decentralization

7. Which of the following allows installing multiple versions of Microsoft Office concurrently on a single desktop?

   a. VMware Workstation

   b. VMware ThinApp

   c. Microsoft Hyper-V

   d. Hardware virtualization software

8. Which of the following virtualization features provides security by preventing the CPU from executing certain instructions?

   a. Hardware virtualization

   b. NX/XD feature

   c. SLAT feature

   d. Dual cores

9. Which of the following virtualization products are data center oriented? (Choose all that apply.)

   a. Microsoft Hyper-V

   b. Oracle VirtualBox

   c. VMware vSphere

   d. VMware Workstation

10. Virtual machine performance can be enhanced by which of the following? (Choose all that apply.)

    a. Adding physical memory to the host computer

    b. Deleting unused virtual machines

    c. Installing a larger hard drive

    d. Using hardware virtualization

11. Which of the following virtualization features allows you to select a saved virtual machine state you want to return to? (Choose all that apply.)

    a. VMware Teams

    b. Snapshots

    c. Undo Disks

    d. Linked clones

12. Which of the following is a file format used to store an image of a CD?

    a. CDR

    b. ISO

    c. WinISO

    d. VCD

13. Which of the following virtual disk types provides the best performance but uses more physical disk space?

    a. Fixed-size

    b. Dynamic

    c. Relative

    d. Physical

14. Which of the following is a virtualization feature commonly used with VDI to reduce the disk space required to host many user virtual desktops? (Choose all that apply.)

    a. Snapshots

    b. Undo disks

    c. Nonpersistent disks

    d. Linked Clones

15. Which of the following network options allows connecting a virtual machine to the Internet without accessing the local network directly?

   a. Shared (NAT)

   b. Local

   c. Bridged

   d. Host only

16. Which of the following products is intended to support VDI?

   a. Hyper-V

   b. VMware Workstation

   c. VMware Horizon

   d. vSphere

17. Which of the following products is used for application virtualization? (Choose all that apply)

   a. VMware ESX Server

   b. Microsoft Hyper-V

   c. VMware ThinApp

   d. Microsoft App-V

18. How are VMware Tools and Microsoft Integration Services added to your virtualization software?

   a. Installed on the host OS

   b. Installed on the guest OS

   c. Added to virtualization hypervisor as a product update

   d. Selected as an option when installing the virtualization software package

19. Which of the following service types supports application running in the cloud?

   a. SaaS

   b. PaaS

   c. IaaS

   d. Hybrid service (HS)

20. Which type of cloud would you use if you wanted to host a Web-based order system but needed additional capacity during peak loads?

   a. Public cloud

   b. Private cloud

   c. Extended private cloud

   d. Hybrid cloud

Case Projects

CASE PROJECTS

Case Project 1-1: Identifying Virtualization Software Features

Using the information in this chapter, fill in the following table of features for each virtualization package:

	VMware Workstation	Oracle VirtualBox	Microsoft Hyper-V
Support for SCSI virtual disks			
Support for ISO image files			
Support for USB devices			
Support for saving machine state			
Support for multiple snapshots			
Support for parenting/ cloning			
Support for shared (NAT) networking			
Support for bridged networking			
Support for teams			
Support for additional virtual machine tools			
Support for non-Windows guest systems			
Support for 64-bit guest OSs			
Requires a 64-bit processor			
Requires each virtual machine OS to have its own license			

Case Project 1-2: Selecting a Virtualization Product for Classroom Use

Superior Technical College's IT Department is planning to use virtual machines in its computer lab. Instructors want to place parent copies of preset computer environments on the classroom server for each unit in a course. Students should be able to build a virtual machine from the parent and then use it for their work in that unit. At the end of the unit, students submit changes they have made, and instructors use students' changes to give them credit for the unit. The lab computers are limited in terms of memory and CPU capability, so instructors are interested in the use of VDI and think clients for the student computers. The college has asked you to recommend a virtualization product and explain how this environment could be set up. Write a brief report recommending a virtualization product and explaining the reasons for your recommendation.

Case Project 1-3: Reducing Server Sprawl

The IT Department at Universal AeroSpace uses three Windows Server 2016 servers: one for the Accounting Department, one for engineering, and one for the Marketing Department. These servers are running on separate systems that are aging and don't have the capability for future expansion. The IT Department wants to purchase new hardware and upgrade to Windows Server 2016. To save costs, they would like to use virtualization to consolidate their servers and provide for high-availability in the event of a hardware failure. As a consultant for Computer Technology Services, you have been asked to write a report that includes which data center virtualization product you recommend and why.

Case Project 1-4: Selecting a VDI Service

The Universal AeroSpace company is planning to implement data center virtualization using VMware vSphere and two Windows servers with a large SAN disk system. Management would like to host applications on the Web to allow staff and students to access technical information from any location using a variety of devices. Because the IT Department is located in a different city, they need to access the virtual server's administrative console remotely. As a consultant for Computer Technology Services, you have been asked to write a report that includes the benefits of using VDI and which VDI product you recommend and why. The report should include a diagram showing the VDI components that will be needed.

Case Project 1-5: Selecting a Cloud Service

Rocky Ridge Enterprises currently uses desktops in a peer-to-peer network to share files and a printer. Management wants to implement a server-based IT system that uses Active Directory and provides more features and security than currently available on the peer-to-peer network. They would also like to have some of this information available online to sales people while on the road. Since they are not sure of their longer term needs, they want to hold their hardware costs to a minimum. Write a recommendation of which type of service you would recommend along with any reasons for making this recommendation.

chapter 2

Working with Oracle VM VirtualBox 5

After reading this chapter and completing the exercises, you will be able to:

- Install Oracle VM VirtualBox 5
- Work with menu options in VirtualBox Manager
- Work with virtual machines in VirtualBox

Since 2007, Oracle has offered a number of virtualization products that they have both acquired and developed. Getting a later start, Oracle virtualization products do not have as large of a market share as VMware or Microsoft, but they have strong support in organizations that are heavy users of Oracle database software. To help support these database needs, Oracle has tuned its virtualization products to be more application oriented. In this chapter we will introduce you to VirtualBox for the desktop. To learn more about other Oracle virtualization products, such as VM Server and Virtual Desktop Infrastructure, see Appendix C.

Installing VirtualBox

VirtualBox includes many of the same features as commercial applications such as VMware Workstation and has the advantage of being free and easy to use. In this chapter, you learn how to install and configure this program and use it to create and work with virtual machines. Installing VirtualBox in Windows is fairly straightforward. However, before beginning, make sure your host computer meets or exceeds the recommended hardware and software requirements listed in Chapter 1. To summarize, VirtualBox requires a recent Intel or AMD x86 CPU; hardware virtualization support is recommended but not required. It requires at least 30 MB disk space and 512 MB of RAM. You should also check memory and disk space requirements for the running guest OSs and add these requirements to the host OS requirements.

Installing VirtualBox in Windows 10

Before installing VirtualBox, you need the setup file (downloaded in Chapter 1). VirtualBox can be installed on Windows XP and newer operating systems, either 32-bit or 64-bit. It will also run on Mac OS X and Linux. It can run virtual machines for almost all Windows OSs as well as Linux. In the following activity, you install VirtualBox on your computer.

Activity 2-1: Installing VirtualBox

Time Required: Approximately 5 minutes

Objective: Install VirtualBox on your host computer.

Description: Superior Technical College is planning to use virtual machines in the general-purpose computer lab so that students can study different operating systems without affecting their desktop computers. The college has elected to use VirtualBox because of its free license. Students can also install VirtualBox on their home computers or laptops to work on projects outside class. As the consultant for this project, you need to gain experience in installing and working with VirtualBox.

1. If necessary, log on to your host computer with your administrative username and password.

2. Open Windows Explorer, and navigate to the folder containing the setup file you downloaded in Chapter 1.

3. Double-click the **VirtualBox-xxxxxx-Win.exe** file to start the VirtualBox Setup Wizard. In the wizard's welcome window, click **Next**.

4. Next you will choose the features to be installed, such as USB and networking support. All options are selected by default, click **Next**.

5. You can choose to create icons for VirtualBox on your desktop or in the Quick Launch Bar and also create file associations so VirtualBox will start automatically when a virtual machine is double-clicked. All options are selected by default, click **Next**.

6. You will receive a warning message that you will temporarily be disconnected from the network during installation, for example aborting any files currently downloading. Once it is safe to proceed, click **Yes**.

7. Click **Install** to begin the installation. The status bar displays the installation progress. If the User Account Control (UAC) message box opens, click **Yes**. In the wizard's welcome window, click **Next**.

8. You may receive a warning about installing device software, such as the "Oracle Corporation Universal Serial Bus." Click **Install**.

9. When the installation is completed, click to uncheck the **Start Oracle VM VirtualBox** check box and then click **Finish**. Stay logged on for the next activity.

Creating a Virtual Machine

After installing VirtualBox, one of your first tasks is creating a virtual machine environment for each guest OS you want to install. You can start the Create Virtual Machine wizard by clicking the New toolbar icon or using the Machine menu in the VirtualBox Manager, explained later in "Working with the VirtualBox Manager."

- *Name*—The name of your virtual machine as it will appear in list in the VirtualBox manager. It should be descriptive, such as "Windows Server 2016 – Domain Controller," in order to show its purpose and differentiate it from other virtual machines. Multiple virtual machines with similar generic names can become confusing.

- *Type*—The operating system type, such as Microsoft Windows, Linux, or Mac OS X. Operating systems will be grouped by type in the VirtualBox Manager.

- *Version*—VirtualBox will customize the virtual machine settings based on which OS version you will install, for example Windows 7. You can choose between 32-bit and 64-bit versions, or choose Other if the version is not listed, such as an upcoming operating system.

Next, the memory size is displayed. VirtualBox will recommend the amount of memory for the virtual machine based on the version selected in the previous step. To adjust the amount of allocated memory, you use the slider bar or enter the specific amount in megabytes. Be sure to leave enough free memory so the host computer performance is not degraded while the virtual machine is running.

The Hard disk window, as shown in Figure 2-1, is displayed with three options used to configure the virtual machine's hard disk.

- *Do not add a virtual hard disk*—A virtual machine can be created without a hard disk; however, it will only be able to boot from a virtual optical disc or from the network. A disk can be added at a later time.

- *Create a virtual hard disk now*—This will create a new virtual hard disk file. See "Creating a Virtual Hard Disk File" below for more details.

- *Use an existing virtual hard disk file*—This will reuse a previously created virtual hard disk. You can choose one VirtualBox remembers from the dropdown list or click the browse button to locate one.

The size of the hard disk is recommended by VirtualBox based on the operating system to be installed.

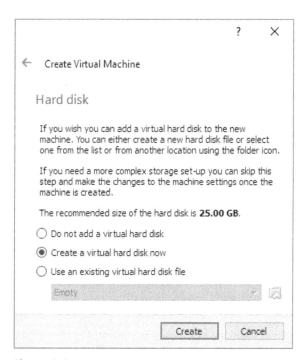

Figure 2-1   The Hard disk window

Source: Oracle Virtual VM VirtualBox 5.0

Creating a Virtual Hard Disk File

When creating a new virtual hard disk file, you will be prompted to choose the file type as shown in Figure 2-2. By default, VirtualBox will use the "VirtualBox Disk Image" format, or VDI. It can also create files compatible with other virtualization software, such as VMDK files from VMware or VHD files from Microsoft.

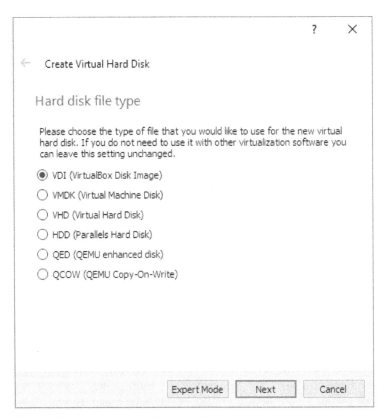

Figure 2-2   The Hard disk file type window

Source: Oracle Virtual VM VirtualBox 5.0

The next step is how the file size should be allocated, as shown in Figure 2-3. The first choice is a **dynamically allocated** hard disk file, which will start out small and grow as is needed up to the maximum specified size. For example, a 20 GB dynamic hard disk with 10 GB of data will only consume 10 GB on the host computer. However, the file will not shrink and will still be 10 GB even if 5 GB of data is deleted.

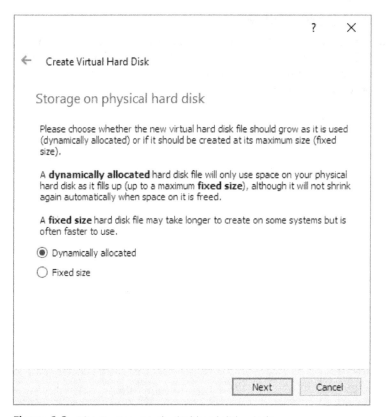

Figure 2-3   The Storage on physical hard disk window

Source: Oracle Virtual VM VirtualBox 5.0

The second choice is a **fixed size** hard disk file, which will immediately consume the full size of the virtual hard disk on your host. Because of this it will take longer to create, but has the advantage of speed over a dynamic hard disk.

Finally the location and size of the virtual hard disk is chosen. The default name of the disk file will be the same as the virtual machine name, but an alternate filename and save location can be chosen. You can change the size of the virtual hard disk from the recommended default by moving the slider or typing in a new size.

The virtual machine will then be created and the wizard will close. You will return to the VirtualBox Manager, where the new virtual machine is now listed.

Activity 2-2: Creating a Virtual Machine for Windows Server 2016

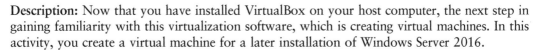

Time Required: Approximately 10 minutes

Objective: Create a new virtual machine.

Description: Now that you have installed VirtualBox on your host computer, the next step in gaining familiarity with this virtualization software, which is creating virtual machines. In this activity, you create a virtual machine for a later installation of Windows Server 2016.

1. If necessary, log on to your host computer with your administrative username and password.

2. Open the VirtualBox Manager by clicking **Start**, scrolling the All apps list to the **Oracle VM VirtualBox** folder, and then the **Oracle VM VirtualBox** icon.

3. Click the **New** toolbar icon, or click **Machine, New** from the menu.

4. In the Name and operating system window, type **Windows Server 2016** for the name. Choose **Microsoft Windows** for the type and **Windows 2012 (64 bit)** for the version.

5. In the Memory size window, type **2048** in the MB box on the right, if necessary, and then click **Next**.

6. In the Hard disk window, click the **Create a virtual hard disk now** option button. Record the recommended size of the hard disk below, and then click **Create**.

---

7. In the Hard disk file type window, click the **VDI (VirtualBox Disk Image)** option button, and then click **Next**.

8. In the Storage on physical hard disk window, click the **Dynamically allocated** option button, and then click **Next**.

9. In the File location and size window, verify the file name and location. Type **25** into the GB file size text box, and then click **Create**.

10. Your new virtual machine is then listed in the VirtualBox Manager with the status "Powered Off." Leave VirtualBox Manager open for the next activity.

Basic Virtual Machine Functions

There are two main ways to start a virtual machine: Click the Start button in the VirtualBox Manager, or double-click the VirtualBox Machine Definition file (.vbox extension) in Windows Explorer.

Before entering data into the guest OS, you need to click inside the virtual machine window to activate it and transfer keyboard and mouse control to the virtual machine. To switch control back to the host computer, press the **Host key**, which is Right Ctrl by default.

When a Windows Server OS starts, you're prompted to press Ctrl+Alt+Del to display the login dialog box. To prevent the host computer's Windows OS from intercepting this key combination, you can click the Input menu, Keyboard, Insert Ctrl+Alt+Del, or use the keyboard shortcut: Right Ctrl+Del.

If you want to use the full screen for a virtual machine, click the View menu, Full-screen Mode. In full-screen mode, you can't access the host computer. You can access the VirtualBox main menu bar by pressing Right Ctrl+Home. To switch out of full screen mode, press Right Ctrl+F.

In the VirtualBox Manager, you can end a virtual machine session in four ways:

- Click Pause from the Machine menu. Use this method when you want to suspend the virtual machine temporarily while you perform other tasks. Pausing the session frees up the processor and memory for other desktop applications. To resume the session, click the Machine menu and Pause again.

- Click Reset from the Machine menu. This option, which is similar to using the reset button on a physical computer, shuts down the virtual machine and performs a restart. You should use this option only when your virtual machine isn't responding because it could result in lost data or system corruption.

- Click ACPI Shutdown from the Machine menu. This will perform a safe and proper shutdown of the Windows guest OS, preventing any loss of data.

- Click the Close button to open a dialog box with "Save the machine state," "Send the shutdown signal," and "Power off the machine." The "Save the machine state" option is useful when you need to exit a virtual machine and don't want to restart the guest OS later; it saves memory and disk contents in their current states. The next time you start the virtual machine it will resume in the same place. The "Send the shutdown signal" option is similar to the ACPI Shutdown method above, it performs a safe shutdown of Windows. "Power off the machine" is similar to Reset above and should only be used when the virtual machine is locked up.

Installing a Guest OS

To work with a virtual machine, you need to install an OS. Installing a guest OS usually involves three main tasks. First, make sure the virtual machine is set to boot from an optical disc before the hard disk. The default boot order is Floppy, Optical, and then Hard Disk. This can be changed in the virtual machine's settings, as shown in Figure 2-4 and described in the upcoming "Working with the Machine Menu" section. A one-time boot device can also be chosen by pressing F12 within a few seconds of powering up the virtual machine.

The second task is to ensure that the optical device is connected to the virtual machine.

 Although OSs are often installed from physical media, in VirtualBox you can also use an ISO image file. ISO image files can be accessed from the host computer's hard drive or a shared network drive and act like physical CD/DVD media, so they're convenient in computer lab environments.

The first time a new virtual machine is started, the Select start-up disk wizard will appear as shown in Figure 2-5.

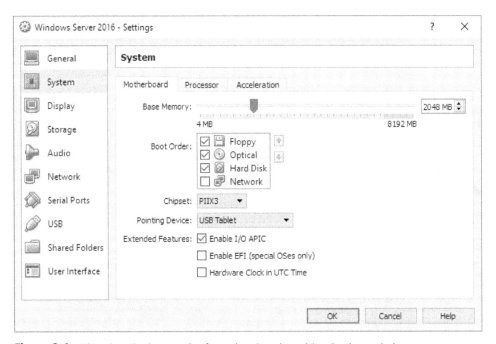

Figure 2-4   Choosing the boot order from the virtual machine Settings window

Source: Oracle Virtual VM VirtualBox 5.0

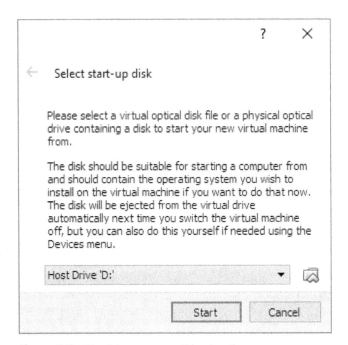

Figure 2-5   The Select start-up disk wizard

Source: Oracle Virtual VM VirtualBox 5.0

You can choose to install from either a physical disc on your host PC or an ISO image file. VirtualBox will provide a list of the physical drives available on the host and their drive letters. To choose an ISO image file instead, click the folder icon to right of the dropdown list and locate the file in the dialog box.

If the wizard is no longer available, the optical device can be changed while the virtual machine is powered down from the Machine menu under Settings, Storage, or the Device menu under Optical Drives on a running virtual machine.

Activity 2-3: Installing Windows Server 2016 as a Guest OS

Time Required: Approximately 30 minutes

Objective: Install Windows Server 2016 as a guest OS.

Description: You're giving a demonstration of using VirtualBox to run Windows Server 2016 on a virtual machine. In this activity, you prepare for the demonstration by installing Windows Server 2016 on the virtual machine you created in Activity 2-2.

1. If necessary, log on to your host computer with your administrative username and password and open the VirtualBox Manager.

2. Click **Windows Server 2016** in the VirtualBox Manager list, and then click the **Start** toolbar button.

3. In the Select start-up disk wizard, choose the appropriate drive letter if you have a physical Windows DVD to install from, otherwise click the icon to the right of the dropdown list to choose an ISO image instead and locate the file.

4. If the Select start-up disk wizard did not appear, click the **Devices** menu, point to **Optical Drives,** and click either **Host Drive** or **Choose disk image** as above. You will need to reset the virtual machine by clicking **Machine,** and then clicking **Reset.** (If prompted, click **Reset** in the confirmation box.)

5. Select settings for language, time and currency format, and keyboard or input method, and then click **Next.**

6. Click **Install now** in the next window.

7. In the Activate Windows window, enter your product key and click **Next.** If you currently don't have a product key, click the **I don't have a product key** link to continue the installation without one. You will be able to enter a product key at a later date.

8. In the Select the operating system you want to install window, you're prompted to choose the Windows Server 2016 edition. If you didn't enter a product key in the previous step, you will be shown both Standard and Datacenter editions, choose Standard. Click **Windows Server 2016 (Desktop Experience),** and then click **Next.**

9. In the License terms window, click the **I accept the license terms** check box, and then click **Next.**

10. In the Which type of installation do you want? window, click **Custom: Install Windows only (advanced).**

11. In the Where do you want to install Windows? window, verify that Drive 0 Unallocated Space is selected, then click **Next** to continue.

12. The Windows installation begins. Typically, the process takes around 15 minutes, and your virtual machine restarts at least once. When the installation is finished, you're prompted to create a password for the administrator account. (Make sure it's at least six characters, contains uppercase and lowercase letters, and includes a number or non-alphanumeric character.) Reenter it into the second password box, and then click **Finish.** Record your password below:

_____

13. Your Windows Server 2016 installation is finished. Log on to the server by using **Right Ctrl+Del** or clicking the **Input, Keyboard, Insert Ctrl+Alt+Del** menu option and entering the password you created in the previous step. Power off the virtual machine by clicking **Start,** followed by **Power, Shut down.** Choose Other (Planned) in the dropdown list and click **Continue.**

14. If you used the Start-up disk wizard and an ISO image, it will automatically be removed. If you choose an ISO manually, you can eject it by clicking the **Machine** menu and then **Settings.** Click **Storage,** then click the ISO image you're using from the Storage Tree. Click the disc icon under Attributes to display a new menu, and then click **Remove Disk from Virtual Drive.** Click **OK.**

15. Leave the VirtualBox Manager open for the next activity.

Working with the VirtualBox Manager

The VirtualBox Manager you have been working with is divided into three main areas (See Figure 2-6). At the top is the menu bar with File, Machine, and Help menus, as well as the toolbar with New, Settings, Discard, and Start icons. Below this on the left is a list of virtual machines that can be used within the manager. The right side contains either detailed information about the currently selected virtual machine, such as memory and attached storage, or its available snapshots.

Working with the Toolbar

The toolbar allows you to create a new virtual machine, and gives quick access to commonly used functions of the currently selected virtual machine.

- *New*—You can use this option to create a new virtual machine with the Create Virtual Machine wizard.

- *Settings*—This option opens the Settings window, where you configure settings like storage and network devices for a selected virtual machine. You will learn more about these settings in "Working with the Machine Menu."

- *Discard*—If a virtual machine was previously saved rather than shut down, this will allow you to discard that saved state and instead boot the virtual machine fresh rather than resuming where you left off.

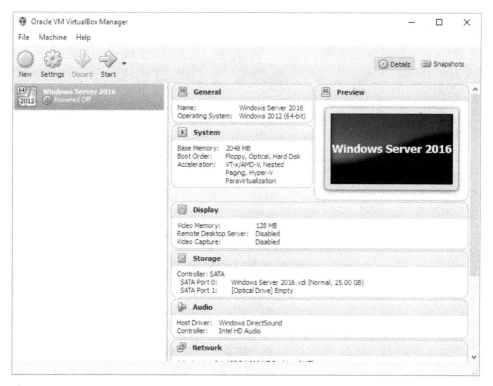

Figure 2-6 The VirtualBox Manager

Source: Oracle Virtual VM VirtualBox 5.0

- *Start*—Powers on the selected virtual machines. Clicking the arrow to the right of this button reveals a menu with three choices: Normal Start (the default), Headless Start, which starts the virtual machine but runs it in the background not displaying the virtual machine, and Detachable Start, which starts normally but gives the option when closing to continue running in the background.

Working with the File Menu

The File menu is mainly used to set global settings, import and export appliances, and manage virtual media images and network operations.

- *Preferences*—This option opens the VirtualBox - Preferences dialog box (see Figure 2-7), where you configure global settings that affect all virtual machines (listed in Table 2-1).

- *Import Appliance*—An appliance is a pre-made virtual machine in Open Virtualization Format (OVF). It will contain an operating system and pre-installed applications and will be ready to run immediately.

- *Export Appliance*—This option will export your virtual machine, with its operating system, applications, and all settings, so it can be easily reused on another host.

- *Virtual Media Manager*—This option opens the Virtual Media Manager, which organizes current and previously used CD/DVD ISOs, hard disk, and floppy disk images. You will learn more about this in "Working with the Virtual Media Manager."

- *Network Operations Manager*—When installing VirtualBox extension packages, this option is used to guide you through the required steps.

- *Check for Updates*—This option checks to see that you have the latest version of the VirtualBox Manager installed.

- *Reset All Warnings*—VirtualBox will give helpful tips and warning messages at the top of the virtual machine window, which can be hidden. This option will restore all of your hidden messages.

- *Exit*—You use this option to exit the VirtualBox Manager. Any active virtual machines will continue to run until their windows are closed.

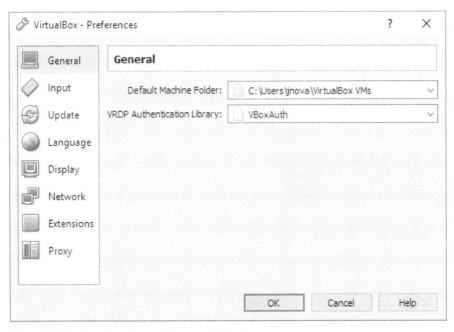

Figure 2-7   The VirtualBox Preferences dialog box

Source: Oracle Virtual VM VirtualBox 5.0

Table 2-1   Settings in the VirtualBox Preferences dialog box

Setting	Description
General	Used to choose the default folder where new virtual machines will be saved, as well as the authentication used with the remote display extension.
Input	Configures the keyboard shortcuts used in both the VirtualBox Manager and also within a running virtual machine guest OS window. You can also specify the Host key.

(continues)

Table 2-1   **Settings in the VirtualBox Preferences dialog box (***continued***)**

Setting	Description
Update	Determines if and how often VirtualBox Manager automatically checks for new updates, and which types of updates should be installed, such as stable releases, new releases, or pre-releases.
Language	The language used in the VirtualBox Manager interface.
Display	Configures the default size of the virtual machine guest OS window, either automatic or a specified height and width.
Network	Sets up host-only networks and NAT networks the virtual machines will be able to access.
Extensions	Manages extensions, which provide additional features and functionality to VirtualBox. For example, a commercial extension can add USB 2.0+ support.
Proxy	Configures an HTTP proxy server if required.

Activity 2-4: Setting Global Preferences

Time Required: Approximately 10 minutes

Objective: Work with global virtual machine preferences.

Description: The instructors at Superior Technical College want you to give a demonstration of using VirtualBox. In this activity, you prepare for the demonstration by working with global preferences in the VirtualBox Preferences dialog box.

1. If necessary, log on to your host computer with your administrative username and password and open the VirtualBox Manager.

2. Click **File, Preferences** from the menu to open the VirtualBox Preferences dialog box.

3. Click **Input** on the left and record the default keyboard shortcuts:

    • VirtualBox Manager: Power Off

    _____

    • Virtual Machine: Host Key Combination

    _____

    • Virtual Machine: Full-screen Mode

    _____

4. To assign a keyboard shortcut to Normal Start under VirtualBox Manager, click the Shortcut box next to Normal Start in the list and type **Ctrl+Z**. Observe the setting change.

5. Click **Update**. Which types of releases are set to be installed automatically?

    _____

6. Click **Display**. What are the available choices for the Maximum Guest Screen Size?

    _____

7. Close the VirtualBox Preferences dialog box by clicking **OK**. Leave the VirtualBox Manager open for the next activity.

Working with the Machine Menu

The Machine menu, used to manage and configure the selected virtual machine, contains the following options:

- *New*—You use this option to open the Create Virtual Machine wizard. It has the same action as clicking the New toolbar icon.

- *Add*—You use this option to add an already existing virtual machine that is on the host PC, but is not yet listed in the VirtualBox Manager. This will be discussed further in "Adding and Removing Virtual Machines."

- *Settings*—You use this option to configure settings for the selected virtual machine as shown in Figure 2-8 and described below. It has the same action as clicking the Settings toolbar icon.

- *Clone*—You use this option to create a clone of your current virtual machine. This will be discussed further in "Creating Clones."

- *Remove*—You use this option to remove a virtual machine from the VirtualBox Manager. You will be prompted to either remove it from the list and keep its files, such as the virtual hard disk file, on the host computer, or to delete all files associated with the virtual machine.

- *Group*—You can use this option to place the selected virtual machines into a new group as it appears in the list, or ungroup them if they are already in a group. This allows you to organize your virtual machines.

- *Start*—You use this option to start the selected virtual machine and opens the guest OS window. It has the same action as clicking the Start toolbar icon.

- *Pause*—You can use this option to temporarily suspend a virtual machine to free up system resources.

- *Reset*—You can use this option to force a virtual machine to reset if it becomes unresponsive, at the risk of data loss or file corruption.

- *Close*—This menu contains options to close a virtual machine by Save State, ACPI Shutdown, or Power Off, as describing previously in "Basic Virtual Machine Functions."

- *Discard Saved State*—You can use this option to discard the previous saved state of a virtual machine so it will perform a clean boot on the next power up rather than resuming. It has the same action as the Discard toolbar icon.

- *Show Log*—You can use this option to display VirtualBox logs generated from a running virtual machine that can be useful in diagnosing technical issues.

- *Refresh*—You can use this option to refresh the accessibility of the selected virtual machines.

- *Show in Explorer*—You can use this option to open a Windows Explorer window at the location the currently selected virtual machine is saved.

- *Create Shortcut on Desktop*—You can use this option to create a shortcut on the host computer's desktop. This shortcut allows you to launch a virtual machine directly without using the VirtualBox Manager.

- *Sort*—You can use this option to sort the group your selected virtual machine is in alphabetically.

The Settings dialog box (see Figure 2-8) includes options for configuring the selected virtual machine. The following list describes these options briefly. Some options will only be available when the virtual machine is powered off.

- *General*—Change the name of the virtual machine. You can also change the type and version, but this has no effect after virtual machine creation and is only cosmetic. Under Advanced you can change the default snapshot save folder, as well as if Shared Clipboard and Drag'n'Drop are enabled. These require Guest Additions, see the upcoming section "Installing Guest Additions on a Virtual Machine." Under the Description tab you can enter notes about your virtual machine and its configuration. The Encryption tab allows you to password protect a virtual machine.

- *System*—Here you can configure the amount of memory a virtual machine has available, as well as the boot device order, chipset and pointing device details, and advanced features like using EFI instead of BIOS. Under the Processor tab you can choose the number of CPU cores to use, as well as how much of the core the virtual machine can use. The default is 100%. PAE/NX support allows a 32-bit OS to access more than 4 GB of RAM. Under the Acceleration tab hardware virtual support can be enabled or disabled. This will be set automatically based on your host computer's available features.

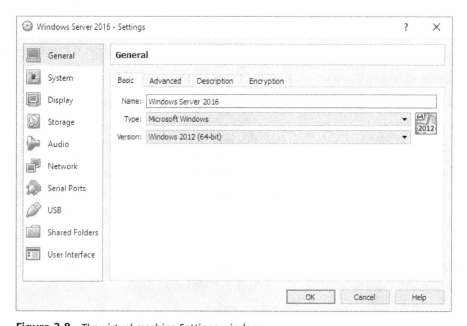

Figure 2-8 The virtual machine Settings window

Source: Oracle Virtual VM VirtualBox 5.0

- *Display*—Here you can choose how much video RAM the virtual machine can use, which determines the maximum screen resolution and number of colors. You can add up to eight virtual monitors, which each appear as its own guest OS window. 2D and 3D hardware acceleration will speed up graphics if you have the Guest Additions installed, see "Installing Guest Additions on a Virtual Machine." Remote Display allows you to access the virtual machine desktop using a Remote Desktop Protocol (RDP) viewer. The Video Capture tab allows you to record the virtual machine's display with various screen size, aspect ratio, and quality settings.

- *Storage*—Here you will see the virtual storage adapters in your virtual machine as well as the assigned image files or devices. An IDE or SATA port can be used for the optical drive, assigned to an ISO image or a CD/DVD drive on the host PC, as well as a SATA port with the virtual hard disk image file. Additional drives can be added and removed, and image files changed here.

- *Audio*—The audio on the virtual machine can be turned on and off, assigned to a specific audio device on the host PC, and set to emulate specific audio hardware.

- *Network*—Here you can configure up to four virtual network adapters for the virtual machine. By default the virtual machine is given one card attached to Network Address Translation (NAT), which gives it access to outside networks such as the Internet. You can also choose to emulate specific models of adapter cards, and choose a specific MAC address.

- *Serial Ports*—Up to four serial ports can be added to the virtual machine. They can be connected to a physical serial port on the host PC, a virtual serial port on the host, a file, or TCP/IP.

- *USB*—USB devices on the host PC can be used by the virtual machine; while doing so they will be unavailable to the host. Only USB 1.1 is supported in the free version of VirtualBox, 2.0 and 3.0 require a VirtualBox extension pack.

- *Shared Folders*—Allow files to be quickly passed between the host and guest OSs using folders specified here. This require Guest Additions, see "Installing Guest Additions on a Virtual Machine."

- *User Interface*—This allows you to customize the menu bar in the VirtualBox Manager, turning off specific menus or hiding individual menu options. You can also show, hide, and re-order the status icons that appear in the bottom right corner of the guest OS window of a running virtual machine.

Activity 2-5: Working with Virtual Machine Settings

Time Required: Approximately 10 minutes

Objective: Work with virtual machine settings.

Description: You're giving a demonstration of using VirtualBox to run Windows Server 2016 on a virtual machine. In this activity, you continue to prepare for the demonstration by working with options in the Settings dialog box.

1. If necessary, log on to your host computer with your administrative username and password and open the VirtualBox Manager.

2. Click the **Windows Server 2016** virtual machine from the list, but leave it powered off.

3. Click **Machine, Settings** from the menu to open the Settings dialog box.

4. Click the **System** option the left, and change the setting to prevent the guest OS from trying to boot from a floppy disk automatically.

5. Click the **Acceleration** tab still within **System** option. Notice that you can toggle hardware virtualization for a specific virtual machine.

6. Click the **Storage** option. From the Storage Tree, click the **CD** icon under Controller: SATA. On the right under Attributes, click the **CD** icon and assign the drive to a physical drive on the host PC.

7. Click the **Audio** option, and disable the sound on this virtual machine. Record below the Audio Controllers that can be emulated:

   _____

8. Click the **Network** option, and under Adapter 1 click **Advanced**. Record below the name and model number of the Adapter Type:

   _____

9. Click **OK** to save your settings. Leave the VirtualBox Manager open for the next section.

Working with Virtual Machines in VirtualBox

When you start a virtual machine, the VirtualBox guest OS window opens, showing the virtual machine's desktop and any graphical desktop displays or messages specific to the OS, as shown in Figure 2-9. In addition, it shows the virtual machine name in the title bar and a menu bar with File, Machine, View, Input, Devices, and Help menus. The File and Machine menus have some of the same options as in the VirtualBox Manager and additional options for managing the virtual machine while it's running, as described in Table 2-2.

The View menu contains options to change to Full-screen mode and change the window size. You can also take a screenshot and start a video capture. The menu bar and status bar can also be customized here. The Input menu allows the keyboard commands to be customized, as well as sending special key combinations like Ctrl+Alt+Del to the virtual machine. Mouse Integration allows the mouse pointer to move seamlessly between the host and guest without having to click within the guest OS window. The Devices menu allows the virtual optical device to be changed, change network settings, connect to USB devices from the host PC, and configure Shared Folders, Shared Clipboard, and Drag and Drop. You can also install the Guest Additions, explained further in "Installing Guest Additions on a Virtual Machine." In the following sections, you learn how to perform common virtualization tasks.

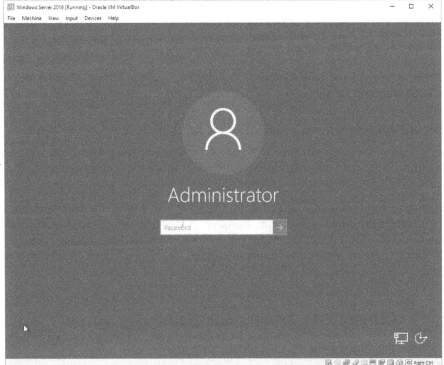

Figure 2-9   The VirtualBox guest OS window

Source: Oracle Virtual VM VirtualBox 5.0

Table 2-2   Machine menu options in the VirtualBox guest OS window

Setting	Description
Settings	Opens the Virtual Machine Settings dialog box described previously. Some options will be disabled as they can't be changed while the virtual machine is running, such as changing the amount of RAM available.
Take Snapshot	Creates a snapshot of the virtual machine's current state. This will be described further in "Using Snapshots."
Session Information	Opens a window with a summary of the virtual machine configuration, as well as runtime information such as the current screen resolution, how much data has been read and written to the virtual hard disk file, and how much network data has been transmitted and received.
Pause, Reset, ACPI Shutdown	Same as the Machine menu options in the VirtualBox Manager.

Adding and Removing Virtual Machines

With workstation virtualization, you can use a virtual machine on several host computers simply by copying its files from one computer to another. For example, your instructor might provide a Windows Server 2016 virtual machine you can use to perform activities in this book. For a copied virtual machine to communicate with other virtual machines on the network it will need a unique MAC address, as explained further in "Configuring Network Settings." To add an existing virtual machine to your computer, follow these three simple steps:

1. Create a folder on your host computer for the virtual machine files, and then copy the virtual hard drive file (.vdi extension by default) and the virtual machine definition file (.vbox extension) to the folder you created. (You can copy the entire virtual machine folder from the source media to your computer.)

2. Start the VirtualBox Manager and click the Machine, Add menu.

3. In the Select a virtual machine file window, navigate to the folder containing the virtual machine files, select the virtual machine definition file (.vbox extension), and click Open.

When you find you no longer need to use a virtual machine, you can remove it from the VirtualBox Manager by clicking Machine, Remove. A dialog box will appear; you can remove the virtual machine only from the Manager, leaving the definition file and virtual hard disk file still on the host to be re-added or moved later. The virtual machine can also be deleted completely to free up space if it will never be needed again.

Activity 2-6: Adding and Removing Virtual Machines

Time Required: Approximately 10 minutes

Objective: Remove and add virtual machines in the VirtualBox Manager.

Description: Being able to add new virtual machines and remove unused virtual machines is an important part of keeping your VirtualBox Manager organized. In this activity, you practice removing and then adding virtual machines to your VirtualBox Manager.

1. If necessary, log on to your host computer with your administrative username and password.

2. Click the **Windows Server 2016** virtual machine from the list, but leave it powered off.

3. Click **Machine, Shown in Explorer**. Record the path to the virtual machine below and close the Explorer window:

_____

4. Click **Machine, Remove** from the menu options. After reading the message in the Question dialog box, click **Remove only** to remove the virtual machine from the manager without deleting its files.

5. To add the virtual machine back to the VirtualBox Manager, click **Machine, Add** from the menu options.

6. In the Select a virtual machine file window, navigate to the folder containing the files for the Windows Server 2016 virtual machine recorded in step 3.

7. Click the **.vbox** file to place the pathname in the File name text box, and then click **Open**.

8. Your virtual machine should be displayed in the VirtualBox Manager. Leave the VirtualBox Manager open for the next activity.

Installing Guest Additions on a Virtual Machine

Guest Additions is installed on a guest OS to add several useful features and allows for better integration of the host and guest PCs:

- *Mouse pointer integration*—This allows the mouse pointer to move seamlessly between the guest OS window and the host computer's desktop without having to release the mouse pointer with the Host keyboard key.

- *Shared folders*—This allows you to transfer files easily between the guest and host by choosing folders on the host that will appear as network shares on the guest. This will be described further under "Working with Shared Folders."

- *Better video support*—Special video drivers on the guest allow for higher and non-standard screen resolutions, and allow hardware acceleration.

- *Seamless windows*—This disables the desktop background on the guest, making an application running on the guest appear seamlessly as if it was running natively on the host computer.

- *Generic host/guest communications*—This permits virtual machine characteristics, as well as generic strings, to be passed between the host and the guest, useful for third-party development.

- *Time synchronization*—This ensures the host and guest computers' system times are in sync.

- *Shared clipboard*—The clipboard of the guest computer is shared with the host, allowing a quick way to transfer data.

- *Automated logins*—This allows VirtualBox to automatically log on as a specified user into a Windows guest OS at startup.

Activity 2-7: Installing Guest Additions on a Virtual Machine

Time Required: Approximately 10 minutes

Objective: Install Guest Additions.

Description: You're giving a demonstration of using VirtualBox to run Windows Server 2016 on a virtual machine. In this activity, you install Guest Additions on your Windows virtual machine.

1. If necessary, log on to your host computer with your administrative username and password and open the VirtualBox Manager.

2. Start the **Windows Server 2016** virtual machine. Log on to the server using **Right Ctrl+Del** or clicking the **Input, Keyboard, Insert Ctrl+Alt+Del** menu option.

3. Click **Devices, Install Guest Additions CD Image** from the VirtualBox guest OS window.

4. In the guest OS, click the **Start** button, then **File Explorer**. Click **This PC** on the left.

5. In the This PC window, double-click the **CD Drive (D:) VirtualBox Guest Additions** icon.

6. Click **Next** in the Oracle VM VirtualBox Guest Additions Setup window. Click **Next** in the Choose Install Location window.

7. Click **Install** in the Choose Components window. If a Windows Security dialog box appears asking to install device software, choose **Install**.

8. Wait for the installation to complete. When asked to reboot your guest OS, click **Finish**.

9. After the virtual machine returns, log on and power it off and then leave the VirtualBox Manager open for the next activity.

Transferring Files with Shared Folders

Guest Additions makes transferring files between the host computer and virtual machines easy by adding drag and drop and shared folder capabilities. To use shared folders, designate a folder on the host computer's hard drive for the virtual machine to access. After you have set up a shared folder, files in it can be shared between a virtual machine and the host computer using a network share in the guest OS. In the following activity, you set up a shared folder on your Windows virtual machine.

Activity 2-8: Working with Shared Folders

Time Required: Approximately 10 minutes

Objective: Use shared folders to transfer files between a virtual machine and the host computer.

Description: Being able to transfer files between a virtual machine and host computer is useful if you've downloaded software updates to your host computer and want to copy them to a virtual machine, for example. In this activity, you set up a shared folder you can use to transfer files.

1. If necessary, log on to your host computer with your administrative username and password and open the VirtualBox Manager.

2. Click the **Windows Server 2016** virtual machine from the list, but leave it powered off.

3. Click the **Settings** toolbar icon to open the Settings window, then click **Shared Folders**. On the right, click the **folder icon with the plus** to open the Add Share dialog box.

4. Click the **down arrow** to the right of the Folder Path, then click **Other** to open the **Select Folder** dialog box.

5. Navigate to the Desktop location on your host computer and click **Select Folder**. To allow the virtual machine to automatically use this shared folder each time it starts, click to check the **Auto-mount** check box, then click **OK**.

6. The shared folder path is displayed in the Folders list. Click the **OK** button to close the Settings window.

7. Start the **Windows Server 2016** virtual machine. Log on to the server using **Right Ctrl+Del** or clicking the **Input, Keyboard, Insert Ctrl+Alt+Del** menu option.

8. In the guest OS, click the **Start** button, **File Explorer**. Click **This PC** on the left.

9. In the This PC window, double-click the new icon under Network locations, it will be named similarly to **Desktop (\\vboxsrv) (E:)**. Verify that you can access the shared folder and see files on your host computer's desktop.

10. Leave the virtual machine running for the next activity.

Transferring Files with Drag and Drop

You have probably used drag and drop to move files. To copy a file or folder to a virtual machine, you simply drag it from the host to a location on the virtual machine. You can copy files and folders from the virtual machine to the host computer, too. For security purposes you can limit transfers to host to guest or guest to host only. By default Drag and Drop is disabled. To enable this feature, click Devices, Drag and Drop in the VirtualBox guest OS window, then click the Bidirectional menu option.

Using Snapshots

Snapshots are used to preserve the current state of a virtual disk so you can return to it later even after many changes to the guest OS. This can be useful if you're installing new software packages or major updates. If there is a problem, you can quickly revert back to the original snapshot to return the virtual machine to fully working again. The number of snapshots is only limited by available disk space on the host. A complex tree of snapshots can be created with different levels, as shown in Figure 2-10.

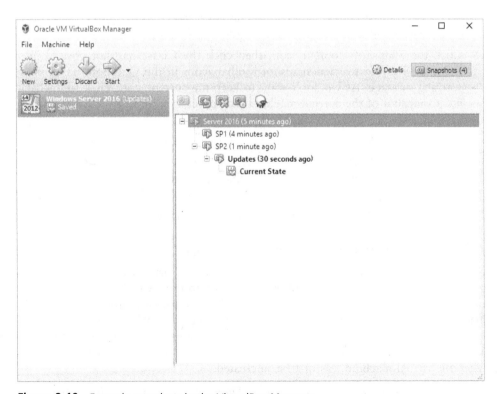

Figure 2-10 Example snapshots in the VirtualBox Manager

Source: Oracle Virtual VM VirtualBox 5.0

Activity 2-9: Working with Snapshots

Time Required: Approximately 10 minutes

Objective: Configure a virtual machine to use snapshots.

Description: Snapshots save changes made to a virtual disk in a separate file. The instructors at Superior Technical College want students to use snapshots at the beginning of each class so they can return their virtual machines to a beginning point in case of a serious error. In this activity, you practice using snapshots on your virtual machine.

1. If necessary, log on to your host computer with your administrative username and password and open the VirtualBox Manager.

2. Click the **Windows Server 2016** virtual machine from the list, but leave it powered off.

3. Click the **Snapshots** button on the far right of the toolbar. Click the **Take a snapshot** icon above the snapshots list.

4. In the Take Snapshot of Virtual Machine dialog box, type **Class** and today's date into the Snapshot Name text box, then click **OK**.

5. Start the **Windows Server 2016** virtual machine. Log on to the server using **Right Ctrl+Del** or clicking the **Input, Keyboard, Insert Ctrl+Alt+Del** menu option.

6. Delete the **SampleData** text file created in the previous activity and empty the Recycle Bin.

7. Power off the virtual machine by clicking **Start**, followed by **Power, Shut down**. Choose **Other (Planned)** in the dropdown list and click **Continue**.

8. Click the **Snapshots** toolbar icon, then click the **Class** snapshot created in steps 3-4. Click the **Restore selected snapshot** toolbar icon. In the Question dialog box, read the warning message. As we don't want to keep the current state, click to uncheck the **Create a snapshot of the current machine state** check box and then click **Restore**.

9. Start the **Windows Server 2016** virtual machine again and log on. Observe that the SampleData file has been restored. Power down the virtual machine.

10. Click the **Snapshots** toolbar icon, then click the **Class** snapshot created in steps 3-4. Click the **Delete selected snapshot** toolbar icon. In the Question dialog box, read the warning message. As we no longer need this snapshot, click **Delete**.

11. Leave the VirtualBox Manager open for the next activity.

Adding and Editing Virtual Hard Disks

In VirtualBox, each virtual machine can have up to 30 virtual hard disks on the SATA controller (by contrast, the IDE controller supports up to four, which typically includes the optical device). Having multiple virtual hard disks can increase storage capacity for virtual machines and help you learn more about disk management. When you use the Create Virtual Hard Disk wizard, you can choose to use an existing hard disk image, or create a new one. This wizard is the same as the one used previously in "Creating a Virtual Hard Disk File" when the virtual machine was first being created.

The Virtual Media Manager, as shown in Figure 2-11, organizes virtual hard disk, optical ISO, and floppy disk images currently and previously used in virtual machines. These will

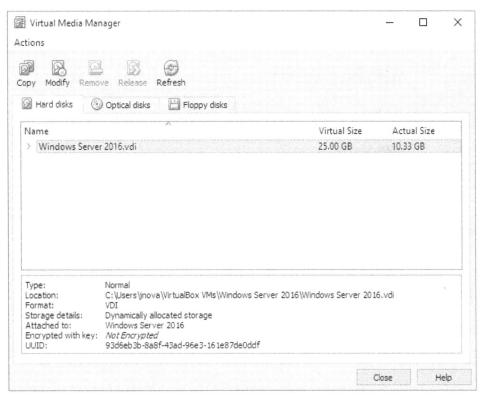

Figure 2-11   The Virtual Media Manager window

Source: Oracle Virtual VM VirtualBox 5.0

appear in the dropdown lists when selecting an image for quick reuse without having to browse to the file. The Manager will list important statistics about your image files, such as if it is dynamic or fixed, and the actual size the image is using on the host in comparison to the virtual hard disk size. Virtual hard disk images can be copied, removed, and modified. When you modify an image, there are five different modes:

- *Normal*—This is the default mode for an image file, the guest OS has full access to read and write to it. When a snapshot is created, the state of a normal disk is also saved along with it, so when reverting back to the snapshot it's fully reset.

- *Writethrough*—Unlike a normal disk, the state of this image is not saved when a snapshot is created, and is not restored when the snapshot is reverted back.

- *Shareable*—Similar to the Writethrough mode, except that the image file can be used by multiple virtual machines at the same time. This type of image must be of a fixed size, it cannot be dynamic.

- *Immutable*—Any changes made to an image in this mode will be lost when the virtual machine is powered down. This is useful as the guest OS can't be permanently damaged by user changes.

- *Multi-attach*—Multiple virtual machines can share a single image file at the same time, with each one storing only the changes unique to that virtual machine.

Some modes can only be set when the image file has been released from its virtual machine, and can then be re-added afterwards.

Activity 2-10: Working with the Virtual Media Manager

Time Required: Approximately 10 minutes

Objective: Set a virtual hard disk image mode to immutable to prevent permanent changes.

Description: A virtual hard disk image in immutable mode will discard any changes made when powered down. The administrators of the general purpose computer lab, which uses virtual machines, want to ensure that changes a student makes, such as installing unauthorized software or getting a virus from a bad Web site, are removed after their session and a pristine virtual machine is available to the next student.

1. If necessary, log on to your host computer with your administrative username and password and open the VirtualBox Manager.

2. Click the **Windows Server 2016** virtual machine from the list, but leave it powered off.

3. In the VirtualBox Manager, click the **File, Virtual Media Manager** menu option.

4. Under the hard disks tab, click the **Windows Server 2016.vdi** file. You can confirm the correct file from the Location field at the bottom of the window, record the location below:

   _____

5. Click the **Release** toolbar icon. Click **Release** in the Question dialog box.

6. Click the **Modify** toolbar icon. In the Modify medium attributes dialog box, click the **Immutable** option button and then click **OK**. Click **Close** in the Virtual Media Manager window.

7. Click the **Settings** toolbar icon, then click **Storage** on the left.

8. In the Storage Tree, click **Controller: SATA**. Click the **Adds hard disk** icon to right. In the Question dialog box, click **Choose existing disk**, then browse to the **Windows Server 2016.vdi** file at the location recorded in step 4 and click **Open**. Click **OK** to close Settings.

9. Start the **Windows Server 2016** virtual machine. Log on to the server using **Right Ctrl+Del** or clicking the **Input, Keyboard, Insert Ctrl+Alt+Del** menu option.

10. To create a text document in the Windows guest OS, right-click the Desktop, point to **New**, and click **Text Document**. Type **Junk** as the document name.

11. Power off the virtual machine by clicking **Start**, followed by **Power, Shut down**. Choose **Other (Planned)** in the dropdown list and click **Continue**.

12. Start the **Windows Server 2016** again, and log on. Observe that the Junk file is no longer on the desktop. Power down the virtual machine.

13. Repeat steps 2 through 6, skipping step 5, and setting the mode back to **Normal** in step 6.

14. Leave the VirtualBox Manager open for the next activity.

Creating Clones

Instead of creating a new virtual machine from scratch each time, installing the operating system and updates, it can be useful to keep a virtual machine as a base and create a copy of it when needed. This can be done by manually copying the virtual machine definition and disk files and adding them to the VirtualBox Manager as described earlier, or preferably using the Clone Virtual Machine wizard.

First you choose the type of clone. A **full clone** is an exact copy, with the new virtual machine getting a copy of all of the virtual disk files in its own folder. A **linked clone** will continue to use the original virtual machine's disk files, only storing the differences, similar to snapshots. You can also choose to reinitialize the network card's MAC addresses in the clone, which is important if you intend to have both virtual machines running at the same time, as covered in the upcoming section "Configuring Network Settings."

Next, you will choose how the snapshots on the cloned virtual machine are handled. Choosing "Everything" will include all of the snapshots on the parent in the clone, while choosing "Current machine state" will only include the current state, no snapshots.

Activity 2-11: Creating a Cloned Virtual Machine

Time Required: Approximately 10 minutes

Objective: Create a clone of your virtual machine.

Description: Cloning a virtual machine is a good way of making a backup. You will create a clone of your Windows Server 2016 virtual machine so you can use it as the basis for future projects without having to create a new virtual machine and install the operating system again.

1. If necessary, log on to your host computer with your administrative username and password and open the VirtualBox Manager.

2. Click the **Windows Server 2016** virtual machine from the list, but leave it powered off.

3. Click the **Machine, Clone** menu option to open the Clone Virtual Machine wizard.

4. In the New machine name window, click the **Reinitialize the MAC address of all networks** check box, then click **Next**.

5. In the Clone type window, click the **Full clone** option button, then click **Clone**. If you have snapshots on this virtual machine, click **Next** and in the Snapshots window, click the **Current machine state** option button, then click **Clone**.

6. The status bar displays the cloning progress. When complete, observe that the new virtual machine appears in the VirtualBox Manager.

7. To delete the new virtual machine, click the clone from the list, then click the **Machine, Remove** menu option. Click **Delete all files** in the Question dialog box.

8. Power off any running virtual machines, and close the VirtualBox Manager.

Configuring Network Settings

VirtualBox provides up to four virtual network adapters that can be configured in several differ-ent ways (see Figure 2-12). You can configure many networking options on a virtual machine while it's running. Each virtual network adapter can be attached in one of the following ways:

- *Not attached*—This option means the virtual machine has a virtual network adapter, but it is not connected, like a disconnected Ethernet cable.

- *NAT (Network Address Translation)*—This default mode allows the guest OS access to the Internet.

- *NAT Network*—This mode simulates a home router, allowing the guest OS access to the network and outside world, but preventing outside systems direct access inside.

- *Bridged Adapter*—This method allows the virtual machine to connect directly to the network card on the host computer, bypassing its networking stack.

- *Internal Network*—This software network can be seen by other virtual machines, but not by the host computer or the outside world.

- *Host-only Adapter*—This connects virtual machines and the host without using the host computer's network adapter.

- *Generic Driver*—This is a custom network type provided by a driver included with VirtualBox or in an extension pack.

Several different virtual network adapters are available. PCNet FAST III is the default for many guest OSs, however Intel PRO/1000 MT Desktop is used for Windows Vista and newer. The MAC (Media Access Control) address is the unique identifier for the network adapter.

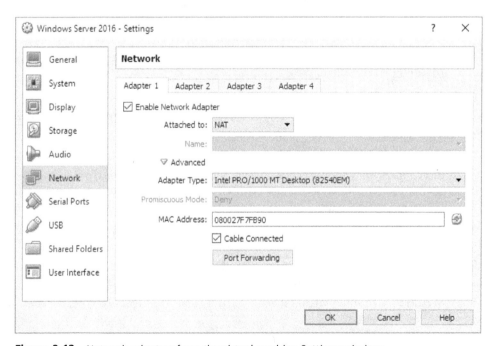

Figure 2-12   Network adapters from the virtual machine Settings window

Source: Oracle Virtual VM VirtualBox 5.0

If another virtual machine has the same MAC address because it was copied manually rather than cloned (without the reinitialize option), there will be network communications issues if they are both running at the same time. VirtualBox can generate a new random MAC address.

Chapter Summary

- VirtualBox requires an x86 processor with 512 MB RAM and 30 MB disk space; the actual requirements depend on the guest OSs you plan to run simultaneously.

- The Create Virtual Machine Wizard is used to create virtual machines or add existing virtual machines to the VirtualBox Manager.

- Creating a virtual machine requires selecting a name and guest OS type, the memory size, selecting the type and size for the virtual hard disk, and the file location.

- Installing a guest OS involves setting the BIOS boot sequence to start from the CD/DVD-ROM drive and connecting the CD/DVD-ROM device or ISO file to the virtual machine.

- An ISO image file can be used instead of physical media to link a virtual CD/DVD device to a virtual machine.

- You use the VirtualBox Manager File menus to change both global and local settings. Global settings that affect all virtual machines can be viewed and modified in the Preferences dialog box.

- Guest Additions adds several features to a guest OS, including shared folders, time synchronization, better video support, and mouse pointer integration.

- You can easily transfer data between a host and virtual machine by setting up Shared Folders, which the virtual machine sees as a standard network share, and by turning on drag and drop support.

- A linked clone can be created to link from a child virtual machine to an existing parent machine.

- Snapshots save the current state of a virtual disk so you can return to it later, removing any changes that have been made since the snapshot was created.

- There are five different virtual hard disk modes including Normal, Writethrough, Shareable, Immutable, and Multi-attach. Normal is the default mode and gives full access. Writethrough is similar to normal except the state is not restored when a snapshot is reverted. Sharable is like writethough but can be used by multiple virtual machines, and must be fixed size. Immutable will lose any changes made when the virtual machine is powered down. Multi-attach allows multiple virtual machines to share a single virtual disk file, each only storing the differences.

- There are seven different networking options including not attached, NAT, NAT Network, Bridged Adapter, Internal Network, Host-only Adapter, and Generic Driver. NAT gives access to the Internet and is the default. NAT Network is like a home router, not allowing incoming traffic. Bridged Adapter lets the virtual machine talk directly to the host network adapter. Internal Network is only seen by other virtual machines. Host-only lets the host and virtual machines communicate without using the host's network adapter, and Generic Driver allows custom network types through third-party add-ons.

Key Terms

dynamically allocated	full clone	linked clone
fixed size	Host key	snapshots

Review Questions

1. What are the minimum hardware requirements for installing VirtualBox?

   a. x86 Intel or AMD processor with 512 MB RAM and 1 GB hard disk space

   b. x64 Intel or AMD processor with 1 GB RAM and 30 MB hard disk space

   c. x86 Intel or AMD processor with 512 MB RAM and 30 MB hard disk space

   d. x64 Intel or AMD processor with 256 MB RAM and 1 GB hard disk space

2. You can add existing virtual machines to the VirtualBox Manager by doing which of the following? (Choose all that apply.)

   a. Using the Virtual Disk Wizard

   b. Using the Create Virtual Machine Wizard

   c. Double-clicking the virtual machine's .vbox file in Windows Explorer

   d. Clicking the Machine, Add option

3. Which option on the guest OS window Machine menu shows total hard disk reads and writes?

   a. Properties

   b. Session Information

   c. Details

   d. Operations

4. How many snapshots can a virtual machine have?

   a. 1

   b. 2

   c. 4

   d. Limited only by available disk space

5. Which of the following is *not* a power option in the guest OS window Machine menu?

   a. ACPI Shutdown

   b. Reset

   c. Turn off

   d. Pause

6. Which tab in the Settings dialog box is used to set the boot device order?
   a. General
   b. System
   c. Hard Drives
   d. Advanced

7. Which of the following drive size types provides the best performance for virtual servers?
   a. Fixed size
   b. Dynamically allocated
   c. Bridged
   d. Shared

8. What is the maximum number of virtual network adapters in VirtualBox?
   a. 1
   b. 2
   c. 4
   d. 8

9. What is the default key for returning keyboard and mouse control to the host computer?
   a. Ctrl+Alt+Insert
   b. Delete
   c. Right Alt
   d. Right Ctrl

10. Which of the following devices can be configured to use an image file? (Choose all that apply.)
    a. Floppy disk
    b. CD/DVD-ROM drive
    c. FireWire port
    d. USB port

11. Which of the following is an advantage of installing Virtual Machine Additions? (Choose all that apply.)
    a. Improved video resolution on the virtual machine
    b. Ability to move the mouse pointer between virtual machines and the host
    c. Shared folders
    d. Automatic software updates

12. Which of the following settings can't be changed when the virtual machine is running? (Choose all that apply.)

    a. Display Scale Factor

    b. Memory

    c. Shared Folders

    d. Sound

13. A snapshot can be used to perform which of the following tasks?

    a. Create a parent virtual machine.

    b. Save the virtual machine state.

    c. Prevent changes to the virtual machine.

    d. Link a virtual hard disk to the host computer's physical disk.

14. Which menu selection do you use to change the way the virtual machine keyboard shortcuts?

    a. File, Keyboard

    b. File, Preferences, Input

    c. Machine, Preferences, Input

    d. Devices, Keyboard

15. Which of the following networking options allows the virtual machine to directly use the host's network adapter?

    a. NAT

    b. Internal Network

    c. Bridged Adapter

    d. Host-only Adapter

16. Which of the following disk modes will discard any changes when powered down?

    a. Fixed

    b. Writethrough

    c. Immutable

    d. Temporary

17. Which of the following disk options is available when using the wizard to create a virtual machine? (Choose all that apply.)

    a. Differencing

    b. Dynamically allocated

    c. Linked

    d. Fixed size

18. Which of the following best describes how to connect an ISO image to a virtual machine?

    a. Clicking the File, Preferences option in the VirtualBox Manager

    b. Clicking the File, Preferences option in the guest OS window

    c. Clicking the Devices, Optical Devices option in the guest OS window

    d. Clicking the Machine, Optical Devices option in the VirtualBox Manager

19. What file extension is used for a VirtualBox disk image file?

    a. ISO

    b. VDI

    c. VDISK

    d. VBOX

20. Which type of cloned virtual machine uses the least disk space?

    a. Full clone

    b. Exact clone

    c. Partial clone

    d. Linked clone

Case Projects

CASE PROJECTS

Case Project 2-1: Documenting Guest Additions

The computer lab staff at Superior Technical College wants you to give a presentation on using Guest Additions. Your presentation should include a handout describing its features (including which guest OSs it can be installed on) and how to use them to improve virtual machine operations in the computer lab.

Case Project 2-2: Using Clones

An instructor at Superior Technical College is developing a Windows server course that includes student projects on server configuration, starting with an existing server and then configuring it to perform certain tasks. Write a brief report explaining how the instructor could use clones.

Case Project 2-3: Comparing VMware Workstation and Oracle VirtualBox

Write a brief report comparing the following features of VMware Workstation with similar features in VirtualBox: snapshots, cloning, and VMware Tools.

chapter 3

Working with VMware Workstation 12 Pro

After reading this chapter and completing the exercises, you will be able to:

- Install VMware Workstation 12 Pro on Windows
- Add virtual machines to the administrative console
- Export, import, and clone virtual machines
- Use the VMware administrative console menus
- Perform common tasks on virtual machines
- Share virtual machines with other hosts
- Use VMware Workstation 12 Player to import virtual machines

As described in Chapter 1, virtualization software consists of both type-1 and type-2 hypervisor products. While personal workstations typically use type-2 hypervisors, a data center often needs to incorporate both types of products for the best results. As the first company to offer commercial virtualization products, VMware is still the leader in virtualization software and offers a wide variety of workstation and server products.

VMware has two major workstation or type-2 virtualization products: VMware Workstation Pro and VMware Workstation Player. VMware Workstation Player offers a free, more limited version of VMware Workstation Pro that is designed for the small business or home user. VMware Workstation Player is great for hosting simple virtual desktops and performing basic virtualization functions. As described in Chapter 1, VMware Workstation Player is often used to host virtual appliances. This chapter focuses on VMware Workstation Pro because it contains the advanced features and high performance most commercial workstation applications need. Because of its advanced features, VMware Workstation Pro is often used by professional developers and administrators to develop and test applications and computer environments on a variety of platforms.

This chapter was written using VMware Workstation 12 Pro. By the time you use this book newer versions of VMware Workstation Pro will no doubt be released. As a result, there may be slight variations in the menu options and window screen shots you will see with the version of VMware Workstation Pro you are using. In this chapter we will use VMware Workstation to refer to both Workstation Pro and Workstation Player. You may wish to refer to Appendix B for more information on Workstation Player.

In Chapter 1, you downloaded the installation files. In this chapter, you learn how to install VMware Workstation 12 Pro, and then use the administrative console to create, configure, and operate virtual machine environments. In addition, you learn how to install and operate a guest OS, manage virtual networks, and use advanced features, such as Unity view, cloning, and snapshot management. At the end of the chapter you will learn the steps necessary to transfer your virtual machine to VMware Workstation 12 Player so you will be able to continue to use them for later chapter activities.

Installing VMware Workstation 12 Pro

In Chapter 1's activities, you downloaded an evaluation for VMware Workstation 12 Pro setup files for installing to Windows. Prior to installing VMware Workstation 12 Pro you need to be sure your workstation meets the requirements shown in Table 3-1.

Table 3-1 VMware Workstation 12 Pro requirements

Memory	2 GB RAM minimum / 4 GB RAM and above recommended
CPU	64-bit x86 Intel Core™ SolProcessor or equivalent, AMD Athlon™ 64 FX Dual Core Processor or equivalent 3 GHz speed or faster
Disk Space	1.2 GB of available disk space for the application. Additional hard disk space required for each virtual machine. Please refer to vendor's recommended disk space for specific guest operating systems

In this section, you will learn how to install the 30-day trial version of VMware Workstation 12 Pro in Windows.

When you install VMware Workstation 12 Pro by default you will also get a copy of VMware Workstation 12 Player. While your trial version of VMware Workstation 12 Pro will expire in 30 days, you **NOTE** will be able to continue to use VMware Workstation 12 Player to work with virtual machines throughout this book. Appendix B contains instructions on how to use with VMware Workstation 12 Player to install and work with virtual machines.

VMware Workstation 12 Pro includes both standard and silent installation methods. With the standard method, the most commonly used, you use a wizard to go through each installation step and select options. The silent method is useful when you need to automate VMware Workstation 12 Pro installations on several computers, such as in a school's computer lab. The following sections show you the steps in each method.

Performing a Standard Installation

A standard installation of VMware Workstation 12 Pro is fairly straightforward because a wizard prompts you for information as it progresses. However, before starting the installation wizard, you should prepare for the process by doing the following:

1. Be sure your computer meets the minimum requirements stated in Chapter 1.

2. Have the VMware Workstation 12 Pro installation file you obtained in Chapter 1 available.

3. Uninstall any existing VMware products, such as VMware Server, VMware Workstation 12 Player, or VMware Virtual Machine Console, as VMware Workstation 12 Pro can't share a host computer with another version of VMware.

4. Determine the path where you want to install VMware Workstation 12 Pro. The default for 64-bit operating systems is C:\Program Files\VMware\VMware Workstation.

5. Determine whether you want to use the typical or custom installation method. With a custom installation, you can find out how much disk space is required for each component or get a description of any icon in the installation list.

Performing a Silent Installation

With a silent installation, you can set installation parameters ahead of time from an administrative computer. After extracting the installation files, you use the Microsoft Installer program, Msiexec.exe, to automate the installation on a different host computer. The unattended installation doesn't use a wizard or GUI and works in the background. This method is useful if you're installing VMware Workstation 12 Pro on several computers or want someone else to perform the installation.

Activity 3-1: Performing a Standard Installation of VMware Workstation 12 Pro

Time Required: 15 minutes

Objective: Perform a standard installation of VMware Workstation 12 Pro.

Requirements: The VMware Workstation 12 Pro setup file you obtained in Chapter 1

Description: Assume that you are an IT technician for a computer support firm. Your manager would like you to use VMware Workstation 12 Pro as a workbench to install, configure, and test the virtual servers that will later be deployed in an organization's data center using VMware vSphere. In this activity, you perform a standard installation of VMware Workstation 12 Pro on your Windows 10 computer.

1. Log on to your Windows host as the local administrator or a user who's a member of the local Administrators group. (Being a member of the Administrators group ensures that you have the rights to change system settings and install the VMware service.)

2. In Windows Explorer, navigate to the folder containing the setup file you downloaded, and double-click the **VMware-workstation-full-12.#.exe** file to start the installation wizard. (The # represents the installation file's version and build number.) If the Windows User Account Control (UAC) message box opens, click **Yes** to continue.

If you are running the file from a network drive, you may receive a security warning message box. Click **Run** to continue.

3. In the Welcome window, click **Next** to display the License Agreement page. Scroll down to review the license agreement, click the **I accept the terms in the License Agreement** check box, and then click **Next** to display the VMware Workstation 12 Pro Custom Setup window.

4. Record the installation path and then click **Next** to accept the default path and display the User Experience Settings window.

5. Verify that the "Check for product updates on startup" option is selected and then click to remove the check mark from the "Help improve VMware Workstation Pro" check box. Click **Next** to display the Shortcuts window.

6. Verify that the "Desktop" and "Start Menu Programs Folder" options are selected and then click **Next** to display the Ready to install VMware Workstation 12 Pro window.

7. Click **Install** to start the installation process. You have a few minutes to take a break while file copying and installation take place.

 During the installation, if you see any Windows Security warning messages asking whether you want to install certain device software, such as the USB controller, click the option to install the software driver and continue the installation.

8. After the installation is complete you will be given an option to enter a license key or finish the installation. If you have a license key, click the **License** button and enter the license key at this time. If you do not have a license key at this time, click the **Finish** button to start a 30-day trial period. If you click Finish, you will also be given a chance to enter the key the first time you start VMware Workstation 12 Pro.

 You can also use the Help menu in the administrative console to enter the serial number at a later time (covered later in "Using the Administrative Console Menus").

9. You have now successfully completed Activity 3-1. You may log off of your computer, or stay logged on for the next activity.

Getting Started with VMware Workstation 12 Pro

After installing VMware Workstation 12 Pro you can immediately begin using it to create and configure virtual machines. In this section you will learn how to use the administrative console to create, copy, and export.

If you did not enter a license during installation, when you first start VMware Workstation 12 Pro the Welcome window showing the VMware Workstation 12 license options will be displayed.

You may now click the option to enter a valid license key or start your 30-day trial. To start the 30-day trial, click the **I want to try VMware Workstation Pro for 30 days** option button and enter your email address in the text box and click **Continue**. After completing the license page, the VMware Workstation 12 Pro administrative console shown in Figure 3-1 will be displayed.

 If a new update is available, you will receive a Software Updates window. Click the **Download and Install** button to install the latest update or version. The update operation may take several minutes. During this process you may need to click "Yes" in response to the User Account Control box. If installing a new version, you will be asked to uninstall the existing VMware Workstation Pro software and then repeat the installation process described in this activity.

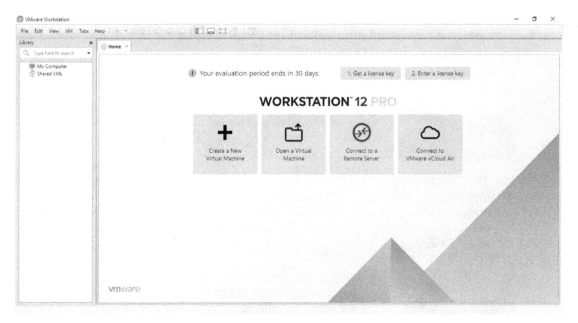

Figure 3-1 VMware Workstation 12 Pro administrative console Home tab

Source: VMware Workstation

Notice that the administrative console window contains a menu line across the top and two main information panes in the body. The left-hand information pane is called the Library pane and is used to display virtual machines you have added to the administrative console arranged in folders. Initially only the Shared VMs and My Computer folders exist in the Library pane. You will learn how to organize your virtual machines into folders later in this chapter. In this book we will refer to the right-hand information pane as the Summary/Console pane, and it contains a Home tab along with tabs for any virtual machines you add to the administrative console. Initially only the Home tab is shown. The top of the Home tab shows the number of days remaining in your evaluation period along with buttons to obtain or enter a license key. The Home tab also includes "Create a New Virtual Machine," "Open a Virtual Machine," "Connect to a Remote Server," and "Connect to VMware vCloud Air" buttons. You will be learning how to use these options in this and later chapters.

Adding Virtual Machines to the Administrative Console

You use the administrative console to create virtual machines, configure settings, and manage virtual machine operations. As shown previously in Figure 3-1, the VMware Workstation 12 Pro administrative console window includes a Library pane and a Summary/Console pane containing the Home tab. A new tab will be created in the Summary/Console pane for each of the virtual machines added to your administrative console.

The Library pane has folders for organizing what's displayed in the tabs, such as virtual machines on the local computer or shared VMs (virtual machines that are available to run on other host computers). When you click a VM or folder from the library pane, a tab for that VM or folder will be added to the right-hand Summary/Console pane. The tabs are used to access and switch between virtual machine user consoles quickly and easily. You can close tabs by clicking the "X" to the right of the tab's name.

Initially, the administrative console has only a Home tab containing useful shortcuts to tasks such as creating a virtual machine or opening an existing virtual machine or connecting to a remote host. To remove a tab, simply right-click it and click Close Tab or click the "X" to the right of the tab name. To add it back, simply click the virtual machine from the Library pane. If you inadvertently close the Home tab, you can restore it by clicking the **Go to Home Tab** option from the Tabs menu.

In this section, you explore the administrative console for VMware Workstation 12 Pro and learn about major global settings and features that affect VMware Workstation 12 Pro's operation.

Creating Virtual Machines

Virtual machines can be added to the administrative console by creating a new virtual machine, the method discussed in this section, or selecting an existing virtual machine, explained later in "Adding Existing Virtual Machines to the Administrative Console."

Before creating a virtual machine, you need to consider factors such as the type of OS the virtual machine will run, name and location of virtual machine files, amount of memory to assign to the virtual machine, network connectivity options, type of virtual disk adapter (SCSI or IDE), disk type (fixed or dynamic), and maximum disk size. In this section, you learn more about these choices and use VMware Workstation 12 Pro to create two virtual machines.

When creating a virtual machine, you have two options: Custom and Typical. Generally, the Custom option is best because it gives you control of all virtual machine settings. You can change default settings and select more options, so it's the one described in detail in this section. The Typical option assumes only one processor with an IDE disk adapter type and a default memory size based on the OS you select.

With the Custom option, the first step is selecting the hardware compatibility option for the virtual machine. The Virtual Machine Hardware Compatibility window allows you to select what versions of VMware will be able to run the new virtual machine along with the hardware limitations the selected compatibility level will have.

In this chapter, VMware Workstation 12 compatibility will be selected to allow the virtual machines to have up to 16 vCPUs, 64 GB of RAM, 10 network adapters, and 8 TB disk size. In addition to VMware Workstation 12, this virtual machine will also be compatible with VMware Fusion version 8. Unless you plan to move the virtual machine to other systems running previous versions of VMware, selecting the most recent version is usually recommended.

The Virtual Machine Hardware Compatibility window also contains a check box for ESX Server compatibility. As described in Chapter 1, ESX Server (also known as vSphere Hypervisor) is VMware's bare metal, type-1 hypervisor. Compatibility with ESX Server is important if you are configuring a virtual server that will be used in the data center.

The next step is selecting an installation method for the guest OS as shown in Figure 3-2.

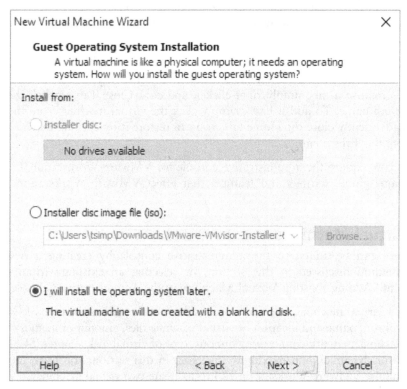

Figure 3-2   New Virtual Machine Wizard - Guest Operating System Installation window

Source: VMware Workstation

Notice that there are three installation options: (1) **Installer disc**, (2) **Installer disc image file (iso)**, or (3) **I will install the operating system later**. The Installer disc and Installer disc image file (iso) options enable you to use **Easy Install** to automate the guest OS installation during the creation of the VM. The Installer disc option requires a physical DVD containing the guest OS to be inserted into the host computer. If your guest OS software is contained in an ISO file, you should select the Installer disc image file (iso) option and then specify the path to the ISO file that contains the disk image. When you select one of these options VMware will detect the OS to be installed and enable Easy Install if possible (available for recent Windows versions and newer Linux builds). As shown in Figure 3-3, when using the Easy Install option you will be prompted for your OS product key and username and password, from that point the installation is automatic.

The "I will install the operating system later" option creates a blank virtual machine with the hardware environment of the guest OS you selected. If you select this option, VMware Workstation 12 Pro displays the Select a Guest Operating System window that is used to set the default VM environment including memory and disk settings. VMware Workstation 12 Pro will then create a new virtual machine that contains a formatted virtual hard drive with no OS. You will then need to use a physical DVD or ISO file to install the guest OS later.

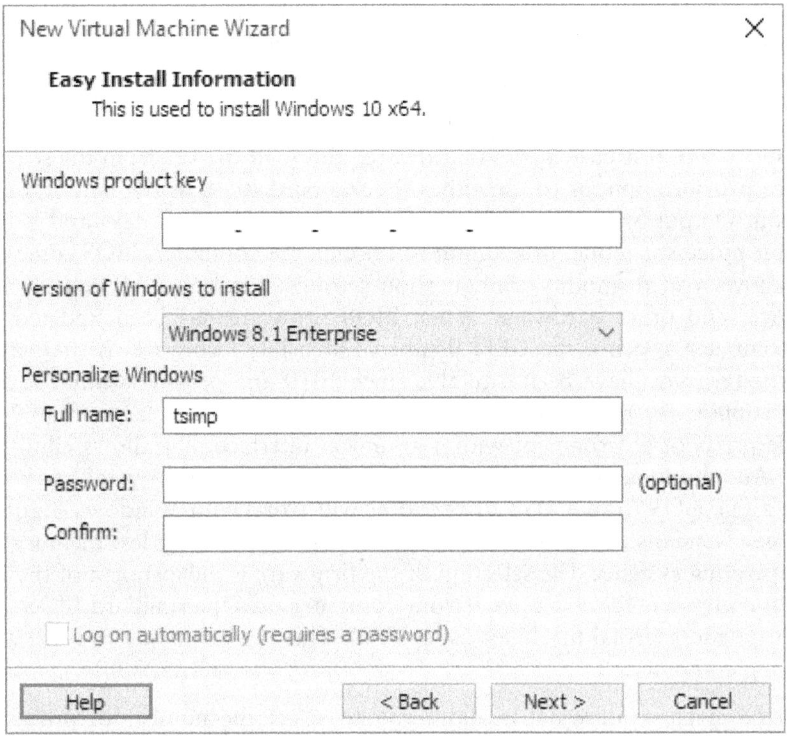

New Virtual Machine Wizard   ✕

   Easy Install Information
        This is used to install Windows 10 x64.

Windows product key

              [-   -   -   ]

Version of Windows to install

              [Windows 8.1 Enterprise   ⌄]
Personalize Windows

   Full name: [tsimp   ]

   Password: [   ]   (optional)
   Confirm: [   ]

        ☐ Log on automatically (requires a password)

[Help   ]   [< Back] [Next >] [Cancel]

Figure 3-3   New Virtual Machine Wizard - Easy Install Information window

Source: VMware Workstation

The guest OS options you can select include Microsoft Windows, Linux, Novell NetWare, Solaris, VMware ESX, and Other. Use the Other option for setting up a VM for special OS environments, such as MS-DOS or FreeBSD. You can also use the VMware ESX option to install VMware's vSphere bare metal hypervisor in a VM for testing and learning. After creating the VM, you do a manual installation of the OS just as you would on a physical computer. You will get the opportunity to use both the installer disk image and manual installation options in the Activities 3-2 and 3-3.

The next step is selecting the virtual machine name and storage location for the configuration and data files. You should enter a name that you will use later for that workstation or server. For example, if you are planning to install a server for the Sales Department you may wish to enter the name SalesServer1. The default location in a Windows 10 host is Documents\Virtual Machines (c:\users*username*\Documents\Virtual Machines*name*). Using this location helps ensure that virtual machine files are kept separate from other users sharing your host computer. Another option is storing files in a separate Virtual Machines folder or on a network drive. A network drive may be useful in an environment when you're working at different host computers or want a backup in case data are lost on the primary host computer. If using a network drive, you will want to be sure you have a high speed (1 Gbps) network connection to provide adequate performance. You can also store files in a shared folder so that you can make the virtual machine available to other users.

If you selected Windows 10 or Windows Server 2008 or later you will be asked to select the firmware type. Just as in a physical computer, firmware is used to initialize devices including the hard disk and video, test basic system hardware, and load the OS from the selected boot device. VMware provides options to use either the standard BIOS or the new EFI firmware. BIOS (Basic Input Output System) has been around since the early PC days and is limited to running in 16-bit processor mode. In addition to booting the computer, BIOS contains a user interface that allows you to modify configuration settings stored in CMOS such as system date, boot device, and other hardware. While BIOS firmware has been updated to work with modern computer systems, the UEFI (Unified Extensible Firmware) is the wave of the future. UEFI-based systems have been available since 2010 and provide a number of advantages including support for newer processors, booting from partitions larger than 2 TB, and a more versatile pre-boot environment with a graphical interface that allows editing of configuration files. An additional advantage of selecting EFI for VMware virtual machines is the ability to boot a guest OS from a USB drive. UEFI will work with Windows 8 and later as well as certain new versions of Linux. BIOS has the advantage of using less memory and supporting older operating systems. The selection of the firmware is independent of the firmware used on the host computer. For example, if your computer uses the standard BIOS firmware, you can still create guest virtual machines using UEFI. This is a great way to learn about EFI with your existing computer.

Next, you will be given windows that allow you to select the number of processors and amount of memory to allocate to the virtual machine. Unless you plan to run the virtual machine on a host computer with multiple processors or a dual-core processor, leave the default setting of one processor and the suggested memory. As described in Chapter 1, selecting multiple virtual processors can actually decrease the guest VM speed depending on the number of VMs and host hardware configuration.

By default, the wizard sets the memory amount to what's recommended for the OS you selected. In addition to the recommended memory size, the Memory for the Virtual Machine window includes recommended maximum and minimum settings. To start with, you should use the recommended setting for the OS you are installing. If the host computer is running multiple virtual machines, make sure it has enough memory for its own OS in addition to the amount for each virtual machine it is simultaneously running. When a VM is put in production, the number of processors and memory can be adjusted if necessary to increase performance.

 As a general rule it is best to start with smaller values and increase as necessary to provide the required performance.

Next, you select the network connection type for the virtual network adapter (see Figure 3-4). The options include Use bridged networking, Use network address translation (NAT), Use host-only networking, or Do not use a network connection.

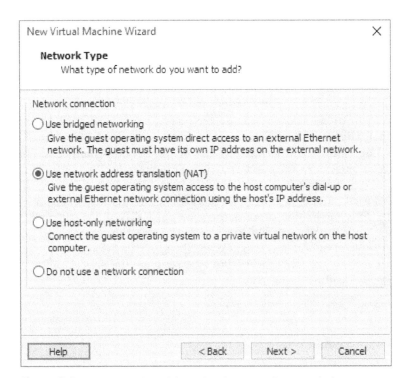

Figure 3-4   New Virtual Machine Wizard - Network Type window

Source: VMware Workstation

As with memory, you can change the network connection type and number of adapters later using the administrative console. Each network connection option can be compared with connecting the virtual machine to a network switch. If you're running multiple virtual machines on the host computer, they must use the same network connection type to communicate with each other. The following list gives you some guidelines for selecting a network connection type:

- *Bridged*—with this option, the virtual machine has direct access to the local area network (LAN) because it shares the host computer's NIC. When using bridged networking, the virtual machine appears as another physical computer on the network.

- *NAT*—this option is a good choice if you want to hide the virtual machine from the main network to increase security and prevent conflicts with other physical machines yet still use the host computer's NIC to access the Internet and other local network resources. With the NAT option, the virtual machine will only directly communicate with the host computer and any other virtual machines that are using the NAT option on the same host.

- *Host-only*—this option limits the virtual machine to communicating only with the host computer and any other virtual machines that are configured to use the Host-only network on that host. Using the Host-only option, the virtual machine will not be able to access the physical network or the Internet. You will be able to experiment with the different network connection types later in this chapter.

After selecting the network connection type, you will see the Select I/O Controller Types window.

This window allows you to change the I/O adapter type for any virtual SCSI adapters you will use in the virtual machine. The IDE adapter is limited to the ATAPI adapter type, but you can select Bus Logic or LSI Logic for the SCSI adapter. You should select an adapter type based on the requirements of the guest OS you will be installing. VMware Workstation 12 Pro offers an LSI Logic SAS mode (default for Windows 10), which uses a serial interface; previous SCSI modes used parallel interfaces. In general, an LSI adapter offers improved performance, but older OSs might not support them or need drivers downloaded from the Avago Technologies (now Broadcom) Web site *(avagotech.com)*. In most cases, you should leave the default setting, unless you know the OS for the guest VM does not support the LSI Logic SAS controller type. After selecting the I/O adapter type, the Select a Disk Type window shown in Figure 3-5 will be displayed.

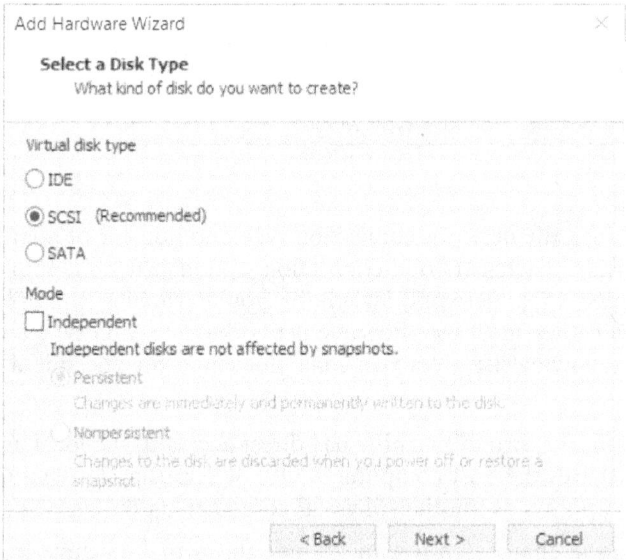

Figure 3-5   New Virtual Machine Wizard – Select a Disk Type window

Source: VMware Workstation

While by default the disk controller type for most server operating systems is SCSI, you can also select IDE or SATA depending on the needs of the guest OS you will be installing in the VM. If your Guest OS does not support the LSI Logic SAS controller type, you may need to select either SATA or IDE as the disk type. Remember, your selection does not depend on the physical hardware of the host, but rather what driver will be used on the guest VM. If possible you should select SCSI (even though your physical computer may use SATA or IDE) to provide the best performance for your VM.

Next, the "Select a Disk" window will be displayed. In addition to the default "Create a new virtual disk" option, this window provides options to use an existing virtual disk file or use the host computer's physical drive. The existing disk option can be useful if you're creating a new virtual machine and want to retain software and data from an existing guest OS. For example, if you're transferring an older virtual machine created with an earlier version of VMware Workstation Pro, you could create a new virtual machine with VMware Workstation 12, and then use the existing disk option to connect the new virtual machine to the hard drive containing the existing guest OS.

The physical disk option installs the virtual machine directly on an unformatted physical hard drive or partition on the host computer instead of on a virtual disk file on a formatted drive. Using the physical disk option can increase virtual disk speed by allowing the virtual machine to read and write directly from a physical disk, instead of using the host computer's file system for disk accesses, as with the other virtual disk options. However, the physical disk option has the disadvantage of making it more difficult to move the virtual machine to another host computer and should be used only when increased disk performance is more important than the virtual machine's mobility.

Although using the physical disk option installs the guest OS on a hard disk, you can't boot the host computer from this drive. VMware Workstation 12 Pro uses a specialized set of drivers that are intended to work with the virtualization software running on the host computer's OS.

After selecting "Create a new virtual disk" you will be asked to specify the Maximum disk size and select an option for how the disk space will be allocated (see Figure 3-6). Possible options include "Allocate all disk space now" along with options on using one or multiple files in storing the virtual disk's data.

- *Allocate all disk space now*—This option sets aside an area of the host computer's hard drive for the virtual machine's use, which reduces disk fragmentation and improves performance. However, it has the disadvantage of taking up more disk space on the host computer. This option is often best used when creating a virtual server to use in a production environment.

- *Store virtual disk as a single file*—Use this option to store the virtual disk on a single file, which takes up less space. This option can be used only with OSs that support file sizes larger than 2 GB.

- *Split virtual disk into multiple files*—This option, the default, is useful if you're going to move a virtual machine by using a FAT32-formatted removable drive that doesn't allow files larger than 2 GB. While it is sometimes easier to move or back up multiple smaller files as compared to a single large file, using multiple smaller files can reduce the virtual machine's performance.

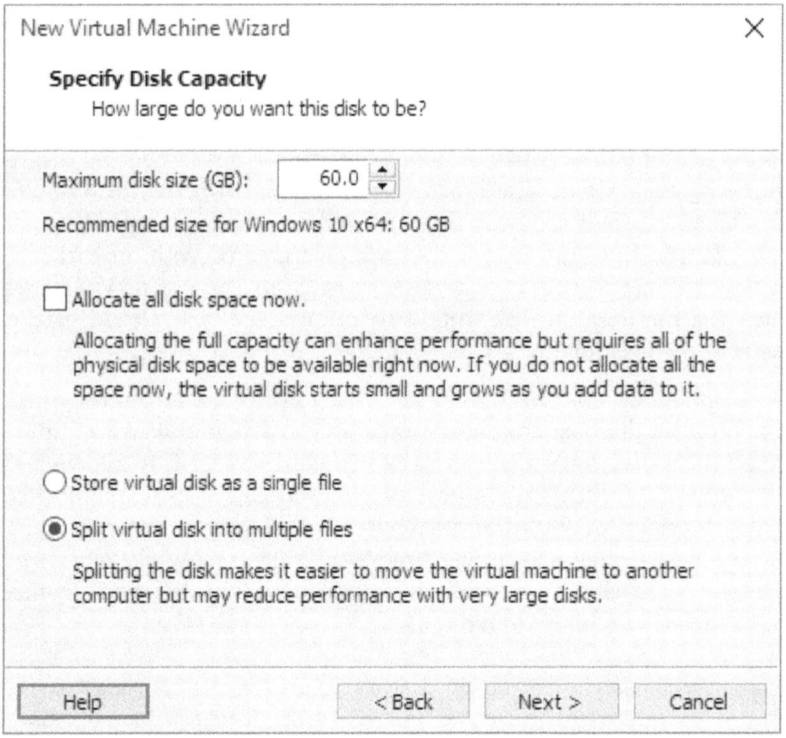

Figure 3-6   New Virtual Machine Wizard – Specify Disk Capacity window

Source: VMware Workstation

After selecting the disk capacity and allocation method, you next see a screen that asks you to enter the name and location of the virtual disk file. By default, the disk file is placed in the same folder as the virtual machine and uses the virtual machine's name with the extension .vmdk. If you're planning to have the virtual machine use multiple disks (for example, servers often use separate drives for the OS and data), you might want to change the default name to include a disk number or other identifier.

After specifying the virtual disk name and location, the final step is reviewing the settings you selected.

The Ready to Create Virtual Machine window also has a Customize Hardware button used to configure more detailed hardware settings, such as adding CD/DVD-ROM drives and ports. If you use the Easy Install option, you will also have a "Power on this virtual machine after creation" check box you can select to start the virtual machine as soon as the wizard is finished. The virtual machine is then created, and the guest OS is installed automatically if you selected the Easy Install option. The new virtual machine will be automatically added as a tab in the administrative console.

In the following activity, you create a virtual machine for a later installation of the Windows Server 2016 guest OS.

Activity 3-2: Creating a Virtual Machine for Windows Server 2016

Time Required: 15 minutes

Objective: Create a virtual machine for a later installation of Windows Server 2016.

Requirements: Completion of Activity 3-1

Description: Now that you have installed VMware Workstation 12 Pro, your next task in to configure and test a Windows Server 2016 server for use by the Superior Technical College. In this activity, you create a virtual machine that you will later use to install the Windows Server 2016 guest OS. You will then test the virtual machine by booting it into the firmware.

1. If necessary, log on to your workstation with your assigned username and password.

2. Start VMware Workstation 12 Pro by using one of the installed shortcuts.

3. If this is the first time you have started VMware Workstation 12 Pro, a Welcome to VMware Workstation 12 Pro window will be displayed asking for your license. Click the **I want to try VMware Workstation Pro for 30 days** option, enter your email address, click **Continue**, and then click **Next** to display the Thank you message page. After reading the information on your evaluation license, click **Finish** to close the Welcome page and display the Home tab and Library pane as shown previously in Figure 3-1.

4. Check the default document path to store virtual machines by clicking **Edit, Preferences** to display the Preferences window and verify that the default path is C:\Users*username* \Documents\Virtual Machines. Briefly look at the options but do not change the defaults. After viewing the options, click **OK** to close the Preferences window.

5. From the Home tab, click the **Create a New Virtual Machine** button to start the New Virtual Machine Wizard.

6. In the Welcome window, click the **Custom** option button, and then click **Next** to display the Choose the Virtual Machine Hardware Compatibility window.

7. In the Hardware compatibility list box, click **Workstation 6.5-7.x** and notice that the Limitations section lists no SATA or EFI support and a 32 GB memory limit. Click **Workstation 12.0** in the list box to change the setting back. Notice Workstation 12.0 has no limitations on SATA and that it supports 64 GB RAM and up to 16 virtual CPUs. Click **Next** to display the Guest Operating System Installation window.

8. In the Guest Operating System Installation window, if necessary, click the **I will install the operating system later** option button, and then click **Next**.

9. In the Select a Guest Operating System window, click the **Microsoft Windows** option button, click the **Version** list arrow, and then click the latest version of the **Windows Server 2016** edition. Click **Next** to display the Name the Virtual Machine window.

The version of Windows Server you select in step 9 should match the ISO file you downloaded in Chapter 1.

10. By default, the virtual machine name matches the OS version, and the virtual machine folder is created in Documents\Virtual Machines. Leave the virtual machine name as **Windows Server 2016**, record the path shown in the Location text box, and then click **Next** to display the Firmware Type window.

---

11. Select the **EFI** firmware type and then click **Next** to display the Processor Configuration window.

12. In the Processor Configuration window, verify that one processor is selected and then click **Next** to display the Memory for the Virtual Machine window.

13. As described earlier in this section, if you have limited memory on your host computer and are planning to run multiple virtual machines at the same time, be sure the total memory doesn't exceed the threshold in the Memory tab of the Preferences dialog box (explained later in "Using the Administrative Console Menus") and then click **Next**.

You can change the amount of memory later, as long as the virtual machine is stopped.

14. In the Network Type window, if necessary click the **Use network address translation (NAT)** option button (unless your instructor specifies another option for your network environment), and then click **Next**. (You can change this option at any time, even while the virtual machine is running.)

15. In the Select I/O Controller Types window, make sure the LSI Logic SAS (Recommended) option button is selected, and then click **Next**.

16. In the Select a Disk Type window, leave the default SCSI (Recommended) option button selected, and then click **Next**.

17. In the Select a Disk window, make sure the Create a new virtual disk option button is selected, and then click **Next**.

18. In the Specify Disk Capacity window, leave the Allocate all disk space now option unchecked, and then enter 120 in the Maximum disk size (GB) text box. If necessary click the **Store virtual disk as a single file** option, leave the Allocate all disk pace now option unchecked, and then click **Next** to display the Specify Disk File window.

Usually, you don't want to select the Allocate all disk space now option unless you're installing a production server and performance is a major concern, so for most virtual machines you should leave the Allocate all disk space now option unchecked.

19. In the Specify Disk File window, verify that the name for the virtual disk file is the same as the virtual machine name entered in step 10, with the .vmdk extension added. After verifying the filename and location, click **Next** to display a Ready to Create Virtual Machine window summarizing your selections.

20. Verify your selections, and then click **Finish**. The virtual machine is created and the administrative console is displayed with a new tab for the virtual machine.

21. To boot your new virtual machine into the EFI firmware, click the **VM** menu, click the **Power** option, and then click **Power On to Firmware**. A Removable Devices message box will be displayed describing the devices that connected to the virtual machine using the Removable Devices menu option. After reading the options, click **OK** to close the message window.

22. Click in the Boot Manager window, then press the **down arrow** key to highlight the **Enter setup** option and press **Enter**.

23. Press **Enter** again to select **Configure boot options** and record the boot configuration options. You will be using the Change boot order option in Activity 3-9 to install Windows Server 2016 guest OS from an ISO image.

24. After viewing the options, press the **Esc** key to return to the Boot Manager screen. Select the **Shut down the system** option to return to the Windows Server 2016 startup tab.

25. You may leave VMware Workstation 12 Pro open for the next activity.

Creating Virtual Machines with Easy Install

VMware Workstation 12 Pro users can use the **Easy Install feature** to automate installing a recent Windows or Linux OS while creating a virtual machine. For example, when installing Linux or Windows 10 guest OS, this feature partitions and formats the drive automatically. The Easy Install utility next installs the Windows or Linux OS optionally using the product key and other details you supply. Finally, Easy Install completes the guest installation by installing VMware Tools, all without any additional user input. In the following activity, you practice using the Easy Install feature to install Ubuntu Linux on a virtual machine.

Activity 3-3: Installing Ubuntu Linux with Easy Install

Time Required: 30 minutes

Objective: Perform an automated installation of Ubuntu Linux on a virtual machine.

Requirements: Completion of Activity 3-1 and the Ubuntu Linux ISO image file (obtained from your instructor or downloaded from the Ubuntu Web site at *www.ubuntu.com*)

Description: One of the concerns when surfing the Web, downloading files, or opening email attachments is the possibility of malware. One way to reduce your risk is to do your Web surfing and email on a virtual machine. Assume that the software development company you work for wants certain users to browse the Web for competitive software products. To help prevent malware from affecting their desktop systems, your IT manager has asked you to create a Linux-based virtual machine that will be used for this task. In this activity, you use VMware's Easy Install feature to create a virtual machine running Ubuntu Linux.

1. If necessary, log on to your workstation with your assigned username and password.

2. If necessary, acquire a copy of the latest Ubuntu desktop software. To obtain the Ubuntu desktop you can go to the Ubuntu Web site (www.ubuntu.com), click the Desktop menu link, and then click the Download Ubuntu button. Save the .iso file in the folder you created in Chapter 1, Activity 1-1.

3. Start VMware Workstation 12 Pro and click the **Home** tab. From the Home tab, click the **Create a New Virtual Machine** button to start the New Virtual Machine Wizard.

4. Click the **Typical** option button, and then click **Next**.

5. In the Guest Operating System Installation window, click the **Installer disc image file (iso)** option button. Click the **Browse** button, navigate to the location of the Ubuntu ISO file, and double-click the file. Verify that VMware has detected the OS and shows that it will use Easy Install. Click **Next**.

6. In the Easy Install Information window, enter your full name, username (must be all lowercase), and password. This information will be used by Easy Install to create the default Ubuntu user account. Click **Next** to display the Name the Virtual Machine window.

7. By default, the virtual machine name matches the OS version, and the virtual machine folder is created in Documents\Virtual Machines. Change the virtual machine name to **UbuntuVM-iii** (where iii represents your initials), and then click **Next** to display the Specify Disk Capacity window.

8. In the Specify Disk Capacity window, accept the recommended disk size in the Maximum disk size (GB) text box, click the **Store virtual disk as a single file** option, and then click **Next**.

9. Verify that the entries in the Ready to Create Virtual Machine window are correct. Verify that the "Power on this virtual machine after creation" option is selected. Click **Finish** to start.

10. The virtual machine is then created, and the automated installation of Ubuntu Linux begins. Read and respond to any messages. During the installation, VMware Tools will be installed along with Ubuntu Linux OS. When the installation is complete, record your Ubuntu username and password below:

_____   _____

11. After the Ubuntu guest is created, click the **VM** menu and click **Settings** to open the Virtual Machine Settings window. Check the settings and verify the following values:

Memory = 1 GB

Processors = 1

Hard Disk = 20 GB

Network Controller = NAT (having NAT will allow the VM to access the Internet using the host as its NAT gateway)

12. Click **Cancel** to close the Virtual Machine Settings window.

13. You now have a Ubuntu virtual desktop system that is ready to play with—See how easy that was!

14. If your desktop host has Internet access, you should be able to log on to your Ubuntu desktop using the password you entered in step 6 and surf the Internet.

15. Click the **VM** menu, click **Power**, click **Shut Down Guest**, and then click the **Shut Down** button to power down your guest VM.

16. This completes Activity 3-3. At this time you should close VMware Workstation 12 Pro, but you may stay logged on to your Windows host for the next activity.

Adding Existing Virtual Machines to the Administrative Console

There are several reasons for adding an existing virtual machine to the administrative console, such as running a virtual appliance, moving a virtual machine to another computer, or distributing a virtual machine to multiple hosts.

As you learned in Chapter 1, a virtual appliance is an application that's already installed on a virtual machine and ready to run. With virtual appliances, an application can be shared among several users without having to install the application software on each physical computer. Of course, you need licenses for all computers running the virtual appliance. After purchasing and downloading a virtual appliance, you copy the virtual machine files to each host computer where you want to run the virtual appliance. Next, you add the virtual appliance to the host computer's VMware Workstation 12 Pro administrative console, as described in this section.

You might need to move a virtual machine to another computer to improve its speed by placing it on a faster host or to continue running a virtual machine if the original host computer fails. Distributing a virtual machine to several hosts is often done in schools and other training environments; for example, you might have several students using the same virtual machine to perform an activity. To move or distribute a virtual machine to other compatible hosts you can simply copy the virtual machine files to the new hosts and then add the virtual machine to the administrative console, as described in this section.

When distributing a virtual machine to multiple computers, be aware of licensing agreement restrictions on using an OS on more than one system. One solution is to get an enterprise license that allows distributing the software to multiple virtual machines.

An important consideration when moving or copying virtual machines is the **universal unique identifier (UUID)** code that VMware assigns to each virtual machine. The UUID identifies the virtual machine and is part of the machine's physical network address (MAC address). When you copy a virtual machine to another host computer, you need to decide whether you want to keep the original computer's UUID. If you're recovering a backup, select the "I moved it" option to keep the original VM's UUID (and MAC address). If you're copying a virtual machine from another source and want to make it a unique machine, select the "I copied it" option to create a new UUID.

You can also add Microsoft Virtual PC virtual machines to the VMware administrative console. Keep in mind, however, that a Virtual PC VM's performance might be slower. To make it run faster, you can convert it to a VMware virtual machine with VMware Converter.

Another option to use when deploying virtual machines on other host environments is exporting and importing virtual machine files using **Open Virtualization Format (OVF)**. As described in Chapter 1, OVF allows you to move a virtual machine from one hypervisor environment to another. Both VMware Workstation 12 Pro and VMware Workstation 12 Player support importing OVF file formats. For example, you can create and configure a Windows Server in VMware Workstation 12 Pro and then use OVF to export the VM files and import them into a host running Windows Hyper-V. Conversely you export the virtual machine files created with Oracle VirtualBox to OVF, and then import the virtual machine's OVF files into VMware Workstation 12 Pro or VMware Workstation 12 Player. In the following activities you will practice using the VMware Workstation 12 Pro administrative console to copy, export, and import virtual machines.

Activity 3-4: Moving an Existing Virtual Machine

Time Required: 15 minutes

Objective: Be able to move an existing VM to another host and add it to the administrative console, and practice removing and adding tabs.

Requirements: Completion of Activity 3-3

Description: Now that you have created and tested the Ubuntu virtual machine on your VMware Workstation 12 Pro, you next will need to move the machine to a production environment. In this activity you will simulate this process by moving your existing Ubuntu virtual machine to a different directory, removing the Ubuntu virtual machine from the administrative console, and then adding it back.

1. If necessary, start your Windows host computer and log on with your assigned username and password.

2. Open File Explorer, and create a directory named **LinuxVMs** on the root of the C drive.

3. Use File Explorer to move the folder named UbuntuVM-iii *(where iii represents your initials)* from your Documents\Virtual Machines folder to your new LinuxVMs folder, and then close Windows Explorer.

4. Start VMware Workstation 12 Pro. Notice that the tab for your UbuntuVM-iii has been removed and that when you click the UbuntuVM-iii machine in the Library pane an "X" icon is displayed along with a File not found dialog box containing Remove and Cancel buttons.

5. Click the **Remove** button from the File not found dialog box to remove the UbuntuVM-iii from the Library pane.

6. The following steps test the process the users will use to add the Ubuntu virtual machine to their VMware Workstation 12 Pro hosts. From the Home tab, click the **Open a Virtual Machine** icon and navigate to the **C:\LinuxVMs\UbuntuVM-iii** folder.

7. Click the UbuntuVM-iii configuration file (extension vmx), and then click **Open** to add the virtual machine to your administrative console.

8. Start UbuntuVM by clicking the **UbuntuVM-iii** tab, and then clicking the **Power on this virtual machine** link.

9. In the "This Virtual Machine might have been moved or copied" dialog box that opens, click the **I Moved It** option button to retain the original virtual machine's UUID code. (This step is important to maintain the machine's MAC address on the network.) Click **Yes** to any connection message and then click **OK** to start UbuntuVM. You can now log on and use the Ubuntu guest system.

10. Shut down the UbuntuVM by clicking the **Shut Down Guest** option from the power button located to the right of the Help menu option and then clicking the **Shut Down** option from the VMware Workstation 12 Pro message box.

11. If the Home tab is removed accidentally, you can add it back easily. To practice this, first, remove the Home tab by right-clicking it and clicking **Close Tab**.

12. Restore the Home tab by pointing to **Tabs** and then clicking **Go to Home Tab**.

13. If you accidently remove a virtual machine tab you can quickly restore it by clicking the VM from the Library pane.

14. This completes Activity 3-4. You may leave VMware Workstation 12 Pro running and stay logged on for the next activity.

Activity 3-5: Exporting and Importing Virtual Machines Using OVF

Time Required: 15 minutes

Objective: Be able to export an existing VM to OVF files and then import the OVF file to create a new virtual machine in a separate Library folder.

Requirements: Completion of Activity 3-4

Description: Now that you have created and tested the Ubuntu virtual machine on your VMware Workstation 12 Pro, you next will need to move the machine to a production environment. In this activity you will simulate this process by moving your existing Ubuntu virtual machine to a different directory, removing the Ubuntu virtual machine from the administrative console, and then adding it back. You also learn how to copy a VM to another host by exporting the files to OVF and then importing the OVF files as a new virtual machine.

1. If necessary, start your Windows host computer and log on with your assigned username and password.

2. Use File Explorer to create a new folder on your C drive named **ExportedVMs**.

3. If necessary, start VMware Workstation 12 Pro and click the UbuntuVM-iii tab to make it active.

4. Open the **File** menu and click the **Export to OVF...** option to display the Export Virtual Machine to OVF window.

5. Navigate to your new C:\ExportedVMs folder and click the **Save** button. A VMware Workstation 12 Pro message box will be displayed showing the status of the Exporting operation. This process will take a few minutes depending on your host's speed. After the process is completed, you will have 3 Open Virtualization Format package files in your ExportedVMs folder. Use Windows Explorer to open your ExportedVMs folder and view the files. These files can be copied to other host computers. Record the file names and sizes below:

_____   _____

_____   _____

_____   _____

6. To import an OVF file to VMware Workstation 12 Pro, click the Home tab and then click the **Open a Virtual Machine** button.

7. Navigate to your C:\ExportedVMs folder and the click the **UbuntuVM-iii.ovf** (Open Virtualization Format) file. Click **Open** to display the Import Virtual Machine dialog box.

8. In the "Name for the new virtual machine" text box, change the name to **UbuntuVM-iii2** and then use the **Browse** button to change the path to your **C:\LinuxVMs** folder and click **OK**.

9. After making these changes, click the **Import** button to display the Importing UbuntuVM-iii2 status window. If you receive a message informing you that the VM does not meet compliance checks, click **Retry** to relax the restriction and start the import process. The import process will take a few minutes. After the process is completed a new tab with the name UbuntuVM-iii2 will be added to your administrative console.

10. Click the Power on button to start the imported UbuntuVM-iii2 virtual machine and click **OK** to close the Removable Devices dialog box.

When starting an imported virtual machine, VMware Workstation 12 Pro will automatically supply a new UUID as it would a new virtual machine.

11. Use the **Shut Down Guest** option to shut down the UbuntuVM-iii2 VM.

12. This completes Activity 3-5. You may leave VMware Workstation 12 Pro running for the next activity.

Using the Administrative Console Menus

The administrative console window is organized into areas which include the toolbar across the top, the Library pane on the left, and the Summary/Console pane containing a Home tab along with tabs for each virtual machine. When you select a VM by clicking the tab, the Summary/Console pane for that virtual machine will be shown to the right of the Library pane. Notice that the Summary/Console pane includes a Devices section showing all the devices for that VM on the left and a small guest console window on the right as shown in Figure 3-7.

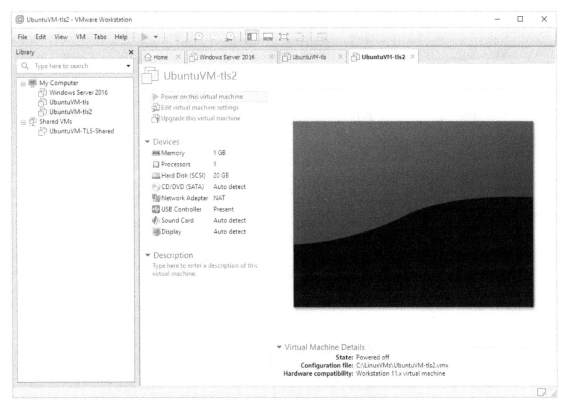

Figure 3-7 Administrative console showing the virtual machine Summary/Console pane

Source: VMware Workstation

Located above the Devices section are links that allow you to power on the virtual machine, edit virtual machine settings, or upgrade the virtual machine. Under the console, the Console/Summary pane shows status information including the virtual machine's current state, compatibility mode, and location of configuration files. When you power on a virtual machine, the Summary/Console pane will be replaced by the guest's operating system console pane. You can switch between the Summary/Console pane and guest console pane using the View menu as described later in this section.

Buttons to the right of the menu bar allow you to change the screen display by hiding the Library or Thumbnail bar, or change to full screen mode. If you start a VM and click the Full Screen mode, the VM's desktop will be enlarged to fill the display. In this section we will explore each of the administrative console's work areas identified previously in Figure 3-7.

The Library Pane

The Library pane shows folders containing virtual machines. By grouping virtual machines in folders you can control and manage multiple virtual machines as a group. Folders and virtual machines that are stored locally are shown under My Computer while shared virtual machines that are available to other hosts are shown under Shared VMs. If you connect to a remote host, the shared VMs on that host will be shown in the Library pane. You can organize virtual machines in the Library pane by creating folders and then dragging and dropping VMs into the folders based on their type or usage. You can also create new VMs in the folder by selecting the folder prior to creating the VM. In addition to organizing VMs, the library folders can be used to manage groups of virtual machines. For example, you can click a folder name and then click the Start button to start all virtual machines in the folder. You will learn how to work with folder groups in the "Working with Virtual Machines" section.

The Menu Tool Bar

The Menu tool bar contains a number of menu options along with buttons that allow you to work with and manage virtual machines along with the VMware Workstation 12 Pro environment. Certain options are grayed out or not available based on the running state of the VM you have selected in the main window. The buttons to the right of the menu options (see Figure 3-7) are shortcuts that allow you to quickly perform certain operations. The Power button allows you to start, pause, or shut down the selected VM. Pausing a VM is similar to hibernating a Windows system. The current state of the VM is saved and the guest OS is shut down. The Interrupt button sends a Ctrl+Alt+Del key sequence to the selected guest VM. You may optionally use this button to log on to a Windows Server or shut down the Ubuntu guest. The clock symbols are used to manage snapshots. You can use these buttons to take a snapshot that saves the state of the selected VM, or return the VM to a saved state. You will work with snapshots in later activities. The Window buttons are used to hide or view the Library and Thumbnail panes. The Screen button may be used to place a VM in full screen mode or return it to window mode. The Unity button is used to invoke VMware Workstation 12 Pro Unity mode. In Unity mode, the guest VM's applications can be run from the host computer. You will learn more about using Unity mode later in this chapter. The final Console button may be used to hide or display the VM's desktop in the main window. If you click the button on a running VM, the guest desktop will be minimized to the size shown in Figure 3-7. You can then view the VM's status information or use the Details pane to view or change settings. After viewing or changing the settings you can click the Console button again to return the guest desktop to the entire main window pane. You can further enlarge the size of your guest desktop by hiding the Thumbnail and Library panes or using the Full Screen button. You will work with these buttons and other options in Activity 3-6.

Certain VM settings such as the amount of memory cannot be changed while the VM is running.

The File Menu The File menu contains the following options:

- *New Virtual Machine*—Use this option to create virtual machines or open another administrative console. You can also use it to create teams.

- *New Window*—Use this option to open another administrative console containing only a Home tab.

- *Open and Close Tab*—Use these options to add and remove virtual machine tabs from the administrative console. With Open, you can browse to a folder containing an existing virtual machine and add it to the administrative console. Close removes the currently selected tab from the administrative console without deleting the virtual machine files. You can later add the VM back using the Open option.

- *Connect to Server*—Use this option to connect to a remote VMware Workstation 12 Pro or VSphere host.

- *Connect to VMware vCloud Air*—Use this option to connect to a cloud-based server and access its virtual machines.

- *Virtualize a Physical Machine*—This option starts the VMware Conversion Wizard. You will need to download and install the converter prior to using this option.

- *Export to OVF*—Use this option to export the selected VM files to the industry standard OVF format. The files can then be distributed to other host computers and imported into their native format. This option is grayed out and not available if the VM is running.

- *Map Virtual Disks*—Use this option to map a drive letter from the host computer to any virtual disk, which is useful for copying files while a virtual machine is shut down.

- *Exit*—Use this option to close the administrative console.

The Edit Menu The Edit menu contains Cut, Copy, Paste, Virtual Network Editor, and Preferences options. You will learn how to use the Virtual Network Editor option to configure your virtual network environment later in this chapter. The Preferences option (see Figure 3-8) includes the following configuration options you can use to customize VMware settings. You will explore these options in Activity 3-6.

- *Workspace*—As shown in Figure 3-8, you can use this option to change the default location for creating or opening virtual machines, set the hardware compatibility level to other versions of VMware Workstation 12 Pro, change startup settings, or set a location for screenshots. You can also use the options under the Virtual machines heading to enable shared folders on all virtual machines or run powered-on virtual machines in the background after closing the administrative console. Running virtual machines in the background is important when using shared virtual machines and you want to save host resources.

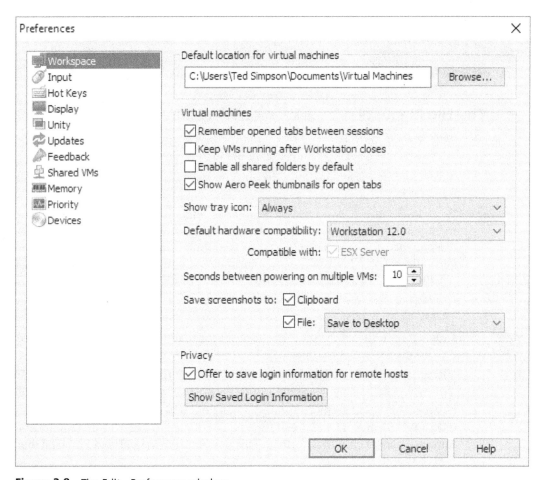

Figure 3-8 The Edit - Preferences window

Source: VMware Workstation

- *Input*—Use this option to control how a virtual machine takes control of the mouse and keyboard. You can also set how the mouse cursor behaves when you're running VMware Tools.

- *Hot Keys*—You can use this option to change the default key combination for switching mouse and keyboard control from a virtual machine to the host computer. The default is the Shift key, but you might need to change it if you're running software on the virtual machine that uses the same keys for an internal function. You can click other keys to set a different key combination.

- *Display*—In this option you control the autofit features that resize virtual machine and application windows automatically. You can also decide how to handle full-screen view, such as stretching or centering the VM window to fit in the host window, or letting the window resize automatically if you're using VMware Tools.

- *Unity*—Unity is a VMware Workstation 12 Pro function that enables you to separate applications from a virtual machine so that they can be run without the VMware interface, as though the applications are running on the host. You can also use this option to change the hot-key combination used for Unity applications. You will learn more about using Unity in the "Working with Virtual Machines" section.

- *Updates*—You can use this option to configure checking for updates of VMware Workstation 12 Pro on the host and automatically updating VMware Tools (discussed later in "Working with Virtual Machines") on the guest OS.

- *Feedback*—Use this option to turn on or off the option of sending anonymous data to VMware to help improve the VMware Workstation 12 Pro products.

- *Shared VMs*—You can use this option to enable or disable sharing VMs on the host computer and select what port number will be used. By default VMware uses port 443 when connecting to a VM from a remote host. You will work with Shared Virtual Machines in the "Working with Virtual Machines" section.

- *Memory*—You can set the maximum amount of RAM used by all running virtual machines and specify whether you want the host computer to swap virtual machine memory to and from the host computer's paging file. The "Fit all virtual machine memory into reserved host RAM" option prevents paging and results in the best virtual machine performance. The disadvantage of using this option is that fitting all virtual machines into physical memory without paging reduces the number of virtual machines you can run at one time.

- *Priority*—Use you can use this option to tune VMware performance. For example, you can change what priority Windows gives a virtual machine's processes. Normal means the virtual machine receives resources equal to all other processes on the host, but this level can be elevated to High to increase VM performance. However, elevating VM performance may slow down other applications on your host computer. You can also decide whether you want to take and restore snapshots in the background so that you can continue working.

- *Devices*—Use this tab to enable or disable the autorun feature on the host computer. By default autorun is disabled as this works best for most virtual machine operations.

The View Menu The View menu contains the following options for controlling how virtual machines are displayed and what menus and options you see in the administrative console:

- *Full Screen*—Use this option to have the selected virtual machine's user console take up the host computer's entire screen. You can exit full-screen mode and return control to the host computer OS by pressing Shift+Enter.

- *Unity view*—Unity is a VMware feature that allows your VM guest applications to be run on the host OS. This option allows you to work with Unity configuration settings. You will learn more about using Unity view later in this chapter.

- *Console View*—Use this option when the virtual machine is running to switch between the Summary/Console pane and guest console pane. As shown previously in Figure 3-7, the Summary/Console pane contains a minimal guest console along with a Devices section showing the settings for memory, hard disk, CD-ROM, Ethernet, USB, and audio. When you start a virtual machine, the pane changes from the Summary/Console pane to a full guest console automatically, showing only the virtual machine's OS console and Library panes. You can use the Console View menu option to change back to Summary/Console pane when you want display or change the virtual machine's settings while the virtual machine is running.

- *Fit Window Now or Fit Guest Now*—Use Fit Window Now to fit the console view into your display, which is useful if you have disabled the Autofit Window setting. Fit Guest Now is used when Autofit Guest is disabled so that you can resize the virtual machine window and remove any unused space in the administrative console.

- *Autosize*—This option contains settings to change how the administrative console and guest OS windows are displayed. Settings include Autofit Guest, Stretch Guest, and Center Guest. In addition, there is a check box you can use to Autofit the VMware Workstation 12 Pro administrative console. You should experiment with these settings to see what works best for your virtual machine.

- *Customize*—Use this option to enable or disable display of the panes and tabs from the administrative console.

The VM Menu The VM menu has options for managing and configuring a virtual machine selected in the main window. To use these options, select a virtual machine's tab in the administrative console. If a tab isn't displayed, select File, Open from the menu. Certain options are grayed out depending on whether that virtual machine is running or not.

You can right-click a virtual machine tab for a quick shortcut to options in the VM menu.

- *Power*—Use this option to start up or shut down your virtual machine. As shown in Table 3-2, there are a few ways you can use to power on or shut down a virtual machine depending on your needs.

Table 3-2 Settings in the VM menu's Power option

Setting	Description	Key Combination
Start Up/Resume Guest	If a virtual machine has been suspended or paused, you can use this option to restart the VM from the exact place you paused it.	Ctrl+B
Power On/Start Up Guest	This option also starts the virtual machine that has been powered off.	Ctrl+B
Power Off/Shut Down Guest	The Power Off option shuts down the virtual machine quickly, much like using the power off button on a physical computer. Using Shut Down Guest is generally preferable to Power Off as it goes through the guest OS shutdown process. You should usually try using the OS's shutdown procedure first to avoid possible data loss or corruption.	Crtl+E

Table 3-2   Settings in the VM menu's Power option (*continued*)

Setting	Description	Key Combination
Suspend/Suspend Guest	This option saves the virtual machine's current configuration so that you can restart it later with the same settings; useful for continuing exactly where you left off.	Ctrl+J
Reset/Restart Guest	This option resets the virtual machine, much like pressing the reset button on a physical computer.	Ctrl+R

- *Removable Devices*—This option will display devices such as the network adapter, printer, sound card, and CD/DVD that can be connected or removed from a virtual machine that is running. The option will be grayed out if the VM is powered down. For example, you can use this option if you want the selected VM to access the physical optical drive or sound card from the host computer.

- *Pause*—Use this option to pause a running VM. You can later use the Resume option from the Power menu to restart the VM exactly where you left off.

- *Send Ctrl+Alt+Del*—Use this option on a running VM to send a Ctrl+Alt+Del key sequence to the guest OS. (You can also use the Interrupt button from the menu bar.)

- *Grab Input*—Select this option to give the currently selected virtual machine keyboard and mouse control. To return control to the host computer, use Ctrl+Alt.

- *Snapshot*—Snapshots are used to save the current state of your virtual machine. The snapshot menu contains options for taking a snapshot, reverting to snapshot, or accessing the Snapshot Manager window. You will be using this menu to perform snapshot operations later in this chapter.

- *Capture Screen*—Use this option from a running VM to take a screenshot of the virtual machine's desktop shown in the current tab. This option is useful when you're creating documentation.

- *Install/Reinstall VMware Tools*—Use this option to install or reinstall VMware Tools in the guest OS of a running virtual machine. The VMware Tools provide additional capabilities such as easily moving the cursor between the guest and the host, and providing increased performance. VMware Tools is installed automatically when you create a new VM using the Easy Install method. You will learn how to install VMware Tools manually in the "Working with Virtual Machines" section.

- *Manage*—Use this option to perform a variety of management options on a virtual machine including creating a clone copy, sharing the VM, cleaning up the virtual disk, and uploading the VM to another host environment. You will learn more about using the Manage options in the "Working with Virtual Machines" section.

- *Settings*—Use this option to open the Virtual Machine Settings dialog box containing Hardware and Options tabs as shown in Figure 3-9.

The Hardware tab contains a list of virtual device options for configuring memory, the hard drive, the CD/DVD-ROM drive, the Ethernet adapter, USB ports, the sound adapter, the display, and processors. You can configure these same settings from the virtual machine's Devices pane in the administrative console (see Figure 3-7). When you click a device from the Devices section of the Summary/Console pane, the Hardware tab shown in Figure 3-9 is displayed.

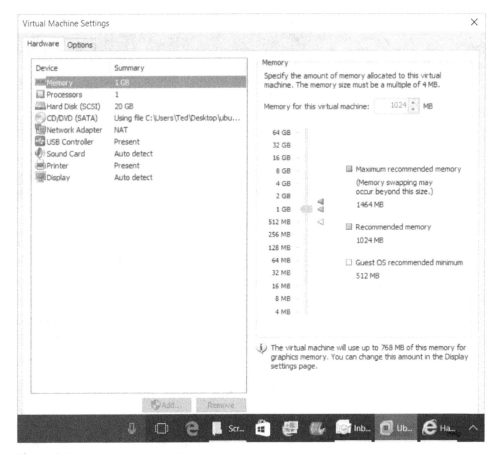

Figure 3-9 Virtual Machine Settings window

Source: VMware Workstation

The virtual machine must be powered off to change memory or hard drive settings, but you can change CD/DVD, network adapter, USB, and sound card settings while the virtual machine is powered on. (Before a USB device is enabled, the virtual machine must be powered on and the USB device must be connected to a USB port on the host computer.) The Hardware tab also includes buttons for adding or removing hardware devices, but the virtual machine must be powered off to use them. You will work more with the Hardware tab in the "Working with Virtual Machines" section.

The Options tab shown in Figure 3-10 provides additional settings you can use to configure VMware Workstation 12 Pro.

- *General*—Use this setting to change the virtual machine name, guest operating system or version, and working directory path where snapshot and suspend files are stored; for example, you might want to store snapshots on a removable drive for backup and portability reasons. You can also select the Enhanced Virtual Keyboard option to

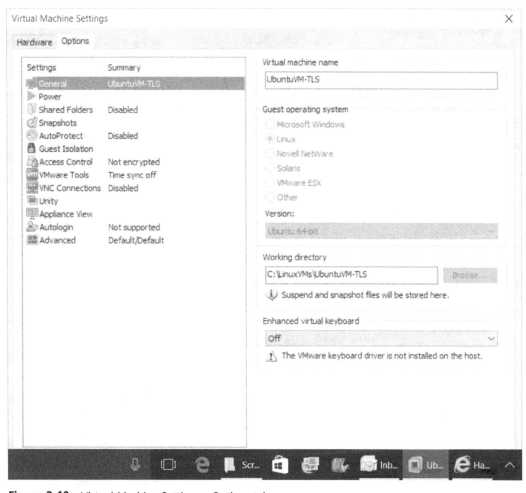

Figure 3-10   Virtual Machine Settings – Options tab

Source: VMware Workstation

enable international or special keyboards or have Ctrl+Alt+Delete display Windows Task Manager in only the guest OS.

- *Power*—Use this setting to change how virtual machines start and shut down. (Refer to the options listed previously in Table 2-1.) You can also select to enter full screen mode after powering on, close after powering off, and report battery information to guest.

- *Shared Folders*—Use this setting to set up access to shared folders on the host computer.

- *Snapshots*—Use this setting to configure how VMware handles snapshots when powering off the virtual machine (see Table 3-3).

Table 3-3   Power off options for snapshots

Option	Description
Just power off	No changes are made to snapshots; it's the default option.
Revert to snapshot	The virtual machine returns its configuration automatically to the last snapshot you made. This option is useful if you have a virtual machine intended to test software installations. After your test is finished, the virtual machine is returned to its original state.
Take a new snapshot	VMware takes a new snapshot when you power off.
Ask me	You can decide whether a snapshot is necessary when shutting down the virtual machine. This option is useful if you make a mistake or something goes wrong because you can revert to the previous snapshot.

- *AutoProtect*—You can use the AutoProtect option to enable VMware to automatically take snapshots at the selected interval. By default VMware will take daily snapshots, saving the snapshots for up to three days.

- *Guest Isolation*—Use this setting to determine whether files can be dragged or pasted between the virtual machine and the host.

- *Access Control*—You can use this setting to turn on encryption and enable restrictions. Restrictions prevent the user from modifying the virtual machine or its settings. This is important when a VM is shared among multiple users.

- *VMware Tools*—Use this setting to enable synchronizing time between the host and guest. You can also use this setting to specify how you want VMware to check for and upgrade VMware Tools: upgrading automatically at the next power on, upgrading manually, or using the application setting in the Updates setting of the Preferences dialog box (the default).

- *VNC Connections*—Use this setting to have the selected virtual machine accessed remotely through Virtual Network Computer (VNC) software, using the selected port and optional password. By default VNC connections are disabled.

- *Unity*—When Unity view is used, you can customize "decorations," such as window borders and colors, in the application window as well as enable or disable the virtual Start menu.

- *Appliance View*—Use this setting to enter version and author information when creating a VM to be used for a virtual appliance.

- *Autologin*—This setting is used with VMs running the Windows guest operating system to automatically log on to Windows after starting the virtual machine.

- *Advanced*—Use this setting to configure default file storage locations and to change process priorities for grabbing input, setting memory page trimming, and configuring boot options. This option also contains a setting to enable or disable Template mode for the selected VM. Templates are important when deploying multiple VMs that all need a similar guest configuration. VMs that are configured as templates cannot be run or changed. Template mode is used to make the VM a master for cloning. You will learn how to create clones from a template VM in the "Working with Virtual Machines" section.

The Help Menu The Help menu contains options for searching help topics, viewing the user manual, checking for updates, and entering the serial number (if you didn't enter this information during installation). If you purchase a full version of VMware Workstation 12 Pro, you can also use this option to enter a new serial number without having to reinstall the software.

Activity 3-6: Working with the Administrative Console Menus

Time Required: 15 minutes

Objective: Practice using menu options in the VMware Workstation 12 Pro administrative console.

Requirements: Completion of Activities 3-4 and 3-5

Description: In this activity, you practice using menu options in the VMware Workstation 12 Pro administrative console.

1. If necessary, start VMware Workstation 12 Pro and click the **UbuntuVM-iii** tab to make it active.

2. Click **Edit, Preferences** from the menu to open the Preferences dialog box. Click the **Updates** tab, and verify that the Software updates options are checked. Click the **Automatically update VMware Tools on a virtual machine** check box to enable automatically updating VMware Tools.

3. Click the **Hot Keys** tab, and record the default hot key setting:

   _____

4. Click the **Workspace** tab, and record the default path to your virtual machine files:

   _____

5. Click **OK** to close the Preferences dialog box. If necessary, click **Yes** to close the UAC dialog box.

6. Click the **VM** menu and click the **Power** option. Record the available options in the space below:

   _____

7. Click the **Start Up Guest** option to start your **UbuntuVM-iii** virtual machine, and if necessary click **OK** to close the Removable Devices dialog box.

8. Click **View, Full Screen** from the menu to switch the view of your virtual machine.

9. Click **View, Autosize** from the menu and experiment with the different view options.

10. Press **Ctrl+Alt+Enter** to switch back and forth between full screen and administrative console views. Notice that you can also use the Full Screen button on the toolbar to switch in and out of full screen mode.

11. Switch out of full screen mode. Click **VM** from the toolbar menu, point to **Power**, and record the options available for powering off or shutting down your UbuntuVM:

    _____

12. Click the **Shut Down Guest** option and then click the **Shut Down** button in the VMware dialog box to shut down the UbuntuVM virtual machine.

13. Click the **VM** menu and record all available power on options:

    _____

14. Use the Power On option to start your UbuntuVM-iii virtual machine. When you see the logon window asking for the username, click the **VM** menu and notice that all items are available.

15. Suspend the virtual machine by clicking **VM** from the menu, pointing to **Power**, and clicking **Suspend Guest.**

16. Click the **VM** menu and record the available Power options:

    _____

17. Click **VM**, point to **Power**, and record any power options that weren't listed in step 6:

    _____

18. Click the **Resume Guest** option and record the results on the following line. Do you think UbuntuVM started faster than it did in step 7? If so, when you're ending a virtual machine session, you might want to suspend the virtual machine instead of powering it off.

    _____

19. Click the **Power Off** option from the toolbar. You should see a warning message asking you to shut down the guest before powering off. This step prevents loss of data and possible corruption of programs or files on the virtual machine. If you're logged off the guest OS, clicking the **Power Off** button and powering off the virtual machine should be safe. However, when possible, using the shutdown procedure is best. To shut down your UbuntuVM-iii, click **Cancel**, click the **arrow** to the right of the Power icon, and then click **Shut Down Guest.** When asked to confirm this action, click the **Shut Down** button to power off the virtual machine.

20. This completes the activities in this section. You may close VMware Workstation 12 Pro.

Working with Virtual Machines

In the following sections, you learn how to apply some of the VMware Workstation 12 Pro options you have learned about to performing a variety of common virtualization tasks, such as starting and stopping virtual machines, configuring virtual devices, installing and working with guest operating systems, and performing tasks such as snapshots and cloning.

Starting and Stopping Virtual Machines

After installing a guest OS, you can begin using the virtual machines much as you would any physical computer. You can start a virtual machine using either the VM menu or the start option from the Tool bar or virtual machine tab. The VM menu includes three major startup options: Start Up Guest, Power On, and Power On to Firmware. If VMware Tools is installed on the guest OS, the Startup Guest option (also referred to as a "soft" power up) will run a script that will renew the IP address during the startup process. The Power On option (also referred to a "hard" power up) simply loads the guest OS, and the Power On to Firmware option will boot the virtual machine to the emulated BIOS. Booting to firmware BIOS is useful if you want to configure BIOS settings on the virtual machine such as the boot sequence. Another option available on Windows guest VMs is the Autologin option, which allows you to enable an automatic logon to the Windows guest. You can select the Autologin option from the Options tab of the Virtual Machine Settings option (refer to VM Options discussed in the previous section). When you enable Autologin you will be asked to enter the log on credentials that will be used to log onto the Windows guest using a local user account.

In some cases you may wish to power on a number of virtual machines at one time. You can do this by placing all the virtual machines under a folder in the Library pane. You can power on all virtual machines listed under that folder by clicking the folder name in the Library pane and then clicking the Power on button.

When working with a Library folder containing multiple virtual machines, only the Power on or "Hard power" option is available. The Startup Guest and Power on to Firmware options are not available when starting multiple virtual machines from a library folder.

The Resume and Resume Guest options are used to start a VM that has previously been suspended or paused. If you plan to restart the guest at the same point you are currently using, use the Suspend or Pause option. Suspending a VM saves all of its current state and then returns the VM to that state when you use the Resume option. There are two suspend options: Suspend and Suspend Guest. The Suspend Guest option will run a VMware Tools script that disconnects the guest VM from the network prior to suspending it. The Suspend process can take a few minutes to suspend and resume a VM. Because it leaves the VM in memory, the Pause option takes less time than the Suspend option and is best used when you want to stop a VM for a few minutes in order to have more processor speed to do some work on the host, or another VM. You can then quickly return back to the paused guest. Be aware that when resuming a virtual machine, the guest will not ask for a logon, but just start back up right where you left off. This could be a security problem if the host is shared with other users.

To shut down a guest you should usually try using the OS's shutdown procedure first to avoid possible data loss or corruption.

There are a number of shutdown options. You can perform the normal shutdown from the guest OS desktop. If it is not feasible to go through the Guest operating system's normal shutdown procedure, the next best option is to use the Shut Down Guest option from one of the power menus mentioned above. VMware's Shut Down Guest option will run a VMware Tools script to disconnect the guest from the network and then trigger the guest OS to perform a normal power off procedure to close files and log off. The Suspend Guest option is only available when VMware Tools has been installed in the guest system. The Power Off option is the last resort as it will essentially perform a hard power off similar to holding the power button down on a physical computer.

As shown in Figure 3-11, VMware Workstation 12 Pro includes a number of services that are automatically started when you boot your host computer.

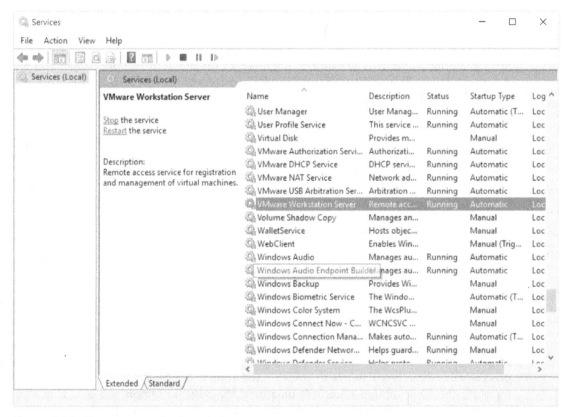

Figure 3-11   Host computer Services window

Source: VMware Workstation

Among the services is the VMware Workstation Server. VMware Workstation Server is a type-2 hypervisor service that is responsible for running virtual machines. This service remains running independent of the VMware Administrative Console. By default, when you close a VM tab or exit the Administrative console while virtual machines are still running, you will see the VMware Workstation 12 Pro dialog box shown in Figure 3-12.

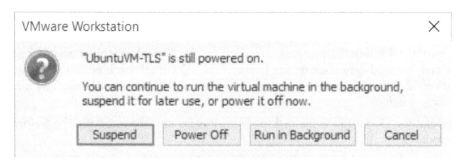

Figure 3-12   VMware Workstation 12 Pro dialog box

Source: VMware Workstation

The Suspend and Power Off buttons shown in Figure 3-12 perform the same power off functions previously described. The **Run in Background** button will close the tab, or VMware Workstation 12 Pro console, while continuing to run the VM in the background. This can be very useful if the VM is performing an ongoing task or if you want to share the VM from a remote host. You can later connect to the background VM by clicking the Virtual machines running icon from the task bar. You will practice running virtual machines in background mode in the following activity.

Activity 3-7: Working with Power Options

Time Required: 15 minutes

Objective: Practice using Power options in the VMware Workstation 12 Pro administrative console.

Requirements: Completion of Activities 3-3, 3-4, and 3-5

Description: In this activity, you will practice running a VM in background and then returning to it.

1. If necessary, start VMware Workstation 12 and then start your UbuntuVM-iii2 virtual machine and log on to Ubuntu using the username and password you set up in Activity 3-3.

2. Get the IP address of your Ubuntu VM by clicking the System Settings icon and then clicking the Network icon. Record the IP address given to your VM below:

_____

3. Close your Ubuntu VM tab by right-clicking the tab and clicking **Close Tab.**

4. When you see the VMware Workstation dialog box as shown previously in Figure 3-12, click the **Run in Background** button.

5. Close the VMware Workstation 12 Pro console.

6. Open a command prompt on your Windows host computer. (Click the Windows button and the enter **cmd** and press Enter.)

7. Enter the command: **Ping ip_address** (where ip_address is the IP address you entered in step 2). You should get a reply from the VM running in background.

8. Restart the Ubuntu VM console by clicking the **Virtual machines** running icon from the task bar and then clicking the **UbuntuVM-iii2** virtual machine. The VMware Workstation 12 Pro administrative console will be reloaded with the UbuntuVM-iii2 desktop console window.

9. Suspend the Ubuntu VM by clicking **VM, Power,** and then clicking the **Suspend Guest** option.

10. This completes Activity 3-7. You can leave VMware Workstation 12 Pro open for the next activity.

Activity 3-8: Working with the Library Pane

Time Required: 15 minutes

Objective: Practice working with the Library pane by creating new folders, moving VMs to a folder, and powering on groups of virtual machines.

Requirements: Completion of Activities 3-3, 3-4, and 3-5

Description: The Library pane allows you to group virtual machines based on their usage. For example, assume that you have a database application that requires multiple Ubuntu servers to be running. Rather than start and stop each VM individually, you can group them in a library folder. In this activity you will create an Ubuntu library, move the Ubuntu VMs to the folder, and then practice starting and stopping them as a group.

1. If necessary, log on to your Windows host and open the VMware Workstation 12 Pro administrative console.

2. In the Library pane, right-click **My Computer** and then click the **New Folder** option from the pull-down menu.

3. Type the name "**Ubuntu Team**" and press **Enter**.

4. Using the Library pane, drag and drop both of your Ubuntu VMs into the Ubuntu Team folder.

5. Click the "+" icon to the left of the Ubuntu Team folder to display the member VMs. A tab will be opened for the Ubuntu Team.

6. With the Ubuntu Team folder highlighted, click the **Power On** button from the menu toolbar. Wait while each of the Ubuntu VMs is powered on.

7. Log on to each of the Ubuntu guest VMs.

8. Click the **Ubuntu Team** folder and then click the **down arrow** to the right of the Power button. Notice that only the Power Off and Suspend options are available as you cannot do a Shut Down Guest on multiple VMs.

9. Click the **Suspend** option. Both VMs will be placed in the Suspend state.

10. This completes Activity 3-8. You can leave the VMware Workstation 12 Pro console open for the next activity.

Configuring Virtual Machine Memory and Virtual CPUs

When a virtual machine is powered off, you can change the amount of RAM or number of virtual processors (vCPUs) it uses. Increasing RAM can make the virtual machine run faster, but you need to be sure you have enough memory available for your host computer to prevent excessive paging, which slows down the entire system. You should have enough physical RAM so that each virtual machine has the recommended minimum memory based on the guest operating system (the recommended minimum for the guest is shown in the Memory pane). To change the RAM amount, double-click Memory in the Devices pane of the virtual machine's tab (or click Memory in the Hardware tab of the Virtual Machine Settings dialog box) to display the Memory page shown previously in Figure 3-9. Use the slider or enter the amount of memory in the memory box, and then click OK to save your changes.

By default a VM is assigned a single processor core. Increasing the number of processors should only be done when the host has more cores than are typically used by all virtual machines running at one time. As described in Chapter 1, assigning an additional processor to a VM can actually decrease a VM's performance. When a VM uses two processors the hypervisor must schedule it during a time that two cores are available. If you are running a single VM on a system that has four cores, increasing the number of processors should increase performance. If you were running three VMs on a processor with four cores, assigning two processors may decrease performance since the VM would have to wait until two cores were both available in order to get scheduled. Since each situation is different, you may need to experiment to see what works best in your environment. You will practice changing memory and processors options for your Windows Server 2016 VM in Activity 3-9.

Working with CD/DVD-ROM Drives and ISO Image Files

By default, a virtual machine is configured to attach the virtual CD/DVD-ROM drive to the secondary IDE controller. If you have multiple CD/DVD-ROM drives on your host computer, VMware might detect a device you don't want to use. To avoid this problem, double-click CD/DVD in the Devices pane of the virtual machine's tab (or on the Hardware tab of the Virtual Machine Settings dialog box) to specify the drive you want your virtual machine to access. You can also connect your virtual machine's CD/DVD-ROM device to an ISO image file while the virtual machine is running or powered off. You will work with connecting an ISO file to a virtual CD device in the "Installing a Guest OS" section.

You can connect a virtual machine to an ISO image file at any time, even while the virtual machine is running.

Installing a Guest OS

In addition to installing a guest OS with the Easy Install feature, as you did earlier, you can install one manually in much the same way you install an OS on a physical computer. One difference when installing an OS on a new virtual machine is that you can use a CD or an ISO image file, but a physical computer (with a blank hard drive) requires installing from physical media. For example, if you're installing Windows Server on a physical computer from a downloaded ISO file, you have to burn a DVD from the ISO image, and then use that DVD for the installation. In the following activity, you modify virtual machine settings and then install Windows Server 2016 on the virtual machine created in Activity 3-2.

Activity 3-9: Installing Windows Server 2016 on an Existing Virtual Machine

Time Required: 30 minutes

Objective: Perform a manual installation of Windows Server 2016 on an existing virtual machine.

Requirements: Completion of Activity 3-2 and the Windows Server 2016 ISO image file downloaded in Chapter 1

Description: Now that you have your Ubuntu servers up and running your next task is to install Windows Server 2016 into the virtual machine you created and then prepare and test it prior to deploying the server for use in the Superior Technical College data center environment. Since VMware's Easy Install option doesn't have the partitioning options you need, you need to perform a manual installation of Windows Server 2016 and manually set the partitions.

1. If necessary, log on to your host computer and start VMware Workstation 12 Pro.

2. Click the **Windows Server 2016** tab to display the summary window.

3. From the summary window, record the current memory size below:

   _____

4. Click the Memory option and increase the memory by up to 1 GB. Be sure to leave 1 GB less than the maximum amount of memory listed in the Maximum recommended memory setting.

5. Click the Processors option and increase the Number of processors to 2.

6. Click the check box to select the **Virtualize Intel VT-xEPT or AMD-V/RVI** option.

7. Configure your virtual machine to use the Windows Server 2016 ISO image file, as described previously in "Working with CD/DVD-ROM Drives and ISO Image Files."

8. Click **OK** to save your changes.

9. Next, you set the virtual machine's firmware to change the settings so the guest VM will boot to the virtual CD/DVD device. Click **VM** on the menu, point to **Power**, and click **Power On to Firmware**. If necessary, click **OK** to bypass any informational messages and continue. When the BIOS screen is displayed, click in this window to transfer keyboard control to the virtual machine.

10. Use the arrow keys to select the **EFI VMware Virtual SATA CDROM Drive** boot option and press **Enter** to display the "Press any key to boot from CD or DVD" message. Press the **Enter** key to start the Windows Setup program from the virtual CD/DVD.

 When using the host computer's physical CD, if the virtual machine doesn't boot from the physical CD/DVD-ROM device, click VM, Removable Devices from the menu to connect to the CD/DVD-ROM drive.

11. Select settings for language, time and currency format, and keyboard method, and then click **Next**.

12. Click **Install now** in the next window.

13. When you see the Activate Windows screen, click the **I don't have a product key** link.

14. Next, you're prompted to enter the Windows Server 2016 edition. Click **Windows Server 2016 Datacenter (Desktop Experience)**, and then click **Next**.

15. In the License terms window, click the **I accept the license terms** check box, and the click **Next**.

16. In the Which type of installation do you want? window, click **Custom: Install Windows only (advanced)**.

17. In the Where do you want to install Windows? window, verify that Drive 0 Unallocated Space is selected, click **New**, change the size to 40,000 MB, then click **Apply**. When a Windows message box is displayed informing you that Windows may create additional partitions, click **OK** to create the new partition and display the partition table. After creating the partition(s), click **Next** to continue.

18. The Windows installation begins. Typically, the process takes around 15 minutes, and your computer restarts at least once, so it is a good time to take a short break. When the installation is finished, the Customize Settings windows will be displayed and you're prompted create a password for the administrator account. (Make sure it's at least six characters, contains uppercase and lowercase letters, and includes a number or non-alphanumeric character.) Record your password below and then click **Finish**.

_____

19. Windows Server requires you to press Ctrl+Alt+Delete key sequence on your keyboard to unlock the server console. To send a Ctrl+Alt+Delete key sequence to the Windows VM, click the **Send Ctrl+Alt+Del to this Virtual Machine** button (located to the right of the power button on the tool bar). After pressing the Ctrl+Alt+Del key sequence button, the Administrator's logon window will be displayed.

20. Enter your password and then click the **blue arrow** icon to log on to your Windows Server 2016. You will next be prompted to select whether or not to allow the PC to be discoverable by other devices on the network. Click **Yes** to display the Server Manager dashboard.

21. The installation of Server 2016 is now finished. Press **Ctrl+Alt** to release the keyboard and mouse back to the host computer. Power off the virtual machine by clicking the **Power** option from the VM menu and then clicking the **Shut Down Guest** option. Click the **Shut Down** button from the VMware Workstation 12 Pro message box to complete the shutdown process.

22. You may leave VMware Workstation 12 Pro open for the next activity.

Working with VMware Tools

VMware Tools consists of utilities and drivers installed in the guest OS that improve performance and add useful management features, such as making it easier to share files and to move control of cursor and keyboard between virtual machines and host windows. If you use the Windows or Linux Easy Install option VMware Tools will be automatically installed along with the OS during the creation of the virtual machine. The install files for VMware Tools are stored and accessed from ISO image files. Each type of OS including Windows, Linux, Solaris, FreeBSD, and NetWare all have ISO image files that are included with the VMware Workstation 12 Pro. The most recent versions of the ISO images are available from the VMware Web site. When you select the option to install or upgrade VMware Tools, the VMware Tools installation wizard compares the ISO images on your local host with the Web site to determine whether it has the most recent version. If you're installing VMware Tools on a Linux virtual machine, refer to the VMware documentation for instructions. In the following activity, you practice installing VMware Tools on your Windows Server 2016 virtual machine.

Activity 3-10: Installing VMware Tools on a Windows Virtual Machine

Time Required: 15 minutes

Objective: Install VMware Tools on an existing virtual machine.

Requirements: Completion of Activity 3-9

Description: In this activity, you learn how to install VMware Tools on your Windows Server 2016 virtual machine.

1. If necessary, open the administrative console and start the **Windows Server 2016** virtual machine. If necessary, click **OK** to close the Removable Devices message box.

2. Click the **Send Ctrl+Alt+Del to this virtual machine** button and then log on to Windows with your administrative username and password (you will need to click inside the virtual machine window in order to enter your password.)

3. When VMware recognizes the guest OS, it will automatically start the VMware Tools Setup wizard. If the wizard does not start automatically, you can manually start the wizard by clicking **VM, Install VMware Tools** from the menu and follow the instructions in the message box to open a Run message box. Enter **D:\setup.exe** (where D: is the drive letter assigned to the drive containing the VMware Tools files) in the Run message box and click **OK**. A message box will be displayed informing you that VMware Tools is installing.

4. Click **Next** when you see the VMware Tools Setup wizard's Welcome window.

5. When you see the Choose Setup Type window, click the **Complete** option button to enable you to run this virtual machine on other VMware products such as vSphere data center, and then click **Next**.

6. In the Ready to install VMware Tools window, click **Install**.

7. When the installation is completed, click **Finish**, and then click **Yes** to restart the virtual machine.

8. Your Windows server will now restart and load VMware Tools.

9. Click the **Shut Down Guest** option from the **VM, Power** menu to safely shut down your virtual machine.

10. You may leave VMware Workstation 12 Pro open for the next activity.

Adding a Virtual Hard Disk

Each virtual machine can have multiple virtual hard disks mapped to files on the host computer's hard drive. You might want several virtual hard disks to learn more about disk management. For example, you could add a drive to a server to practice mirroring disk partitions. To create a new virtual disk, open the Virtual Machine Settings window, Hardware tab, shown previously in Figure 3-9.

From the Hardware tab, click the Add button to display a list of virtual device types. Click Hard Disk from the Hardware types pane and then click Next to display the Select a Disk Type window shown previously in Figure 3-5. The default disk type for most guest operating systems is SCSI, but you can select IDE (also called PATA) or SATA depending on the OS version. For example, if installing an older guest OS such as Windows XP, you may wish to select an IDE disk as the IDE driver is standard in earlier versions of Windows XP. In addition to selecting a disk type, you can optionally select to have the virtual disk act in independent mode. One of the differences between independent mode virtual disks and standard disks is that independent mode virtual disks are not included in snapshots. Independent mode disks can also be configured as either persistent or nonpersistent. Changes made to a nonpersistent disk are not saved when the virtual machine is powered down. Nonpersistent disks are useful in virtual desktop (VDI) environments to prevent users from modifying a shared virtual machine. Nonpersistent disks also save storage space in VDI environments by allowing multiple VMs to share a disk. In Chapter 9 you will learn more about how to use nonpersistent disks when planning and implementing VDI environments. In the following activity, you learn how to add a hard disk to one of your virtual machines.

Activity 3-11: Adding a Hard Disk to a Windows Virtual Machine

Time Required: 15 minutes

Objective: Use the administrative console to add a hard disk to a virtual machine.

Requirements: Completion of Activity 3-10

Description: One of the configuration tasks you need to perform on the new server is to set up a separate disk for data storage. In this activity you will use VMware Workstation 12 Pro to create a new virtual hard disk and then format it for your Windows Server 2016 server.

1. If necessary, log on to your host computer and start VMware Workstation 12 Pro.

2. Click the **Windows Server 2016** tab and make sure the virtual machine is powered off.

3. Click the **Edit virtual machine settings** link from the status pane. In the Hardware tab, click the **Add** button. If a UAC message box opens, click **Yes** to continue and display the Hardware Type window.

4. In the Hardware Type window, click to select **Hard Disk**, if necessary, and then click **Next**.

5. In the Select a Disk Type window, verify that the **SCSI (Recommended)** option button is selected, and then click **Next** to display the Select a Disk window.

6. In the Select a Disk window, verify that the Create a new virtual disk option button is selected and then click **Next** to display the Specify Disk Capacity window.

7. In the Specify Disk Capacity window, enter **100 GB** in the Maximum disk size (GB) text box. Make sure the Allocate all disk space now check box is *not* selected, and then click to select the **Store virtual disk as a single file** option. Click **Next** to display the Specify Disk File window.

 Allocating all disk space now is also referred to as **thick provisioning** and while thick provisioning enhances performance, it also will use up unnecessary disk space. You will learn more about thick and thin provisioning in Chapter 4.

8. In the Specify Disk File window, you may enter a name and location for the virtual disk file. By default the new disk file will be stored in the same folder as your Windows Server 2016 virtual machine. For this activity, record the disk file name and location below and then click **Finish** to place the file in your virtual machine folder.

_____

9. In the Virtual Machine Settings Hardware pane, click **OK** to save your changes. When you start this virtual machine, you can initialize and format the new hard disk.

10. Start the **Windows Server 2016** virtual machine, and log on with your administrative username and password.

11. If necessary, open Server Manager by clicking the Server Manager icon from the task bar. Click the File and Storage Services option under the Dashboard and then click **Disks** to display a Disks window.

12. Right-click the Offline disk and then click the **Bring Online** option from the pull-down menu and click **Yes** when you see the Bring Disk Online dialog box.

13. Right-click **Disk 1** again, and select the **Initialize** option from the pull-down menu. Click **Yes** again when you see the Initialize Disk message box warning you that all data will be erased.

14. Right-click **Disk 1** and click the **New Volume ...** option from the pull-down menu to start the New Volume Wizard, and then click **Next** to display the Select the server and disk window.

15. Verify that the new Disk 1 is selected and then click **Next** to display the Specify the size of the volume window.

16. Record the maximum size below and then click **Next** to display the Assign to a drive letter or folder window.

_____

17. Record the default drive letter and click **Next** to display the Select file system settings window.

_____

18. Select the NTFS file system, enter the name **User Data 1** for the disk volume's name, and click **Next** to display the Confirm selections window.

19. Verify your settings and then click **Create** to create and format the new volume.

20. After the volume is successfully created, click **Close**. You may now close the Server Manager window.

21. Open File Explorer and verify that you now have an E drive mapped to your User Data 1 volume.

22. Shut down your Windows Server 2016 by clicking the **Windows** button, and then clicking **Shut down** from the Power option. You will need to select a reason for this shutdown and click **Continue**.

23. You have now completed Activity 3-11. You may leave VMware Workstation 12 Pro open for the next activity.

Configuring Virtual Network Options

In a physical network, a **switch** is a device that uses ports to connect multiple NICs to the same network. Most modern switches inspect each frame's MAC address to determine which port the frame is sent to. Virtual networks use software to emulate switches; you can use these **virtual switches** to configure a variety of virtual networks for different purposes. As shown in Figure 3-13, VMware Workstation provides support for three basic types of virtual switches.

A **bridged switch** includes the host computer's NIC, allowing the virtual machine to be part of the physical network. A **host-only switch** isolates the virtual machine from the physical network but allows communication with the host computer. By default, VMware Server sets up three virtual switches named VMnet0, VMnetl, and VMnet8. Two virtual adapters—Local Area Connection 2 and Local Area Connection 3—connect the host computer's NIC to VMnetl and VMnet8 for communication with virtual machines without using the physical network. VMnet0, called a **bridged network**, contains a virtual bridge connecting it to the host computer's NIC, so a virtual machine connected to VMnet0 can send frames to the host computer as well as to other physical computers on the external network.

The VMnet1 switch is called a host-only switch because it doesn't contain a bridge to the host computer's NIC; therefore, it restricts virtual machines to communicating only with other virtual machines connected to that switch and to the host computer, which is connected to the VMnet1 switch through the Local Area Connection 2 virtual adapter.

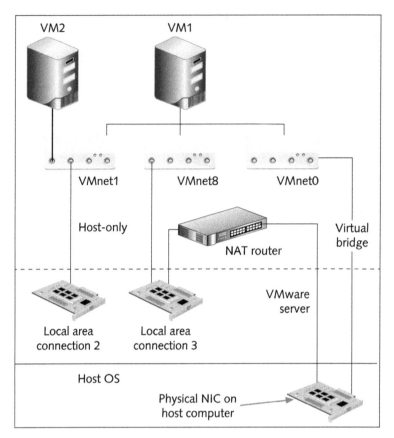

Figure 3-13 Virtual network configurations

Source: VMware Workstation

The VMnet8 switch connects the virtual machine to the host computer via a Network Address Translation (NAT) router. The NAT router enables virtual machines connected to VMnet8 to access the external network by using the host computer's IP address. You learn more about using virtual switches in Chapter 4.

You have several options for configuring network access for virtual machines. In VMware Workstation 12 Pro, each virtual machine on a Windows host can have up to ten virtual network adapters. The standard VMware Workstation switch connections are Bridged (which is VMnet0), NAT (VMnet8), and Host-only (VMnet1). You can also use the Custom option (see Figure 3-14) to connect the network adapter to one of 20 virtual network switches.

The bridged network option (VMnet0) provides a connection between the virtual network adapter and the host computer's physical network card, making the virtual machine appear as another physical device on the network. When using this option, the VM will get its IP address from the DHCP server running on the physical network and appear to other devices as another device. You should use this option with caution, as it can create extra network traffic, create security issues, and interfere with other network communication.

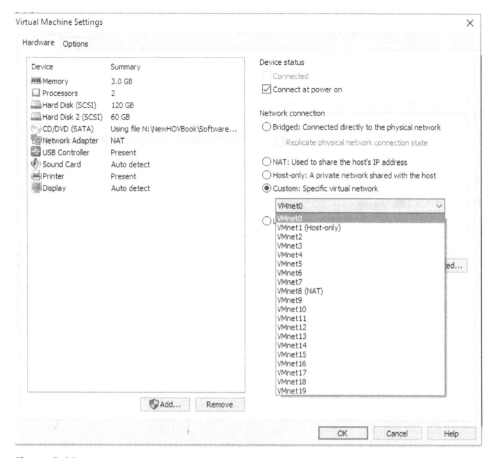

Figure 3-14   VMware Workstation 12 Pro custom network options

Source: VMware Workstation

The default virtual network configuration is the **NAT switch.** The virtual network adapter is connected to an internal virtual network (VMnet8) that includes itself, the host computer, and any other virtual machines running on the host that are configured to use NAT. As mentioned previously, with the NAT option, the host computer acts as a NAT router allowing the guest VM to access outside networks, such as the Internet, without actually being connected to the physical network.

You can use the Virtual Network Editor option from the Edit menu to change the default network configuration including the ip_network address range used by the virtual network switch.

The host-only option (VMnet1) limits communication to the host computer and any other virtual machines configured to use VMnet1. When using host-only or NAT, the VM will get its IP address from the internal DHCP service running on the VMware host computer.

To see how to use the Network Editor to change the default NAT address for both VMware Workstation 12 Pro and VMware Workstation 12 Player, refer to Appendix B. Your instructor may assign you an additional activity to practice using the Network Editor.

Using Snapshots in VMware Workstation 12 Pro

You use snapshots to save a virtual machine's current state so that you can return to it later. VMware Workstation 12 Pro allows you to save multiple snapshots and use Snapshot Manager to return the machine to any saved state. To take a snapshot, simply click the **Take a Snapshot of this virtual machine** button from the toolbar or select VM, Snapshot, Take Snapshot... from the menu. To view all existing snapshots, click the Manage Snapshot button from the tool bar or select VM, Snapshot, Snapshot Manager (Ctrl+M) from the menu (see Figure 3-15).

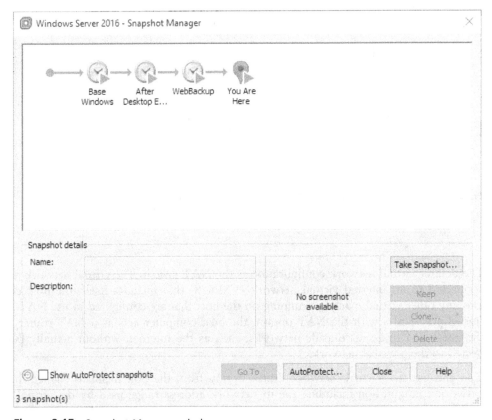

Figure 3-15   Snapshot Manager window

Source: VMware Workstation

To set your machine back to a previous snapshot, simply select the corresponding icon from the Snapshot Manager window and click the Go To button. In the following activity, you practice working with Snapshot Manager.

Activity 3-12: Working with Snapshot Manager

Time Required: 15 minutes

Objective: Use Snapshot Manager to restore a virtual machine to previous saved states.

Requirements: Completion of Activity 3-11

Description: In this activity, you create a snapshot tree of your Windows Server 2016 virtual machine, and then practice restoring the virtual machine to specific states.

1. If necessary, log on to your Windows host and start VMware Workstation 12 Pro.

2. In the administrative console, click the **Windows Server 2016** tab to make this virtual machine active, if necessary.

3. Click **VM** from the menu, point to **Snapshot,** and click **Take Snapshot.** Name the snapshot **BaseMachine** and then click the **Take Snapshot** button.

4. Start your Windows Server 2016 VM and log on as Administrator.

5. Use File Explorer to create a folder named **Backup** on your Windows Server 2016 virtual machine file system in the root of the C drive.

6. Copy the contents of the **C:\Windows\Web\Wallpaper** folder on the Windows Server 2016 virtual machine to the Backup folder.

7. In the administrative console, click **VM,** point to **Snapshot,** and click **Take Snapshot.** Name the snapshot **WebBackup** and then click the **Take Snapshot** button.

8. Use File Explorer to create a second folder named **FileBackup** on the root of your Windows Server 2016 guest's C drive.

9. Select any three files from the Windows folder and copy them to the **FileBackup** folder.

10. In the administrative console, click **VM** from the menu, point to **Snapshot,** and click **Take Snapshot.** Name the snapshot **WebFileBackup** and click the **Take Snapshot** button.

11. Close the File Explorer window.

12. Click **VM** from the menu, point to **Snapshot,** and click **Snapshot Manager.** Record the items in your snapshot tree:

_____

13. In Snapshot Manager, click **BaseMachine** and then click the **Go To** button and click **Yes** to acknowledge the warning that the current state will be lost. If necessary, power on the restored virtual machine.

14. Open Snapshot Manager to view the snapshot location your machine is currently in. Use Windows Explorer to verify that neither the Backup or FileBackup folder exists. Record your results:

_____

15. In Snapshot Manager, switch to each snapshot, and check the status of the Backup and FileBackup folders. Record your results:

_____

_____

16. When you're finished, switch back to the BaseMachine snapshot and leave the virtual machine running.

Transferring and Sharing Files

When working with virtual machines it is often convenient to transfer files between the host and guest environments. For example, if you are using a virtual machine to surf the Internet and download files, after checking the files for any malware you may want to transfer the clean file to your host computer. One advantage of using a type-2 hypervisor like VMware Workstation is the ability to use the host computer's operating system environment to exchange files. VMware Workstation 12 Pro provides three major methods you can use to share or transfer files between virtual machines and the host computer: dragging and dropping files, using shared folders, or mapping virtual disks. If you are simply transferring one or more files between the host and a guest VM, the easiest way is to simply drag and drop, or copy and paste, the selected file(s) from one environment to the other. In other situations it may be more efficient and fast to simply share files with the guests. For example, assume your host computer has a number of application installation files and you want to install one or more applications on the guest OS. Rather than copying the installation file to the guest and then running it, you could simply share the folder containing the installation setup files and then run the desired setup program from the guest VM. With shared folders, you can specify which folders on the host computer are available to the virtual machine and restrict them to read-only access, if necessary. When you start a virtual machine, you can access a shared folder as though it were any other network share. You can also map a drive letter on the host computer to any virtual disk, which is an easy way to transfer files without powering on the virtual machine. In the following activity, you enable shared folders for a Windows virtual machine.

Both shared folders as well as dragging and dropping files require VMware Tools to be installed on the guest operating system. You will practice transferring files between the host and your Windows Server 2016 virtual machine.

Activity 3-13: Transferring and Sharing Virtual Machine Files

Time Required: 15 minutes

Objective: Use drag and drop along with shared folders to transfer files between a virtual machine and a host computer.

Requirements: Completion of Activity 3-11

Description: Assume that you are configuring the virtual Windows Server 2016 server for use in the Superior Technical College virtual network. Part of this process requires you to transfer certain standard files to the server along with installing some applications. In this activity you will practice performing both drag and drop as well as sharing a folder with the Windows Server 2016 virtual machine.

1. If necessary, log on to your Windows 10 host computer and then start VMware Workstation 12.

2. If necessary, start your Windows Server 2016 virtual machine.

3. Create a folder named **WebFiles** on the root of your Windows Server 2016 C drive and then open a window to the WebFiles folder.

4. On the host computer, navigate to the **C:\Windows\Web\Screen** folder.

5. Adjust window sizes so you can see both the host computer C:\Windows\Web\Screen window and VMware Workstation 12 Pro console.

6. Click and hold one of the files in the host computer window and then drag and drop it to the virtual machine WebFiles window to copy it.

 Another option available with type-2 hypervisors is the ability to share a folder on the host computer with a virtual machine. In the following steps you will use VMware Workstation 12 Pro to share the desktop **NOTE** on your host computer with the Windows Server 2016 VM.

7. To share a folder, start by clicking **VM, Settings** from the menu, and then click the **Options** tab.

8. Click the **Shared Folders** item on the left. Under Folder sharing on the right, click the **Always enabled** option button to enable sharing, and then click the **Add** button to start the Add Shared Folder Wizard.

9. In the wizard's welcome window, click **Next**.

10. In the Name the Shared Folder window, click the **Browse** button to the right of the Host path text box, scroll up and click **Desktop**, and then click **OK** to return to the Name the Shared Folder window.

11. Enter **My Host Desktop** in the Name field and then click **Next** to display the Specify Shared Folder Attributes window. Notice that this window also allows you to make the contents of the shared folder read-only, preventing the guest from adding, changing, or deleting files from the folder.

12. In the Specify Shared Folder Attributes window, verify that the Enable this share check box is selected, and click **Finish** to complete the wizard. Click **OK** to close the Virtual Machine Settings dialog box.

13. From your Windows Server 2016 guest, click **Start, File Explorer**, right-click **Network**, and click **Properties**. From the Network and Sharing Center, click **Change advanced sharing settings,** and under Private profile click **Turn on network discovery**. Repeat this process to turn on network discovery for the Guest and Public profile and then click the **Save changes** button. Close the Network and Sharing Center window.

14. From File Explorer, click to expand the **Network** option and then click the **vmware-host computer** to display a folder named Shared Folders. Click to expand **Shared Folders**. You should now be able to access any files or folders you have added to your host computer's desktop. You can now view files on your host computer's desktop and copy files between it and the virtual machine using this shared folder.

15. Power off your virtual machine. You may leave VMware Workstation 12 open for the next activity.

Using Unity View

Unity view is a VMware Workstation feature that enables you to run virtual machine guest applications from the host OS. By using Unity you can access the guest's Start menu directly from the host to start an application. While the application appears to be running on the host, it is actually running in the virtual machine. The guest OS must be running a recent version of VMware Tools to use Unity view. In the following activity you will enable Unity view and learn how to run a virtual application directly from the host computer.

Activity 3-14: Using Unity View to Share Applications with the Host

Time Required: 10 minutes

Objective: Use Unity view in VMware Workstation 12 to access virtual machine applications from the host computer.

Requirements: Completion of Activity 3-11

Description: Some programmers in the IT Department want to run applications installed on their virtual machines on their host computers, too. In this activity, you test the Unity view feature of VMware Workstation 12 to learn more about it.

1. If necessary, start the Windows Server 2016 virtual machine, and log on.

2. To enable Unity view, click **View, Unity** from the VMware Workstation 12 menu line.

After enabling Unity view, any applications running in the guest OS are placed in Unity mode automatically. In addition, a start button with the name of your virtual machine (Windows Server 2016) appears above the start button in your host OS.

3. Click **Windows Server 2016**, point to **Programs**, point to **Windows Accessories**, and click **Notepad**.

4. Notepad appears in your host OS, but it's actually running in the guest OS. A border also appears around the window, and a VMware icon is shown on the right side of the title bar.

5. To exit Unity view, restore the VMware Workstation 12 Pro window, and then click the **Exit Unity** button in the center of the window. (You can't access the virtual machine from the VMware Workstation 12 Pro console while in Unity view.) Notice that Notepad is still running on the Windows Server 2016 guest VM.

6. Exit Notepad and use the **Shut Down Guest** option of the VM, Power menu to shut down the Windows Server 2016 VM. You may leave VMware Workstation 12 Pro running for the next activity.

Cloning Virtual Machines in VMware Workstation 12 Pro

As explained in Chapter 1, by cloning virtual machines, you can base a virtual machine on an existing parent machine or a snapshot of a parent. As you will learn in Chapter 9, cloning can be very useful when implementing a Virtual Desktop Infrastructure (VDI). Cloned machines can be full clones or linked clones. A **full clone** is a complete copy of the parent virtual machine, so it can operate independently of the parent machine's files. As described in Chapter 2, linked clones share the base virtual machine files with the parent or snapshot. Multiple linked clones can be based on the same parent, saving a lot of memory when you have several virtual machines that share similar configurations. Any changes made to each of the linked clones are stored in separate files on the host computer. When using linked clones, the parent VM or snapshot that a linked clone is based on must be available on the host's local or network drive. To ensure the parent or snapshot is not deleted or changed, you should enable the Template option on the parent VM. Linked clones are the most useful because they're easy to create and take up much less disk space than full clones on the host computer. Linked clones are very important when implementing a Virtual Desktop Infrastructure as described later in Chapters 4 and 9. In the following activity, you will practice creating two linked clones from your Ubuntu virtual machine.

Activity 3-15: Cloning the UbuntuVM Virtual Machine

Time Required: 15 minutes

Objective: Create a linked clone of an existing virtual machine.

Requirements: Completion of Activity 3-8

Description: The IT instructors at Superior Technical College want to create a clone of the virtual machine they've created for a Linux class so that students can use it. In this activity, you demonstrate how to use the clone feature to create virtual machines that share a common parent.

1. If necessary, power off the UbuntuVM-iii.

2. Click the **UbuntuVM-iii** in the Library pane. Click on the **Edit virtual machine settings** link in the Summary/Console and then click the **Options** tab. Turn on the Template option by clicking the **Advanced** option and then clicking the **Enable template mode (to be used for cloning**) option from the Settings pane. Click **OK** to save your changes and close the Virtual Machine Settings window.

3. When creating clones from a Template VM, the clone must be created from a snapshot. Take a snapshot of the UbuntuVM-iii machine and name the snapshot **UbuntuClone-Base**, giving a description that states the snapshot is the base for linked clone.

4. Click **Manage, Clone** from the **VM** menu to start the Clone Virtual Machine Wizard, and then click **Next**.

5. In the Clone Source window, verify that existing snapshot "UbuntuCloneBase" is selected and then click **Next**.

 The current state in the virtual machine option is available only when the Template option is not enabled. If you create a linked clone using "The current state in the virtual machine" option, a snapshot will automatically be taken and the linked clone will be associated with the snapshot.

6. In the Clone Type window, verify that the **Create a linked clone** option button is selected and then click **Next**.

7. In the Name of the New Virtual Machine window, type **UbuntuVM-iii-Clone1** for the clone name.

8. Use the **Browse** button to navigate to the **LinuxVMs** folder you created on the host computer's C drive and then use the **Make New Folder** button to create a new folder named **UbuntuVM-iii-Clone1** (where iii represents your initials). After selecting the UbuntuVM-iii-Clone1 folder, click **Finish** to create the clone. Notice how fast the linked clone is created.

9. Click **Close** to exit the wizard. The clone is now available as a tab in the administrative console.

10. Power on the clone and record your results:

    Clone 1 results: _____

11. Click the **UbuntuVM-iii** tab in the administrative console, then repeat steps 4-10 to create another clone named UbuntuVM-iii-Clone2 and power it on.

    Clone 2 results: _____

12. Power off both Ubuntu clones. You may leave VMware Workstation 12 Pro open for the next activity.

13. Use File Explorer to check the space required by each of your Ubuntu clones. Record how little space they use below.

    Clone 1 folder size: _____

    Clone 2 folder size: _____

Configuring Ports

VMware Workstation 12 Pro provides support for printers and USB controllers found in most desktop computers. If a virtual machine is the active window when you insert a USB device, by default the virtual machine will take control of the USB port. If you want to connect a USB device to the VM manually, you need to turn off the automatic detection option by opening the Settings window from the powered down VM, clicking the **USB Controller** option, and then removing the check from **Automatically connect new USB devices** (the virtual machine must be powered down to change this setting). Administrators can manually connect USB devices after they are inserted into the host computer. To manually connect a USB flash drive from a virtual machine, insert the USB drive into the host computer and then from the VM menu, click the **Removable Devices** menu option. Next, click the USB flash drive listed at the bottom of the pull-down menu and click **Connect**. A message box will be displayed informing you that the USB device is about to be unplugged from the host computer. Click **OK** to continue. The USB flash drive will now be disconnected from your Windows host and connected to the Windows Server 2016 VM. To disconnect the flash drive, from the VM menu, click the **Removable Devices** menu option and then click the USB flash drive listed at the bottom of the pull-down menu and click **Disconnect** (**Connect to host**). The USB flash drive will now be disconnected from your VM and connected to the Windows host computer.

VMware Workstation 12 Pro Tools also contains a nice feature that allows VMs to use printers that are installed on the host computer. When you install VMware Tools on a Windows guest, the host's current printers are added to the virtual machines devices using virtualized serial ports.

Initially virtual machines have no COM or LPT ports, but you can add a virtual COM or LPT port if you want the virtual machine to communicate with a device attached to a serial COM port. When adding a port, you can have the output sent to a text file on the host computer's hard drive or to the device based on the settings. Sending COM or LPT output to a text file is handy for testing device output because you can view the file in Notepad on the host computer.

Your instructor may assign an activity to practice working with virtual ports and connecting to USB devices and printers to a virtual machine.

Sharing Virtual Machines

If you have virtual machines that you want to access from multiple VMware Workstation 12 Pro hosts, you can either place the virtual machine files on a shared network drive, or share the virtual machine from the parent host computer. Typically sharing a virtual machine provides better performance and management. Sharing a VM can be very useful if you work from multiple computers or if you have other people that are working with you on a project. For example, assume that you will be working with another Windows Server 2016 specialist to help configure the server. You can perform the following steps to allow the Windows Server expert to work with your existing virtual machine.

1. Power down your existing Windows Server VM.

2. From the Library pane, drag and drop the Windows Server virtual machine to the Shared VMs folder. When you see the Welcome to the Share VM Wizard click **Next** to display the Share Virtual Machine Wizard window.

3. Notice that you can either move the virtual machine or make a full clone copy. In this scenario you would want to move the virtual machine so that both you and the Windows Server expert will be working on the same VM. You should also note the default location of the shared virtual machine is in the C:\Users\Public\Documents\Shared Virtual Machines folder, which is a default shared area of your Windows host computer.

4. Click **Finish** to move the virtual machine and display a status window. After closing the status window the VM should show under Shared VMs folder.

5. You can now power on the shared VM and have the Windows server expert use the **Connect to a Remote Server** option on their copy of VMware Workstation 12 Pro to enter the IP address and username of your VMware Workstation 12 Pro console. After connecting to your VMware Workstation 12 Pro the shared Windows VM appear under the Shared VMs folder of the Windows server expert's workstation.

 Your instructor may assign an activity to have you practice sharing a virtual machine with another workstation.

Converting a Physical Computer to a VM

VMware Converter is a powerful tool that can be used to convert an existing physical computer to a VM or used to convert virtual machines created with other virtualization software to VMware-formatted machines. To convert a physical computer to a virtual machine, click the Virtualize a Physical Machine option from the File menu and then download and install VMware Converter as a separate standalone product. You can use this feature to convert an existing machine, such as a server, to a virtual machine without having to reinstall the server's OS and all the applications and features. Using this product is outside the scope of this chapter's activities, but is included as an optional Case Project at the end of the chapter.

Working with VMware Workstation 12 Player

As mentioned at the beginning of this chapter, VMware Workstation 12 Player is installed along with VMware Workstation 12 Pro. Since the version of VMware Workstation 12 Pro will expire in 30-days, you will need to either get a VMware Workstation 12 Pro license or use VMware Workstation 12 Player to complete the VMware activities in later chapters. If you will be using VMware Workstation 12 Player, you can refer to Appendix B for more information on working with virtual machines. To start VMware Workstation 12 Player and move your existing Windows Server 2016 virtual machine you can follow the steps shown below:

1. Start VMware Workstation 12 Player by using the Start button and scrolling down to expand the VMware heading and clicking on the VMware Workstation 12 Player link.

2. Click the **Open a Virtual Machine** link and navigate to the folder containing your Windows Server 2016 VM you created in Activity 3-2 and open that folder.

3. Double-click the **Windows Server .vmx file** to add the Windows Server 2016 VM to your Windows VMware Workstation 12 Player console.

4. Start your Windows Server 2016 VM by clicking the **Play virtual machine** link

5. Verify your Windows Server 2016 VM is running.

6. Power down the Windows Server 2016 machine.

7. While it is not necessary for other activities in this book, if you like, you can repeat steps 2-6 to add and test the other virtual machines you created with VMware Workstation 12 Pro.

8. After you have completed moving virtual machines to VMware Workstation 12 Player, close VMware Workstation 12 Player.

Congratulations, you have now completed all the activities in Chapter 3 and may shut down your Windows 10 workstation.

Chapter Summary

- VMware Workstation 12 Pro includes VMware Workstation 12 Player. VMware Workstation 12 Player is intended for running virtual appliances or non-commercial applications. VMware Workstation 12 Pro is intended for professional use and has many powerful virtualization features, including Easy Install for installing a guest OS automatically and Unity view. Other features include snapshot management and cloning.

- When creating virtual machines, VMware Workstation 12 Pro provides an Easy Install option that will install the guest OS during the creation of the virtual machine, simplifying the process of getting a guest OS up and running.

- The Edit menu gives you access to the Preferences dialog box, which contains Workspace, Input, Hot Keys, Display, Unity, Updates, Feedback, Shared VMs, Memory, Priority, and Devices tabs.

- VMware Workstation 12 Pro includes support for up to 10 virtual networks, including VMnet0 (bridged), VMnet1 (host-only), and VMnet8 (shared/NAT).

- The Virtual Machine Settings dialog box from the VM menu contains Hardware and Options tabs. Use the Hardware tab to configure or add hardware devices. In the Options tab, you can change the virtual machine name as well as power and snapshot options.

- When creating a virtual machine, you need to select the OS version, amount of RAM, disk adapter type (SCSI or IDE), and disk size type (fixed or dynamic).

- A virtual machine's CD/DVD device can be configured in the Hardware tab of the Virtual Machine Settings dialog box. You can attach a virtual CD-ROM device to the host computer's physical CD-ROM drive or an ISO image file.

- Snapshots can be used to save a virtual machine state and then revert to it later. VMware Workstation 12 Pro uses Snapshot Manager for displaying multiple snapshots in a hierarchical tree structure.

- In VMware Workstation 12 Pro, you can share and transfer files between host and virtual machine by dragging and dropping, enabling shared folders, and mapping a virtual disk to a drive letter.

- With VMware Converter, you can create VMware virtual machines from physical computers and convert virtual machines created with other virtualization software to VMware-compatible machines.

Key Terms

bridged network	host-only switch	switch
bridged switch	NAT switch	universal unique identifier
Easy Install	Open Virtualization Format	(UUID)
full clone	(OVF)	virtual switch

Review Questions

1. Which of the following shows the minimum RAM and CPU requirements for installing VMware Workstation 12 Pro?

    a. 1.5 GHz Intel or AMD processor with 2 GB RAM

    b. 500 MHz Intel or AMD processor with 1 GB RAM

    c. 2 GHz Intel or AMD processor with 3 GB RAM

    d. 500 MHz Intel or AMD processor with 256 MB RAM

2. Which of the following are advantages of using the UEFI firmware? (Choose all that apply.)

    a. It is necessary to use the UEFI firmware to take advantage of multiple virtual processors.

    b. It is necessary to use the new UEFI firmware if you are booting from disk partitions larger than 2 TB.

    c. The new UEFI firmware will allow a VMware Workstation 12 Pro guest computer to boot from the host computer's USB drive

    d. The new UEFI firmware is necessary to boot your virtual machine from a .iso image file.

3. You can open a new Home tab in VMware's administrative console by using which of the following menus?

    a. VM

    b. Tab

    c. File

    d. View

4. The Map or Disconnect Virtual Disks menu option can be used to do which of the following?

    a. Share the host computer's physical drive with the guest OS.

    b. Map a drive letter on the host computer to a shared virtual disk on the virtual machine (only when the VM is powered on).

    c. Map a drive letter on the host computer for accessing files on a virtual disk when the virtual machine is powered on.

    d. Map a drive letter on the host computer for accessing files on a virtual disk when the virtual machine is powered off.

5. Which of the following is the virtual network for bridging to the host computer's NIC?

    a. VMnet0

    b. VMnet1

    c. VMnet2

    d. VMnet8

6. Which virtual network is used for allowing the virtual machine to access outside networks, using NAT on the host computer?

    a. VMnet0

    b. VMnet1

    c. VMnet2

    d. VMnet8

7. Which tab in the Preferences dialog box is used to set a virtual machine's default hardware compatibility to VMware Workstation 12 Pro?

    a. Input

    b. Workspace

    c. Priority

    d. Tools

8. Which tab in the Preferences dialog box contains the default location for storing virtual machine files on the host computer?

    a. Devices

    b. Workspace

    c. Files

    d. Tools

9. Which of the following power options is preferred to power off a VM because it works through the guest OS shut down process?

    a. Shut Down Guest

    b. Reset

    c. Power off

    d. Close guest

10. Which of the following products can import virtual machines using OVF? (Choose all that apply.)

    a. VMware Workstation 12 Player

    b. VMware ACE

    c. VMware Workstation 12 Pro

    d. VMware Converter

11. After VMware Tools has been installed, which of the following methods can you use to share files between the host computer and virtual machine? (Choose all that apply.)

    a. Dragging and dropping

    b. Using shared folders

    c. Using the VM, Copy menu choice to transfer files from the host

    d. Mapping a drive from the host computer to the virtual disk

12. Prior to creating a linked clone from a parent, which of the following should you do? (Choose all that apply.)

    a. Back up the parent

    b. Enable the Template setting on the parent

    c. Take a snapshot of the parent

    d. Share the parent VM

13. Which disk size type offers the best use of disk space?

    a. Fixed

    b. Dynamic

    c. Bridged

    d. Shared

14. Which of the following is not a power option in the VM menu?

    a. Power on/Start up Guest

    b. Suspend/Suspend Guest

    c. Snapshot/Snapshot Guest

    d. Reset/Restart Guest

15. Which key combination is used to return keyboard and mouse control to the host computer when VMware Tools is not installed?

    a. Ctrl+Alt+Del

    b. Ctrl+Alt+Insert

    c. Ctrl+Alt

    d. Ctrl+Alt+Enter

16. Which of the following can be configured to use an ISO image file?

    a. Floppy drive

    b. CD/DVD-ROM drive

    c. Virtual hard drive

    d. USB port

17. Which of the following is an advantage of installing VMware Tools? (Choose all that apply.)

    a. Improved performance on the host computer

    b. Capability to move the mouse pointer between virtual machines and the host

    c. Drag and drop files

    d. Automatic software updates

18. Which of the following VM menu items allows you to change the Hardware Compatibility settings?

    a. Settings

    b. VMware Tools

    c. Manage

    d. It cannot be changed once a guest OS is installed

19. How do you start Snapshot Manager? (Choose all that apply.)

    a. Click Snapshot Manager from the VM menu.

    b. Click VM, click Snapshot, and then click Snapshot Manager.

    c. Click the Snapshot Manager button from the toolbar.

    d. Click Edit, click Snapshot, and then click Snapshot Manager.

20. How do you run a virtual machine in background? (Choose all that apply.)

    a. Select the Start in Background option from the Power menu.

    b. Turn on Unity view.

    c. Start a Shared VM and then exit VMware Workstation 12 Pro.

    d. Start a Virtual Machine and then select the Run in Background option when you exit VMware Workstation 12 Pro.

Case Projects

CASE PROJECTS

Case Project 3-1: Researching Virtual Appliances

Your organization is investigating virtual appliances to run certain applications and has asked you to prepare a report for management. They would like to know what virtual appliances may be available to implement network storage. Use the Internet to find a source of virtual appliances and use the information to write a report describing what virtual appliances are, how the company could benefit from using them, along with a few examples of available virtual appliances. You may wish to refer to articles in Infoworld by going to Infoworld.com and searching for articles on Virtual Appliances for VMware.

Case Project 3-2: Documenting Snapshots and Cloning for a School Lab

The IT instructors at Superior Technical College are planning to use virtual machines in a Windows Server 2016 course. The course is divided into four units, with several activities planned for each unit. Students' virtual machines are checked and graded at the end of each unit. The problem is that errors made in early units could make it difficult to perform certain tasks in later units. Create a short report explaining how instructors could use a combination of snapshots and linked clones so that students can have a new virtual machine for each unit of the class.

Case Project 3-3: Cloning a Physical Computer

Now that you have configured the Windows Server 2016 virtual server for use in the Superior Technical College IT virtual network, IT management would like to virtualize two existing servers. In this project you are to describe the steps necessary to perform this process by using VMware Converter to virtualize your physical desktop system. This process will involve the following steps:

Download and install the VMware Converter software.

Record the steps you use to create a virtual machine from your physical desktop.

chapter 4

Data Center Virtualization and Cloud Computing

After reading this chapter and completing the exercises, you will be able to:

- Describe the need for virtualization in data center and cloud environments
- Describe and compare hardware performance features found in VMware and Hyper-V
- Describe the VMFS file system used by VMware and compare it to Microsoft NTFS
- Identify the data storage features found in VMware and Hyper-V data center virtualization products
- Identify the types of networks needed to support data center virtualization.
- Identify the network components and features used in data center virtualization including virtual switches, port groups, virtual adapters, and NIC teaming

As described in Chapter 1, virtualization software consists of both type-1 and type-2 hypervisor products. In Chapters 2 and 3 you learned how to use both Oracle VirtualBox and VMware Workstation type-2 virtualization products to perform a number of common personal desktop virtualization tasks. While workstation virtualization products provide flexible platforms that are great for developing, running, and testing applications as well as configuring server environments, they are not designed to provide the high speed fault tolerant environments needed to run servers in the data center. Dedicated type-1 (bare metal) hypervisors are designed to deliver the performance and specialized features required in today's data center and cloud computing environments. Some features that are part of data center virtualization products you will encounter in this chapter include scalability of CPUs and memory for high performance, load balancing among multiple VMs, rapid provisioning of new virtual servers using templates, clustering of hosts for high availability, cloud-based services, and security.

In this chapter we will look at each of these features and how they are implemented in both VMware vSphere and Microsoft Hyper-V.

Data Center Virtualization and Cloud Computing

Over the past few years virtualization has matured from being used primarily on the desktop to a technology that plays an important role in most data centers as well as being the foundation of cloud computing services. **Hyperconvergence** is a term used to describe today's virtualized data centers. Hyperconvergence can be defined as the process of using hypervisor software to converge CPUs, memory, storage, and networking into pools of resources that can be accessed through applications running on virtual machines. In hyperconverged data centers, the virtual machines become the focus of the system and are used by servers and workstations to access resources, applications, and data across virtualized network systems. The term **software-defined data center (SDDC)** is often used to describe a hyperconverged data center in which all the hardware resources are abstracted into a virtualized pool of resources that can be assigned to virtual machines. Rather than using expensive proprietary devices such as brand name switches and SAN storage systems, each with its own administrative console, an SDDC uses commodity hardware that can be virtualized and then managed using a centralized administrative console.

Today IT Departments and organizations are increasingly using hyperconverged data centers to deploy mission-critical, or tier-1, applications such as large online transaction processing (OLTP) databases and online transaction analysis (OLTA) systems that can use more than 16 processors and large amounts of memory. In addition to supporting these resource demanding online applications, data centers are now starting to implement Virtual Desktop Infrastructure environments along with cloud computing. You will learn more about hyperconvergence and cloud-based environments in Chapter 10.

As described in Chapter 1, Virtual Desktop Infrastructure (VDI) environments use a lot of system resources and put heavy loads on the host computers. In addition to supporting the processing requirements, data center virtualization systems must be able to provide consistent performance by balancing workloads among multiple hosts, and providing high availability, failover clustering, and security. **High availability** is the process of maintaining access to a virtual machine if a host system fails or is brought down for planned maintenance. Both VMware and Microsoft Hyper-V provide powerful type-1 virtualization products that can support these data center and cloud computing requirements.

Appendix C provides coverage on how virtualization and cloud computing services help provide disaster recovery and high availability in today's software-defined data centers.

To start with, all data center virtualization products gain speed by using type-1 or bare metal hypervisors. As described in Chapter 1, bare metal hypervisors install directly on the computer hardware, eliminating the overhead of having a host OS. This means that virtual servers and desktops installed in VMs running on type-1 hypervisors run as fast as they would if the server were installed directly on the hardware. In some cases, the VMs can even provide better, more consistent performance than a direct hardware installation by utilizing a number of specialized data center virtualization features discussed later in this chapter. Because they are installed on the host computer hardware, you will need to check the compatibility list of the hypervisor product you are installing to be sure it will support the host computer's hardware including CPU, amount of memory, disk system, and network adapters.

Data center virtualization products also include high scalability features that can handle up to 64 virtual CPUs and 4 TB of memory. As mentioned in Chapter 1, new host computer CPUs and motherboards are being designed with more cores and special features such as SLAT and hardware virtualization. In addition to the host's support of CPU features, modern guest operating systems such as Windows 7, Server 2008 and later support a feature called **Enlightened I/O** that allows the guest OS to communicate directly with the hypervisor, providing additional features and improved performance. Data center virtualization products are designed to take advantage of all these hardware capabilities as well as provide load balancing and fault tolerance features that can be used to migrate VMs between different hosts to provide high availability and balance processing power.

Another advantage of virtualizing a data center is the added backup and disaster recovery capabilities and services virtualization provides. When using virtual servers, you can backup and entire server and all its data by coping the virtual disk files to another location. If the virtual server crashes, or the host computer suffers a hardware failure, you can quickly restore the backup onto another computer and continue running. Hypervisors also provide services that allow backups of running servers as well as replicate data between virtual machines running on different hosts. Both VMware and Microsoft offer a variety of backup and recovery software and services for their virtualization products. Appendix C covers backup and disaster recovery concepts along with high availability clusters that support moving virtual machines between host computers in the event of hardware failure or scheduled host maintenance. In addition to providing backup and recovery services at the local data center, virtualized data centers also can be linked to cloud-based services that allow rolling virtual machines over to cloud-based systems in the event of system failures or bottlenecks. You will learn more about using cloud-based disaster recovery services in Chapter 10 and Appendix C.

VMware vSphere Performance Features and Products

The vSphere product can be divided into three major components including the vSphere ESXi hypervisor, vSphere Client, and vCenter Server. Over the years, VMware has used a number of product names for their type-1 hypervisors including ESX, ESXi , and most recently the term vSphere Hypervisor to refer to the free ESXi version. Up through version 4 of vSphere, VMware used ESX (short for Elastic Sky X) as their type-1 hypervisor. These older ESX hypervisors had built in GUI consoles to provide management functions. With vSphere version 5, VMware redesigned their hypervisor to provide improved performance and reliability, removing the GUI console in the process and naming the new hypervisor ESXi. With vSphere 6, VMware introduced a new free version of the hypervisor called vSphere Hypervisor, although most sources still refer to it as an ESXi hypervisor.

For the purposes of this book we will be using the term "ESXi hypervisor" when referring to both the licensed ESXi and the free vSphere hypervisor. We will use the term "free vSphere Hypervisor" when specifically installing or addressing capabilities or limitations of the free hypervisor version.

The core of the vSphere ESXi hypervisor is the VMKernel, and it controls all virtual machine access to the host computer's hardware providing storage, network, and management services to both the host computer and all VMs. The vSphere Client is a management console that runs on a Windows desktop and provides management and configuration for the free vSphere hypervisor. There is also a Web-based version of vSphere Client that allows remote administration of ESX servers (the Web client is not available for the newer licensed ESXi hypervisors or the free vSphere Hypervisor). While vSphere Client allows management of a single instance of an ESXi hypervisor or free vSphere Hypervisor, vCenter Server is designed to work with multi-host environments and provide services such as distributed virtual network switches, clustering, high availability, and migration of virtual machine environments among multiple ESXi hypervisors. The vCenter Web client is a browser-based client that is used to manage vCenter Server environments. As mentioned earlier, VMware provides both licensed and free versions of the vSphere ESXi hypervisor as shown in Table 4-1.

Table 4-1   vSphere versions and features

Platform	Resource	Free vSphere Hypervisor with vSphere Client	Licensed vSphere ESXi with vCenter Server
Host	Logical processors	480	480
	Physical memory	6 TB	6 TB
	Virtual CPUs per host	4096	4096
	SLAT support	Yes	Yes
	Ballooning support	Yes	Yes
	Transparent Page Sharing (TPS)	Yes	Yes
	Memory compression	Yes	Yes
Virtual Machine	vCPUs per VM	8	128
	Active VMs per host	1024	1024
	Guest NUMA support	Yes	Yes
	Memory per VM	4 TB	4 TB
	Hot add support	No	Yes
Cluster	Max nodes	N/A	64
	Max VMs	N/A	8000
Features	vCenter Server	N/A	Yes
	Load balancing	N/A	Yes
	High availability	N/A	Yes

The first thing to look at in the table is the support of CPUs. Notice both the free and licensed versions of vSphere will support up to 480 CPU cores per host computer. For all practical purposes this is more than enough. The difference comes in the number of vCPUs that can be supported by each virtual machine. Notice that the free version of vSphere can support 8 vCPUs per guest, whereas the licensed version can support 128 vCPUs on each guest VM. For smaller data centers supporting 8 vCPUs per VM is very reasonable, but as mentioned earlier, large online database applications can require 16 or more CPUs per server. In addition, larger data center applications will require services such as clustering to provide fault tolerance and high availability.

Notice that when it comes to memory utilization and management both versions are essentially the same. They can both support up to 6 TB of physical memory per host, 4 TB of memory for each VM, and both support memory management features including Second Level Address Translation (SLAT), ballooning, and **Non-Uniform Memory Access (NUMA)**. As described in Chapter 1, SLAT is a memory management feature built into most CPUs to reduce the overhead associated with software-managed page tables. Also described in Chapter 1, ballooning is a software technique VMware uses to free up unused memory in a VM by inflating a special driver that is part of VMware tools. Inflating the driver causes the VM to release unused pages of memory back into the free pool.

NUMA is a memory management protocol used in multiprocessing environments. Using NUMA, a CPU can access its own local memory faster than memory that is shared with other processors. This provides faster performance in virtual environments as each VM can be assigned a processor and dedicated memory.

Other helpful features built into vSphere include Transparent Page Sharing and memory compression. When running multiple VMs in a data center environment, it is not uncommon to have multiple copies of an OS such as Windows Server 2016 running on the same host. The VMware **Transparent Page Sharing** (**TPS**) feature allows identical pages of memory to be shared between VMs, reducing the amount of paging that is needed when running multiple copies of a guest OS. TPS also decreases the amount of physical memory needed to run the VMs along with providing improved performance.

While using balloon drivers and Transparent Page Sharing is usually sufficient to reduce memory contention on an ESXi hypervisor, during heavy utilization page swapping can still affect performance. When physical memory is needed the ESXi hypervisor will move inactive pages in a VM's memory to a page file created for that specific VM. Moving pages to and from disk takes time, and the ESXi hypervisor is able to use the **memory compression** feature to reduce the amount of swapping to and from disk by compressing unused memory pages and then decompressing them when they are needed. Memory compression works by scanning a page of memory and then replacing strings of repeating characters with a code. The compressed memory pages are then stored in a per-VM memory cache, which provides much faster access time than using the standard uncompressed disk swap file.

Hot add support allows vSphere to dynamically change a guest VM's number of vCPUs or memory size while the guest is running. This feature is only available on VMs that are running guest OS's capable of handling dynamic addition of CPUs and memory.

As you can see from the features section of Table 4-1, the free version of vSphere hypervisor does not include vCenter Server. A vSphere license is required to use vCenter Server and provide for more advanced features such as clustering, load balancing, and high availability.

While the free vSphere Hypervisor and the licensed ESXi hypervisor are essentially the same product, applying the license will unlock API (Application Program Interface) features in the free ESXi hypervisor **NOTE** that are necessary to support vCenter Server.

In the following activity you will download the free version of the vSphere Hypervisor so you can install and use it in later activities to get some experience with vSphere features. In Chapter 7 you will work with vSphere Client to manage the free vSphere hypervisor data centers, and then in Chapter 8 you will learn how to perform more advanced virtualization functions using a trial version of the licensed vCenter Server.

Activity 4-1: Downloading the Free vSphere Hypervisor and vSphere Client

Time Required: 15 minutes

Objective: Download free versions of vSphere v6 ESXi Hypervisor and vSphere Client.

Requirements: A MyVMware account

Description: Rocky Ridge Forest Products is in the process of setting up a virtual data center to manage their business. In Chapter 3 you created and configured a Windows Server 2016 server using VMware Workstation. Now that the server is running in a test environment, your next task will be to host the virtual server in a production network using vSphere. In this activity you will download the free vSphere Hypervisor and Client using your MyVMware account created in Chapter 1.

1. If necessary, start your Windows workstation and open a Web browser to VMware. com.

2. If necessary, modify the browser settings to ask you for the download path.

3. Point to Login, click **My VMware** and then log on using the account you created in Chapter 1.

4. On the right side of the page under the Quick Links heading, click the **All Downloads** link.

5. Under the Other Downloads heading located on the right side of the page, click the **Trial and Free Products** link.

6. Scroll down to the bottom of the page, then under the Download Free Products section click the **vSphere Hypervisor (64 bit)** link. Click the **Register** button and fill in the required fields on the Accept End-User License Agreement page, click to agree to the terms of the license agreement, and click **Continue.**

7. Under the Download Packages heading, click the **Manually Download** button to the right of the ESXi ISO image (Includes VMware Tools) option.

8. Verify that the Save file option is selected and then click **OK** to start the download. If asked, enter the path you created in Activity 1-1.

9. After the download is complete, download vSphere Client by clicking the **Manually Download** button to the right of the VMware vSphere Client 6 option (the current client 6 version number will be displayed).

10. Verify that the Save file option is selected and then click **OK** to start the download. If asked, enter the path you created in Activity 1-1.

11. You may now return to the My VMware page and log off.

12. You may leave your browser open for later activities.

Microsoft Hyper-V Performance Features and Products

Over the years Microsoft has provided a number of virtualization products including Virtual PC 2007, Virtual Server, Virtual PC (a Windows 7 version), and most recently Hyper-V. Up until Hyper-V, all Microsoft virtualization products were based on type-2 hypervisors. Hyper-V first came out as a type-1 hypervisor with Windows Server 2008. Since then there have been a number of Hyper-V releases, including a version that comes free with Windows 8 and Windows 10 Professional and later. Table 4-2 contains a list of Hyper-V versions and their capabilities.

Table 4-2   Hyper-V versions and features

Platform	Resource	2008 R2 Hyper-V	2016 Hyper-V
Host	Logical processors	64	512
	Physical memory	1 TB	24 TB
	Virtual CPUs per host	512	2048
Virtual Machine	vCPUs per VM	4	64 for gen 1, 240 for gen 2
	Active VMs per host	384	1024
	Memory per VM	64 GB	1 TB for gen 1, 12 TB for gen 2
Cluster	Max nodes	16	64
	Max VMs	1000	8000

Microsoft also provides a System Center that may be used to manage multiple hosts. Like VMware's vCenter, Microsoft's System Center is a licensed product that includes a Virtual Machine Manager (VMM) application that is used for the management of multiple Hyper-V systems.

In Chapter 7 you will work with System Center to manage multiple Hyper-V hosts.

In addition to managing multiple Hyper-V hosts, System Center uses Virtual Machine Manager (VMM) to provide advanced capabilities such as clustering and high availability. Hyper-V requires the host CPU to support both SLAT and hardware virtualization (called VT on Intel and AMD-V on AMD). Be sure these features are enabled prior to installing Hyper-V. Windows Server 2016 Hyper-V contains a number of new features. In the following activity you will check your system to see that it meets Server 2016 Hyper-V requirements and then document some of the new features.

Activity 4-2: Verifying Hyper-V Requirements and Features

Time Required: 15 minutes

Objective: View new Hyper-V features and check for system compatibility.

Requirements: Windows Server 2016 installed on your host computer

Description: Superior Technical College has recently purchased a new computer system that has an AMD FX-6300 six-core processor with 8 GB RAM. They have installed Windows Server 2016 and want to be sure it will meet system requirements for Hyper-V. In addition, they are in the process of deciding whether to use Hyper-V or vSphere for the virtual data center. In this activity you will check to see that the new server meets Hyper-V requirements and then document some features of Hyper-V that will be important to their virtual data center.

1. If necessary, boot your computer to Windows Server 2016 and sign on as administrator.

2. Open a command prompt by clicking the **Start** button, typing **cmd,** and clicking the **Command Prompt** option.

3. Enter the command **Systeminfo** and press **Enter** (if a Hypervisor such as VMware is installed or if the Hyper-V role is enabled the Hyper-V requirements will not be shown.).

4. Record the five Hyper-V requirements below along with whether or not your computer meets each requirement.

_____

_____

_____

_____

_____

5. You will need a standard user account to use the Edge Web browser from the server console. If you have a standard user account on this server or have installed Active Directory, skip to step 9 and sign in using a standard user account.

6. Click **Start,** click **Windows Administrative Tools,** double-click **Computer Management,** and then from the left pane, expand **Local Users and Groups** and click **Users.**

7. From the **Action** menu, click **New User...,** enter a username and password, and click to remove the check from the **User must change password at next logon** option. Click **Create,** then close the Computer Management and Administrative Tools windows.

8. Click **Start,** click your Administrator username, and then click **Sign out.**

9. Sign in using your standard username and password.

10. Check requirements on the Web site by opening an Edge browser window and entering the URL https://technet.microsoft.com/en-us/library/mt608570.aspx

11. In the left pane, click **System requirements**. In the space below describe whether the system purchased by Superior Technical College meets memory and processor requirements shown.

_____

12. Superior Technical College would like to be able to perform the following functions on the virtual data center. Click the **What's new in Hyper-V** link and indicate below what Hyper-V feature will support the functions listed:

   • Adjust the amount of memory used by a VM while it is running: Yes or No

   • Set up a lab where students can use a virtual machine as a host for educational purposes: Yes or No

   • Create checkpoints for running VMs for backup purposes: Yes or No

   • Change the size of virtual hard disks while the VM is running: Yes or No

   • Protect virtual machines from tampering or stealing of data by either another virtual machine or by the administrator: Yes or No

13. Close your browser window and log off the Server 2016 computer.

Data Center Storage Systems

As described in Chapter 1, a virtual machine is stored as a set of files. In this section you will learn about data storage systems and features and how they are implemented to provide more hyperconverged environments in both VMware vSphere and Microsoft Hyper-V products. Each virtual machine needs several files including its virtual disk, configuration data, and several control and swap files. A **data store** is a generic term often used for a container or storage volume that holds the virtual machine files. As compared to workstation virtualization, data stores for data center environments require a number of additional capabilities including larger storage capacities, faster speed, and higher reliability and fault tolerance. Type-2 virtualization systems such as VMware Workstation and Oracle VirtualBox are limited to using the host operating system's file storage system, whereas data center virtualization products such as vSphere and Hyper-V use specialized disk management formats along with network storage systems such as Storage Area Networks (SAN) to provide a number of high speed, high availability storage solutions for data stores.

In the past virtualization typically involved virtualizing the servers to save costs by reducing the number of physical computers in the data center, thus lowering hardware, power consumption, and cooling costs. Today's hyperconverged or software-defined data centers also require virtualization of storage and networking systems to increase performance and provide a more flexible and scalable data center. **Storage tiering** is an example of a data center storage technology that can further increase performance by dividing storage devices into tiers based on access speed. A virtual machine manager can then dynamically move VMs that require a lot of disk I/O to higher speed storage tiers running on fast devices such as SSD drives. In addition to storage speed, today's data centers are experiencing a rapidly growing need for storage capacity to support large database and Virtual Desktop Infrastructure environments. One way to help tame the storage capacity monster is through data deduplication. Large storage applications often include a lot of data that are duplicated in different locations. A good example of this is Virtual Desktop Infrastructures, where many identical operating systems exist on multiple desktop environments. **Data deduplication** is the process of storing just one copy of the data sector and then using reference pointers to access this data from other locations.

Types of Storage Systems

A type-1 hypervisor accesses its data stores using either the host computer's directly attached disk drive(s) or through a Network Attached Storage (NAS) system. While local storage works well to store virtual machine files in smaller data centers, it does not offer more advanced features such as clustering, load balancing, and high availability that are available in network-based storage systems. As a result, in larger data centers local storage is most often used to boot the hypervisor and store ISO images, VM templates, and archived virtual machines.

If using a local hard drive, the hypervisor must be compatible with the host computer's disk adapter.

Most data centers use network storage systems for their data stores. As mentioned earlier, network storage systems have the advantage of sharing virtual machine files among multiple host computers thus providing clustering, fault tolerance, and load balancing features. As described in Chapter 1, network storage systems can be classified as Network Attached Storage (NAS) or Storage Area Network (SAN). Figure 4-1 shows an example of a virtual data center using both NAS and SAN shared storage. You will be implementing a similar shared storage environment in Chapters 7 and 8. As shown in Figure 4-1, in a NAS environment, the NAS disk controller uses its own format to store and retrieve disk information based on file name. In addition to its internal file storage format, the NAS system uses an access protocol to provide shared access to its file system across the network. NAS systems can provide a number of network access protocols including NFS (often used by Linux systems), AFP (Apple), and CIFS (Microsoft). VMware ESXi Hypervisor uses the NFS v3 protocol to access files on a NAS system while Hyper-V may use either CIFS or NFS.

Storage Area Network (SAN) When using directly attached disks or SAN storage, a type-1 hypervisor can use its own file system format and directly manage the files in its data store. VMware uses a file system called **VMFS** to manage its data store while Hyper-V uses NTFS. Storage Area Networks (SAN) are more expensive to implement than NAS, but because the data stores on a SAN are directly formatted and managed by the hypervisor, SAN can provide higher speed performance than NAS along with more advanced features such as clustering and dynamic storage allocation.

SAN systems are based on either Fibre Channel or iSCSI. The original **Fibre Channel** (still used on mainframe computers) requires a separate fiber-based network with its own specialized switches, controllers, and storage system forming what is called a **fabric**.

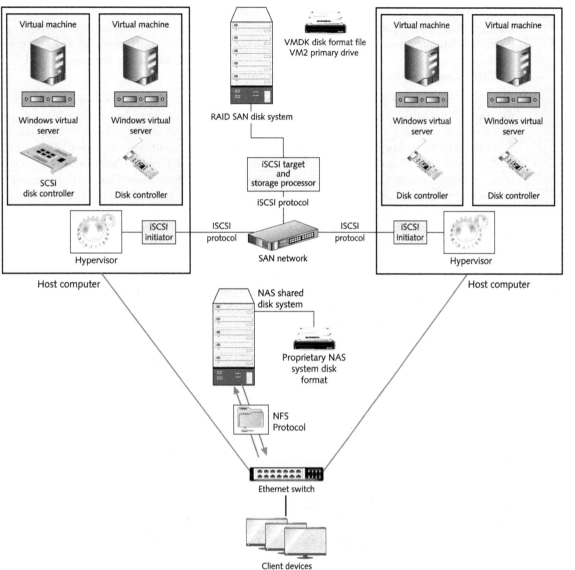

Figure 4-1 NAS and SAN Shared Storage environments

 The term "fiber" is often used in networking while the term "fibre" is typically used to define a SAN-based storage system the uses fiber networking.

Fibre Channel over Ethernet (FCoE) is a modification of the Fibre Channel protocol that encapsulates Fibre Channel traffic within Ethernet packets, allowing Fibre Channel devices to operate on standard Ethernet networks.

Because of the cost and special requirements needed for Fibre Channel, iSCSI-based SANs are more commonly used in many virtualized data centers. Figure 4-1 also includes an iSCSI SAN consisting of several components. Entities on the iSCSI network are referred to as nodes. Each node (target or initiator) must have an iSCSI Qualified Name (IQN) or Extended Unique Identifier (EUI). The iSCSI target is an array of physical disks that are organized into one or more logical unit numbers (LUNs), which are then connected to a TCP/IP network using one or more Storage Processors (SP).

The iSCSI initiator on the host hypervisor system connects to the iSCSI storage target across the TCP/IP network. The iSCSI initiator can be either a hardware-based **host bus adapter** (**HBA**) or a software initiator. The iSCSI initiator transmits iSCSI commands across the TCP/IP network to find an iSCSI target. The target then presents one or more LUNs to the initiator and the initiator makes a connection to the iSCSI target. The connection process often involves using **CHAP (Challenge-Handshake Authentication Protocol)** to create a secure connection by encrypting the logon process using a private or secret key. After the connection is established, the initiator can send SCSI commands to read and write data to the iSCSI data store in much the same way it would access a local SCSI drive.

Clustering As shown in Figures 4-2 and 4-3, server clustering is a process that takes advantage of network storage devices such as SAN to allow multiple servers to share access to common files and applications. By having two or more servers share access to an application and its data, clustering provides users with continuous access to applications and data in the event of a server or network failure.

The process of using clustering to provide continuous access to application data in the event of a failure is referred to as high availability. For example, Figure 4-2 shows a two-server

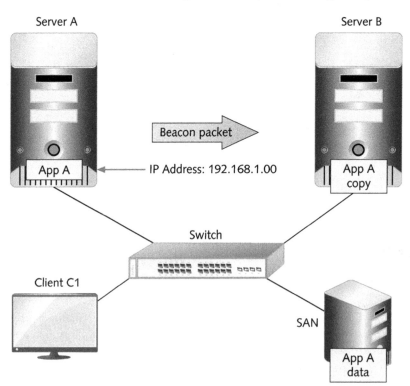

Figure 4-2 Two-server cluster with server A hosting application A and server B as backup server

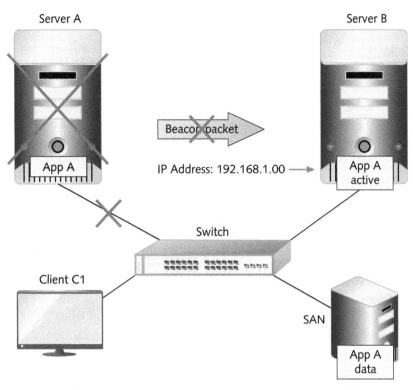

Figure 4-3 Two-server cluster with server A down and server B hosting application A

cluster hosting with server A hosting an application named App A. Both Server A and Server B have access to application App A and its data through a shared SAN network drive. In this example, application App A has been configured as a clustered application with its own IP address. If Server A goes down, as shown in Figure 4-3, Server B will no longer see its beacon and will start hosting application App A using the same IP address as used by Server A. Client C1 continues to access App A without interruption. To make this happen, Server A and Server B must be part of the same cluster and application App A needs to be configured as a clustered application with its own unique IP address.

Activity 4-3: Setting up a Windows iSCSI Target Server

Time Required: 15 minutes

Objective: Set up a Windows Server 2016 to be an iSCSI target.

Requirements: Completion of Chapter 3, Activity 3-11. In this activity, you will use the Windows Server 2016 installation you made in Activity 3-9 of Chapter 3 to set up an iSCSI target. If you do not have your Windows Server 2016 VM transferred to VMware Workstation 12 Player, you can follow the procedure at the end of Chapter 3 to import your Windows Server 2016 VM into VMware Workstation 12 Player, or follow the procedure in Appendix B to install a new Windows Server 2016 virtual machine using VMware Workstation 12 Player.

Description: Assume you are a technician for a consulting company called Computer Technology Services. One of your clients has recently asked your firm to setup a SAN using one of their Windows Server 2016 systems as the iSCSI target. In this activity you will prepare for this job by configuring your Windows Server 2016 virtual machine as an iSCSI target.

1. If necessary, boot to your Windows computer and log on.

2. Open VMware Workstation 12 Player (or VMware Workstation 12 Pro) and click your Windows Server 2016 virtual machine you created in Chapter 3, Activity 3-9. Use the Manage option of the Player menu to open the Virtual Machine Settings window and then click the **Network Adapter**. If necessary, change the Network Adapter connection to **NAT** and then click **OK** to save your changes and close the Virtual Machine Settings window.

3. Start the Windows Server 2016 virtual machine and then log on using your administrator account.

4. Open a command prompt window (click the Start button, type **CMD** and press **Enter**). Type the command **IPCONFIG** and press **Enter** to list the current IP address of your Windows Server 2016. Note that the address consists of four numbers (called octets) separated by periods. The first three octets from the left represent the NAT subnet and the last octet is your unique server's address. You will need to use the NAT subnet on all devices connected to the VMware NAT switch. Record the IP address below:

   IP Address: _____

   NAT Subnet: _____

   Subnet Mask: _____

   Default Gateway: _____

5. In this step you will set a fixed IP address of 101 for your server on the VMware NAT subnet and then record that address for use in later activities. Open File Explorer, right-click **Network**, and click **Properties**. Click the **Change adapter settings** link and then right-click your **Ethernet0** adapter and click **Properties**. Click the **Internet Protocol Version 4(TCP/IPv4)** option and click the **Properties** button to display the Internet Protocol Version 4(TCP/IPv4) window. Click the **Use the following IP address** option button and then enter the three values of the NAT subnet followed by **101** in the last octet. Enter the Subnet Mask and Default Gateway values you recorded in step 4. At this time, we will leave the DNS server settings on automatic. Click **OK** to save your changes and then close all the network properties windows. Record the IP address information you entered for your Windows Server 2016 system below:

   IP Address: _____

   Subnet Mask: _____

   Gateway: _____

6. If necessary, start Server Manager and click the **Add roles and features** link.

7. Click **Next** to begin.

8. Verify that the Role-based or feature-based installation option is selected and then click **Next**.

9. Select your server from the server pool and click **Next**.

10. Expand both File and Storage Services and File and iSCSI Services options.

11. Click to select the **iSCSI Target Server** option, verify that the Include management tools (if applicable) option is selected, click the **Add Features** button, and then click **Next**.

12. Click **Next again** to select the .NET Framework 4.6 Features option.

13. Click **Install** to start the installation process.

14. Click **Close** after the installation is completed and return to the Server Manager main menu.

15. On the left side of the Dashboard, click to expand **File and Storage Services**.

16. From the left pane, click the iSCSI link and then click the **To create an iSCSI virtual disk, start the New iSCSI Virtual Disk Wizard** link.

17. Click the **Type a custom path** option, type **c:\iscsi\vdisk01**, and click **Next**.

18. In the Specify iSCSI virtual disk name page, type **iSCSI vDisk 01** and click **Next** to display the Specify iSCSI virtual disk size page.

19. Verify that the Dynamically expanding option is selected, then type **100** (or the largest value you can given your virtual disk size) in the Size field and click **Next**.

20. Verify that the New iSCSI target option is selected and then click **Next**.

21. Type **xxx-iSCSI-FileCluster** (where xxx represents your initials) in the Name field and click **Next** (no spaces are allowed in the Name field).

22. In the Specify access servers page, click **Add** to display the Select a method to identify the initiator page. This page is important as it allows you to select which computers can use this iSCSI target.

23. Click the **Enter a value for the selected type** option, select IP Address, and then type your NAT subnet (from step 4) followed by **141** in the last octet of the Value field (for example, enter 192.168.###.141 where ### is your NAT network address) and click **OK**.

24. Repeat step 23 to add another machine with an IP address of **142** into the Value field.

25. Click **Next** to display the Enable Authentication page.

26. Click the **Enable CHAP** check box and then enter the username and 12-character password you want to use for this iTarget. Record the username and password below:

    Username: _____

    Password: _____

27. Click **Next** to display the Confirm selections page. After verifying the selections, click **Create** to create the virtual disk.

28. Click **Close** to return to the Server Manager.

29. You can edit the iSCSI Target by clicking the iSCSI option to display the iSCSI targets on your server. Right-click the **iSCSI cluster** and click **Properties** to display the Properties window. Verify your settings and then close the window.

30. You have now completed this activity. You will work more with this iSCSI target in later chapters.

VMware vSphere Storage Features

As described in the previous section, type-1 hypervisors such as vSphere ESXi use their own file system to format and manage data stores on both local and SAN storage devices.

NAS storage devices format and manage their internal storage using their own disk system and then present the data to the network using a file sharing protocol such as NFS or CIFS.

VMware uses a file system called VMFS to format and manage data stores on both local and shared SAN storage including Fibre Channel and iSCSI. VMFS is a high performance clustered file system designed to maximize support of virtual machines and provide virtualization features such as the ability to dynamically increase data store capacity while virtual machines are running, use sub-lock addressing to make efficient use of storage for small files, and provide for virtual disk files up to 2 TB in size. While VMFS is used to format and manage the physical data store, the virtual disk files used by the virtual machines are stored using a special VMDK file format. Because the .vmdk virtual disk file has its own format, it can be moved to different physical disk systems. For example, a .vmdk disk file can be moved from a drive formatted for VMFS to a NAS device whose hard drive uses the NTFS format.

In addition to being efficient and scalable, VMFS is the foundation for VMware's distributed infrastructure services. Allowing multiple hosts to simultaneously read and write to shared networked storage devices enables virtualization features such as clustering of virtual machines across different servers, migration of running virtual machines from one host to another without down time, and automatic restarting of failed virtual machines on a separate host.

Clustering and other advanced features involving multiple vSphere hosts require obtaining a licensed version of vSphere that includes vCenter Server.

Clustering and High Availability Prior to VMware implementing high availability through the clustering of virtual hosts, applications and servers had to be specifically configured to support clustering. VMware clustering eliminates this extra setup by providing the infrastructure necessary for high availability and load balancing by clustering multiple vSphere hosts. The goal behind VMware's High Availability feature is to provide continuous access to any application running on the clustered VMs with minimum or no special cluster configuration of the application or guest servers. As shown in Figure 4-4, to provide high availability to applications running on any VM requires just two VMware ESXi hosts to be configured in a cluster sharing a common VMFS data store and network connectivity.

As with server clustering, to provide high availability within a cluster, all hosts in that cluster must be in constant communication through the transmission of a beacon. Each host transmits a beacon at regular intervals throughout the network indicating they are up and running. When a host's beacon is not received within a specified time period, that host is considered down or offline and another host will spring into action using the shared SAN

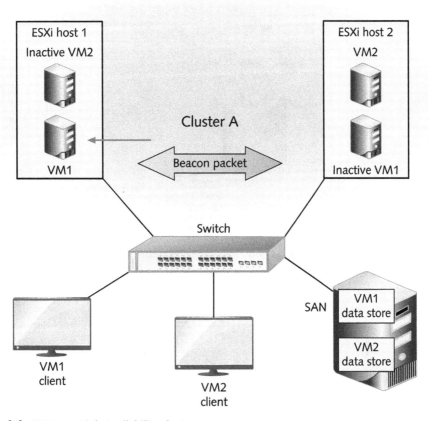

Figure 4-4 VMware High Availability cluster

to bring up the VMs from the failed host. Capacity can be reserved on each ESXi host to ensure there are enough resources to bring up the clustered VMs in the event of a host failure elsewhere in the cluster. You can learn more about clustering and high availability in Appendix C.

Another VMware feature that is also closely tied to clustering is VMware Fault Tolerance or **VMware FT**. VMware FT is VMware's answer to being able to run mission-critical applications on virtual machines. When VMware FT is enabled for a VM, a second copy of that VM is kept running on a second vSphere host and kept updated in real time using VMware's vLockstep technology. If the original VM fails, the FT copy is already running and up-to-date so that it can take over transparently with no downtime or disruption of service.

vMotion VMware's **vMotion** feature is similar to High Availability in that it allows the movement of a running VM from one ESX host to another without interruption. The difference is that with vMotion the migration of the virtual machine does not depend on failure of a vSphere host, but can be done for other reasons such as maintenance, upgrading of a vSphere host, or to improve performance in the event one of the hosts is experiencing heavy processing loads. To perform vMotion, a network connection or a port must be dedicated to the vMotion process and both hosts must share the same data network switch and data store location as shown in Figure 4-5.

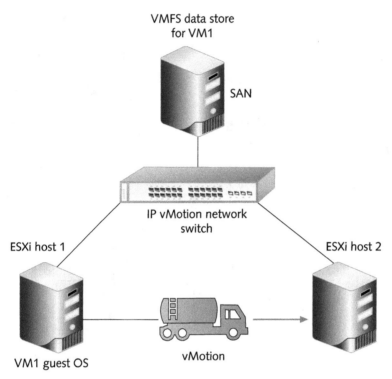

VMFS data store
for VM1

SAN

IP vMotion network
switch

ESXi host 1

ESXi host 2

VM1 guest OS

vMotion

Figure 4-5   VMware vMotion service

While vMotion can "hot migrate" a running VM from one ESXi host to another, the VM's data store stays on the shared drive and is not moved. Storage vMotion (svMotion) is similar to vMotion in that it moves the VM from one host to another, but it differs in that it not only transfers the VM to a different host, Storage vMotion also moves the files from one data store to another as shown in Figure 4-6.

Distributed Resource Scheduler (DRS) is an advanced vSphere feature that runs on vCenter Server and takes advantage of vMotion to balance workloads across multiple ESXi hosts. DRS works by using vCenter Server to constantly monitor the performance of each ESXi host in a cluster and how each VM is impacting that workload. Based on these data, DRS calculates the impact of moving certain VMs to other hosts in order to better balance the work load. You can configure DRS to run in automatic, semi-automatic, or manual mode. In automatic mode, DRS will automatically move VMs to other ESXi hosts based on a preset performance threshold rating. In semi-automatic and manual mode, DRS will make suggestions on which VMs to move for optimal performance. In semi-automatic mode DRS will choose the host for you whereas in manual mode you are prompted to select a host to run the VM on. When you start a VM, DRS provides a service that will suggest the optimal host in a cluster to start the VM on, thus reducing the need to move a VM to another host.

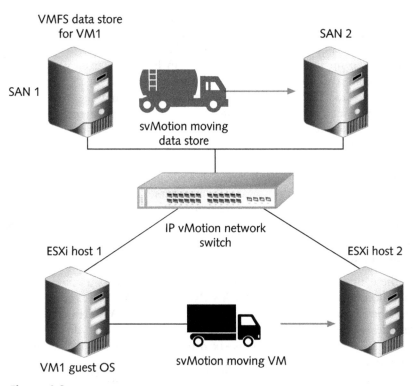

Figure 4-6 VMware Storage vMotion service

A new feature of DRS is the ability to set rules regarding separating certain VMs on different ESXi host computers in order to increase redundancy. For example, you can set rules preventing two domain controller VMs from residing on the same host. Using rules, you can help ensure that if a host fails, at least one domain controller VM will be available on the network.

In addition to standard DRS, vSphere 5 and later provides an advanced feature called storage DRS. Storage DRS takes advantage of storage tiering to specify speeds of different storage devices. For example, tier-1 storage would be located on high speed drives such as SSD. This type of high speed storage would be suitable for mission-critical database applications that need high speed access, a host cache, or a VM's boot disk. Storage DRS monitors the disk reads and writes to determine the storage usage. It will then use sVMotion to move virtual machines to higher of lower storage tiers based on their needs.

Some higher end SAN storage system vendors provide a dynamic tiering option within their storage systems that can perform the tiering process independent of VMware DRS.

Virtual SAN Fibre Channel and iSCSI SAN devices can be very expensive and provide limited scalability. To help solve these issues, a number of venders offer software-based

SAN systems that utilize free disks on multiple servers to create a networked SAN volume. Starting with vSphere v5.1 VMware offers a VMware Storage Appliance (VSA) feature that forms shared storage by pooling the capacity of disks directly attached to clustered ESXi hosts. The free disks from up to three ESXi hosts can be placed in a VSA storage cluster that can then be made available through vCenter to other hosts in the data center. Data stores can then be created on the VSA clusters and shared using the NFS protocol. VSA relies on a Linux appliance to manage the storage capacity, performance, and data redundancy of the hard disks that are installed on the ESXi hosts. Each ESXi host in the VSA cluster must have the Linux VSA appliance installed. In addition, in order to manage VSA clusters, vSphere requires a special plug-in for vCenter Server called VSA Manager. Once the plug-in is installed you can use vCenter Server to manage, monitor, maintain, and troubleshoot VSA clusters. While for many smaller data centers VSA was a good alternative to a dedicated SAN, VSA relies on Linux appliances and plug-ins making it more difficult and complex to implement. Additionally, VSA clusters are accessed using the NFS protocol similar to a NAS environment, restricting use of certain advanced features such as Storage DRS as well as limiting performance.

To overcome these limitations, in vSphere v6 VMware provided a more integrated and robust SAN solution called Virtual SAN or VSAN. VMware VSANs consist of a cluster of ESXi hosts that contribute unused SSD and spinning disks to a SAN array. Each VSAN cluster must have at least one SSD drive for caching and at least one hard disk for data storage. A VSAN cluster can consist of as many as six drives. Not all hosts in the cluster need to contribute disk space but instead can access data shares on the cluster. Clusters are managed directly from vCenter Server along with the Web client. Currently VMware supports third-party data deduplication on storage arrays, but does not yet offer a built-in deduplication feature for VSAN. In the near future VMware plans to include data deduplication, which will help reduce storage usage within VSAN clusters. In Case Projects 4-1 and 4-2 you can gain more information and experience by accessing VMware online labs and videos to learn more about how implement VSAN capability within vSphere version 6.

Activity 4-4: Installing the vSphere Hypervisor (ESXi)

Time Required: 15 minutes

Objective: Install the free ESXi Hypervisor within VMware Player 12.

Requirements: Completion of Activity 4-1 along with VMware Player installed from Chapter 3

Description: Rocky Ridge Forest Products is in the process of setting up a virtual data center to manage their business. In Chapter 3 you created and configured a Windows Server 2016 server using VMware Workstation. Now that the server is running in a test environment, your next task will be to host the virtual server in a production network using vSphere. In this activity you will install the free vSphere ESXi Hypervisor that you downloaded in Activity 4-1.

1. If necessary, start your Windows workstation and start VMware Player 12.

2. Click **Create a New Virtual Machine**.

3. Click the **Installer disk image file (iso)** option, and click the **Browse** button.

4. Navigate to the folder where you stored the vSphere Hypervisor file downloaded in Activity 4-1 and select the **ESXi iso** file.

5. Click **Next** to display the Name the Virtual Machine screen. Type **ESXi6-xxx** (where xxx represents your initials) after the default server name and click **Next**.

6. In the Specify Disk Capacity window, leave the default of 40 GB and then click the **Store virtual disk as a single file** option and click **Next**.

7. Click **Finish** to start the installation process.

8. After installing the hypervisor files, you will see the Welcome to VMware ESXi 6.0 Installation message box. To reduce overhead and provide maximum performance, the ESXi 6.0 hypervisor does not have a GUI interface, but instead works with what is called the DCUI command line interface. You will now use this interface to complete the installation process.

9. If necessary, click anywhere in the ESXi VM window to transfer the keyboard control to the ESXi VM. (You can return to the Windows desktop by pressing Ctrl+Alt.)

10. When asked, press **Enter** to continue and display the license agreement.

11. Press **F11** to accept the license agreement and start the scanning process to find a local disk drive. The virtual disk you created for this VM should be displayed.

12. Press **Enter** to accept the local disk drive selected by the scanning process and continue.

13. Choose your keyboard layout, or press **Enter** to accept the US Default keyboard and continue.

14. In the Enter a root password window, enter a password you want to use for the "root" user. Record the password you use below:

Since ESXi is based on the Linux kernel, it uses the default name "root" for the administrative user.

15. After entering the password twice, press **Enter** to display the Confirm Install message box, and then press **F11** to continue the installation process. This process may take a few minutes, so you may wish to take a quick stretch break.

16. When the installation process finishes, the Installation Complete message box will be displayed. If you are using DVD media, you should now remove the DVD from the drive. If you are using an ISO file, press **Ctrl+Alt** to return to the Windows desktop, click the **Player** menu, point to **Manage**, and click the **Virtual Machine Settings...** option. Click **CD/DVD** setting and then change the connection to the **Use physical drive** option and click **OK**.

17. Return mouse and keyboard control to the ESXi virtual machine and press **Enter** to reboot the ESXi host.

18. When the host restarts, press **F2** to display the Authorization Required dialog box.

19. Leave the Login Name as "root," press the **Tab** key, type the password you recorded in step 14, and press **Enter** to log on and display the System Customization menu box shown in Figure 4-7.

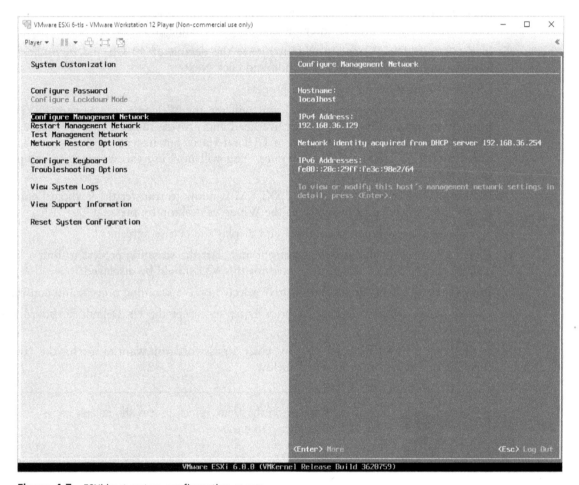

Figure 4-7   ESXi host system configuration menu

Source: VMware vSphere 6.0 ESXi.

 You will be using some of these options to establish the management network in the next activity.

20. To shut down an ESXi hypervisor, press the **Esc** key, press **F12**, and then confirm you are the root user by entering your password.

21. Press the **F2** key to properly shut down the host and exit VMware Workstation 12 layer. This completes the activities for this section. If necessary, close VMware Workstation 12 Player and any open windows.

Microsoft Hyper-V Storage Features

Microsoft Hyper-V offers many of the same storage options as VMware including clustering using NAS, Fibre Channel, and iSCSI. Table 4-3 shows a comparison of features between Hyper-V and vSphere. In this section we will look at each of these features and see how they compare.

Table 4-3   Hyper-V and vSphere storage features

Storage Feature	Hyper-V 2012R2 and later	Free vSphere ESXi Hypervisor with vSphere Client	Licensed vSphere with vClient Server
iSCSI/Fibre Channel support	Yes	Yes	Yes
Clustering and high availability	Yes	No–requires vCenter Server	Yes
Virtual machine migration	Yes	No–requires vCenter Server	Yes–vMotion and sVMotion
Storage Tiering	Yes–called Multipathing	No	Yes - VSAN
Native 4-KB disk support	Yes	No	No
Storage virtualization	Yes	No	Yes VSAN
Storage tiering	Yes	No	Yes
Data deduplication	Yes	No	Available for backups Support for third-party storage vender
Offloaded Data Transfer (ODX)	Yes	No	No
Online checkpoint merge	Yes	Yes	Yes
Online virtual disk resize	Yes	Grow only	Grow only
Hypervisor disk format	NTFS ReFS	VMFS	VMFS
Virtual machine disk format	VHD VHDX	VMDK	VMDK

As shown in the table, all versions of both Hyper-V and vSphere support iSCSI and Fibre Channel storage options. VMware requires the licensed vCenter Server to perform more advanced storage functions such as clustering, vMotion, and load balancing. As described in the previous section, virtual machine migration allows a VM to be moved between host computers to provide for high availability and load balancing. Both the licensed version of vSphere 6 and Windows Server 2012 R2 Hyper-V and later support clustering and high availability features. VMware's Distributed Resource Scheduler (DRS), described in the previous section, provides a unique load balancing process. While Hyper-V has similar capability using third-party products, it does not provide all the features of DRS.

Both vSphere and the later versions of Hyper-V support the live migration of virtual machines between hosts by either moving the VM files to another data store or between clustered hosts that share the same data store.

As described in the previous section, storage tiering is a process of dividing network storage into tiers based on access speeds. High speed storage devices that use SSD drives are classified as tier-1 storage. When multiple VMs are sharing access to network storage devices, it is important to ensure that VMs running mission-critical applications get prioritized access to storage system. This process can be performed by both the hypervisor and the storage system working together. Storage vendors may provide a storage tiering option called multi-pathing within their network storage solutions. Both Hyper-V and the licensed version of vSphere support storage tiering. Hyper-V aggregates physical disks into pools of storage called Spaces. Starting with Server 2012 R2, tiering was introduced for Spaces, allowing VMs to be moved into tier-1 or high speed storage for increased performance. VMware's vSphere 6 release also provides the capability of aggregating SSD and HDD disks with the VSAN 6.0 feature. Currently VSAN has the advantage of using RAID to allow the creation of highly available storage across multiple hosts.

As of this writing, Hyper-V has the advantage of supporting 4-KB disk sectors in virtual disks. Support for 4-KB disk sectors lets the VM take advantage of the emerging storage hardware that provides for increased capacity and reliability. You may expect that VMware will be adding this feature in future releases.

Storage virtualization is the process of creating iSCSI and NAS storage from existing host computers. VMware has provided this capability since vSphere v5.0 using virtual SANs based on the Linux VSA clusters as described in the previous section. More recently with vSphere v 6.0, VMware has provided an advanced storage virtualization capability using VSAN clusters. Microsoft Hyper-V implements this capability using Storage Spaces.

As described earlier, storage deduplication is important to reduce storage requirements for large database applications, Virtual Desktop Infrastructures (VDI), and backups. While VMware can perform deduplication to save space on backups, it relies on the storage vendor to provide this capability on the data volumes. Windows Server 2012 R2 Hyper-V and later can implement deduplication using the host server. This provides for a more economical solution to reducing storage requirements. Using deduplication for virtual desktops or VDI environments can provide storage saving ranging as high as 95%, making this a very attractive capability when implementing Virtual Desktop Infrastructures (VDI) as described in Chapter 9.

VMware uses VMFS for formatting the data store and VMHD for its virtual disks. Both of these file systems are highly tuned for the virtual environment. While the Windows Server 2012 R2 Hyper-V still uses the NTFS format for accessing hard drives, with 2012 R2 Hyper-V now uses a new more advanced virtual hard disk format called VHDX for the virtual disks. VHDX provides improvements over the older VHD format used by earlier releases of Hyper-V by providing increased storage capacity (up to 64 TB per VM disk), improved performance, and security.

Offloaded Data Transfer (ODX) is a feature provided by Hyper-V and the licensed version of vSphere 6.0 that improves VM performance by allowing the hypervisor to offload storage related tasks to the SAN device making the host CPU(s) more available for more VM usage.

Both vSphere 6.0 and Hyper-V provide checkpoint merge capability which allows a snapshot to be applied to a running VM without the need to shut down and restart as would typically be done when using type-2 workstation hypervisors such as VMware Workstation or Oracle VirtualBox. Another nice feature of both Hyper-V and vSphere is the ability to increase the storage capacity of a VM while it is running. Hyper-V gets a one-up in this department as it can also decrease the storage capacity of a virtual disk while the VM is running. Being able to add and remove capacity on the fly is an important feature when implementing a hyper-converged data center, as it allows the central storage pool to be a resource that is assigned to VM based on needs of applications running on the virtual machine. If a VM no longer needs storage capacity, it is an advantage to be able to release that capacity back to the storage pool so it can be assigned to other or new virtual machines.

Activity 4-5: Working with Server 2016 Hyper-V Storage Systems

Time Required: 15 minutes

Objective: Configure a volume using the new Microsoft ReFS storage system.

Requirements: Windows Server 2016 installed on your computer; free disk space

Description: At a recent conference, the IT administrator learned about Microsoft's new ReFS storage system and would like to know more about how it would benefit Hyper-V virtual machines. In this activity you will identify some of the new features of ReFS and then set up a demonstration volume on your Server 2016 disk.

1. If necessary, boot to your Windows Server 2016 server and sign in using your standard user account.

2. Open the Edge browser and go to the http://www.tech-coffee.net/why-using-refs-with-hyper-v-2016/ Web site.

3. Read the article and summarize at least two points that benefit Hyper-V virtualization below:

   1. _____

   2. _____

4. Sign in to your Windows Server 2016 system as Administrator.

5. Open the Computer Management window by clicking **Start, Windows Administrative Tools,** and then double-clicking **Computer Management.**

6. From the left pane, click **Disk Management** to display the current disk configuration.

7. Right-click an unallocated section of a disk and then click the **New Simple Volume** option to display the New Simple Volume Wizard Welcome window.

8. Click **Next** to display the Specify Volume Size window.

9. In the Simple volume size in MB field, enter a capacity of **15,000** or more and then click **Next** to display the Assign Drive Letter or Path window.

10. Verify that the Assign the following drive letter option is selected and click **Next** to display the Format Partition window.

11. Click the **down arrow** in the File System field and click to select the **ReFS** file system.

12. Verify that the Perform a quick format option is checked and then click **Next** and click **Finish** to format the drive using the new ReFS format.

13. Close the Computer Management and Administrative Tools windows and sign off your Windows Server 2016 system. You may optionally use this new ReFS volume to create a Virtual Machine in Chapter 6.

Virtual Network Systems

Virtualization of the network is necessary to achieve a more hyperconverged, or software-defined, data center. **Network functions virtualization (NFV)** refers to virtualization of traditional networking devices such as network adapters, switches, routers, and load balancers. In addition, NFV often includes security enhancements such as firewalls, intrusion detection or prevention systems (IDS/IPS), and antivirus management. To provide the infrastructure needed in a hyperconverged data center, type-1 virtualization products provide a richer set of networking virtualization features than found in type-2 workstation virtualization products. For example, data center virtualization products provide for teaming of NICs on the host to increase speed and fault tolerance. They also provide separate networks for management, data, and hypervisor functions such as the migration of a VM from one host to another. Another rapidly expanding technology that is closely related to virtualization and part of hyperconvergence is software-defined networking. In this section you will learn about networking features that are needed to implement data center virtualization environments in both VMware and Hyper-V products. You will also be introduced to NFV features found in hyperconverged data centers and software-defined networking.

Virtual Network Adapters

Physical computers use network interface cards (NICs) to transmit and receive data on a network. The hypervisor emulates a NIC's functions and provides the guest OS with a software driver for this virtualized NIC, which is called a **virtual network adapter**. Virtual network adapters gain access to the outside network by being assigned to a switch that is connected to the physical NIC. The physical NIC can be assigned to a single virtual network adapter or shared by multiple virtual adapters, depending on the configuration of the virtual machine.

Both physical and virtual network adapters transfer data between network computers in packets of data bits called frames. In addition to data, frames include a **Media Access Control (MAC) address** used to identify the sender and receiver. Network adapters receive frames by "listening" to network transmissions and checking each frame's MAC address. When a network adapter "sees" a frame with its MAC address, it transfers data bits from that frame into memory and then notifies the OS that the frame has been received. The OS then transfers data from the network adapter to an application, based on the information in the frame.

To send and receive frames, network adapters, both physical and virtual, must be assigned MAC addresses. A MAC address consists of six bytes and is expressed as a hexadecimal number, such as 00:0C:29:B3:53:65. (Two hexadecimal characters equal 1 byte.) With physical NICs, the manufacturer assigned the MAC address. The first three hexadecimal numbers represent the manufacturer's ID, and the last three hexadecimal numbers represent the NIC's serial number. With virtual machines, you can have a MAC address generated randomly by the host computer or assign one manually.

When you have virtual machines running on multiple host computers connected to the same physical network, you might want to assign MAC addresses manually to ensure that virtual machines aren't assigned the same MAC address accidentally.

Virtual machines access the physical network using the host computer's physical network adapters that are assigned to a virtual switch. In Chapter 1 you learned that simple virtual switches such as those used with type-2 hypervisors can be host-only, bridged, or NAT. Both bridged and NAT switches utilize one of the host's physical NICs. In a virtual data center, host computers can run several virtual machines that need to access the physical network. Having only one physical network adapter can be a bottleneck when it is being shared by multiple virtual machines. In addition, host computers in a virtual data center often use some type of shared network storage. To provide better performance and security, the host computer should use a separate network adapter to connect to the shared storage as well as additional adapters for management and VM data. This means that to provide access and sufficient bandwidth for all the network traffic a host will require a number of physical network adapters or use multi-port network cards.

When using multi-port cards or multiple adapters, each port on the NIC requires a unique MAC address.

While VMware compatible multi-port adapters can be rather expensive, using multi-port network adapters reduces the number of expansion slots needed on the host's motherboard. The disadvantage of using a single multi-port NIC is that it presents a single point of failure in the event the NIC card fails. In order to provide more fault tolerance, a host computer should have at least two multi-port NICs to provide redundancy in the event of a NIC failure. In the following activity you will get a chance to view some of the various multi-port network adapters on the market and document prices and features.

Your instructor may choose to assign the following activity as a homework project or perform it as a demonstration.

Activity 4-6: Recommending vSphere Compatible Adapters

Time Required: 15 minutes

Objective: Given a scenario, document prices on three vSphere 6.0 compatible network adapters.

Requirements: Access to the Internet

Description: Assume you are an IT consultant for Computer Technology Services and you have been asked to provide prices on three network adapters for the ESXi host you are installing for the Rocky Ridge Forest Products company. Initially the ESXi host will run two Windows servers that will need access to the local network as well as the Internet.

In addition, the host will be using an iSCSI SAN and management network, which must be attached to a separate physical network switch to provide enhanced performance and security. In this activity you will use the VMware vSphere compatibility guide along with Newegg to recommend a solution that will provide at least two separate network connections from the host to the physical network.

1. Log on to your Windows host as the local administrator, and use a Web browser to access google.com.

2. Search for "**VMware I/O compatibility guide**" and open the corresponding .pdf file.

3. Save the VMware I/O compatibility guide file in the folder you created in Activity 1-1.

4. Use the Find function to locate all Broadcom network cards in the PDF file.

5. In a separate window, go to the www.newegg.com site (or another site your instructor recommends).

6. Find all Broadcom network cards and sort them by price.

7. In the space below, record the three lowest price Broadcom network cards along with their price, speed, number of ports, and any other distinguishing features.

Broadcom Card Model	Price	Speed	Ports	Other Features

8. Close the windows and exit your Internet browser.

Using TCP/IP with Virtual Machines

Transmission Control Protocol/Internet Protocol (TCP/IP) was developed in the 1960s to support communication between mainframe computers in government agencies and educational institutions. This suite of protocols is responsible for formatting frames and routing them between networks. Because TCP/IP was developed to connect many independent organizations, it was designed to support communication between diverse computers and OSs.

Most private and public networks, including the Internet and virtual networks, use TCP/IP to send and receive frames. TCP/IP uses its own address scheme, separate from MAC addresses, to deliver frames. Today there are two major protocols in use on public and private networks. IPv4, which was the original Internet address system, uses 32-bit addresses as shown in Figure 4-8, and is still in use on most computer networks and is used to configure virtual machines in this book. While IPv6, which uses a 128-bit address and provides many features to enhance security and performance, is slowly gaining ground. For the purposes of this book we will focus on IPv4.

IPv4 Addressing Although MAC addresses are used to transmit frames between NICs attached to the same network switch, they aren't suitable for moving data across large and complex network systems, such as the Internet. For efficient communication among many computers attached to multiple network switches, TCP/IP requires another address system, called IP addressing. Each computer attached to a network is called a host and is assigned a unique address consisting of a network ID and a host ID. As shown in Figure 4-8, each IPv4 address consists of 32-bit binary numbers, divided into four groups of 8 bits each (called octets) that are separated by periods; this formatting is called dotted decimal notation.

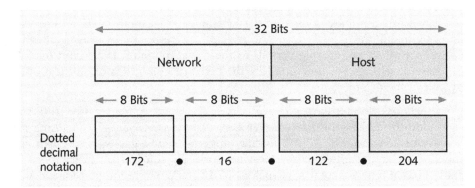

Figure 4-8   IPv4 addressing

The network ID is the same for all computers on a network. The host ID represents a network device and must be unique for each entity on the network. IP addresses are divided into three major classes. In a Class A address, the first octet represents the network ID, and the last three octets represent network devices. In a Class B network, the first two octets are the network ID, and the last two octets are the host ID. Class C addresses are intended for small networks, with only one octet reserved for host IDs and three octets used for the network ID.

IPv4 addresses also use a special number called a **subnet mask** to determine which part of the IP address is the network ID and which part is the host ID. A simple subnet mask consists of 255 in each position representing part of the network ID and 0 in each position representing the host ID. For example, the standard subnet mask used by a Class A network is 255.0.0.0, and Class B and C subnet masks are 255.255.0.0 and 255.255.255.0, respectively.

In addition, TCP/IP includes **private IP addresses**, which are reserved for use on private internal networks and aren't routed across the Internet. All address classes have a range of private IP addresses, as shown in Table 4-4. The Class A address 127.0.0.1 is reserved as a **loopback address** (also called the local host address), used to test IP communication software by sending frames to receiving software on the same host computer. A frame sent to the loopback address never actually leaves the host computer's NIC.

Table 4-4   Private IP addresses by class

Class	Private IP Address Range
A	10.0.0.0 to 10.255.255.0
B	172.16.0.0 to 172.31.0.0
C	192.168.1.0 to 192.168.254.0

The DHCP Service To communicate by using TCP/IP, each network device needs at least the following information: an IP address, a subnet mask, and a default gateway (address of the router for sending packets outside the local network). You can configure this information manually or automatically by using DHCP or Automatic Private IP Addressing (APIPA). When using DHCP, one computer on the network is configured to run the DHCP service. When a client computer configured to obtain its IP address automatically starts, it broadcasts a request packet on the local network, asking for IP address configuration information. If the DHCP server is available, it responds by leasing IP settings (IP address, subnet mask, and leasing period) to the client computer to be used for a specified period. These IP settings are configured by the network administrator and can also include IP addresses of the default gateway and the DNS server.

If the local network doesn't have a DHCP server, the client computer uses APIPA to assign itself a random IP address in the range 169.254.0.1 to 169.255.255.254, using a Class B subnet mask of 255.255.0.0. APIPA doesn't supply a default gateway, so client computers are limited to communicating on the local network. As you learned in Chapters 2 and 3, workstation-based type-2 hypervisors such as VMware Workstation and Oracle VirtualBox can optionally provide a DHCP service to the virtual machines they host. However, type-1 data center products such as vSphere and Hyper-V do not have a built in DHCP server and instead rely on other network devices to provide DHCP to the hosted virtual machines.

As network adapters communicate using MAC or physical addresses, in order to send a packet from one IP device to another, the sender has to obtain the MAC address associated with the receiver's IP address. To find a MAC address of a receiver, a device first uses the IP mask to determine the network address of the receiver. If the receiving device is on a different IP address, the sending device transmits the packet to its default gateway or router. If the receiving device has the same network IP address as the sender, the sending device will use the **Address Resolution Protocol** (**ARP**) to broadcast the IP address of the receiver on its local network and wait for the receiving device to return its MAC address. It then creates a data frame, which it transmits to the receiver.

Understanding Virtual Switches

In a physical network, a **switch** is a device that uses ports to connect multiple NICs to the same network. Most modern switches inspect each frame's MAC address to determine which port the frame is sent to. Broadcast frames are sent to all ports that are part of the network segment or logical network (or broadcast domain). Virtual networks use hypervisor software to simulate switches; you can use these **virtual switches** to configure a variety of virtual networks for different purposes. Virtual network switches typically divide traffic into a few different types to enable better utilization of the network. Traffic types include virtual machine data that is passed between VMs and out to the physical network, management operations, and kernel traffic. Kernel traffic is used by the hypervisor for system functions such as accessing iSCSI or NFS storage, migrating virtual machines between hosts, and performing fault tolerant operations. Each of these different traffic types can be assigned to its own virtual switch, or a single virtual switch can host traffic of different types.

In order to help separate network traffic, both physical and virtual switches support the concept of logical networks or Virtual LANs (VLANS). To allow more devices to communicate efficiently and securely on a network switch it is often important to divide the ports of the switch into separate VLANs. VLANs allow the ports on a switch to be divided into logical groupings such that the ports in the **VLAN** act as a separate logical network called a **broadcast domain**. Devices that are part of a broadcast domain can send packets directly to each other using MAC addresses.

Each VLAN is given a unique number called a tag. This tag is attached to each packet and is used by the switch to determine what ports can receive the packet. For example, in Figure 4-9 there are 4 VLANs.

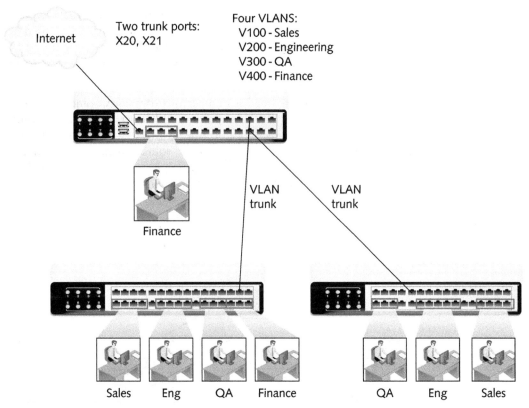

Figure 4-9 Traditional network switch configuration

The Sales VLAN is tagged as 100, Engineering is 200, Quality Assurance is 300, and Finance is tagged as 400. A **trunk** is a special port that connects two switches. A trunk can be configured to pass packets from several different VLAN tags. Trunks are necessary for devices connected to different switches to participate in a VLAN.

Using VLANs provide the following benefits:

- Create logically grouped networks.
- Improve performance by confining broadcast traffic to a subset of switch ports.

- Improve security by preventing traffic on one VLAN from being monitored or accessed from machines that are connected to other logical networks or VLANs.

- Save cost by partitioning the network without the overhead of adding specialized router equipment.

You will use VLAN in later chapters to configure virtual network switches.

Introduction to Software-Defined Networking

Software-defined networking (SDN) is not directly a part of virtualization, but instead is a way of managing the flow of data across complex switched network environments that can include both physical and virtual switches. In traditional networking, each switch is its own world with its data ports assigned to various VLANs and trunk ports used to connect switches. Because traditional networks have a "switch-based" view of the traffic flow, traffic bottlenecks occurring on certain trunk ports can slow down network access to many users and applications as shown in Figure 4-9.

Companies such as Cisco have provided a number of proprietary solutions to help manage traffic on their switches, but these can be expensive and limited to a certain vendor. Other protocols such as software-defined networking offer a more hyperconverged network management environment in which a centralized, open source manager is used to configure switches in order to provide the best data flow. To implement software-defined networking, switches and the management console must support a common protocol used to communicate traffic flow from the switch as well as allow the management console to configure traffic flow across the trunks. As shown in Figure 4-10, **OpenFlow** is a common open source protocol used to communicate between the switches and management server.

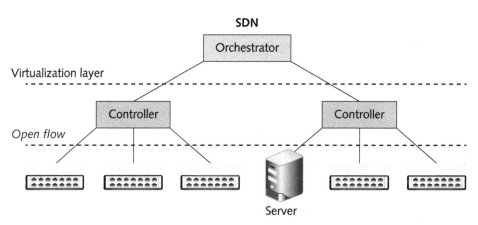

Figure 4-10 Using software-defined networking for configuring and monitoring network traffic control

OpenFlow is an open source protocol that is rapidly becoming the software-defined networking standard many switches support. Virtualization companies such as VMware and Microsoft are working with network venders such as Cisco to help build software-defined data centers that use OpenFlow to manage both physical and virtual networking using centralized management consoles.

Virtual Networking in vSphere

Both vSphere and Hyper-V have similar virtual network functions. In this section we will focus on how networking is implemented in vSphere. In the Hyper-V section we will compare the virtual networking function in vSphere to how Hyper-V handles its virtual network environment.

A vSphere virtual switch is a software construct implemented in the VMKernel of the ESXi Hypervisor. vSphere has two major types of virtual switches based on the version of vSphere: standard switches (available on all versions) and distributed switches (available only on licensed or vCenter versions). While a **standard switch** is limited to accessing only VMs running on the same host that the switch is on, a **distributed switch** can be accessed from VMs running on any host managed by the vCenter Server. One of the major advantages of distributed switches is that they enable a virtual machine to maintain a consistent network configuration as it migrates from one host to another. If you are planning to implement vMotion or VMware FT on a virtual machine, you will need to assign these services to separate port groups on a distributed switch so they can be shared among all hosts in the cluster.

Ports on a standard vSphere virtual switch can be either VM data ports, VMKernel ports, or Uplink ports. For example, Figure 4-11 shows an example of a virtual network switch divided into port groups for Production, Marketing, a DMZ (Demilitarized Zone) along with Kernel port groups for Management, and iSCSI SAN access.

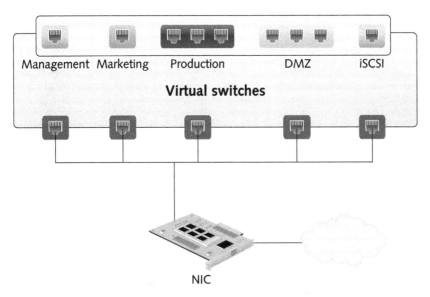

Figure 4-11   Logical VLAN port groups

VMKernel port groups are reserved for use by the hypervisor. The management network port is used by the administrative console to interact with the host's hypervisor and the iSCSI network is used by the hypervisor to communicate with the SAN. In addition to these Kernel ports, separate ports also must be created for vMotion and Fault Tolerance functions.

To connect the virtual switch to the physical network, one or more NICs must be assigned to each switch using the uplink ports (see Figure 4-12). The process of assigning multiple NICs

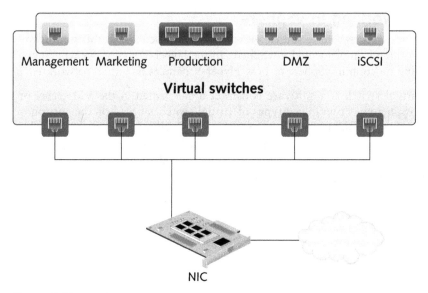

Figure 4-12 Configuring multiple virtual switches based on traffic type

to a virtual switch type is called **teaming**. Teaming two or more NICs to the same virtual switch provides for increased performance as well as fault tolerance.

 While you can have two or more NICs mapped to a single virtual switch, each NIC can only be assigned to a single virtual switch.

When configuring virtual networking on a host, you can either create separate virtual switches for each type of network traffic as shown in Figure 4-12, or you can create a single switch with multiple port groups as shown in Figure 4-11.

Since a NIC can be assigned to only one virtual switch, you would need to have five NICs to implement the switch configuration shown in Figure 4-12. Rather than installing five separate NICs in the host computer, it would be more efficient to purchase one or two multi-port NICs. In addition to allowing traffic to be grouped by type, port groups also allow assigning network policies. Policies are an important part of managing a hyperconverged data center. vSphere provides for three types of network policies: security, traffic shaping, and NIC teaming. The security policy gives the administrator the option of disallowing certain behaviors that might compromise security such as changing the MAC address of a virtual machine, forging the source MAC address of data frames sent from the VM, or setting the virtual adapter to promiscuous mode in order to view all traffic on the virtual switch.

A traffic-shaping policy can be used in cases where the administrator wants to protect bandwidth of a virtual machine or port group in an oversubscribed network. Traffic shaping can be useful to provide the performance necessary to support applications such as VoIP and video.

The NIC teaming policy enables the administrator to distribute network traffic among multiple network adapters to enhance performance. While default NIC teaming policies are set for the entire standard switch, these defaults can be overridden at the port group level in order to reroute traffic for load balancing and failover situations.

One of the challenges and expenses of setting up a vSphere ESXi host computer is obtaining the network adapters that are compatible with the ESXi Hypervisor. In order to eliminate the need to have several expansion slots on your host's motherboard, many NIC today provide multiple network ports, allowing you to use one NIC for multiple virtual switches. In the following activity you will explore some of the NIC options that are compatible with vSphere ESXi hosts.

Activity 4-7: Configuring the ESXi Management Network

Time Required: 15 minutes

Objective: Configure your ESXi hypervisor to use the management network.

Requirements: Completion of Activity 4-3 along with VMware Player installed from Chapter 3

Description: Now that you have installed ESXi Hypervisor and obtained a multi-port compatible NIC, your next task will be to set up and test the management network. You will then use this network in Activity 4-8 to access your ESXi host from the vSphere Client software.

1. If necessary, start your Windows workstation and start VMware Player 12.

2. Add a second bridged network adapter to your ESXi VM. Click to select your ESXi-xxx virtual machine, click the **Player** menu, point to **Manage**, and click **Virtual Machine Settings**. Click the **Add** button, select **Network Adapter**, and click **Next**. Click the **Bridged** option and click **Finish**. Click **OK** to close the Virtual Machine Settings window.

3. Start your ESXi host, press **F2**, and log on using your "root" user account and password. The System Customization menu shown previously in Figure 4-7 will be displayed.

4. Use the down arrow key to select the **Configure Management Network** option and press **Enter**.

5. With **Network Adapters** selected, press **Enter** a second time to display the available network adapters. Notice that you can select multiple adapters to provide fault tolerance and load balancing.

6. Select the network adapter you added in step 2 and then press the **spacebar** to toggle the NIC as selected.

7. Press **Enter** to save your changes and return to the Configure Management Network menu.

8. Scroll down to IPv4 Configuration and press **Enter** to display an IPv4 Configuration dialog box.

9. Notice that by default the ESXi host is using a DHCP address to get the address shown. In the space below, record the IP address information of your ESXi host on the management network and then press **Enter** to return to the Configure Management Network menu.

IP Address of your ESXi host: _____

Subnet Mask: _____

Default Gateway: _____

10. Use the **DNS Configuration** option and then scroll down and select the **Use the following DNS server addresses and hostname** option. Change the hostname to the server name you used for the VM in Activity 4-3. Record the DNS information and name of your host below and then press **Enter** to save the change and return to the Configure Management Network menu.

Primary DNS server: _____

Hostname: _____

11. Press **Esc** to close the Configure Management Network menu and display the Confirmation dialog box. Press the **Y** key to apply the changes and restart the management network. Record the IP address assigned to your ESXi6-xxx host in on the line below:

IP Address of your ESXi host: _____

12. Press **Ctrl+Alt** to return control to your Windows 10 workstation.

13. Open a command prompt window and enter the command: **Ping ip_address** (where ip_address is the address you entered in step 11). Record your results below:

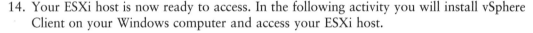

_____

_____

14. Your ESXi host is now ready to access. In the following activity you will install vSphere Client on your Windows computer and access your ESXi host.

Activity 4-8: Installing and Testing the vSphere Client

Time Required: 15 minutes

Objective: Install vSphere Client and then use it to access and create a new network switch.

Requirements: Completion of Activity 4-7

Description: Now that you have tested your ESXi host on the management network, in this activity you will install vSphere Client you downloaded in Activity 4-1 and use it to view your ESXi host configuration.

1. If necessary, start your Windows workstation and navigate to the folder where you downloaded the vSphere Client installation file in Activity 4-1.

2. Double-click the file **VMware-viclient-all-6.0.0-xxx.exe** (where xxx is the build number of the installation file) and then click the **Run** button to start the installation wizard if necessary.

3. If necessary, click **Yes** when you see the User Account Control dialog box.

4. Select the language and click **OK** to extract the software and display the Welcome window.

5. Click **Next** to display the End User License Agreement window. Click the **I accept the terms in the license agreement** option and click **Next** to select the destination folder. Click **Next** to leave the default folder and then click **Install** to perform the installation process.

6. After the installation is complete, click the **Finish** button to return to the Windows Desktop. Close any unneeded windows.

7. If necessary, open VMware Player and start your ESXi host.

8. Double-click the **VMware vSphere Client** icon from the desktop to display the ESXi host login window.

9. Enter the IP address of your ESXi host you recorded in step 11 of Activity 4-7 along with the "root" username and password and click the **Login** button. When you see the Security Warning message box, click **Ignore** to continue.

10. Close the VMware Evaluation Notice dialog box.

11. Double-click Inventory if necessary. Click the **Configuration** tab and then click the **Networking** link as shown in Figure 4-13.

12. Notice that the management network and the VM network are currently both using the same switch. This can create a single point of failure and cause performance degradation. The management network is using a VMKernel port while the VM Network is using a standard port group. To improve performance and reliability, the management network should be moved to a separate virtual switch or another adapter port added to VSwitch0. These operations can be performed using the **Add Networking** link in the upper right of the window. You will learn how to perform these and other vSphere networking configuration options in Chapters 7 and 8.

Figure 4-13 vSphere Client Networking window

Source: VMware vSphere Client 6.0

13. Click the **Summary** tab to get an overview of the ESXi host configuration.

14. Click the **Virtual Machines** tab to see any virtual machines currently assigned to this ESXi host.

15. Click the **Performance** tab to view a graph of the ESXi host performance.

16. Click **Home** in the Navigation Bar to return to the opening window.

17. Click **File, Exit** to exit vSphere Client.

18. Return to your ESXi host VM running on VMware Player and click in the VM window to transfer control to the VM.

19. Shut down the ESXi host by pressing the **Esc** key, pressing the **F12** key, and then entering your password in the Authentication Required dialog box.

20. Press **F2** to shut down the host and close VMware Player. You have now completed this activity.

Virtual Networking in Hyper-V

Just as in vSphere, Hyper-V uses virtual network adapters that connect to a virtual switch. As shown in Figure 4-14, Hyper-V offers three types of virtual switches: Private, External, and Internal.

A **Private virtual switch** is a switch that limits communication to only virtual machines running on that host. Guest operating systems that are connected to the same Private Virtual Network can communicate with each other, but they cannot communicate with the Host operating system and the Host operating system cannot connect to the VMs on the Private Virtual Network. Private Virtual Networks are great if you need total isolation from all other Virtual Networks and the host computer. They can present problems if you need to copy files to a virtual machine since there is no connectivity to any physical network or to the Host operating system.

An **internal virtual switch** is similar to a Private Virtual Network in that it isn't bound to any physical NIC. The Internal Virtual Network is an isolated virtual switch like the Private Virtual Network, but in the case of the Internal Virtual Network, the Host operating system has access to the guest virtual machines through the Internal Virtual Network virtual switch. However, there is no DHCP-like functionality with this virtual switch (as there is with some instantiations of VMware Workstation), so if you want to communicate with virtual machines that are connected to the Internal Virtual Network switch, you are going to need to assign an IP address to the virtual NIC that's associated with that Internal Virtual Network for the Host operating system that is valid on the virtual network to which you are trying to connect.

An **external virtual switch** is different from the other switches because this type of virtual switch is associated with physical network adapters. You can have one External Virtual Network for each physical NIC that's installed on the Hyper-V server. The External Virtual Network switch appears to take the place of the physical NIC on the Hyper-V server—so that if you were to look at the configuration of the former NIC, it would appear to not have any IP addressing assigned to it. Instead, a virtual NIC is added to the Network Connections window and that virtual NIC is connected to the External Virtual Network switch. It is the virtual NIC which has the IP addressing assigned to it that allows it to communicate with the physical network.

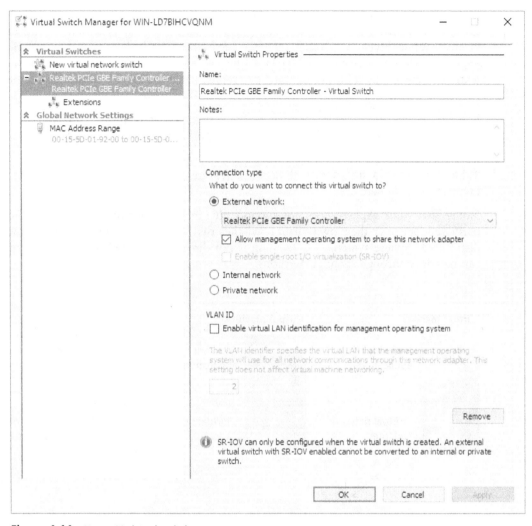

Figure 4-14 Hyper-V virtual switches

Source: Microsoft Windows Server 2016 Hyper-V

Network adapters can be added to external switches using Hyper-V Manager. In order to add a network adapter to a virtual switch, the network adapter must first be made available for placement. Network adapters on a Hyper-V host can be made available for use in virtual switches by using Hyper-V Manager to access the properties of the adapter and selecting either *Available for placement* or *Used by management*. Adapters that are marked as Available for placement may be connected to an external virtual switch and then used to connect virtual machines on that switch to the physical network. Adapters that are marked as Used by Management are used for communication between the Virtual Machine Manager (VMM) console and the Hyper-V host. Network adapters that are marked for Management may also be used in migrating virtual machines and load balancing.

Hyper-V switches are more like Workstation in that they offer fewer options such as port groups and traffic types. For example, Hyper-V does not offer distributed switches or port groups. While Hyper-V virtual switches have more limited configuration options than vSphere, they are extensible. A Hyper-V **Extensible switch** is designed to support additional features through the addition of third-party plug-ins. Figure 4-15 shows an example of an extensible Hyper-V switch connected to the physical network.

Possible extensions include security systems such as firewalls and malware protection, along with networking capabilities such as support for OpenFlow management to support software-defined networking.

Table 4-5 shows a list of virtual network features and how they are supported by both Hyper-V and vSphere 6.0.

Notice that while vSphere does not support plug-in extensions to their virtual switch, third-party vendors offer their own virtual switches that can be substituted for the standard and distributed vSphere switch. NIC teaming is not directly supported by Hyper-V switches but can be added through switch extensions.

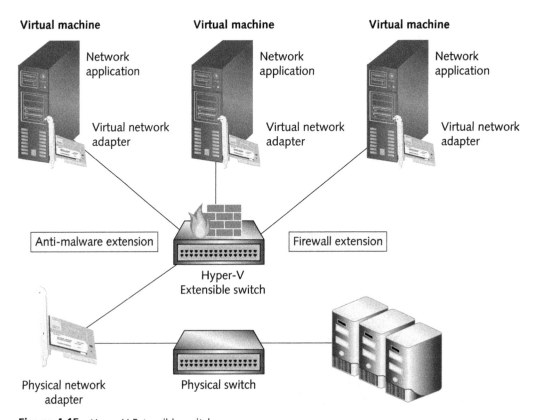

Figure 4-15   Hyper-V Extensible switch

Table 4-5 Comparison of networking features in vSphere and Hyper-V

Networking Feature	Hyper-V 2012R2 and Later	vSphere Free	vSphere Licensed
Extensible network switch	Yes	No	Replaceable by third-party
NIC Teaming	Available through switch extensions	Yes	Yes
Port groups	No	Yes	Yes
Private VLANs	Yes	No	Only through vCloud or third-party
Port monitoring	Yes	Per port group	Yes
Port mirroring	Yes	Per port group	Yes
Distributed switch	Using third-party extension	No	Yes
Security policy	DHCP snooping guard	Yes	Yes

With Server 2008, Hyper-V started as a more limited data center hypervisor designed to provide a means to run multiple servers on a single host. With Hyper-V Server 2008 R2 and now Windows Server 2016 releases, Microsoft has added functionality to make it competitive with vSphere. While VMware currently holds a strong market share lead in data center virtualization products, we can expect to see Hyper-V continue to grow its market share in the future. In Chapters 5 and 6 you will be working with Hyper-V and Virtual Machine Manager to implement many of the data center virtualization features that have been described in this chapter.

Virtualization Security

Just as in traditional data centers, software-defined data centers are subject to a number of security risks including accidental data loss, insider data theft, hacker attacks, and malware. While virtualization helps to provide better fault tolerance and data recovery through clustering and backup, it also adds additional software layers to the system, increasing the attack surface. In this section we will introduce you to some of the security threats and prevention measures including operational security, hacker attacks, and malware awareness.

Implementing Operational Security

A key aspect of operational security is securing the host to control who has access to the virtual disk files. At the simplest level, an insider could possibly steal data by obtaining a copy of the virtual machine's hard disk and then accessing the data using a cloned virtual machine at home. Just as in a physical server environment, in a software-defined data center the host computers need to be kept in physically secured areas with access limited to just the people who need it. Since a lot of administration is done remotely using server consoles such as vSphere Client or Virtual Machine Manager (VMM), usernames and passwords for the host must be kept secure. Passwords need to changed regularly and be complex, consisting of a combination of at least eight numbers, upper- and lowercase characters, and symbols.

It is also important to isolate console management activity to a separate network or VLAN. Separating management traffic helps to prevent packet sniffer software running on a VM or other physical computer from scanning the network and pulling off un-encrypted data packets.

Running a graphical user interface (GUI) on the host hypervisor is also something to avoid as running a GUI decreases performance and can make it easier for an intruder to gain access to the hypervisor either from the console or through some security flaw in the GUI software. With ESXi Hypervisor, VMware eliminated the GUI console providing just a minimal command interface such as you experienced when installing ESXi hypervisor in Activity 4-4. When using Hyper-V, host performance and security can be improved by installing only the server core, which does not include the GUI environment. Other important parts of operational security include separation of duties, establishing a change configuration policy, and virtual machine monitoring.

Separation of duty involves defining specific tasks and who is responsible for them. Unfortunately, this process can involve some political battles between various administration groups who feel it is part of their job security to manage the host environment. For example, do network administrators manage virtual switches and other virtual network system, or should the virtualization team handle this? Whatever the final decision, administrators should be given only the rights they need to perform their assigned duty or task. Higher end management of the system such as configuring global hypervisor settings should involve more than one person to prevent security breaches.

Just as in physical data centers, a change configuration policy is necessary to establish a process by which any changes or software patches are applied. Without a proper change configuration policy, updates and modifications may be applied in a haphazard manner. creating cracks in the security system. Major goals of any change configuration policy include consistency and documentation. Given the vast array of settings that pertain to VM management, monitoring, and network control, it is critical that any changes be evaluated and agreed upon before being implemented. Microsoft uses Update Manager to help keep host computer software updated. VMware offers two products to help in managing updates and patches. VMware Go is a cloud-based service that allows small organizations to set up a central management system that communicates with the VMware cloud to scan and patch hosts and virtual machines. Larger organizations may use VMware Update Manager (VUM) to automate and streamline patching and upgrading ESXi systems.

Virtual machine monitoring involves tracking virtual machine creation and operation. Virtual machines can be deployed in just a few minutes (for example, short term testing VMs). Virtual machines created on-the-fly may not be patched, updated, or properly configured. These virtual machines may be subject to security flaws that can affect the entire software-defined data center. For this reason, it is important to monitor virtual machine creation and operation in order to prevent or reduce VM sprawl. Another concern is monitoring network traffic on virtual networks. In many virtual environments, traffic on the virtual network is not being monitored. Not monitoring virtual machine traffic can be very dangerous in terms of preventing data sniffing and other security breaches. One way to monitor virtual network traffic is to run an application on a virtual machine to act as an **Intruder Detection System (IDS)**. The IDS will look at all packets on the virtual network in order to determine such things as whether a virtual machine is infected by a worm, is launching a denial of service attack, or is scanning open ports. The downside of monitoring a network is the decrease in performance experienced by running IPS applications on virtual machines.

Preventing Hacker Attacks

Like thieves and vandals, the goal of a hacker is to break into your data facility in order to steal information or damage your system. Many hackers today are not just thugs and robbers, but very professional people that do hacking for a living. Other hackers may be actual terrorists or governmental spies. The holy grail for any hacker is to gain control of administrative console to a server or host computer. The first step to prevent hacking is to be sure to use secure passwords that are at least eight characters in length and consist of a combination of upper- and lowercase letters along with numbers and special symbols and are changed on a regular basis. Next is to implement proper firewalls. Hackers typically employ a process that consists of reconnaissance, scanning, exploitation, and pivoting as illustrated in Figure 4-16.

4

In the **reconnaissance phase** the attacker would search for information about the target using publicly available sources such as Web sites or Facebook pages. The goal of this stage is to learn about the target's people, systems, and applications. The best way to protect your system from hacker reconnaissance is to limit the information that is available on Web sites to only what is necessary. Because reconnaissance is done from the outside using techniques such as DNS queries, WHOIS records, and examining Web sites, virtualization of the data center does not directly affect the security process. One piece of information that may help a hacker is learning whether or not your site is virtualized and what virtualization software is being used. For this reason, it is a good idea to have administrators use a different username and email address on VMware and other forum sites.

In the **scanning phase,** the hacker often uses tools such as Network Mapper (NMAP) to look for open network ports and other vulnerable aspects of the system or applications including whether the system is real or virtual. This information will be used to determine the best attack method. Clues such as open ports, running services, MAC addresses, and the values

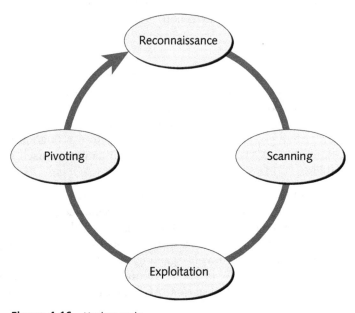

Figure 4-16 Hacker cycle

contained in data packet fields can all aid the hacker in learning about the system and its vulnerabilities. One of the best ways to protect your system from scanning is to block access to the local network using firewalls and Intruder Protection Systems (IPS).

In the **exploitation phase** hackers use the information they have gathered to actively attack the system and applications using the vulnerabilities they have discovered in the scanning phase. The best defense against exploitation is implementing good operational security including keeping software up to date through proper change management policies, using secure passwords, separation of duties, implementation of firewalls and intruder detection systems (IPS and IDS), and following anti-malware practices.

Pivoting is simply the act of gaining access to systems and applications in order to establish a "beachhead." Often beachheads may simply be scanner software running on a virtual machine that has been infected by a virus or worm. From the beachhead, begin the cycle again in order to further infiltrate the system. Good hackers can pivot through several systems to get to the data they are looking for.

Hacker attacks on virtual systems are best prevented by using intruder protection systems to monitor the virtual network traffic and incorporating firewalls in the virtual network switches. Microsoft has opened the door to improving network monitoring by allowing third-party venders to write extensions to virtual switches. Extensions can include firewalls as well as intruder detection systems. Windows Server 2016 Hyper-V contains a new feature called Shielded virtual machines, which encrypts the data and state of the shielded virtual machine to make it harder for Hyper-V administrators and malware on the host to inspect, tamper with, or steal data. When using the shielded option, Hyper-V administrators can't see the video output and disks, and the virtual machines can be restricted to run only on known, healthy hosts, as determined by a Host Guardian Server. VMware has a product called TrustPoint that also provides a number of features to increase virtual security including monitoring the network to detect unmanaged virtual machines, identifying and containing unfolding hacker attacks, and improving threat detection.

Malware Awareness

The term malware is used to encompass a variety of nasty software including viruses, worms, bots, rootkits, and spyware. In most cases the same type of anti-malware practices used on physical servers and workstations also apply to virtualized data center. Today some malware is virtualization aware, allowing it to act differently when running on a guest system. For example, when running on a virtual guest, the malware may refuse to run (a good thing), or since many security professionals use VMs to analyze malware, it can make itself harder to detect and analyze (a bad thing).

One of the latest types of virtualization aware malware is known as VM Escape. This type of malware will take advantage of flaws in the hypervisor device drivers, such as a virtual network adapter, to gain access to the hypervisor kernel. Once this occurs the malware is capable of spreading directly to other guests or stealing information by directly reading from virtual disk files. **Directory traversal attacks** involve gaining access to the underlying host through flaws in the hypervisor. For example, in 2008, researchers at Core Security discovered a flaw in certain versions of VMware Workstation, ACE, and Player that could allow a hacker to exploit the VMware Shared Folders feature to read or write to any of the underlying host OS disks.

Rootkits are viruses that are operating at the same privilege as the hypervisor and have methods to hide from detection by anti-virus software. Blue Pill is an example of a rootkit virus that takes advantage of virtualization. Blue Pill works by exploiting the SVM/Pacifica virtualization capabilities built into AMD processors in order to create a rogue hypervisor that encapsulates the running Windows virtual machine and virtualizes it. Since the operating system is now running on top of the rootkit hypervisor, the Blue Pill malware has full control of everything within the guest OS. Like all rootkits, Blue Pill is very difficult to detect unless using special anti-virus scanners, such as the Samsara rootkit detection software.

Worms are malware that scan systems for open ports and then attempt to copy themselves to other systems using security flaws in the operating system or drivers. The Storm worm is a nasty example of malware that can detect whether it's running in a VM and then attempt to exploit vulnerabilities in the host or hypervisor.

Just as in physical data centers, one of the best defenses against malware is keeping the system updated with all patches by implementing a configuration change policy and running virus scanning software on the host and VMs. One difference with virtualized data centers is, when performing malware scans on a number of guest virtual machines, it is important to factor in the impact these scans will have on the performance of the underlying host. In the following activity you will view firewall settings on your ESXi host and then download a network monitoring toolkit. You will learn more about implementing network monitoring and other operational security measures for Hyper-V and VMware in later chapters.

Activity 4-9: Checking Virtualization Security Settings

Time Required: 15 minutes

Objective: Use vSphere Client to check firewall settings on the ESXi host you installed.

Requirements: Completion of Activity 4-8

Description: Management at Rocky Ridge Forest Products would like to have you document the existing firewall settings on the ESXi management network and enable the iSCSI service. In this lab activity you will document the firewall settings on your ESXi host and enable the iSCSI client.

1. If necessary, log on to your Windows workstation and start VMware Workstation 12 Player and launch the ESXi host you installed in Activity 4-7.

2. Start your vSphere Client and sign into your ESXi host using the procedure you learned in Activity 4-8.

3. From the Home screen, click the **Inventory** icon in the upper left of the screen.

4. Click the **Configuration** tab and then click **Security Profile** from the Software pane. The Firewall section displays the Incoming and Outgoing ports that will be allowed on the management network.

5. Click the **Properties** link to the right of the Services heading and document the first of the running services in the space below:

_____

6. Click **OK** to close the Services Properties dialog box and then click the **Properties** link to the right of Firewall heading.

7. Click the **vSphere** Web client and answer the following questions:

Is the Web client available on this version of ESXi hypervisor?

_____

What IP addresses are available: _____

8. Scroll down the list and click to place a check in the **Software iSCSI client** check box. You can later restrict this to use only the iSCSI target you install.

9. Click **OK** to save your settings.

10. This completes the activities for this chapter. You can now close your vSphere Client and shut down the ESXi hypervisor using the procedure you learned in Activity 4-7.

Chapter Summary

- Prior to virtualization, the typical server was using only 15% of its capacity, resulting in a lot of extra facility and equipment costs. Online applications brought a new demand for scalable and reliable services that were difficult and expensive to implement using legacy equipment and infrastructure. Data center virtualization started as a means to more efficiently utilize computer resources.

- As virtualization technology and products have improved, data centers have begun to take advantage of virtualization to abstract other resources including storage and networking. Today the term hyperconvergence applies to the process of using virtualization to consolidate data center resources into pools that can be allocated to services running on virtual machines. The virtual machines rather than the individual resource become the focus of the software-defined data center. Hyperconvergence of a software-defined data center involves virtualizing the processing, storage, and networking components. In this chapter we looked at each of these virtualization areas and how the hyperconvergence of these components is being handled by both VMware in their vSphere products and Microsoft using their Hyper-V solutions.

- In addition to hyperconvergence of resources, data center virtualization offers a number of services that provide load balancing and high availability including virtual switches, storage area networks (SAN), clustering, Distributed Resource Scheduler (DRS), and vMotion services to move virtual machines between hosts.

- While virtualization offers many advantages for the data center, the extra software layers created by the hypervisors also increase the attack surface and therefore administrators need to take extra security precautions.

- Operational security includes monitoring the virtual network as well as separation of job duties to prevent any one administrator from having unnecessary rights that could be misused or accidently fall into the hands of a hacker. Security measures to protect the virtual data center from hacking should include implementing strong passwords that are changed on a regular basis, a change policy that ensures host computers and guest virtual machines are kept current with the latest security patches, firewalls to restrict access to and from virtual networks, monitoring virtual network traffic using intruder detection software installed on the virtual network switches or VMs, regular backups, and encryption of data using features such as Microsoft's Shielded virtual machines or VMware TrustPoint.

■ Malware takes a variety of forms including viruses, worms, Trojans, rootkits, and spyware. Today, viruses are becoming virtualization aware, enabling them to act differently on virtual guest operating systems. VM Escape malware will look for security flaws in the hypervisor or virtual drivers that enable them to gain root level access to the host and other guest VMs.

■ Scanning needs to be carefully planned and implemented to ensure host performance is not adversely affected when several VMs are performing virus scans. To help prevent malware it is important that all updates are applied to the host and guest machines as well as following safe computing habits, and operational security measures.

Key Terms

Address Resolution Protocol (ARP)

broadcast domain

CHAP (Challenge-Handshake Authentication Protocol)

data deduplication

data store

directory traversal attacks

Distributed Resource Scheduler (DRS)

distributed switch

Enlightened I/O

exploitation phase

Extensible switch

external virtual switch

fabric

Fibre Channel

Fibre Channel over Ethernet (FCoE)

high availability

host bus adapter

hyperconvergence

internal virtual switch

Intruder Detection System (IDS)

loopback address

Media Access Control (MAC)

memory compression

network functions virtualization (NFV)

Non-Uniform Memory Access (NUMA)

Offloaded Data Transfer (ODX)

OpenFlow

private IP addresses

pivoting

Private virtual switch

reconnaissance phase

scanning phase

software-defined data center (SDDC)

software-defined network (SDN)

standard switch

storage tiering

subnet mask

teaming

Transparent Page Sharing (TPS)

trunk

virtual network adapter

virtual switches

VLAN

VMFS

vMotion

VMware FT

Review Questions

1. The process of using hypervisors to create pools of resources containing processors, storage, and networking that can be assigned to virtual machines is called what?

   a. Software-defined networking

   b. Virtualization

   c. Hyperconvergence

   d. Cloud computing

2. Which of the following is an example of a tier-1 application?

   a. Word processing

   b. Payroll system

   c. A large online database ordering system

   d. Web site

3. Which of the following features allows a virtual machine to communicate directly with the hypervisor, providing enhanced features?

   a. NUMA

   b. Enlightened I/O

   c. Data deduplication

   d. Distributed Resource Scheduler (DRS)

4. Which of the following is a memory management technique used in multiprocessing to allow a CPU faster access to local memory?

   a. Memory compression

   b. NUMA

   c. SLAT

   d. Transparent Page Sharing (TPS)

5. Which of the following will reduce the amount of paging needed when hosting the same guest OS on multiple VMs?

   a. Memory compression

   b. NUMA

   c. SLAT

   d. Transparent Page Sharing (TPS)

6. _____ is a generic term often used for a container or storage volume that holds virtual machine files.

   a. Tier

   b. Data store

   c. SAN

   d. LUN

7. _____ is the process of storing just one copy of a data sector and then using pointers to access the data from other locations.

   a. Memory compression

   b. Data deduplication

   c. Tiering

   d. Clustering

8. Which of the following increases performance by dividing storage into separate sections based on access speed?

   a. Memory compression

   b. Data deduplication

   c. Storage tiering

   d. Clustering

9. Which of the following are advantages of using shared SAN storage? (Choose all that apply.)

   a. Clustering

   b. Higher speed

   c. Less expense

   d. Load balancing

10. Which of the following are characteristics of a NAS device? (Choose all that apply.)

    a. They often use NFS protocol to communicate with the host.

    b. They use the host's disk format to format the NAS hard disks.

    c. They use their own format (independent of the host hypervisor) to format their disks.

    d. They use the iSCSI protocol on the network.

11. SAN systems are based on which of the following protocols? (Choose all that apply.)

    a. iSCSI

    b. NFS

    c. Fibre Channel

    d. FCoE

12. A host bus adapter or HBA is often used with _____.

    a. an iSCSI target

    b. an iSCSI client as a hardware-based initiator

    c. a multi-port network adapter

    d. a SCSI hard disk controller

13. Which of the following are the most common benefits of clustering? (Choose all that apply.)

    a. High availability

    b. Access speed

    c. Load balancing

    d. Storage capacity

14. Which of the following file systems does VMware ESXi Hypervisor use to format a data store on a SAN hard drive?

    a. VMFS

    b. NFS

    c. VMDK

    d. VHD

15. Which of the following VMware services uses vLockstep technology to keep two virtual machines synchronized in order to provide high availability for mission-critical applications?

    a. VMware FT

    b. Distributed Resource Scheduler (DRS)

    c. vMotion

    d. sVMotion

16. Which of the following vSphere services monitors host and virtual machine performance in order to recommend when and where to move a virtual machine for load balancing?

    a. VMware FT

    b. Distributed Resource Scheduler (DRS)

    c. vMotion

    d. sVMotion

17. Which of the following is the phase in which a hacker establishes a beachhead on the target system in order to launch additional attacks on the host?

    a. Reconnaissance phase

    b. Scanning phase

    c. Pivoting phase

    d. Exploitation phase

18. Which of the following switch types allows connection of virtual machines across different hosts?

    a. Standard switch

    b. External switch

    c. Distributed switch

    d. Extensible switch

19. Which of the following switch types allows third-party plug-ins?

    a. Standard switch

    b. External switch

    c. Distributed switch

    d. Extensible switch

20. Which of the following is the first network type you need to configure when setting up an ESXi host?

    a. VM network

    b. Storage network

    c. Management network

    d. Kernel network

21. Which of the following Microsoft Hyper-V switch types does not allow virtual machines to communicate with the host OS?

    a. Private switch

    b. External switch

    c. Internal switch

    d. Extensible switch

22. What Microsoft Windows Server 2016 Hyper-V feature will help protect VMs from data thefts?

    a. Extensible switch

    b. TrustPoint

    c. Shielded virtual machines

    d. Virtual machine lock

23. Which type of malware can gain access to data on other virtual machines?

    a. Storm worm

    b. Super bot

    c. VM escape

    d. Blue Pill rootkit

24. Which of the following are operational security measures that help virtualization security? (Choose all that apply.)

    a. Separation of duties

    b. Change policy

    c. Network monitoring policy

    d. Risk management policy

25. Which of the following security policies would best protect the virtual network from hacker attacks? (Choose all that apply.)

    a. Separation of duties

    b. Firewall policy for the virtual network switch

    c. Virtual network monitoring

    d. Anti-malware scanning policy

Case Projects

CASE PROJECTS

Case Project 4-1: Setting up a VSAN Cluster in vSphere 6.0

Assume you are a technician for Computer Technology Services and your manager, Lucas Mikkelson, has asked you to give a report at the upcoming IT conference on VMware's new VSAN product. In this project you are to view the VMware online video (see link give below) to prepare a 10-minute PowerPoint presentation on this new vSphere feature.

https://www.youtube.com/watch?v=1EDWKE93ivw&list=PLjwkgfjHppDv RITFUQNQNrKOREXbj-lbN&index=48

Case Project 4-2: VMware Virtual SAN Online Lab

Time Required: 60 minutes

As an alternative to creating an expensive iSCSI RAID server, your boss would like you to explore the possibility of using vSphere's VSAN feature to set up a cluster of vSphere hosts that share their SSD and hard drives. In this activity you will use the My VMware account you created in Chapter 1 to perform the following VMware's VSAN online lab.

1. Log on to your Windows computer, open a Web browser, and go to VMware.com.

2. Point to Login, click MyVMware and log on using the name and password you created in Chapter 1.

3. Scroll down and click the **VMware Hands-on Labs** link. If necessary, click the **Labs** icon from the left-hand pane and then click the **SDDC** link located under the All Labs heading.

4. Scroll down and click the **Enroll** button located in the Virtual SAN 6.x from A to Z lab box. If necessary, register for the lab by entering your MyVMware username and password.

5. Click the **Start This Lab** button and read the Lab Overview information.

6. When you see the Module 1 screen, perform each of the lessons shown.

7. Write a brief report describing the benefits of a VSAN along with the basic steps needed to setup a simple VSAN environment.

Case Project 4-3: Comparing vSphere and Microsoft Hyper-V

Assume that a local school district is looking at virtualizing their data center. Currently they have three Windows Server 2016 servers set up in a domain structure for administrative use. In addition, they have two Linux-based Web servers that run Web services including a Web proxy used to filter Internet access. They have asked your firm, Computer Technology Services, to compare the features of vSphere and Hyper-V to see which hypervisor solution will work best for them. In this project you should use the Internet to find some comparisons between Hyper-V and vSphere v6.0. While you should try to find the most current information, some possible links for information are given below:

- https://redmondmag.com/articles/2015/05/01/vsphere-vs-hyperv.aspx
- Use Google to search for:
  windows_server_2012_r2_server_virtualization_white_paper.pdf

Your report should compare Hyper-V and vSphere in the following categories:

Scalability

Security

Virtual machine support

Virtual networking

Storage capability (support for NAS, iSCSI, Fibre Channel, and scalability of storage capacity)

High Availability features (clustering, migration, high availability, load balancing)

Case Project 4-4: Documenting Latest Security Threats

Management at Superior Technical College would like you to report on one or more of the latest virtualization malware or security threats. In this project you are to use the links below to prepare a report that describes how the Storm worm and how other malware may use virtualization. In addition to these sites, use Google or some other research tool to gather more information regarding techniques to secure the software-defined data center.

http://isc.sans.org/diary.html?storyid=3190

http://www.symantec.com/connect/blogs/does-malware-still-detect-virtual-machines

Case Project 4-5: Documenting Features of VMware TrustPoint

Management at Rocky Ridge Forest Products are considering purchasing VMware TrustPoint and would like you to report on the security features this product would provide along with its cost. In this project you are to write a brief report that outlines the security benefits of TrustPoint along with any costs.

1. Open VMware.com, point to Products, and then click **Products**.

2. Click **TrustPoint**.

3. Create a report that summarizes the security benefits of TrustPoint.

4. What is the cost of a TrustPoint license?

5. Is there a trial version available?

chapter 5

Working with Microsoft Hyper-V

After reading this chapter and completing the exercises, you will be able to:

- Install the Hyper-V role on a Windows Server 2016 host computer
- Work with settings in Hyper-V Manager
- Work with virtual machines in Hyper-V

Hyper-V, Microsoft's latest virtualization product, is built into Windows Server 2016. Microsoft has focused on performance by requiring 64-bit processors with hardware virtualization support. Depending on the server edition you choose, you're given a number of licenses to run virtual Windows servers at no additional cost. It can also be installed on a Windows 8 or Windows 10 Professional or Enterprise edition desktop. In this chapter, you learn how to add the Hyper-V server role to your server and use Hyper-V Manager to create and use virtual machines.

Installing Hyper-V

In this section, you learn how to install and configure the Hyper-V server role on a Windows Server 2016 host computer and use it to create virtual machines. Before getting started, make sure your host computer meets or exceeds the recommended hardware and software requirements for Hyper-V described in Chapter 1. If you haven't yet installed Windows on your host computer, review the following section to select the edition of Windows Server that best supports the features and licensing you need for virtual servers.

Choosing a Windows Server 2016 Edition

Several editions of Windows Server are available. The operating system can be installed without out a user interface, similar to earlier Server Core installations. A command-line interface is used and the server must be managed from another machine. You can also choose a version with the Desktop Experience which provides the typical Windows graphical user interface.

Almost all editions include Hyper-V with the exception of Essentials. Choosing the correct edition is important to ensure that it supports your licensing needs. Here are some of the most common editions of Windows Server 2016:

- *Standard and Datacenter Editions*—Standard provides two licenses for virtual servers where Datacenter allows installing an unlimited number of virtual servers. Datacenter editions also support Storage Spaces Direct, a high availability directly attached storage system as well as Storage Replica, a disaster recovery feature.

- *Hyper-V Server*—This special edition of Windows Server, available free from Microsoft, runs only Hyper-V; it doesn't run additional services, such as DHCP. It can only use a command-line interface and must be managed from another machine. It does not include any licenses.

Server software tends to be expensive, but some businesses and schools can get unlimited free licenses for Windows Server through a paid subscription to Microsoft's MSDN program. If you're a student with a valid school email address, you can get a free license for Windows Server 2016 Standard edition through the Microsoft DreamSpark program at *https://www .dreamspark.com*, which is enough for the activities in this book. Keep in mind that this version is limited to only a single license for installing a virtual machine.

There are other legitimate ways to acquire a copy of Windows Server 2016 at no cost. You can download a free trial version of Windows Server 2016 from the Microsoft Web site that runs for 180 days before requiring activation. With this download, you can install the

Standard or Datacenter edition. Microsoft also documents a method for pushing the activation time beyond 180 days using the *slmgr.vbs –rearm* command.

Installing the Hyper-V Server Role

To install Hyper-V, you need a 64-bit version of Windows Server 2016 and a processor that supports Second Level Address Translation (SLAT) and hardware virtualization. In AMD processors, this hardware virtualization feature is called AMD-V; Intel processors refer to this feature as VT. You can verify that your processor supports one of these extension sets by using CoreInfo, as described in Chapter 1. Hyper-V also requires NX bit (No eXecute) or Enhanced Virus Protection support, a security feature that prevents malicious software from inserting executable code into sections of memory intended for data storage. This feature is called **Data Execution Prevention (DEP)** in Windows.

5

Even if your CPU supports hardware virtualization, this feature may be disabled in the motherboard's BIOS. DEP/NX bit support might be disabled, too. You can usually enter the system's BIOS at startup by pressing F2 or Delete, and you must do a cold boot for these settings to be applied. If you can't find these options and you know your processor supports them, you might need to do a BIOS update. Refer to your computer manual or the motherboard manufacturer's Web site for more details.

Activity 5-1: Installing the Hyper-V Server Role

Time Required: 10 minutes

Objective: Install the Hyper-V server role.

Requirements: A PC running Windows Server 2016

Description: In this activity, you use Server Manager to add the Hyper-V server role to your Windows Server 2016 host computer.

1. If necessary, log on to the host computer with your assigned administrative username and password.

2. If Server Manager is not running, click **Start** and then click **Server Manager**.

3. In the Server Manager window, click **Manage** in the upper right corner, then click **Add Roles and Features**.

4. In the Before you begin window, click **Next**.

5. In the Select installation type window, make sure the Role-based or feature-based installation option button is selected, then click **Next**.

6. In the Select destination server window, click **Next**.

7. In the Select server roles window, click to check **Hyper-V**, and then click **Add Features** in the confirmation dialog box. Click **Next**.

8. In the Select features window, click **Next**.

9. The Hyper-V welcome window contains a description of Hyper-V and some notes. Click **Next**.

10. In the Create Virtual Switches window, you can choose the physical network adapters that virtual servers have access to. This will be configured later in "Configuring Networks with Virtual Switches," click **Next**.

11. In the Virtual Machine Migration window, you choose if Hyper-V can transfer running virtual machines between physical servers. Leave the option unchecked and click **Next**.

12. In the Default Stores window, you choose the paths for the virtual machine configuration and hard disk files. Click **Next**.

13. On the Confirm installation selections window, click **Install**.

14. Wait for the installation to finish, then click **Close**.

15. To restart the server click **Start**, followed by **Power, Restart**. Choose **Other (Planned)** in the dropdown list and click **Continue**.

16. After your computer restarts, log on with your Administrator account. Stay logged on for the next activity.

Creating a Virtual Machine

Although you can attempt to install almost any guest OS in Hyper-V with various degrees of success, Microsoft officially supports and certifies only the following guest Windows OSs in 32-bit or 64-bit forms:

- Windows Server 2016
- Windows Server 2012/R2
- Windows Server 2008 SP2/R2 SP1
- Windows Home Server/Small Business Server 2011
- Windows 10
- Windows 8/8.1
- Windows 7 (except Home edition)
- Windows Vista SP2 (except Home edition)

 Some OSs, such as Windows 7 and Server 2008, have kernels designed to work with virtualization software, a feature known as **Enlightened I/O**. With this feature, the guest OS can communicate more directly with Hyper-V for improved performance.

After installing Hyper-V, one of the first tasks is creating a virtual machine. To open Hyper-V Manager, first open Server Manager. Click Start, Server Manager. Click Tools in the upper right corner, then click Hyper-V Manager. Then select the host computer in the left pane under Hyper-V Manager to specify which virtual machines you're managing.

To create a virtual machine, click the New link in the Actions pane, and then click Virtual Machine to start the New Virtual Machine wizard. In the Specify Name and Location window, enter the virtual machine's name. It should be descriptive, such as "Windows Server 2016—Domain Controller," to differentiate from other virtual machines and show its purpose. Accept the default location or specify a new location (see Figure 5-1). Checkpoints are also saved in this location.

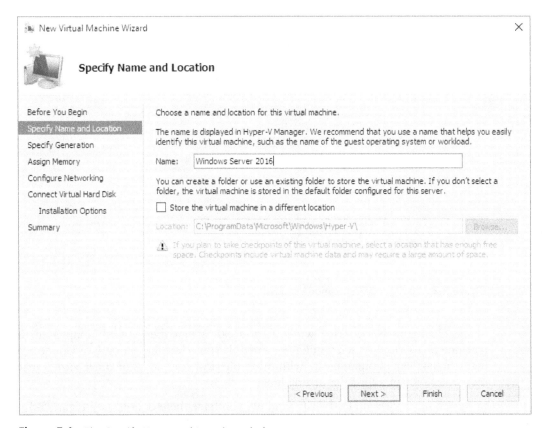

Figure 5-1   The Specify Name and Location window

In the Specify Generation window, you choose between a first- or second-generation virtual machine (see Figure 5-2). First available in Server 2012 R2, second-generation virtual machines support UEFI as well as newer virtualization features such as advanced security and more modern virtualized hardware devices. Only 64-bit guest operating systems are supported (generation one supports 32-bit or 64-bit). Once a virtual machine is created you cannot change its generation.

Next, in the Assign Memory window, you specify the amount of memory for the virtual machine. Usually, you should enter more than the recommended minimum for the guest OS you plan to install because there can be performance issues if you don't leave enough memory for the host computer. Dynamic Memory is a more efficient way of allocating memory. Rather than taking all memory specified immediately, when enabled this feature will only use as much memory as is needed, within ranges you specify.

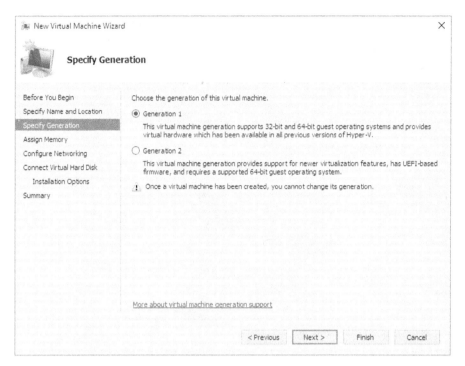

Figure 5-2   The Specify Generation window

In the Configure Networking window, you can assign the network adapter in the virtual machine to a virtual switch you have created. If you select the option Not Connected, the virtual machine can't communicate with other physical computers or other virtual machines on the host. You can adjust this setting later.

In the Connect Virtual Hard Disk window, you have these options (see Figure 5-3):

- *Create a virtual hard disk*—With this option, you enter a name for the hard disk file (with a .vhdx extension, earlier versions used .vhd), specify the file location, and enter the disk size. Microsoft recommends a 127 GB file, and the default disk type is dynamic. As you've learned, a dynamic disk takes up only the physical hard drive space that's required (typically 10 to 12 GB for a Windows Server installation) and can grow as needed up to the maximum size you specify. You can change a dynamic disk's maximum size later, if necessary.

- *Use an existing virtual hard disk*—With this option, you can use a virtual hard disk file that's already been created.

- *Attach a virtual hard disk later*—With this option, a virtual hard disk file isn't associated with the virtual machine. You can't install a guest OS until you attach a virtual hard disk.

In the Installation Options window (see Figure 5-4), you prepare the virtual machine for the guest OS you plan to install. You can choose to handle the installation yourself later, or select an option for installing from a physical DVD drive on the host computer or an ISO

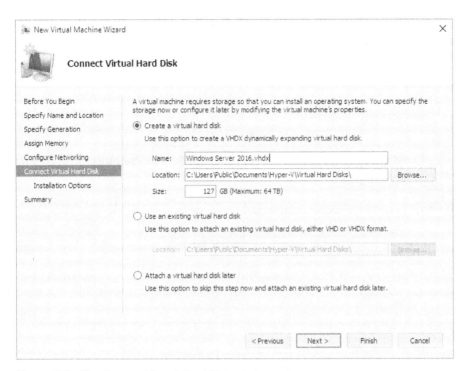

Figure 5-3   The Connect Virtual Hard Disk window

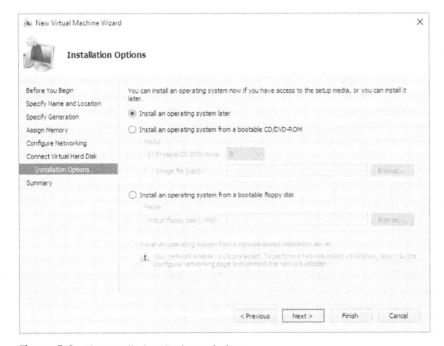

Figure 5-4   The Installation Options window

image file, which contains a complete image of a CD or DVD. You can also install from a virtual floppy disk file (.vfd, generation one virtual machine only) or a network server, if you're using a remote installation service.

Finally, review your installation options in the Completing the New Virtual Machine Wizard window. After clicking Finish, the new virtual machine is then listed in the Virtual Machines pane of Hyper-V Manager.

Activity 5-2: Creating a Windows Server 2016 Virtual Machine

Time Required: 15 minutes

Objective: Create a virtual machine.

Requirements: Completion of Activity 5-1

Description: Now that you have installed the Hyper-V server role, the next step is to create a virtual machine. In this activity, you create one for a later installation of Windows Server 2016.

1. If necessary, log on to the host computer with your administrative username and password.

2. If Server Manager is not running, click **Start** and then click **Server Manager**.

3. Click **Tools** in the upper right corner, then click **Hyper-V Manager**.

4. In the Actions pane on the right, click the **New** link and then click **Virtual Machine** to start the New Virtual Machine wizard.

5. In the Before You Begin window, click **Next**.

6. In the Specify Name and Location window, type **Windows Server 2016** in the Name text box. Verify that the default location is C:\ProgramData\Microsoft\Windows\ Hyper-V. (If you want a different location, you can click the "Store the virtual machine in a different location" check box and browse to another folder, but leave the default location for this activity.) Click **Next**.

7. In the Specify Generation window, click the **Generation 2** option button, then click **Next**.

8. In the Assign Memory window, accept the default 1024 MB for the Startup memory setting. Click to check the **Use Dynamic Memory for this virtual machine** box, and then click **Next**.

9. In the Configure Networking window, click the **Connection** list arrow, click **Not Connected**, and then click **Next**.

10. In the Connect Virtual Hard Disk window, click the **Create a virtual hard disk** option button. Accept the default name, which is based on the virtual machine name, and the default location, C:\Users\Public\Documents\Hyper-V\Virtual Hard Disks. Accept the default disk space, 127 GB, and then click **Next**.

11. In the Installation Options window, verify that the Install an operating system later option button is selected, and then click **Next**.

12. In the Completing the New Virtual Machine Wizard window, review the summary of your selected installation options, and click **Finish**. Your virtual machine is then listed in the Virtual Machines pane of Hyper-V Manager. Leave Hyper-V Manager open for the next activity.

Working with Hyper-V Manager

Hyper-V Manager has the standard Microsoft Management Console (MMC) interface used in many Windows management tools. It's divided into three main sections. In the left pane is the list of physical Hyper-V servers you're managing. Clicking a server displays a window similar to the one in Figure 5-5. In the middle, you see the Virtual Machines pane, listing the virtual machines being managed on that server, as well as the Checkpoints pane and details pane. The details pane contains Summary, Memory, Networking, and Replication tabs with quick information about the virtual machine's settings and current usages. In the Actions pane on the right is a list of links for creating and modifying virtual machines, virtual switches, and virtual disks. Most of the links in this pane are also available on the menu bar.

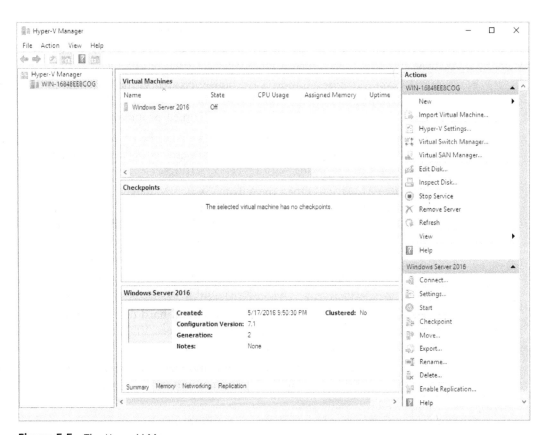

Figure 5-5 The Hyper-V Manager

Working with the Actions Pane

The Actions pane contains links to configure and use Hyper-V and actions to control the currently selected virtual machine. If you don't have a server selected in the left pane, you see the following limited list of actions:

- *Connect to Server*—Use this option to add Hyper-V servers to the console. By default, the local computer is already available, but you can browse to other servers in your workgroup or in Active Directory and manage them remotely. This option is especially useful for managing installations without a GUI.

- *View*—This option opens a menu containing only the Customize option, which displays check boxes for hiding or showing parts of the console, such as the console tree, toolbar, Actions pane, and menus.

- *Help*—Displays the help file for the MMC and Hyper-V. You can browse for articles on topics such as creating virtual machines and troubleshooting, and use the Search tab to find articles containing specific words.

When you select a virtual machine, the top half of the Actions pane refreshes to show new options for configuring Hyper-V, creating virtual machines, and managing virtual disks. The options described in the previous list remain, and the following list explains the new options that are available:

- *New*—Open a menu where you can choose to create a virtual machine with the New Virtual Machine wizard, create a virtual hard disk with more advanced options (such as fixed and differencing disks), and create a virtual floppy disk.

- *Import Virtual Machine*—Import a previously created virtual machine to the current server's inventory, with the option to reuse the original virtual machine's unique ID, depending on whether the virtual machine is copied or moved.

- *Hyper-V Settings*—Open the Hyper-V Settings dialog box where you can set global options, such as file paths and mouse and keyboard settings. You learn more about this dialog box later in "Working with Hyper-V Settings."

- *Virtual Switch Manager*—Open the Virtual Switch Manager dialog box where you can create external, internal, or private networks to control how virtual machines communicate with each other and the physical network. You learn more about this dialog box later in "Configuring Networks with Virtual Switches."

- *Virtual SAN Manager*—Create a direct connection to a Fibre storage area network (SAN). A SAN is a high-speed network of storage devices like disk arrays or tapes that the operating system sees as a local device and is usually better at disaster recovery.

- *Edit Disk*—Start a wizard for compacting a virtual hard disk, converting a dynamic disk to a fixed disk, changing the disk format between VHD and VHDX, or expanding a virtual hard disk to increase its maximum size.

- *Inspect Disk*—Select a virtual hard disk file and view its settings, such as disk type, filename and location, maximum size, and amount of disk space being used on the host.

- *Stop Service*—Stop the Hyper-V service temporarily.

- *Remove Server*—Remove the currently selected server from the manager. You can add it back later with the Connect to Server option, even if you've removed the local computer where you're currently running Hyper-V Manager.

- *Refresh*—Redraw the contents of all windows.

The bottom half of the Actions pane, named for the currently selected virtual machine, contains the following commands:

- *Connect*—Open the Virtual Machine Connection window in which the guest OS runs. This window is described in more detail later in "The Virtual Machine Connection Window."

- *Settings*—Configure virtual hardware, such as memory, firmware, and processors. You can also configure some management options, such as checkpoint locations and automatic start and stop actions. These settings are described more in "Working with Virtual Machine Settings."

- *Start*—Power on the virtual machine; this option doesn't open a Virtual Machine Connection window.

- *Checkpoint*—Take a snapshot of the virtual machine's current state, which appears in the Checkpoints pane.

- *Move*—Move a virtual machine (even while running if live migrations is enabled) or a virtual disk file to a new location on the server or in shared storage.

- *Export*—Export the virtual machine's settings, hard disk files, and checkpoints to the location you specify.

- *Rename*—Change the virtual machine's display name.

- *Delete*—Delete the virtual machine's configuration file from the host computer. The virtual disk file remains intact, however.

- *Enable Replication*—Start the Enable Replication wizard. Replication allows a virtual machine on the host to have an exact replica elsewhere on the local network, or across the Internet, which can be used if the primary virtual machine goes down.

Working with Hyper-V Settings

Options in the Hyper-V Settings dialog box (as shown in Figure 5-6) apply to all virtual machines on the server. The Server section contains the following options:

- *Virtual Hard Disks*—This is the default path where virtual disk files are saved (C:\Users\Public\Documents\Hyper-V\Virtual Hard Disks).

- *Virtual Machines*—This is the default location where virtual machine configuration files are saved (C:\ProgramData\Microsoft\Windows\Hyper-V).

- *Physical GPUs*—The video card's graphical processing unit (GPU) can be used in virtual machines allowing hardware accelerated video and 3D rendering using Microsoft RemoteFX. This requires the Remote Desktop Virtualization role be added to the server.

- *NUMA Spanning*—NUMA (Non-Uniform Memory Architecture) is a hardware architecture where a host PC's memory and processors are split up into nodes. By allowing spanning, a virtual machine can use memory from another node if its own node is full.

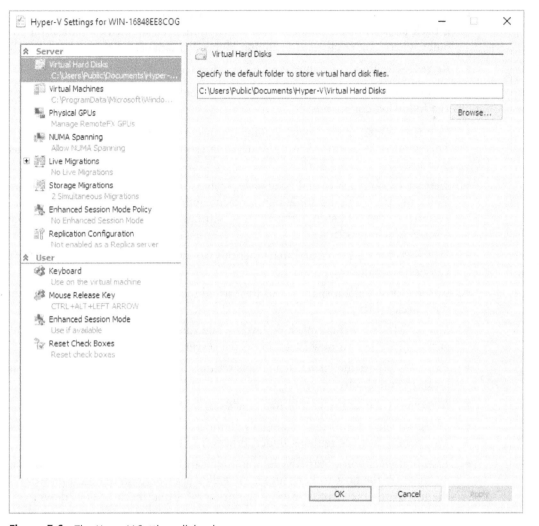

Figure 5-6   The Hyper-V Settings dialog box

- *Live Migrations*—This feature allows a virtual machine to be moved from one host to another while it's still running without interruption. The number of simultaneous migrations allowed can be set, as well as where migrations can come from on the network.

- *Storage Migrations*—Similar to Live Migrations, this moves only the storage of your virtual machine while it's running, not the entire virtual machine. The number of simultaneous storage migrations can also be set.

- *Enhanced Session Mode Policy*—This allows local resources on the host computer, such as audio, printers, and USB devices, to be redirected to and used by the virtual machine.

- *Replication Configuration*—Configure the host as a replica server, choosing if a secure connection is required and which port is used, and also which servers will be allowed to use it.

The User section contains the following options:

- *Keyboard*—Specify how key combinations, such as Alt+Tab to switch tasks, are handled in a Virtual Machine Connection window. You can send keystrokes to the physical computer, to the virtual machine (the default), or to the virtual machine only when it's in full-screen mode.

- *Mouse Release Key*—Assign a key combination that transfers mouse control from the Virtual Machine Connection window to the host OS. This setting is especially important when Integration Services hasn't been installed on the virtual machine. By default, the setting is Ctrl+Alt+left arrow, but you can choose from several other combinations.

- *Enhanced Session Mode*—When enabled, enhanced session mode will automatically be used when it's available in the guest operating system.

- *Reset Check Boxes*—This option clears the "Do not show this again" check boxes in many wizard windows and confirmation messages so that they're displayed again.

Activity 5-3: Setting Global Hyper-V Options

Time Required: 10 minutes

Objective: Practice using global settings in Hyper-V.

Requirements: Completion of Activity 5-2

Description: The instructors at Superior Technical College want you to give a demonstration of using Hyper-V. In this activity, you prepare for the demonstration by investigating the global settings in Hyper-V Manager.

1. If necessary, log on to the host computer, open Hyper-V Manager, and click the host computer in the left pane.

2. Click the **Hyper-V Settings** link in the Actions pane to open the Hyper-V Settings dialog box.

3. In the Server section, click **Virtual Hard Disks** and record the default location for storing virtual hard disk files:

_____

4. Click **Virtual Machines** and record the default location for storing virtual machine configuration files:

_____

5. Click **Live Migrations** and record the default number of simultaneous migrations allowed:

_____

6. In the User section, click **Keyboard**. Review how the key combinations can be handled when a virtual machine is being interacted with.

7. Click **Mouse Release Key**. Record the key combinations that are available:

_____

8. Click **Reset Check Boxes,** and on the right, click the **Reset** button to have "Do not show this page again" check boxes displayed again.

9. Click **OK** to close the Hyper-V Settings dialog box, and leave Hyper-V Manager open for the next activity.

Working with Virtual Machine Settings

Each virtual machine has its own Settings dialog box that can be opened from the Actions pane, where you can configure virtual hardware and some management options, as shown in Figure 5-7.

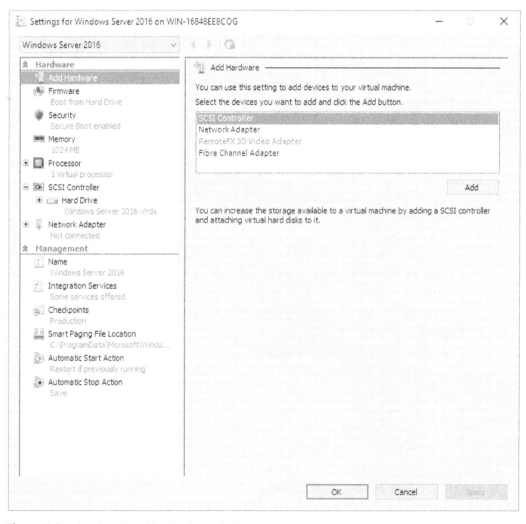

Figure 5-7   The virtual machine Settings window

The Settings dialog box is divided into two sections: Hardware and Management. The Hardware section contains the following options:

- *Add Hardware*—You use this option to add hardware devices to a virtual machine, such as a SCSI controller so that you can add hard drives for more storage. (The boot drive must still be on an IDE controller for a generation one virtual machine.) You can also add a network adapter and 3D video adapter for RemoteFX support. A legacy network adapter can be added to generation one virtual machines.

- *BIOS or Firmware*—Generation one virtual machines simulate an older style BIOS and only allow you to configure the order in which devices are checked to find a boot device. A generation two virtual machine simulates the newer style EFI firmware with additional security features.

- *Security*—Only available on generation two virtual machines, you have the option to enable Secure Boot, which blocks unauthorized software and operating systems from running at boot. You can also enable Trusted Platform Module (TPM) support, special hardware that handles cryptographic keys. Finally, you can enable Shielding, which disables some management features.

- *Memory*—You can choose the amount of memory assigned to the virtual machine. If dynamic memory is being used you can specify the minimum and maximum range, as well as a buffer and the priority the virtual machine is assigned memory over others.

- *Processor*—Specify the number of processors or cores your virtual machine uses. You can also balance performance with other virtual machines by selecting the minimum and maximum amount of the host's CPU that's available.

- *IDE Controller*—Only available to generation one virtual machines, virtual IDE devices are attached to two separate IDE controllers, 0 and 1. Typically, the virtual hard disk is on controller 0, and the virtual DVD drive is on controller 1. You can add new drives by mapping hard drives to virtual hard disk files and the host's physical drive or an ISO image file to the virtual DVD drive.

- *SCSI Controller*—Similar to an IDE controller, a single SCSI controller supports more devices with up to 64 locations, as opposed to only two devices per IDE controller. Only generation two virtual machine SCSI controllers support virtual DVD drives.

- *Network Adapter*—Specify which virtual network or physical NIC the virtual machine uses to communicate. You can also choose a dynamic MAC address or enter a static address, assign the adapter to a VLAN, and limit network bandwidth.

- *COM 1 and COM 2*—Only available on generation one virtual machines, you can use a virtual COM port that communicates with the host computer through a named pipe (a method of accessing physical ports as though they're files) on the local machine or over the network.

- *Diskette Drive*—Only available on generation one virtual machines, this selects a virtual floppy disk (.vfd) file to use in the virtual machine's floppy drive. To create a .vfd file, click New, Floppy Disk in the Actions pane.

You can set the following options in the Management section:

- *Name*—Enter the virtual machine's display name as well as descriptive notes that are displayed in the details pane.

- *Integration Services*—This option contains a list of services Hyper-V can use with the virtual machine. These services must be installed and supported by the guest OS, using Integration Services, and include Operating system shutdown, Time synchronization, Data Exchange, Heartbeat, Backup (volume shadow copy), and Guest services.

- *Checkpoints*—Choose the type of checkpoints to be used, either the standard checkpoint which saves the current memory and disk states, including running applications, or production checkpoint which does not save running application but can be more reliable (see the upcoming section "Using Checkpoints" for more details). You can also specify the folder where checkpoints for this virtual machine are saved, which is based on the setting in the Hyper-V Settings dialog box.

- *Smart Paging File Location*—The default location the smart paging file is saved, normally where virtual machine configuration files are located, and is used to facilitate virtual machine dynamic memory.

- *Automatic Start Action*—Configure what the virtual machine does when the host computer starts. You can have the virtual machine not load automatically, start automatically if it was running when the service stopped (the default), or always start automatically. If it's set to start automatically, you can enter a delay in seconds to make sure servers start in the correct order. Automatic starting is useful to ensure that virtual servers come back online if a physical server has to restart.

- *Automatic Stop Action*—Configure what a virtual machine should do when the host computer shuts down. You can select Save the virtual machine state (similar to hibernation in Windows), Turn off the virtual machine (like turning off a physical power switch, so it could cause data loss), or Shut down the guest operating system. The last option requires installing Integration Services.

Activity 5-4: Working with Virtual Machine Settings

Time Required: 10 minutes

Objective: Configure a virtual machine in the Settings dialog box.

Requirements: Completion of Activity 5-3

Description: In this activity, you continue preparing for the demonstration by working with options in the Settings dialog box.

1. If necessary, log on to the host computer, open Hyper-V Manager, and click the **Windows Server 2016** virtual machine in the Virtual Machines pane in the middle.

2. Click the **Settings** link under Windows Server 2016 in the Actions pane to open the Settings dialog box.

3. In the Hardware section, click **Firmware**. Record the order in which boot devices are tried:

_____

4. Click **Integration Services**. Record which service is not enabled by default:

_____

5. In the Management section, click **Name**. In the Notes text box, type your first and last name.

6. Click **Automatic Start Action**. Record what the virtual machine does by default when the host computer starts:

_____

7. Click **Automatic Stop Action**. Record what the virtual machine does by default when the host computer shuts down:

_____

8. Click **OK** to close the Settings dialog box. In the Windows Server 2016 pane in the middle, confirm that your name appears next to "Notes" in the summary tab in the details pane. Leave Hyper-V Manager open for the next activity.

5

The Virtual Machine Connection Window

The Virtual Machine Connection window is where you interact with a virtual machine and use the guest OS. To open this window, click the Connect link in the Actions pane. As shown in Figure 5-8, the Virtual Machine Connection window includes a menu bar, a toolbar, and a status bar. If you connect to a virtual machine that isn't running, you get a message stating that it's turned off with information on how to start it. The status bar at the bottom shows the virtual machine's current state, such as off or running; the progress of certain commands; and icons to indicate whether the window has mouse and keyboard control and whether it's running on a secure connection.

The File menu contains the Settings command, which opens the same Settings dialog box for a virtual machine you used in Activity 5-4. Some options are disabled if the virtual machine is running. The Exit command closes the Virtual Machine Connection window, but it doesn't power off the virtual machine. If the virtual machine is running when you exit, it continues to run in the background, and its status is shown in the Virtual Machines pane. You can connect to it again later.

All the following Action menu items are also available on the toolbar:

- *Ctrl-Alt-Delete*—Send a virtual Ctrl+Alt+Delete keystroke to the guest OS. In Windows, this keystroke opens Task Manager or a logon window on a Windows Server.

- *Start*—Power on the virtual machine and load the guest OS.

- *Turn Off*—This command, only available on the toolbar, is similar to using the physical power button on a computer, could cause data loss or corrupted files. Unless the guest OS has locked up, avoid using this option.

- *Shut Down*—To shut down a guest OS, you should use the shutdown procedure, such as Start, Power, Shut down in Windows. If you have the Operating System Shutdown

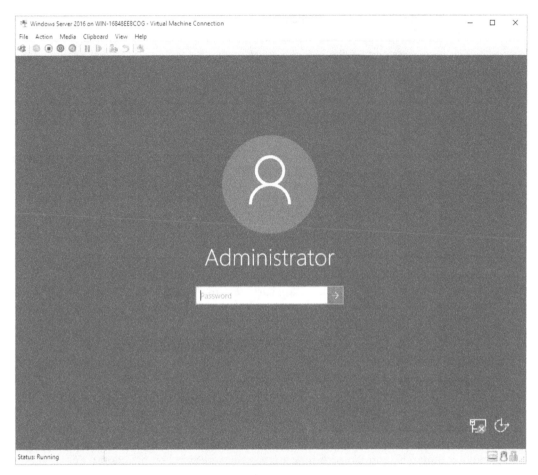

Figure 5-8   The Virtual Machine Connection window

service (an Integration Services feature) enabled on the virtual machine, this command automates a safe shutdown procedure.

- *Save*—Similar to the hibernate feature on physical computers, this command saves the virtual machine's state and memory to a file and then powers off. The next time you start the virtual machine, you can continue from where you left off.

- *Pause*—With this command, the virtual machine isn't powered off and its state isn't saved. This command simply suspends the virtual machine temporarily and is replaced with the Resume command for bringing the virtual machine back to an active state.

- *Reset*—This command, which is similar to using the reset button on a physical computer, can result in data loss or corruption and shouldn't be used on a Windows guest OS unless the virtual machine isn't responding.

- *Checkpoint*—Use this command to take a snapshot of the virtual machine's current state, which is then listed in the Checkpoints pane.

- *Revert*—Return the virtual machine to the state saved in the most recent checkpoint. You're prompted to confirm this command in case it's selected in error.

The Media menu contains the following commands:

- *DVD Drive*—Assign the host's physical DVD drive to the virtual machine with the Capture option (generation one virtual machine only), or use the Insert Disk option to browse to an ISO image file. After a drive or image file is connected, you have options to release a physical drive and eject an ISO image.

- *Diskette Drive*—Only available on generation one virtual machines, this assigns or ejects a virtual floppy disk file. Using a physical floppy drive on your host computer isn't possible in Hyper-V; only image files are supported.

The Clipboard menu (only available when the virtual machine is powered on) contains two commands: Type clipboard text (also available with the Ctrl+V keyboard shortcut), which pastes the host's Clipboard contents to the virtual machine, and Capture screen, which places a screen capture of the virtual machine on the Clipboard. You can paste this screen capture into a graphics editor, such as Microsoft Paint.

The View menu contains the Full Screen Mode command (also available with the Ctrl+Alt+Break keyboard shortcut) to maximize the Virtual Machine Connection window and hide the host OS interface. You can use the keyboard shortcut to exit this mode. This menu also contains an option to toggle the toolbar on or off, and use an enhanced session.

Working with Virtual Machines in Hyper-V

In the following sections, you learn how to perform virtual machine tasks, such as starting and stopping a virtual machine, installing a guest OS, using different virtual disk types, managing virtual machines, making checkpoints, and configuring virtual networks.

Basic Virtual Machine Functions

You can start a virtual machine with one of several methods. Click the Start link in the Actions pane to power on the virtual machine and have it run in the background. To interact with the guest OS, double-click its name under Virtual Machines, or click the Connect link to open a Virtual Machine Connection window. If you connect to a virtual machine that isn't running, click the Start toolbar button in the Virtual Machine Connection window to power it on. When a Windows Server 2016 system starts, you're prompted to press Ctrl+Alt+Delete to display the sign in screen. Because this key combination opens Task Manager in the host OS, use the Ctrl+Alt+End key combination or the Ctrl-Alt-Delete toolbar button.

Before interacting with the guest OS, click inside the Virtual Machine Connection window to activate it. The host computer then passes keyboard and mouse control to the virtual machine. To transfer control back to the host computer, press Ctrl+Alt+left arrow.

Full-screen mode hides the host desktop so that the guest OS fills the entire screen. To enable this view, click View, Full Screen Mode from the menu in the Virtual Machine Connection window. To view the host desktop again, press Ctrl+Alt+Break.

To suspend a virtual machine temporarily, click Action, Pause from the Virtual Machine Connection menu or click the Pause toolbar button. No settings are saved, and the virtual machine isn't powered off. To suspend a virtual machine long term, click Action, Save from the Virtual Machine Connection menu or click the Save toolbar button. The virtual machine's memory and state are written to a file on the host computer, and the virtual machine is powered off. The Action, Start menu command (or the Start toolbar button) resumes the virtual machine where it left off. You can use the Action, Reset menu command (or the Reset toolbar button) to force a virtual machine to restart, but as mentioned previously, you should use this option only as a last resort.

When you have finished using a virtual machine, you have several options. If you simply close the Virtual Machine Connection window, the virtual machine continues to run in the background, and you can connect to it later. If you use the Turn Off toolbar button, the virtual machine is powered off immediately as if the power plug was pulled, which might cause data loss or file corruption. You should try the guest OS shutdown procedure first, such as Start, Power, Shut down for Windows; the virtual machine powers off automatically when the shutdown procedure is finished. Finally, if you have Integration Services installed and the Operating System Shutdown service enabled, clicking the Shut Down toolbar button issues a shutdown signal to the virtual machine, and it automatically logs off and powers off safely.

Using ISO Image Files and Physical Media

ISO image files can be accessed from the host computer's hard drive or a shared network drive, so they're convenient in computer lab environments. There are several differences between generation one and generation two virtual DVD drives. A new generation one virtual machine will always include a DVD drive on the IDE controller, and that drive can be attached to a DVD drive on the host so physical media can be used. A new generation two virtual machine will not have a virtual DVD drive if you choose the "Install an operating system later" option in the final step of the New Virtual Machine wizard, but one can be added in the virtual machine settings. A generation two virtual machine uses the SCSI controller for virtual DVD drives, and cannot be attached to a physical drive on the host.

To add a missing DVD drive to a generation two virtual machine, follow these steps:

1. In the bottom half of the Actions pane, under the virtual machine name, click Settings. In the Hardware section of the Settings dialog box, click SCSI Controller.

2. Click DVD Drive from the list, then click Add. Click Apply.

3. Click Firmware in the Hardware section, under Boot order click the DVD Drive, and click Move Up so it appears before the Hard Drive in the list. Click OK.

Follow these steps to configure your virtual machine to use an ISO image file:

1. In the bottom half of the Actions pane, under the virtual machine name, click Settings. In the Hardware section of the Settings dialog box, click DVD Drive.

2. If you're using an ISO image file, click the Image file option button, and then browse to select the file. If necessary, first copy the ISO image file to a folder on the host computer or map a drive to the shared folder containing the ISO image file.

3. If you're using a DVD in the host computer's drive on a generation one virtual machine, click the Physical CD/DVD drive option button, and then select the correct drive letter in the dropdown box.

Installing a Guest OS

Now that you're familiar with Hyper-V Manager's menus and settings, the next step is installing a guest OS. In the next activity, you install Windows Server 2016 on the virtual machine you created earlier.

Activity 5-5: Installing Windows Server 2016 as a Guest OS

Time Required: 30 minutes

Objective: Install Windows Server 2016 on a virtual machine.

Requirements: Completion of Activity 5-2, Windows Server 2016 Installation Media

Description: You need to give a demonstration of using Hyper-V to run Windows Server 2016 on a virtual machine. In this activity, you prepare for the demonstration by installing Windows Server 2016 on the virtual machine you created in Activity 5-2.

1. If necessary, log on to the host computer and open Hyper-V Manager.

2. Click the host computer in the left pane, and click the **Windows Server 2016** virtual machine in the Virtual Machines pane.

3. In the Actions pane under Windows Server 2016, click the **Settings** link.

4. In the Settings dialog box, click **DVD Drive**. If you don't see a DVD Drive, follow the steps in the previous section to add one. Click the **Image file** option button. Click the **Browse** button, navigate to the folder containing the ISO image file, click the file, and then click **Open**. Click **OK** to close the Settings dialog box.

5. In the Actions pane under Windows Server 2016, click the **Connect** link to open the Virtual Machine Connection window.

6. In the Virtual Machine Connection window, click the **Start** toolbar button. The virtual machine powers on. Press a key within a few seconds when the "Press any key to boot from CD or DVD" message appears. If you see the Virtual Machine Boot Summary, press a key to reboot and try again.

If you get an error message when you start the virtual machine, make sure you have DEP and hardware virtualization enabled. Refer to "Installing the Hyper-V Server Role" earlier in this chapter for more details.

7. Select settings for language, time and currency format, and keyboard or input method, and then click **Next**.

8. Click **Install now** in the next window.

9. In the Activate Windows window, enter your product key and click **Next**. If you currently don't have a product key, click the **I don't have a product key** link to continue the installation without one. You will be able to enter a product key at a later date.

10. In the Select the operating system you want to install window, you're prompted to choose the Windows Server 2016 edition. If you didn't enter a product key in the previous step, you will be shown both Standard and Datacenter editions, choose Standard. Click **Windows Server 2016 Standard (Desktop Experience)**, and then click **Next**.

11. In the License terms window, click the **I accept the license terms** check box, and then click **Next**.

12. In the Which type of installation do you want? window, click **Custom: Install Windows only (advanced)**.

13. In the Where do you want to install Windows? window, verify that Drive 0 Unallocated Space is selected, then click **Next** to continue.

14. The Windows installation begins. Typically, the process takes around 15 minutes, and your virtual machine restarts at least once. When the installation is finished, you're prompted to create a password for the administrator account. (Make sure it's at least six characters, contains uppercase and lowercase letters, and includes a number or nonalphanumeric character.) Reenter it into the second password box, and then click **Finish**. Record your password below:

_____

15. Your Windows Server 2016 installation is finished. Log on to the server by using **Ctrl+Alt+End** or clicking the **Ctrl-Alt-Delete** toolbar button and entering the password you created in the previous step. Power off the virtual machine by clicking **Start**, followed by **Power, Shut down**. Choose Other (Planned) in the dropdown list and click **Continue**.

16. Your Windows Server 2016 installation is finished. To eject the ISO image from the virtual DVD drive, click the **Media** menu, then **DVD Drive** and click **Eject**.

17. Leave the Hyper-V Manager open for the next activity.

Using Integration Services

Integration Services consists of a set of drivers optimized for the guest OSs that Hyper-V supports. These drivers have been designed to work in a virtual environment, replacing the generic mouse, keyboard, video, network, and SCSI controller drivers provided by the guest OS. A virtual machine can function without them, but performance suffers.

As mentioned, one useful feature is enhanced mouse support, which enables you to move between the virtual machine and host without using a key combination. With Operating System Shutdown, you can use the Shut Down toolbar button to power off a virtual machine safely, similar to using the guest OS shutdown procedure. The Time Synchronization feature synchronizes the virtual machine and host system clocks automatically. The Data Exchange feature enables the virtual machine and host computer to read a specific region of each other's Registries (HKEY_LOCAL_MACHINE\SOFTWARE\Microsoft\Virtual Machine \Guest\Parameters) to pass information back and forth. With the Heartbeat feature, Hyper-V can ping a virtual machine periodically to make sure it's still functioning correctly. The backup (volume shadow copy) feature allows backup agents using the Volume Shadow Copy Service (VSS) to back up a running virtual machine as well as applications running on the virtual machine that support VSS. Finally, Guest Services allows files to be copied into running virtual machines across the Hyper-V Virtual Machine Bus (VMBus) regardless of its virtual network configuration. You can selectively choose which services can be used by a virtual machine under its settings in the Hyper-V Manager.

In previous versions of Hyper-V the Integration Services installer was included as an ISO image that was installed manually from the Actions menu. Starting with Windows Server 2016, the latest Integration Services drivers are installed automatically through Windows Update, ensuring the guest and host will always have the same version and not be mismatched.

Adding and Removing Virtual Machines

With virtualization software, you can move a virtual machine between several host computers, even if they have different hardware. You can move a virtual machine in several ways. You can copy the virtual hard disk file from one host to another; the default location is C:\Users\Public\Documents\Hyper-V\Virtual Hard Disks. Using the New Virtual Machine wizard, when prompted to connect to a virtual hard disk, select the "Use an existing virtual hard disk" option button, and browse to the file you copied. A new virtual machine is created with the existing virtual hard disk file.

Another method is clicking the Export link in the Actions pane. You must enter a path to export the virtual machine to. The export progress in displayed in the Status column of the Virtual Machines pane, and you can cancel the export while it's in progress.

After the export is finished, you can move the folder containing the virtual hard disk file, configuration file, and checkpoints to a new host computer. Click the Import Virtual Machine link in the Actions pane and browse to the folder with the exported virtual machine. There are three import types:

- *Register the virtual machine in-place*—This assumes the virtual machine files are already in their correct destination and will not copy them. It will re-use the unique ID of the exported virtual machine.

- *Restore the virtual machine*—This will copy the virtual machines into your default configuration and hard disk folders, which is useful if your virtual machine is being imported over the network or from removable storage. It will re-use the unique ID of the exported virtual machine.

- *Copy the virtual machine*—This will copy the virtual machine similar to the Restore option above, but will create a new unique ID. This is useful when using a base virtual machine as a template.

If you no longer want to use a virtual machine, you can remove it from Hyper-V Manager with the Delete link in the Actions pane. This command deletes the virtual configuration file but retains the virtual hard disk file. If you're sure you won't use the virtual hard disk file again, you can delete it manually. In the following activity, you practice removing and adding virtual machines.

Activity 5-6: Adding and Removing Virtual Machines

Time Required: 10 minutes

Objective: Export, remove, and then add a virtual machine to Hyper-V Manager.

Requirements: Completion of Activity 5-5

Description: Being able to add and remove virtual machines is an important part of keeping Hyper-V Manager organized and balancing the load among virtual machines. In this activity, you practice exporting, removing, and then adding a virtual machine.

1. If necessary, log on to the host computer and open Hyper-V Manager.

2. In the Virtual Machines pane, click **Windows Server 2016**. Make sure this virtual machine is powered off.

3. In the Actions pane, under Windows Server 2016, click the **Export** link to open the Export Virtual Machine dialog box.

4. Click the **Browse** button. Click **Documents** on the left, and then click the **Select Folder** button.

5. Click the **Export** button in the Export Virtual Machine dialog box. This process takes several minutes; the progress is shown in the Status column of the Virtual Machines pane.

6. On the host computer, click **Start, File Explorer** and then click **Documents**. Navigate to the **Windows Server 2016** folder, and verify that the export was successful. This folder should contain a Virtual Machines folder, a Virtual Hard Disks folder, and a Snapshots (previous name for checkpoints) folder. Leave the window open.

7. In Hyper-V Manager, click the **Delete** link under Windows Server 2016 in the Actions pane. In the Delete Selected Virtual Machines confirmation dialog box, click **Delete**. Verify that Windows Server 2016 is no longer listed in the Virtual Machines pane.

8. In the Computer window, navigate to the **C:\Users\Public\Public Documents\Hyper-V \Virtual hard disks** folder. Click the **Windows Server 2016.vhdx** file and press **Delete**. When prompted to confirm the deletion, click **Yes**. The virtual machine has now been removed from the host's hard drive as well as Hyper-V Manager.

9. In Hyper-V Manager, click the **Import Virtual Machine** link in the Actions pane to start the Import Virtual Machine wizard.

10. In the Before You Begin window, click **Next**.

11. In the Locate Folder window, click **Browse** and then click **Documents**. Select the **Windows Server 2016** folder and click the **Select Folder** button. Click **Next**.

12. In the Select Virtual Machine window, click **Next**.

13. In the Choose Import Type window, choose the **Restore the virtual machine (use the existing unique ID)** option button, and then click **Next**.

14. In the Choose Folders for Virtual Machine Files window, click **Next**.

15. In the Choose Folders to Store Virtual Hard Disks window, click **Next**.

16. In the Completing Import Wizard window, review the summary of your selected import options, and click **Finish**.

17. The import may take several minutes. Verify that Windows Server 2016 is listed in the Virtual Machines pane. Power on and connect to the virtual machine to confirm that it's functioning correctly.

18. Power off the virtual machine by clicking the **Shut Down** toolbar button, and then close the Virtual Machine Connection window. Leave Hyper-V Manager open for the next activity.

Using Checkpoints

As you've learned in previous chapters, checkpoints are a powerful feature of virtualization software that enable you to save a virtual machine's current state so that you can revert to it later. Checkpoints are especially useful when you're installing new applications, updates, or making configuration changes on a virtual machine; if there are any problems, you can undo the changes quickly. There are two types of checkpoints:

- *Standard*—This saves the memory and disk state of the virtual machine, allowing the virtual machine to resume exactly where it was created with no unsaved work lost.

- *Production*—This saves the virtual machine state, but ignores any open applications. If you have a document open, any changes since the last save will be lost. This uses the Volume Shadow Copy Service (VSS) in the guest OS. Windows will cold boot when a production checkpoint is applied. This can be more reliable because a standard checkpoint has the effect of moving back in time which can disrupt important services on a server. This is the default checkpoint type, but it can changed in the virtual machine's settings.

To create a checkpoint, simply click the Checkpoint toolbar button in the Virtual Machine Connection window, or click the Checkpoint link in the Actions pane in Hyper-V Manager. The checkpoint is then listed in Hyper-V Manager's Checkpoints pane. You can create checkpoints of virtual machines that are running or powered off. Each subsequent checkpoint you create saves only the changes made since the previous checkpoint, and you can revert to any earlier stage by selecting that checkpoint. Any unsaved changes are lost when the earlier checkpoint is restored.

Activity 5-7: Creating and Restoring Checkpoints

Time Required: 15 minutes

Objective: Create a checkpoint, and use it to restore a virtual machine to a previous state.

Requirements: Completion of Activity 5-5

Description: Using checkpoints before performing a potentially dangerous task is a good way to make sure you can undo changes quickly if problems occur. In this activity, you create a base checkpoint, make a change to the server configuration, restore the base checkpoint, and then revert to the checkpoint with the configuration change.

1. If necessary, log on to the host computer and open Hyper-V Manager.

2. In the Virtual Machines pane, click **Windows Server 2016**. Make sure this virtual machine is powered off.

3. In the Actions pane, under Windows Server 2016, click the **Checkpoint** link.

4. Click the new **Windows Server 2016** checkpoint listed in the Checkpoints pane. The Actions pane now shows options to manage checkpoints. Click the **Rename** link, and change it to **Windows Server 2016–Base Installation**.

5. In the Virtual Machines pane, click the **Windows Server 2016** virtual machine. Power on and connect to the virtual machine, and log on to the guest OS with your Administrator account.

6. In Server Manager, click **Local Server.** Click **Enabled** next to Remote management. In the Configure Remote Management dialog box, click to uncheck **Enable remote management of this server from other computers**, then click **OK**. Notice Remote management is now disabled in Server Manager.

7. In the Virtual Machine Connection window, click the **Checkpoint** toolbar button. When prompted for a checkpoint name, type **Windows Server 2016–Updated Configuration**, and then click **Yes**. In the Virtual Machine Checkpoint dialog box, click **OK**.

8. Leave the virtual machine running. In Hyper-V Manager, review the Checkpoints pane. It should be similar to Figure 5-9.

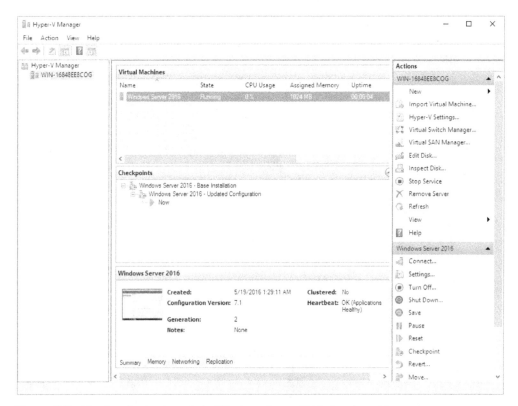

Figure 5-9   Viewing checkpoints of the Windows Server 2016 virtual machine

9. Click the **Windows Server 2016–Base Installation** checkpoint, and then click **Apply** in the Actions pane. In the warning message that the current state will be lost, click **Apply**.

10. The Windows Server 2016 virtual machine is powered off automatically and the checkpoint is applied. Power on the virtual machine again, and log on with your Administrator account. In Server Manager, click **Local Server** and notice that Remote management is now enabled again. This shows a successful rollback to the point before the setting was changed.

11. Leave the virtual machine running. In Hyper-V Manager, click **Windows Server 2016– Updated Configuration** in the Checkpoints pane, and then click **Apply** in the Actions pane. In the warning message that the current state will be lost, click **Apply**.

12. The virtual machine is powered off and the checkpoint is applied. Power on the virtual machine again and log on. Notice in Server Manager, Local Server the Remote management is disabled again, and that you can switch between the two checkpoints (before and after the configuration change). Power off the virtual machine by clicking the **Shut Down** toolbar button, and then close the Virtual Machine Connection window.

13. To restore the virtual machine to before this activity, click the **Windows 2016–Base Installation** checkpoint, and then click **Apply** in the Actions pane. In the warning message that the current state will be lost, click **Apply**. Remove the checkpoints by clicking the **Windows 2016–Base Installation** checkpoint, and then clicking **Delete Checkpoint Subtree** in the Actions pane. In the Delete Checkpoint Tree dialog box, click **Delete**. Leave Hyper-V Manager open for the next activity.

Adding Virtual Hard Disks

You can add virtual hard disks to increase a virtual machine's storage capacity, improve file system organization, and experiment with disk configurations. You can create a stand-alone virtual disk by clicking New, Hard Disk in the Actions pane and assigning it to a virtual machine's settings later, or you can start the New Hard Disk wizard from the virtual machine's Settings dialog box when configuring hard disk controllers (see Figure 5-10). When you add hard disks, you can also specify advanced disk types, such as fixed and differencing disks.

A dynamically expanding disk is the default disk type in Hyper-V. A maximum size is set for the disk, typically 127 GB, but the disk file is only as large as needed; it can grow up to the maximum disk size. However, performance suffers when the disk is resized dynamically as the guest OS writes to it.

On the other hand, a fixed disk always takes up the disk space specified as its maximum size immediately. For example, a 127 GB virtual hard disk creates a 127 GB file on the host computer, even if the guest OS uses only 10 GB and the remaining space is empty. This disk type boosts performance but uses more disk space.

Hyper-V supports two different disk file formats, VHD (.vhd) and the newer VHDX (.vhdx) introduced in Windows Server 2012. A VHDX file can have a capacity of up to 64 TB versus a 2 TB limit on VHD files. A VHDX also supports 4 KB logical sector sizes for increased performance on modern drives, and is better at preventing data loss due to unexpected shutdowns. The Edit Disk wizard can convert a disk file between these two formats.

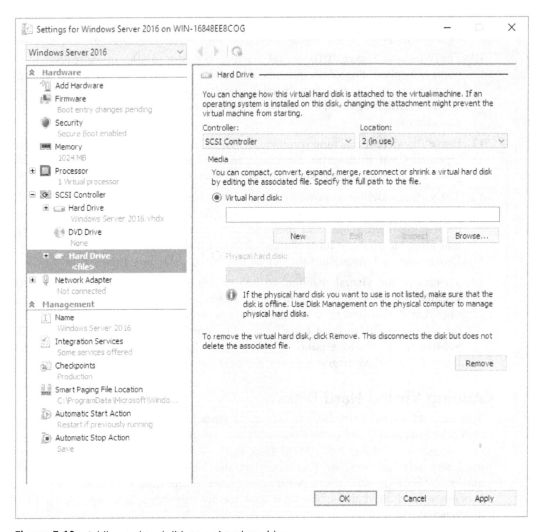

Figure 5-10 Adding a virtual disk to a virtual machine

A differencing disk is tied to another hard disk, and only changes between the two disks are saved in the differencing disk file. This disk type is useful if you have several small servers: You can create a parent virtual hard disk with a guest OS installed, and then have other child virtual machines share that virtual hard disk file. Because these child virtual machines don't need to store a complete guest OS installation, they take up less disk space.

Activity 5-8: Adding a Virtual Hard Disk

Time Required: 10 minutes

Objective: Add a virtual hard disk for increased storage.

Requirements: Completion of Activity 5-7

Description: In this activity, you use the New Virtual Hard Disk wizard to add a hard disk to the Windows Server 2016 virtual machine.

1. If necessary, log on to the host computer and open Hyper-V Manager.

2. In the Virtual Machines pane, click **Windows Server 2016**. Make sure this virtual machine is powered off.

3. In the Actions pane, under Windows Server 2016, click the **Settings** link.

4. In the Hardware section of the Settings dialog box, click **SCSI Controller**. Click **Hard Drive**, and on the right, click the **Add** button.

5. A virtual hard disk is added to the SCSI controller. In the Media section on the right, click the **New** button to start the New Virtual Hard Disk wizard. Click **Next** in the Before You Begin window.

6. In the Choose Disk Type window, verify that the Dynamically expanding option button is selected, and then click **Next**.

7. In the Specify Name and Location window, type **Data Disk.vhdx** in the Name text box. Accept the default location, and then click **Next**.

8. In the Configure Disk window, verify that the Create a new blank virtual hard disk option button is selected, and the disk size is 127 GB. Click **Next**.

9. In the Summary window, click **Finish** to create the virtual disk. Click **OK** to close the Settings dialog box.

10. Power on and connect to the Windows Server 2016 virtual machine, and log on to the guest OS with your Administrator account.

11. In Server Manager in the guest OS, click **File and Storage Services** in the left pane, then click **Disks** under Volumes.

12. Under DISKS, if disk number 1 has a status of Offline, then right-click Number **1**, the new virtual disk, and click **Bring Online**. In the Bring Disk Online dialog box, click **Yes**.

13. Right-click number **1** again, and click **Initialize**. In the Initialize Disk dialog box, click **Yes**.

14. Right-click number **1** again, and click **New Volume**. Click **Next** in each step of the New Volume wizard, accepting the defaults, and click **Create**. Creating and formatting the disk takes a few moments; when it's finished, click **Close**.

15. Verify that a new hard disk is now online under DISKS. Typically, a new hard disk is assigned to drive letter E under VOLUMES. Click **Start, File Explorer** and then click **This PC** to confirm the new drive is available.

16. Power off this virtual machine by clicking the **Shut Down** toolbar button, and then close the Virtual Machine Connection window. Leave Hyper-V Manager open for the next activity.

Using Differencing Disks

Hyper-V uses differencing disks to share a virtual hard disk file between two virtual machines; the child differencing disk contains only the differences from the parent. To add a differencing disk, you use the New Hard Disk wizard, but you select the Differencing disk option button and browse to the parent virtual disk file. In the following activity, you create a child virtual machine by using a differencing disk.

Activity 5-9: Creating a Child Virtual Machine with a Differencing Disk

Time Required: 15 minutes

Objective: Create a child virtual machine by using a differencing disk.

Requirements: Completion of Activity 5-8

Description: A differencing disk allows a child virtual machine to store only the differences from the parent virtual disk, which saves disk space because you don't have the overhead of storing the guest OS. In this activity, you create a child virtual machine with a differencing disk.

1. If necessary, log on to the host computer and open Hyper-V Manager.

2. In the Virtual Machines pane, click **Windows Server 2016**. Make sure this virtual machine is powered off.

3. Refer to Activity 5-2 for the steps to create a virtual machine. Name this virtual machine **Windows Server 2016 Child**, and in the Connect Virtual Hard Disk window, click the **Attach a virtual hard disk later** option button.

4. In the Virtual Machines pane of Hyper-V Manager, click the **Windows Server 2016 Child** virtual machine. In the Actions pane, under Windows Server 2016 Child, click the **Settings** link.

5. In the Hardware section of the Settings dialog box, click **SCSI Controller**, and then click **Hard Drive**. On the right, click the **Add** button.

6. A virtual hard disk is added under the SCSI Controller. In the Media section on the right, click the **New** button to start the New Virtual Hard Disk wizard. Click **Next** in the Before You Begin window.

7. In the Choose Disk Format window, click the **VHDX** option button, and then click **Next**.

8. In the Choose Disk Type window, click the **Differencing** option button, and then click **Next**.

9. In the Specify Name and Location window, type **Windows Server 2016 Child.vhdx** in the Name text box, and then click **Next**.

10. In the Configure Disk window, you're prompted to specify the location of the parent virtual hard disk file. Click **Browse**, navigate to the **Virtual Hard Disks** folder in C:\Users\Public\Public Documents\Hyper-V\Virtual hard disks, double-click the **Windows Server 2016.vhdx** file in the Open dialog box, and then click **Next**.

11. In the Summary window, click **Finish** to create the virtual hard disk. Click **OK** to close the Settings dialog box.

12. Power on **Windows Server 2016 Child** and connect to the virtual machine to confirm that it's functioning correctly. Power off this virtual machine by clicking the **Shut Down** toolbar button, and then close the Virtual Machine Connection window.

13. On the host computer, click **Start, File Explorer**. Click **This PC** in the File Explorer window and navigate to the **Windows Server 2016** virtual machine folder, which is in C:\Users\Public\Public Documents\Hyper-V\Virtual hard disks.

14. Right-click **Windows Server 2016.vhdx** and click **Properties**. In the Properties dialog box, note the file size. Do the same with the **Windows Server 2016 Child.vhdx** file. Notice that even though both virtual machines have fully functional guest OSs installed, the parent virtual machine uses much more disk space than the child does. Record the file sizes below:

_____

15. Close the File Explorer window and both Properties dialog boxes, and leave Hyper-V Manager open for the next activity.

Editing Virtual Hard Disks

After creating a virtual hard disk, you can edit it in various ways. You can compact it to regain space on a dynamic disk after files have been deleted in the guest OS. You can also convert a dynamic disk to a fixed size disk, or between VHD and VHDX file formats. You can also increase the maximum size of a fixed or dynamic disk. In the next activity, you learn how to compact a virtual hard disk.

Activity 5-10: Compacting a Virtual Hard Disk

Time Required: 10 minutes

Objective: Compact a virtual hard disk to reduce its file size.

Requirements: Completion of Activity 5-5

Description: In this activity, you use the Edit Virtual Hard Disk wizard to compact the virtual hard disk on the Windows Server 2016 virtual machine.

1. If necessary, log on to the host computer and open Hyper-V Manager.

2. In the Virtual Machines pane, click **Windows Server 2016**. Make sure this virtual machine is powered off.

3. In the Actions pane, under Windows Server 2016, click the **Settings** link.

4. In the Hardware section of the Settings dialog box, under SCSI Controller click **Hard Drive (Windows Server 2016.vhdx)**. On the right, click the **Edit** button under Media to start the Edit Virtual Hard Disk wizard.

5. In the Before You Begin window, click **Next**.

6. In the Locate Virtual Hard Disk window, click **Next**.

7. In the Choose Action window, verify that the Compact option button is selected, and then click **Next**.

8. In the Summary window, click **Finish** and then click **OK** to close Settings. Leave Hyper-V Manager open for the next activity.

Configuring Networks with Virtual Switches

You use the Virtual Switch Manager to create virtual switches that control how virtual machines communicate with each other, the host computer, and outside the network (such as with the Internet). You can create three types of virtual networks, as shown in Figure 5-11. The external type is connected to a physical network adapter in your host computer and allows virtual machines to access other computers outside the host. The internal and private network types aren't connected to a physical network adapter and can't communicate outside the host. The private type is the most restrictive; a virtual machine can't even communicate with the host computer, only other virtual machines. You can also have multiple networks set up to allow specific virtual machines to communicate with each other. In the following activity, you will create a virtual switch the Windows Server 2016 virtual machine can use to access the Internet.

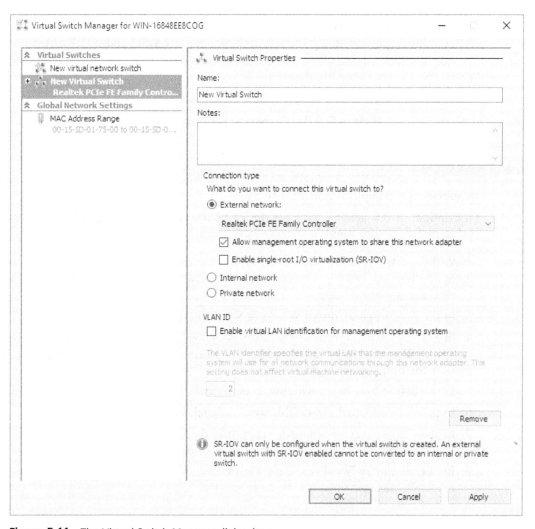

Figure 5-11   The Virtual Switch Manager dialog box

Activity 5-11: Working with Virtual Networks

Time Required: 10 minutes

Objective: Place a virtual machine on an external network virtual switch.

Requirements: Completion of Activity 5-5, an Internet connection

Description: To enable your Windows Server 2016 access to the Internet so it can download updates, in this activity you will create an external network connected to the physical network adapter in the host computer and assign the virtual machine's network adapter to it. Connectivity will be tested with the ping command, which sends packets to a server that will then send back an acknowledgement.

1. If necessary, log on to the host computer and open Hyper-V Manager.

2. In the Virtual Machines pane, click **Windows Server 2016.** Power on and connect to this virtual machine, and log on to the guest OS with your Administrator account.

3. In the Server Manager window, click **Tools** in the upper right corner, then click **Windows PowerShell.**

4. At the prompt in the PowerShell window, type **ping google.com.** The response "Ping request could not find host google.com" reflects that the virtual machine currently doesn't have Internet access (but note that not all Web sites respond to ping requests).

5. Leave the virtual machine running. In Hyper-V Manager, click **Virtual Switch Manager** in the Actions pane.

6. On the left, verify that New virtual network switch is selected. On the right, verify that External is selected in the Create virtual switch section, and then click the **Create Virtual Switch** button.

7. In the Name text box, type **Internet.** Verify that the External network option button is selected in the Connection type section, and that the correct network adapter on the host computer with Internet access is selected in the dropdown list. Click **OK,** then click **Yes** in the Apply Networking Changes dialog box to close the Virtual Switch Manager dialog box.

8. In the Actions pane, under Windows Server 2016, click the **Settings** link. In the Hardware section of the Settings dialog box, click **Network Adapter.**

9. On the right, click the **Virtual switch** list arrow, and click **Internet.** Click **OK** to close the Settings dialog box.

10. In the Virtual Machine Connection window for Windows Server 2016, you may be asked if you want to allow your PC to be discoverable by other PCs and devices on the network. If so, click **Yes.**

11. Type **ping google.com** into the PowerShell window again. This time you should see four replies from the Google servers, confirming that the virtual machine now has Internet connectivity.

12. Power off this virtual machine by clicking the **Shut Down** toolbar button, and then close the Virtual Machine Connection window and Hyper-V Manager.

Chapter Summary

- You should choose an edition of Windows Server 2016 that meets the features and licensing needs for your virtual servers.

- Using Hyper-V requires a 64-bit processor as well as hardware virtualization support. Some computers have this feature disabled in the BIOS, and it must be enabled.

- Hyper-V is a server role that's installed in Server Manager. For guest OSs, Hyper-V officially supports Windows Server 2008 and newer, and Windows Vista and newer on the desktop.

- VHDX is an improved hard disk file format, supporting up to 64 TB versus only 2 TB for VHDs, with improved performance and file recovery.

- Two generations of virtual machines can be created. Generation one virtual machines use IDE controllers, support 32- or 64-bit operating systems, use BIOS, and support virtual floppy disks and COM ports. Generation two virtual machines have improved performance, support only 64-bit operating systems, only support SCSI controllers, and use EFI firmware with optional Secure Boot.

- The Hyper-V Actions pane is used to change both global settings for Hyper-V and settings for specific virtual machines.

- The Virtual Machine Connection window enables you to interact with the guest OS on a virtual machine.

- Integration Services adds drivers optimized for virtualization. It enhances mouse support and adds the following features that you can enable for specific virtual machines: Operating system shutdown, Time synchronization, Data Exchange, Heartbeat, Backup (volume shadow copy), and Guest services.

- There are two types of checkpoints. A production checkpoint will not save the state of currently running applications and cold boots when resuming which is more reliable with server services. A standard checkpoint saves the memory and disk states and resumes in the exact place it left off.

- The Edit Virtual Hard Disk wizard is used to compact a virtual hard disk, convert a dynamic disk to a fixed disk or between VHD and VHDX formats, or increase a disk's maximum size.

- You can use differencing disks to link a child virtual machine to a parent virtual machine; only the differences between the two are saved to reduce the use of disk space.

- Virtual switch types include external, which allows a virtual machine to access computers outside the host; internal, which limits access to the host and other virtual machines; and private, which allows access only to other virtual machines, not the host computer.

Key Terms

DEP (Data Execution Prevention)   Enlightened I/O

Review Questions

1. What are the advantages of a VHDX hard disk file format over a VHD? (Choose all that apply.)

   a. Increased capacity

   b. Improved file recovery

   c. Increased performance on modern drives

   d. Higher security

2. How do you set the startup device order for a virtual machine?

   a. Start the virtual machine and press F2 to enter the BIOS.

   b. Start the virtual machine and press Delete to enter the BIOS.

   c. Configure the virtual machine's firmware or BIOS settings in Hyper-V Manager.

   d. A virtual machine's startup device order is fixed and can't be changed.

3. Which disk types can you create with the New Virtual Hard Disk izard? (Choose all that apply.)

   a. Differencing

   b. Undo

   c. Fixed

   d. Dynamically expanding

4. Which virtual network type doesn't allow a virtual machine to communicate with the host computer?

   a. Internal

   b. Bridged

   c. External

   d. Private

5. Which of the following is a feature of Integration Services? (Choose all that apply.)

   a. Easier transfer of keyboard and mouse control between the virtual machine and host computer

   b. Synchronization between the virtual machine and host computer's system clocks

   c. Drag and drop files between the virtual machine and the host computer

   d. Automatic guest OS shutdown from a toolbar button

6. What is the default key combination to transfer mouse control from a virtual machine to the host?

   a. Ctrl+Alt+Shift

   b. Ctrl+Alt+left arrow

   c. Ctrl+Alt

   d. Ctrl+Alt+spacebar

7. How many free licenses does Windows Server 2016 Standard edition offer for virtual machines?

    a. 1

    b. 2

    c. 4

    d. Unlimited

8. Which disk type usually results in the smallest virtual hard disk file size?

    a. Dynamically expanding

    b. Fixed

    c. Parent disk

    d. Differencing

9. Which of the following is a requirement for installing the Hyper-V server role in Windows Server 2016? (Choose all that apply.)

    a. A 32-bit or 64-bit processor

    b. A 64-bit processor

    c. Hardware virtualization support built into the processor

    d. 8 GB RAM

10. Which of the following is *not* an action a virtual machine can take when the host starts?

    a. Ask me to start this virtual machine

    b. Start automatically if it was running when the Hyper-V service stopped

    c. Nothing

    d. Always start this virtual machine automatically

11. Which of the following is *not* a device that can be added to a virtual machine?

    a. RemoteFX 3D video adapter

    b. Network adapter

    c. USB controller

    d. SCSI controller

12. Which of the following Virtual Machine Connection toolbar buttons should you normally use to shut down a Windows virtual machine?

    a. Turn Off

    b. Shut Down

    c. Reset

    d. Pause

13. Which of the following virtual devices can use an ISO file?

   a. DVD drive

   b. Floppy disk drive

   c. Hard drive

   d. COM port

14. Which of the following is *not* an option in the Edit Virtual Hard Disk wizard?

   a. Create a differencing disk to save only file changes.

   b. Compact a virtual disk to free up space.

   c. Expand the capacity of a virtual disk.

   d. Convert a dynamic disk to a fixed size.

15. Which of the following can't be created by using the New link in the Hyper-V Manager's Actions pane?

   a. Floppy disk

   b. Virtual switch

   c. Virtual machine

   d. Hard disk

16. The Smart Paging File is associated with which feature?

   a. Dynamic hard disk file

   b. Fixed hard disk file

   c. Dynamic memory

   d. Checkpoints

17. The Data Exchange feature in Integration Services does which of the following?

   a. Allows dragging and dropping files between the host and virtual machine

   b. Allows physical drives on the host to appear as network shares on the virtual machine

   c. Allows the host and virtual machine to share the clipboard

   d. Allows the host and virtual machine to communicate through their registries

18. Which virtual devices are not available on a generation two virtual machine? (Choose all that apply.)

   a. COM ports

   b. EFI

   c. IDE controller

   d. SCSI DVD drives

19. Which Windows Server 2016 edition supports Hyper-V? (Choose all that apply.)

  a. Standard edition

  b. Enterprise edition

  c. Datacenter edition

  d. Foundation edition

20. Which key combination can be used to emulate Ctrl+Alt+Delete on the virtual machine?

  a. Ctrl+Alt+End

  b. Ctrl+Alt+Insert

  c. Ctrl+Alt+Break

  d. Ctrl+Alt+left arrow

Case Projects

CASE PROJECTS

Case Project 5-1: Selecting Server Hardware

Currently, Superior Technical College has three physical servers that it plans to replace with Windows Server 2016 virtual machines. In addition, it plans to buy a high-speed computer to host the virtual machines. The Windows Server 2016 virtual machines each require 4 GB RAM and one virtual hard disk of 100 GB+ of very fast storage to be used for the Windows Server 2016 OS files. A 6 TB virtual hard disk will be attached to one of the virtual machines for user data. For this project, write a brief report describing the hardware requirements for the host computer to support these three Windows Server 2016 virtual machines.

Case Project 5-2: Comparing Server Virtualization Features

Write two brief reports, one describing an IT environment in which Hyper-V is more suitable than VMware vSphere for virtualization software and one describing an IT environment in which VMware vSphere is the best choice. Your reports should discuss the following virtualization features to support the choice of virtualization software for the environment:

- Snapshot/Checkpoint support
- Licensing requirements
- Host OS requirements

chapter 6

Working with Virtual Machine Manager

After reading this chapter and completing the exercises, you will be able to:

- Install Microsoft Virtual Machine Manager 2016
- Work with the VMM Console

With Microsoft Virtual Machine Manager 2016, administrators have centralized management over Microsoft Hyper-V, VMware ESX, and Citrix XenServer virtual servers. You can manage virtualization resources for multiple servers and create hardware and software profiles for templates to generate virtual machines to any specification quickly.

Installing Virtual Machine Manager

Microsoft System Center Virtual Machine Manager 2016, known as **Virtual Machine Manager (VMM)**, is a tool for centralized management of virtual machines and virtualization resources. In this section, you learn how to install and configure VMM components on your Windows Server 2016 host computer.

The Virtual Machine Manager Components

Virtual Machine Manager has three major components: VMM Management Server, VMM Console, and VMM Local Agent.

VMM Management Server The **VMM Management Server** controls the core functions of Virtual Machine Manager and consists of the following:

- *VMM Service*—This service allows VMM components to communicate with each other and with the host computers being managed to facilitate file transfers, issue commands, monitor server status, and move virtual machines.

- *Database server*—The **database server** uses a SQL Server database to store VMM's settings. VMM no longer supports Express editions of SQL Server.

- *Library server*—The system running VMM Server is also the default library server. A **library server** consists of standard Windows network shares (called library shares) used to store resources for creating virtual machines, such as virtual hard disk and floppy disk files, ISO image files, virtual machine templates, and hardware and guest OS profiles. In large networks, you can create multiple library servers on different computers.

VMM Console The **VMM Console** is used to perform administrative tasks, such as managing, creating, and deploying virtual machines, managing host and library servers, and working with configuration settings. You can install multiple consoles on different computers on the network, although they can manage only one VMM server at a time.

VMM Local Agent Any host computer managed by VMM must have a **VMM Local Agent** installed to enable it to communicate with VMM. Installation takes place automatically when a host is added to the VMM Administrator Console and is in the Active Directory domain, or it can be done manually. The VMM Local Agent can be installed on any Windows 8 or newer OS or a computer running Hyper-V or VMware ESX Server.

Software and Hardware Requirements

Before you can run VMM, you must install the prerequisite software and services. If any required component isn't detected during installation the Setup program gives you details on how to acquire them. The following are required to run VMM:

- *Windows Server 2016*—The 64-bit version of the Standard or Datacenter Edition (with Desktop Experience) needs to be installed.

- *Microsoft .NET Framework 3.5 and 4.6*—Both versions need to be installed. While the 4.6 framework is installed by default with Windows Server 2016, the 3.5 version will need to be installed manually.

- *Microsoft SQL Server 2012 or 2014*—This database server software will need to be downloaded separately at Microsoft.com. VMM will not work with free Express editions.

- *Windows Assessment and Deployment Kit for Windows 10*—This software works with Windows image files and will need to be downloaded separately from Microsoft.com.

Table 6-1 shows the hardware requirements for each component.

Table 6-1   Hardware requirements for VMM components

Component	Processor (Min)	Processor (Rec)	RAM (Min)	RAM (Rec)	Hard Drive Space (Min)	Hard Drive Space (Rec)
Server	8 Cores 2.0 GHz	16 Cores 2.66 GHz	4 GB	16 GB	4 GB	10 GB
Console	2 Cores 1.0 GHz	2 Cores 2 GHz	4 GB	4 GB	10 GB	10 GB
Database server	8 Cores 2.8 GHz	16 Cores 2.66 GHz	8 GB	16 GB	50 GB	200 GB
Library server	4 Cores 2.8 GHz	4 Cores 2.66 GHz	2 GB	4 GB	Varies based on files stored	Varies based on files stored

Installing the Active Directory Role

The VMM Management Server must be installed on a computer that is a member of an Active Directory domain. The VMM can be installed into a separate forest, however you will need to use a two-way trust between the cross-forest domains as one-way trusts are not supported in VMM.

Activity 6-1: Installing the Active Directory Role

Time Required: 10 minutes

Objective: Install the Active Directory role.

Requirements: A Windows Server 2016 PC

Description: In this activity, you use Server Manager to add the Active Directory role to your Windows Server 2016 host computer, a prerequisite for the VMM.

1. If necessary, log on to the host computer with your assigned administrative username and password.

2. If Server Manager is not running, click **Start** and then click **Server Manager**.

3. In the Server Manager window, click **Manage** in the upper right corner, then click **Add Roles and Features**.

4. In the Before you begin window, click **Next**.

5. In the Select installation type window, make sure the Role-based or feature-based installation option button is selected, then click **Next**.

6. In the Select destination server window, click **Next**.

7. In the Select server roles window, click to check **Active Directory Domain Services**, and then click **Add Features** in the confirmation dialog box. Click **Next**.

8. In the Select features window, click **Next**.

9. The Active Directory Domain Services window contains a description of Active Directory and some notes. Click **Next**.

10. On the Confirm installation selections window, click to check **Restart the destination server automatically if required**, then click **Yes** in the confirmation dialog box.

11. Click **Install**. Wait for the installation to finish, then click the **Promote this server to a domain controller** link.

12. In the Deployment Configuration window, choose the **Add a new forest** option button, and then type **stc.local** into the Root domain name text box. Click **Next**.

13. In the Domain Controller Options window, type your administrator password into the Password and Confirm password text boxes, then click **Next**.

14. In the DNS Options window, you may see a warning that delegation for this DNS server cannot be created, click **Next**.

15. In the Additional Options window, click **Next**.

16. In the Paths window, note the default folder locations and click **Next**.

17. In the Review Options window, confirm your settings by clicking **Next**.

18. In the Prerequisites Check window, your system's hardware and software are scanned to see whether it can run Active Directory Domain Services. If your system fails the check, follow the instructions to make the necessary updates. Otherwise, when all prerequisite checks pass click **Install**.

19. Wait for the installation to finish, the server will then automatically restart.

20. Log on with your administrator account. Stay logged on for the next activity.

Downloading Virtual Machine Manager

Microsoft offers a free 180-day trial version of VMM. The download, SCVMM_EN.exe, is a self-extracting executable that creates the installation files. VMM requires 1 GB hard disk space for the compressed files and an additional 1.2 GB for the extracted installation files. You might want to place the installation files on a network drive or removable media for easier installation of components on other computers.

Activity 6-2: Downloading Virtual Machine Manager

Time Required: 15 minutes

Objective: Download Virtual Machine Manager.

Requirements: Access to the Internet; 3 GB hard disk space

Description: In this activity, you download the VMM software from the Microsoft Web site and extract the installation files.

1. If necessary, log on to the host computer with your assigned administrative username and password.

2. By default, the Microsoft Edge Web browser cannot be run on a Windows Server 2016 PC under an administrator account, and user accounts are not allowed to log on locally to an Active Directory Domain Controller. The easiest solution is to download the Google Chrome or Mozilla Firefox browser on another PC and install it onto your Windows Server 2016 host. Alternatively, you can use the Internet Explorer browser by clicking **Start, Windows Accessories,** and then click **Internet Explorer.** If enhanced security in the browser blocks the site, click **Add** and **Close** at each prompt to allow access.

3. Start your Web browser and navigate to **www.microsoft.com.**

4. In the Search text box, type **technet evaluation center** and press **Enter.** Click the first result.

5. Click **Evaluate Now** in the navigation bar and click **System Center 2016** in the menu. Click the **Download link** button if necessary, then click the **Sign in** button.

6. On the Sign in page, enter your Microsoft account email address and password and click **Sign in,** or click **Create one** if you need to create a new account.

7. Click the **Register to continue** button, complete the form, and then click **Continue.** Click the **Download** button next to the file SC2016_SCVMM.EXE and save it to your desktop.

8. When the download is finished, double-click the **SCVMM_EN.exe** file, then click **Run.**

9. In the Welcome to the SCVMM Setup Wizard window, click **Next.**

10. In the License Agreement window, click the **I accept the agreement** option button, then click **Next.**

11. In the Select Destination Location window, accept the default path unless otherwise instructed, click **Next.**

12. In the Ready to Extract window, click **Extract.** After it finishes, click **Finish.** Stay logged on for the next activity.

Downloading and Installing SQL Server 2014

SQL Server 2014 is a required prerequisite for the VMM and needs to be downloaded from the Microsoft Web site. The free Express edition can no longer be used with the VMM, however a free 180-day trial version is available.

Activity 6-3: Downloading and Installing the SQL Server 2014

Time Required: 30 minutes

Objective: Download and install the SQL Server 2014.

Requirements: Access to the Internet; 2.1 GB hard disk space; Windows Server 2016 installation media

Description: In this activity, you download then install the SQL Server 2014, a prerequisite for VMM. You will also be installing the Microsoft .Net Framework 3.5.

1. If necessary, log on to the host computer with your assigned administrative username and password.

2. To confirm the required prerequisite Microsoft .Net framework 3.5 is installed, start Server Manager: click **Start** and then click **Server Manager.**

3. In the Server Manager window, click **Manage** in the upper right corner, then click **Add Roles and Features.**

4. In the Before you begin window, click **Next.**

5. In the Select installation type window, make sure the Role-based or feature-based installation option button is selected, then click **Next.**

6. In the Select destination server window, click **Next.**

7. In the Select server roles window, click **Next.**

8. In the Select features window, check the **.Net Framework 3.5 Features** box and click **Next.** If the box is already checked, you can click **Cancel** and proceed to step 11.

9. On the Confirm installation selections window, if you see a "Do you need to specify an alternate source path?" warning, click the **Specify an alternate source path** link at the bottom of the window. In the Path text box, enter the path to your Windows Server 2016 installation media drive letter or network location along with the \Sources\SxS folder, then click **OK.**

10. Click **Install.** Wait for the installation to finish, then click **Close** and exit Server Manager.

11. Start your Web browser and navigate to **www.microsoft.com.**

12. In the Search text box, type **technet evaluation center** and press **Enter.** Click the first result.

13. Click **Evaluate Now** in the navigation bar and click **SQL Server 2014 SP2** in the menu. Click the **Download** link button if necessary, then click the **Sign in** button if not currently signed in.

14. If required, on the Sign in page, enter your Microsoft account email address and password and click **Sign in,** or click **Create one** if you need to create a new account.

15. Click the **ISO option button** under file type, then click the **Register to continue** button, complete the form, and then click **Continue.** Click the **Download** button next to the file SQLServer2014SP2-FullSlipstream-x64-ENU.iso and save it to your desktop.

16. When the download is finished, double-click the **SQLServer2014SP2-FullSlipstream-x64-ENU.iso** to mount the ISO file into a virtual DVD drive. Double-click the **setup.exe** file.

17. In the SQL Server Installation Center window, click **Installation** in the left pane, then click the **New SQL Server stand-alone installation or add features to an existing installation** link on the right to open the SQL Server 2014 Setup window.

18. In the Product Key window, if you don't have a product key available click the **Specify a free edition** option button and confirm Evaluation is selected in the dropdown list, then click **Next**.

19. In the License Terms window, click to check the **I accept the license terms** check box, then click **Next**.

20. In the Global Rules window, any issues preventing the installation of SQL Server will be displayed. When everything passes, the next step is shown.

21. In the Microsoft Update window, click **Next**.

22. In the Product Updates window, the next step is shown after checking for updates.

23. In the Install Setup Files window, wait for the files to be finished copying and setup will automatically proceed to the next step.

24. In the Install Rules window, any issues preventing the installation of SQL Server will be displayed. When everything passes, click **Next**.

25. In the Setup Role window, confirm the SQL Server Feature Installation option button is selected, then click **Next**.

26. In the Feature Selection window, click the **Database Engine Services** check box under Instance Features and **Management Tools–Complete** under Shared Features. Note the default installation paths, then click **Next**.

27. In the Instance Configuration window, click **Next**.

28. In the Server Configuration window, click the dropdown list in the Account Name column under SQL Server Database Engine, then click **Browse**. In the Select User, Computer, Service Account, or Group window, click **Advanced**, then click **Find Now**. Click **System** under Search results, then click **OK**. Click **OK** to close the Select User, Computer, Service Account, or Group window, then click **Next**.

29. In the Database Engine Configuration window, click the **Add Current User** button, then click **Next**.

30. In the Ready to Install window, review your settings and then click **Install**.

31. Wait for the installation to finish, then click **Close**. Stay logged on for the next activity.

Downloading and Installing the Windows ADK

The Windows Assessment and Deployment Kit (ADK) for Windows 10 is a required prerequisite for the VMM and needs to be downloaded from the Microsoft Web site. The ADK contains a collection of tools used to test and customize Windows images.

Activity 6-4: Downloading and Installing the Windows ADK

Time Required: 15 minutes

Objective: Download and install the Windows ADK.

Requirements: Access to the Internet; 3.4 GB hard disk space

Description: In this activity, you download the install the Windows ADK for Windows 10 on your Windows Server 2016 host computer, a prerequisite for the VMM.

1. If necessary, log on to the host computer with your assigned administrative username and password.

2. Start your Web browser and navigate to **www.microsoft.com**.

3. In the Search text box, type **windows adk 10** and press **Enter**. Click the first result.

4. Click the **Get Windows ADK for Windows 10** button and save the file to your desktop.

5. When the download is finished, double-click the **adksetup.exe** file, then click **Run** if prompted.

6. In the Specify Location window, confirm the Install the Windows Assessment and Deployment Kit option button is selected and click **Next**.

7. In the Windows Kits Privacy window, choose either option and then click **Next**.

8. In the License Agreement window, click **Accept**.

9. In the Select the features you want to install window, click to select the **Deployment Tools** and **Windows Preinstallation Environment (Windows PE)** check boxes. Un-check all other options and click **Install**.

10. Wait for the installation to finish, then click **Close**. Stay logged on for the next activity.

Creating the VMM Service Account

When installing VMM, you'll be asked to provide a VMM service account in the Administrators group. This account cannot be changed after installation without uninstalling and reinstalling and should be used only for VMM. Specifying your administrator account as the service account will cause some operations to fail if attempted while you are logged on under that account. This should also be a domain account to allow high availability and shared ISO images.

Activity 6-5: Creating the VMM Service Account

Time Required: 10 minutes

Objective: Create a new user account to be used as the VMM service account.

Requirements: None

Description: In this activity, you create a new user account, vmmservice, and add it to the administrators group. This account will be chosen when VMM is installed.

1. If necessary, log on to the host computer with your assigned administrative username and password.

2. If Server Manager is not running, click **Start** and then click **Server Manager**.

3. In the Server Manager window, click **Tools** in the upper right corner, then click **Active Directory Users and Computers**.

4. In the Active Directory Users and Computers window, click **stc.local** in the left pane, then double-click **Users** on the right.

5. Click the **Action** menu, point to **New**, and then click **User**.

6. In the New Object–User dialog box, First name text box, type **vmmservice**.

7. In the User log on name text box, type **vmmservice**, then click **Next**.

8. In the Password and Confirm password text boxes, enter your administrator password. Click to uncheck the **User must change password at next logon** check box, and click to check the **Password never expires** check box, then click **Next**.

9. In the summary window, click **Finish** to create the account and close the dialog box.

10. Right-click the new **vmmservice** user account from the list and click **Add to a group** from the menu.

11. In the Select Groups window, click **Advanced**, then click **Find Now**. Under Search results, click **Administrators**, then click **OK** to close the Advanced dialog box, and again to close the Select Groups window.

12. Click **OK** on the successfully completed dialog box and then close the Active Directory Users and Computers window.

13. Close Server Manager and stay logged on for the next activity.

Installing Virtual Machine Manager

The VMM components can be installed on multiple servers, but for the purposes of this book, you install them on the host computer you used in Chapter 5, where Hyper-V is installed. Running all components on a single server is typical for small businesses. Running the setup.exe file starts the Setup program; Figure 6-1 shows the first window.

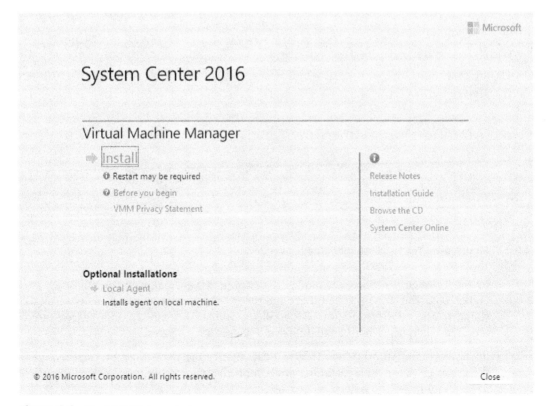

Figure 6-1 The VMM Setup window

Installing VMM Management Server and Console To start the installation, click Install under the Virtual Machine Manager heading shown in Figure 6-1. Previously installed separately, the VMM Management Server and Console are now installed together. After stepping through some initial windows for product registration, license agreements, privacy, and updates, you come to the Installation Location window, where you specify the location to install VMM. The default path is C:\Program Files\Microsoft System Center 2016\Virtual Machine Manager. In the Database configuration window, shown in Figure 6-2, you can enter the name of the computer running SQL Server, which can be the same computer that VMM is being installed to. A new database is created by default, but an existing database can also be specified.

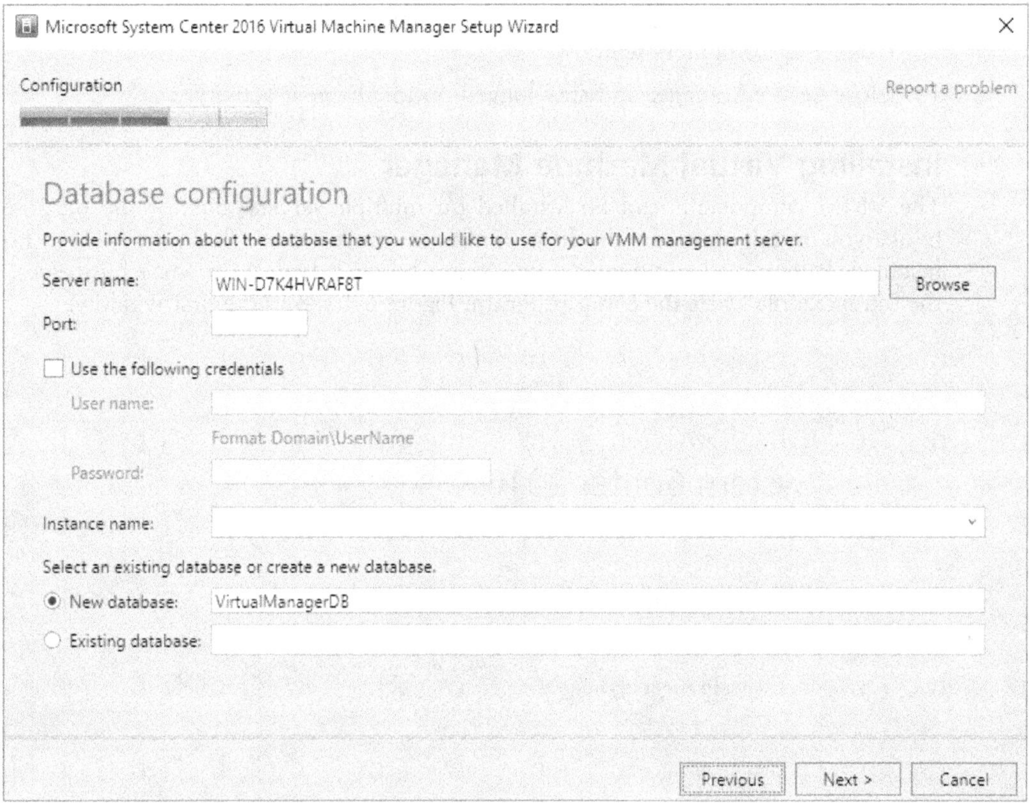

Figure 6-2   The Database configuration window

In the Configure service account and distributed key management window, as shown in Figure 6-3, you choose which account the VMM Service will use. This setting cannot be changed after the installation is complete, and a Domain account is recommended and required when using high availability and shared ISO images.

In the Port configuration window you can specify the ports used by each feature. Typically these can be left at their defaults, and cannot be changed without re-installing VMM. Port 5986 should not be assigned to any feature.

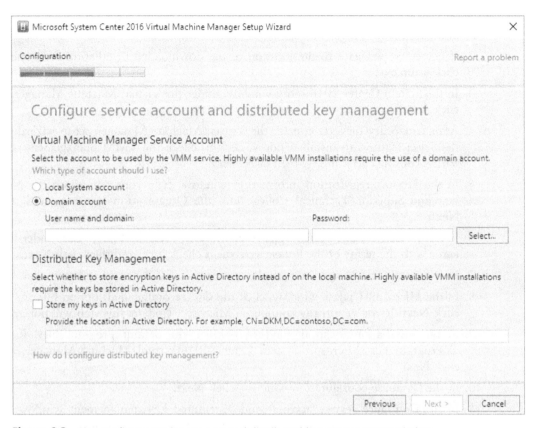

Figure 6-3   The Configure service account and distributed key management window

In the Library configuration window you create a library share or use an existing one on another server. When creating a library share, you enter the name of the network share, the location on the host where library files will be stored (by default a hidden folder, \Program Data\Virtual Machine Manager Library Files), and a description of the share. After the default library share is created it can't be deleted or moved, so make sure it's in the right location.

In the Installation summary window, review your selections, and click Install to begin the VMM installation. When it's finished, Setup can optionally open Windows Update to check for updates and open the VMM Console.

Activity 6-6: Installing Virtual Machine Manager

Time Required: 15 minutes

Objective: Install the VMM Management Server and Console components.

Requirements: Completion of Activities 6-1 through 6-5

Description: In this activity, you install the VMM Management Server and Console components on your Windows Server 2016 host computer.

1. If necessary, log on to the host computer with your assigned administrative username and password.

2. If necessary, navigate to the location of the downloaded installation files, and double-click **setup.exe**.

3. In the System Center 2016 setup window, under the Virtual Machine Manager heading, click **Install**.

4. After temporary files are copied, the Virtual Machine Manager Setup wizard starts. In the Select features to install window, click to check the **VMM management server** and **VMM console** check boxes, then click **Next**.

5. In the Product registration information window, type your name into the **Name** text box and **Superior Technical College** into the Organization text box, and then click **Next**.

6. In the Please read this license agreement window, click the **I have read, understood, and agree with the terms of the license agreement** check box, and then click **Next**.

7. In Diagnostic and Usage Data window, review the information and then click **Next**.

8. In the Microsoft Update window, click the **On (recommended)** option button, and then click **Next**. If you've already configured Microsoft Update, this step will not appear.

9. In the Installation location window, confirm the default program files' location at C:\Program Files\Microsoft System Center 2016\Virtual Machine Manager, and then click **Next**.

10. In the Database configuration window, click **Next**.

11. In the Configure service account and distributed key management window, confirm the Domain account option button is selected, then type **stc\vmmservice** into the Username and domain text box, and administrator password into the Password text box. Click **Next**.

12. In the Port configuration window, note the ports used and click **Next**.

13. In the Library configuration window, click **Next**.

14. In the Installation summary window, review your settings and click **Install**.

15. Wait for the installation to finish, click to uncheck the **Check for the latest Virtual Machine Manager updates** and **Open the VMM console when this wizard closes** check boxes, and then click **Close**. Click **Close** on the System Center 2016 installer and stay logged on for the next activity.

Working with the VMM Console

The VMM Console is the main VMM tool administrators use to manage resources on all virtual server hosts. It also serves as a front end for specialized commands, called **cmdlets**, running in Windows PowerShell.

Windows PowerShell is an advanced command-line interface, similar to Linux shells, with more features than the standard command prompt window. When you perform a function in the VMM Console, it actually runs cmdlets in PowerShell behind the scenes. Many functions in the console allow you to view or modify the commands sent to PowerShell. You can also open a PowerShell window and enter these commands manually.

To start the VMM Console, use the Start menu or the Virtual Machine Manager Console desktop icon created during installation. When you open the console, a Connect to Server dialog box opens, asking which VMM server you want to administer. By default, localhost:8100 is displayed; localhost is a Windows DNS name referring to the current computer, and 8100 is the port specified for administrative communication when you install VMM Management Server. You can make this computer the default server so that you aren't prompted to connect each time you start the console.

After connecting to a server, the main VMM Console opens (see Figure 6-4). Across the top of the window is the ribbon that organizes the current commands available to perform tasks based on the workspace you are viewing and what you have selected, which is further split into tabs. Below the ribbon in the left pane is a list of the nodes for the current workspace, and below that you can choose a workspace. To the right is the results pane of the current workspace. The following workspaces are available in the console:

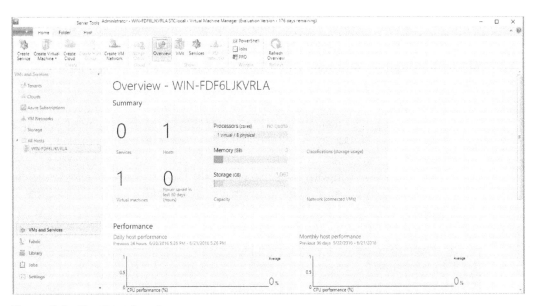

Figure 6-4   The VMM Console

- *VMs and Services*—You use this workspace to add, remove, create, configure, and monitor virtual machines services on virtual machine hosts and in private clouds.
- *Fabric*—This workspace manages the infrastructure needed to share storage devices over the network: the servers, networking, and storage resources.
- *Library*—The library stores all the virtualization resources VMM uses. You can use this workspace to configure guest OS and hardware profiles; create and modify virtual machine templates; access ISO files, virtual disk files, and virtual machine files; and add library servers and library shares.

- *Jobs*—A **job** is typically created when you perform any task in VMM and is based on a script that calls cmdlets to run in PowerShell. In this workspace you can monitor, restart, and stop jobs and see the results of jobs.

- *Settings*—This workspace contains options for configuring global VMM settings. It includes the following nodes: General, User Roles, Run As Accounts, Servicing Windows, Configuration Providers, System Center Settings, Console Add-ins, and Microsoft Azure Site Recovery.

The VMs and Services Workspace

The VMs and Services workspace allows you to manage your virtual machines and contains six nodes. The Tenants node organizes virtual machines you host for your tenants, also referred to as customers or clients. The Clouds node displays the virtual machines within your private cloud, taking advantage of the cloud model using on-premises hardware. Under the Azure Subscriptions node you can manage your Microsoft Azure cloud-based instances, connecting to virtual machines over the Internet and performing simple power and restart actions. The VM Networks node displays the available virtual networks and their IP address pools. The Storage node shows the disk information for your virtual machines, such as the type (for example, fixed or dynamic), total capacity, available space, and use of storage arrays. The All Hosts node allows you to configure and interact with all hosts being managed by the VMM Management Server and their virtual machines.

Although the ribbon is customized to show tasks available based on your current node, they all share the following commands:

- *Create Service*—A service is a collection of virtual machines designed to work together and be managed as a single unit. For example, a company may need to host an app that requires a database, Web, and application servers.

- *Create Virtual Machine*—Create a new virtual machine from scratch or based on an existing virtual machine, a template, or virtual hard disk. You can also convert a virtual machine created with other virtualization software that is compatible with Microsoft virtualization.

- *Create Cloud*—Start a wizard that brings together all of the resources and settings needed to create an on-premises private cloud.

- *Create Host Group*—Create a group combining related hosts to simplify management of a large number of servers.

- *Create VM Network*—Start a wizard to create a virtual machine network that operates on your logical network.

- *Assign Cloud*—Assign the selected private cloud to an existing user role, or create a new role and then assigns it.

- *Overview, VMs, Services, VM Networks*—Choose which information will be displayed about the selected host in the results pane: a summary of the server's hardware and current performance, a list of running services and virtual machines, and the current virtual networks configuration.

- *PowerShell*—Open a Microsoft PowerShell window, which can be used to run VMM cmdlets directly from the command line.

- *Jobs*—Display a summary of the most recently run jobs.

- *PRO*—Performance and Resource Optimization (PRO) settings are available only when you have installed System Center Operations Manager and configured it to work with VMM. This tool generates tips labeled as Warning or Critical and can be configured to run automatically. Possible tips include reconfiguring a virtual machine's hardware when it's underperforming or moving a virtual machine to another host when its current host is running low on resources.

Working with All Hosts The All Hosts node, shown previously in Figure 6-4, displays a list of all hosts managed by VMM Management Server and the results pane displays the virtual machines they are hosting. Clicking a virtual machine provides additional information. Under Virtual machine information the status is shown: whether it's running or stopped, the owner, the number of processors, and total memory. Logical networks and Network adapters show which network adapters the host is connected to and the logical networks in use. Storage shows the number of virtual disks in use, as well as their total capacity and free space. The Recent Job tab shows the name of most recent job the host performed and whether it was successful or not.

Adding a Host to the VMM Console Even though you have installed VMM Management Server on an active Hyper-V host, it isn't managed by VMM yet. The first task you need to perform is adding this host to the VMM Console. In the VMs and Services workspace, right-click All Hosts and choose Add Hyper-V Hosts and Clusters to start the Add Resource wizard.

In the Resource Location window (see Figure 6-5), you can choose from four locations: a Windows Server host in a trusted Active Directory domain, an untrusted Active Directory domain, a perimeter network, or a physical computer to be provisioned as a host. A perimeter network is one that isn't in Active Directory; to use a host in a perimeter network, you must install the VMM Local Agent manually from the VMM installation files. A computer in an Active Directory domain has the VMM Local Agent installed automatically through the network when it's added. Then you enter the username and password of the administrator account on the host.

In the Discovery Scope window, you specify the search scope used to locate your potential virtual hosts. If you know the names of the hosts you can type them in directly, or create an Active Directly query. In the Target Resources window, a list of computers in Active Directory as well as the virtualization software (if any) they're running within the scope is displayed. If a computer isn't running virtualization software, the Hyper-V server role is installed automatically.

In the Host Settings window, you can select the group you want to add the host to; by default, it's added to the global All Hosts group. You can also reassociate the host with VMM, which enables you to reassign selected hosts to the current VMM Server system if they had been managed by another one.

You can also select the locations for storing virtual machines created on this host. Note that these locations must already exist; they aren't created automatically.

In the Summary window, review your selections. You can click the View Script button to see the script that runs in PowerShell to perform the task you just created in the wizard. Clicking the Finish button creates a new job and runs it immediately. Figure 6-6 shows the progress of this job.

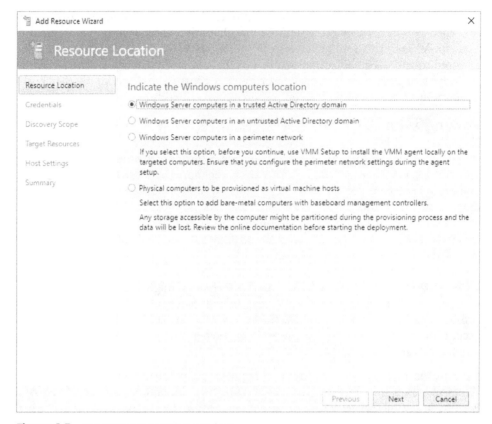

Figure 6-5   The Resource Location window

Figure 6-6   The Jobs dialog box

Activity 6-7: Adding a Host to the VMM Console

Time Required: 10 minutes

Objective: Add a host computer to the VMM Console.

Requirements: Completion of Activity 6-6

Description: In this activity, you add the Hyper-V host created in Chapter 5 (or the role will be installed automatically) so that you can manage it in the VMM Console and access its resources.

1. If necessary, log on to the host computer with your assigned administrative username and password. Double-click the **Virtual Machine Manager Console** desktop icon to open the VMM Console.

2. In the Connect to Server dialog box, confirm that localhost:8100 is displayed in the Server name text box, and click to select the **Automatically connect with these settings** check box so that you aren't prompted in the future. Click **Connect**.

3. Click the **VMs and Services workspace** button at the lower left, and then right-click **All Hosts** and choose **Add Hyper-V Hosts and Clusters** from the menu to start the Add Resource wizard.

4. In the Resource Location window, click the **Windows Server computers in a trusted Active Directory domain** option button, then click **Next**.

5. In the Credentials window, click the **Manually enter the credentials** option button and type your administrator account name, **stc\administrator**, into the User name text box and password in the Password text box, and then click **Next**.

6. In the Discovery Scope window, click the **Specify an Active Directory query to search for Windows Server computers** option button, then click **Generate an AD query**. In the Find Computers dialog box, click **OK** to close the dialog box, and then click **Next**.

7. In the Target Resources window, the names of computers in your Active Directory domain that are running virtualization software are displayed in the Discovered computers list. If you get a warning message about no computers being found, click **Refresh**. Click the check box before the name of your Hyper-V server (should be the same as the computer where you're running the VMM Console), and then click **Next**.

To find your computer name, right-click **Start**, and then click **System**. Look in the "Computer name, domain, and workgroup settings" section.

8. In the message box stating that Hyper-V is installed if the selected server isn't running it, click **OK**.

9. In the Host Settings window, verify that All Hosts is selected in the Host group drop-down list, and then click **Next**.

10. In the Summary window, review your settings, and then click the **Finish** button. The Jobs dialog box shows the progress of this task, which takes several minutes. When it's finished, close this dialog box.

11. The host should be listed in the VMs and Services workspace under All Hosts. Leave the VMM Console open for the next activity.

Interacting with a Virtual Machine Within the All Hosts node, selecting VMs in the Show group of the ribbon displays all virtual machines managed by VMM in the results pane, organized by their host groups (see Figure 6-7). The Virtual Machine tab is added to the ribbon when a virtual machine is selected, with the following options:

- *Create*
  - *Clone*—Create a copy of a virtual machine. You can modify the virtual machine's hardware but not the guest OS files. The cloned virtual machine has the same computer name as the original, which could lead to conflicts. Therefore, renaming the computer in the clone's OS is recommended.

  - *Create VM Template*—Create a virtual machine template based on another virtual machine or a hardware or guest OS profile. This task is covered in more detail later in "Creating a Virtual Machine Template."

- *Shut Down*—To shut down a guest OS, you should use its shutdown procedure, such as Start, Power, Shut down in Windows. If you have the Operating System Shutdown service (a Virtual Guest Services feature) enabled on the virtual machine, this command automates a safe shutdown procedure.

Figure 6-7 A virtual machine in VMs and Services workspace

- *Power On*—Start the virtual machine and load the guest OS.

- *Power Off*—Similar to using the power button on a physical computer, this command could cause data loss or corrupted files. Unless the guest OS has locked up, avoid using this command.

- *Pause/Resume*—Unlike the Save state command, the virtual machine isn't powered off and its state isn't saved. It's simply suspended temporarily. Click Resume to bring the virtual machine back to an active state.

- *Reset*—This command, which is similar to using the reset button on a physical computer, can result in data loss or corruption and shouldn't be used on a Windows guest OS unless the virtual machine isn't responding.

- *Save State*—Similar to the hibernate feature on a physical computer, this command saves the virtual machine's state and memory to a file and then powers it off. The next time you start the virtual machine, you can continue from where you left off.

- *Discard Saved State*—Power off a virtual machine that's in a saved state and discard the state.

- *Migrate Storage*—Move a virtual machine to a new storage location on the host.

- *Migrate Virtual Machine*—Move a virtual machine from one host to another.

- *Store in Library*—Remove the virtual machine from its host and store it on a library server.

- *Create Checkpoint*—Create a checkpoint for the virtual machine's current state by performing a complete backup, including the virtual hard disk. You can then use the checkpoint to return to this state later. If the virtual machine is running when you create a checkpoint, it's powered off and then restarted.

- *Manage Checkpoints*—You can create a checkpoint, restore a previous virtual machine state from a checkpoint, or delete a checkpoint. If you remove a checkpoint, all checkpoints created after it are removed, too.

- *Refresh*—Refresh the results pane with the latest information.

- *Repair*—If a virtual machine fails, this command offers three possible fixes: Retry the last job that failed again, return the virtual machine to the state before the failed job, or ignore if you've solved the problem (such as a file the virtual machine uses being moved on the host).

- *Install Virtual Guest Services*—After installing a supported OS, use this command to mount the ISO image containing Virtual Guest Services on the virtual machine.

- *Manage Protection*—Enabling Protection allows the virtual machine to be synced with the Microsoft Azure Site Recovery Vault and be used as a failover.

- *Connect or View*

  o *Connect via Console/RDP*—Connect to the virtual machine by using the Virtual Machine Viewer (Console), similar to the Virtual Machine Connection window in the Hyper-V Manager, or using Remote Desktop (RDP), to interact with the guest OS.

- *View Networking*—Open Network Configuration view, which shows a graphical representation of hosts, virtual machines, network adapters, and network connections.

- *Delete*—Delete a virtual machine's configuration and virtual disk files permanently. To remove a virtual machine from a server without deleting it, you can store it in the library instead.

- *Properties*—View a virtual machine's settings, including hardware configuration, checkpoints, automatic startup and shutdown options, and storage options.

Basic virtual machine operations work the same way they do in Hyper-V Manager. After you select a virtual machine, clicking Power On starts it. The pane at the bottom of the window provides a quick overview of the virtual machine's status and configuration as well as recent jobs and CPU performance. To interact with the guest OS, choose either Connect via Console (Virtual Machine Viewer, as shown in Figure 6-8) or Connect via RDP (Remote Desktop Protocol must be enabled within the guest OS) under the Connect or View command in the ribbon.

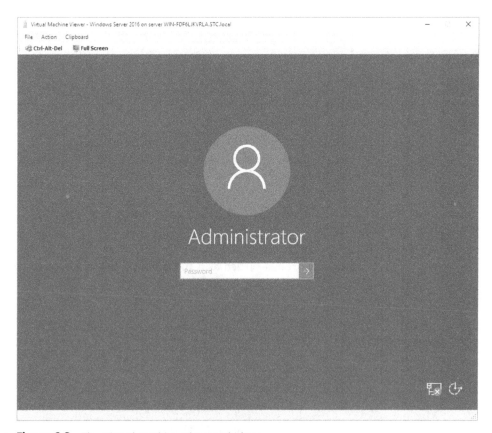

Figure 6-8 The Virtual Machine Viewer window

In this window, you can reconnect to a virtual machine if the connection is lost, send a Ctrl+Alt+Delete keystroke to the guest OS (which you can also do by pressing Ctl+Alt+End), or switch to full-screen mode. To leave full-screen mode, click the Restore Down icon on the standard Remote Desktop toolbar. The Type clipboard text command (also available with the Ctrl+V keyboard shortcut) pastes the host's Clipboard contents to the virtual machine. Note that closing the Virtual Machine Viewer doesn't power off the virtual machine. It continues running in the background until you power it off.

Activity 6-8: Interacting with a Virtual Machine

Time Required: 10 minutes

Objective: Interact with a virtual machine.

6

Requirements: Completion of Activity 6-6

Description: In this activity, you start the virtual machine you created in Chapter 5 by using the Virtual Machine Viewer.

1. If necessary, log on to the host computer with your assigned administrative username and password. Double-click the **Virtual Machine Manager Console** desktop icon to open the VMM Console.

2. Click the **VMs and Services workspace** in the lower left, and then click the **All Hosts** node. Click **VMs** under Show in the ribbon.

3. In the results pane, click the **Windows Server 2016** virtual machine.

4. Click **Power On** from the ribbon under the Virtual Machine tab to start the virtual machine.

5. Click **Connect or View** from the ribbon, then click **Connect via Console** from the menu to open the Virtual Machine Viewer window.

6. When you see the "Press Ctrl+Alt+Delete to unlock" prompt, click **Ctrl-Alt-Del** on the toolbar and log on.

7. Close the Virtual Machine Viewer window. At the bottom of the results pane in the VMM Console, note under Virtual machine information that the virtual machine is still running.

8. Click **Shut Down** from the ribbon to power off the virtual machine. In the warning dialog box that opens, click **Yes** to continue.

9. It might take a minute or two for the virtual machine to shut down safely, and then its status changes to Stopped. Leave the VMM Console open for the next activity.

The Fabric Workspace

The **Fabric** workspace, as shown in Figure 6-9, manages the servers, networking, and storage resources that make up the infrastructure to deploy private clouds.

The Servers node allows you to select a VMM host and power it up or down remotely, as well as restart or reset it. The server can be placed in maintenance mode, with the virtual machines either moved to another host in the cluster or put in a saved state and suspended. A host can be added to a host group or removed from a cluster, and you can open a Remote Desktop connection to the server.

Figure 6-9   The Fabric workspace

The Fabric ribbon contains the following commands by default while on the Servers node:

- *Create*—In addition to services and virtual machines, a Hyper-V cluster can be created in the Fabric workspace allowing for high availability, keeping virtual machines online by shifting to a new host if their original VMM host stops responding.

- *Add Resources*—Add additional resources, such as Hyper-V and VMware ESX hosts and clusters, VMware vCenter servers, and PXE, Library, and Update servers.

- *Compliance*—Show the compliance status of VMM servers, including if they have all Windows Update patches required as defined in a baseline when using Windows Server Update Services (WSUS).

- *Scan*—Perform a scan to check for any compliance changes.

- *Remediate*—When a machine is found to be non-compliant, Remediate gives the option to install the required updates, and also to override the baseline and not require a patch.

The Networking node manages the logical networks and switches used to create virtual machine networks, and all of the resources needed to build them, for example IP and MAC address pools, load balancers, and port profiles and classifications. The Fabric ribbon contains the following commands by default while on the Networking node:

- *Create Logical Network*—Create a logical network, a simplified way of representing a physical network by its purpose, for example the "Backend."

- *Create VM Network*—Create a virtual machine network, allowing for multiple networks to sits on top of a logical network with options for isolation.

- *Create IP Pool*—Create a pool of IP addresses, as well as gateways, DNS, and WINS servers that are available to logical networks. Pools can be assigned to specific host groups.

- *Create MAC Pool*—Create a pool of Media Access Control (MAC) addresses that uniquely identify network adapters and can be used when creating new virtual network devices.

- *Create VIP Template*—Create VIP (Virtual IP) templates used to configure hardware load balancers. The port the traffic will use is specified, and can either apply to any balancer or a specific model and maker.

- *Create Logical Switch*—Creates a logical switch, like a physical switch that routes traffic around the network, with much more customization possible beyond the external, internal, and private standard switches of Hyper-V.

The Storage node allows you to create custom classifications for different storage resources based on their performance, and organize storage space into units abstracted from the physical drives beneath, assigning them to different hosts. The Fabric ribbon contains the following commands by default while on the Storage node:

6

- *Create Storage Classification*—Create user-defined labels for different types of storage, typically based on performance. For example, you classify a mechanical hard drive "Bronze," an SSD "Silver," and a RAID "Gold."

- *Create Logical Unit*—A piece of a storage pool made up of a collection of physical disks, and defined only by name and size that can them be assigned to host groups.

- *Create File Share*—A file share can be created from a storage pool, local path, or volume. It can include resiliency, such as single or dual parity, and redundancy, such as two-way or three-way mirroring.

- *Create Storage QoS Policy*—Create Quality of Service (QoS) policies by assigning storage classifications to actual performance metrics, for example maximum bandwidth and IOPS (Input/Output Operations Per Second).

- *Allocate Capacity*—Allocate storage pools and logical units to VMM host groups.

The Library Workspace

The Library workspace, as shown in Figure 6-10, allows you to manage your library servers and their resources, such as templates, profiles, and virtual hard disks, and includes seven nodes. The Profiles node allows you to create and modify your application, guest OS, hardware, physical computer, SQL Server, and VM shielding profiles, which contain all of the configuration settings you can apply to a new virtual machine or template. For example, the **guest OS profile** is a collection of OS settings, such as product keys, passwords, and workgroups or domains and a **hardware profile** is a collection of hardware settings, such as amount of memory, processor requirements, and DVD drives.

The Equivalent Objects node allows you to designate resources, such as a common virtual hard disk file stored on different hosts at different sites, as equivalent so a single template can be used and VMM decides which equivalent resource to use based on the placement rules, for example location, in the profile or template. The Cloud Libraries node displays the resources available in private cloud libraries and are typically read-only to most users; they require administrators to make new resources available. In the Self Service User Content node users with the self-service user role can create their own resources, such as

Figure 6-10   The Library workspace

virtual hard disk files, ISO files, and templates, to build their own virtual machines and services.

The Library Servers node contains a list of all library servers managed by VMM, names of their library shares, and the virtual machines, profiles, and templates they contain. The Stored Virtual Machines and Services section can be used to store virtual machines that are not in use, and is also the default location where self-service user-created resources are stored. The Orphaned Resources section contains templates that reference resources that are no longer available to VMM because the library share they were located on has been removed. The Update Catalog and Baselines node stores resources associated with Windows Server Update Services (WSUS) when you use VMM to manage Windows OS updates, such as the baseline configurations specifying the updates required to be compliant and the update files themselves.

Although the ribbon is customized to show tasks available based on your current node, they all share the following commands:

- *Create Service Template*—Create a new service using the Service Template Designer.

- *Create VM Template*—Create a template used when deploying new virtual machines, configured individually or based on the pre-configured profiles for hardware, guest OS, and more (explained in "Creating a Virtual Machine Template").

- *Create*
  - *Application Profile*—Instructions to create Microsoft Server App-V, Microsoft Web Deploy, and Microsoft SQL Server applications.

- o *Capability Profile*—Defines which resources are available to a virtual machine, such as maximum memory, total number of processors, and types of virtual disk files allowed.

- o *Guest OS Profile*—Creates a profile containing OS settings that can be used with a template when creating a virtual machine (discussed in "Creating a Guest OS Profile").

- o *Hardware Profile*—Creates a profile containing hardware settings that can be used with a template when creating a virtual machine (covered in "Creating a Hardware Profile").

- o *Physical Computer Profile*—Creates a profile defining the hardware and OS when converting another physical computer on the network to a Hyper-V host.

- o *SQL Server Profile*—Creates a profile used when deploying a service with a customized SQL Server instance

- o *Baseline* – Creates a baseline, specifying the required Windows update a virtual machine must have to be compliant when using Windows Server Update Services.

- • *Add Library Server*—Create additional library shares on the VMM. The resources on the new share are added immediately, and then updated at the interval you specify with the Library Settings command.

- • *Import Template*—Import the template that was previously created on another VMM Management Server.

- • *Import/Export Physical Resource*—Transfer resources such as ISO images, scripts, virtual hard disks, answer files, and keys between the libraries of different VMM Management Servers.

- • *Import Shielding Data*—Import the encrypted Shielding Data file containing sensitive information used to shield a virtual machine by its creator.

- • *Library Settings*—Determine how often the library refreshes, indexing new files, which defaults to once an hour but can be disabled completely as well. You can refresh immediately with the Refresh button under the Folder tab on the ribbon.

When you click a template in the results pane, the Template tab on the ribbon adds the following options:

- • *Create Virtual Machine*—Create a virtual machine based on an existing virtual machine or a template in the library; you can use an existing virtual hard disk file or a new one.

- • *New VM Template*—This is the same as the command discussed previously.

- • *Disable/Enable*—Temporarily disable a file in the library so that it can't be used in new virtual machines, profiles, or templates. After it's disabled, you can use this command to enable the resource again.

- • *Delete*—Remove the virtual disk file from the library and physically delete the file from the server.

- • *Properties*—View the virtual disk file's settings, including size, capacity, installed OS, the virtualization software used to create it, and any dependencies.

When you click a virtual hard disk file in the results pane, the VHD tab on the ribbon is very similar to that used for templates above, but adds the following additional options:

- *Mark Equivalent*—Select multiple disk files and mark them equivalent so they can be used interchangeably.

- *Open File Location*—Open the Windows folder where library files are stored.

Creating a Hardware Profile As mentioned, a hardware profile is a collection of virtual hardware devices that make up a virtual machine. By using a profile, you can create virtual machines with the same hardware specifications easily, and you can maintain multiple profiles for different types of virtual machines. After entering the profile's name and description, you can configure the following settings and devices in the General and Hardware Profile tabs (see Figure 6-11):

Figure 6-11 The New Hardware Profile dialog box

- *Generation*—Choose between a first or second generation virtual machine. Second generation virtual machines support UEFI as well as newer virtualization features such as advanced security and more modern virtualized hardware devices. Only 64-bit guest operating systems are supported (generation one supports 32-bit or 64-bit).

- *Cloud Capability Profiles*—Specify if the profile will validate against the Hyper-V or ESX Server capability profiles.

- *Processor*—Specify the number of processors or cores the virtual machine uses, and whether it can be migrated to another host with a different processor version to compatibility.

- *Memory*—Specify the amount of memory assigned to the virtual machine, up to the maximum amount.

- *Floppy Drive*—Only available to generation one virtual machines, select a virtual floppy disk (.vfd) file or assign it to the physical floppy drive on the host.

- *Video Adapter*—Only available to generation one virtual machines, select between a standard video adapter, or a Microsoft RemoteFX 3D adapter allowing for multiple monitor support and setting a maximum resolution.

- *COM 1 and COM 2*—Only available to generation one virtual machines, this is a virtual COM port that communicates with the host through a named pipe (a method of accessing physical ports as though they're files) or over the network.

- *IDE Devices*—Only available to generation one virtual machines, this shows the total number of IDE devices connected to the virtual machine. You don't configure hard drives in the Hardware profile, only virtual DVD drives.

- *Virtual DVD drive*—By default, the hardware profile includes a DVD drive. A generation one virtual machine attaches the drive to the IDE bus, whereas a generation two uses a SCSI adapter. A DVD drive can be connected to a physical drive on the host or an ISO image in the library.

- *SCSI Adapters*—By default a single SCSI adapter is attached to the virtual machine, which will host virtual hard disk files once a virtual machine has been created based on the profile.

- *Network Adapters*—Select the network the virtual machine is connected to and the IP address it will use, either static or dynamic, as well as a static or dynamic MAC address.

- *Fibre Channel Adapters*—Configure adapters used for a Fibre storage area network (SAN). A SAN is high-speed network of storage devices like disk arrays or tapes that the operating system sees as a local device and is usually better at disaster recovery.

- *Checkpoints*—Enable or disable checkpoints and choose the type of checkpoints to be used, either the Standard checkpoint, which saves the current memory and disk states, including running applications, or Production checkpoint, which does not save running application but can be more reliable

- *Availability*—Choose if a virtual machine will be highly available; this places the virtual machine on a server that is part of a cluster. The priority the virtual machine is started or placed on a node can be set to either high, medium, or low.

- *Firmware*—Allows you to set the status of the Num Lock key at startup. On second generation virtual machines, Secure boot can also be configured to block unauthorized software and operating systems from running at boot.

- *CPU Priority*—Specify the priority the virtual machine has to the host's CPU: low, normal, high, or custom. Reserve control further refines this with minimum and maximum percent CPU cycle usage.

- *Virtual NUMA*—Non-Uniform Memory Access is a hardware architecture where a host PC's memory and processors are split up into nodes. By allowing spanning, a virtual machine can use memory from another node if its own node is full.

- *Memory Weight*—Similar to CPU Priority, but for memory, this helps VMM decide which virtual machines get priority access to memory when resources are low.

In addition to the basic hardware listed, you can add devices, such as network adapters or DVD drives, by clicking the New toolbar button. You can also remove devices from the profile by clicking the Remove toolbar button.

Activity 6-9: Creating a Hardware Profile

Time Required: 10 minutes

Objective: Create a hardware profile.

Requirements: Completion of Activity 6-7

Description: In this activity, you configure a hardware profile that you use later with a guest OS profile to create a virtual machine template.

1. If necessary, log on to the host computer with your assigned administrative username and password. Double-click the **Virtual Machine Manager Console** desktop icon to open the VMM Console.

2. Click the **Library** workspace in the lower left, and then click the **Profiles** node.

3. From the ribbon, click **Create**, then click **Hardware Profile** from the menu to open the New Hardware Profile dialog box.

4. In the General tab, type **Light-duty Hardware** in the Name text box and **This profile is for applications that don't require many resources and run in low priority** in the Description text box. Confirm Generation 1 is selected in the Generation dropdown list and then click the **Hardware Profile** tab.

5. In the General section, click **Memory** and type **2048** in the Virtual machine memory text box.

6. In the Advanced section, click **CPU Priority**, and then click the **Low** option button.

7. In the Advanced section, click **Memory Weight**, and then click the **Low** option button.

8. In the Bus Configuration section, click **Virtual DVD drive**. Record below which channel the drive is currently using.

   _____

9. Click **OK** to close the New Hardware Profile dialog box and create the profile. Make sure the profile is listed in the Library workspace under the Profiles node, and leave the VMM Console open for the next activity.

Creating a Guest OS Profile A guest OS profile is a collection of settings for customizing the OS. With a profile, you can reuse the same settings on other virtual machines easily. After entering the profile's name, description, and choosing the compatibility (Windows, Windows (Shielded), or Linux) in the General tab, you can configure the following settings in the Guest OS Profile tab, shown in Figure 6-12:

- *Operating System*—Specify the version of the OS used with this profile. Almost every version of Windows, starting with Windows XP, is supported, and you can select 32-bit or 64-bit editions.

- *Identity Information*—Specify the computer name. By default, it's an asterisk, which means the computer is assigned a random name. If you enter a name, you might want

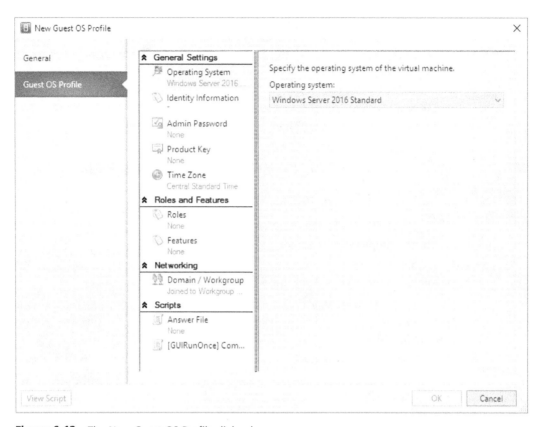

Figure 6-12   The New Guest OS Profile dialog box

to omit it from the network to prevent possible conflicts with other virtual machines on the network using the same name. You can also enter your name and organization to register the OS.

- *Admin Password*—Choose to have no administrator credentials be required, specify the local administrator's password, or use the credentials from a previously configured Run As account.

- *Product Key*—Enter the Windows product key; you can have this information supplied in the Sysprep answer file (if you use one).

- *Time Zone*—Specify your local time zone.

- *Roles*—Install server roles, such as Active Directory Domain Services or a DHCP server, automatically on virtual machines running Windows Server 2008 R2 or newer.

- *Features*—Install server features, such as the .Net Framework 3.5 or the Telnet client, automatically on virtual machines running Windows Server 2008 R2 or newer.

- *Domain/Workgroup*—A virtual machine can start in the default workgroup (called WORKGROUP), or you can specify an Active Directory domain for it to join. To specify a domain, supply the domain name and the username and password of a user account with the right to join domains.

- *Answer File*—Assign a Sysprep answer file for virtual machines running Windows XP or Server 2003 or an Unattend.xml file for virtual machines running Windows Vista or Server 2008 or newer. Answer files, which are optional, are scripts used to perform customized unattended installations of Windows.

- *[GUIRunOnce] Commands*—This setting specifies commands Windows should run the first time a user logs on. These commands customize the virtual machine by running additional applications or scripts or modifying the Registry.

Activity 6-10: Creating a Guest OS Profile

Time Required: 10 minutes

Objective: Create a guest OS profile.

Requirements: Completion of Activity 6-7

Description: In this activity, you configure a guest OS profile that you use later with a hardware profile to create a virtual machine template.

1. If necessary, log on to the host computer with your assigned administrative username and password. Double-click the **Virtual Machine Manager Console** desktop icon to open the VMM Console.

2. Click the **Library** workspace in the lower left, and then click the **Profiles** node.

3. From the ribbon, click **Create**, then click **Guest OS Profile** from the menu to open the New Guest OS Profile dialog box.

4. In the General tab, type **Windows Server 2016 Base** in the Name text box and **This profile is for Windows Server 2016 virtual machines not in a domain** in the Description text box, and then click the **Guest OS Profile** tab.

5. Click **Operating System**, and then click **Windows Server 2016 Standard** in the Operating system dropdown list.

6. Click **Admin Password**, and click the **Specify the password of the local administrator account** option button and type **Password01** in the Password text box and again in the Confirm text box.

7. Click **Product Key**. In the Product Key text box, type the Windows Server 2016 product key, if you have one; otherwise, type **11111-11111-11111-11111-11111**

8. Click **Domain/Workgroup**, and verify that the Workgroup option button is selected.

9. Click **OK** to close the New Guest OS Profile dialog box and create the profile. Make sure the profile is listed in the Library workspace under the Profiles node, and leave the VMM Console open for the next activity.

Creating a Virtual Machine Template A template is used to create virtual machines with a specific configuration. It can be combined with pre-configured specifications defined in hardware and guest OS profiles and a virtual disk file or another virtual machine in the library to create virtual machines for specific purposes.

To create a template, select the Library workspace, choose the Templates node and start the Create VM Template wizard with the Create VM Template button on the ribbon. In the Select Source window, you can select from two possible sources. The first is an existing template or virtual disk file in the library. A virtual disk file should have an OS installed, but the computer identification information should be removed with Microsoft's Sysprep tool. Sysprep doesn't run automatically when you select this option; you must run it manually.

The second source option is an existing virtual machine. If you use this option and the virtual machine is deployed on a host, the virtual machine no longer functions as a standalone virtual machine because VMM runs Sysprep automatically when creating the template, so its identification information is removed. If you select this option, you're prompted to make a clone of the virtual machine first. To do this, click Clone under Create after selecting the virtual machine in the VMs and Services workspace.

6

In the Identity window, enter the template's name and description. Next, in the Configure Hardware window, you specify virtual hardware devices for the template. All the options for creating a hardware profile are also available in this window. If the source is a virtual hard disk file, you can configure hardware devices in this window. If you selected a virtual machine as a source, these options are disabled. With either source, you can select a previously created hardware profile from the library in the dropdown list at the top. If you don't use an existing profile or modify an existing one, you can click the Save As toolbar button to add the new profile to the library for future use.

In the Configure Operating System window, select an existing guest OS profile from the library or create or modify one, saving it to the library if you want. This window includes all the options available when creating a guest OS profile.

If you selected a virtual disk file as the source, you proceed to the Summary window and don't have to select a library server or share path. Otherwise, the Select Library Server window is displayed, and you select a library server where you save virtual machines created with this template.

In the Select Path window, you specify the library share where you want to save virtual machines. After clicking browse, you can expand the tree view of each share and click the Explore directory link to open the Windows folder containing the share's files to see what else is stored there.

In the Summary window, review your selections. You can click the View Script button to see the script for creating this template, or click the Create button to run the new job and create the template.

Understanding Host Ratings When you select the host where you plan to deploy a virtual machine, the server is assigned a rating between zero and five stars that indicates how well the virtual machine will function on this host. The rating is determined by the resources the virtual machine needs and the available resources on the host (CPU use, free memory, disk I/O, and network utilization). These ratings are also used when VMM is determining whether virtual machines should be moved to other hosts to optimize performance.

Activity 6-11: Creating a Virtual Machine Template

Time Required: 30 minutes

Objective: Create a virtual machine template.

Requirements: Completion of Activities 6-9 and 6-10, a Windows Server 2016 virtual machine as created in Chapter 5

Description: In this activity, you create a template, using a cloned virtual machine.

1. If necessary, log on to the host computer with your assigned administrative username and password. Double-click the **Virtual Machine Manager Console** desktop icon to open the VMM Console.

2. Click the **VMs and Services** workspace in the lower left, and then click the **All Hosts** node.

3. In the results pane, click the **Windows Server 2016** virtual machine. Click **Create** from the ribbon, then click **Clone** from the menu to start the Create Virtual Machine wizard.

4. In the Identity window, type **Windows Server 2016–Clone** into the Virtual machine name text box, then click **Next**.

5. In the Configure Hardware window, click **Next**.

6. In the Select Destination window, confirm the Place the virtual machine on a host option button is selected as well as **All Hosts** from the Destination dropdown list. Click **Next**.

7. In the Select Host window, click the name of your VMM server. Note the host rating, and then click **Next**.

8. In the Select Path window, click **Next**.

9. In the Select Networks window, click **Next**.

10. In the Add Properties window, click **Next**.

11. In the Summary window, click **Create** to create the clone and close the dialog box. The Jobs dialog box shows the progress of this task, which takes several minutes. When it's finished, close this dialog box.

12. Click the **Library workspace** in the lower left, and then click the **Templates** node.

13. From the ribbon, click **Create VM Template** to start the Create VM Template wizard.

14. In the Select Source window, click the **From an existing virtual machine that is deployed on a host** option button, then click **Browse** to open the Select VM Template Source dialog box.

15. Click **Windows Server 2016–Clone** from the list. Click **OK** to close the dialog box, then click **Next**.

16. In the Virtual Machine Manager dialog box, review the warning message about user data being lost, then click **Yes** to continue.

17. In the Identity window, type **Windows Server 2016 Light-duty** in the VM Template name text box and **Created with Light-duty hardware and Windows Server 2016 Base profiles** in the Description text box, and then click **Next**.

18. In the Configure Hardware window, click **Light-duty hardware** in the Hardware profile dropdown list. Review the hardware settings, and then click **Next**.

19. In the Configure Operating System window, click **Windows Server 2016 Base** in the Guest OS profile dropdown list. Review the OS settings, and then click **Next**.

20. In the Select Library Server window, click the name of your VMM server and click **Next**.

21. In the Select Path window, click **Browse** to open the Select Destination Folder dialog box. Click **MSSCVMMLibrary** under your server. Click **OK** to close the dialog box, then click **Next**.

22. In the Summary window, review your settings, and then click the **Create** button.

23. The Jobs dialog box opens, showing the progress of your task, which may take several minutes. After it's finished, close this dialog box. The new profile should be listed in the Library workspace under the Templates node. Leave the VMM Console open for the next activity.

Creating a Virtual Machine from a Template With a template, you can generate virtual machines running guest OSs quickly. To create a virtual machine from a template, click the VMs and Services workspace and click Create Virtual Machine to start the Create Virtual Machine wizard. You can use an existing virtual machine, a template, a virtual hard disk, or a blank virtual hard disk file as the source. If you create a virtual machine from a template, you can change the hardware and guest OS options you selected when you created the template. However, if the source is an existing virtual machine or a virtual disk file, you can modify only the hardware settings. To use a virtual disk file as the source, it must be stored in the library.

After selecting the existing template option, select the source template from the library. In the Identity window, enter the virtual machine's name and description.

Next, in the Configure Hardware window, review the settings, which are based on the template you selected. However, you can change these settings, if necessary, and save them as a new hardware profile. You can also add hard disks to the virtual machine, which isn't possible when the template is created.

The Configure Operating System window also displays settings from the template, and you can create a profile based on any modifications you make here. You must enter a valid product key for the guest OS, or the creation of the virtual machine fails.

In the Select Destination window, you have the option of placing the virtual machine on a private cloud, a host, or storing it in the library. When creating a virtual machine from a template, you cannot use the last option.

In the Select Host window, you select the host for the virtual machine. If the new virtual machine exceeds the host's total resources, you must select another host. Unlike Hyper-V, VMM assumes that all virtual machines on a host run simultaneously, so you can't create a virtual machine if it exceeds the host's total resources when combined with other virtual machines, even if these virtual machines aren't currently running. Because each virtual machine created in Chapter 5 uses 1 GB memory and you're creating more in this chapter, you might need to specify a lower amount of memory per virtual machine. To adjust the memory setting for the Windows Server 2016 and Windows Server 2016 clone virtual machines, select them in the VMs and Services workspace and click Properties, Hardware Configuration.

In Configuration Settings, you can review values that will be used for your new virtual machine based on your template, for example the randomly generated computer name. In the Select Networks window, you assign each virtual network adapter to a virtual network, or you can leave adapters disconnected.

In the Add Properties window, you specify how the virtual machine responds when the host computer is turned on or off. Important servers can be started automatically, with an optional delay to make multiple virtual machines start in a specific order. By default, when the host shuts down, the virtual machine is put into a saved state.

Activity 6-12: Creating a Virtual Machine with a Template

Time Required: 30 minutes

Objective: Create a virtual machine with a template.

Requirements: Completion of Activity 6-11

Description: In this activity, you use the template that uses the hardware and guest OS profiles created earlier based on a clone of the Windows Server 2016 virtual machine to create a new virtual machine.

1. If necessary, log on to the host computer with your assigned administrative username and password. Double-click the **Virtual Machine Manager Console** desktop icon to open the VMM Console.

2. Click the **VMs and Services** workspace in the lower left, and then click the **All Hosts** node.

3. Click the **Create Virtual Machine** button on the ribbon to start the Create Virtual Machine wizard.

4. In the Select Source window, click the **Use an existing virtual machine, VM template, or virtual hard disk** option button, and then click **Browse**. In the Select Virtual Machine Source dialog box, under Type: VM Template, click **Windows Server 2016 Light-duty**. Click **OK**, and then click **Next**.

5. In the Virtual Machine Identity window, type **Grades Server** in the Virtual machine name text box, and **Grading Software: Windows Server 2016 Light-duty** in the Description text box, and then click **Next**.

6. In the Configure Hardware window, verify that the settings you configured for the Light-duty Hardware profile are listed, then click **Next**.

7. In the Configure Operating System window, verify that the OS is set to Windows Server 2016 and the product key and administrator password used are as configured in the guest OS profile (Windows Server 2016 Base). Click **Next**.

8. In the Select Destination window, verify that the Place the virtual machine on a host option is selected and the Destination dropdown list has **All Hosts** selected. Click **Next**.

9. In the Select Host window, click your VMM server, and then click **Next**.

10. In the Select Path window, verify that the default virtual machine path is C:\Program-Data\Microsoft\Windows\Hyper-V, and then click **Next**.

11. In the Configure Settings window, click **Operating System Settings** and type **GradesSrv** in the Computer name text box, then click **Next**.

12. In the Select Networks window, in the Virtual Network column and the Network Adapter 1 row, click the "**...**" button to change the setting to the name of the host's network adapter in the Select a VM Network dialog box, then click **OK**. Click **Next**.

13. In the Add Properties window, review the actions the virtual machine will take when the host starts and stops, and then click **Next**.

14. In the Summary window, review your settings, and then click the **Create** button. The Jobs dialog box opens, showing the task's progress (which will take several minutes). After the job is finished, close this dialog box.

During Step 1.7 in the Jobs dialog box, "Customize virtual machine," the process stalls if you aren't using a valid Windows product key. This is as far as you can proceed, and you need to cancel the job. Not having this virtual machine doesn't affect completing the remaining activities, however.

15. The virtual machine is created and listed in the VMs and Services workspace under the All Hosts node. Leave the VMM Console open for the next activity.

The Jobs Workspace

The Jobs workspace displays the status of all jobs over the past 90 days, and these jobs can be sorted and filtered. It contains two nodes: Running for active jobs, and History for those that have completed. Most tasks in VMM, from a simple library refresh to creating a virtual machine, run as a job in the background. You can use the Jobs workspace to open a job in a separate status window or monitor a job's progress. Clicking a job shows the status of each step in the details pane (see Figure 6-13). From the ribbon you can restart a failed job or cancel one that's currently running. Some jobs are completed successfully but marked as "Completed w/ Info." Clicking the Details tab displays a warning message and possible solutions for solving the problem. Hosts and virtual machines also have a Recent Job section in their details so that you can review the results of the most recent task.

The Settings Workspace

When you select the Settings workspace, the following nodes available (see Figure 6-14):

- *General*—Configure global VMM options related to the library, remote control, and diagnostics and usage data, among others.

- *User Roles*—Display the user roles available in each profile. You can add Active Directory user accounts to a role or create a new role with access to specific hosts and

Figure 6-13 The Jobs workspace

Figure 6-14 The Settings workspace

rights to certain virtual machine functions, such as creating virtual machines based on approved templates.

- *Run As Accounts*—Manage stored account credentials. Any time VMM requires the user to enter a login and password, a Run As account defined here can instead be chosen.

- *Servicing Windows*—Define a period of time when a resource will be unavailable, for example to perform regular maintenance or install updates. These windows can be assigned to hosts, virtual machines, or services.

- *Configuration Providers*—Display a list of configuration providers that are currently installed. These plugins allow the VMM to communicate with devices such as a load balancer.

- *System Center Settings*—View reports generated by System Center Operations Manager (a Microsoft tool for performance and event monitoring), if it's installed.

- *Console Add-ins*—Manage third-party add-ins that are designed to add additional features to the VMM Console, for example manage specific vendor hardware devices.

- *Microsoft Azure Site Recovery*—Configure settings related to Azure Site Recovery, which replicates virtual machines and handles failover in the event of a failure.

6

Also available within the Settings workspace is the Backup command. A SQL Server database stores all the configuration information VMM uses. Backing up this information in addition to virtual machines and files in the library helps prevent downtime resulting from a system failure. If you prefer, you can use a dedicated SQL Server backup utility, such as SQL Server Management Studio, instead of this backup function in VMM.

When you perform a backup, you're asked for a location to store it, either on a network share or a local computer that SQL Server can access. A restore function isn't built into the VMM Console. To recover a backup, run SCVMMRecover.exe (in the Bin subfolder of the VMM installation folder).

In the Settings workspace view, you can click General node to see several options in the results pane for configuring VMM global settings, described in the following sections.

- *Diagnostic and Usage Data Settings*—This program helps Microsoft improve its software by collecting information anonymously on how you use its products and your hardware and software configurations. This setting is configured when you install VMM Server, but you can use this option to opt into or out of the program at any time.

- *Database Connection*—You use this option to view information about the database storing VMM settings, such as the database server name instance name, and SQL Server database name (VirtualManagerDB, by default). These fields are for informational purposes only and can't be changed.

- *Library Settings*—VMM automatically checks library share locations once an hour for new files moved there manually (in other words, outside the VMM Console). You can enable or disable these checks and set the interval in hours at which the library is refreshed. To force an immediate update, use the Refresh button from the Folder tab in the Library workspace.

- *Remote Control*—You use this option to configure the VMConnect port used to provide desktop access to virtual machines.

- *Network Settings*—Choose how logical networks are matched, for example by DNS suffix or switch name, and the alternative if a match cannot be made. You can also enable or disable the automatic creation of logical networks when a host network adapter isn't assigned one.

- *Host Guardian Service Settings*—You can configure settings related to shielded virtual machines and guarded hosts such as the Key Protection Server URL and Code Integrity policies.

Configuring User Roles Clicking the User Roles node in the Settings workspace displays all roles available. By default, the only role is the Administrator role (based on the Administrator profile type), with domain administrator accounts as members. Users assigned this role have full access to all VMM resources. Other roles include Fabric Administrator (Delegated Administrator), which has access only to selected host and library servers. A Read-Only Administrator cannot modify any resources. A Tenant Administrator can manage their self-service users and create and manage their own virtual machines. Along with the Application Administrator (Self-Service User), they can be further refined to allow or prevent certain actions, such as starting or stopping a virtual machine or only creating virtual machines from templates. Clicking a role displays which user accounts are members. Table 6-2 shows which capabilities can be configured for each role.

Table 6-2   User role capabilities

	Fabric Admin (Delegated Admin)	Read-Only Admin	Tenant Administrator	Application Admin (Self-Service User)
Library Servers	X	X		
Networking			X	X
Resources			X	X
Permissions			X	X
Run As accounts	X	X		

To create a role, start the Create User Roles wizard by clicking Create User Role from the ribbon on the User Roles node of the Settings workspace. Enter a name and description, and then select which profile type the role is based on. You can't create new roles based on the Administrator profile type. You can only add new users to the existing Administrator role.

In the Members window, you specify which user accounts or groups in the domain you're adding to the new role. In the Select Scope window, select the cloud resources they will have rights to.

In the Library Servers window, access can be given to specific library servers. In the Networking window you can specify which virtual networks the role will be able to use.

In the Run As accounts window, a user can be given rights to use specified Run As accounts. You can also create a new Run As account directly from this step.

For roles based on the Delegated or Read-Only Administrator, you move to the Summary window next. For roles based on the Self-Service User and Tenant Administrator, you can configure permissions.

In the Virtual Machine Permissions window, you can give role members access to all virtual machine functions, or you can choose tasks from the following list:

- *Author*—Users can create virtual machine and service templates.

- *Checkpoint*—Users can create, merge, or optionally only restore previous checkpoints.

- *Deploy*—Users can create a virtual machine from virtual hard disks, or optionally only from templates.

- *Deploy shielded*—Users can create a shielded virtual machine.

- *Local Administrator*—Users can set the virtual machine's administrator password when creating a virtual machine, which gives him or her administrator rights.

- *Pause and resume*—Users can pause and resume a virtual machine.

- *Receive*—Users can receive resources from other self-service users.

- *Remote connection*—Users can connect to a virtual machine and interact with the guest OS.

- *Remove*—Users can remove a virtual machine, which deletes the configuration file.

- *Save*—Users can save virtual machines and services.

- *Share*—Users can share resources with other self-service users.

- *Shut down*—Users can shut down a virtual machine.

- *Start*—Users can start a virtual machine.

- *Stop*—Users can stop a virtual machine.

- *Store and re-deploy*—Users can store virtual machines into the library and later retrieve them.

Activity 6-13: Creating a User Role

Time Required: 10 minutes

Objective: Create a user role.

Requirements: Completion of Activity 6-7

Description: In this activity, you create a role based on the Self-Service User role and add your administrator account to it. This role will have access to the library server and most virtual machine tasks.

1. If necessary, log on to the host computer with your assigned administrative username and password. Double-click the **Virtual Machine Manager Console** desktop icon to open the VMM Console.

2. Click the **Settings** workspace in the lower left, and then click the **User Roles** node.

3. Click the **Create User Role** button on the ribbon to start the Create User Role wizard.

4. In the Name and description window, type **Developer** in the Name text box and **For debugging purposes** in the Description text box, and then click **Next**.

5. In the Profile window, click the **Application Administrator (Self-Service User)** option button, and then click **Next**.

6. In the Members window, click the **Add** button to open the Select Users, Computers, or Groups dialog box. In the Enter the object names to select text box, type **administrator**, click **OK** to close the dialog box, and then click **Next**.

7. In the Scope window, click **Next**.

8. In the Networking window, click the **Add** button to open the Select VM Networks dialog box. Click your network adapter, then click **OK**. Click **Next**.

9. In the Resources window, click the **Add** button to open the Add resources dialog box. Click **Windows Server 2016 Light-duty** under Type: VM Template, then click **OK**. Click **Next**.

10. In the Permissions window, click the **Select all** button. Click to clear the **Remove** and **Local Administrator** check boxes, and then click **Next**.

11. In the Run As accounts window, click **Next**.

12. In the Summary window, review your settings and then click the **Finish** button. The Jobs dialog box opens, showing the task's progress (which will take only a few seconds). After the job is finished, close this dialog box.

Chapter Summary

- Virtual Machine Manager consists of three major components: VMM Management Server, VMM Console, and VMM Local Agent.

- The pre-requisites to install VMM are a SQL Server 2012 or 2014, which requires the .Net Framework 3.5, and the Windows Assessment and Deployment Kit (ADK) for Windows 10. The server needs to be a member of Active Directory, and a special VMM service account should be created.

- VMM Management Server controls the core functions of Virtual Machine Manager and consists of the VMM Service, the Database Server service, and the library server, which consists of standard Windows network shares for storing virtualization resources (such as ISO images, templates, hardware and guest OS profiles, and virtual disk files).

- The VMM Console is used to perform administrative tasks, such as managing, creating, and deploying virtual machines, managing host and library servers, and working with configuration settings. It serves as a front end to cmdlets running in Windows PowerShell.

- Any host computer managed by VMM must have a VMM Local Agent installed to enable it to communicate with VMM.

- The VMM Console has the following workspaces: VMs and Services, Fabric, Library, Jobs, and Settings. Each workspace is further split into different nodes, and features a ribbon that shows relevant tasks to what's currently being worked on.

- The VMs and Services workspace is used to add, remove, create, configure, and monitor virtual machines and services on virtual machine hosts and in private clouds.

- A host rating, consisting of zero to five stars, determines how well a virtual machine will work on a new host. These ratings also determine whether virtual machines should be moved to other hosts to optimize performance.

- The Fabric workspace contains the infrastructure needed to share storage devices over the network: the servers, networking, and storage resources.

- The Library workspace stores all the virtualization resources VMM uses. You can use this workspace to configure guest OS and hardware profiles; create and modify virtual machine templates; access ISO files, virtual disk files, and virtual machine files; and add library servers and library shares.

- A hardware profile is a configuration file used to create virtual machines; it contains hardware settings for a virtual machine's processor, amount of memory, and other hardware settings.

- A guest OS profile is a configuration file used to create virtual machines; it includes settings such as the computer name, OS product key, and administrator password.

- A template is used to create virtual machines with a specific configuration. You can select a virtual disk file or an existing virtual machine as the template source. Templates can also be combined with hardware and guest OS profiles.

- When creating a template, you must run the Microsoft Sysprep tool on the virtual disk file or virtual machine to remove the computer identification information. Sysprep runs automatically when an existing virtual machine is the template source, so make sure you create a clone of the virtual machine before selecting it as the source.

- In the Jobs workspace you can monitor, restart, and stop jobs and see the results of jobs. A job is based on a script that runs cmdlets. The details pane shows each step of a job along with its status.

- You use the Setting workspace to configure global VMM settings, such as user roles, and Run As accounts.

- You can add Active Directory user accounts to a user role or create a new role with access to specific hosts and rights to certain virtual machine functions. By default, the only user role is Administrator, with domain administrator accounts as members. Other roles include Fabric Administrator (Delegated Administrator), Read-Only Administrator, Tenant Administrator, and Application Administrator (Self-Service User). Administrators can specify which tasks the last two groups of users are allowed to perform.

Key Terms

cmdlets	job	VMM Console
database server	library server	VMM Local Agent
Fabric	template	VMM Management Server
guest OS profile	Virtual Machine Manager (VMM)	
hardware profile		

Review Questions

1. Which of the following is a workspace in the VMM Console? (Choose all that apply.)

   a. Library

   b. Fabric

   c. Servers

   d. Jobs

2. Which setting can't be configured in a hardware profile?

   a. Processor

   b. Hard drive

   c. Memory

   d. Virtual DVD drive

3. Which of the following statements about templates is true? (Choose all that apply.)

   a. They can be created with a hardware profile.

   b. They can be created with a guest OS profile.

   c. They can be created from a virtual disk file in the library.

   d. They can be created from a virtual disk file on a host.

4. Which resource can't be stored in the library?

   a. VMM configuration

   b. ISO image

   c. Virtual machine

   d. Virtual disk file

5. Which user roles can be assigned permissions to only perform specific tasks? (Choose all that apply.)

   a. Fabric Administrator (Delegated Administrator)

   b. Tenant Administrator

   c. Application Administrator (Self-Service User)

   d. Read-Only Administrator

6. Which of the following statements about host ratings are true? (Choose all that apply.)

   a. Ratings are set as one through five stars.

   b. Ratings can be weighted based on CPU, memory, disk I/O, and network use.

   c. Ratings can use load balancing as a determining factor.

   d. Ratings can use resource management as a determining factor.

7. Which of the following is *not* a valid user role?

    a. Administrator

    b. Application Administrator (Self-Service User)

    c. Domain Administrator

    d. Fabric Administrator (Delegated Administrator)

8. When creating a template with an existing virtual machine as the source, you can't configure hardware devices during the template creation. True or False?

9. Which VMM component can be installed on a Windows 10 computer?

    a. VMM Management Server

    b. VMM Console

    c. VMM Local Agent

    d. Library server

10. VMM can manage virtual servers created with which of the following virtualization products? (Choose all that apply.)

    a. Microsoft Hyper-V

    b. Citrix XenServer

    c. Oracle VirtualBox

    d. VMware ESX Server

11. Which of the following is *not* a prerequisite for installing VMM?

    a. Windows ADK

    b. Microsoft .NET Framework 3.5

    c. Hyper-V

    d. SQL Server 2014

12. Which of the following fixes can you attempt when using the Repair action? (Choose all that apply.)

    a. Ignore the error.

    b. Retry the last job that failed.

    c. Return to a previous state before the failed job.

    d. Delete the damaged object.

13. What does the Sysprep tool do?

    a. Defragment a virtual disk file.

    b. Remove unique identification information from a computer.

    c. Convert a physical computer to a virtual machine.

    d. Move a virtual machine from one host to another.

14. Which of the following isn't a permission that can be assigned to a User Role?

    a. Author

    b. Local Administrator

    c. Initialize

    d. Remote connection

15. Which of the following is *not* a component of VMM Server?

    a. VMM Service

    b. Library server

    c. Configuration server

    d. Database server

16. Which of the following are profile types that can be created? (Choose all that apply.)

    a. Hardware

    b. SQL Server

    c. Capability

    d. Features

17. Which of the following is *not* a setting in a guest OS profile?

    a. IP address

    b. Computer name

    c. Product key

    d. Time zone

18. Windows PowerShell uses which of the following?

    a. Scriptlets

    b. Cmdlets

    c. Commandlets

    d. Powerlets

19. Which port does VMM Server use to communicate with the VMM Console?

    a. 80

    b. 8080

    c. 8100

    d. 443

20. At what interval does VMM scan for changes in library shares?

    a. Every 30 minutes

    b. Once an hour

    c. Every 12 hours

    d. Once a day

Case Project

Case Project 6-1: Creating Hardware Profiles

Superior Technical College has started using VMM to manage its virtual servers and wants to create templates to make deploying virtual machines easier. The administrator has asked you to write a report recommending hardware profiles that can be used to create templates for deploying the new DHCP server, file server, SQL Server database server, and Web server. Write a report, explaining your reasons for choosing certain hardware profiles for these virtual servers.

6

chapter 7

Working with VMware vSphere

After reading this chapter and completing the exercises, you will be able to:

- Describe the vSphere versions and how they fit into the VMware products
- Install and configure vSphere components including the ESXi hypervisor and vSphere Client and virtual machine remote console
- Create and configure virtual switches
- Configure ESXi storage options and perform data store backups
- Create and configure virtual machines
- Manage virtual machines and ESXi Hosts

The race is on with VMware in the lead, but Microsoft is rapidly gaining ground with Hyper-V being part of its popular Windows Server releases. With each release, Microsoft continues to improve its product making it more competitive with VMware's vSphere. In Chapter 4 you learned why virtualization and hyperconvergence of resources are playing a major role in today's data centers and how VMware and Microsoft are offering competitive products and services that meet these data center virtualization needs. Hyper-V is the basis of Microsoft's data center virtualization software, and in Chapters 5 and 6 you have been able to work with Hyper-V to perform a variety of virtualization tasks. As you learned in Chapter 1, starting in 1998 VMware was the first company to offer commercial virtualization software and has been the leader in developing and marketing innovative and advanced virtualization features ever since. Today, vSphere is the foundation of VMware's data center virtualization products, and in Chapter 4 you had the opportunity to download and install the free version of vSphere and the vSphere Client. In this chapter you will continue to build on your vSphere knowledge and skills by using the vSphere Client to configure and work with the free ESXi hypervisors in order to create, configure, and manage virtual machine environments. In Chapter 8 you will plan and implement a multi-host vSphere environment using the licensed version of vCenter Server along with the vSphere Web client.

Planning a vSphere Installation

Having practical experience learning a new technology, such as through internships while you're a student, enhances your ability to learn the topic. In this book you will gain some practical experience with vSphere 6 by playing the role of a student intern for the fictitious Universal AeroSpace (UAS) Corporation. By helping to set up vSphere for this company's virtual data center, you'll learn how to apply virtualization by gaining hands-on experience hyperconverging services and resources.

For the purposes of this book we will assume that UAS is a small manufacturing firm founded in late 1990s to design and manufacture specialized parts for the aerospace industry. The company's strength has been designing and manufacturing components using high-strength alloy materials.

As a result of a proposal drafted by the Sales and Engineering Departments, the corporation was recently awarded a contract with a major space exploration company to design and build components for their re-usable manned spacecraft. As a result of this contract, Universal AeroSpace has been expanding its operation, including hiring additional design engineers and office staff. Assume that currently UAS employs about 25 people in the manufacturing facility, 5 engineers, and another 15 people in the sales and business office. In the past they have been outsourcing their Web services, but now plan to host their own Web site on a Linux server as well as use a Windows server for their business applications and data. While they are willing to accept a few hours downtime in the event of a computer failure, UAS management wants to be able to continue operations of both the Web site and business server within a couple hours. To reduce the cost of having additional technical staff, UAS has selected your company to set up and maintain its IT system. Your supervisor has designed the system shown in Figure 7-1, which uses the free version of vSphere to meet the initial needs of their virtualized data center. As shown in the diagram, the virtual data center will contain two ESXi hosts that

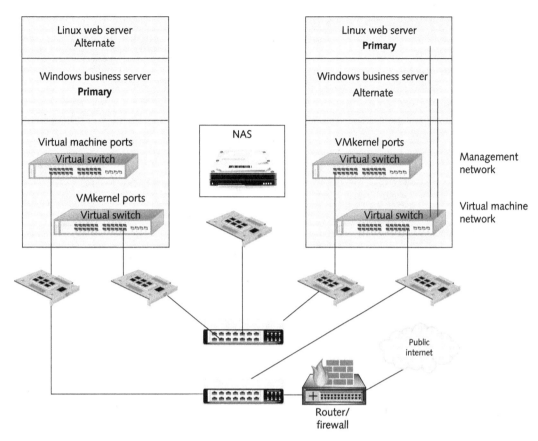

Figure 7-1   Universal AeroSpace virtual data center design

will be used to run their Windows and Linux server environments. In addition Universal AeroSpace will be using one of its older servers as a NAS device. Having two ESXi hosts and a shared NAS will enable the company to move the virtual machines between hosts to help maintain operations whenever one of the host computers is down or needs upgrading. Notice that there are two networks, one for the management and NAS data and the other for virtual machine user traffic. Separating the network helps improve reliability, security and performance. In Chapter 8 you will learn how to add a virtual machine to the management network switch as well as how to migrate the virtual machines between hosts. Your first task will be to use VMware Workstation 12 Player to create a test or sandbox environment to develop, test, and demonstrate the feasibility of the data center plan.

vSphere ESXi Hypervisor Installation and Configuration

In Chapter 4 you downloaded and installed the free version of vSphere ESXi hypervisor and then used the vSphere Client to review the default ESXi host's configuration. As in Chapter 4, in this section we will continue to use VMware Workstation 12 Player to practice working with vSphere. Using VMware Workstation 12 Player gives you the ability to create a virtual "sandbox" that can be used to learn about vSphere without the need for extra computers and network equipment. The major disadvantage to using VMware Workstation 12 Player is that by default it limits the virtual machines on the ESXi host to using 32-bit guest operating systems. For this reason we will be using Windows 10 as our guest operating system for testing purposes. In this section you will continue to build on your vSphere skills by installing two ESXi hypervisors and then learn how to use the command line environment to access and configure your ESXi hosts. If you have not done so, you should perform Activities 4-1 and 4-8 from Chapter 4 to install and configure your initial ESXi host.

Activity 7-1: Installing the Universal AeroSpace ESXi Servers

Time Required: 30 minutes

Objective: Install two ESXi free hypervisors within VMware Workstation 12 Player for the Universal Aerospace virtual data center.

Requirements: Completion of Activity 4-1

Description: VMware Workstation 12 Player is a convenient way to set up and test vSphere virtual data center environments. In this activity you will use the free vSphere hypervisor you downloaded in Chapter 4 to install two vSphere hosts for use in setting up and testing the UAS vSphere data center.

1. If necessary, start your Windows workstation and start VMware Workstation 12 Player.
2. Click **Create a New Virtual Machine.**
3. Click the **Installer disk image file (iso)** option, and click the **Browse** button.
4. Navigate to the folder where you stored the ESXi server file downloaded in Activity 4-1 and select the ESXi iso file.
5. Click **Next** to display the Name the Virtual Machine screen. Type **UAS-vHost1-xxx** (where xxx represents your initials) as the default server name and click **Next.**
6. In the Specify Disk Capacity window, change the default of 40 GB to **120 GB,** then click the **Store virtual disk as a single file** option and then click **Next.**
7. Verify that the Power on this virtual machine after creation option is checked and then click **Finish** to start the installation process. During the installation VMware Player will display a message line at the bottom of the screen informing you to install the ESXi server as you would on a physical machine and that you need to click in the virtual screen to send keystrokes.
8. If you see the Removable Devices dialog box, you may click the **Do not show this hint again** option and then click **OK.**
9. After installing the hypervisor files, you will see the Welcome to VMware ESXi 6.0 Installation message box. Click the **I Finished Installing** button from the VMware Workstation 12 Player message line.
10. Click anywhere in the ESXi VM window to transfer the keyboard control to the ESXi VM. A message will be displayed informing you to press Ctrl+Alt to return the keyboard to your local computer.

11. Press **Enter** to continue and display the license agreement.

12. Press **F11** to accept the license agreement and start the scanning process to find a local disk drive.

13. When you see the Select a Disk to Install or Upgrade window, press **Enter** to accept the local disk drive selected by the scanning process and continue.

14. Choose your keyboard layout, or press **Enter** to accept the US Default keyboard and continue.

15. In the Enter a root password window, enter a password you want to use for the "root" user twice. Record the password you use below:

_____

Since ESXi is based on the Linux kernel, it uses the default name "root" for the administrative user.

16. After entering the password twice, press **Enter** to complete the scanning process and display the Confirm Install message box. When you see the Confirm Install message box, press **F11** to continue the installation process. This process may take a few minutes, so you may wish to take a quick stretch.

17. When the installation process finishes, the Installation Complete message box will be displayed. If you are using DVD media, you should now remove the DVD from the drive. If you are using an ISO file, press Ctrl+Alt to return to the Windows desktop, click the **Player** menu, point to **Manage**, and click the **Virtual Machine Settings...** option. Click the **CD/DVD** setting and then change the connection to the Use physical drive option and click **OK**.

18. Click in the virtual machine window to return mouse and keyboard control to the ESXi virtual machine and press **Enter** to reboot the ESXi host.

19. When the host restarts, press **F2** to display the Authorization Required dialog box.

20. Leave the Login Name as "root," press the **Tab** key, type the password you recorded in step 15, and press **Enter** to log on and display the System Customization menu shown previously in Chapter 4, Figure 4-8.

To reduce overhead and provide maximum performance, the ESXi 6.0 hypervisor does not have a GUI interface, but instead works with what is called the DCUI interface (described in the following section). You will be using the DCUI menu to establish the Management network in later activities.

21. Press the **Esc** key to exit the System Configuration menu. To shut down the ESXi host, press **F12**, and then confirm you are the root user by entering your password as described in step 20.

22. Press the **F2** key to properly shut down the host.

23. Repeat steps 1 through 22 to install a second ESXi host VM named **UAS-vHost2-xxx** (where xxx represents your initials).

    Record the password you used for your UAS-vHost2-xxx host below:

    _____

24. This completes this activity. You may leave your VMware Workstation 12 Player instances running for the next activity.

Working with the ESXi Consoles

There are a number of client options for working with the vSphere environment. The ESXi host has a very minimal user interface in order to increase the hypervisor's performance and security. The two major console interfaces used to work with an ESXi host are the **Direct Console User Interface (DCUI)** and the vSphere remote command line interface (vCLI). DCUI is a text-based menu environment that you used in Chapter 4 to initially set up your first ESXi host. While the DCUI menu is easy to use when performing basic configuration, it requires working directly from the ESXi console and is limited in management options. While the vCLI client allows managing the host from another computer, the command line environment is very cryptic and difficult to use. To perform more complex configuration and management activities VMware provides two GUI consoles: the vSphere Client and the Web client. You downloaded, installed, and used the vSphere Client in Activity 4-8 of Chapter 4 to view the configuration of your ESXi host.

 You will be using the vSphere Client to perform most of the activities in this chapter. If you have not done so, perform steps 1-6 of Activity 4-8 to install the vSphere Client on your local computer.

The Web client provides an HTML-based console you can use from remote locations to perform management functions. The Web client requires connecting to a Web server running on a host computer. Since the basic ESXi host does not run a Web server, using the Web client requires installing the licensed version of vSphere which includes a Web service built into the vCenter Server. In a more complex or licensed vSphere data center the vCenter Server plays the central role of managing the vSphere ESXi hypervisors. When using vCenter Server, the Web client will first connect to vCenter Web server and then it will manage access to the individual hosts as shown in Figure 7-2.

You will learn how to install and use vCenter Server and the Web client to manage a licensed multi-host vSphere environment in Chapter 8.

As mentioned earlier, the VCLI client is a way to directly manage an ESXi server from another computer using text-based or DOS commands. Table 7-1 shows some VCLI commands and their usage.

An ESX/ESXi system grants access to its resources when a known user with appropriate permissions logs on to the system with a password that matches the one stored for that user. The vicfg-user command supports creating, modifying, deleting, and listing local direct

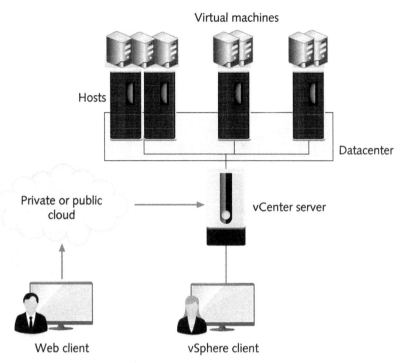

Figure 7-2   Web client and vCenter Server

Table 7-1   Sample VCLI commands

Command	Description	Options
vicfg-user <options>	Creates, modifies, deletes, and lists local direct access users and groups of users	**--addgroup | -g <group_list>** Comma-separated list of groups to add the user to. **--adduser | -u <user_list>** Comma-separated list of users to add to a specified group.
vicfg-ipsec	Supports setup of IPSec	**--add-sa <sa>** Adds a security association. Use this option together with the --sa-src, --sa-dst, --sa-mode, and other parameters to create a security association. The last parameter is always the name of the association. **--add-sp <sp>** Adds a security policy. Use this option together with the <--sp-src>, --sp-dst, --src-port, --dst-port and other parameters to create a security policy. You must associate this policy with a named security association. The last argument is always the name of the security policy.
vicfg-vmknic	Adds, deletes, and modifies virtual network adapters (VMkernel NICs)	**--add | -a** Adds a VMkernel NIC to the system. You must specify the IP address using --ip, the netmask, and the port group name. When the command completes successfully, the newly added VMkernel NIC is enabled. You cannot specify the dvsName and dvportId parameters with this option. **--delete | -d <port_group>** Deletes the VMkernel NIC on the given port group. The port group name is the same as the VMkernel NIC name.

(continues)

Table 7-1   Sample VCLI commands (*continued*)

Command	Description	Options
vicfg-vswitch	Adds or removes virtual switches or vNetwork Distributed Switches, or modifies switch settings	**--add | -a <switch_name>** Adds a new virtual switch. **--add-pg | -A <portgroup> <vswitch_name>** Adds a port group to the specified virtual switch.
vmkfstools	Creates and manipulates virtual disks, file systems, logical volumes, and physical storage devices on ESX/ESXi hosts	**--help** Prints a help message for each command-specific and each connection option. Calling the script with no arguments or with --help has the same effect. **--vihost | -h <esx_host>** When you execute a vCLI with the --server option pointing to a vCenter Server system, use --vihost to specify the ESX/ESXi host to run the command against.

access users and groups of users on an ESX/ESXi host. You cannot run this command against a vCenter Server system. The following command would add a user with login ID user27:

vicfg-user <conn_options> -e user -o add -l user27 -p 27_password

Before you can use vCLI, you need to download and install the client on another computer or virtual machine. Working with the vCLI client is outside the scope of this book, but your instructor may assign an optional activity to download and install the vCLI client.

Configuring the Virtual Network Environment

Now that the ESXi hosts have been installed, the next step will be to establish the virtual network environment. As shown previously in Figure 7-1, UAS is planning to have two separate physical networks, one for the management and NAS, and the other for virtual machine data and communications.

Configuring Virtual Switches

The fundamental component of a virtual network is the virtual switch. As described in Chapter 4, the virtual switch is a software component within the hypervisor's VMkernel that provides networking connectivity for virtual machines as well as handling the hypervisor's traffic including management and network storage operations. vSphere provides both standard and distributed virtual switch types. Standard switches exist only within a single vSphere hypervisor. Distributed switches can be shared among multiple associated vSphere hosts, providing consistent network configuration, such as IP address and gateway, when a virtual machine is transferred between hosts using vMotion.

Using distributed switches requires the licensed version of vCenter Server. You will work with vCenter Server to implement a distributed switch in Chapter 8.

Traffic is handled through the virtual switch by using port groups. As illustrated previously in Chapter 4, Figure 4-11, virtual switches have three types of ports: virtual machine ports, VMkernel ports, and uplink ports.

Virtual machine ports are used to handle traffic between virtual machines and between virtual machines and the physical network. Virtual machine ports can be divided into port groups to separate traffic and provide more control options.

When using distributed switches, port groups are shared among all associated hosts.

VMkernel ports include the management network port used to connect to remote consoles such as the vSphere Client, as well as ports for network storage, vMotion migration, and fault tolerance. Each VMkernel port must be configured with its own IP address and gateway. Uplink ports are used to connect one or more physical network adapters to the virtual switch. While a virtual switch does not need to be uplinked to the physical network, two virtual switches cannot share the same physical network adapter. When two or more physical network adapters are connected to the same switch they can be "teamed" using network policies to increase performance and provide fault tolerance in case one network adapter or physical switch fails. Figure 7-3 shows an example of five different virtual switch configurations.

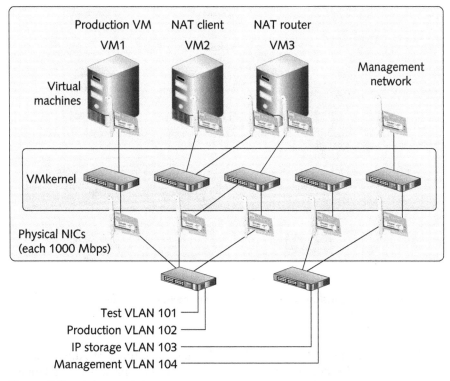

Figure 7-3   vSphere switch types

Starting from the left, the first switch shows an example of a standard virtual switch with a single physical adapter connected to the uplink port. This switch is being used only by VM1.

The next switch is an internal-only standard virtual switch, which is not uplinked to any physical network. This switch allows virtual machines in a single ESXi host to communicate directly with other virtual machines connected to the same standard virtual switch. For example, VM2 and VM3 can use this switch communicate with each other. The third example shows two physical adapters teamed to a single switch in order to provide automatic distribution of packets with a failover policy that maintains the physical connection in the event an uplink port is not working. In this example, VM2 can communicate to the outside world by using VM3 as its NAT gateway. Switch 4 is an example of a standard virtual switch that is used by the VMkernel for accessing iSCSI or NAS-based storage. The rightmost or fifth switch is a standard virtual switch that is used by the VMkernel to allow remote management capabilities.

You can use the vSphere Client to create, remove, or change switch properties. By default a standard virtual switch has 120 ports, but you can modify this number to increase it up to a maximum of 4,088. As shown in Figure 7-4, you can also use the vSphere client to view or change the speed and duplex properties of the physical adapter.

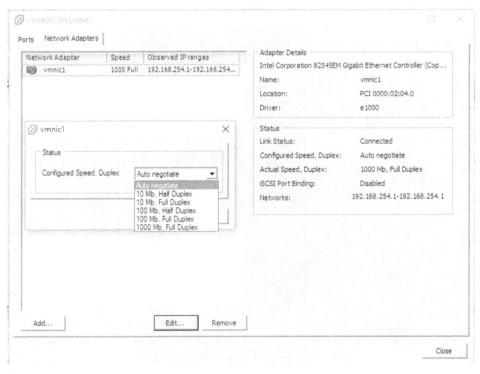

Figure 7-4 Changing the physical adapter properties on the host computer

Source: VMware

If using a Gigabit Ethernet adapter you should leave these settings at Auto negotiate as they are part of the latest IEEE 802.3 Ethernet standard. Since Gigabit Ethernet adapters are now common equipment on most host computers you should rarely need to modify this setting.

Virtual switches also support VLAN tagging as described in Chapter 4. VLANs can be configured at the port group level, allowing you to separate virtual machines into different broadcast domains in order to achieve increased performance and security. When using VLANs on your virtual switches, one of the host's physical network adapters must be defined as a static trunk port on the physical switch. The **trunk port** is used by the physical switch to pass packets from multiple VLANs to the host using VLAN tags. Once the packets arrive at the host the host will use the tag to send the packet to the appropriate port group. No VLAN configuration is required in the virtual machine as the ESXi host will handle tagging and untagging packets as they go through the virtual switch.

The design of our virtual network depends on many factors, which include how much physical network equipment is available, how much network bandwidth is required for the virtual machine applications, and whether to use networking features such as NIC teaming and VLANs. Because the virtual networking environment rests on the physical network infrastructure, as a vSphere administrator you will need to discuss your networking needs and plan with your network administration team.

As you can see from Figure 7-1, the UAS network plan involves two separate physical networks, one for normal data traffic and the other for use by management and network storage. To gain more experience with virtual switches and configuring a management network, in the following activities you will configure the management network on both hosts.

7

Activity 7-2: Adding a Management Network Adapter

ACTIVITY

Time Required: 10 minutes

Objective: Use the VMware Player console to add a second adapter to your ESXi hosts.

Requirements: Completion of Activity 7-1

Description: The first step in setting up a vSphere data center is to configure the ESXi hosts to use the management network. In order to set up a test or sandbox environment using VMware Workstation 12 Player, we will simulate the network environment by using the NAT network adapter switch for the Management network. In this activity you will add a second NAT adapter to your ESXi virtual machines for the management network.

1. If necessary start your Windows workstation and start VMware Workstation 12 Player.

2. Click on the **UAS-vHost1-xxx** virtual machine from the Home pane, then click **Edit Virtual Machine Settings** link to display the Virtual Machine Settings Hardware tab window.

3. Next, you will add a second NAT network adapter that will be used for the virtual machine network. Click the **Add** button, then select **Network Adapter** from the Add Hardware Wizard Hardware Type options and click **Next** to display the Network Adapter Type window. To allow the virtual machines to directly access the physical network, if necessary click to select the **NAT** option and click **Finish** to add the second NAT adapter. and return to the Virtual Machine Settings Hardware tab window.

4. Click **OK** to save your changes and return to the VMware Player main window.

5. Repeat steps 2-4 for your UAS-vHost2-xxx ESXi host.

6. Leave your VMware Workstation 12 Player open for the next activity.

Activity 7-3: Configuring the ESXi Host Management Network

Time Required: 15 minutes

Objective: Use the DCUI console to configure management networks on ESXi hosts.

Requirements: Completion of Activity 7-2

Description: Now that you have configured the virtual hardware environment for both your host virtual machines, in this activity you will use the DCUI console to configure both your virtual ESXi hosts to use the second NAT adapter for the management network.

1. Start your UAS-vHost1-xxx ESXi host, click in the VM window, and press **F2**. Log on using your "root" user account and password. The System Customization menu will be displayed.

2. Use the down-arrow key to select the **Configure Management Network** option and press **Enter** to display the Configure Management Network window as shown in Figure 7-5.

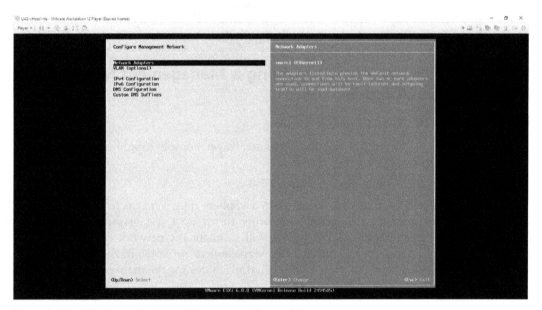

Figure 7-5 ESXi Host - Configure Management Network Menu

Source: VMware

3. With **Network Adapters** selected, press **Enter** a second time to display the available network adapters. Using this page you can select one or more adapters for your management network. Having multiple adapters helps to provide fault tolerance and load balancing for the management network.

The first and second adapters in the list correspond to the first and second network adapters listed in the VMware Workstation Player's Virtual Machine Settings, Hardware tab window.

4. Press the space bar to remove the check from the first adapter (vmnic0) and then use the down arrow to move to the second, vmnic1 adapter. Press the spacebar to toggle on the check mark on the second (vmnic1) adapter.

5. Press Enter to save your changes and return to the Configure Management Network menu.

6. Use the down arrow to select the **IPv4 Configuration** option and press Enter.

7. Use the down arrow to select the **Set static IPv4 Address** option and press the spacebar.

8. Use the down arrow to select the IPv4 address, then press the right arrow key, press backspace key to delete the last octet of the address and then enter 141. Press **Enter** to save your settings and return to the Configure Management Network menu. Record the IPv4 address information below:

   IPv4 Address: _____

   Subnet mask: _____

   Default gateway: _____

9. Press **Esc** and then press the **Y** key to save your changes and return to the System Customization menu.

10. Select the **Restart Management Network** option and press **Enter**. Press **F11** to restart the network. Press **Enter** to return to the System Customization menu. Record the IP address assigned to your UAS-vHost1-xxx host on the line below:

    IP Address of your UAS-vHost1-xxx host: _____

11. Press **Esc** to close the System Customization menu.

12. Press **Ctrl+Alt** to return control to your Windows 10 workstation.

13. Start another copy of VMware Workstation 12 Player (the free VMware Player can only run one VM at a time).

14. Start your UAS-vHost2-xxx host, press **F2**, and log on using your "root" user account and password. The System Customization menu shown previously in Chapter 4, Figure 4-8 will be displayed.

15. Repeat steps 2-11 to configure the management network on your UAS-vHost2 ESXi host system using **142** as the last octet of the IP address. Record the IP address for your UAS-vHost2 system below:

    IP Address of your UAS-vHost2-xxx host: _____

16. Press **Ctrl+Alt** to return control to your Windows 10 workstation.

17. Open a Command Prompt and enter the command: **Ping ip_address** (where ip_address is the address you entered for your UAS-vHost1 system in step 8). Record your results below:

    _____

    Enter the command: **Ping ip_address** (where ip_address is the address you entered for your UAS-vHost2 system in step 15). Record your results below:

    _____

    Your ESXi hosts are now ready to work with. You may leave your ESXi hosts and VMware Player running. In the following activity you will use the vSphere Client on your Windows computer to work with virtual switch configuration.

Activity 7-4: Working with Virtual Switches

Time Required: 20 minutes

Objective: Use the vSphere Client you installed in Activity 4-8 to set up the virtual switch structure on your UAS hosts.

Requirements: Installation of vSphere Client from Chapter 4, Activity 4-8 and completion of Activity 7-3

Description: Now that you have configured the management network on both your ESXi hosts, in this activity you will use vSphere Console to create a new switch and then configure the virtual switches to remove virtual machine traffic from the Management switch and configure the virtual machine port groups on the new virtual machine switch.

1. From your Windows desktop, launch the vSphere Client.

2. When you see the VMware vSphere Client login window, enter the IP address of your UAS-vHost1-xxx system you recorded in step 8 of Activity 7-3, the username **root**, the password you used for your UAS-vHost1-xxx host, and then click **Login**. When you see the Certification Warning dialog box, click **Ignore** to sign in and then if necessary click **OK** to close the evaluation license dialog box and display the vSphere Client Getting Started page.

If you receive the Security Warning dialog box, click to check the Install this certificate and do not display any security warnings for *ip_address* and then click Ignore to continue. You will receive a 60 day expiration warning, this is common for the free version and the evaluation license will not expire. Click OK to continue.

3. Click the **Configuration** tab, and then click the **Networking** option from the left Hardware pane to display the existing virtual switch.

4. Click the **Properties** option located on the right side of the Standard Switch: vswitch0 to display the Ports screen as shown in Figure 7-6.

5. To remove the virtual machine data network from this management switch, click the **VM Network** option, click **Remove**, and then click **Yes** when you see the confirmation dialog box. Click **Close** to return to the Networking Configuration tab.

6. You should now have only one VMkernel port on vswitch0 with vmnic1 as the physical adapter.

7. Click the **Properties** link to the right of your vSwitch0, then click the **Management Network** configuration and record the Port Properties in the space below:

Network Label: _____

VLAN ID: _____

vMotion: _____

Management traffic: _____

iSCSI port binding: _____

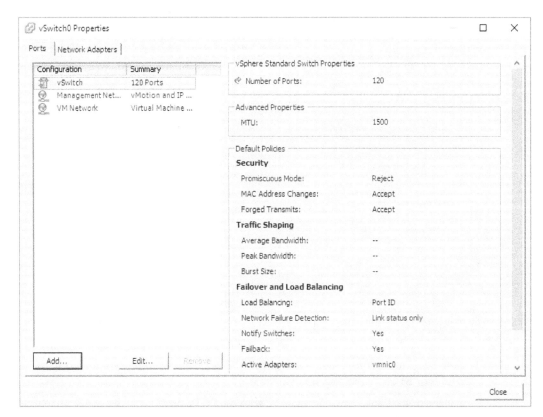

Figure 7-6 vSphere client networking configuration port screen

Source: VMware

8. Click **Close** to return to the Configuration page.

9. To create a new standard switch for virtual machine data and communications, click the **Add Networking** option on the right side of the Networking window to display the Connection Type window. Verify that the **Virtual Machine** connection option is selected and then click **Next** to display the Virtual Machines–Network Access window.

10. Verify that the **Create a vSphere standard switch** option is selected and that the switch will be connected to the vmnic0 network. After verifying the configuration, click **Next** to display the Port Group Properties window. Record the data below:

    Network label: _____

    VLAN Id: _____

11. Click **Next** to display the Ready to Complete window. Verify the configuration of your VM Network switch and then click **Finish** to create the switch and display the Networking Configuration window as shown in Figure 7-7. Verify that the Management Network switch is displayed and that it contains only one VMkernel Port.

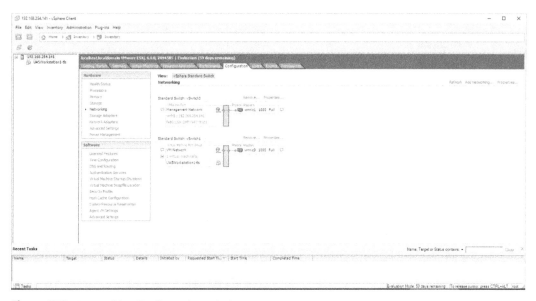

Figure 7-7   Networking Configuration window

Source: VMware

12. You have now completed configuring the virtual switches on UAS-vHost1-xxx. Click **File, Exit** to close the vSphere Client.

13. Repeat steps 1 through 12 to configure your UAS-Host2-xxx switches to match the ones you configured for your UAS-vHost1 host.

14. This completes Activity 7-4. If you like you may leave your vSphere Client active to work with virtual switch policies in the next section. If you have completed your sessions at this time, close vSphere Client and power down your ESXi host by clicking in the host's virtual machine console, pressing **F12**, and entering your root username and password. You can then press **F2** to safely power down your UAS-vHost2-xxx virtual machine.

Virtual Network Switch Policies

Virtual network **switch policies** allow the administrator to set up rules and procedures to manage how virtual network resources are used. Virtual switches provide for three types of network policies: security, traffic shaping, and NIC teaming. These policies can be defined for the entire virtual switch, or can be defined for individual ports or port groups including the VMkernel ports. When a policy is defined for an individual port, the settings of the policy will override the default policy defined for the virtual switch.

Security Policy   Security policies can be defined at both the standard virtual switch level and the port group level. Remember that security policies defined at the port group level override switch-based policies. The network security policy allows the administrator to set the following security exceptions:

- *Promiscuous Mode*—When set to Reject, placing a guest adapter in promiscuous mode has no effect on which frames are received by the adapter (default is Reject).

- *MAC Address Changes*—When set to Reject, if the guest attempts to change the MAC address assigned to the virtual NIC, it stops receiving frames (default is Accept).

- *Forged Transmits*—When set to Reject, the virtual NIC drops frames that the guest sends, where the source address field contains a MAC address other than the assigned virtual NIC MAC address (default is Accept).

In general, these policies give you the option of disallowing certain behaviors that might compromise security. For example, a hacker might use a promiscuous mode device to capture network traffic for unscrupulous activities. Or someone might gain unauthorized access by spoofing a device's MAC address in order to impersonate the node. You can set Promiscuous Mode to Accept in order to use a network monitor application in a virtual machine that analyzes or sniffs packets, such as a network-based intrusion detection system (IDS) as described in Chapter 4. Set MAC Address Changes and Forged Transmits to Reject in order to help protect against certain attacks launched by a rogue guest operating system which has spoofed the MAC address of another device. You may need to leave MAC Address Changes and Forged Transmits at their default value of Accept if you are running applications that change the mapped MAC address, as do some guest operating system-based firewalls.

Traffic-Shaping Policy Traffic-shaping policies are used to help prioritize network traffic in order to ensure time sensitive applications such as VOIP get the necessary bandwidth. The ESXi host shapes only outbound traffic by establishing parameters for three traffic characteristics: average bandwidth, peak bandwidth, and burst size. Just as with security policies, you can establish a traffic-shaping policy at either the virtual switch level or the port group level with settings at the port group level overriding settings at the virtual switch level.

- *Average Bandwidth*—Establishes the number of kilobits per second to allow across a port, averaged over time. The average bandwidth is the allowed average load.

- *Peak Bandwidth*—The maximum number of kilobits per second to allow across a port when it is sending a burst of traffic. This number tops the bandwidth that is used by a port whenever the port is using its burst bonus.

- *Burst Size*—The maximum number of kilobytes to allow in a burst. If this parameter is set, a port might gain a burst bonus if it does not use all its allocated bandwidth.

Whenever the port needs more bandwidth than specified in Average Bandwidth, the port might be allowed to temporarily transmit data at a higher speed if a burst bonus is available. This parameter tops the number of kilobytes that have accumulated in the burst bonus and thus transfers at a higher speed.

NIC Teaming Policy NIC teaming policies enable you to determine how network traffic is distributed between adapters and how to reroute traffic in the event of an adapter failure. NIC teaming policies include load-balancing and failover settings. While default NIC teaming policies are set for the entire standard switch, these default settings can be overridden at the port group level. The policies shown are what is inherited from the settings at the switch layer. At the port group level for Production, you can select one of the policy exceptions and override the default selection. In the following activity you will explore the teaming policy as well as work with other security policy settings.

Activity 7-5: Working with Network Policies

Time Required: 15 minutes

Objective: Use the vSphere Client you installed in Activity 4-8 to configure and view network policies.

Requirements: Installation of vSphere Client from Activity 4-8 and completion of Activity 7-5

Description: To help manage network traffic, management at UAS would like you to set up the following policies on both of the ESXi hosts:

- Reject Promiscuous Mode and all MAC address changes and forged transmits on the VMkernel Management and VM network switches.
- Document NIC teaming and Traffic Shaping options on the Management switch.
- Add a port group to the virtual machine switch that has the promiscuous mode. This port group will be used to connect an Intruder Detection network monitor application.

1. If necessary launch VMware Workstation 12 Player and start your UAS-vHost1-xxx virtual machine.
2. If necessary, from your Windows desktop, launch the vSphere Client, and sign in to your UAS-vHost1-xxx host as described in step 2 of Activity 7-4.
3. Click the **Configuration** tab and then click **Networking** from the left Hardware pane to display your virtual switches.
4. Click the **Properties** link to the right of your management switch (vSwitch0) to display the Properties window as shown previously in Figure 7-6.
5. Click to select the **Management Network** port group and then click the **Edit** button to display the Properties page.
6. Click the **Security** tab to display the security policy settings and, if necessary, change the policies to **Reject** Promiscuous Mode, **Reject** the MAC Address Changes, and **Reject** Forged Transmits as shown in Figure 7-8.
7. Next, click the **Traffic Shaping** tab and record its status along with the parameters you can change below:

   Status: _____

   Parameters that can be changed: _____

8. Click the **NIC Teaming** tab and record the Active adapters, Failback setting, and Load balancing information below:

   Load balancing:

   _____

   Failback:

   _____

   Active and Unused adapters:

   _____

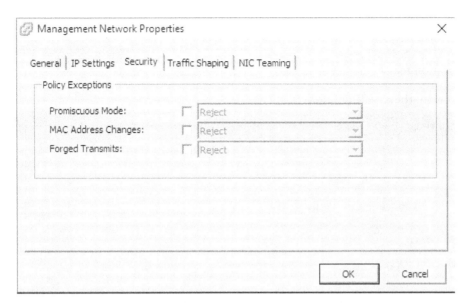

Figure 7-8   Vswitch0 Management Network security policies

Source: VMware

9. Click **OK** to close the window and then click **Close** to return to the Networking window displaying both your switches.

10. Click the **Properties** button to the right of your new VM Network virtual machine switch (vSwitch1).

11. To add a new port group click the **Add** button, verify that the Virtual Machine connection type is selected, and then click **Next** to display Port Group Properties frame. Change the label to **Promiscuous ports** and then click **Next** to display the Ready to Complete window.

12. Verify the settings and then click **Finish** to complete the operation, and then click **Close** to return to the Networking window.

13. Follow the procedure you used in step 6 of this activity to change the security policy on the Promiscuous ports group to accept promiscuous mode and reject the other policies.

14. Click **OK** to save your changes and return to the Networking Configuration window.

15. Repeat steps 1-14 to configure the switches on your UAS-vHost2 ESXi server.

16. You have now completed the activities in this section.

17. You can now close your vSphere Client and properly shut down your ESXi virtual machines.

Working with Virtual Machines

As you have learned in preceding chapters, a virtual machine is a set of virtualized hardware on which a supported guest operating system and its applications run through the use of the hypervisor, making the guest OS unaware that it is running on virtualized hardware. The use of a uniform hardware environment makes the virtual machine portable across vSphere hosts. The vSphere ESXi hypervisor configures the virtual machine's environment using a number of configuration files as described in Table 7-2.

Table 7-2   Virtual machine configuration files

Configuration file	Description
VM_name.vmx	Virtual hardware configuration information
VM_name.vswp	Swap file used to swap memory pages for the virtual machine when it is running
VM_name.nvram	BIOS file
VM_name.log	Log files for the virtual machine
VM_name.rdm.vmdk	Raw Device Map (RDM) pointer file
VM_name.vmdk	Disk descriptor file
VM_name-_vmdk	Disk data file
VM_name.vmss	Snapshot state file
VM_name.vmsd	Snapshot data file

The VMware ESXi host stores these files in a data store located on the local host's hard drive or on a shared network drive. When naming virtual machines, it is best to avoid using special characters, including spaces, in the virtual machine name as this can interfere with the hypervisor's access to the configuration files.

If the virtual machine is converted to a template, a virtual machine template configuration file (.vmtx) replaces the virtual machine configuration file (.vmx).

If the virtual machine has more than one disk file, the file pair for the second disk file and later is named <VM_name>#.vmdk and <VM_name>#-flat.vmdk, where # is the next number in the sequence, starting with 1. For example, if the virtual machine named Test has two virtual disks, this virtual machine has the files Test.vmdk, Test-flat.vmdk, Test_1.vmdk, and Test_1-flat.vmdk.

Six of the archive log files are maintained at any one time. For example, -1.log to -6.log might exist at first. The next time an archive log file is created (for example, when the virtual machine is powered off and powered back on), the following occurs. -2.log to -7.log are maintained (-1.log is deleted), then -3.log to -8.log, and so on.

A virtual machine can have other files such as snapshot files when snapshots are taken, raw device mapping (RDMs are described in the next section) files, or a change tracking file if the VM is backed up with the VMware Data Recovery appliance A virtual machine may also have a lock file if it resides on an Network File System (NFS) data store.

Virtual Hardware Components

The virtual machine environment consists of a number of virtualized hardware components that are configured in the virtual machine files including CPU, memory, virtual disk, and network interface card.

When you create a new virtual machine, the vSphere Client interface will provide a default memory size for your virtual machine at the time it is created. This memory size can be changed later up to a maximum memory size of a virtual machine running on the free vSphere hypervisor of 4 TB. Depending on the design of CPU on the host computer, virtual machines running on the free vSphere hypervisor can have up to 8 virtual CPUs (vCPU). The licensed version can have up to 128 vCPUs. Since many guest operating systems and applications are not enhanced by adding additional CPUs, creating virtual machines with multiple CPUs is the exception rather than the rule.

Most virtual machines have at least one virtual disk. When you add the first virtual disk, the virtual machine wizard implicitly adds a virtual SCSI adapter for its disk interface. The ESXi host offers a choice of adapters: BusLogic Parallel, LSI Logic Parallel, LSI Logic SAS, and VMware Paravirtual. The Virtual Machine Creation wizard in the vSphere Client selects the type of virtual SCSI adapter, based on the choice of guest operating system.

Although you can select to place a virtual disk in an alternate location, by default the virtual disk file is given the name of the virtual machine with the .vmdk extension and stored in the same folder as the other virtual machine configuration files. Typically you would select a VMFS data store to hold the new, blank virtual disk, and specify the disk's size. When creating a virtual disk, three virtual disk types are available. The defaults are Thick Provision Lazy Zeroed, Thick Provision Eager Zeroed, and Thin Provision. A special disk mode called "independent" exists. The independent mode has two options: persistent and nonpersistent. As described in Chapter 1, a persistent disk preserves any changes made while the virtual machine was running whereas with a nonpersistent disk all changes made during a session are discarded.

The other major virtualized hardware component is the virtual machine's network adapter. Based on the guest operating system you select, the following network adapter options might be available for your virtual machine:

1. *Flexible network adapter*—This functions as a vlance adapter if VMware® ToolsTM is not installed in the virtual machine and functions as a vmxnet driver when VMware Tools is installed in the virtual machine:

   - *vlance*—An emulated version of the AMD 79C970 PCnet32 LANCE NIC, an older 10 Mbps NIC with drivers available in most 32-bit guest operating systems, except Windows Vista and later.

   - *vmxnet*—A virtual network adapter that has no physical counterpart, this adapter is optimized for performance in a virtual machine. Because operating system vendors do not provide built-in drivers for this card, you must install VMware Tools to make available a driver for the vmxnet network adapter.

2. *e1000, e1000e*—e1000 is an emulated version of the Intel 82545EM Gigabit Ethernet NIC, with drivers available in most newer guest operating systems, including Windows XP and later and Linux versions 2.4.19 and later. It is the default adapter type for virtual machines that run 64-bit guest operating systems. e1000 is required for VLAN guest tagging support. e1000e is an emulated version of the Intel 82574L Gigabit Ethernet NIC. Whether the e1000 driver or the e1000e driver is loaded depends on the physical NIC adapters that are used.

3. *vmxnet2 (Enhanced vmxnet)*—The vmxnet2 adapter is based on the vmxnet adapter. But the adapter provides high-performance features commonly used on modern networks, such as jumbo frames and hardware off-loads.

4. *vmxnet3*—The vmxnet3 adapter is the next generation of a paravirtualized NIC designed for performance. It is not related to vmxnet or vmxnet2. The vmxnet3 adapter offers all the features available in vmxnet2 and adds several features, like multiqueue support (called Receive-Side Scaling in Windows), IPv6 offloads, and MSI/MSI-X interrupt delivery. vmxnet3 devices support fault tolerance and record/replay. This virtual network adapter is supported only for a limited set of guest operating systems and is available only on virtual machines with hardware version 7.

While the virtual CPU, virtual memory, virtual disk, and NIC are the minimum requirements for most virtual machines, often it is important to access other devices such as a virtual CD/DVD drive, a USB port, as well as some other generic device such as tape backup systems, plotters, and scanners.

Just as in other virtualization platforms you have worked with, you can map the virtual machine's CD/DVD drive either to a physical drive or to an ISO file for your CD/DVD drive. An ISO file is a byte-for-byte copy of a CD or DVD that has been "ripped": its file system is copied byte-for-byte to the disk surface. These virtual CDs/DVDs can be accessed remotely and are usually faster than physical CDs/DVDs.

vSphere 6 supports USB 3.0 devices in virtual machines, allowing devices such as smart-card readers and flash drives to be attached. Since USB devices cannot be connected directly to the ESXi host computer, connecting a USB drive to your virtual machine requires connecting the USB device to a desktop computer running the VMware vSphere® Web Client application or the vSphere Client. The virtual machine can then access the USB device from the client computer.

Virtual Machine Consoles

Unlike virtual machines running on a type-2 hypervisor, vSphere virtual machines must be accessed from another computer or device. There are a few different ways to access the virtual machine in order to install and operate the guest operating system. The first way is by using the vSphere Client to connect to the ESXi host and connecting to the virtual machine's desktop. You would normally use this method to initially install the guest OS on the virtual machine. Once the guest is installed and running, you can connect to its desktop using a Remote Desktop connection (such as Microsoft's Remote Desktop Connection) or though the VMware View software. You will learn how to use VMware View to connect to virtual desktops in Chapter 9.

Creating Virtual Machines

You can use the Create New Virtual Machine wizard from the vSphere Client to create and manage virtual machines. To create a virtual machine using vSphere Client, select the New Virtual Machine option from your ESXi host's Inventory window. When the wizard starts it first asks you to select either a typical or custom installation. While the typical installation works for many basic VMs, the custom provides more options such as the number of vCPUs, number and type of virtual network adapters, and SCSI disk controller type. Selecting these options when you create the VM can save you time as compared to making changes later.

If you choose the typical configuration, the Create New Virtual Machine wizard prompts you for information such as virtual machine name, the location of the data store on which to store the virtual machine's files, the guest operating system to be installed into the virtual machine, and the size and type of the virtual disk file. You can select from the following three major virtual disk file types:

- *Thick Provision Lazy Zeroed*—Space required for the virtual disk is allocated during creation. Data remaining on the physical device is not erased during creation, but is zeroed out on demand at a later time on first write from the virtual machine.

- *Thick Provision Eager Zeroed*—Space required for the virtual disk is allocated during creation. Data remaining on the physical device is zeroed out when the disk is created. If you select this check box, this virtual machine can take advantage of VMware vSphere® Fault Tolerance (discussed in a later module).

- *Thin Provision*—A thin provisioned disk uses only as much data store space as the disk initially needs. If the thin disk needs more space later, it can expand to the maximum capacity allocated to it.

7

Table 7-3 identifies the differences between the virtual disk options including the time it takes to create the virtual disk type, how block allocation and zeroing is performed, and how the virtual disk would be laid out on disk.

Table 7-3   Virtual disk file types

	Thick (Lazy Zeroed)	Thick (Eager Zeroed)	Thin Provision
Creation time	Fast	Slow in proportion to disk size	Fastest
Block allocation	Fully preallocated	Fully preallocated	Allocated and initialized on demand after first write to a disk block.
Virtual disk layout	Higher chance of contiguous file blocks for faster access	Higher chance of contiguous file blocks for faster access	Layout varies according to dynamic state of host's volume
Zeroing of allocated blocks	File blocks are zeroed when disk is first written to	File blocks are allocated and zeroed out when the disk is created	File blocks are zeroed out as the blocks are allocated

Thin provisioning enables virtual machines to use storage space as needed, further reducing the cost of storage for virtual environments considerably. Thin provisioning is often used with storage array deduplication to improve storage use and to backup virtual machines. Thin provisioning can be configured to provide alarms and reports to track current usage of storage capacity as well as allowing a storage administrator to optimize the allocation of storage for virtual environments. As shown in Figure 7-9, when using thin provisioning

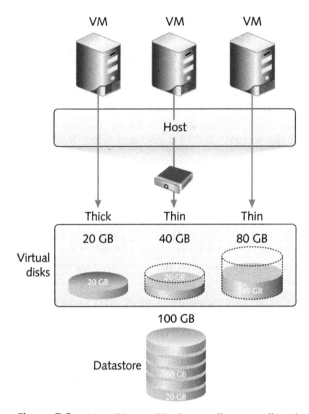

Figure 7-9   Using thin provisioning to allow overallocation of host disk space

administrators can make maximum use of available storage space by employing overallocation. **Overallocation** is the process of assigning more disk space to your virtual disks than you have space available on the VMFS data store.

If you choose the custom configuration, the Create New Virtual Machine wizard prompts you for more information, like the virtual machine version and specifics about the virtual hardware. The custom wizard also gives you the options of creating a new virtual disk, using an existing virtual disk, using no disk at all, or creating a **Raw Device Mapping (RDM)** connection.

Using the custom feature also allows you to set advanced options, such as enable and configure independent mode for disks. When using the independent disk mode the disk can be either persistent or nonpersistent, as shown in Figure 7-10. As mentioned earlier, the persistent option commits changes immediately and permanently writes them to the disk. The nonpersistent option discards changes when the virtual machine is powered off or reverted to a snapshot.

The Independent disk mode allows you to create either Persistent or Nonpersistent virtual disks. Nonpersistent virtual disks are useful when sharing a virtual machine among multiple users as any changes made by one user will not be saved and therefore will not affect other users of the virtual machine.

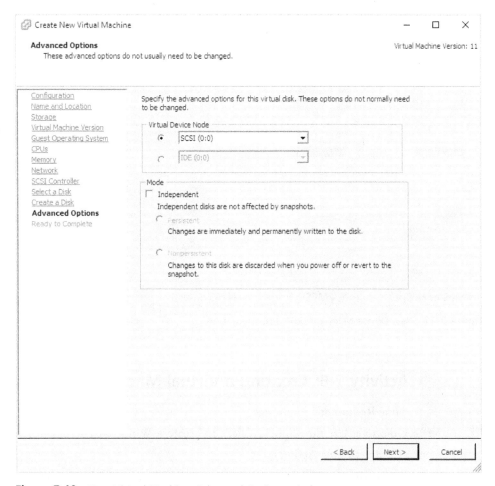

Figure 7-10 New Virtual Machine–Advanced Options window

Source: VMware

You will often need to add or configure virtual devices after creating the virtual machine. For example, you can attach an ISO image to the virtual CD/DVD drive after the virtual machine is created. These kinds of configuration settings can be managed from the virtual machine settings menus. You will learn how to perform these configuration settings in later activities.

As illustrated in Figure 7-11, a Raw Device Mapping is a file stored in a VMFS volume that acts as a proxy or go-between for a physical storage device.

Instead of storing virtual machine data in a virtual disk file stored on a VMFS data store, when using an RDM disk the guest operating system stores data directly on a the host computer's storage (local or SAN). Storing the data this way may provide faster data access and is useful if you are running applications in your virtual machines that must know the physical characteristics of the storage device. An RDM is recommended when a virtual machine must interact with data on the actual local disk on the SAN. This condition is the case when you make disk array snapshots or have a large amount of data that you do not want to move onto a virtual disk as part of a physical to virtual conversion.

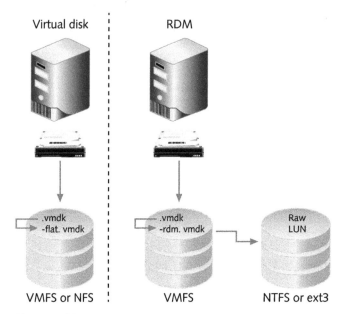

Figure 7-11 Raw Device Mapping (RDM) configuration

Activity 7-6: Creating a Virtual Machine

Time Required: 15 minutes

Objective: Use the vSphere Client to create a Windows 10 virtual machine.

Requirements: Completion of Activity 7-4

Description: To test the virtual data center you are building on VMware Workstation 12 Player, your next step will be to create virtual machines. In this activity you will use your vSphere Client to create a new Windows 10 virtual machine.

1. If necessary log on to your desktop computer and start VMware Workstation 12 Player.

2. Start your UAS-vHost1-xxx virtual machine.

3. From your Windows desktop, start the vSphere Client and sign into your UAS-vHost1-xxx host.

4. From the opening Inventory window, click the **Virtual Machines** tab to open the Virtual Machines window.

5. Right-click in the open space and click the **New Virtual Machine...** option to start the Create New Virtual Machine wizard.

6. Click to select the **Custom** option and then click **Next**.

7. In the Name text box enter **UASWorkstation1-xxx** (where xxx represents your initials) and click **Next** to display the Storage window showing the data store located on your host's local drive.

8. Click **Next** to select the default data store and display the Virtual Machine Version window.

9. Verify that the latest virtual machine version (11) is selected and then click **Next** to display the Guest Operating System window.

10. Click the **list arrow,** then scroll down and select the **Microsoft Windows 10 (32-bit) OS** and click **Next** to display the CPUs window.

Because by default an ESXi host running on VMware Player can only support 32-bit guest operating systems, in this activity we will create a 32-bit virtual machine.

11. Click **Next** to select just one vCPU for this virtual machine and display the Memory window.

12. If necessary, change the default memory to 1 GB and, then click **Next** to display the Create Network Connections window as shown in Figure 7-12.

Figure 7-12   Create New Virtual Machine – Network window

Source: VMware

13. Verify that only one E1000E virtual adapter is selected for use on the VM Network switch you created in Activity 7-4 and then click **Next** to display the SCSI Controller window. (If you have more than one virtual machine port group you can use the pull down menu to select the port group you want used by this virtual machine.)

14. Record the selected SCSI adapter type below and then click **Next** to display the Select a Disk window.

    LSI Logic SAS: _____

15. Verify that the Create a new virtual disk option is selected and then click **Next** to display the Create a Disk window.

    Click the **Thin Provision** option, change the disk capacity to 15 GB, verify that the virtual disk is stored in the same location as the other virtual machine files, and then click **Next** to display the Advanced Options window.

 If you do not have sufficient disk space for the size you specify for the VM's disk space, you will receive a warning message informing you that you are overcommitting the host's disk space. If you receive this warning message, click OK to continue.

16. Leave the default options as shown in the Advanced Options window and record the two options available under the Independent Mode setting on the line below. After recording the Independent Mode options, click **Next** to display the Ready to Complete window.

    _____

    _____

17. Verify your settings and then click **Finish** to create the new virtual machine and add it to the Virtual Machines window.

18. This completes Activity 7-6. You may leave VMware Player and your vSphere Client open for the next activities.

Activity 7-7: Installing a Guest Operating System

Time Required: 15 minutes

Objective: Use the vSphere Client to install the Windows 10 operating system.

Requirements: Completion of Activity 7-6. A copy of Windows 10 iso installation iso file

Description: To test the virtual data center your manager has told you to install a version of Windows 10 on the virtual machine you created. Since UAS is in the process of obtaining the latest version of Windows Sever, this will allow you to demonstrate the virtual data center. In this activity you will use Windows vSphere Client to access your virtual machine and install the Windows 10 operating system from an iso image file provided by your instructor (see the end of chapter projects to download the Windows 10 iso).

1. If necessary log on to your desktop computer and start VMware Workstation 12 Player.

2. If necessary, start your UAS-vHost1-xxx virtual machine and the vSphere Client and sign into your UAS-vHost1-xxx host. If necessary, click on the **Virtual Machines** tab of the Inventory window.

3. From vSphere Client Virtual Machines window, double-click your **UASWorkstation1-xxx** to select it and display a properties window and then click the **Summary** tab to display the virtual machine settings along with a Commands frame as shown in Figure 7-13.

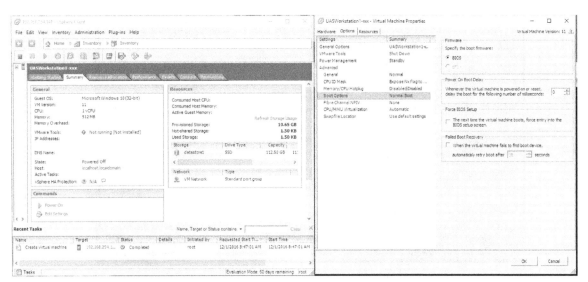

Figure 7-13 Virtual Machine Settings window

Source: VMware

4. To set your virtual machine's BIOS to boot from the CD drive, click the **Edit Settings** from the Commands frame, and then click **OK** when you see the Restricted Virtual Machine Settings dialog box. Next, click the **Options** tab and click **Boot Options** to display the boot options window. Click to place a check in the **Force BIOS Setup** section, and then click **OK** to save your settings and close the window (See Figure 7-13).

The Restricted Virtual Machine Settings dialog box informs you that the client has restricted editing capabilities on version 9 and higher VMs. This is due to using the free client, click **OK** to close the dialog box. This message will not be displayed when using the licensed version with the vCenter Server in Chapter 8.

5. Click the **Power On** option and as soon as the **Open Console** link appears in the Command pane, click it to open the console window and display the Phoenix BIOS Setup screen shown in Figure 7-14.

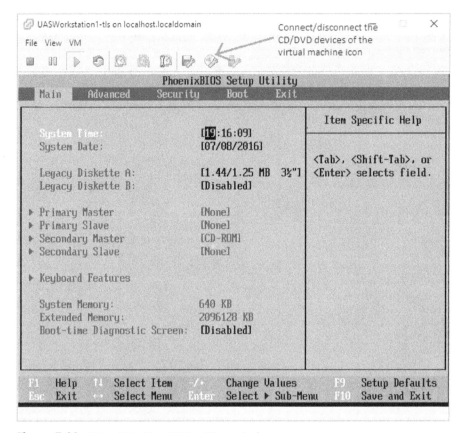

Figure 7-14 Virtual Machine BIOS settings window

Source: VMware

6. Press **Ctrl+Alt** to return control to your local desktop.

7. Click the **Connect/disconnect the CD/DVD devices of the virtual machine** icon and select the option to **connect CD/DVD drive 1 to an ISO image on the local disk**.

8. Browse to the folder containing your Windows 10 iso image file and click **Open** to select it.

9. Click in the virtual machine window and then use the arrow keys to select the **Boot** menu.

10. Use the down arrow to point to the CD-ROM device and then use the + key to move the CD-ROM drive to the top of the list.

11. Press **F10**, then press **Enter** to exit the Setup Utility and reboot your virtual machine. The Windows 10 installation process will start.

12. Perform a standard Windows 10 Pro installation and record any parameters you select along with your password in the space below:

_____

If you do not have a license key, select the Skip link and continue. You can enter a product key later or continue to use the evaluation copy for the length of the course.

13. After installation is complete, you can proceed to use this virtual machine to test your virtual network environment.

14. You may leave your vSphere Client open for the next activity.

Activity 7-8: Viewing Virtual Machine Settings

Time Required: 15 minutes

Objective: Use the vSphere Client to view and document virtual machine configuration parameters.

Requirements: Completion of Activity 7-7

Description: Now that the virtual machine is installed you next need to prepare a demonstration to UAS management. In this activity you will use the vSphere Client to view and document configuration parameters for the virtual machine you installed the Windows 10 guest OS on in Activity 7-7.

1. If necessary log on to your desktop computer and start VMware Workstation 12 Player.

2. If necessary, start your UAS-vHost1-xxx virtual machine and the vSphere Client and sign into your UAS-vHost1-xxx host.

3. If necessary, click the **Virtual Machines** tab from the main vSphere Client window.

4. Double-click your **UASWorkstation1-xxx** virtual machine to display the Summary tab window shown previously in Figure 7-13.

5. Click each of the tabs to view its settings.

6. Right-click your **UASWorkstation1-xxx** virtual machine from the left-hand pane and then click **Edit Settings** to display the Virtual Machines Properties window (if necessary, click **OK** to close the Restricted Virtual Machine Settings message box) as shown in Figure 7-15.

7. Notice that this windows is very similar to the VMware Workstation Hardware Settings window and allows you to change memory, CPUs, Network Adapters, and other hardware options. In this case, if necessary, edit the memory to 1 GB.

8. Click the Network Adapter and record the MAC address and adapter type below:

   MAC address: _____

   Adapter type: _____

   Network Connection: _____

9. Click the **Options** tab and then click **VMware Tools** link. Notice that VMware Tools are installed by default. In the Advanced section, click to select the **Check and upgrade Tools during power cycling** option.

10. Click **OK** to save your settings and close the Properties window.

11. This completes the activities for this chapter. Close your vSphere Client and use the **F12** key to properly power down your UAS-vHost1-xxx and UAS-vHost2-xxx virtual machines as described previously.

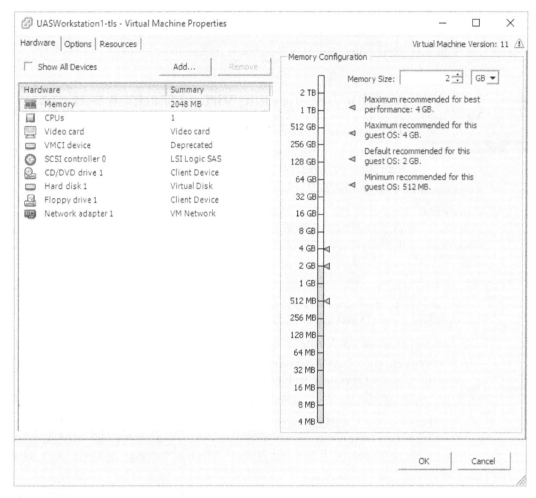

Figure 7-15   Virtual Machine Properties window

Source: VMware

In Chapter 8 you will continue to work with the UAS virtual data center you started in this chapter by installing the licensed version of vCenter Server and the vCenter Web client.

Chapter Summary

- VMware has been a leader in data center virtualization products since the 1990s, with vSphere the being the flagship data center virtualization product.

- VMware offers free versions of the vSphere hypervisor and client, which is a great way for a company to get started with the process of creating a software designed data center. The best way to learn about any new product or technology is to apply it in a business setting. In this chapter you have been introduced to vSphere by applying it to a simulated business situation using a sandbox environment created through the VMware Workstation 12 Player.

- The key components in setting up a virtual data center are establishing the network environment and creating virtual machines. In this chapter you worked with VMware Workstation 12 Player to create a network environment consisting of two simulated physical networks. You then used the DCUI client on the ESXi host to establish a network dedicated to management and VMkernel operations.

- The vSphere Client is the graphical user tool needed to configure and manage the virtual data center. In this chapter you were able to use vSphere Client to create and configure virtual network switches as well as apply network policies to increase security and enhance performance.

- In this chapter you learned about the many options that are available when planning virtual machines including CPUs, memory, virtual network adapters, and virtual disk types. The vSphere Client is also the tool needed to create and manage virtual machines.

- In this chapter you learned how to create and access a Windows guest virtual machine and configure its settings. In Chapter 8 you will continue your vSphere journey by using the vCenter Server to manage more complex virtual data center environments.

Key Terms

Direct Console User Interface (DCUI)	switch policies	Thin Provision
overallocation	Thick Provision Eager Zeroed	trunk port
Raw Device Mapping (RDM)	Thick Provision Lazy Zeroed	

Review Questions

1. Which of the following is a disadvantage of using VMware Player to host a "sandbox" vSphere virtual data center?
   a. vSphere hosts cannot access the local network.
   b. Virtual machines running on the ESXi hosts are limited to 32-bit guest OS.
   c. You need to install the 32-bit vSphere version.
   d. Virtual machines running on the virtualized ESXi hosts are limited to 4 GB of RAM.

2. Which of the following consoles are used on the ESXi host when installing the free vSphere ESXi host?
   a. vSphere Client
   b. VCLI
   c. DUCI
   d. Web Client

3. Which of the following consoles may be used by the free vSphere ESXi host? (Choose all that apply.)

   a. vSphere Client

   b. VCLI

   c. DUCI

   d. Web Client

4. Which of the following is a remote command line client?

   a. vSphere Client

   b. VCLI

   c. DUCI

   d. vClient

5. Which of the following are used for management of the ESXi host as well as for accessing shared storage?

   a. Distributed switches

   b. VMkernel ports

   c. Uplink ports

   d. System port groups

6. Which of the following is true about a standard virtual switch?

   a. It cannot be used for VMkernel traffic.

   b. It can be shared among multiple ESXi hosts.

   c. It can be connected to multiple NICs.

   d. It can share a NIC with another virtual switch.

7. Which of the following is true about using VLANs with virtual switches? (Choose all that apply.)

   a. VLANs require the use of distributed switches.

   b. It requires the guest OS to be VLAN aware.

   c. VLANs can be configured at the port group level.

   d. One of the Host's physical NICs must be defined as a static trunk port.

8. Which of the following virtual networks is configured using the DCUI client?

   a. VMkernel network

   b. Management network

   c. Virtual Machine network

   d. VLAN network

9. Which of the following is a network switch security policy?

   a. Firewall

   b. Burst mode

   c. Promiscuous mode

   d. NIC Teaming

10. Which of the following is NOT an option of the traffic-shaping network policy?

    a. Burst mode

    b. Promiscuous mode

    c. NIC teaming

    d. Peak bandwidth

11. Which of the following is a virtual machine virtual disk file?

    a. Windows10.vmx

    b. Windows10.vmhd

    c. Windows10.vmdk

    d. Windows10.vswp

12. Which of the following commands would be used to create a new group named Managers?

    a. vicfg-user

    b. vicfg-group

    c. viGrp-add

    d. vmkfstools-grp

13. By default a Windows guest VM will use which of the following types of disk adapters?

    a. SCSI

    b. VDI

    c. IDE

    d. SATA

14. Which of the following virtual network adapters is typically used by default when creating a virtual machine for use with Windows 8 or later operating systems?

    a. e1000

    b. vmxnet2

    c. vmxnet3

    d. vlance

15. Which of the following clients can be used to access a virtual machine's desktop? (Choose all that apply.)

    a. vSphere Client

    b. VMware View

    c. DCUI

    d. Remote Desktop

16. Which of the following clients is designed for use in Virtual Desktop Infrastructures?

    a. vSphere Client

    b. VMware View

    c. DCUI

    d. Remote Desktop

17. Which of the following disk types allows for virtual disk overcommitment?

    a. Persistent

    b. Lazy Zeroed

    c. Thin provisioned

    d. Independent

18. Which of the following disk types allows for persistent and nonpersistent disk types?

    a. RDM

    b. Lazy Zeroed

    c. Thin provisioned

    d. Independent

19. Which disk type allows the virtual machine to store data directly on the host's VMFS disk volume?

    a. RDM

    b. Lazy Zeroed

    c. Thin provisioned

    d. Independent

20. What is one of the first functions you need to do when installing a guest OS in a virtual machine from a local computer? (Choose all that apply.)

    a. Select the network adapter.

    b. Change the BIOS boot sequence of the virtual machine.

    c. Point the virtual CD drive to the location of the installation file on local computer.

    d. Point the virtual CD drive to the installation file on the host computer's VMHD.

Case Projects

Case Project 7-1: Downloading the Windows 10 ISO File

In order to test the data center on your VMware Workstation 12 Player "sandbox" your manager has asked you to download the Windows 10 iso file. You can then use the Windows 10 workstation to test the virtual machine environment prior to rolling it out on actual hardware using the Windows Server 2016.

Open a Web browser (Edge) to go to https://www.microsoft.com/en-us/software-download/windows10

Click the **Download tool now** button and download Windows 10 iso file to the folder you created in Activity 1-1.

Case Project 7-2: Installing a Third ESXi Host

Universal AeroSpace would like to have a third ESXi host system to provide the organization with more high availability and load balancing options in the future. In this case project you are to follow the process you learned in Activities 7-1 and 7-2 to create an ESXi host virtual machine named UAS-Host3-xxx (where xxx represent your initials). Your UAS-Host3 host should have a 100 GB hard drive and two NAT network adapters. Follow the procedure from Activity 7-3 to configure the Management Switch on your UAS-vHost3-xxx host to use the second NAT adapter with a host IP address "143" and record the following information:

IP Address of VMkernel Storage port: _____

IP Address of your UAS-vHost3-xxx host: _____

Subnet Mask: _____

Default Gateway: _____

Case Project 7-3: Creating a Second Virtual Switch for Virtual Machine Traffic for Universal AeroSpace Virtual Data Center

Follow the procedure you used in Activity 7-4 to create a new virtual switch on your UAS-vHost3 ESXi host and configure it to use the first NAT adapter. Record the following information:

Switch name: _____

Physical adapter: _____

Port Group name: _____ Security Mode and Status:_____

Case Project 7-4: Implementing NIC Teaming for Failover

One of the strengths of virtual switches is their ability to connect to multiple NICs and then use the additional NICs for load balancing and fault tolerance. In this project you are to document how to add NIC teaming to the management network switch.

Step 1: Add an additional virtual adapter to your VMware Workstation 12 Player. After adding the adapter, restart your UAS-vHost3-xxx virtual machine.

Step 2: Launch vSphere Client and add the new adapter to your management switch. Document the procedure you use below:

_____

_____

_____

_____

Case Project 7-5: Creating a Virtual Machine

In this project you are to use the procedure you learned in Activity 7-6 to create and run an Ubuntu virtual machine on your UAS-vHost3-xxx host. Record the process you use along with your results below:

_____

_____

_____

_____

chapter 8

Working with VMware vCenter Server

After reading this chapter and completing the exercises, you will be able to:

- Describe the purpose of vCenter Server and its components
- Install vCenter Server appliance
- Use vCenter Server to configure and manage a virtual data center
- Set up an iSCSI data store
- Perform common virtual machine management tasks
- Migrate virtual machines manually using vMotion
- Create a High Availability cluster
- Apply basic roles and permissions

In Chapter 7 you learned how the free vSphere version could be used to set up a virtual data center that can be used for small scale virtualization environments. As an organization grows, the need for more advanced virtualization features such as centralized management of virtualized components, easy migration of virtual machines, load balancing, and fault tolerance become more valuable. VMware's licensed version of vSphere is based around vCenter Server as the management center. In this chapter you will learn about the components that make up vCenter Server and be able to install and use it to create a virtual data center consisting of the hosts and virtual machines you created in Chapter 7. You will then learn how to manage the virtual data center, configure security, and manage virtual machines including migration using the new Web Client along with the vSphere Client you are familiar with from Chapter 7.

Implementing Shared Storage

One of the goals that management at Universal AeroSpace would like to implement is the ability to keep their virtual servers running in the event a host computer needs to be brought down for maintenance or experiences a hardware failure. Using the free version of vSphere, the best way and lowest cost way to do this is implement a NAS or SAN device. As described in Chapter 4, there are two major forms of network shared storage systems, Network Attached Storage (NAS) and Storage Area Network (SAN). Most SANs use the iSCSI protocol and while they provide more features and performance, they are more costly and complex to implement than a NAS. UAS plans to obtain an iSCSI server, purchase the licensed version of vSphere, and implement a SAN in the future. In the interim, they would like to use their existing Windows Server 2016 as a NAS server to provide shared storage to the virtual data center. In the future the NAS device will be used to store virtual machine templates and other work files. In the following activities you will implement a NAS system on your Windows Server 2016 virtual machine and then use it to implement a network storage system for the UAS virtual data center.

Activity 8-1: Installing NFS File Sharing on Your Windows Server 2016 Virtual Machine

Time Required: 15 minutes

Objective: Add an NFS file server role to Windows Server 2016 and then use it to share a directory.

Requirements: Completion of Chapter 4, Activity 4-3 (if you do not have a Windows Server 2016 virtual machine on VMware Workstation 12 Player, follow the instructions in Appendix B to create a Windows Server 2016 VM on VMware Player). Your Windows Server should have a fixed IP address on your NAT network as described in Chapter 4, Activity 4-3.

Description: Now that you have demonstrated how the free version of vSphere can be used to host virtual machines, UAS management would like to make the virtual machines available to multiple host computers. In this activity you will install the NFS server on a Windows Server 2016 machine and use it to share a directory on the network.

1. Open VMware Workstation 12 Player and click to select your Windows Server 2016 VM you created in Chapter 4. Click the **Edit virtual machine settings** link to display the Virtual Machine Settings window.

 If you do not have a working Windows Server 2016 VM from Chapter 4, you should following the instructions in Appendix B to create and install Windows Server 2016 on VMware Workstation 12 Player.

2. Verify the Network Adapter is set to your Management network (NAT). If necessary, click the **Network Adapter** setting and then click to change the LAN adaptor to NAT and return to the Virtual Machine Settings window.

3. Add a new hard disk drive to be used for your NAS storage by clicking the **Add** button from the Virtual Machine Settings window. Verify that the **Hard Disk** hardware type is selected and then click **Next**. Select the default options to create a new SCSI hard disk of at least 60 GB capacity. Click to select the Store virtual disk as a single file and then click **Finish** to create the new hard disk.

4. Start Windows Server VM and then log on as Administrator. If necessary start Server Manager, click **Local Server,** and click to expand the **File and Storage Services**. Click **Disks** to display your new disk drive which should be displayed as Offline. Right-click the drive and click the **Bring Online** option and click **Yes** to the message dialog box.

5. Right-click the new drive and select **New Volume...** option to start the New Volume Wizard. Use the wizard to create a 60 GB NTFS volume using the default settings. When you create the new volume you can close all windows. Record the drive letter assigned to the new volume in the space below:

   New volume drive letter: _____

6. Open a command prompt and enter **IPCONFIG** to display the IP address settings. You will need to record what address your VMware Workstation 12 Player is using for the NAT network. Record the IP address values shown below:

   IP Address: 192.168._____._____

   Subnet Mask: _____._____._____._____

   Default Gateway: 192.168._____._____

7. If necessary start the Server Manager application, click the **Add roles and features** link, and click **Next** to display the Select installation type page.

8. Verify that the Role-based or feature-based installation option is selected and click **Next** to display the Select destination server page.

9. Verify that your Windows Server 2016 is selected and click **Next** to display the Select server roles page.

10. Click to expand the **File and Storage Services** and **File and iSCSI Services** links.

11. Click to place a check in the **Server for NFS** option to display the Add Roles and Features Wizard

12. Verify that the Include management tools (if applicable) option is selected and then click the **Add Features** button to return to the Select server roles page.

13. Click **Next** twice to display the Confirm installation selections page.

14. Confirm your selection of Server for NFS and click **Install** to perform the feature installation. Monitor the progress of your installation on the Feature installation progress bar.

15. Wait until you see "Installation succeeded on *your_server_name*" and then click **Close** to return to the Server Manager dashboard. You can now close Server Manager.

16. Start File Explorer and open a window to your new drive letter you recorded in step 5.

17. Create a folder named **SharedVMs** on your new drive.

18. Right-click the **SharedVMs** folder and then click **Properties** to display the Properties window.

19. Click the **NFS Sharing** tab and then click the **Manage NFS Sharing** button to display the NFS Advanced Sharing window and then click the **Share this folder** option to display the window shown in Figure 8-1.

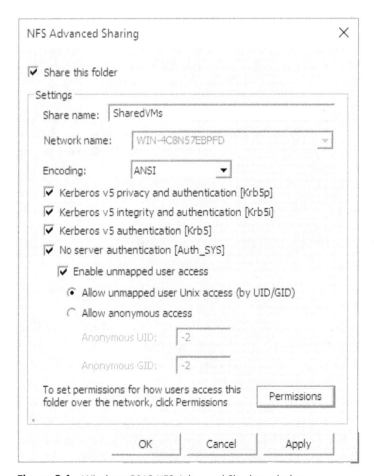

Figure 8-1 Windows 2016 NFS Advanced Sharing window

20. Click the **Permissions** button to display the NFS Share Permissions window.

21. Change the Type of access to **Read-Write** and then click to put a check in the **Allow root access** check box (it is necessary to allow the ESXi host to access the share as the root or administrative user).

22. Click **OK** to save your changes and return to the NFS Advanced Sharing window.

23. Click **OK** to save your changes and return to the SharedVMs Properties window.

24. Click **Close** and then close File Explorer.

25. You have created an NFS shared storage area for use with your vSphere system. You may leave your Windows Server 2016 virtual machine open for the next activity.

Activity 8-2: Connecting Your ESXi Hosts to the NAS Storage Server

Time Required: 15 minutes

Objective: Connect ESXi servers to a NAS storage device.

Requirements: Completion of Activity 8-1

Description: The next step is to add the shared storage device as a data store on your ESXi servers. In this activity you will use the vSphere Client to add the shared storage device to both your UAS hosts.

1. If necessary open an instance of VMware Workstation 12 Player and start your Windows Server 2016 VM.

2. Open a second instance of VMware Workstation 12 Player and click to select your UAS-vHost1-xxx host.

3. Click the **Edit virtual machine settings** option to display the Hardware devices.

4. Verify that you have currently have two Network Adapters as shown below:
   - Network Adapter NAT
   - Network Adapter NAT

5. To add a third network adaptor to be used in a later activity for iSCSI storage on the NAT network, click **Add**, select **Network Adapter**, and click **Next**. Verify that NAT is selected and click **Finish** to add another NAT adapter to the host. Click **OK** to close the Virtual Machine Settings dialog box. You should now have three network adapters all connected to the NAT network.

6. Repeat steps 2-5 for your UAS-vHost2-xxx host. Each of your host virtual machines should now have three NAT adapters.

7. Start both your UAS-vHost1-xxx and UAS-vHost2-xxx virtual machines. And wait for both hosts to start before proceeding to step 8.

8. From your Windows 2016 virtual machine, test communications with your ESXi server by opening a command prompt window and entering the command: **Ping** *ip_address* (where *ip_address* is the IP address of your UAS-vHost1-xxx machine) and pressing **Enter**.

If you do not get a response, check the IP address of both machines and be sure that they are both using the VMware NAT adapter configuration. In this chapter we are connecting all virtual networks through the NAT switch to simulate a single corporate network that may use VLANs to divide network traffic types. Using different adapter types such as Bridged and Host-Only would require a more complex networking infrastructure.

9. Start vSphere Client and log on to your UAS-vHost1-xxx host (if necessary click **Ignore** when you see the certificate warning message).

10. Click the **Configuration** tab and then in the left Hardware pane, click the **Storage** option to display the existing data stores. Record the existing data store name and capacity below:

   Data store name and capacity: _____

11. Click the **Add Storage** link in the upper right corner of the window to display the Add Storage window showing Disk/LUN and Network File System options.

12. Click to select the **Network File System** option and then click **Next** to display the Locate Network File System window as shown in Figure 8-2.

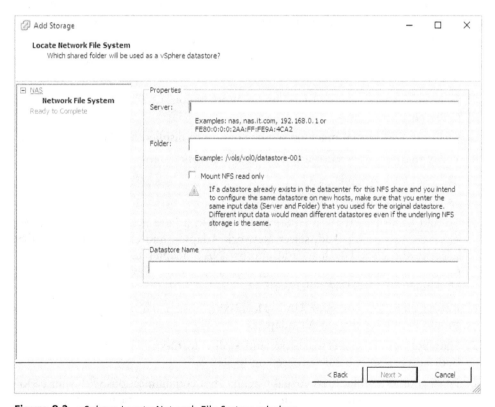

Figure 8-2 vSphere Locate Network File System window

Source: VMware vSphere Client

13. In the Server field, enter the IP address of your Windows Server 2016 computer that you recorded in step 6 of Activity 8-1.

14. In the Folder field, enter **SharedVMs,** the name you gave your shared NFS file system.

15. In the Datastore Name field, enter **UAS Shared Virtual Machines and Templates** and click **Next** to display the Ready to Complete window.

16. Verify your entries and then click **Finish** to add the SharedVMs data store to your Storage window. Notice that the drive type says "Unknown." This is because the NFS server takes care of the storage formatting. The ESXi host makes requests for data. The NFS server will process the request and get the data using its own disk format. When working with a local or iSCSI drive, the ESXi host will use its own VMFS disk access to retrieve the data.

17. Close your vSphere Client session.

18. Repeat the process described in steps 9-16 for UAS-vHost2-xxx.

19. Close your vSphere Client but leave all your virtual machines running for the next activity.

Activity 8-3: Moving an Existing Virtual Machine from Local Data store to Shared VM Drive

Time Required: 15 minutes

Objective: Move a virtual machine from a local data store to the shared NAS device.

Requirements: Completion of Activity 8-2

Description: Now that you have both your ESXi hosts connected to the same NAS storage device, the next step is to move the virtual machine from UAS-vHost1-xxx to the shared storage so it is accessible to both hosts. In this activity you will use the vSphere Client to move your UASWorkstation1-xxx virtual machine to the shared NAS device.

1. If necessary, open an instance of VMware Workstation 12 Player and start your Windows Server 2016 virtual machine.

2. Open a second instance of VMware Workstation 12 Player and start your UAS-vHost1-xxx virtual machine. Open a third instance of VMware Workstation 12 Player and start your UAS-vHost2-xxx virtual machine.

3. Wait for all virtual machines to start and then open the VMware vSphere Client and log on to your UAS-vHost1-xxx host. (If asked click **Ignore** in the Security Warning dialog box and then click **OK** to close the VMware Evaluation Notice dialog box.)

4. Click the **Configuration** tab and click **Storage** from the left Hardware pane.

5. Right-click **datastore1** and then click the **Browse Datastore...** option to view the data stores as shown in Figure 8-3.

Figure 8-3 vSphere Datastore Browser window

Source: VMware vSphere Client

6. Click your UAS-Workstation1-xxx data folder to select it and then click the **Move a file from this datastore to another location accessible to vCenter** icon (located to the left of the red "X" icon).

7. Read the Confirm Move message in the dialog box and summarize what it says below:

_____

_____

8. After reading the Confirm Move message, click **Yes** to display the Move Items To... window.

9. Click your **UAS Shared Virtual Machines and Templates** in the Datastore pane to select it as the destination folder.

10. Click the **Move** button to start the moving process. A Moving... status box will be displayed indicating how long the move will take. After the move is completed (about 5 minutes); close the Datastore Browser window for datastore1.

11. Click the **Virtual Machines** tab and right-click your existing UASWorkstation1-xxx virtual machine.

12. Click the **Remove from Inventory** command and then click **Yes** when you see the Confirm Remove message box.

13. You can now add the virtual machine to either of your ESXi hosts. To add the UASWorkstation1-xxx virtual machine from the UAS Shared Virtual Machines data store to your UAS-vHost2-xxx inventory, close the vSphere client.

14. Start vSphere Client and login to your UAS-vHost2-xxx host. (If asked click **Ignore** in the Security Warning dialog box and then click **OK** to close the VMware Evaluation Notice dialog box.)

15. Click the **Configuration** tab and then click the **Storage** option from the left Hardware pane.

16. Right-click the **UAS Shared Virtual Machines and Templates** data store and then click the **Browse Datastore...** option.

17. Double-click the UASWorkstation1-xxx folder to open it.

18. Right-click the **UASWorkstation1-xxx.vmx** configuration file and then click the **Add to Inventory** option to start the Add to Inventory wizard.

19. Click **Next** to accept the existing name "UASWorkstation1-xxx" to display the Resource Pool window showing the IP address of your UAS-vHost2-xxx host selected.

20. Click **Next** to select your UAS-vHost2-xxx host and display the Ready to Complete window.

21. Verify the settings and click **Finish** to add the UASWorkstation1-xxx VM to your host.

22. Close the Datastore Browser window.

23. Click the **Virtual Machines** tab. Your UASWorkstation1-xxx VM should now appear in the list. You can now launch the virtual machine using your UAS-vHost2-xxx hypervisor. In the space below record how the capability to run the UASWorkstation1-xxx VM from the NAS drive could benefit the UAS organization.

_____

_____

24. You can now close the vSphere client as this concludes the activities in this section. In the following section you will implement vCenter Server and then use it to import your hosts and associated resources such as virtual switches and shared storage to create a virtual data center for Universal AeroSpace. You may now close your vSphere Client session and shut down the ESXi hosts using the proper shutdown procedure.

In this section you created an NFS 3 Network File System and connected it to both your ESXi hosts. In Chapter 4, Activity 4-3, you created an iSCSI target on your Windows Server 2016 Virtual Machine. You will use this iSCSI target in the next section to add an iSCSI shared storage device to your virtual data center.

Working with vCenter Server

In addition to being a management center for vSphere data center, vCenter Server is actually the master of the data center and needs to be performing an active role in the day-to-day operation of the ESXi hosts. Because of the interactive role it plays, you could say the vCenter Server is more important to the function of the data center than any of the ESXi host systems. When a host goes down, it is vCenter Server that will manage the migration of virtual machines to other hosts. In addition to watching over the ESXi hosts while the administrator sleeps, vCenter Server also monitors performance of the virtual machines and virtual networks in order to provide load balancing and other services.

The vCenter Server system consists of a variety of services that are divided into two major components: the VMware Platform Services Controller and the vCenter Server. The VMware platform services consist of vCenter Single Sign On, the License service, the Lookup service, and VMware Certificate Authority. The vCenter services include the vCenter Server itself, the Web Client, an Inventory database service, the Auto Deploy service, and Syslog services. The Platform Services Controller can be either installed on the same machine as the vCenter Server, called the **Embedded Platform Services Controller**, or installed separately on a different system and referred to as the **External Platform Services Controller**. A single vCenter Server with an Embedded Platform Services Controller can connect up to 1,000 hosts and manage 10,000 powered-on virtual machines. However, to provide redundancy and efficiency, large virtual data centers that are spread over large geographic regions often consist of multiple vCenter Servers that are arranged to provide performance and management with an External Platform Services Controller as shown in Figure 8-4.

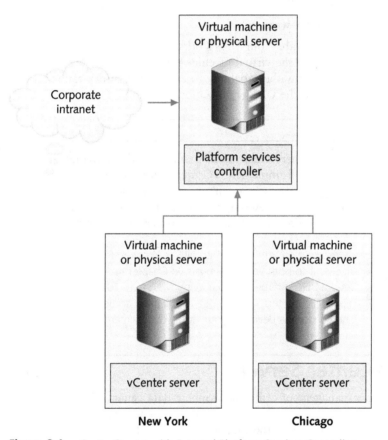

Figure 8-4 vCenter Servers with External Platform Services Controller

As shown in Figure 8-4, in large data centers consisting of multiple vCenter Servers, the platform services are usually installed in an External Platform Services Controller located on a dedicated computer. Having an External Platform Services Controller to work with multiple vCenter Servers is more efficient than embedding all these services in each of the vCenter Server systems.

Figure 8-5 shows an illustration of using the vCenter Server virtual data center components with an Embedded Platform Services Controller. Universal AeroSpace is planning to use this type of configuration. In the following section you will learn how to install vCenter Server with an Embedded Platform Services Controller for your Universal AeroSpace virtual data center.

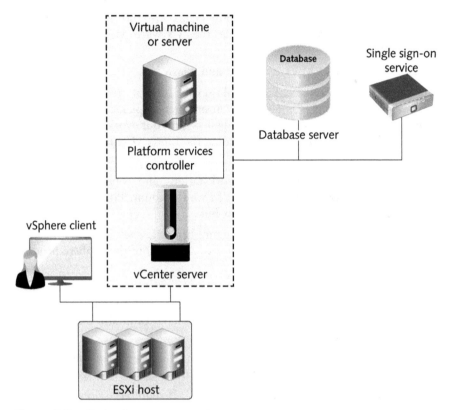

Figure 8-5 vCenter Server components

Installing vCenter Server

In addition to selecting an embedded or external platform service, there are two major ways to implement vCenter Server. It can be installed on a Windows server that is a member of an Active Directory domain, or as a stand-alone Linux appliance. If your organization currently has an active domain with multiple Windows servers, installing the Windows version is the best alternative. Since vCenter Server cannot be installed on an Active Directory domain controller, it usually means the organization would have at least three Windows servers, two domain controllers and at least one member server. If you have a smaller or non-Windows Active Directory network, such as our Universal AeroSpace case project, installing the Linux appliance is the most straightforward as it does not require an Active Directory domain. In the following activity you will download the vCenter Server Linux appliance iso file using your MyVMware Web site. Since this is a large download, your instructor may supply you with a path to the iso file that you can use.

Activity 8-4: Downloading VMware vCenter Linux Appliance Installation File

Time Required: 30 minutes

Objective: Use your MyVMware account to register for a trial vSphere product and then optionally download the vCenter Server Linux appliance. (You can also download the VMware-VCSA-all-6.0.0-3634788.iso file from the VMware Academy by selecting the VMware vCenter Server 6 Standard product.)

Requirements: An active MyVMware account and password

Description: Universal AeroSpace has been sold on the idea of creating a virtual data center and wants your firm to set up vCenter Server in order to implement the many vSphere data center features available. In this activity you will begin your work by registering for a trial copy of vSphere and then optionally downloading the Linux vCenter Server appliance installation file.

1. If necessary, start your Windows workstation and open a Web browser to VMware.com. Then log on to your MyVMware account. Point to the **Products** menu and then click the **Trial and Free Products** link.

2. Under the Datacenter and Cloud Infrastructure heading, click the **VMware vSphere with Operations Management** link to display information about the vSphere product registration options.

3. Click the **Go to Downloads** link under the Download Evaluation Product heading and then click the **Installation & Use Cases** step to display information and videos regarding the vSphere with Operations Management product. You can also use this page to download documentation and setup instructions.

4. To register and download the product, click the **License & Download** step and then click the **Register** button to display the Accept End-User License Agreement page.

5. Enter the required information (displayed in red). If required, select minimum values in the "Number of Employees" and "Number of x86 and/or blade servers in your environment" fields and then select **No, I'm still learning** in the "Do you have an active virtualization or cloud initiative" field. Click the **NAS** and **SAN-iSCSI** storage type options in the "Type of storage used" field.

6. After entering the required information, scroll down and check the **I agree to the terms and conditions outlined in the Evaluation End User License Agreement** option and then click the **Start Free Trial** button to display the Product Evaluation Center for VMware vSphere and vSphere with Operations Management page.

You will receive an email that contains an Access My Evaluation! link. Click the **Access Now** button in the email to go to the VMware vSphere and vSphere with Operations Management page.

7. If necessary, click to expand the **Download VMware vCenter Server** option and then click to expand **Download vCenter Server for Linux**. View the process of downloading

the file. If you already have access to the vCenter Server Appliance file, skip to step 10 to complete this activity.

8. Click the **Manually Download** button to the right of the **VMware vCenter Server Appliance option**.

9. Use the **Save As** option to save the iso file in the folder you created in Chapter 1, Activity 1-1. This is a large download so you may wish to take a break during this process.

10. After completing the download, you may sign off MyVMware and close your browser window.

The vCenter Server appliance is a virtual machine that will run on one of your ESXi host computers. The installation process runs from a Windows workstation and then remotely creates a virtual machine on the selected host and installs the virtual appliance to run on that VM. The computer that will host the vCenter Server appliance will need a minimum hardware configuration as shown in Table 8-1.

Table 8-1   vCenter Server appliance minimum hardware requirements

Hardware Component	Minimum Requirement
CPU	2 cores required NX/XD bit enabled in BIOS Intel VT-x or AMD RVI
Memory	4 GB minimum
LAN	One or more Gigabit Ethernet controllers
Disk	120 GB SCSI drive

Since the lab activities in this book are designed to run the ESXi hosts from the VMware Workstation 12 Player VM, you will need to make sure the virtual machine that hosts your UAS-vHost1-xxx ESXi host has the virtual hardware needed to support the vCenter Server appliance. In the following activity, you will use VMware Workstation 12 Player to check and if necessary upgrade your virtual machine hardware settings.

Activity 8-5: Modifying Hardware Settings to Meet vCenter Requirements

Time Required: 10 minutes

Objective: Use VMware Workstation 12 Player to verify and update virtual machine hardware settings to meet vCenter requirements.

Requirements: Completion of Activity 8-4

Description: Given the current size of the proposed Universal AeroSpace virtual data center, management has instructed you to install the virtual machine that will host the vCenter Server appliance on the computer that currently runs the UAS-vHost1-xxx virtual machine. In this activity you will simulate upgrading the UAS-vHost1-xxx computer by upgrading the

VMware Workstation Player virtual machine to meet the hardware requirements shown previously in Table 8-1. In addition to the other changes, you will need to add a Virtual Machine port to your management virtual switch. This port will be used by vCenter Server to manage the ESXi hosts.

1. If necessary, start your Windows workstation, open VMware Workstation 12 Player, and click your UAS-vHost1-xxx virtual machine to select it.

2. If necessary, power down your UAS-vHost1-xxx virtual machine and then click the **Edit virtual machine settings** link to display the Hardware tab of the Virtual Machine Settings window.

3. Click the **Memory** device and then change the memory size to 12 GB (if your desktop has 16 GB of RAM you may want to give your ESXi host 16 GB to provide better performance).

4. Click Processors and if necessary set the number of cores to **2**.

5. Click the **Hard Disk (SCSI)** device and if necessary use the **Expand** button to set the size to 120 GB.

6. For the purposes of the labs in this chapter, verify that all Network Adapters are set to NAT. (For the purposes of this book activities, the NAT network will act as the corporate network environment.)

7. Click **OK** to save your changes.

8. Click the **Play virtual machine** link to start your UAS-vHost1-xxx virtual machine.

9. After your UAS-vHost1-xxx virtual machine is running, start your vSphere Client and login to your UAS-vHost1-xxx host.

10. Click the **Configuration** tab and then click the **Networking** option to display the Networking window.

In order to install the vCenter Server on your UAS-vHost1-xxx ESXi host, you will need to add a virtual machine port to your vSwitch0 management switch. Having a virtual machine port on the management switch will allow the vCenter virtual machine to communicate with the ESXi host systems.

11. To add a virtual machine port to your management switch, click the **Properties** link to the right of the vSwitch0 to display the vSwitch0 Properties window.

12. Verify that vSwitch0 is selected and then click the **Add** button to start the Add Network wizard.

13. Verify that Virtual Machine connection type is selected in the Connection Types pane and then click **Next** to display the Connection Settings window.

14. Change the name to **VM Mgmt Network** and click **Next** to display the Ready to Complete window.

15. Verify your settings and then click **Finish** to add the VM Mgmt Network port group and return to the vSwitch0 Properties window.

16. Click **Close** to return to the Configuration options window and then close your vSphere client.

17. You have now completed the steps in this activity; you may wish to leave your virtual machines running for the next activity.

Installing vCenter Server Appliance In addition to the Platform Services Controller, the most important part of the vCenter system is the database. The vCenter database is used to store information on all the inventory components that make up the virtual data center. Smaller organizations such as our example Universal AeroSpace company can use the built-in PostgreSQL database. Larger installations will need to set up a database system such as Microsoft SQL Server to manage all the objects. In the following activity you will install the vCenter Server Linux appliance using the built-in PostgreSQL database and Embedded Platform Services Controller.

The installation of the vCenter Server Linux appliance can be performed from a Windows 10 workstation by mounting the iso file and then installing the Client Integration plug-in from the DVD image. After the plug-in is installed, you can run the installation from a Web browser. To start the installation, you will need to sign in to your ESXi host by providing its IP address and root user password. During the installation, the vCenter Server Appliance will set up a Single Sign On (SSO) domain with the default administrator name of "administrator@domain_name". For the purposes of our activities, the recommended domain name will be "UAS-xxx.local" where xxx represents your initials. In the following activity you will install the vCenter Appliance and set up a Single Sign On domain.

Activity 8-6: Installing the VMware vCenter Linux Appliance

Time Required: 30 minutes

Objective: Use the vCenter Linux Appliance file you obtained in Activity 8-4 to install an instance of vCenter Server.

Requirements: Completion of Activities 8-4 and 8-5

Description: Now that the hardware has been upgraded to support the vCenter Server Linux appliance, in this activity you will use your Windows 10 workstation along with the iso file you obtained from Activity 8-4 to install the vCenter Server appliance as a virtual machine running on your UAS-vHost1-xxx host.

1. If necessary, start your UAS-vHost1-xxx virtual machine. (This host will be used to host the vCenter Server Linux VM.)

2. Map the iso file you obtained in Activity 8-1 to your Windows 10 computer DVD drive by opening File Explorer, and navigating to the folder that contains the vCenter Server Appliance iso file. Right-click the iso file and then click **Mount** to mount the file as your DVD drive.

3. If necessary, use File Explorer to open a window to the newly mounted DVD drive.

4. Start the Client Integration plug-in installation navigating to **the vcsa-ui-installer\win32** folder and then double-clicking **installer.exe** to start the vCenter Server Appliance 6.5 Installer.

5. Click on the **Install** option to install a new vCenter Server appliance. Notice that this is a two stage process. The first stage deploys the new appliance to the ESXi host and the second stage will setup the deployed appliance.

6. Click **Next** to start the deployment process.

7. Click to accept the license agreement and then click **Next** to display the deployment type window as shown in Figure 8-6.

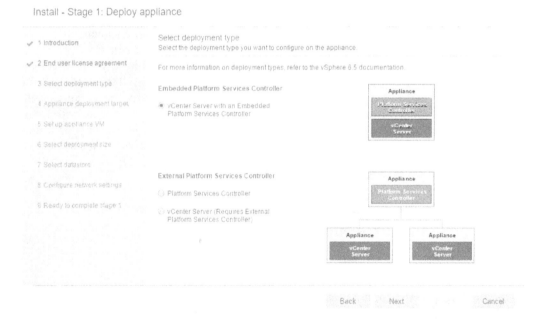

Figure 8-6   vCenter Appliance Deployment—Connect to target server

Source: VMware vSphere

8. Verify that **the vCenter Server with an Embedded Platform Service Controller** option is selected and click **Next** to display the Appliance deployment target window.

9. Enter the IP address of your UAS-vHost1-xxx host along with the user name "root" and password and then click **Next**. If a Certification Warning dialog box is displayed, click **Yes** to continue and display the Install - Stage 1: Deploy vCenter Server with an Embedded Platform Services Controller – Setup appliance VM window.

10. In the VM name field, enter **UASxxx-vCenter1** (where xxx represents your initials) and then enter the password you will use for the root Linux user on your vCenter virtual

server (the password must be at least eight characters long and contain numbers along with upper and lower case letters and at least one special character. If it meets the requirements, you may wish to use the same password as you use for your UAS-vHost1 system.). Record the appliance name and password for your Linux root user below:

Appliance name: _____

Linux root user password: _____

11. Click **Next** to continue to the Select deployment size window as shown in Figure 8-7.

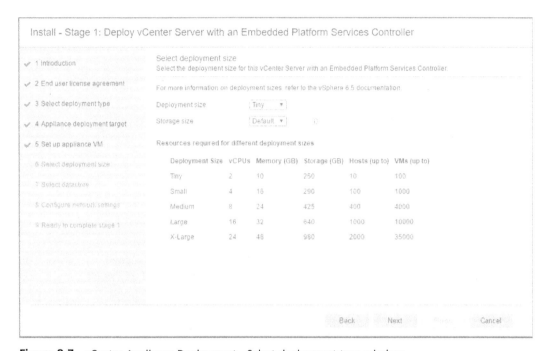

Figure 8-7   vCenter Appliance Deployment—Select deployment type window

Source: vSphere Server Setup

12. Verify that the Tiny Deployment size is selected along with the Default storage size and then click Next to display the Select datastore window. Record the datastore Name, type, capacity, and Thin provisioning specifications below:

_____   _____   _____

13. Leave the default datastore1 selected, click to select the **Enable Thin Disk Mode** option, and then click **Next** to display the Configure Network Settings window shown in Figure 8-8. These are the settings that will be used by your vCenter Server appliance virtual machine.

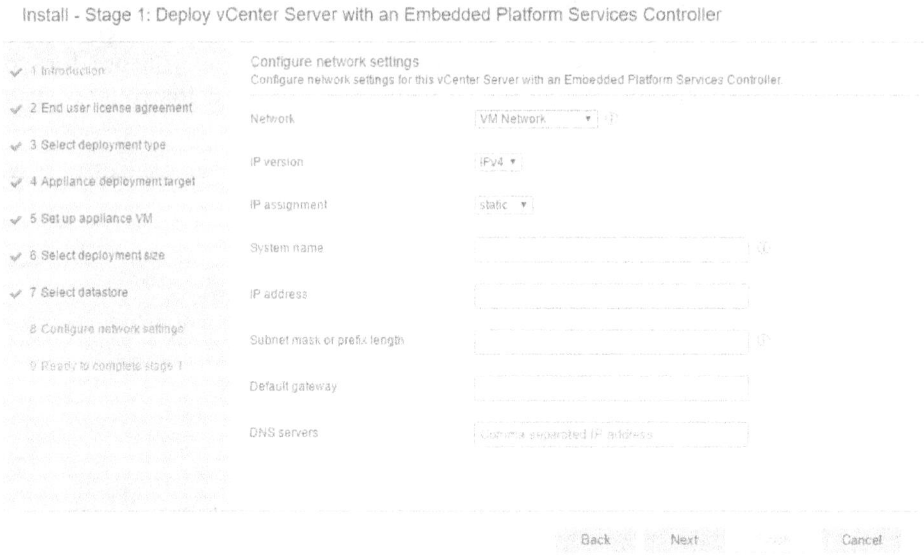

Install - Stage 1: Deploy vCenter Server with an Embedded Platform Services Controller

	Configure network settings
✓ 1 Introduction	Configure network settings for this vCenter Server with an Embedded Platform Services Controller.
✓ 2 End user license agreement	Network — VM Network
✓ 3 Select deployment type	
✓ 4 Appliance deployment target	IP version — IPv4
✓ 5 Set up appliance VM	IP assignment — static
✓ 6 Select deployment size	System name
✓ 7 Select datastore	IP address
8 Configure network settings	Subnet mask or prefix length
9 Ready to complete stage 1	Default gateway
	DNS servers — Comma separated IP address

Back   Next   Cancel

Figure 8-8   vCenter Appliance Deployment—Create new SSO domain

Source: vSphere Server Setup

14. Click the pull-down arrow in the Network field to select the port group you created for the Management network in Activity 8-5 (*VM Mgmt Network*).

15. Enter the static IP address **192.168.###.151** in the Network address and System name fields (where ### is the subnet used by your NAT network for the server management network). This address/system name will be used to access the vCenter Server running on the NAT network (you may get this subnet address represented with the "###" from looking the ESXi server screen). Record the network address you enter below:

    IP address used in place of the FQDN name. 192.168._____._____

    Enter Subnet mask: 255.255.255.0

    Enter Network gateway: 192.168.###.2 (Same as used on your ESXi host)

    (where ### is the ESXi host subnet)

16. Enter DNS server **192.168.###.2** (the same address as your gateway) and click **Next** to display the Ready to complete stage 1 window.

17. Verify your settings and then click **Finish** to deploy the vCenter server on your UAS-vHost1-xxx host. Depending on the speed of your system, this process will take several minutes so it's a good time to take a stretch.

18. When you see the "You have successfully deployed vCenter Server with an Embedded Platform Services Controller" message, click **Continue** to proceed to the Stage 2 – Set Up vCenter Server Appliance with an Embedded PSC startup window and then click **Next** to display the Appliance configuration window.

19. In the Time synchronization mode field, use the pull-down menu to select the **Synchronize time with ESXi host** option, verify that the SSH access is set to Disabled, and then click **Next** to display the Single Sign-on Option (SSO) window as shown in Figure 8-9.

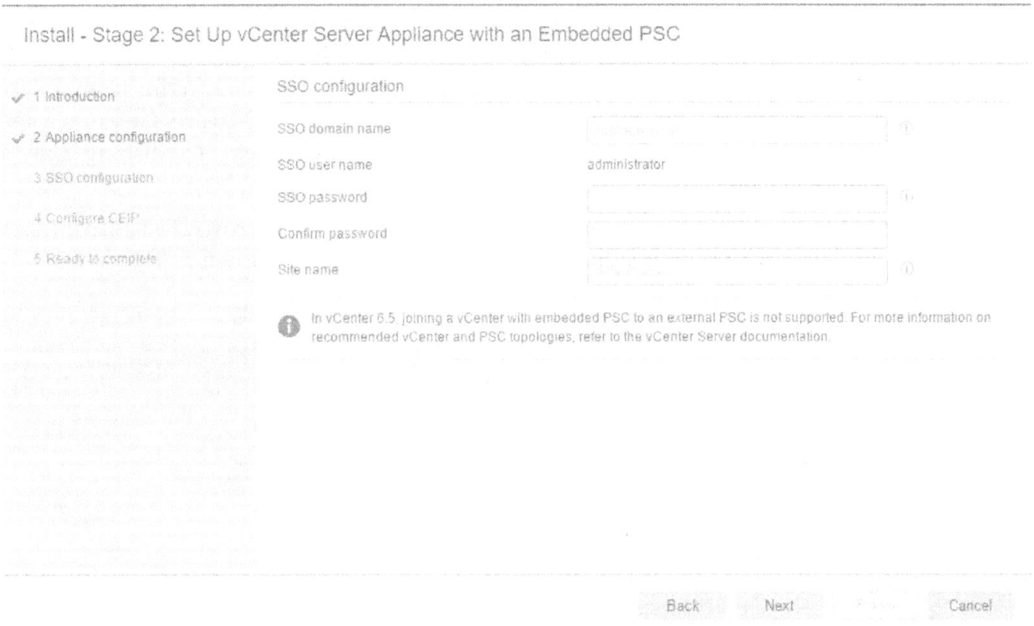

Install - Stage 2: Set Up vCenter Server Appliance with an Embedded PSC

✓ 1 Introduction

✓ 2 Appliance configuration

3 SSO configuration

4 Configure CEIP

5 Ready to complete

SSO configuration

SSO domain name

SSO user name   administrator

SSO password

Confirm password

Site name

ℹ In vCenter 6.5, joining a vCenter with embedded PSC to an external PSC is not supported. For more information on recommended vCenter and PSC topologies, refer to the vCenter Server documentation.

Back   Next   Cancel

Figure 8-9   vCenter Appliance Deployment – Network Settings

Source: vSphere Server Setup

20. Enter a domain name UASxxx.local (where xxx represents your initials) and UASxxx as your SSO site name along with a password for your vCenter administrator account. Record the information you enter below and then click Next to validate your entry and continue to display the Configure CCIP (Customer Experience) window.

Administrator username: <u>administrator</u>

vCenter password: _____

SSO domain name: _____

SSO site name: _____

21. Since this is an educational system, you may click to remove the check from the **Join the VMware Customer Experience Improvement program** check box and then click **Next** to display the Ready to complete page.

22. Verify your entries and then click **Finish**. When you see the Warning dialog box informing you not to pause or stop the install from completing click **OK** to start the configuration process. This process will take at least 15 to 20 minutes, so it's a good time to take a break before starting the next step.

23. When you see the Complete window informing you that you have successfully setup this appliance, click the https://ip_address:443/vspher-client link to display the VMware vCenter Single Sign-On window. (Use the required process on your Web browser version to bypass any certificate warning messages. If using the Edge browser, click **Yes** when you see the "Did you mean to switch apps pop-up".)

24. After entering the information, click **Next**. You will receive a warning message stating that an IP address was provided for the FQDN name. Click **OK** to continue and display the Customer Experience page. Since this is an educational system, you may click to remove the check from the **Join the VMware Customer Experience Improvement program** check box and then click **Next** to display the Ready to Complete page.

25. Point to the Home icon to the right of the vmware vSphere Web Client window heading and then click the **Home** link to display the Home tab shown in Figure 8-10.

Figure 8-10 vCenter Home page

Source: VMware vCenter Server

26. Save this page in your favorites for easy access in the future.

27. Log off by clicking the **Logout** option from the dropdown menu next to your administrator name and then close the Web Client. You may leave your virtual machines running for the next activity.

Using the Web Client As you can see from Figure 8-10, the Web Client enables you to manage data center inventory objects such as hosts, clusters, networks, and virtual machines.

When you use the Web Client to log on to vCenter Server, the Home page is displayed. The default layout is the Home page with a menu bar, a navigation bar, a search box, and panels. The Home page has divisions for major Client functions: Inventory, Monitoring, and Administration. When you log off of the Web Client, it retains the view that was displayed when it was closed and returns you to that view the next time you log on.

As you can see from the message at the top of the Web Client page, one of the first functions you may need to manage is licensing. In the vCenter environment, license reporting and management are both centralized. All product and feature licenses are encapsulated in 25-character license keys that are managed and monitored from vCenter Server using the Web Client. License information can be viewed by product, license key, or asset:

- *Product*—A license to use a vSphere software component or feature, for example, evaluation mode and vSphere 6 Enterprise Plus.
- *License key*—The serial number that corresponds to a product.
- *Asset*—A machine on which a product is installed. For an asset to run certain software legally, the asset must be licensed.

You can split some license keys by applying them to multiple assets. For example, you can split a four-CPU license by applying it to 2 two-CPU hosts. vCenter Server can also manage licenses for older hosts (ESXi 3.x/ESXi 3.5 hosts), but a special VMware License Server is required for legacy host license management. For more about licensing, see the vSphere Installation and Setup Guide at http://www.vmware.com/support/pubs/vsphere-esxi-vcenter-server-pubs.html.

In the next section you will learn how to use the Web Client and vSphere Client to create a new data center and work with inventory objects.

Because of the importance of the vCenter Server you will want it to start running when you start the ESXi host computer. In the following activity you will configure your UAS-vHost1-xxx host to automatically start your vCenter Server virtual machine.

Activity 8-7: Configuring Your Host to Automatically Start vCenter Virtual Machine

Time Required: 10 minutes

Objective: Use the vSphere Client to access your UAS-vHost1-xxx virtual machine and configure a virtual machine to start automatically when the host boots.

Requirements: Completion of Activity 8-6

Description: Since the vCenter Server is such an important part of managing and monitoring the virtual data center it is important that it is running along with the host computers. In this activity you will use the vSphere Client to access your UAS-vHost1 host and configure it to automatically start your vCenter Server.

1. Start your vSphere Client (the client you used in Activity 8-2 and 8-3) and log on to your UAS-vHost1-xxx host using its IP address and root name and password.

2. Click the **Configuration** tab and then click **Virtual Machine Startup/Shutdown** from the left Software pane.

3. In the upper right corner of the page, click the **Properties** link to display the Virtual Machine Startup and Shutdown window as shown in Figure 8-11.

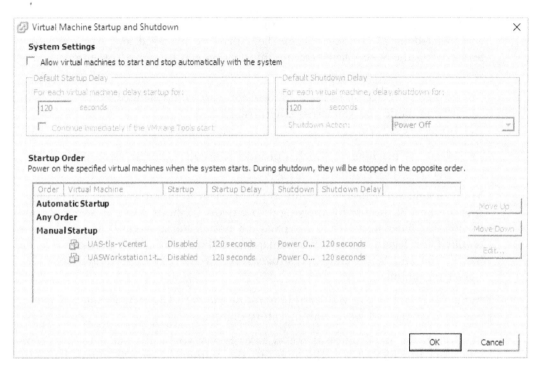

Figure 8-11 Virtual Machines Startup and Shutdown window

Source: vCenter Server Web Client

4. Click the **Allow virtual machines to start and stop automatically with the system** check box to enable the startup options.

5. Click to select your UAS-xxx-vCenter1 virtual machine and then use the **Move Up** button until the vCenter virtual machine is listed under the **Automatic Startup** heading.

6. Click **OK** to save your changes and return to the Configuration tab.

7. Close your vSphere Client and perform a normal shutdown procedure on your UAS-vHost1-xxx host system.

Creating a vCenter Server Virtual Data Center

As shown in Figure 8-12, vCenter Server and ESXi hosts are accessed through the Web Client using vpxa and **hostd** agents running on the ESXi host and the vpxd daemon running on the vCenter Server.

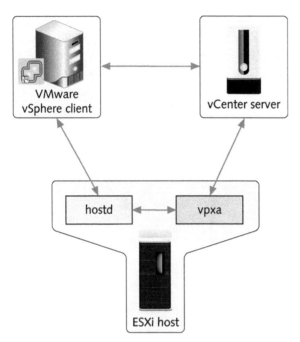

Figure 8-12   Web Client and vSphere Client access process

The **hostd agent** runs directly on the ESXi host and is responsible for managing most of the operations on the ESXi host. It is aware of all virtual machines that are registered on the ESXi host, the storage volumes visible by the ESXi host, and the status of all virtual machines. Most all commands or operations come down from vCenter Server through hostd—for example, creating, migrating, and powering on virtual machines, and so on.

The **vpxa agent** acts as an intermediary between the vpxd process, which runs on vCenter Server, and the hostd process to relay the tasks to perform on the host.

When you are logged on to the vCenter Server system using the Web Client, vCenter Server passes commands to the ESXi host through the vpxa process. The vCenter database is also updated. If you are using the vSphere Client to communicate directly with an ESXi host, such as we did in Chapter 7 and earlier in this chapter, communications go directly to the hostd process and the vCenter database is not updated. For this reason after installing vCenter Server it is important to make all changes using the vCenter Web Client.

As shown in Figure 8-13, the vCenter inventory is a hierarchy of objects arranged in folders starting with the virtual data center.

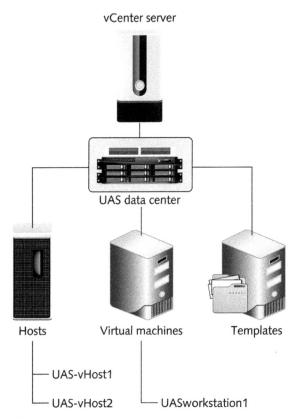

Figure 8-13 vCenter Server object single data center hierarchy

These objects are either containers of other objects, such as folders, or objects that you manage. Hosts, virtual machines, templates, clusters, resource pools, data stores, or networks can all be objects in the vCenter inventory. The inventory hierarchy is used to group your objects in a meaningful way and provides a natural structure on which to apply permissions. In the example shown in Figure 8-13, hosts, virtual machines and templates are placed in separate folders. The organization system you use will be dependent on how the objects are used and managed. For example, an advantage of organizing objects into folders is that you can create a structure on which appropriate access can be assigned to administrators. On the other side of the coin you need to design your inventory hierarchy with care as too many folders and too complicated a hierarchy can make management difficult.

vCenter Server can be used to manage one or more data centers as shown in Figure 8-14. Large companies might use multiple data centers to represent organizations or business units in the company.

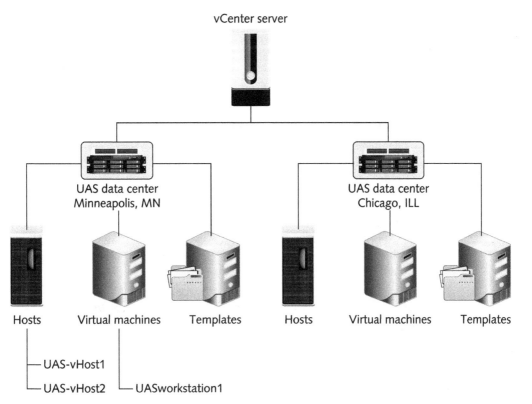

vCenter server

UAS data center
Minneapolis, MN

UAS data center
Chicago, ILL

Hosts   Virtual machines   Templates   Hosts   Virtual machines   Templates

── UAS-vHost1

── UAS-vHost2   ── UASworkstation1

Figure 8-14   vCenter multi-datacenter hierarchy

In the figure, data centers are based on their geographical location. Each geographical location might have and be responsible for its own team of IT administrators, its own set of customers, and its own set of ESXi hosts, virtual machines, networks, and data stores. The topmost object in the vCenter Server inventory is called the root object, represented by a back-slash (\). The root object is the vCenter Server system itself and cannot be removed from the inventory.

Inventory objects can interact in data centers but have limited interaction across data centers. Certain operations can be performed between data centers and others. For example, you can clone a virtual machine from one data center to a different data center, but you cannot use vMotion to migrate a virtual machine from a host in one data center to a host in another in a different data center. You will learn more about how to migrate virtual machines between hosts later in this chapter.

In addition to managing the vCenter Server from the Web Client you can also manage your data center from the vSphere Client we used in Chapter 7. The vSphere Client allows you to connect to vCenter Server or directly to ESXi host. As mentioned earlier, when using vCenter Server if possible you should always connect to a host through the vCenter Server in order to properly manage the database inventory. In the following activity you will use the vSphere Client to connect to your vCenter Server and create a new data center for the UAS company.

Activity 8-8: Creating a New Data Center Using the vSphere Client

Time Required: 10 minutes

Objective: Use the Web Client to access the vCenter Server appliance and create a new data center.

Requirements: Completion of Activity 8-6 and Activity 8-7

Description: The management at Universal AeroSpace is anxious to get started with their new virtual data center. In this activity you will first use the Windows based vSphere client to verify that the vCenter server appliance VM is running and then use the vCenter Web Client to access your vCenter Server appliance and create a new data center for Universal AeroSpace.

1. If necessary, start your UAS-vHost1-xxx host computer.

2. Start your vSphere Client (the client you used in Activities 8-2 and 8-3) and log on to your UAS-vHost1-xxx host computer using its IP address and root username and password.

You can use either the Windows-based vSphere Client or the vCenter Web client to create and manage data centers. Since VMware no longer supports the Windows vSphere Client, it is recommended to use the vCenter Web client when managing the vSphere environment. In this activity you will see how you can use the Windows-based vSphere Client can be used access the vCenter Server and perform certain basic function such as creating the data center. Because of its more advanced features, you will be using the vCenter Web Client for performing vSphere management tasks in future activities.

3. Verify that your UAS-xxx-vCenter1 virtual machine is running by clicking the **Virtual Machines** tab.

4. After you have verified that the vCenter virtual machine is powered on, close the vSphere Client window.

5. Open a Web browser and enter **https://ip_address** (where ip_address is the IP address of your vCenter Server) or use the shortcut (bookmark) you saved earlier. If necessary accept the CA warning message and launch the VMware client integration plug-in to display the VMware vCenter Single Sign-On page.

6. Enter the administrator username and password for your vCenter server and click the **Login** button to display the initial Navigator page. (You may need to click the option to run the VMware Client Integration plug-in again.)

7. If necessary, click the **Getting Started** tab and then click the **Create Datacenter** link to display the New Datacenter dialog box.

8. Enter **UAS Primary Datacenter** (or another **name** of your preference) as the new data center name and click **OK**. The new datacenter will now appear in the Navigator pane.

9. This completes Activity 8-8, but you can stay logged in to the vCenter Web client to start working with your new data center in the next activity.

Working with the Virtual Data Center

The Web Client divides the work space into Inventories, Monitoring, and Administration panels. In this section we will look at the various icons and options available to work with objects in the Inventories panel. It is important to organize objects using containers or folders as shown previously in Figure 8-13. For example, in your UAS data center we may want to create a container for hosts and another container for virtual machines. In the following activity you will work with the Web Client to set up a virtual data center for UAS network.

Activity 8-9: Setting up UAS Data Center

Time Required: 10 minutes

Objective: Use the Web Client to set up and document a data center by adding ESXi hosts.

Requirements: Completion of Activity 8-8

Description: Your manager has asked you to set up an initial data center to demonstrate the capability of using vCenter for Universal AeroSpace management. In this activity you will add your existing UAS-vHost1-xxx and UAS-vHost2-xxx systems to the vCenter Server and then document that the vCenter inventory has been populated with the host resources. **8**

1. If necessary, open a Web browser to your vCenter client and then logon using your administrator user name and password.

2. Go to the Home page by pointing at the house icon to the right of the vSphere Web client title and clicking the **Home** link.

3. Next, we want to create container objects for the hosts and VMs. To create a container object for the hosts, click the **Hosts and Clusters** icon, then right-click your **UAS Primary Datacenter** and click the **New Folder** option from the dropdown menu.

4. Click the **New Host and Cluster Folder** option, then enter the name **UAS-Hosts** and click **OK** to create the new folder. The UAS-Hosts container should now appear under the UAS Primary Datacenter. (You may have to click to expand and display the contents of the UAS Primary Datacenter.)

 It may take some time for the folders to appear under the data center. One way to force them to appear is complete creating the UAS-VMs folder in step 7 and then logout and log back in. The folders should then appear when you expand your data center.

5. Return to the Home page by clicking the Home icon in the title bar and then clicking the **Home** link in the Navigator field.

6. To create a folder for your virtual machines, click the **VMs and Templates** icon, right-click the UAS Primary Datacenter object, point to the **New Folder** link, and then click the **New VM and Template Folder** option.

7. Enter **UAS-VMs** as the New Folder name and click **OK**.

8. Double-click UAS Primary Datacenter to display the UAS-VMs folder. In the Navigator field, click the back arrow until you return to the home page.

9. Next, we will add your UAS-vHost1-xxx host to the data center by clicking the **Hosts and Clusters** icon and then if necessary double-click the UAS Primary Datacenter to show the subfolders.

10. Right-click the **UAS-Hosts** folder and then click the **Add Host** option to display the Add Host window.

11. Enter the IP address of your UAS-vHost1-xxx host in the Host name or IP address field and click **Next** to display the Connection Settings pane.

12. Enter the root username and password and click **Next**. If necessary, click **Yes** to respond to the Security Alert and display the Host summary window.

13. Verify your host settings and click **Next** to display the Assign license window. Verify that Evaluation License is displayed and then click **Next** to display the Lockdown mode window.

14. Verify that the **Disabled** option is selected and click **Next** to display the VM location window. (This screen is used to allow you to select a folder for the VMs.)

15. Click **Next** to display the Ready to complete window as shown in Figure 8-15. Verify the selections and then click **Finish** to add the host to the inventory.

Figure 8-15   Web Client - Add Host - Ready to Complete window

Source: vCenter Server Web Client

16. Be sure your UAS-vHost2-xxx virtual machine is running and then repeat steps 10-15 to add your UAS-vHost2-xxx to the UAS-Hosts folder.

NOTE You can ensure an ESXi server is running by clicking its console and pressing the F2 key. When asked, log on using the root user's password to view the configuration menu. You can then press Esc to close the configuration menu page.

17. You should now be able to expand the UAS-Hosts folder in the UAS Primary Datacenter to display the IP address of both your ESXi hosts. (Your hosts may initially show up as "disconnected".)

18. To view information about a host, click the IP address of a host system and then click the **Summary** tab and check the connection state. If necessary, expand the **Hardware** tab and verify the hardware settings you made for this host. Do this for both your host systems.

19. Click your UAS-vHost1-xxx ESXi system and click the **Configure** tab. Click **VM Startup/Shutdown** to view the startup process for each virtual machine on this host. Verify that the vCenter virtual machine is set to start automatically.

20. Return to the Home page by clicking the Home icon and then clicking the **Home** link. In the following steps you will document the items that currently exist in your UAS Datacenter inventory.

21. Click the **VMs and Templates** icon and then, if necessary, expand your UAS Primary Datacenter to display the existing virtual machines. Record the virtual machines in your data center inventory below:

_____

_____

22. Click your UAS-xxx-vCenter1 virtual machine to display the Summary window.

23. If necessary expand the VM Hardware section and record memory utilization statistics shown below:

Memory Available: _____

Memory Active: _____

24. Click the **Configure** tab and click **Edit**. Notice that you can now manage the VMs from vCenter Server rather than connecting separately to each host. Click the **Network Adapter** and record the network options below along with which switch the VM is connected to:

Network Adapter 1 Switch: _____

Adapter Type: _____

25. Click **Cancel** and then return to the vCenter Home page. Click the **Storage** icon and if necessary expand your UAS Primary Datacenter to view the data stores listed in the Inventory. Click the **Summary** tab. Click each data store and then if necessary, click to expand the **Details** pane and record the data store's name, type, and number of hosts in Table 8-2:

Table 8-2   Data stores

Data Store Name	Data Store Type	Number of Hosts

26. Return to the Web Client Home page and click the **Networking** icon, then expand your UAS Primary Datacenter to show all the switch groups. Click each switch listed under your UAS Primary Datacenter, click the **Summary** tab, and record the virtual switch name and number of hosts below:

Switch Name   **Number of Hosts**

_____   _____

_____   _____

_____   _____

27. You have now completed this activity; if you like you can leave your browser open for the next activity.

Working with iSCSI Shared Storage

As you saw from the previous section, when you add hosts to the vCenter Server data center, the host's resources such as virtual machines, virtual switches, and data stores are also brought forward into the data center inventory. Certain shared devices such as NAS and iSCSI storage devices are accessed and managed by vCenter through the ESXi host. Other devices such as distributed switches and clusters are examples of inventory items that are available to the ESXi hosts, but are managed directly by vCenter Server. As described in Chapter 4, iSCSI devices act more like local disks providing vSphere the ability to create and format data stores on iSCSI devices using the VMware VMFS file system.

An iSCSI SAN consists of an iSCSI storage system, which contains one or more Logical Unit Numbers (LUNs) and one or more storage processors (SPs). Communication between the host and the storage array occurs over a TCP/IP network as shown in Figure 8-16.

An initiator can be hardware-based, called a host bus adapter (HBA), or the initiator can be software-based, known as the iSCSI software adapter. A **software iSCSI initiator** is VMware code built in to the VMkernel. The initiator enables your host to connect to the iSCSI storage device through standard network adapters. The software iSCSI initiator handles iSCSI processing while communicating with the network adapter. With the software iSCSI initiator, you can use iSCSI technology without purchasing specialized hardware.

An initiator connects to an iSCSI target by performing the following steps:

• The initiator finds one or more targets and establishes a connection using the target's connection requirements.

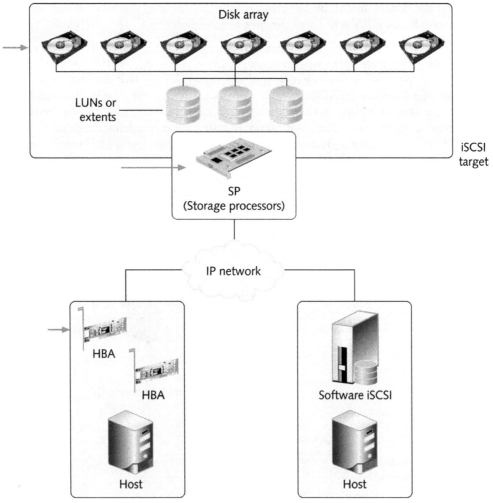

Figure 8-16   iSCSI objects

- A target presents LUNs to the initiator.
- The initiator sends SCSI commands to a target.

The ESXi host supports two iSCSI target-discovery methods:

- *Static discovery*—The initiator does not have to perform discovery. The initiator knows in advance all the targets that it will contact and uses their IP addresses and domain names to communicate with them.

- *Dynamic discovery*—When the initiator contacts a specified iSCSI server, it sends the SendTargets request to the server. The iSCSI server then responds by supplying a list of available targets to the initiator.

The names and IP addresses of these targets appear as static targets in the vSphere Client. You can remove a static target that was added by dynamic discovery. If you do remove the target, the target might be returned to the list during the next rescan operation, if a hardware-based HBA is reset, or the host is rebooted.

The IP networks that the iSCSI technology uses to connect to remote targets do not encrypt the data that they transport. So you must ensure the security of the connection by running the iSCSI on a separate network and implementing CHAP for a secure login. **CHAP (Challenge Handshake Authentication Protocol)** uses a three-way handshake algorithm to verify the identity of your host and, if applicable, of the iSCSI target when the host and target establish a connection. The verification is based on a predefined private key, also called a CHAP secret, that the initiator and target share. When using hardware-based HBA, ESXi supports CHAP authentication at the adapter level, so all targets receive the same CHAP secret from the iSCSI initiator. For software-based iSCSI adapters, ESXi supports CHAP on a per-target level. After the connection is established, the initiator transmits SCSI commands over the IP network to the target service as shown in Figure 8-17.

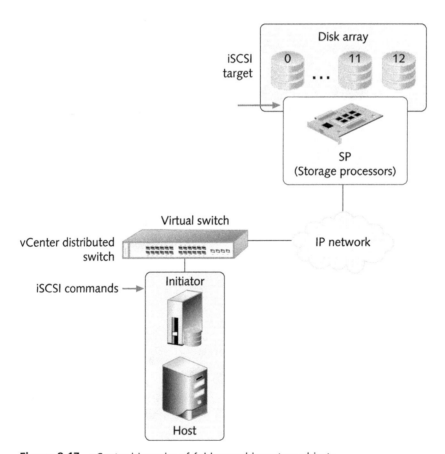

Figure 8-17 vCenter hierarchy of folders and inventory objects

As mentioned previously, a recommended security process is to use a separate network for iSCSI traffic. Rather than create and configure virtual switches on each host for iSCSI traffic, you can use a distributed switch created and configured from vCenter Server and then add it to each host that will access the iSCSI storage devices. In the following activity you will use the Web Client to create a distributed switch that can be connected to either host and then used to access a shared iSCSI target from both your hosts.

Activity 8-10: Adding a Distributed Switch to a Data Center

Time Required: 10 minutes

Objective: Use the Web Client to add a distributed switch to your UAS data center.

Requirements: Completion of Activity 8-9 (you will need to have an unassigned network adapter for your distributed switch, and three NAT network adapters on each of your ESXi hosts; if necessary, bring down your host computers and then follow the instructions in Activity 8-1 to add another NAT adapter to each host)

Description: Now that you have demonstrated how a virtual data center can be centrally managed using vCenter Server and the Web Client, Universal AeroSpace has invested in an iSCSI server and would like you to add it to the inventory on a virtual network that is accessible to all hosts. In this activity you will create a distributed switch for shared storage use and then add the switch to both the UAS hosts.

1. If necessary perform Chapter 4, Activity 4-3 to set up the iSCSI target server on your Windows Server 2016 VM.

2. If necessary, start an iteration of VMware Workstation 12 Player for each of the following virtual machines:

   Windows Server 2016

   UAS-vHost1-xxx

   UAS-vHost2-xxx

3. Wait for all virtual machines to start and then open a browser window and log on to your vCenter Server Web Client.

4. Click the **Global Inventory Lists** icon and if necessary click the Summary tab to display the Summary window

5. Click the **Create a new distributed switch** option from the Actions menu to display the New Distributed Switch window.

6. In the Name field, change the name to **UAS Network Storage** and click to select your UAS Primary Datacenter.

7. Click **Next** to validate your entry and display the Select version window.

8. Change the Distributed switch to version 5.5 and then click **Next** to display the Edit settings window shown in Figure 8-18.

9. Change the number of uplinks to 1 and change your Port group name to **iSCSI Storage Network**. Click **Next** to display the Ready to complete window.

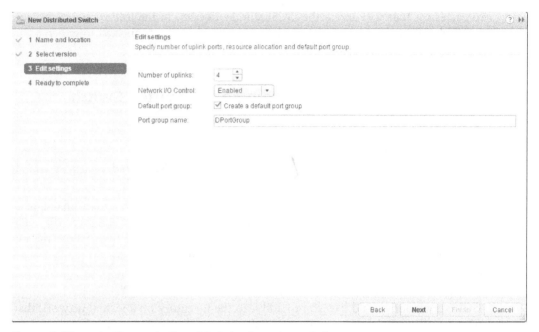

Figure 8-18 Web Client - Distributed Switch Edit settings window

Source: vCenter Server Web Client

10. Review your selections and then click **Finish** to create the distributed switch and return to the Summary window.

11. Under the Global Inventory Lists heading, scroll down and click the **Distributed Switches** option to display the Objects window containing your new distributed switch.

12. Click your **UAS Network Storage** switch and click the **Summary** tab to display the Distributed Switch Summary window.

13. Click the **Manage** tab and view the configuration options.

14. Click the **Getting Started** tab and then click the **Add and manage hosts** option from the Basic Tasks menu to display the Add and Manage Hosts window. Verify that the Add hosts option is selected, click **Next** to display the Select hosts window.

15. Click the **+New hosts...**link to display your existing hosts.

16. Click in the appropriate check box to select your UAS-vHost1-xxx host ip_address, click **OK**, and verify that your UAS-vHost1-xxx ip_address is listed with a status of Connected in the Select hosts window.

17. Click **Next** to add the distributed switch to your host and display the Select network adapter tasks window.

18. Verify that Manage physical adapters and Mange VMKernel adapters options are selected and then click **Next** to display the Manage physical network adapters window showing the physical adapters available on your host similar to the one shown in Figure 8-19.

Figure 8-19   Web Client Manage physical network adapters window

Source: vCenter Server Web Client

19. Click to select an unused NAT adapter under your UAS-vHost1-xxx ip_address and then click the **Assign uplink** icon, and click **OK** when you see the Select an Uplink dialog box to assign the Uplink 1 and return to the Manage physical network adapters window with the adapter now showing under the On this switch heading.

If you receive a Warning that one or more hosts have no assigned physical network adapters, be sure you have clicked the **Assign uplink** icon after selecting your network adapter. You must also be sure to select an unassigned network adapter on your selected host. If necessary, follow the procedure in Activity 8-1 to verify that you have 3 NAT adapters on each of your host computers.

20. Click **Next** to display the Manage VMkernel network adapters window. Under your UAS-vHost1 ip_address heading, click the **On this switch** heading and then click the **+New Adapter** icon to display the Select target device window.

21. Click the **Browse** button to display the network port groups. Click your **iSCSI Storage Network** group, click **OK**, and click **Next** to display the Port properties window.

22. Click to select the **Management** and **vMotion** check boxes and then click **Next** to display the IPv4 settings window.

23. Verify that the default Obtain IPv4 settings automatically is selected and then click **Next** to display the Ready to complete window.

24. Verify the settings and click **Finish** to return to the Manage VMkernel network adapters window.

25. Click **Next** display the Analyze impact window and verify that No Impact is displayed in the Status column.

26. Click **Next** to display another Ready to complete window. After verifying the settings, click **Finish** to complete the process and return to the Getting Started window.

27. Repeat steps 14–26 to add your UAS-vHost2-xxx ip_address to the distributed switch.

28. Use the Navigator window to return to the vSphere Web Client home page. You may leave your Web Client logged on for the next activity.

Activity 8-11: Adding iSCSI Shared Storage to a Data Center

Time Required: 10 minutes

Objective: Add an iSCSI target and storage device to your data center.

Requirements: Completion of Activity 8-10 (you will also need an iSCSI target role installed on your Windows Server 2016 VM; if necessary repeat Chapter 4, Activity 4-3 to create an iSCSI target and record its IP address before performing this activity)

Description: Now that you have demonstrated how a virtual data center can be centrally managed using vCenter Server and the Web Client, Universal AeroSpace has invested in an iSCSI server and would like you to add it to the inventory on a virtual network that is accessible to all hosts. In this activity you use the distributed switch to add the iSCSI LUN to your ESXi host computers.

1. Get the following information from Chapter 4, Activity 4-3. (If you created a new Windows Server 2016 machine for this chapter in Activity 8-1, perform the process described in Chapter 4, Activity 4-3 at this time to set up an iSCSI target and record the information you use below.)

   a. IP address of Windows Server 2016 iSCSI Target VM: _____

   b. IP addresses of allowed initiators: _____ _____

   c. CHAP username and password: _____ _____

2. If necessary, open a Web browser to your vCenter Server Web console and log on using your administrator username.

3. Click **Hosts and Clusters**.

4. Select your UAS-vHost1-xxx host under the UAS-Hosts folder, click the **Configure** tab, and then click the **Storage** tab.

5. If necessary, click the **Storage Adapters** option to display the existing storage adapters.

6. Click the **plus** symbol and select the **Software iSCSI adapter** option, then click **OK** when you see the message box.

7. Scroll down and click to select the **vmhba##** (where ## is a number such as 33) adapter under the iSCSI Software Adapter heading.

8. On the Details pane, click the **Targets** tab, and then click the **Dynamic Discovery** button to display the iSCSI server list.

9. Click the **Add** button to display the Authentication Settings window, and then click to remove the check from the **Inherit settings from parent** check box to display the Authentication settings window.

10. Using the information you recorded in step number 1, enter the ip_address of your Windows Sever 2016 VM in the iSCSI Server field.

11. In the Authentication Method field drop-down list, click the **Use unidirectional CHAP unless prohibited by target** setting.

12. In the outgoing CHAP credentials fields, enter the user **Name** and **Secret** password you recorded in step 1. When your Add Send Target Server window appears similar to the window shown in Figure 8-20 (your user name may be different), and click **OK**.

Figure 8-20 Web Client—Authentication Settings window

Source: vCenter Server Web Client

13. Close the rescan recommended message box and then click the **rescan** icon in the Storage Adapters menu bar (the fourth icon from the left) to rescan the storage adapter and then click the **Devices** tab to display the iSCSI storage devices similar to the one shown in Figure 8-21.

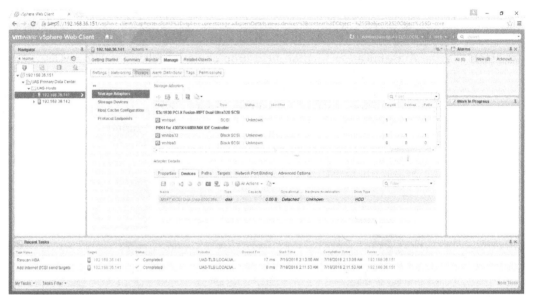

Figure 8-21   Web Client—iSCSI Storage Devices window

Source: vCenter Server Web Client

14. Click the iSCSI storage device and then, if necessary, click the **Attach** option from the All Actions menu (the Attach option may be grayed out if the device is attached by default). The disk will now be connected to your host computer.

15. Repeat steps 4–14 to connect the iSCSI device to your UAS-vHost2-xxx host.

16. Use the Navigator field to return to the Home window. In order for the iSCSI storage device to be used by vSphere, you will need to create and format one or more data stores on the device as described in the following section.

17. You may leave your browser open for the activities in the following section.

Working with the VMFS File System Data Stores

Before you can use an iSCSI storage device, you need to create a VMFS data store on the device. As you learned in Chapter 4 and Chapter 7, VMFS is the file system used by ESXi hosts for formatting local or iSCSI data stores. Because the VMFS file system is optimized for storing and accessing large files like virtual disks (which can be up to 64 TB) and memory images, they are ideally suited as repositories for the files of virtual machines. While you can use an NFS data store to store your virtual machines, the maximum size is limited by the NAS device and not all functions are supported.

As you learned in Chapter 7, using thin-provisioned virtual disks for your virtual machines is a way to make the most of your data store capacity. While you can use over-allocation to put more virtual disks on a data store than the physical size, if your data store is too small, it can become overcommitted when the thin-provisioned virtual disks end up using most of their allotted disk space. When a data store reaches capacity, alarms can be set to allow the vSphere Client to prompt you to provide more space on the underlying VMFS data store while it freezes the virtual machine until more space is added. To prevent this from happening, you should use the storage reports to check disk space usage on a regular basis by using the Show all Datastores report in the Storage Views tab.

To solve disk space issues you can expand the data store space or use VMware vSphere Storage vMotion (described later in this chapter) to move virtual machines to other data stores. Data stores are placed on iSCSI extents. An **extent** is a partition on a storage device (called a LUN in iSCSI terminology). A VMFS data store can be dynamically expanded by either adding more extents to the data store or expanding the storage used on an existing extent.

Extents can be added to any VMFS data store up to a maximum of 32 extents per data store. One reason for adding an extent to the data store is to create a VMFS data store that is bigger than the original extent. For example, assume that you have a data store that consists of one 5 TB extent and you run out of space in this data store. In order to add more files to this data store, you will need to extend the size of the data store by adding more extents to the data store from the iSCSI target server. The other option is to increase the size of the VMFS data store in its existing extent. Only extents with free space immediately after them are expandable. As a result, rather than adding new extents, you may be able to expand the existing extent so that it fills the available adjacent space. For example, assume that the storage administrator has given you a 1 TB extent on a LUN for the VMFS data store. When the VMFS data store fills up the storage administrator may be able to use management tools to expand the iSCSI LUN to 10 TB. After the underlying extent is increased, you could dynamically expand the VMFS data store using the free space now available in the extent. In the following activity you will create a VMFS data store in the iSCSI extent you connected to in the previous activity.

Activity 8-12: Creating iSCSI VMFS Data Stores

Time Required: 15 minutes

Objective: Create an iSCSI shared data store that is accessible from multiple hosts.

Requirements: Completion of Activity 8-11

Description: Now that you have attached each of your hosts to the iSCSI target, you next need to set up a shared data store. In this activity you will create a data store that is available to all your ESXi hosts.

1. If necessary start your virtual machines and then login using your vCenter Web Client and go to the Home page.

2. Click the **Storage** icon, then click the Summary tab if necessary to display all existing data stores in your inventory. Record your existing data stores below:

_____

3. Right-click your **UAS Primary Datacenter,** point to **Storage,** click the **New Datastore** option to display the New Datastore window, then click **Next** to display the Type window.

4. Verify that the VMFS type option is selected and click **Next** to display the Name and device selection window.

5. Enter the name **iSCSI Datastore1** and then select the IP address of your UAS-vHost1-xxx host in the Select a host to view its accessible disks/LUNs field.

6. Click to select the iSCSI LUN you added in Activity 8-11 and click **Next** to display the Partition configuration window. Change the Datastore Size field to be 80 GB as shown in Figure 8-22.

Figure 8-22   Web Client—Partition configuration window

Source: vCenter Server Web Client

7. Click **Next** to accept the default settings and display the Ready to Complete window.

8. Verify your settings and click **Finish** to create the new data store underneath your UAS Primary Datacenter.

9. Click **iSCSI Datastore 1,** click the Hosts tab, and verify that both your ESXi hosts are connected to this shared data store.

10. This completes the activities for this section. You may now log off of your Web Client and follow the normal shutdown procedure for each of your virtual machines.

Working with vSphere Virtual Machines

Many of the same tasks that you have learned to work with virtual machines using VMware Workstation Pro or Oracle VirtualBox can be used with vSphere. In this section we will look at some of the more specialized features of vSphere, including creating templates and migrating virtual machines between hosts.

Cloning Virtual Machines and Using Templates

In Chapter 7 you learned how to create virtual machines to run in ESXi hosts. In this section we will look at how to simplify the creation of new virtual machines by using templates and cloning.

Using Templates A template is a master copy of a virtual machine that can be used to create and provision new virtual machines. The template image often includes:

- A guest operating system
- A set of applications
- A configuration specification that provides settings to the new guest OS

Creating templates makes provisioning virtual machines faster and less error prone than provisioning physical servers or creating new virtual machines from scratch. While templates can coexist with virtual machines in the inventory, it is often helpful to place them in separate folders, possibly on a NAS device, in order to allow you to organize template collections and access them from multiple hosts. You can create a template by either cloning an existing virtual machine to a template or by converting an existing virtual machine to a template. Some administrators prefer to convert existing virtual machines into templates without the need to make a full copy of the virtual machine files and the creation of a new object.

When you use the Clone an existing virtual machine to a template option, the original virtual machine is retained and you are given the following format choices for the template's virtual disks:

- Same format as source
- Thin provisioned format
- Thick Provisioned Lazy Zeroed format
- Thick Provisioned Eager Zeroed format

When you convert an existing virtual machine to a template, the original virtual machine is replaced by the template and you are not offered a choice of formats, instead the template simply uses the existing virtual machine's disk format.

By default, when you deploy a virtual machine from a template, you will be given the chance to add the new virtual machine to the folder that you select during the creation process. In addition you will be given the option to modify the guest operating system from a specification file as described later in this section.

Cloning Existing Virtual Machines Cloning an existing virtual machine is an alternative to deploying a virtual machine from a template. Cloning a virtual machine creates a duplicate of the virtual machine with the same configuration and installed software as the original. After creating the clone, you can customize the guest operating system of the clone to change the virtual machine name, network settings, and other properties. Customizing the guest operating system prevents conflicts that might occur when a virtual machine and a clone with identical guest operating system settings are deployed simultaneously. To clone a virtual machine, you must be connected to vCenter Server. You cannot clone virtual machines if you connect the VMware Web Client directly to a VMware vSphere ESXi host. While the virtual machine being cloned can be powered on or powered off, it is best to power off a virtual machine to be sure all data file are closed so they can be properly copied.

When you clone an existing virtual machine or deploy a new virtual machine from a template you may need to change the guest operating system information, including name, network settings, and license information. This can be done using a set of specifications from the vSphere customization database as illustrated in Figure 8-23.

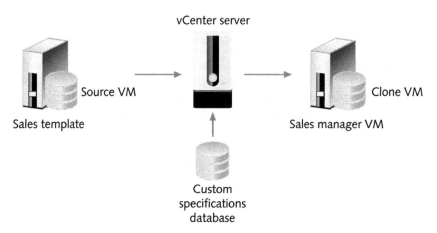

Figure 8-23   Deploying a new virtual machine from a template using custom specifications

Earlier Windows operating systems prior to Windows Vista required running a special "Sysprep" program on the guest virtual machine prior to cloning or creating a template from it. Newer Windows guest operating systems can now be customized by the Web Client when the new virtual machine is deployed or cloned. If the guest operating system is running VMware Tools, you can specify the customization settings by selecting a customization file during the cloning or deployment process. In the following activities you will create a customization file and then use it in the cloning and template deployment process.

Activity 8-13: Creating a Customization Specification

Time Required: 15 minutes

Objective: Create a virtual machine from a template or clone.

Requirements: Completion of Activity 8-12

If necessary, start each of the following virtual machines in a separate VMware Workstation 12 Player instance:

Your UAS-vHost1-xxx host

Your UAS-vHost2-xxx host

Your Windows Server 2016 VM

Description: As you know from previous experience, creating new virtual machines from scratch can be a time consuming and potentially error prone process. Universal AeroSpace would like to be able to rapidly provision virtual machines in the future to facilitate implementation of a Virtual Desktop Infrastructure (described in Chapter 9). In this activity, you learn how to clone an existing virtual machine as well as create templates and then use them to create new virtual machines.

1. Wait for all your virtual machines to start, then open the Web Client window to your vCenter Server and log on to vCenter.

2. Under the Operations and Policies section heading, click the **Customization Specification Manager** icon to open the Customization Specification Manager.

3. Click the **Create a new specification** icon in the upper left of the screen to display the New VM Customization Spec window.

4. Verify that the Windows option is listed in the Target VM Operating System field and that the option Use custom SysPrep answer file is NOT checked. Enter the name **UAS Workstation** in the Customization Spec Name field and click **Next** to display the Set Registration Information window.

5. Enter your name in the Name field and **UAS** in the Organization field, and then click **Next** to display the Computer Name window shown in Figure 8-24.

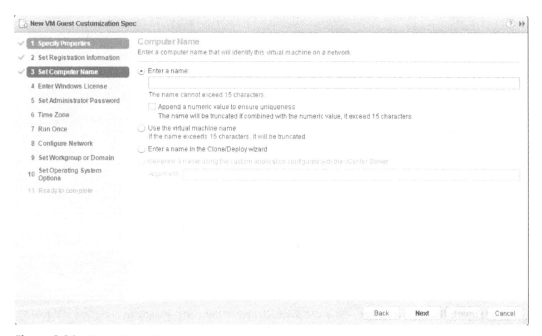

Figure 8-24   Web Client—Computer Name window

Source: vCenter Server Web Client

6. Click the **Use the virtual machine name** option and then click **Next** to display the Enter Windows License window.

7. At this time leave the Product Key field blank, click to remove the check from the **Include Server License Information** field, and click **Next** to display the Set Administrator Password window. Enter a password in the **Password** and **Confirm password** text boxes and record the password you enter below. Click to place a check in the **Automatically logon as administrator** check box and verify that this is only done once.

   Password:_____

8. Click **Next** to display the Time Zone window. Select your time zone and click **Next** to display the Run Once window. You can use this window to enter a command that the guest OS will run when it first starts. At this time, we will leave this screen blank and click **Next** to display the Configure Network window.

9. Notice that you can use this field to either take the default DHCP settings for the new guest OS, or configure specific IP address information. At this time leave the Use standard network setting for the guest default option selected and click **Next** to display the Set Workgroup or Domain window. Leave the default Workgroup option selected and record the default Workgroup name below:

   Workgroup name:_____

10. Click **Next** to display the Set Operating System Options window. Leave the default setting to Generate New Security ID (SID) and click **Next** to display the Ready to complete window similar to the one shown in Figure 8-25.

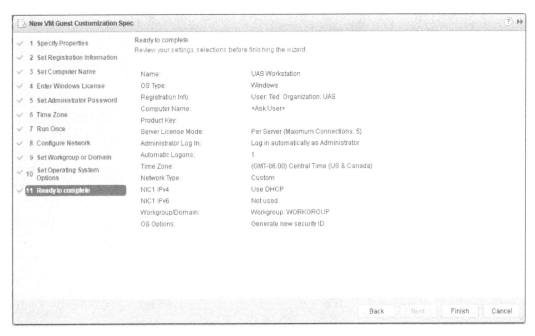

Figure 8-25 Web Client—New VM Guest Customization Spec—Ready to Complete window

Source: vCenter Server Web Client

11. Verify your selections and click **Finish** to create the specification and add it to the Customization Specification Manager window. You will use this specification in the following activity to create new virtual machines using the cloning and template deployment processes.

12. Click in the Navigator window to return to the Home page.

13. You may stay logged into your vCenter Web client for the next activity.

Activity 8-14: Creating a Template from a Virtual Machine

Time Required: 15 minutes

Objective: Create a template from an existing virtual machine.

Requirements: Completion of Activity 8-13

Description: As you know from previous experience, creating new virtual machines from scratch can be a time consuming and potentially error prone process. Universal AeroSpace would like to be able to rapidly provision virtual machines in the future to facilitate implementation of a Virtual Desktop Infrastructure (described in Chapter 9). There are two ways to create a template: convert an existing virtual machine to a template or clone a virtual machine to a template. In this activity you will learn how to convert an existing virtual machine to a template and then place that template in a new folder within your UAS Primary Datacenter.

1. If necessary, start each of the following virtual machines in a separate VMware Workstation 12 Player instance and then wait for the virtual machines to initialize (this may take several minutes depending on the speed of your computer).

   Your UAS-vHost1-xxx host

   Your UAS-vHost2-xxx host

   Your Windows Server 2016 VM

2. If necessary, open the vCenter Web Client and log on to vCenter.

3. When you see the vCenter Home page, click the **VMs and Templates** icon to display your existing VMs and folders.

4. Create a new folder for your templates by right-clicking the **UAS Primary Datacenter**, pointing to **New Folder**, and clicking **New VM and Template Folder** to display the New Folder... dialog box. Type **UAS Workstation Templates** in the Enter a name for the folder text box and click **OK** to create the folder.

5. If necessary, expand the UAS-VMs folder within your UAS Primary Datacenter and then right-click your **UASWorkstation1-xxx** VM, point to the **Template** menu, and then click the **Convert to Template** option.

6. Click **Yes** when you see the Confirm Convert dialog box. Within seconds the virtual machine will be converted to a template.

7. To move the template to your UAS Workstation Templates folder, right-click the **UASWorkstation1-xxx** template and click the **Move to...** option to display the Move To... window. If necessary, expand VM Folders and to select your UAS Workstation Templates folder.

8. Click **OK** to move the template to your UAS Workstation Templates folder.

9. If necessary click to expand your UAS Workstation Templates folder and then rename the UASWorkstation1-xxx by right-clicking the template and clicking **Rename**.

10. Enter **UAS Workstation Template** as the new name and click **OK** to change the name.

11. Use the Navigator window to go back to the vCenter Home page. You may leave your Web Client open for the next activity.

Activity 8-15: Creating Virtual Machines from Templates

Time Required: 15 minutes

Objective: Create a new virtual machine from a template.

Requirements: Completion of Activity 8-14

Description: Templates can greatly increase the efficiency of creating new virtual machines as well as provide a common set of applications and configurations. In this activity, you learn how to create a new virtual machine by using the template from Activity 8-14.

1. If necessary, from the Home page, click the **VMs and Templates** icon and then if necessary click to expand the **UAS Workstation Templates** folder.

2. Right-click your **UAS Workstation Template** and then click the **New VM from this template** option to display the Select a name and folder window.

3. Type **UASxxx Sales Workstation1** (where xxx represents your initials) in the Enter a name for the virtual machine field.

4. Expand your UAS Primary Datacenter and click to select your **UAS-VMs** folder, then click **Next** to display the Select a compute resource window.

5. Expand your UAS-Hosts folder and select the IP address of your UAS-vHost1-xxx host, then click **Next** to display the Select storage window.

6. Click to select your **iSCSI Datastore**, and then in the Select virtual disk format field, use the dropdown menu to select the **Thin Provision** disk format.

7. Click **Next** to display the Select clone options window. Record the three clone options below:

_____   _____   _____

8. Click the **Customize the operating system** option and click **Next** to display the Customize guest OS window. Click your **UAS Workstation** specification and click **Next** to display the Ready to Complete window similar to the one shown in Figure 8-26.

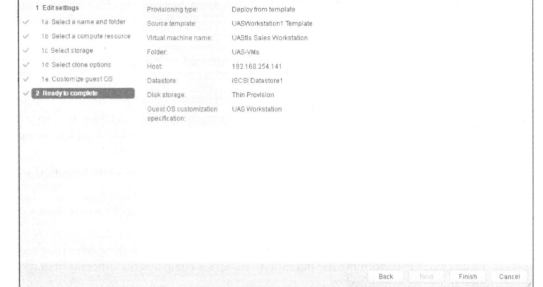

Figure 8-26 Web Client—Deploy from template—Ready to Complete window
Source: vCenter Server Web Client

9. Verify your options and click **Finish** to create the new virtual machine in the iSCSI data store.

10. Monitor the status of creating your new virtual machine in the Recent Tasks pane. It may take several minutes to complete the operation. After completion, your new UASxxx Sales Workstation1 should appear in your UAS-VMs folder.

11. Click your new VM, if necessary click the Summary tab, and then click the **Powered Off** link to power it on (you may see a message informing you it is not connected to a network, this should be OK after you power on the VM).

12. If you receive a message informing you that VMware Tools is not installed, click the option to Install VMware tools and then click the Mount button to mount the virtual CD drive containing the VMware setup files.

13. Open your remote console and click the **Send Ctrl+Alt+Delete** button to log in.

14. Start File Explorer on your VM, open This PC, double-click the VMware Tools drive and run the Setup program to perform a typical installation of VMware Tools on your UASxxx Sales Workstation VM. After the installation is complete, power down your UASxxx Sales Workstation1 VM.

15. When the task is completed you may stay logged in to the vCenter Web Client for the next section. If you have completed your work, close the Web client and properly shutdown your virtual machines.

In the next section you will learn how you can migrate virtual machines between hosts to increase fault tolerance and perform load balancing.

Migrating Virtual Machines between Hosts

It is often necessary to move virtual machines from one host to another for maintenance, load balancing, or fault tolerance purposes. In vCenter Server, you can perform the following types of migrations:

- *Cold*—Migrate a virtual machine that is powered off to a different shared data store or a data store that is accessible by only one host.

- *Suspended*—Migrate a virtual machine that is suspended to a different host or data store.

- *VMware vSphere vMotion*—Migrate a powered-on virtual machine to a new host. Virtual machine migration can be used to balance server load and for planned maintenance or upgrades to physical servers.

- *VMware vSphere Storage vMotion*—Migrate a powered-on virtual machine to a new data store. Storage vMotion is discussed in this lesson.

- *Enhanced vMotion*—Migrate a powered-on virtual machine to a new data store and a new host.

A major factor behind the decision to use a particular virtual machine migration technique is the purpose for performing the migration. Table 8-3 compares the different migration techniques and what is required to perform them.

Table 8-3   Migration type comparison

Migration Type	VM Power State	Change Host	Change Storage	Across Data Centers	CPU
Manual–Cold	Off	Yes	Yes	Yes	Different CPUs allowed
Manual–Suspended	Suspended	Yes	No	Yes	Same CPU
vMotion	On	Yes	No	Yes	Same CPU
Storage vMotion	On	NA	Yes	No	Will stay on same host
Enhanced vMotion	On	Yes	Yes	No	Same CPU

For example, you might need to bring a host down for maintenance and have some down time to move the virtual machines. In this case the simplest solution is to perform a manual migration. If you need to keep the virtual machines running while the migration is taking place, you will need to use vMotion to migrate the virtual machines instead of using a manual migration which requires the virtual machines to be in a cold or suspended virtual machine state. If you need to move a virtual machine's files to a different data store to better balance the disk load or transition to a different storage array, then Storage vMotion is the best method.

Some migration techniques, such as vMotion migration, have special hardware requirements that must be met to function properly. Manual techniques that migrate a cold migration suspended virtual machine do not have special hardware requirements to function properly.

Migration of a running virtual machine with vMotion is also called a hot migration because it allows migration of a virtual machine without powering it off.

Using vMotion As mentioned earlier, vMotion can migrate running virtual machines from one host to another with no disruption or downtime. In addition, vMotion can be used along with VMware's Distributed Resource Scheduler (DRS) to migrate running virtual machines from one host to another to help balance processing and storage loads. When using standard vMotion, the entire state of the virtual machine is moved from one host to another while the data storage remains in the same data store. The virtual machine state includes the current memory content along with the other information that defines and identifies the virtual machine. Moving a running VM means the memory contents—including transaction data and whatever operating system memory is used along with applications—must be moved between host hypervisors through the use of a memory swap file. For vMotion to work, both hosts need access to the virtual machine's memory swap file by storing it in a shared storage drive. The definition and identification information stored in the state includes the data that maps to the virtual machine hardware elements, such as: BIOS settings, devices, CPU, and MAC addresses for the network adapter card(s).

Figure 8-27 shows the configuration necessary to perform a vMotion migration of a running virtual machine.

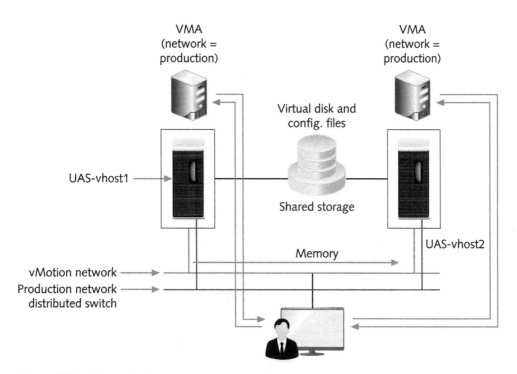

Figure 8-27 Using vMotion

In the figure, the source host is UAS-vHost1 and the target host is UAS-vHost2. As you can see from the figure, both the source host and the target host must have shared access to the data store holding the virtual machine's files. The actual vMotion migration would consist of the following three steps:

1. The virtual machine's memory state is copied over the vMotion network from the source host to the target host. Users continue to access the virtual machine and, potentially, update pages in memory. A list of modified pages in memory is kept in a memory bitmap on the source host.

2. After most of the virtual machine's memory is copied from the source host to the target host, the virtual machine is quiesced. No additional activity occurs on the virtual machine. In the quiesce period, vMotion transfers the virtual machine device state and memory bitmap to the destination host.

3. Immediately after the virtual machine is quiesced on the source host, the virtual machine is initialized and starts running on the target host. A Reverse Address Resolution Protocol (RARP) request notifies the subnet that virtual machine A's MAC address is now on a new switch port.

In the following activity you will gain experience with migrating virtual machines between hosts by performing a basic manual migration of a cold virtual machine. Appendix C provides additional coverage of providing Disaster Recovery and High Availability. You may wish to review that appendix at this time and then perform the following activity to practice migrating virtual machines between hosts and working with simple clusters.

Activity 8-16: Manually Migrating a Virtual Machine and Using Clusters to Improve High Availability

Time Required: 15 minutes

Objective: Migrate a virtual machine from one host to another and then create a host cluster.

Requirements: Completion of Activity 8-15

Description: Assume that your UAS-vHost1-xxx computer needs to be brought down and updated. Prior to doing this the servers and virtual machines need to be transferred to another host so that the office will continue to operate. In this activity you will move your UASWorkstation2-xxx host from UAS-vHost1-xxx to your UAS-vHost2-xxx and then create a cluster for your ESXi host systems.

1. If necessary and start an iteration of VMware Workstation 12 Player for each of the following virtual machines:

   Windows Server 2016

   UAS-vHost1-xxx

   UAS-vHost2-xxx

2. Wait several minutes for all virtual machines to initialize.

3. Open your vCenter Web Client and log on to display your Home page.

4. Click the **Hosts and Clusters** icon and then expand your UAS Primary Datacenter and UAS-Hosts folder.

5. Expand the ip_address of your UAS-vHost1 host to display your virtual machines.

6. Record the virtual machine names below:

_____

7. Right-click your **UASxxx Sales Workstation 1** virtual machine and click **Migrate** to display the Select the migration type window and record the options below:

_____

8. Verify that the **Change compute resource only** option and click **Next** to display the Select a compute resource window showing both your ESXi hosts.

9. Select the ip_address of your UAS-vHost2-xxx host and click **Next** to display the Select network window as shown in Figure 8-28.

Figure 8-28 Web Client—Hosts and Clusters—Select Network
Source: vCenter Server Web Client

10. Click the dropdown menu from the Destination Network column and record the possible destination networks available on the target host.

_____

11. Select your VM Network as shown in Figure 8-28 and click **Next** to display the Ready to complete window.

12. Verify your settings and click **Finish** to migrate the virtual machine.

13. You can now start your UASxxx Sales Workstation1 virtual machine and open a console window.

14. When you have completed testing the workstation, power it off and return to the vCenter Web Client. When the maintenance is complete on UAS-vHost1, the UASWorkstation2-xxx VM can be migrated back to that host.

15. As described in Appendix C, an important high availability feature of vSphere is implementing clusters. To create a cluster, return to the Home page, click the **Hosts and Clusters** icon, click the **UAS Primary Datacenter**, and if necessary click the **Getting Started** tab to display the Basic Tasks menu.

16. Click the **Create a cluster** option to display the New Cluster window (see Figure 8-29) and enter the name **UAS Host Cluster** in the Name field. Notice that the cluster can support a number of load balancing and high availability options.

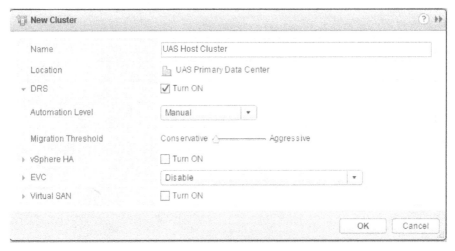

Figure 8-29 Web Client—Hosts and Clusters—New Cluster window
Source: vCenter Server Web Client

17. DRS is an option you can use to improve virtual machine performance by balancing processing loads between hosts. To implement DRS among hosts in this cluster click the **Turn ON** check box to select the **DRS** option and then use the dropdown menu to select **Manual** as the Automation Level and record the other automation levels options below.

_____

18. Change the Migration Threshold to **Conservative** and then click **OK** to display the cluster in your UAS Primary Datacenter.

19. You can either add a new host to the cluster, or move an existing host into the cluster. In the following steps you will move both your existing ESXi hosts to the cluster.

20. If necessary expand the UAS-Hosts folder for your UAS Primary Datacenter, right-click the ip_address of your UAS-vHost1-xxx host, and click the **Move to...** option to display the Move to ... window.

21. Expand your UAS Primary Datacenter, click your new UAS Host Cluster, and click **OK** to display the UAS Cluster–Move Host into This Cluster window shown in Figure 8-30.

What would you like to do with the virtual machines and resource pools for 192.168.254.141?

- Put all of this host's virtual machines in the cluster's root resource pool. Resource pools currently present on the host will be deleted.

- Create a new resource pool for this host's virtual machines and resource pools. This preserves the host's current resource pool hierarchy.

    Resource Pool Name   Grafted from 192.168.254.141

Figure 8-30 Web Client—Hosts and Clusters—Resource pool window
Source: vCenter Server Web Client

22. Verify that the default option to put all the host's resources into the cluster is selected and then click **OK** to move the host.

23. Repeat steps 20-22 to move your UAS-vHost2-xxx and all its resources into the cluster.

24. You can now practice using VMware High Availability as described in Appendix C.

25. This completes the activities for this section. You may leave your Web Client and virtual machines running for the next section.

Implementing Access Control Security

In Chapter 7 you learned how security policies could be applied to networks to implement access security rules including firewalls. Another major security action that you will need to perform as a vSphere administrator is to implement access permissions that allow you to separate job duties required to maintain the virtual data center. Access permissions can be accomplished by using a combination of lockdown mode along with the access control system.

As you saw when creating a cluster in Activity 8-16, you can increase the security of your ESXi hosts by putting them in lockdown mode. When you enable lockdown mode, no users have authentication permissions directly on the ESXi hosts, forcing all operations to be performed through vCenter Server. This means that when a host is in lockdown mode standard users cannot run commands from the command-line interface (vCLI) or directly on the DCUI host console. The root user is still authorized to log on to the direct console user interface (DCUI) when lockdown mode is enabled.

Authorization to perform tasks in vCenter Server is governed by an access control system that allows the vCenter Server administrator to specify in detail which users or groups can perform which tasks on which objects using the following terms and concepts:

Privilege—The ability to perform a specific action or read a specific property. Examples include powering on a virtual machine and creating an alarm.

Role—A collection of privileges. Roles provide a way to aggregate all the individual privileges that are required to perform a higher-level task, such as administering a virtual machine.

Object—An entity upon which actions are performed.

User or group—A user or group who can perform the action.

A permission is the combination of a role, a user or group, and an object. Roles are also configured on the ESXi host, similar to vCenter Server roles, which define things that the user is authorized to do on that host. For example, a user can be granted the ability to start a virtual machine. In the following activity you will create a user and then give that user access to power on a virtual machine.

Activity 8-17: Working with Users and Permissions

Time Required: 15 minutes

Objective: Create a new user and grant them access to a virtual machine.

Requirements: Completion of Activity 8-16

Description: An important part of implementing security is to establish separation of duties. Universal AeroSpace wants to add the ability to have some of their office staff perform certain routine tasks on the data center. In this activity you will add a user to your data center and give that user permissions to power on a virtual machine.

1. If necessary and start an iteration of VMware Workstation 12 Player for each of the virtual machines listed below:

   Your UAS-vHost1-xxx and UAS-vHost2systems

   Your Windows Server 2016 VM

2. Give the machines time (at least a few minutes) to initialize and then start a Web browser and log on to your vCenter Web Client to display the Home window.

3. Under the Administration heading, click the **Roles** icon, and then under Single Sign-On click the **Users and Groups** option to display the Users tab . Record the users with first names below:

   _____

4. Click the + symbol to display the **New User** window. Enter your username and password (password must meet minimum requirements shown by on the (i) icon), and click **OK** to add the user.

5. In the Navigator heading, click to return to the Home tab.

6. Click the **VMs and Templates** icon, expand the UAS-VMs folder in your UAS Primary Datacenter a and then click your **UASxxx Sales Workstation 1** virtual machine.

7. Click the **Permissions** tab and click the **plus sign** to display the Add Permission window.

8. Under the left Users and Groups pane, click the **Add** button to display the Select Users/Groups window.

9. At the top of the window, click to change the domain to your **UASxxx.local** domain name.

10. Click to select your username and then click the **Add** button to insert the name in the Users field. Click **OK** to add the new user and return to the Add Permission page as shown in Figure 8-31.

Figure 8-31 Web Client—Permissions—Select Users/Groups window

Source: vCenter Server Web Client

11. In the top right pane, click **Virtual machine user (sample)** to display the assigned role.

12. View the permissions and then click **OK** to save your permission settings. You can now return to the Home page window.

13. This completes the activities for this chapter. In later chapters you will continue to work with your vSphere data center to implement a Virtual Desktop Infrastructure and incorporate cloud computing features.

Chapter Summary

- In this chapter you learned how to use vSphere to implement a virtual data center using vCenter Server to manage virtualized resources such as shared storage and distributed switches.

- An important part of a virtual data center is being able to access virtual machines in the event of a hardware failure or other downtime. Implementing shared storage devices allows vSphere hosts to share access to a virtual machine. In this way if one host is down, another host that has access to the shared storage can run the VM with very little down time. In this chapter you set up both NAS and iSCSI storage devices on a Windows Server and then connected them to your ESXi hosts.

- While small virtual data centers can be implemented using the free version of vSphere, the real power of vSphere comes through using vCenter Server. vCenter Server is much more than just a management tool, it is the vSphere component that monitors, coordinates, and manages all resources in the virtual data center.

- vCenter Server includes three other major components, the Embedded Platform Services Controller, database system, and Web client.

- The Embedded Platform Services Controller contains all the support services such as inventory service, log services, and deployment that are used by all instances of vCenter Server. The Embedded Platform Services Controller can either be installed in the same computer as vCenter Server or exist on a separate system. Larger data centers with multiple vCenter Servers would use an External Platform Services Controller installed on one or more systems.

- The database system is used by vCenter Server to store information on all the data center inventory resources. The database that is included with vCenter Server can handle up to 1000 hosts and several thousand virtual machines.

- The vCenter Server contains secure Web services that can be accessed from a standard browser known as the Web client. In this chapter you used the Web client to perform all vCenter functions. vCenter Server can be installed on an existing Windows Server that is a member of an Active Directory domain or be installed as a Linux virtual appliance.

- In this chapter you learned how to download a copy of the vCenter Server appliance and then install it in a virtual machine running on one of your ESXi hosts. You then used the Web Client to access the vCenter Server and set up a data center that included your two hosts and all their virtualized resources such as the NAS shared data store.

- In this chapter you also used the Web Client to create a distributed switch that could be connected to multiple hosts as well as implement an iSCSI shared storage that included a VMFS data store. VMFS is the native data store used by vSphere hypervisors and provides special features that support large virtual disk files and higher performance and reliability.

- Virtual machines are the way in which resources in a virtual data center are used by applications and users. In this chapter you learned how vCenter Server can be used to store and manage virtual machines.

- When multiple virtual machines will be using the same guest operating system, using templates and cloning can save a lot of time as well as ensure all machines use a standard configuration.

- VMware Tools (which you used in previous chapters) is an important part of the cloning process as it allows you to apply a set of specifications to the new virtual machine including a computer name, license, and network settings.

- In this chapter you learned how to create a template by cloning an existing virtual machine and then use that template along with a set of specifications to create new virtual machine and store them in data center folders.

- Another important part of a virtual data center is providing access to virtual machines independent of a single host computer. vSphere accomplishes this through the process of migrating virtual machines between hosts. Manual migration is the simplest, but requires advanced planning and cannot be performed on machines that are running. Services like vMotion and Storage vMotion (sVMotion) are more difficult to implement, but allow running virtual machines (Hot VMs) to be moved from one host to another without any down time. In this chapter you manually migrated a cold (powered down) virtual machine from one host to another. In the following chapters you will continue to learn how to use other migration and high availability tools to implement more complex data centers.

Key Terms

CHAP (Challenge Handshake Authentication Protocol)

dynamic discovery

Embedded Platform Services Controller

extent

External Platform Services Controller

hostd agent

software iSCSI initiatory

static discovery

vpxa agent

Review Questions

1. A single vCenter Server can manage a maximum of how many powered-on virtual machines?

    a. 100

    b. 500

    c. 1000

    d. over 5000

2. Which of the following are **not** components of vCenter Server? (Choose all that apply.)

    a. Web Client

    b. Embedded Platform Services Controller

    c. vSphere Client

    d. PostgreSQL database

    e. SQL database

3. The vCenter Server appliance requires the use of which of the following? (Choose all that apply.)

    a. Microsoft Active Directory

    b. Linux

    c. Virtual machine running on ESXi host

    d. MySQL database

4. Which of the following processes runs on the vCenter Server system and communicates with a processes running the ESXi server?

    a. vpxa

    b. vpxd

    c. hostd

    d. vclientd

5. Which of the following clients can be used to connect to vCenter Server? (Choose all that apply.)

    a. Web Client

    b. vSphere Client

    c. vCLI

    d. DHCP

6. Which of the following can be iSCSI initiators? (Choose all that apply.)

    a. HBA

    b. iSCSI Software adaptor

    c. Distributed switch

    d. Extent

7. Which of the following initiators is built into the VMkernel?

    a. HBA

    b. iSCSI Software adaptor

    c. Distributed switch

    d. LUN

8. Which of the following is often used for secure login to an iSCSI target?

   a.   Active Directory

   b.   Kerberos

   c.   CHAP

   d.   Software initiator

9. Which of the following refers to logical unit on an iSCSI target?

   a.   Data store

   b.   Extent

   c.   Volume

   d.   HBA

10. Which of the following discovery methods was used in this chapter to find an iSCSI target?

    a.   Static discovery

    b.   Dynamic discovery

    c.   CHAP discovery

    d.   both static and dynamic

11. Which of the following virtual disk format types can be used to implement overallocation?

    a.   Thick provisioned

    b.   RDM

    c.   Thin provisioned

    d.   Independent disks

12. If an existing data store on an iSCSI SAN fills up, which of the following can you do to expand the data store? (Choose all that apply.)

    a.   Move the data store to a larger device.

    b.   If the extent that contains the data store has free space, you can expand the extent thereby increasing the size of the data store.

    c.   Add more extents to the data store.

    d.   You're doomed, quick apply for a new job.

13. Which of the following are valid ways to create a new template? (Choose all that apply.)

    a.   Convert an existing virtual machine to a template.

    b.   Clone an existing virtual machine to make a new template.

    c.   Select the Template option when you create a new virtual machine.

    d.   Migrate a virtual machine to the template folder.

14. Which of the following options allow you to change the disk format on the template from thin provisioned to thick provisioned? (Choose all that apply.)

    a. Convert an existing virtual machine to a template.

    b. Clone an existing virtual machine to make a new template.

    c. Select the Template option when you create a new virtual machine.

    d. Migrate a virtual machine to the template folder.

15. Which of the following are required to automatically customize a Windows 10 guest OS when creating a new virtual machine from a template? (Choose all that apply.)

    a. Create a customized specification for the guest OS.

    b. Run Sysprep on the template OS.

    c. Install VMware Tools on the template OS.

    d. Create new template from a cloned copy of the original.

16. Which of the following are true when performing the manual migration method? (Choose all that apply.)

    a. The machine can be in a suspended state.

    b. You can migrate the machine to a host with a different CPU.

    c. You can migrate a suspended virtual machine to a new storage location.

    d. You can migrate using vMotion.

17. When migrating a virtual machine using vMotion, which of the following is true?

    a. You can change the host computer.

    b. You can change the storage location.

    c. You can have a different CPU type.

    d. You can migrate the virtual machine between data centers.

18. Which of the following is an option you can select when creating a new cluster?

    a. DRS

    b. Virtual SAN

    c. vMotion

    d. Storage vMotion

19. Which of the following would provide load balancing within a cluster?

    a. DRS

    b. Virtual SAN

    c. vMotion

    d. Storage vMotion

20. Which of the following vCenter Home menu icons would you use to add a new user to your vCenter domain?

    a. vCenter Inventory Lists

    b. Hosts and Clusters

    c. Roles

    d. System Configuration

Case Projects

CASE PROJECTS

Case Project 8-1: Adding Your UAS-vHost3 Host to the UAS Virtual Datacenter and Distributed Switch

To allow managing the new UAS-vHost3 system, Universal AeroSpace has asked you to add the UAS-vHost3 system to its virtual data center. In this project you are to follow the procedure from Activity 8-9 and Activity 8-10 to add your UAS-vHost3 to the virtual data center and then connect it to the distributed switch using the new adapter you set up in Project 8-2. Document your work and report on your results.

8

- Add a NAT network adapter to your UAS-vHost3 virtual machine that can be used by the iSCSI distributed switch.

- Follow the instructions in Activity 8-10 to add your UAS-vHost3 to the distributed switch.

- Follow the procedure used in Activity 8-12 to add your UAS-vHost3 host as a user of the iSCSI shared storage.

Case Project 8-2: Using a Template to Create New Virtual Machines

Universal AeroSpace is planning to implement a Virtual Desktop Infrastructure for its business users. To do this, the company will need a number of Windows 10 workstations. In this project you are to use the template you created in this chapter to create a new Windows 10 virtual machine on your UAS-vHost3 system. Test your new Windows 10 system and create a report to management that documents the steps you used.

Case Project 8-3: Migrating a Virtual Machine

Now that Universal AeroSpace has its new host up and running, management would like to migrate the workstation virtual machines to this host. In this project you are to use the migration process you learned in this chapter to migrate the new virtual machine you created in Case Project 8-2 to your UAS-vHost1 system and then test it. Write a report on the procedure you use and record your results.

Case Project 8-4: Providing Separation of Duties

Universal AeroSpace would like to create a user account for its administrator that will grant that person read permissions for the virtual data center. In this project you are to create a user account (you provide the name) that has read permission to the data center. Test your account by logging onto vCenter Server and viewing the inventory. Write a report the describes the process and results.

chapter 9

Implementing a Virtual Desktop Infrastructure

After reading this chapter and completing the exercises, you will be able to:

- Describe the origins of Virtual Desktop Infrastructure and its benefits to the virtual data center
- Identify the challenges of VDI and how they have been met by new VDI technology
- Identify the components of a Virtual Desktop Infrastructure and describe their functions
- List and describe the VDI products from VMware and Microsoft
- Install VDI components for VMware and Microsoft products
- Deploy a virtual desktop using VMware and Microsoft products

For many early cultures the circle is a special, even sacred, symbol because it represents the cyclical nature of life and the Cosmos. While IT is a relatively young field, it also exhibits a cyclical nature. In the early days of computing, all applications were run on central mainframe computers connected to a network of relatively dumb terminals used to input and access information. More recently, microcomputers have distributed this processing power out to the desktop allowing users to run applications on their local systems independent of a central mainframe. In this distributed processing system, a central server is used to store shared data and applications across a network. The drawback to the distributed processing model is that having independent workstations often makes inefficient use of CPU, memory, and storage resources. In addition, there is a large "cost of ownership" factor when you consider the time and money it takes to manage all the independent workstations and keep them up-to-date. The latest trend is to centralize the processing back into the data center using technologies such as thin clients, terminal services, and most recently Virtual Desktop Infrastructure. In this chapter you will learn about the benefits, challenges, and components involved in setting up a basic Virtual Desktop Infrastructure for an organization.

Introduction to Virtual Desktop Infrastructure

Virtual Desktop Infrastructure has its roots in terminal service products. Terminal service products such as Citrix allow a server to run applications that are accessed using thin clients. Similar to the days of mainframe computers, thin clients act as terminals to the application, allowing the application to run on the server rather than the local desktop. Running applications on the server provides better management and security as well as allowing lower powered clients to run applications that would not install on the client computer due to out of date hardware or operating system. Terminal servers still play an important role in virtualized data centers, allowing users access to applications from a variety of devices including Web browsers.

As IT Departments virtualized servers using ESXi hosts, they also deployed a limited number of Windows virtual desktops for special purposes such as developer workstations or to deliver an application environment to a remote location. These virtual desktops could then be accessed using **Microsoft Remote Desktop Protocol** (**RDP**) on the user client computers. In this way, VDI originated from the VMware community requesting ways to deploy larger numbers of remote desktops to serve an ever-growing demand for a variety of user needs.

VMware along with a number of independent software companies recognized an opportunity to develop a Virtual Desktop Infrastructure and began building VDI solutions. One of these companies was a UK firm named Propero. Propero had originally competed with Citrix in the server-based terminal services market, but saw the opportunity and began to specialize in the desktop virtualization market by developing software that allowed IT Departments to blend access to terminal service applications and virtual desktops in a single Web interface. VMware saw the value in what Propero was doing and decided to jump-start its VDI solution by acquiring Propero in April of 2007. Early versions of VMware's VDI lacked a number of features previously found in the Propero products. Early versions of VDI focused primarily around a management component called a connection broker. As shown in Figure 9-1, a connection broker provides a way to connect thin clients to their assigned virtual desktops based on username and then manages and tracks these connections in a database for auditing and control purposes. Notice that the virtual desktops are stored in desktop pools on a shared SAN device, allowing them to be run by any available host.

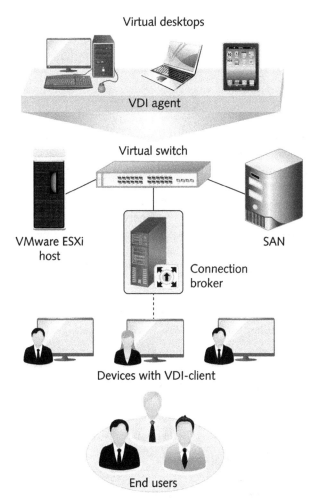

Figure 9-1   Simple Virtual Desktop Infrastructure using connection broker to connect users to their assigned desktop VM

In addition to the connection broker, SAN, and host systems, a basic VDI environment needs to have agent and client software as shown in the figure. The **agent software** is installed on each virtual desktop and communicates through the **connection broker** to the client running on the user computer. The client software logs on to the connection broker and then gets a list of virtual desktops that are available to that user. Virtual desktop machines are stored in groups called pools or collections. In addition to all the components, VDI needs an administrative console and control center. VMware incorporates its vCenter server administrative console in order to quickly provision virtual desktops based on standard desktop configuration templates. Microsoft VDI incorporates RDS into the Server Manager. Today VDI has grown to include not only desktop systems, but applications as well.

VDI Challenges and Features

While running a limited number of virtual desktops is fairly straightforward, implementing a large number of desktops for an entire department poses a number of challenges including storage space, load balancing, application management, and fault tolerance. In this section we will look at each of these challenges and how they have been addressed in modern virtual desktop environments.

Storage As shown in Figure 9-1, rather than storing virtual desktop systems on specific hosts, virtual desktop VMs are typically stored on shared NAS or SAN storage devices. Storing virtual desktop files on shared storage allows them to be run on different hosts based on processing loads and availability. For example, a few virtual desktops each occupying 40 GB of SAN disk space does not tax the storage budget, but if you scale that solution to 100 or more desktop VMs you can quickly tie up over 4 TB of expensive SAN storage. Fortunately, a number of solutions are available to decrease the amount of virtual storage needed to support a Virtual Desktop Infrastructure. The first of these solutions is using non-persistent desktops to allow users to share a virtual machine. This solution works well in school environments, where you may have hundreds of students but only a fraction will be using the system at any given time. When a student signs in they check out any available virtual desktop. When they are finished using the desktop they sign out and the desktop is returned to its original state, ready for the next student.

Another option is using "linked clones," also called **Differencing Disks** in Hyper-V. As shown in Figure 9-2, a linked clone is a virtual machine that is generated from a parent machine but only contains a subset of the files needed to make it a unique user environment.

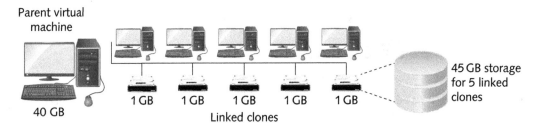

Figure 9-2   Linked clones sharing a single parent to save disk space

Linked clones allow you to have a single 40 GB parent for each unique user group or department and then create linked clones using only one gigabyte for each user's clone. Just like full clones, linked clones can be either persistent or non-persistent. When using non-persistent clones, users can share a clone just as with a full desktop system. When a user logs off, the clone is returned to its original state. Another advantage to linked clones is that only the parent needs to be changed when updating software or applications.

A similar option to linked clones is VMware's instant clone desktop feature known as pooled virtual desktops in Hyper-V. When using instant clone desktops the user desktop is created "on the fly" from a master that is running on the host hypervisor. Because they are created in memory, instant clone desktops do not require any disk storage, but are non-persistent as they are deleted from memory after the user ends their session.

Load Balancing Running too many virtual desktops on a single host can cause performance issues. For a truly responsive and low-risk environment each host's CPU and memory should remain below 60%–70% utilization depending upon the application and user requirements. You can monitor host memory and CPU utilization using an administrative console such as vCenter Web Client.

Enabling load balancing typically involves creating clusters that contain multiple hosts. The virtual desktops are stored on shared storage that is available to all hosts in the cluster. You can then either manually monitor host performance or set up an automated system such as VMware's DRS (Distributed Resource Scheduler) to automatically monitor host performance and if necessary use a service such as vMotion to move virtual desktops from heavily used hosts to hosts that have more capacity.

Fault Tolerance and High Availability Another important challenge in large virtual desktop environments is using fault tolerance techniques to maintain user desktop operation in the event of a host hardware or network failure. Both VMware and Microsoft offer high availability options that allow virtual machines (both servers and virtual desktops) to be migrated to other hosts in a cluster in the event of a host hardware failure. Network redundancy can be accomplished by using multiple network adapters in each host attached to separate physical switches.

User Data Management When sharing virtual desktops or clones in an organizational setting, an important aspect is preserving the user environment or profile. Microsoft servers provide the capability for users to move their profile between desktops through the use of roaming profiles. To ensure that the user environment is maintained across multiple sessions on different desktops, the profile is typically stored in a central location and cached on the local desktop. In order for user profiles to work properly the shared folder containing the profile must be available, the user needs appropriate permissions, and there needs to be sufficient space for the user's personal files. To help facilitate this process, VMware provides a **User Environment Management** (UEM) component that can automate the setup of roaming user profiles across virtual desktop systems. You will learn about implementing user profiles in the VMware and Microsoft sections of this chapter.

Application Management Making applications available to user desktop is another major concern of implementing a Virtual Desktop Infrastructure. Traditionally applications are installed on desktop images that are then applied to physical computers. There are a few problems associated with using this approach on a virtual desktop. The first, of course, is the storage requirement to have the same application installed on many desktops. When applications can be removed from the desktop, the number of images that need to be maintained can be reduced and applications delivered only to users based on their access permissions. The second challenge is the possibility of interference among applications that use some of the same desktop resources. Using application virtualization solves these problems by separating the applications into independent files, eliminating possible conflicts that can occur when you install multiple applications directly into the desktop OS. A third challenge is the need to update applications on many desktops as patches or new versions become available. The application development life cycle is another example of a cyclic process consisting of testing, deploying, upgrading, and removal steps. This process can be very time-consuming when it has to be repeated on multiple desktop images. To simplify the task of installing and managing applications, both VMware and Microsoft have application virtualization packages that are intended to work with the VDI environment. **Application virtualization** is a form of packaging an application that isolates the application's files from the underlying operating system, preventing interference among applications. In addition to saving disk space and preventing application conflicts, another big benefit to implementing application virtualization is the ability to tie applications to users versus the more traditional approach of installing applications into desktop images. VMware has two application virtualization packages called ThinApp and Vapp that are used to virtualize applications for deployment on virtual desktops. Microsoft offers similar application virtualization solutions called RemoteApp and App-V.

VDI Products

While there are a number of VDI products on the market, the undisputed product leaders are from VMware and Microsoft. VMware's latest VDI product is Horizon 7. Horizon is based on the earlier VMware View product line, but includes a number of enhancements and features. Microsoft provides a competitive VDI product line called Microsoft Virtual Desktop Infrastructure (very creative). Both products have many similar features and components. In this chapter you will learn about the components and features of each product as well as practice using each product to set up and manage a simple VDI environment. To gain experience with the new VMware Horizon 7 features and products you should perform Case Project 9-1 to use the VMware Horizon 7 online lab.

Working with VMware Horizon 7

VMware Horizon 7 provides a number of components and features that are designed to implement a scalable Virtual Desktop Infrastructure across multiple platforms and operating systems. Universal AeroSpace would like to get experience implementing a basic VDI environment for their Sales Department users. Since Sales Department users are often mobile in their work, using a VDI environment will make it easier for them to access their desktops from various locations using a variety of devices including laptop computers and tablets. In this section you will learn about the major components that make up a Horizon 7 VDI environment as well as how to use these components to implement a simple Virtual Desktop Infrastructure for the Universal AeroSpace simulation you have been working on in Chapters 7 and 8.

VMware Horizon Components

Figure 9-3 illustrates the essential components found in the VMware Horizon 7 product.

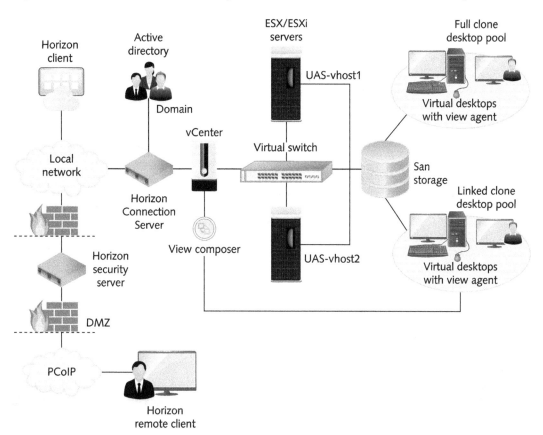

Figure 9-3 VMware Horizon 7 Basic Virtual Desktop Infrastructure components

The core of the Horizon virtual desktop system is the ESXi hypervisors that actually run the virtual desktop VMs. Just as with other vSphere environments, vCenter server is the central management component for administrating the virtual data center and implementing, managing, and monitoring features such as clustering, vMotion, DRS (Distributed Resource Scheduler), Networking, and Storage. The Horizon Virtual Desktop Infrastructure product is a set of components that work with the existing vSphere data center environment to make deploying, managing, and operating virtual desktops both feasible and affordable. As shown in the diagram, the central components of a Horizon VDI is the Horizon Connection Server and Horizon administrative Web console. Using the Horizon administrative console, you can create pools consisting of full desktop clones and then entitle users to run these desktops through a client installed on their device of preference. Each virtual desktop must be running the Horizon agent in order to communicate with the Horizon Connection Server and then connect to the client software running on the user's device. In addition to the basic or essential components shown in the diagram, Horizon consists of a number of other components and features to make the VDI more scalable and affordable. In this section we will look at each of the required and optional components as well as download the essential components so you can implement a simple VDI environment for your simulated Universal AeroSpace organization.

The Horizon Connection Server

As mentioned earlier, the **Horizon Connection Server** is the central component of the Horizon Virtual Desktop Infrastructure. The roles of the Horizon Connection Server include the following:

- Manage connections between Horizon clients and Horizon-managed desktops running the Horizon agent software.
- Authenticate user connection requests and provide access to assigned desktops.
- Host the Horizon administrative console.
- Work with VMware vCenter to manage, deploy, and maintain virtual desktops.

There are a number of Horizon Connection Server types available. The first connection server installed is referred to as a Horizon standard connection server (or just the **connection server**). As the number of virtual desktops increases, additional connection servers may be needed to provide the necessary performance. Up to six additional replica connection servers can be installed in a single Horizon VDI environment. While a connection server can handle up to 2000 clients, a second connection server is typically recommended to provide fault tolerance in the event the primary connection server is down. The hardware and software requirements for installing the connection server are shown in Table 9-1.

Table 9-1   Horizon Connection Server requirements

Component	Minimum Requirement	Recommended
Processor	Pentium IV 2.0 GHz or higher	4 CPUs
Memory	4 GB RAM or more	A minimum of 10 GB RAM for deployments of 50 or more desktops
Networking	100 Mbps NIC	1 Gbps NIC
Hard disk capacity	40 GB	60 GB
Operating system	Windows Server 2008 R2 or higher member server (Cannot be installed on domain controller)	Windows Server 2012 or later

In addition to the Standard and Replica connection server types, VMware Horizon also supports a Security server type that is used to create secure connections between remote clients and the internal connection server as shown in Figure 9-3.

Some of the features and functions of the Security Server include:

- Providing remote Horizon clients with their own dedicated connection broker.
- Setting up connections between remote Horizon clients and internal desktops.
- Authenticating user connection requests.
- Enabling optional RADIUS and RSA two-factor user authentication.

- Enabling placement of server in a DMZ (Demilitarized Zone).
- Able to be installed on a server that is independent of Active Directory.

A major part of the Horizon Connection Server is the administrative console shown in Figure 9-4.

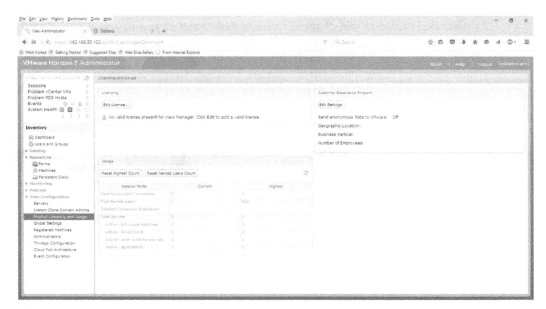

Figure 9-4   VMware Horizon 7 administrative Web console showing the License Window

Source: VMware Horizon 7

The administrative console communicates with both vCenter server and the Horizon Connection Server to enable the administrator to perform setup, configuration, and monitoring of the Horizon VDI environment. You will work with the Horizon administrative console to configure the connection server later in this section. While virtual desktops appear in vCenter Server the same as other typical virtual machines, it is important that all changes to the virtual desktops are done only through the Horizon administrative console in order to properly maintain information that Horizon stores in the database located on the Horizon Connection Server.

Horizon Agent and Client

The Horizon agent must be installed on any guest operating systems that will be used as virtual desktops. In addition to being installed on virtual machines, the agent can also be installed on physical desktops enabling them to be added to pools and managed from the Horizon Connection Server and accessed from Horizon clients. The agent is also responsible for enabling video access using a variety of display protocols including the original Remote Desktop Protocol (RDP), and the newer **PCoIP (PC over IP)** protocol. PCoIP is the preferred display protocol as it is designed to work efficiently with high definition graphics used in today's desktops. While RDP was based on bitmaps and bitmap caching, PCoIP is based on compressing and sending pixels in a manner similar to what is used on HDTV. PCoIP is a lossless protocol by default, meaning it builds the display without losing any of the definition or quality. In addition to allowing remote client connections and different display formats, the Horizon agent enables other functions such as user profiles, access to client devices such as USB drives and printers.

Horizon Composer

As described earlier in this chapter, using linked clones is an important part of reducing the storage requirements needed to run a large number of virtual desktops. Composer is the optional component of VMware Horizon that may be used to create a pool of linked-clone virtual desktops based on a parent virtual machine. Composer can either be installed on a dedicated virtual or physical server or on an existing vCenter virtual machine. The hardware requirements for installing Horizon Composer are shown in Table 9-2.

Table 9-2 Horizon Composer hardware requirements

Component	Minimum Requirement	Recommended
Processor	1–4 GHz x64	2 CPUs
Memory	4 GB RAM	8 GB RAM
Networking	100 Mbps	1 Gbps NIC
Disk capacity	40 GB	60 GB

An alternative to using linked clones is to use the new Horizon instant clone feature, which allows virtual desktop clones to be created on the fly from a running parent VM. In the following activity you will use your MyVMware account to download and register the essential components needed to set up a simple Virtual Desktop Infrastructure demonstration for the Universal AeroSpace organization.

Activity 9-1: Downloading Essential VMware Horizon Components

Time Required: 20 minutes

Objective: Register and download the VMware Horizon 7 components needed to implement a simple Virtual Desktop Infrastructure.

Requirements: A MyVMware user account and password

Description: Your manager would like you to set up a VMware Horizon virtual desktop demonstration system to allow Universal AeroSpace the opportunity to learn how this technology could be used by their Sales Department to provide client flexibility. In this activity you will access your MyVMware account and then download and register the essential Horizon components described in this section.

1. If necessary, start your Windows 10 workstation and log on using your administrator account.

2. Start File Explorer and optionally create a sub-folder in your downloads folder on your Windows 10 workstation named **VMware_Horizon** to contain the VMware Horizon files.

3. Open a Web **browser, go to my.vmware.com,** and log on using your MyVMware user-name and password.

4. Point to **Products** and **then** under All Products and Programs, click **Trial and Free Products.** Click the + symbol to expand the Desktop and Application Virtualization heading.

5. Click **VMware Horizon 7.**

6. Click the **Download Free Trial** link under the Download Evaluation Product heading.

7. Click the **Register** button.

8. Fill out the required information, selecting the minimum values in **each category.**

9. Click the **I agree to the terms and conditions outlined in the Evaluation End User License Agreement** check box and then click the **Start Free Trial** button. You will be given a list of license keys for Horizon products.

 If you are using an account that has an expired trial license you will be taken directly to the "How to Buy" option and not be able to download the trial software. In this case you will need to create a new account and then repeat steps 4-9.

10. Scroll down and click the **Manually Download** button to the right of the Horizon 7 View Connection Server (64-bit) and save the file to your VMware_Horizon folder.

11. Click the **Manually Download** button to the right of the Horizon 7.0 View Agent (32-bit) heading and save the file to your VMware_Horizon folder. (We need the 32-bit agent to install on your 32-bit Windows 10 virtual machines.)

12. Return to the opening myvmware page and click the **All Downloads** link. Scroll down to the Desktop & End-User Computing heading and then click the **View Download Components** link to the right of VMware Horizon (with View).

13. Under the VMware Desktop Clients heading, click the **Horizon Clients download page** link.

14. Scroll down and click the **Go to Downloads** link to the right of the VMware Horizon client for 64-bit Windows.

15. Click the **Download Now** button and then save the client file in the folder you created in step 2.

16. Verify that the file downloads correctly and then return to your myvmware home page.

17. Click the **My Evaluations** link and then click to expand your VMware Horizon 7 evaluation product.

18. Record the license key for your Horizon 7 Enterprise product below:

_____

19. Log off of your VMware account and close your Web browser.

20. You may leave your computer running for the activities in the next section.

Installing and Configuring a VMware Horizon 7 Connection Server

The major component needed to implement a basic VMware Horizon Virtual Desktop Infra-structure is the connection server. The connection server contains the Horizon administrator

Web console as well as connections to the vCenter server using the management network. The connection server uses Microsoft Active Directory to authenticate users and store basic event information and therefore must be installed on a Windows server that is a member of an Active Directory domain as shown in Figure 9-5.

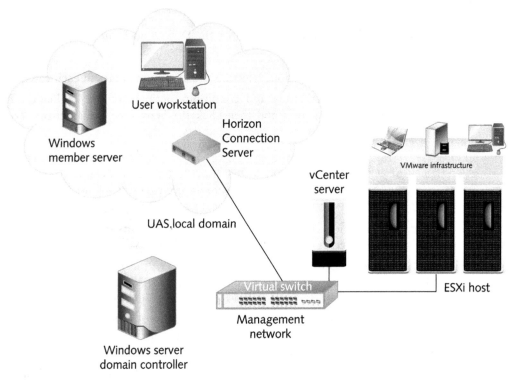

User workstation

Horizon
Connection
Server

Windows
member server

vCenter
server

VMware infrastructure

UAS.local domain

Virtual switch

ESXi host

Management
network

Windows server
domain controller

Figure 9-5   Sample Windows domain for UAS demonstration project

Notice that virtual desktop systems need to be domain members but that the vSphere environment is outside the domain connected by the network management switch through the vCenter server. To install the connection, you first need to set up an Active Directory server with at least one member server to host the Horizon Connection Server. After installing the connection server on the Windows member server you next need to configure the connection server to connect with the vCenter server. By default the domain administrator will also be the Horizon administrator. To delegate tasks you will probably want to create a separate account in Active Directory and then give that account rights to manage the Horizon VDI environment.

In the following four activities you will first install Microsoft Active Directory on your existing Windows Server 2016 server and then install a second Windows server and make it member server of the domain. After setting up the member server you will install Horizon Connection Server and then configure the server to work with your vCenter environment.

Activity 9-2: Installing Active Directory

Time Required: 20 minutes

Objective: Install Active Directory services on an existing Windows Server 2016 server.

Requirements: An existing Windows Server 2016 virtual machine with a static IP address and iSCSI data store from Chapter 8 Activity 8-12

Description: In order to demonstrate the VMware Horizon VDI system to the Universal AeroSpace Sales Department you will need to promote your existing Windows Server 2016 server (the one you used for the iSCSI and NAS storage) to a domain controller and create a domain named UASxxx (where xxx represent your initials). In this activity you first prepare your Windows server by checking its IP information and then promote the server to be the domain controller for your test system.

If your Windows server is already an Active Domain Controller from a previous activity you can record your server's IP address and domain name in steps 3 and 13 and then skip this activity.

1. If necessary, launch VMware Workstation Player 12 and start your Windows Server 2016 virtual machine.

9

When starting your virtual machines you should always start the Windows Server 2016 prior to starting your ESXi hosts. This is necessary for the ESXi hosts to be able to connect to the iSCSI datastore.

2. Log on to your Windows Server 2016 VM using your administrator username and password.

3. Open a command prompt window, then enter the command **IPCONFIG** and record your IP address information below:

   IP address: _____

   Subnet Mask: _____

   Default Gateway: _____

4. Return to Server Manager, and then click **Add roles and features** to start the Add Roles and Features wizard. After the wizard starts, click **Next** to display the Select installation type window.

5. Verify that the **Role-based or feature-based installation** option is selected and then click **Next** to display the Select destination server window.

6. Verify that your server is selected and then click **Next** to display the Select server roles window.

7. Click the **DNS Server** role and click **Add Features**.

8. Click to select the **Active Directory Domain services** option and then click the **Add Features** button to return to the Select server roles window.

9. Click **Next** to display the Select features window showing the NET Framework. Click **Next** to accept the defaults and read the information on the DNS Server window. Click **Next** to display the Active Directory Domain Services window.

10. Read the information on Active Directory and then click **Next** to display the Confirm installation selections. Verify that your selections are correct and then click **Install** to start the installation process. Click the Close button when the **Installation succeeded** message appears to return to the Server Manager window.

11. Click **AD DS** in the left pane, then click the **More** link at the right end of the Configuration required for Active Directory Domain Services message.

12. Click the **Promote this server to a domain controller** link to display the Deployment Configuration window.

13. Click the **Add a new forest** option, enter **UASxxx.local** (where xxx represents your initials) in the Root domain name field, and click **Next** to display the Domain Controller Options window. Record the name of you use for your Root domain: _____

14. Enter a password in the DSRM fields and record the password you use below:

    DSRM Password: _____

15. Record the default settings below and then click **Next**.

    Forest level: _____

    Domain level: _____

    Domain Name System (DNS) server selected? _____

    Global Catalog (GC) selected? _____

16. When you see the DNS delegation zone warning, click **Next** to continue. Record the NetBIOS name shown in the Additional Options window and click **Next** to display the Paths window.

    NetBIOS name: _____

17. Record the paths below and then click **Next** to display the Review Options window.

    Database folder: _____

    Log files folder: _____

    SYSVOL folder: _____

18. Verify your selections and then click **Next** to verify your options in the View Results pane. Record your results below:

    _____

19. Click **Install** to promote your server to a domain controller and view the progress and informational messages. During the process your system will sign you out and restart. The password used with local administrator will become the domain administrator's password.

20. When the system reboots you can log on using your new UASxxx\Administrator account.

21. Your system is now ready to install the connection server on a Windows server that is a member of your new domain.

22. You may leave your virtual machines running for the next activity.

Activity 9-3: Installing a Windows Member Server

Time Required: 20 minutes

Objective: Install Windows Server 2008 R2 or later on a new virtual machine and add it to the domain you created in Activity 9-2.

Requirements: Completion of Activity 9-2 and Windows Server 2008 R2 or later installation files

Description: Now that you have created an Active Directory, your next step is to set up a Windows member server that can host the VMware Horizon Connection Server. In this activity you will create another virtual machine for Windows Server 2016. You will then make the new Windows server a member of your UASxxx domain.

1. If necessary, start your Windows Server 2016 domain controller and log on as administrator.

2. If necessary, start both your UAS-vHost1 and UAS-vHost2 virtual machines.

3. Follow the instructions in Appendix B to use VMware Workstation 12 Player to create a Windows Server (2008 R2 or later) virtual machine on the NAT network that uses the following fixed IP address information and record the addresses you use below:

   IP Address: 192.168.###.102

   (where ### is the subnet from the IP address you recorded in step 3 of Activity 9-2).

   Record the IP address of your member server: _____

   Subnet Mask: Same as use recorded in step 3 of Activity 9-2.

   Default gateway: Same as you recorded in step 3 of Activity 9-2.

   DNS servers: Same as you recorded in step 7 of Activity 9-2.

As of this writing Windows Server 2016 was not compatible with VMware Horizon Connection Server. This should be changed when Windows Server 2016 becomes finalized.

4. If necessary, start your new Windows Server virtual machine and log on as the local administrator.

5. From Control Panel, open the Network and Sharing Center window. Click the **Change advanced sharing settings,** turn on **Network Discovery** and **file and printer sharing** for network connection, and then save your changes and close all Network and Sharing Center windows

6. Open File Explorer, right-click **This PC,** and click **Properties** to display the System window.

7. Click the **Change settings** link to the right of the Computer name, domain, and work-group settings heading.

8. Click the **Change** button to the right of the "To rename this computer or change its domain or workgroup, click Change" heading to display the Computer Name/Domain Changes dialog box.

9. Click to select the **Domain** option button, then enter **UASxxx** (where xxx represents your initials) in the Domain text box, click **OK**, enter your domain administrator username and password, and click **OK**. After a few minutes you should receive the "Welcome to the UASxxx.local domain" dialog box.

10. Click **OK** to close the dialog box and then click **OK** again, close all windows, and click **Restart Now** to restart your Windows member server.

11. You may leave all your virtual machines running for the next activity.

Activity 9-4: Installing VMware Horizon Connection Server

Time Required: 15 minutes

Objective: Install VMware Horizon 7 connection server on your Windows member server.

Requirements: Completion of Activity 9-3

Description: Now that you have set up your Active Directory domain and added a member server you are ready to install the VMware Horizon Connection Server. In this activity you will use the VMware Horizon directory you shared on your Windows 10 desktop to run the VMware Horizon 7 installation file. You will map a drive to the shared folder containing your Horizon installation files and then install the connection Server on your Windows server.

1. If necessary start all your virtual machines.

2. If necessary, enable **Shared Folders** in Virtual Machine Settings on your Windows member Server virtual machine, by clicking **Manage** from the **Player** menu and then clicking the **Virtual Machine Settings...** option to open the Hardware tab of the Virtual Machine Settings window. Click the **Options** tab, click **Shared Folders**, and then click the **Always enabled** option and then click **OK** to save the settings and close the Virtual Machine Settings window.

3. Map a drive to the VMware_Horizon folder you shared on your Windows 10 workstation and open that folder or alternately copy and paste the VMware-viewconnectionserver installation file from the shared folder of your Windows 10 workstation to the desktop of your Windows member server VM.

4. Double-click the **VMware-viewconnectionserver-x86_64-7.0.1-####.exe** file and click **Run** to start the installation wizard and display the Welcome window. Click **Next** to display the License Agreement window.

5. After reading the license agreement, click the **I accept the terms in the license agreement** option and then click **Next** to display the Destination Folder window.

6. Click **Next** to accept the default destination and display the Installation Options window.

7. Verify that the Horizon 7 Standard Server is selected along with Install HTML Access and then record the other Horizon Connection Server types and default IP protocol options below:

   Horizon Connection Server Options: _____, _____, _____

   IP protocol: _____

8. Click **Next**, and then enter a data recovery password and reminder in the appropriate fields. Record your password information below and then click **Next** to display the Firewall Configuration window.

   Data recovery password: _____

   Reminder: _____

9. Verify that the Configure Windows Firewall automatically option is selected and then click **Next** to display the Initial Horizon 7 Administrators window.

10. Click the **Authorize the local Administrators group** option and then click **Next** to display the User Experience Improvement Program window.

11. Since you are a student in the program, you may click to remove the check from the **Participate anonymously in the user experience improvement program** check box and then click **Next** to display the Ready to Install the Program window.

12. Click the **Install** button to start the installation process and monitor the progress.

13. After the installation is complete, click to remove the check from the Read me option and then click the **Finish** button to return to the member server's desktop.

14. You may leave your virtual servers running for the next activity.

Activity 9-5: Configuring Horizon 7 Connection Server

Time Required: 10 minutes

Objective: Configure the connection server to work with your vCenter server.

Requirements: Completion of Activity 9-4

Description: Now that the Horizon Connection Server has been successfully installed on the Windows member server, the next step is to configure the connection server to work with your vCenter environment. In this activity you will log on to the connection server and then connect it to your vCenter server.

1. If necessary, start a VMware Workstation 12 Player sessions for both your UAS-vHost1 and UAS-vHost2 virtual machines and wait a few minutes for both to initialize.

2. If necessary, start your Windows domain controller and member server.

3. From your desktop Windows 10 computer, open a Web browser and enter the following URL to open a browser session for your Horizon Connection Server:

https://*ip_address*/admin (replacing *ip_address* with the IP address of your member server that you recorded in step 3 of Activity 9-3).

 The Web page requires loading a pop-up. We have had the best success when using Mozilla Firefox or Google Chrome. If prompted, click the option to install Flash and then reboot the browser. Because https required an SSL certificate, you may see a message indicating that your connection is not private or secure (the message will vary based on the browser you are using). If this happens, click the **Advanced** button and then click the **Add Exception** button and then click the Confirm the security exception button or click the option to Proceed to ip_address (unsafe) link.

4. When you see the VMware Horizon 7 Administrator login window, enter the Active Directory administrator username (Administrator) and password and then click **Log In** to display the View Administrator console with the Licensing and Usage window as shown previously in Figure 9-4.

5. At this point you can click the **Edit License** button and enter the Horizon 7 license you recorded in Activity 9-1.

6. Under the **View Configuration** heading, click the **Servers** link to display the Servers.

7. With the vCenter Servers tab highlighted, click the **Add** button to display the Add vCenter Server window as shown in Figure 9-6.

Add vCenter Server		
Add vCenter Server	vCenter Server Information	
VC Information	**vCenter Server Settings**	**vCenter Server Settings**
View Composer		Before you add vCenter Server to View, install a valid SSL certificate signed by a trusted CA. In a test environment, you can use the default, self-signed certificate that is installed with vCenter Server, but you must accept the certificate thumbprint.
Storage	Server address:	
Ready to Complete	User name:	
	Password:	
	Description:	
		Provide the vCenter Server FQDN or IP address, user name, and password.
	Port: 443	
	Advanced Settings	**Concurrent Operations Limits**
	Specify the concurrent operation limits.	Max concurrent vCenter provisioning operations: the maximum number of concurrent VM cloning and deletion operations on this vCenter server (full clones).
	Max concurrent vCenter provisioning operations: 20	
	Max concurrent power operations: 50	Max concurrent power operations: the maximum number of concurrent VM power-on, power-off, reset, and configuration operations (full clones and linked clones).
	Max concurrent View Composer maintenance operations: 12	
	Max concurrent View Composer provisioning operations: 8	Max concurrent View Composer maintenance operations: the maximum number of concurrent View
	Max concurrent Instant Clone	
		Next > Cancel

Figure 9-6   VMware Horizon Connection Server vCenter Server Information window

Source: VMware Horizon 7

8. Enter the IP Address of your vCenter Server followed the username and password you established in Chapter 8 (administrator@UASxxx.local). Enter your name in the Description box and click **Next** to verify your vCenter Server connection. Since we have not established certificate services for our test environment, during this process you will receive an Invalid Certificate Detected warning message. To bypass this message, you may need to click the option to **View Certificate** and then click the button to **Accept** in order to continue and display the View Composer Settings window. Record the three View Composer installation options below:

_____, _____, _____

9. Since VMware Horizon Composer is not yet installed, verify that the **Do not use View Composer** option is selected and then click **Next** to display the Storage window. Record the default storage settings below: _____

_____ Cache size: _____

10. Click **Next** to display a Ready to Complete window similar to the one shown in Figure 9-7.

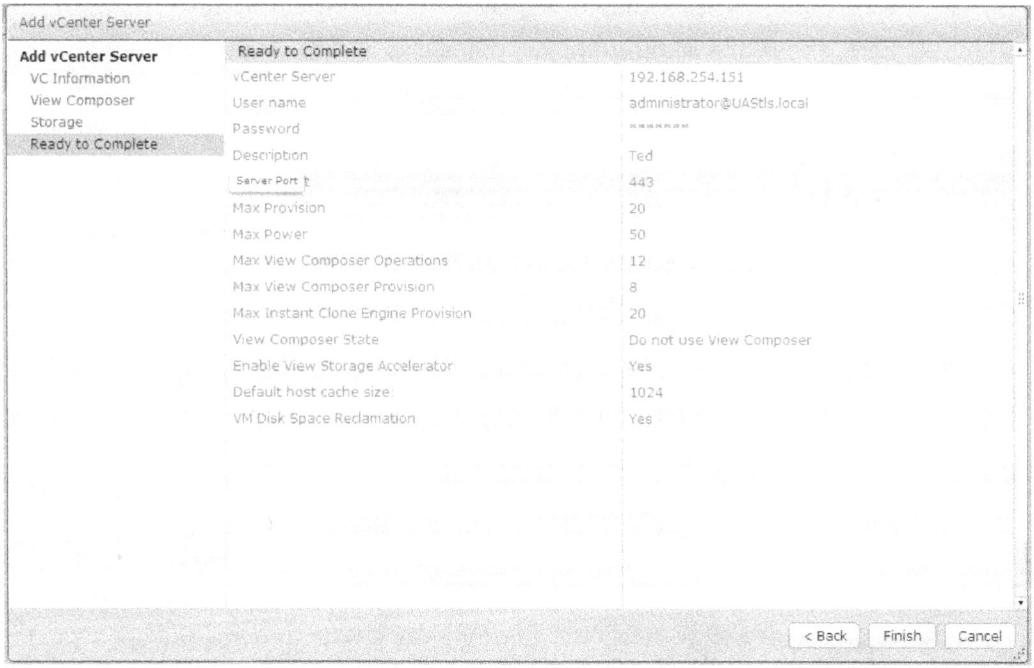

Add vCenter Server		
Add vCenter Server	Ready to Complete	
VC Information	vCenter Server	192.168.254.151
View Composer	User name	administrator@UAStls.local
Storage	Password	******
Ready to Complete	Description	Ted
	Server Port	443
	Max Provision	20
	Max Power	50
	Max View Composer Operations	12
	Max View Composer Provision	8
	Max Instant Clone Engine Provision	20
	View Composer State	Do not use View Composer
	Enable View Storage Accelerator	Yes
	Default host cache size:	1024
	VM Disk Space Reclamation	Yes

< Back   Finish   Cancel

Figure 9-7 VMware Horizon Connection Server Storage Settings window

Source: VMware Horizon 7

11. Verify your settings and click **Finish** to add your vCenter server to the Horizon administrative console.

12. The Basic configuration for the Horizon 7 is now complete. You may now Log off of the VMware Horizon 7 Administrator and leave all your virtual machines running for the next activity in which you will setup the Active Directory user accounts needed to deploy the Sales virtual desktops.

Activity 9-6: Setting up Active Directory Users and Groups

Time Required: 20 minutes

Objective: Add desktop users to Active Directory.

Requirements: Completion of Activity 9-3

Description: In this activity you will create a sales remote users group and manager user in Active Directory.

1. If necessary, start your Windows Server 2016 domain controller and log on as administrator.

2. If necessary, start Server Manager, click the **Tools** link, and click the Active Directory Administrative Center option to display the Overview window.

3. On the left pane, click your **UASxxx (local)** domain option, and then in the center pane, scroll down and click to select the **Users** folder. From the right hand Tasks pane click **New** and then click **Group** to display the Create Group window.

4. Enter **Sales Users** as the group name and click **OK** to create the group and return to the Administrative Directory Administrative Center window.

5. From the right hand Tasks pane click **New** and then click **User** to display the Create User window.

6. Enter **Lucas** in the first name and **McMann** in the Last name. Enter **LucasM** in the User UPN logon name and then enter a password in the password fields. Under password options, click to select the **Other password options** option button and then record the UPN logon name and password below:

   UPN Logon Name: _____   Password: _____

7. From the left pane, click the **Member Of** link, then click the **Add** button and then use the **Advanced** and **Find Now** buttons to add the new user to both the **Remote Desktop Users** and the **Sales Users** groups.

8. After adding the new users to the two groups, click **OK** to display the Members window.

9. Click **OK** to save the changes and return to the Active Directory Administrative Center window.

10. Repeat steps 5–9 to create the following demo user accounts and add them to both the **Sales Users** and **Remote Desktop Users** groups:

    Kellie Thori

    Eric Simonsen

    Kari Simons

11. You may now close the Active Directory Administrative Center window.

12. If you like, you may leave all virtual machines running for Activity 9-7. If you have completed your work, log off of your Windows Server and properly power down all your virtual machines.

Deploying a Virtual Desktop

Deploying a virtual desktop involves preparing one or more desktop virtual machines for use as desktop master templates, creating one or more desktop pools, creating user virtual machines using the template masters, adding user virtual machines to the appropriate pool, and entitling users to the virtual desktop. In the following sections and activities, you will learn what is involved in performing each of these steps and then apply what you have learned to creating virtual desktops you can demonstrate for the Universal AeroSpace project.

Preparing Desktop Virtual Machine Template The first step in deploying a Virtual Desktop Infrastructure is to prepare one or more virtual machines with the necessary settings and software it will need to become a template for deploying virtual desktops in the connection server desktop pool. You can do this either by creating a new virtual machine and installing a guest OS, or by cloning a template or existing virtual machine. If creating clone machines from templates, you should first set up a Customization Specification similar to the one you created in Chapter 8 to define virtual machine settings including Active Directory and other installation options. After you have created the desktop virtual machine that is part of your Active Directory, you will next need to install the Horizon agent and then use it to create a template you can use to create additional machines for other users. For example, to set up a demonstration for Universal AeroSpace your manager has asked you to have two virtual machines for the Sales Department. One virtual machine will be used by the sales manager, Lucas, and the other machine will be shared by the two sales technicians, Eric and Kellie. In the following activities you will create a customization specification for your Sales desktop systems and then use your existing UAS Workstation virtual machine to create clones for the sales virtual desktop systems. You will next prepare the Sales clone by installing the Horizon 7 agent and adding the machine to Active Directory.

Activity 9-7: Creating a Customization Specification for the Sales Desktops

Time Required: 10 minutes

Objective: Create a customization specification for use with creating virtual desktop clones.

Requirements: Completion of all activities through Activity 9-6

Description: The process of creating clone computers can be more consistent and simplified by using customization specifications. These specifications can also be used to automate the creation of user desktops. In the following activity you will use the procedure you learned in Chapter 8 to create a customization template for the Sales Department virtual desktops.

1. If necessary, log on to your Windows 10 desktop and start the following VMware Workstation 12 Player sessions:

    Both your UAS-vHost1-xxx host UAS-vHost2-xxx virtual machines

    Windows Server 2016 domain controller (also your NAS/iSCSI server)

    Windows member server

2. Start your Web browser, enter the URL for your vSphere Web Client, and log on using your vCenter administrator name and password.

3. If necessary, use the Home link to return to the home page and then click the **Customization Specification Manager** icon to display your existing customization specifications.

4. Click the **Create a new specification** icon from the top left side of the window to display the New VM Guest Customization Spec window.

5. Verify that Windows is displayed in the Target VM Operating System field and then enter **Sales Virtual Desktop Spec** in the Customization Spec Name text box along with a brief description stating that this specification is to be used to create virtual desktops for the Sales Department.

6. Click **Next** to display the Set Registration Information window. Enter your name in the Name field and **UASxxx** in the Organization field, and click **Next** to display the Computer Name window and record 3 computer name options below.

_____

_____

_____

7. Click the **Use the virtual machine name** option button and then click **Next** to display the Enter Windows License window.

8. Click to remove the check from the **Include Server License information** check box. You may either enter a license supplied by your instructor or leave the Product Key field blank to use the machine for the evaluation period. Click **Next** to display the Set Administrator Password window.

9. Enter a password for the local administrator account and record that password below. Verify that the **Automatically logon as Administrator** check box is selected with the number of times set to 1, and then click **Next** to display the Time Zone window.

Administrator password: _____

10. Select your time zone region and click **Next** to display the Run Once window.

11. Leave the Run Once window blank and click **Next** to display the Configure Network window.

12. Leave the default **Use standard network settings...** selected and click **Next** to display the Set Workgroup or Domain window.

13. Click the **Windows Server Domain** option button and then enter your domain name (see step 13 of Activity 9-2) in the Windows Server Domain text box. Enter **Administrator** in the Username field and then enter your domain administrator's password in the Password and Confirm Password test boxes (this is the same password and user you used to add your member server in Activity 9-3). Record the entries you make below and then click **Next** to display the Set Operating System Options window.

Windows Server Domain: _____

Username: _____

Password: _____

14. Verify that Generate New Security ID (SID) is selected and then click **Next** to display the Ready to Complete window.

15. Verify the settings on the Ready to complete window and then click **Finish** to create your new Sales Virtual Desktop Specification.

16. In the Navigator field, click the **Home** option to return to the vCenter home window.

17. You may stay logged on to your vCenter Web client and leave your virtual machines running for the next activity.

Activity 9-8: Creating a Sales Clone from an Existing Virtual Machine

Time Required: 10 minutes

Objective: Configure a virtual machine to be used in a desktop pool.

Requirements: Completion of Activity 9-7

Description: Create a clone of your existing UASWorkstation virtual machine that can be modified for later use as a template for your VMware Horizon desktop pool.

1. If necessary, log on to your Windows 10 desktop and start the following VMware Workstation 12 Player sessions:

   Both your UAS-vHost1-xxx host UAS-vHost2-xxx virtual machines

   Windows Server 2016 domain controller (also your NAS/iSCSI server)

   Windows member server

2. If necessary, start your Web browser, enter the URL for your vSphere Web Client, and log on using your vCenter administrator name and password.

3. If necessary use the Home link to return to the home page and then click the VMs and Templates icon and if necessary click to expand your UAS Workstation Templates folder.

4. Right-click your UAS Workstation Template and click the **New VM from This Template...** option to display the Select a name and folder window. Enter **UAS Sales Desktop Master** in the name field and select your UAS-VMs folder. Click **Next** to display the Select a compute resource window.

5. If necessary, click to expand all folders, then click the ip_address for your UAS-vHost1 host and click **Next** to display the Select storage window.

6. Click to change the Select virtual disk format to **Thin Provision** as shown in Figure 9-8.

7. Click your **datastore1** datastore and then click **Next** to display the Select clone options Window and record the three clone options below:

   _____, _____, _____

8. Click to select the **Customize the operating system** option and then click **Next** to display the Customize guest OS window.

9. Select the **Sales Virtual Desktop Spec** customization option you created in the previous activity and then click **Next** to display the Ready to complete window.

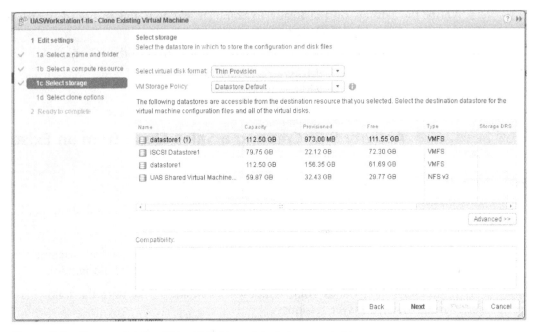

Figure 9-8 Clone an Existing Virtual Machine—Select storage window

Source: VMware vCenter Web Client

10. Verify your settings and then click **Finish** to create the Sales Desktop Master clone in your UAS-vHost1 datastore. You may wish to take a short break at this time as creating a new virtual machine from the template will take several minutes to complete.

 You may receive an error message informing you that the Windows 9 guest is not supported in this configuration due to not having VMware tools installed. You will install VMware tools and complete this customization in Activity 9-9.

11. Use the Navigator to return to the Home window.

12. You may stay logged in for the next activity where you will configure your new Sales Desktop Master VM for deployment.

Activity 9-9: Adding Your Sales Workstation Master VM to Your Active Directory Database

Time Required: 15 minutes

Objective: Configure a virtual machine to be used in manual deployment pool.

Requirements: Completion of Activity 9-8 (connection to Internet to be used by your virtual machines). Internet connection to access your "myvmware" account.

Description: This is the first of two activities necessary to prepare your Sales Desktop VM to be used as a template for the Horizon desktop pool. In this activity you will increase the disk capacity of your Sales Desktop Master and then prepare it to be used as a template for the desktop pool.

1. If necessary, log on to your Windows 10 desktop and start the following VMware Workstation 12 Player sessions:

   Both your UAS-vHost1-xxx host and UAS-vHost2-xxx virtual machines

   Windows Server 2016 domain controller (also your NAS/iSCSI server)

   Windows member server

2. If necessary, open a Web browser to your vCenter Web Client and log on as administrator.

3. Click the **VMs and Templates** icon and then expand your virtual data center to view all virtual machines.

4. Click your UAS **Sales Desktop Master** virtual machine and then click the **Edit virtual machine settings...** link from the Getting Started tab.

5. Increase the size of the virtual hard disk to **20 GB**.

6. Click the **VM Options** tab, and then click to expand the **VMware Tools** heading to display the VMware Tools options shown in Figure 9-9.

Figure 9-9 vCenter Web Console—VM Options window

Source: VMware vCenter Web Client

7. Click the **Synchronize guest time with host** option and then click **OK** to save your changes and return to the Getting Started window.

8. Click the Settings gear icon in the bottom right corner of the VM image, then click **Install Remote Console**. Next, click the **Save File** button in the Opening VMware-VMRC.msi dialog box. Wait for the file to download, then click the downloaded file to display the VMware Remote Console Setup dialog box.

9. Click the **Next** button in the VMware Remote Console Setup dialog box to start the wizard. Next click the check box to agree to the terms of the license agrement, and then click **Next** to proceed to the Destination Folder window.

10. Click **Next** to accept the default destination folder. (May click to remove checks from the "Check for product updates on startup" and "Help improve VMware Remote Console in the User Experience Settings window), and then click **Next** to go to the Ready to install VMware Remote Console window.

11. Click **Install**, then if necessary click **Yes** in the User Account Control dialog box. Click **Finish** when the install is complete.

12. Right-click your UAS **Sales Desktop Master**, click **Power**, and then click **Power On** to start your virtual machine; wait a few minutes for it to power on. If you receive a Power On Recommendations window, click **OK** to select the recommended host and record your selection below:

_____

13. If asked, click the option to Install VMware Tools and click **Mount** button.

14. From the Summary tab, click the Settings gear icon in the bottom right corner of the VM image and then click the **Launch Remote Console** link. If necessary, click the **Connect Anyway** when you see the Invalid Security Certificate dialog box.

If you see an External Protocol Request dialog box (may vary depending on your browser version), click the **Launch Application (on Continue)** button to enable the application plug-in.

15. If you see the Invalid Security Certificate message, click the option to connect to your virtual machine and then log on to your UAS Sales Desktop Master workstation.

16. Perform the following steps to increase the size of your C drive to 20 GB. Open File Explorer, right-click **This PC**, and click **Manage**. Click **Disk Management** to display the Unallocated disk space you added in step 5. Right-click in your C drive click the **Extend volume...** option to start the Extend Volume wizard. Click **Next** and then click **Finish** to add all 10 GB to your existing C drive and then close the Computer Management window.

17. Perform the steps below to install VMware Tools and add the workstation to your UAS domain.

The clone was not added to the domain because the DNS server settings were not established in the UASWorkstation VM.

18. If necessary, open File Explorer on your UAS Sales Desktop Master VM, right-click **Network**, and click **Properties**. Click **Change adapter settings**, right-click your Ethernet adapter, and click **Properties**.

19. Click **Internet Protocol Version 4 (TCP/IPv4)** and click **Properties**.

20. Click the **Use the following DNS server addresses** option button and then change the IP address of your Preferred DNS server to be the IP address of your Windows Server 2016 domain controller you recorded in step 3 of Activity 9-2. Click **OK** to save the change and then click **Close**. You may now close all your network configuration windows.

21. If necessary, open File Explorer, right-click **This PC**, and click **Properties**.

22. Under Computer name, domain, and workgroup settings, click the **Change settings** link to display the System Properties window. Click the **Change** button to the right of the "To rename this computer or change its domain or workgroup" heading to display the Computer Name/Domain Changes window.

23. Click the **Domain** option button, then enter the name of your domain (**UASxxx.local**) in the Domain text box and click **OK**.

24. You will see a dialog box asking for you to enter the name and password of a user that has authority to add this computer to the domain. Enter the administrator username and password for your UASxxx.local domain and click **OK** to add your Sales workstation to your UASxxx domain and display the Welcome to the UASxxx.local domain dialog box. Click **OK** to close the dialog box, and display a message stating you must restart your computer to apply these changes. Click OK to close the message box and then close any open windows. Click the **Restart Later** button as you will next install VMware Tools prior to restarting your Sales workstation.

25. If necessary open File Explorer and open the VMware Tools DVD drive and double-click the **Setup** program and follow the default prompts to install VMware Tools on your UAS Sales Desktop Master guest OS. When you see the Completed the VMware Tools Setup Wizard dialog box, click **Finish** and then click **Yes** to restart your UAS Sales Desktop Master workstation.

26. Leave all your virtual machines running and your remote console open for the next activity.

Activity 9-10: Preparing Your Sales Virtual Master for Use as a Deployment Template

Time Required: 10 minutes

Objective: Configure a virtual machine to be used in a Horizon deployment pool and then use it as a template.

Requirements: Completion of Activity 9-9 (you will need a connection to the Internet which will be used by your virtual machines, and a copy of the Horizon client downloaded on a shared folder from Activity 9-1)

Description: The second step in deploying virtual desktop is to create a template that can be used to create a pool of virtual machines. To create a virtual desktop template you will need to install the Horizon agent on your sales virtual machine master and then enable the necessary Active Directory remote users. After completing the installation of the Horizon agent and any other software required by the users, the virtual machine is ready to be converted to a template. In this activity you will complete the configuration your Sales Desktop Master for desktop deployment, move the virtual machine to your shared NAS device and then convert it to a template.

1. Log on to your Sales Desktop Master using your domain administrator username and password (click **Other user** and enter **UASxxx\administrator**). (Note that it will take a few minutes to prepare your new desktop profile.)

2. Next we need to enable Remote Desktop and assign the Sales group as remote desktop users. Start File Explorer, right-click **This PC**, and click **Properties** to display the System window.

3. Click the **Remote settings** link to display the System Properties window.

4. Click the **Allow remote connections to this computer** option and if necessary click **OK** when you see the Remote Desktop dialog box. Click the **Select Users...** button to display the Remote Desktop Users window.

5. Click **Add** and then click the **Advanced** button to display the Select Users or Groups window.

6. Click the **Find Now** button to display a list of users and groups.

7. Scroll down and double-click the **Sales Users** group to select it.

8. Click **OK** three times to save your changes and then close all the open windows.

9. In the following steps you will install the View Agent on the virtual machine so it can communicate with the connection server. Map a drive from your Sales Master virtual machine to your Sales Master Desktop VM: click **Start** and enter **\\ip_address** (where ip_address is the IP address of your Windows 10 workstation i.e.: 192.168.xxx.1). Enter your Windows workstation username and password. After logging on, you will see a list of shared folders. Double-click the folder containing the files you downloaded in Activity 9-1.

10. Double-click the VMware-viewagent-7.0.1 installation file to start the installation wizard. If you see a Security Warning dialog box, click **Run** and wait for the Welcome window.

11. Click **Next** to display the License Agreement window.

12. Click the **I accept the terms in the license agreement** option and then click **Next** to display the Network protocol configuration window.

13. Click the **IPv4** option and then click **Next** to display the Custom Setup window shown in Figure 9-10.

14. Click the down arrow to the left of the VMware Horizon View Composer option and then click the **This feature will not be available** option.

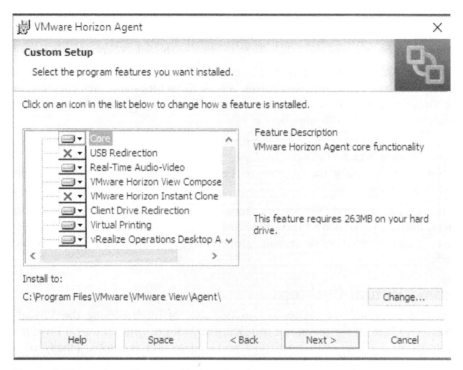

Figure 9-10   Horizon Client Installation wizard—Custom Setup window

Source: VMware Horizon 7

15. List the first five features that will be available in the space below:

_____

_____

_____

_____

_____

16. Click **Next** and then click the **Install** button to install the Horizon agent on the Sales Master virtual machine.

17. After installation is complete, click **Finish** and then click **Yes** to restart the Sales Desktop Master virtual machine.

18. Log on to the Sales Desktop Master using your administrator username and verify that the system is running. Try logging on with the user names you created in Activity 9-6.

19. Power down the Sales Desktop Master virtual machine.

20. From the vCenter Web Client's home page, click the **VMs and Templates** icon and if necessary click to expand your UAS-VMs folder.

21. Move your virtual machine to the NAS storage device by right-clicking the UAS Sales Desktop Master VM and then clicking the **Migrate...** link. Click the **Change Storage only** option button and then click **Next** to display the Select Storage window.

22. Click your UAS Shared Virtual Machines and Templates storage area and click **Next** to display the Ready to complete window. Verify the settings and then click **Finish** to move the virtual machine to your NAS device. It will take a few minutes to move the virtual machine to your NAS storage device.

23. Wait for the preceding task to complete and then right-click your newly configured **Sales Desktop Master** virtual machine, point to **Template** to display the Template options and then click the **Convert to Template** option and click **Yes** to convert your VM to a template.

24. This completes the activities for this section. You may now log off of your vCenter Web client, but you may wish to leave your virtual machines running for then activity. If you have completed your work session, properly log off and power down all your virtual machines.

Accessing Virtual Desktops

Planning and preparing the system is a major part of implementing the Virtual Desktop Infrastructure. Once all the pieces are in place, you will get your return on investment (ROI) by the speed with which you can deploy and update user desktops. Finally the time has arrived to see the fruit of your labors! Now that you have prepared a template that can be used to create virtual desktops, you will be able to perform the following steps to make the desktops available to the users:

- Create one or more desktop pools.
- Entitle users or groups to use the pools.
- Create virtual machines and add them to the appropriate desktop pools.
- Install the Horizon client on the devices that will be used to access the virtual desktops.
- Test your system.

Desktop pools are the collections of virtual desktops that are managed by Horizon Connection Server. Desktop pools define the resources that will be used by the virtual machines including the host hypervisor, networks, and data stores. When defining a desktop pool you can select either a specific host hypervisor or a cluster such as you created in chapter 8. When using a cluster, the virtual desktops can be moved between hosts based on host availability or performance.

As illustrated previously in Figure 9-3, there are two major types of desktop pools: full clone pools and linked-clone pools. Full clone pools contain complete virtual machines that can be assigned to user accounts or made available for use by all users of the pool. You can either create automated or manual full clone pools. In a manual pool, the virtual desktops VMs are created from a template and then configured and added to the pool individually. In an automated desktop pool, the administrator supplies the Horizon administrative console a list of machine names along with a template. The Horizon administrative console then automatically creates and configures clones for each of the virtual desktops named. Creating automatic desktop pools can save a lot of administrative time when you need to create many virtual desktops. Manual pools are best used when creating a small group of customized desktops. In the following lab activities you will use VMware Horizon administrative console to create an automatic desktop pool for the sales users, create and add two virtual desktops to the pool, and entitle the users to their assigned desktops. You will then install the Horizon 7 client on your desktop and test your virtual desktop implementation.

Activity 9-11: Creating an Automatic Desktop Pool

Time Required: 10 minutes

Objective: Create a desktop pool for full virtual machines.

Requirements: Completion of Activity 9-10

Description: The basic preparations are over and finally you will get a chance to actually work directly with VMware Horizon to deploy a simple virtual desktop environment. In this activity you will create an automatic desktop pool and then use your Sales Desktop Master template to create virtual desktops in the pool and assign them to users in the Sales Department.

1. If necessary, log on to your Windows 10 desktop and start the following virtual machines:

   Windows Server 2016 domain controller

   Windows member server

   UAS-vHost1 and UAS-vHost2

2. If necessary, access your VMware Horizon 7 administrator Web page by opening a Web browser, then entering the URL: **https://*ip_address*/admin** (where ip_address represents the IP Address of your Windows member server), and then logging on using your UAS domain administrator username and password.

3. If necessary, expand the **Catalog** heading and click **Desktop Pools** to display the Desktop Pools window.

4. Click the **Add** button to display the Add Desktop Pool window shown in Figure 9-11.

5. Verify that the Automated Desktop Pool option is selected and then click **Next** to display the User assignment window.

6. Click **Floating** and describe how a floating pool is used in the space below:

   _____

7. Click **Dedicated,** verify that the **Enable automatic assignment** option is selected, and then click **Next.**

8. Verify that your vCenter server is selected and then click **Next** to display the vCenter Server window.

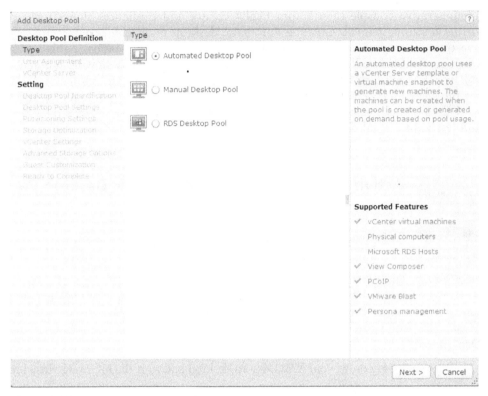

Figure 9-11 Add Desktop Pool window

Source: VMware Horizon 7

9. Verify that your vCenter server IP address is selected and then click **Next** to display the Desktop Pool Identification window.

10. Enter **SalesDesktopPool** in the ID windows and **Sales Desktop Systems** in the Display name field. Leave the Access group field as root (/) and then click **Next** to display the Desktop Pool Settings window shown in Figure 9-12.

11. Under Remote Settings, click to the **Immediately** option in the Automatically log off after disconnect field.

12. Click the arrow to the right of the Default display protocol and list the available protocols below:

_____

_____

_____

13. Scroll down and click to set **HTML Access** as **Enabled** and then click **Next** to display the Provisioning Settings window shown in Figure 9-13.

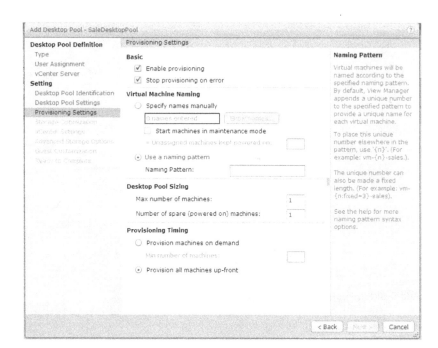

Figure 9-12   Add Desktop Pool - Desktop Pool Settings window

Source: VMware Horizon 7

Figure 9-13   Add Desktop Pool—Provisioning Settings window

Source: VMware Horizon 7

14. Click to remove the check from the **Stop provisioning on error** check box and then click the **Specify names manually** option button and click **Enter names...** to display the Enter Machine Names dialog box.

15. Enter the following machine names in the Enter Machine Names dialog box.

    SalesMgr

    SalesTech

16. After both virtual desktops have been entered, click **Next** to verify the entries. When the names have been entered successfully, click **Finish** to close the pane and return to the Provisioning Settings window.

17. Verify that the **Provision all machines up-front** option button is selected and then click **Next** to display the Storage Policy Management window. Since you do not have a Virtual SAN, the field will be grayed out. Click **Next** to display the vCenter Settings window as shown in Figure 9-14.

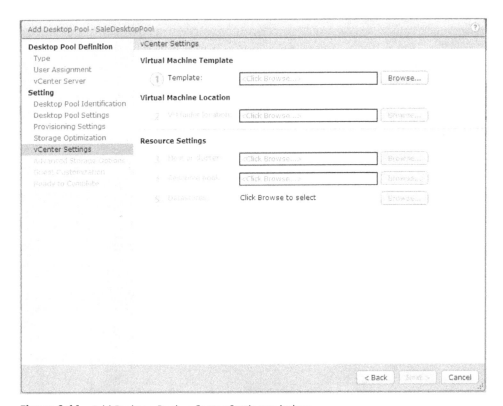

Figure 9-14   Add Desktop Pool—vCenter Settings window

Source: VMware Horizon 7

18. Click the **Browse** button to the right of the Template field and select your **UAS Sales Desktop Master,** and then click **OK** to return to the vCenter Settings window.

19. Click the **Browse** button to the right of the VM Folder Location field and then click to select your **UAS-SalesDesktops,** and then click **OK** to return to the vCenter Settings window.

20. Click the **Browse** button to the right of the Host or cluster field, then select either your UAS Host Cluster (if enabled) or your **UAS-vHost1** IP address and click **OK** to return to the vCenter Settings window.

21. Click the **Browse** button to the right of the Resource Pool field, then select either your UAS Host Cluster (if enabled) or the IP address of your UAS-vHost1 host and then click **OK** to return to the vCenter Settings window.

22. Click the **Browse** button to the right of the Datastores field, then click to select **datastore1** and then click **OK** to return to the vCenter Settings window.

23. Click **Next** to display the Advanced Storage Options window shown in Figure 9-15.

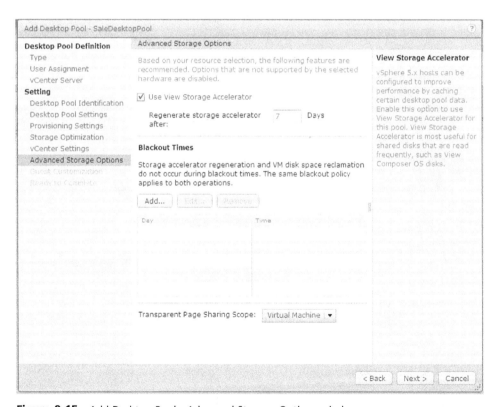

Figure 9-15 Add Desktop Pool—Advanced Storage Options window

Source: VMware Horizon 7

24. Verify that the **Use View Storage Accelerator** option is selected and then click the **Add** button to set a Blackout time from 8:00–10:00 Monday through Friday. Click **OK** and then click **Next** to display the Guest Customization window.

25. Since you will need to manually configure the systems for the sales users, for this pool, if necessary, click the **None—Customization will be done manually** option and click **Next** to display the Ready to Complete window.

26. Review and confirm your settings and then click **Finish** to create SalesDesktopPool and provision the virtual desktops. This process can take several minutes, and you can observe the status of the provisioning process by double-clicking the new SalesDesktop-Pool and then clicking on the Summary or Inventory tab.

Activity 9-12: Entitling Users to Their Assigned Desktops

Time Required: 20 minutes

Objective: Entitle users to use Sales pool and then assign a user to a virtual desktop.

Requirements: Completion of Activity 9-11

Description: The next step is to entitle users to the desktop pool and individual workstations. To allow users to share a workstation, you can entitle a group to use the desktop pool and then leave one or more desktops unassigned. When a user from the group logs on, they will be allowed access to any available desktops that are not specifically assigned to a user's account. To start with, UAS would like to have the sales manager, Lucas McMann, assigned to the SalesMgr workstation. Other Sales Department users will share access to the SalesTech virtual desktop system. In this activity you assign the Sales group to the desktop pool and then assign Lucas to the SalesMgr virtual desktop system.

1. If necessary, open a browser window for your Horizon Web page and log on as administrator.

2. Under Catalog heading, click the **Desktop Pools** link to display the existing Desktop Pools window showing your SalesDesktopPool.

3. Double-click your **SalesDesktopPool** to display a Summary window similar to the one shown in Figure 9-16 (your Summary window should show an Automatic Desktop Pool type).

4. Click the **Entitlements...** button and then click the **Add entitlement...** option to display the Add Entitlements window. Click the **Add** button to display the Find User or Group window as shown in Figure 9-17.

5. Click the down arrow to the right of the Domain field and select your **UASxxx.local** domain.

6. Click to remove the check from the **Users** check box and then click the **Find** button.

Figure 9-16 SalesDesktopPool Summary window

Source: VMware Horizon 7

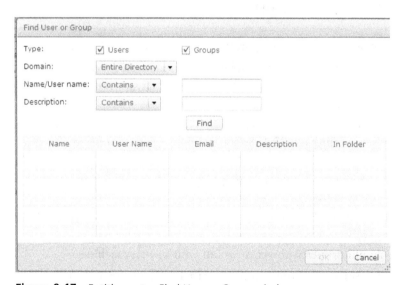

Figure 9-17 Entitlements—Find User or Group window

Source: VMware Horizon 7

7. Scroll down and click the **Sales Users** group, and then click **OK** to add Sales Users to the Entitlements window.

8. Click **OK** to save the changes and return to the Summary window. Click the **Inventory** tab to display your virtual desktop systems.

9. Right-click the **SalesMgr** virtual machine and then click the **Assign user...** option to display the Find User window.

10. Click to select your **UASxxx.local** domain and click the **Find** button to display a list of users in your domain. Notice that no groups are shown since a group cannot be assigned to a virtual desktop.

11. Click your **Lucas McMann** user account and click **OK** to add Lucas to the Users column.

12. After completing this process you are ready to test your virtual desktops. Leave your View Administrator and other virtual machines running for the next activity.

Activity 9-13: Installing Horizon Client

Time Required: 10 minutes

Objective: Install the VMware Horizon client for Windows.

Requirements: Completion of Activity 9-12

Description: Now that you have created a desktop pool and added virtual machines and entitled users, it is time to install the Horizon client on your desktop so you can test your Horizon VDI system. In this activity you will install the Horizon 7 client on your Windows 10 desktop.

1. If necessary, expand the View Configuration heading and click **Servers**.

2. Click the **Connection Servers** tab to display your connection server name.

3. Click your connection server and then click the **Edit** button to display the Edit Connection Server Settings window shown in Figure 9-18.

4. In the External URL field, replace the server name with the IP Address of your Windows member server (https://192.168.###.102:443). The address in the PCoIP Secure Gateway field will change automatically to show the ip_address.

5. When you have changed all names to IP addresses, click **OK** to save your changes and return to the Servers window.

6. Log off of your VMware Horizon administrative console and close your Web page.

7. Since you will have to reboot your workstation to install the VMware Horizon client, at this time you should properly power down all your virtual machines.

8. From your Windows 10 desktop computer start File Explorer and open the folder you created in Activity 9-1 containing your VMware Horizon installation files.

9. Double-click the **VMware-Horizon-Client-x86_64-4.1.0-##** file name and if requested, click **Yes** in the User Account Control dialog box to display the VMware Horizon Client Setup window and record the current settings under the Typical option below:

_____, _____, _____

10. Verify that the Typical setup option is selected and then click the **I Agree & Install** button to start the installation wizard. The installation will take place automatically.

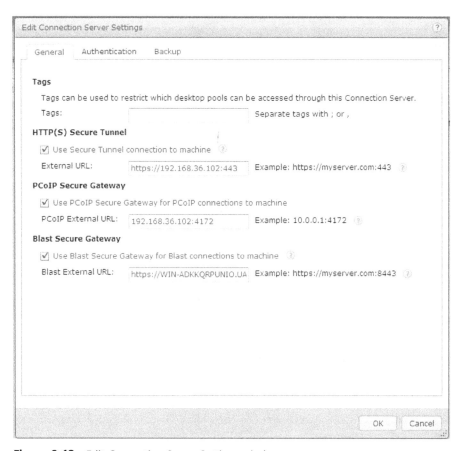

Figure 9-18   Edit Connection Server Settings window

Source: VMware Horizon 7

11. Click **Finish** after the installation is complete and then restart your Windows 10 workstation.

12. Start the following virtual machines and wait several minutes for them to initialize:

    Windows Server 2016 Domain controller

    Windows Member server (contains the VMware Horizon Connection Server)

    Your UAS-vHost1 and UAS-vHost2 host virtual machines

13. Leave your virtual machines running for the next activity.

Activity 9-14: Testing Connections to Your Virtual Desktops

Time Required: 10 minutes

Objective: Use the VMware Horizon client to test access to your virtual desktops with the user accounts you created in Activity 9-10.

Requirements: Completion of Activity 9-13

Description: Finally it's show time. In this activity you will demonstrate how Lucas, Kellie, and Eric can all access their virtual desktop systems using the Horizon client installed on their device.

1. Use the Start button to display your applications, and then click the **VMware Horizon Client** application to open the VMware Horizon Client page.

2. Click the **New Server** button, enter the IP address of your Windows member server (that contains the VMware Horizon Connection Server), and click **Connect**. If you are presented with a certificate warning message dialog box, click to **Continue** and display the Login window.

 Notice that the "https:" is crossed out. This is because no valid certificate was used to log on.

3. Enter KellieT in the User name box and then enter the password for Kellie that you recorded in Activity 9-6 and then click the **Login** button.

4. Double-click the Sales Desktop Pool icon and record your results.

5. Test your virtual desktop by creating a folder on the desktop named **Kellie Folder**. Record your results below:

_____

6. Click **Options** from the menu bar and then click **Disconnect and Log off** to terminate your session.

7. Start the VMware Horizon Client, double-click the Horizon Connection Server icon, and log on as LucasM. Double click the Sales Desktop and record your results below:

_____

8. Create a folder on the desktop named LucasM Folder.

9. Click **Options** from the menu bar and then click **Disconnect and Log off** to terminate your session.

10. Open your Horizon Web console and if necessary log on as the Administrator.

11. If necessary, expand the **Catalog** heading and click **Desktop Pools**. Double-click your SalesDesktopPools and then click the **Inventory** tab.

12. Right-click your **SalesTech** virtual desktop and then click **Enter Maintenance Mode** and click **OK**. Users are not allowed to access desktops that are in Maintenance Mode. When in maintenance mode you can use the vCenter Web console to make changes to the disk or other settings.

13. Right-click your **SalesTech** virtual machine and then click the **Exit Maintenance Mode** and click **OK** to return the desktop to operational mode.

14. Start the Horizon client and log on using your EricS user name and password. Open the desktop and notice that the folder created by KellieT does not appear on the desktop.

15. Click **Options** and then click the **Disconnect and Log Off** option to exit your session.

16. This completes the activities in this section. You should now log off of all your virtual desktops and properly close all your VMware Workstation 12 Player sessions. In the next section you will learn how to work with Microsoft Virtual Desktop Infrastructure (VDI) and learn about some of its similarities and differences.

Working with Microsoft Virtual Desktop Infrastructure

Remote desktops have a long history in Microsoft operating systems. Terminal Services was introduced with Windows NT and allows users to connect to a server that would run their applications and provide an individual desktop and file storage. Beginning with Windows Server 2008 this technology is now known as Session Virtualization and has been joined by Virtual Desktop Infrastructure (VDI) to become **Remote Desktop Services (RDS)**.

Microsoft Virtual Desktop Infrastructure Components

There are five major components that make up the Virtual Desktop Infrastructure, as shown in Figure 9-19, consisting of the following:

- *RD Connection Broker*—Connects users to virtual machines, reconnects them as needed, and balances performance by choosing virtual machines from different servers when possible.

- *RD Web Access*—Provides a Web portal that allows users to easily access their virtual machines from a browser.

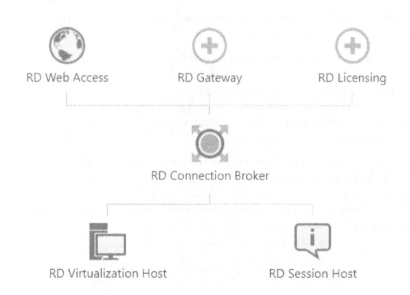

Figure 9-19 The components of Remote Desktop Services

Source: Windows Server 2016

- *RD Virtualization Host*—Manages the Hyper-V servers that will be hosting the virtual machines used for VDI.

- *RD Gateway*—Enables secure access to virtual machines over the Internet without the need to use a VPN, this component is optional.

- *RD Licensing*—Manages the Virtual Desktop Access (VDA) and Software Assurance (SA) licenses authorizing use of operating systems on virtual desktops.

Although not part of VDI, a sixth component of RDS is the RD Session Host, providing server desktops as Terminal Services did rather than virtual machines.

Installing Microsoft Virtual Desktop Infrastructure

The individual RDS components can be installed on multiple servers, but for the purposes of this book they will be installed on a single server. All of the components will be installed on to a separate Windows Server 2016 host computer rather than the one created previously in Chapters 5 and 6, as RDS cannot be installed onto a Domain Controller. The new RDS server will need to be a member of Active Directory, and can join the STC domain hosted by the earlier server (which will then need DHCP). Refer to Activity 5-1 to install the Hyper-V role on the new server.

To start the installation of Remote Desktop Services, first open the Server Manager. Click Start, Server Manager. Click Manage in the upper right corner, then click Add Roles and Features.

The Add Roles and Features wizard will be familiar at this point in the book, previously used to install Hyper-V, Active Directory, and other server roles. However, this time after the Installation Type window, as shown in Figure 9-20, you will choose the Remote Desktop Services installation option. This special option will install and configure all of the required individual roles (components) noted above.

Next, in the Select deployment type window, as shown in Figure 9-21, you will choose the deployment type. The Quick Start option will install all components onto a single server and create a collection without any options for modifications, providing a live Virtual Desktop Infrastructure when the wizard completes. You will be using a standard installation, the current best practice, which allows full customization and multiple servers, and you will create the collections afterwards.

In the Select deployment scenario window, as shown in Figure 9-22, you choose either virtual machine-based desktops or session-based desktops. You will be installing virtual machine-based desktops. Although the wizard only allows you to choose one option, you can install and use both by re-running the wizard afterwards, or adding the RD Session Host role through the normal Add Roles option.

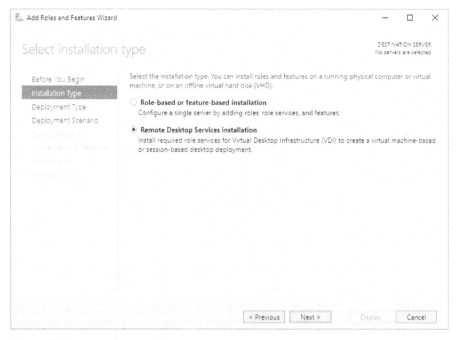

Figure 9-20   The Select installation type window

Source: Windows Server 2016

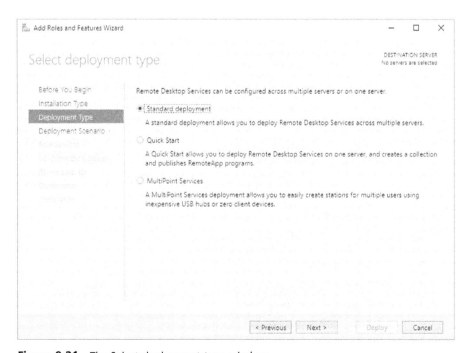

Figure 9-21   The Select deployment type window

Source: Windows Server 2016

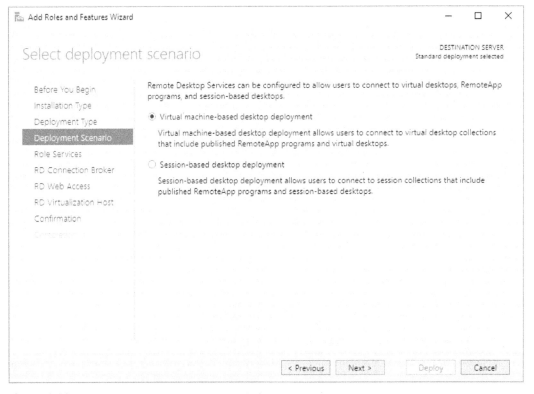

Figure 9-22 The Select deployment scenario window

Source: Windows Server 2016

Next, the Review role services window will list the RDS roles being installed as shown in Figure 9-23. All installations will get the Connection Broker and Web Access, and then either the Virtualization or Session Host based on deployment scenario.

In the next three steps you choose which servers to install the Connection Broker, Web Access, and Virtualization Host services. A check box lets you easily install Web Access onto the same server as the Broker, a common scenario. When choosing a Virtualization Host, it can be set to create a new virtual switch.

Next, in the Confirmation window you review your selections. Selecting "Restart the destination server automatically if required" is recommended. Then you proceed to the Completion window, where each component's installation progress is displayed. The server will reboot several times, resuming the wizard.

Once installed, you can access Remote Desktop Services from the new selection in the left pane of the Server Manager, as shown in Figure 9-24.

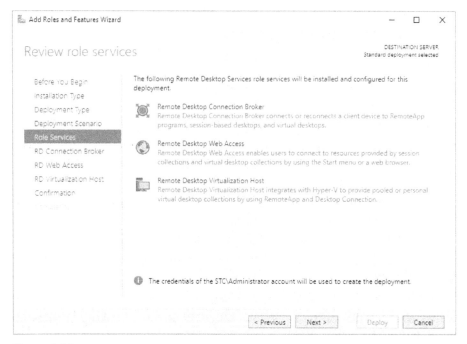

Figure 9-23 The Review role services window

Source: Windows Server 2016

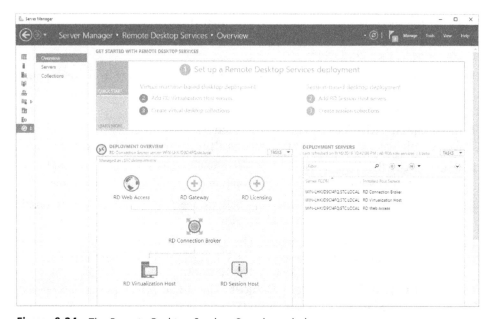

Figure 9-24 The Remote Desktop Services Overview window

Source: Windows Server 2016

Activity 9-15: Installing Microsoft Virtual Desktop Infrastructure

Time Required: 20 minutes

Objective: Install the components of RDS required for Virtual Desktop Infrastructure.

Requirements: A Windows Server 2016 PC with the Hyper-V role that is in Active Directory

Description: In this activity, you use Server Manager to add and configure the components required for VDI to a new Windows Server 2016 host computer that is part of Active Directory. Refer to Activity 5-1 to install the Hyper-V role.

1. If necessary, log on to the host computer with your assigned domain administrative username and password.

2. If Server Manager is not running, click **Start** and then click **Server Manager**.

3. In the Server Manager window, click **Manage** in the upper right corner, then click **Add Roles and Features**.

4. In the Before you begin window, click **Next**.

5. In the Select installation type window, select the **Remote Desktop Services installation** option button, then click **Next**.

6. In the Select deployment type window, make sure the Standard deployment option button is selected, then click **Next**.

7. In the Select deployment scenario window, select the **Virtual machine-based desktop deployment** option button, then click **Next**.

8. In the Review role services window, note that the Remote Desktop Connection Broker, Web Access, and Virtualization Host will be installed and review the summary of each component, then click **Next**.

9. In the Specify RD Connection Broker server window, select your server under **Server Pool**, then click the button with the arrow so the computer appears under **Selected**, and then click **Next**.

10. In the Specify RD Web Access server window, click to check the **Install the RD Web Access role service on the RD Connection Broker server** check box, then click **Next**.

11. In the Specify RD Virtualization Host server window, select your server under **Server Pool**, click the button with the arrow so the computer appears under **Selected**, then click **Next**.

12. On the Confirm selections window, click to check the **Restart the destination server automatically if required**, then click **Deploy**.

13. Wait for the installation to finish. The server will then automatically restart several times, and complete after you log on. Stay logged on for the next activity.

Configuring the Connection Broker The virtual machines that are created for your collections are stored in Active Directory and should be stored in their own Organizational Unit (OU). After creating this OU, RDS needs permission to add new computers to it. This can be done manually, or more simply by letting the Configuration wizard create a PowerShell script you can run on the domain controller to do it for you, as shown in Figure 9-25.

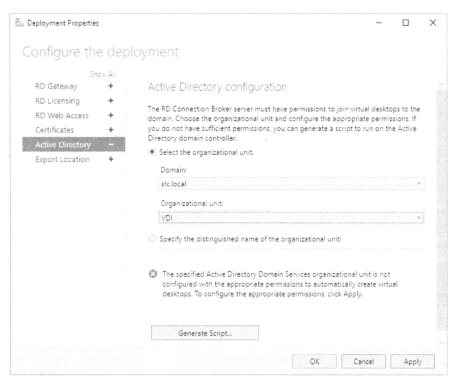

Figure 9-25   The Configure the deployment wizard

Source: Windows Server 2016

Activity 9-16: Configuring the Connection Broker

Time Required: 10 minutes

Objective: Configure Active Directory for use with RDS.

Requirements: Completion of Activity 9-15

Description: In this activity, you create an organizational unit to hold collection virtual machines and set permissions to allow RDS to add them there.

1. If necessary, log on to the domain controller computer with your assigned domain administrative username and password.

2. If Server Manager is not running, click **Start** and then click **Server Manager.**

3. In the Server Manager window, click **Tools** in the upper right corner, then click **Active Directory Users and Computers.**

4. In the left pane, click **stc.local.**

5. Click the **Action** menu, point to **New**, then click **Organizational Unit.**

6. In the New Object—Organizational Unit dialog box, Name text box, type **VDI.**

7. Click **OK** on the successfully completed dialog box and then close the Active Directory Users and Computers window.

8. Log on to the host computer with your assigned domain administrative username and password.

9. In the Server Manager window, click **Remote Desktop Services** from the left pane.

10. In the Overview window, click **Collections** from the left pane.

11. In the Collections window, click the **TASKS** dropdown menu in the upper right corner, then click **Edit Deployment Properties** to open the Configure the Deployment wizard.

12. Click **Active Directory** in the left plane. Select **stc.local** from the **Domain** dropdown list, and the select **VDI** under the Organizational unit dropdown list.

13. Notice the warning at the bottom of the window regarding missing permissions. Click the **Generate Script...** button to open the Configuration Script window.

14. With the text selected, right-click in the window and choose **Copy** from the menu. Close the Configuration script window, then close the Configure the Deployment wizard and Server Manager.

15. Click **Start, Windows Accessories,** and then click **Notepad**.

16. Click the **Edit** menu, then click **Paste**.

17. Click the **File** menu, then click **Save**. Choose a network location or removable storage, and type **Delegate-ControlToConnectionBroker.ps1** into the **File name** text box, then click **Save**.

18. Copy the file over the network or directly with removable storage to the PC running Active Directory.

19. Right-click the **Delegate-ControlToConnectionBroker.ps1** file, then choose **Run with PowerShell** from the menu. If prompted, press **Y** and hit **Enter** at the Execution Policy Change message.

20. After the script runs, you will briefly see a blue window, return to Remote Desktop Services on the RDS host computer and repeat steps 8 through 11.

21. Notice the wizard now reports Active Directory is now configured with the appropriate permissions. Click **OK**.

22. Leave the Server Manager open for the next activity.

Creating Virtual Desktops

VDI offers two different types of virtual desktops, each of which is stored in collections. Virtual machines in a **pooled virtual desktop collection** all share the same master image, and any changes made to the virtual machine are reverted when the user logs off; only the user profile is stored. This has the advantage of using less storage space and being easier to maintain.

With a **personal virtual desktop collection**, individual virtual machines are assigned to users that serve as their own private, persistent desktops. They can install their own applications and have full administrative access. Creating complete virtual machines for each user will use considerably more storage space, and deploying a new application across an organization must be done to each individual virtual machine versus updating a single master image used by a pooled collection.

Preparing the Virtual Desktop Template Virtual Desktop Infrastructure within RDS is designed to be used with desktop operating systems such as Windows 8 or Windows 10, and not server operating systems like Windows Server 2016 used in previous Hyper-V virtual machines in this book. Next, you will create a Windows 10 iso file using the Windows Media Creation Tool and create a new Windows 10 virtual machine using Hyper-V.

Activity 9-17: Installing Windows 10 as a Guest OS

Time Required: 30 minutes

Objective: Acquire the Windows 10 iso image and install it in a virtual machine.

Requirements: Windows 10 installation media

Description: In this activity, you use the Windows Media Creation Tool to download an iso image for Windows 10 to create a virtual machine that will be used as a virtual machine template.

1. If necessary, log on to the host computer with your assigned administrative username and password.

2. By default, the Microsoft Edge Web browser cannot be run on a Windows Server 2016 PC under an administrator account, and user accounts are not allowed to log on locally to an Active Directory Domain Controller. The easiest solution is to download the Google Chrome or Mozilla Firefox browser on another PC and install it onto your Windows Server 2016 host. Alternatively, you can use the Internet Explorer browser by clicking **Start, Windows Accessories**, and then click **Internet Explorer**. If enhanced security in the browser blocks the site, click **Add** and **Close** at each prompt.

3. Start your Web browser and navigate to **www.microsoft.com**.

4. In the Search text box, type **media creation tool** and press **Enter**. Click the first result.

5. Click the **Download tool now** button and save the file to your desktop.

6. When the download is finished, double-click the **MediaCreationTool.exe** file, then click **Run**. Click **Yes** if the User Account Controls dialog box if prompted.

7. In the Applicable notices and license terms window, click **Accept**.

8. In the What do you want to do? window, choose **Create installation media for another PC**, then click **Next**.

9. In the Select language, architecture, and edition window, click to uncheck the **Use the recommended options for this PC** check box, and choose the **Windows 10** edition and **32-bit (x86)** Architecture options, then click **Next**.

10. In the Choose which media to use window, choose **ISO file**, then click **Next**.

11. In the Select a path dialog box, type **Windows10-32.iso** into the **File name** text box, then click **Save**.

12. Wait for the download to complete, then click **Finish**.

13. Follow the steps in Activity 5-2 to create a new virtual machine named **Windows 10**, Generation 1, with 2048 MB of Startup memory and connected to a new virtual switch.

14. Follow Activity 5-5 to install the new virtual machine, choosing **Windows 10 Pro** edition.

15. When the installation is finished, in the Get going fast window, click **Use Express Settings**.

16. In the Who owns this PC? Window, select **I own it,** then click **Next**.

17. In the Keep it simple with your Microsoft account window, click **Skip this step**.

18. In the Create an account for this PC window, enter **student** into the **User name** text box, then click **Next**.

19. In the Meet Cortana window, click **Not now**.

20. Your Windows 10 installation is finished. To eject the iso image from the virtual DVD drive, click the **Media** menu, then **DVD Drive** and click **Eject**.

21. Power down the virtual machine and close the Hyper-V Manager window.

When creating pool collections RDS will use existing virtual machines as templates that have been specially prepared using the System Preparation Tool (Sysprep). This software removes all system-specific information from the OS, such as the computer name, the unique computer security identifier (SID), and driver cache.

After powering on and logging on to your virtual machine, Sysprep can be started by typing %windir%\system32\sysprep\sysprep. exe into the Windows Run dialog box as shown in Figure 9-26.

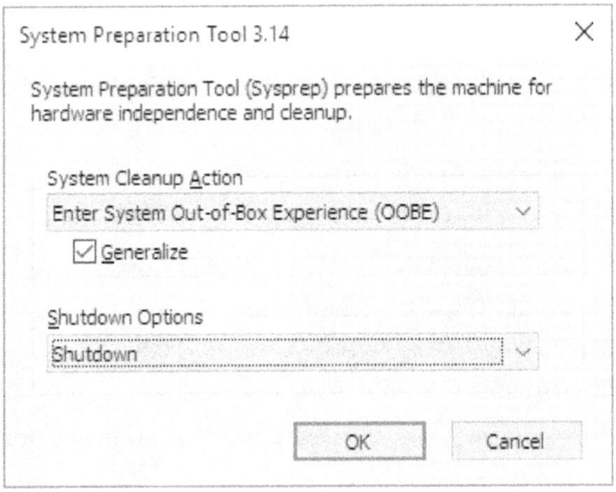

Figure 9-26   The System Preparation Tool dialog box

Source: Windows Server 2016

Choose the System Out-of-Box Experience (OOBE) option from the dropdown list, which allows for tasks such as creating user accounts and naming the computer like a new PC installation. The second option, System Audit Mode, allows applications and drivers to be installed and is used to test the installation.

Next enable the Generalize option, which removes the SID, computer name, and all other unique data such as logs and restore points.

Finally, choose the Shutdown option from the Shutdown Options dropdown list. The virtual machine must not be booted again directly, as that will remove the generalization. RDS will use checkpoints to preserve the clean state of the virtual machine.

Activity 9-18: Running Sysprep on the Guest OS

Time Required: 15 minutes

Objective: Use the Sysprep tool on the Guest OS.

Requirements: Completion of Activity 9-17

Description: In this activity, you use Sysprep to remove all unique information from your Windows 10 virtual machine (to create one refer to Activities 5-2 and 5-5) so it can be used as a template for RDS collections.

1. If necessary, log on to the host computer and open Hyper-V Manager.

2. In the Virtual Machines pane, click **Windows 10**. Power on and connect to this virtual machine, and log on to the guest OS with your Administrator account.

3. Right-click **Start**, then click **Run**. In the Run dialog box type **%windir%\system32 \sysprep\sysprep.exe** and click **OK**.

4. In the System Preparation Tool, under the System Cleanup Action dropdown list ensure Enter System Out-of-Box Experience (OOBE) is selected.

5. Click to check the **Generalize** check box.

6. In the Shutdown Options dropdown list, choose **Shutdown**, then click **OK**.

7. Wait for the process to finish; the virtual machine will power down automatically.

8. Close the Virtual Machine Connection window and stay logged on for the next activity.

Creating a Pooled Virtual Desktop Collection After choosing Remote Desktop Services in the Server Manager, you choose Collections on the Overview window. You begin creating your new collection under TASKS, Create Virtual Desktop Collection. This wizard can create both pooled and personal virtual desktop collections and the process is very similar. You will be creating a pooled collection. After reviewing the prerequisites in the Before you begin window, as shown in Figure 9-27, you choose a name for your collection.

In the Specify the collection type window, as shown in Figure 9-28, you choose between a pooled or personal virtual desktop collection. A checklist below the types shows the capabilities of each when selected. You will use the automatically create and manage virtual desktops option. An unmanaged virtual desktop must be created manually and you will need to create the virtual machines and checkpoints yourself instead of it being created automatically from a template.

Next, you choose the template located on the RD Virtualization Host running Hyper-V that will be the basis for the virtual desktop, which is the Windows 10 VM you created in a previous activity. In the Specify the virtual desktops window you choose if you will provide an answer file, a file containing information on how to configure a new windows installation, or if you will provide it directly in the next step.

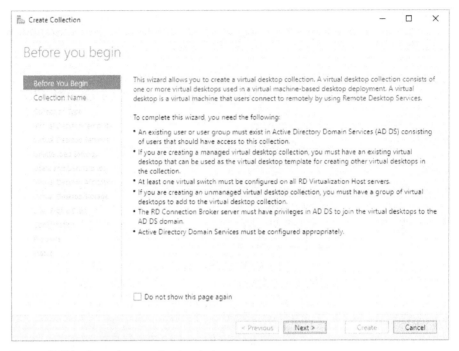

Figure 9-27 The Before you begin window

Source: Windows Server 2016

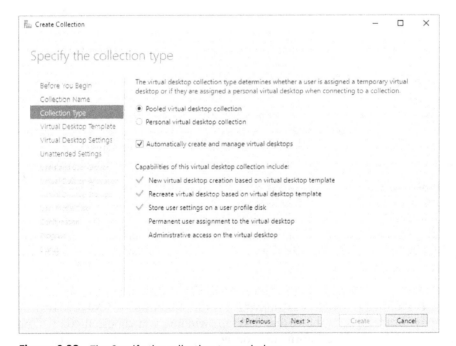

Figure 9-28 The Specify the collection type window

Source: Windows Server 2016

In the Specify the unattended installation settings window, you choose the correct time zone and the Active Directory domain name and organizational unit virtual machines will be stored in, choosing the VDI OU created in a previous activity.

In the Specify users and user groups window, you can choose which user groups can access the collection. The number of virtual desktops can be specified, as well as the naming scheme by choosing a prefix and suffix. A prefix of "PoolVM-" and suffix of "0" will create a series of virtual machines named PoolVM-0, PoolVM-1, PoolVM-2, and so on.

When multiple Virtualization Hosts are available you can specify which server gets how many of the new virtual desktops to fine tune performance.

In the Specify virtual desktop storage window, you can choose where the virtual desktops will be stored: on each individual Virtualization Host, on a network share, or on a Cluster Shared Volume (CSV). An option to automatically roll back virtual desktops is on by default, but can be turned off.

In the User Profile Disks window, you choose if you want RDS to maintain user profiles which are preserved for users even when the virtual machine is rolled back, offering features such as a customized desktop. This can be disabled completely, or it can be managed by another software package.

After confirming your settings, the creation of the collection will begin. You can see a progress bar showing that the virtual machines are being exported from the template and then created. If you switch to Hyper-V while this is occurring, as shown in Figure 9-29, you can see the tasks the wizard is performing as it creates, boots, and configures the new virtual desktops.

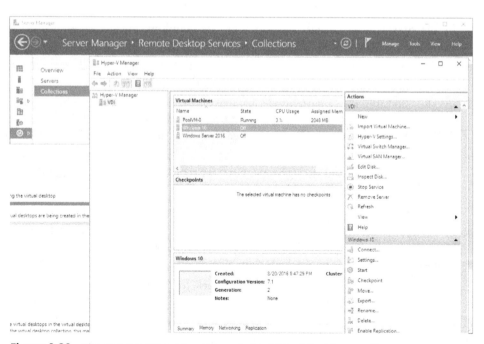

Figure 9-29 The Hyper-V Manager window during Virtual Desktop creation

Source: Windows Server 2016

Activity 9-19: Creating a Pooled Virtual Desktop Collection

Time Required: 10 minutes

Objective: Create a pooled virtual desktop collection.

Requirements: Completion of Activity 9-18

Description: In this activity, you use Server Manager to create a pooled virtual desktop collection using the Windows 10 virtual desktop created in the previous activity.

1. If necessary, log on to the host computer with your assigned administrative username and password.

2. If Server Manager is not running, click **Start**, then click **Server Manager**.

3. In the Server Manager window, click **Remote Desktop Services** from the left pane.

4. In the Overview window, click **Collections** from the left pane.

5. In the Collections window, click the **TASKS** dropdown menu in the upper right corner, then click **Create Virtual Desktop Collection** to open the Create Collection wizard.

6. In the Before you begin window, review the prerequisites, then click **Next**.

7. In the Name the collection window, type **Virtual Desktops Pool** into the Name text box, then click **Next**.

8. In the Specify the collection type window, make sure the Pooled virtual desktop collection option button is selected, and Automatically create and manage virtual desktops is checked. Review the capabilities of a pooled collection, then click **Next**.

9. In the Specify the virtual desktop template window, click the **Windows 10** virtual machine, then click **Next**.

10. In the Specify the virtual desktop settings window, confirm the Provide unattended installation settings option button is selected, then click **Next**.

11. In the Specify the unattended installation settings window, choose the correct region under **Time zone**. Under **Active Directory domain name**, choose **stc.local**. Under **Active Directory Domain Services organizational unit** (OU) choose **VDI**, then click **Next**.

12. In the Specify users and user groups window, replace the contents of the **Prefix** text box with "**PoolVM**" and then click **Next**.

13. In the Specify virtual desktop allocation window, click **Next**.

14. In the Specify virtual desktop storage window, ensure Store on each RD Virtualization Host server option button is selected and Automatically roll back the virtual desktop when the user logs off is checked, then click **Next**.

15. In the Specify user profile disks window, click to uncheck the **Enable user profile disks** check box, then click **Next**.

16. In the Confirm selections window, review your choices and then click **Create**.

17. In the Progress window, wait for the export and creation of virtual desktops to complete, then click **Close**.

Accessing Virtual Desktops

Virtual desktops can be accessed through a Web interface provided automatically by the RD Web Access component at https://hostname/rdweb. You can also access this URL under the deployment properties window. Because a self-signed security certificate is used by default, a security warning will be displayed that the Web site is not trusted. Next, you are prompted to log on with your username and password. A list of the available collections is then displayed as shown in Figure 9-30.

Figure 9-30 The Work Resources web site

Source: Windows Server 2016

Clicking one will open a Remote Desktop Connection window, as shown in Figure 9-31, which can be configured to allow the virtual machine access to different resources: drives, the clipboard, printers, audio recordings, and supported plug and play devices. Once satisfied, click Connect.

The RD Connection Broker will then choose a virtual machine from the selected pool based on load if multiple Hyper-V servers are being used. For pooled collections, if you previously disconnected from your last session it can be resumed where you left off, otherwise if it was shut down a new virtual machine is automatically created off of the template to present a fresh desktop. For virtual machines in a personal collection, the last state will always be saved.

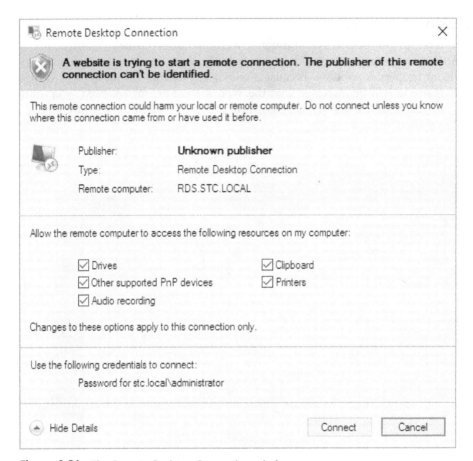

Figure 9-31 The Remote Desktop Connection window

Source: Windows Server 2016

Activity 9-20: Accessing Virtual Desktops

Time Required: 15 minutes

Objective: Use the RD Web Access Web site to launch a virtual machine from a collection.

Requirements: Completion of Activity 9-19

Description: In this activity, you use Internet Explorer to launch virtual machines from your pooled virtual desktop collection. You will also test different ways of closing the Remote Desktop Connection window and how it affects the virtual machines.

1. If necessary, log on to the host computer with your assigned administrative username and password.

2. Start the Internet Explorer browser by clicking **Start**, click **Windows Accessories**, and then click **Internet Explorer**.

3. Navigate to **http://*hostname*/rdweb,** where *hostname* is the name of the computer with the RD Web Access role, for example "http://rds.stc.local/rdweb".

4. When the There is a problem with this Web site's security certificate error message appears in the browser, click **Continue to this website** (**not recommended**). If enhanced security in the browser blocks the site, click **Add,** and then click **Add** and **Close** in the Trusted Sites dialog box.

5. In the sign in window, type **stc.local\administrator** into the Domain\user name text box, and your password into the Password text box, then click **Sign in.**

6. In the Connect to a remote PC window, click **Virtual Desktops Pool.**

7. In the Remote Desktop Connection dialog box, note the resources the virtual machine will have access to, then click **Connect.**

8. A Remote Desktop session will automatically start and you will be logged on to the virtual machine after a slight delay.

9. Once on the virtual machine desktop, click and drag the Recycle Bin icon to the center the screen.

10. Click **Start, Power, Disconnect** to close the Remote Desktop Connection window but leave the virtual machine still running.

11. In the Connect to a remote PC window in Internet Explorer, click **Virtual Desktops Pool** and **Connect** again.

12. Notice the virtual machine desktop appears much quicker, and everything is as it was left.

13. Click **Start, Power, Shutdown** to power off the virtual machine.

14. In the Connect to a remote PC window in Internet Explorer, click **Virtual Desktops Pool** and **Connect** again.

15. When the desktop appears, notice the Recycle Bin icon is back in its original location showing that a new virtual machine has been created for this session.

16. Click **Start, Power, Shutdown.** Close the Internet Explorer Web browser.

9

Chapter Summary

- Nature seems to support a cyclical, repetitive process. Virtual Desktop Infrastructure is an example of how data processing has moved from centralized systems to distributed processing and then back again to centralization of computing resources. The ability to host computing resources holds many advantages including mobility, device independence, and fault tolerance.

- The two major providers of desktop virtualization products are VMware and Microsoft. VMware provides the Horizon suite of desktop virtualization products while Microsoft offers similar features in its Virtual Desktop Infrastructure in RDS.

- A Virtual Desktop Infrastructure requires certain base components such as a connection server (or broker) to provide access from user clients to desktop virtual machines.

In addition, each desktop virtual machine requires an agent to communicate between the virtual machine and the user client and connection broker.

- To provide storage efficiency, a desktop environment must limit the amount of storage used by each virtual desktop. Storage solutions include using clones that are linked to a parent image, providing instant desktop clones that exist only in memory, and using non-persistent disks.

- In this chapter you learned how to set up a basic virtual desktop environment using both VMware Horizon and Microsoft VDI products.

Key Terms

agent software
application virtualization
connection broker
desktop pools
Differencing Disks
Horizon Connection Server

PCoIP (PC over IP)
personal virtual desktop collection
pooled virtual desktop collection

Remote Desktop Services (RDS)
User Environment Management (UEM)

Review Questions

1. Which of the following techniques can be used to reduce storage requirements when implementing virtual desktops?

    a. Templates

    b. Linked clones

    c. Non-persistent disks

    d. Desktop pools

2. Which of the following VDI components runs on the virtual desktop system?

    a. Template

    b. Thin client

    c. VDI Agent

    d. Broker

3. Which of the following is NOT a component of a Virtual Desktop Infrastructure?

    a. Templates

    b. Thin client

    c. VDI Agent

    d. Broker

4. Which of the following challenges does application virtualization best help to solve?

    a. Storage space

    b. Preventing interference between different applications

    c. Reducing administrative overhead

    d. All of above

5. _____ is a VMware VDI component that helps manage user profiles when sharing a virtual desktop.

    a. ThinApp

    b. Linked clone

    c. UEM

    d. Connection Broker

6. The _____ VDI component is used to connect a user to the Broker.

    a. Template

    b. Thin client

    c. VDI Agent

    d. User Environment Manager (UEM)

7. Which of the following VMware Horizon components can be used to create a desktop pool for linked clones?

    a. Connection server Web console

    b. Composer

    c. User Environment Manager

    d. Template

8. Which of the following can be used to install the Horizon Connection Server?

    a. Windows domain member server

    b. Windows domain controller

    c. Windows 8 or later

    d. vCenter server

9. Which of the following are valid Horizon Connection Server types? (Choose all that apply.)

    a. Standard

    b. Replica

    c. Security

    d. Broker

10. How many replica connection servers can be part of a Horizon Virtual Desktop Infrastructure?

    a. 2

    b. 5

    c. 6

    d. 1

11. Which of the following client video options is a lossless protocol that best supports multimedia?

    a. PCoIP

    b. RDP

    c. HDPC

    d. VMware Blast

12. In which of the following environments can Horizon Composer be installed? (Choose all that apply.)

    a. Dedicated windows member server

    b. Windows 8 or later

    c. vCenter server

    d. Windows Domain controller

13. When deploying Horizon virtual desktops for a department, which of the following should you do first?

    a. Create a desktop pool.

    b. Create a template.

    c. Create the virtual desktop systems.

    d. Install the client on the virtual desktop to be used for a template.

14. Which of the following is not a component of Microsoft RDS?

    a. RD Virtualization Host

    b. RD Connection Broker

    c. RD Delegator

    d. RD Session Host

15. Which of following is not a function the Sysprep tool performs?

    a. Removes the security identifier

    b. Removes event logs

    c. Removes the computer name

    d. Removes any user-installed applications

16. Which of the following is a capability of a Microsoft pooled virtual desktop collection? (Choose all that apply.)

    a. Permanent user assignment to the virtual desktop

    b. Administrator access on the virtual desktop

    c. Recreates virtual desktops based on a template

    d. Stores user settings on a user profile disk

17. Which of the following components is not required for a production Microsoft VDI deployment?

    a. RD Connection Broker

    b. RD Licensing

    c. RD Gateway

    d. RD Virtualization and RD Session hosts

18. What is the name of the software from Microsoft that creates OS installation media?

    a. ISO Creator

    b. Windows Creator

    c. Media Creation Tool

    d. OS Creation Tool

9

19. What was the former name for Remote Desktop Services before it included VDI?

    a. Thin Client Services

    b. Terminal Services

    c. Client Services

    d. Terminal Infrastructure

20. What is the name of the application that views Microsoft virtual desktops?

    a. Remote Desktop Viewer

    b. Virtual Desktop Connection

    c. Remote Desktop Connection

    d. Virtual Machine Viewer

Case Projects

CASE PROJECTS

Case Project 9-1: VMware Horizon 7 New Features Overview

VMware has hands-on labs you can use to work with products.

1. Log on to your myvmware account.

2. Point to the Products link and then click Trial and Free Products link to display the Select a Product Trial page.

3. Scroll down and expand the Desktop and Application Virtualization heading.

4. Click VMware Horizon 7 link to display the Try VMware Horizon for Free page.

5. Click the **Go to Lab** link under the Hosted Evaluation option to display the Hosted Lab page.

6. Click the **Launch** button to display the Accept End-User License Agreement page. Fill in the necessary information and click the **I'm not a robot** button to select a set of images that show you are not an automated robot. Then click the **I agree to the terms and conditions** option and click the **Start Free Trial** button to load your virtual lab environment (you may need to click to allow pop-ups from vmware in your browser window).

Go through the New Features Overview module and write a brief report or PowerPoint presentation highlighting at least two new features of VMware Horizon 7 you find most useful.

Case Project 9-2: VMware Horizon 7 Instant Clones Trial Lab

Follow the procedure in Case Project 9-1 to go through the Instant Clones module (about 30 minutes).

> *Write a brief report that briefly describes each of the steps in this module and your experience with it. Do you feel you could implement the Instant Clones demo for your UAS virtual desktop system? Briefly explain why or why not.*

Try an additional module of your choice and write a brief report describing the steps you used.

Case Project 9-3: Creating a Virtual Desktop Pool for Engineering Department

Now that Universal AeroSpace is convinced that implementing a Virtual Desktop Infrastructure is the way they wish to proceed, their next objective is to create virtual desktops for the managers who often work from home or from tablet computers. In this project you are to apply what you have learned in this chapter to perform the following tasks:

- Create an Active Directory group named UAS_Mgr along with three management users named Mary Smith, Bill Carson, and John Carr.
- Create a vSphere folder for Manager VMs.
- Prepare a Windows 10 Manager template that is part of Active Directory and contains a copy of the Horizon agent.
- Create an automatic desktop pool with two virtual desktops named Mgr1 and Mgr2. Have the desktop pool computers stored on your iSCSI storage.

- Entitle the desktop pool to be used by the UAS_Mgr group.
- Experiment with using the DRS capability of your UAS Cluster to move the virtual machines between hosts and report on your results.

Case Project 9-4: Comparing the Differences between Session and Virtual Desktops

Microsoft RDS can deliver both session and virtual desktops to users. Write a brief report showing the advantages and disadvantages of each of these technologies.

Case Project 9-5: Comparing VMware Horizon and Microsoft VDI Products

Now that you have had a chance to get some familiarity with both VMware Horizon and Microsoft VDI, in this project you are to write a brief report that describes what you feel and the advantages and disadvantages of each product based on your experience. At the end of the report indicate which product you preferred and why.

9

chapter 10

Introduction to Cloud Computing

After reading this chapter and completing the exercises, you will be able to:

- Describe basic cloud computing types and models including IaaS, PaaS, and SaaS
- Describe the major applications of cloud computing in data centers including hosting a virtual data center, extending a data center, and providing disaster recovery options
- Describe the components necessary to host a private cloud environment using VMware and Hyper-V platforms
- Create a cloud-based virtual data center for a small organization
- Describe the steps and components necessary to extend a virtual data center using VMware and Microsoft cloud platforms
- Describe the procedures and options involved in developing a backup and disaster recovery procedure for a local virtual data center
- Describe the process of implementing disaster recovery solutions and the options provided by cloud computing
- Describe the steps and components needed to implement a cloud-based disaster recovery system using VMware vCloud
- Describe the components of OpenStack architecture and how OpenStack products are being used and marketed by many major companies

Our perception of things changes over time, and certainly that is true of cloud computing. Perhaps the poetic words Joni Mitchell wrote of clouds in the lyrics "Rows and flows of angel hair; ice cream castles in the air; and feather canyons everywhere; I've thought of clouds that way; But now they only block the sun; they rain and they snow on everyone" can also be applied to use of clouds in cloud computing. In earlier days, IT people used the cloud symbol to illustrate a mysterious process that connected two devices for communication. Today, the cloud is rapidly becoming the source of many services that truly do "rain" down on most everyone.

Our perception of cloud computing itself has changed from being a way of making resources such as servers and applications available across the Internet to being a new way of automatically providing on-demand provisioning of information systems by the consumer. At the foundation of the process is the virtualization or hyperconvergence of computing resources. There has come to be a dizzying array of products and services from VMware, Microsoft, Amazon Web Services (AWS), and other open source organizations that are designed to support the rapidly growing and developing cloud computing market. One important application of cloud computing services is disaster recovery or DR systems. In this chapter, we will examine more of the mysteries of cloud computing and how cloud computing is playing a rapidly growing role along with virtualization to implement reliable and scalable data centers that provide both flexible and cost effective solutions to today's information processing needs. The first section will overview what cloud computing is today and describe its major applications. We will then look at major cloud service products and platforms such as VMware, Microsoft, and OpenStack. The purpose of this chapter is to introduce you to some basic cloud fundamentals so that you can start your journey to the cloud, where truly the sky is the limit.

Introduction to Cloud Services

From its beginning, as a way to represent the public switched telephone network used to connect devices across long distance, the cloud symbol has matured to represent the Internet and its associated Web services. Today the term **cloud computing** represents a form of processing that provides on-demand services based on a virtualized set of resources that are independent from the physical location you are in.

To understand this new paradigm of cloud computing, we need to review the process of computing today as illustrated in Figure 10-1.

At the top of the stack we have the end user or consumer. In the past, the end user of computing services was typically performing data processing applications such as accounting, word processing, engineering, weather forecasting, or calculating the trajectory to the moon. While these "practical" computing applications are still in demand, the Internet opened up a whole new world of online applications including ecommerce, gaming, streaming media, and most recently social media. Today's consumer is mobile, wanting access to their applications from almost any location and from a variety of devices including phones, tablets, and laptop computers. Another important trend in today's office is **BYOD (Bring Your Own Device)**. Bringing in additional devices can tax the internal server and network infrastructure. Cloud computing provides a way in which the businesses and organizations can extend their data center to handle extra loads without adding more hardware.

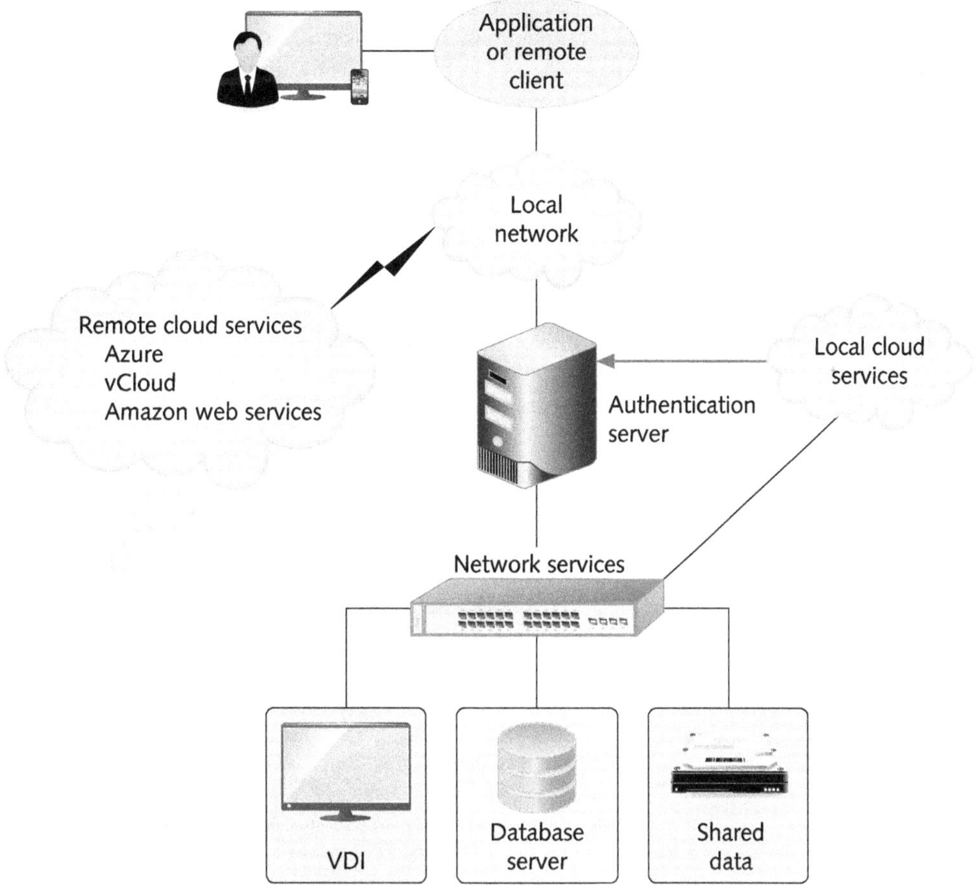

Application
or remote
client

Local
network

Remote cloud services
Azure
vCloud
Amazon web services

Local cloud
services

Authentication
server

Network services

VDI

Database
server

Shared
data

Figure 10-1 Data processing components

The next component is the application or client that provides the user interface or UI. In a distributed computing environment, the application and UI run as software on the device. To run the application software, the device needs a compatible operating system such as Windows, Mac OS, or Linux. The application or client connects to a server running at the data center. This connection can be across the Internet or local network (LAN). The server supports the backend process to access database and network services. This is where cloud computing first comes into the picture. In traditional environments the IT Department manages the data center and is responsible for provisioning new servers and other computing resources. In this environment a consumer needs to submit a request for additional services to the IT Department, which then responds to the request based on their schedule and priorities. For example, prior to virtual data centers, a request for a new Web server could involve budgeting the hardware and then allocating time for the IT staff to install and provision the system. Cloud computing changes this paradigm by allowing the consumer to provision additional IT resources (processing, memory, and storage) within the limits and budget provided by the IT Department. The consumer is charged for the resources they use, which can be expanded or contracted by the consumer based on their needs. To learn more about cloud computing, perform Case Project 10-1 to access the VMware Education center and view an introductory video.

The **National Institute of Standards and Technology (NIST)** defines cloud computing as "a model for enabling ubiquitous, convenient, on-demand network access to a shared pool of configurable computing resources (for example, networks, servers, storage, applications, and services) that can be rapidly provisioned, and released with minimal management effort or service provider interaction."

The NIST definition of cloud computing also includes several essential characteristics as shown in Table 10-1.

Table 10-1   Characteristics of cloud computing

Characteristic	Description
On-demand self-service	The ability for consumers to quickly provision virtual machines with the hardware and software resources they need automatically without waiting for outside assistance.
Broad network access	Access to services over the network using a Web browser and standard interfaces from any location with a variety of devices including desktop, laptop, and tablet computers.
Resource pooling	The ability to group resources and make them available to users on demand in a shared, multi-tenant fashion. Examples of resources include processors, memory, storage, network bandwidth, and virtual machines.
Elasticity	Allows resources to be managed by the consumer and quickly scaled out to provide more capability or quickly scaled in to release unneeded capacity and costs.
Pay-as-you-go	Allows consumers to pay only for the resources they use. Typically cloud service providers have a monthly charge based on processor, memory, and storage used. Consumers can elastically change the resource usage to increase or decrease their usage as their needs change.
Reliability and redundancy	Provides the capability for redundancy and fault tolerance through the use of virtual machines, as well as load balancing and disaster recovery. Small businesses and organizations benefit from the backup services available from cloud providers. Data stored on cloud servers is much less vulnerable to loss due to hardware failures or local disasters such as fire or storms.

As described in Chapter 1 (see Figure 1-11), NIST has defined three major classes of cloud computing including IaaS (Infrastructure as a Service), PaaS (Platform as a Service), and SaaS (Software as a Service). While they offer certain software platform capabilities, both VMware vCloud and Microsoft Azure are generally classified as IaaS cloud platforms.

There are four major applications for IaaS clouds, which include implementing a cloud-based data center, hosting private cloud services, extending the organization's data center to provide additional capacity as needed, and providing disaster recovery services. We will be describing and working with all four of these applications in this chapter.

Building a Cloud-Based Data Center

Many small startup businesses and organizations need computing resources to run business applications such as accounting, inventory, sales, and database management software as well as share documents among users. Today many of these organizations are using some form of NAS to share files with applications and data often stored on individual workstations.

In many cases they have minimal or no disaster recovery plan or are paying an outside consultant to provide these services. In addition, these organizations can also benefit from having access to mobile/device independent applications. As these businesses develop, they need to be able to grow their computing resources while holding costs to a minimum. These types of businesses and organizations are ideal candidates for using cloud services. A number of companies provide a variety of cloud data center options including Amazon Web Services, Microsoft Azure, and VMware vCloud. In this chapter you will learn how to use Microsoft Azure to create a virtual data center for a small organization.

Extending the Data Center

As demand for IT services grows, a company or organization will eventually be faced with the need to expand their data centers either by adding additional hardware or by extending the data center using cloud-based services. Extending the data center into the cloud provides a few advantages including paying only for the resources needed, providing load balancing during peak loads, improving reliability, and providing "Anytime, Anywhere, Anydevice" access to users. For example, an organization has to compute and process a lot of information during certain peak periods such as end of month or during special events and sales. This processing requires addition computing power; the more the power the faster the results are completed and the better response time users experience. In the past data centers needed to provide extra hardware that was not used except during peak loads. Cloud computing can provide such "burst" computing capacity on demand to its users, when they need it the most. The organization can provision virtual machines or instances in the cloud, scale them based on the randomness of their demand, and then destroy all the instances once the job is done. This entire process can also be automated to make the computation far easier and effective during a peak load period. Since cloud computing provides pay-as-you-go services, an organization only has to pay for the extra capacity they actually use. Both VMware and Microsoft offer connection services that allow an organization to extend their vSphere or Hyper-V data center to include virtual machines running on a cloud-based virtual data center. You will learn about these products and how to use them in this chapter.

Hosting Private Cloud Services

One of the features of cloud computing is the ability for an organization to provide consumers and users with on-demand IT services and resources through the use of **private clouds**. Consumers can be either within the organization or an organization can host cloud services for use by outside entities. One reason to host internal private cloud services is for development and testing purposes. Organizations can host their development centers on-premises and test the applications on the cloud by provisioning virtual machines quickly, using them to develop or deploy applications, testing the applications, and then remove the entire infrastructure when it is no longer needed.

Both VMware and Microsoft offer proprietary products that allow organizations to create their own private cloud environments based on vSphere and Hyper-V platforms. Examples of organizations that host cloud services for the public include Amazon Web Services, VMware vCloud Air, and Microsoft Azure. In this chapter you will be working with VMware and Microsoft products that allow an organization to provide on-demand services to its own users as well as host virtual data centers for other organizations. In addition to the proprietary cloud hosting software from VMware and Microsoft, an open standard named OpenStack is gaining a lot of ground as a private and public cloud hosting platform that is not tied to a specific vender. Due the growing popularity of OpenStack, both Microsoft and VMware are providing support. Later in this chapter we will review the basic components of OpenStack.

Implementing Disaster Recovery

Disaster recovery involves making regular backups along with a procedure to restore that data if and when an incident occurs. Incidents can be as simple as a user accidently deleting a file to a full-fledged disaster that results in the loss of an entire data center. A good disaster plan has to provide for all of these contingencies. Prior to cloud computing, organizations would provide regular data and server backups with off-site locations to store backup data as well as provide a plan to restore data including replacement of hardware and moving to another alternate location. Many organizations today use the cloud as a mechanism for disaster recovery. Using the cloud, organizations can create stand-by infrastructure environments that can be used to perform either hot or cold migrations on demand. A cloud hot migration disaster recovery service can be configured to provide continuous, uninterrupted service even if the on-premises data center is completely lost. Clouds today use a variety of techniques to achieve this, such as live virtual machine replication, templates, and cloning. These cloud-based disaster recovery services are classified as **RaaS (Recovery as a Service)** and they allow organizations to replicate data between the local data center and a virtual data center within the cloud. You will get a chance to work with VMware's vCloud disaster recovery system later in this chapter.

VMware Cloud Services

VMware cloud services can generally be divided into two major categories: vCloud Air and vCloud Suite. **vCloud Air** is a public IaaS cloud environment that consumers can use to create and manage their own virtual data centers extend existing in house data centers, or provide disaster recovery services. In addition to providing cloud services through vCloud Air, VMware offers software that organizations can install in their vSphere environments to host their own private cloud services. In this section you will first learn about the vCloud software products that organizations can install in their vSphere environments to offer private cloud services. The second part of this section focuses on using vCloud Air cloud services made available from VMware.

Implementing VMware Private Cloud Services

The two primary products that are part of VMware's private cloud software suites are vCloud Director and vCloud Suite. **vCloud Director** allows an organization to host their own cloud environments that may be used by internal or external consumers to build virtual data centers using the organization's local vSphere environment as illustrated in Figure 10-2.

While implementing vCloud Director is beyond the scope of this chapter, you can do Case Project 10-1 at the end of the chapter to access the VMware Education center and learn more about the vCloud Director components and how vCloud Director can be used to create private cloud environments.

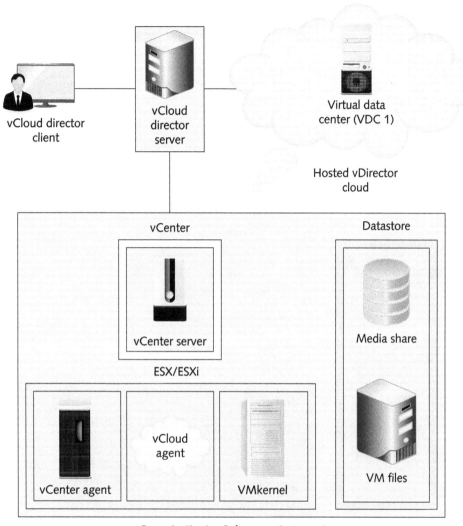

Organization's vSphere environment

Figure 10-2 vCloud Director server installed in vSphere infrastructure

As shown in Table 10-2, vCloud Suite contains a few different **vRealize** software products that an organization can install in their vSphere environment to host on-demand cloud services and monitor and manage the virtualized infrastructure.

You may have noticed the vRealize Operations icon is shown in your vSphere Web console. While it is not installed as part of vSphere Server, clicking this icon will allow you to install the vRealize Operations component that can be used to monitor the performance of your virtual data center. Figure 10-3 shows an example of using vRealize Operations performance check.

Table 10-2 **VMware vCloud suite components**

Component	Functional Description
VMware vRealize™ Operations	Performance, capacity, and configuration management for vSphere environments. You can use vRealize operations to track VM usage statistics and use them to manage resource allocation.
VMware vRealize Automation	Self-service and policy-based infrastructure and application provisioning for vSphere environments. You can use vRealize Automation to provide on-demand cloud services to consumers through the use of catalogs.
VMware vRealize Business	Automated costing, usage metering, and service pricing of virtualized infrastructure for vSphere environments.

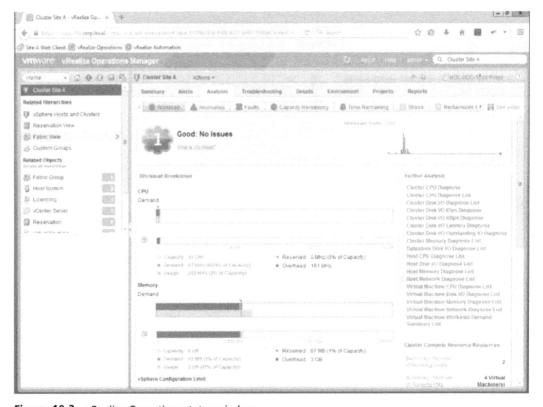

Figure 10-3 vRealize Operations status window

Source: VMware vRealize Web Console

vRealize Business and vRealize Automation are additional products that can also be downloaded and installed as separate components of your vSphere infrastructure. In this chapter we will be focusing on the use of vRealize Automation as it allows an organization to offer on-demand cloud services to users.

Using vRealize Automation to Deliver On-Demand Cloud Services While

we normally think of the cloud as a set of services that are located "out there" on the

Internet, cloud computing actually represents a model that uses virtual machines to provide on-demand services and virtualized resources to users independent of user location or client operating system. This on-demand processing can take place either across the Internet or within a local area network. This brings the perception of cloud computing down to earth, in that implementing on-demand cloud services does not require use of the Internet but can be implemented using vSphere on the local area network. To realize the benefits of the on-demand cloud computing model, an organization will need to install VMware's vRealize Automation product in their vSphere environment. As shown in Figure 10-4, vRealize

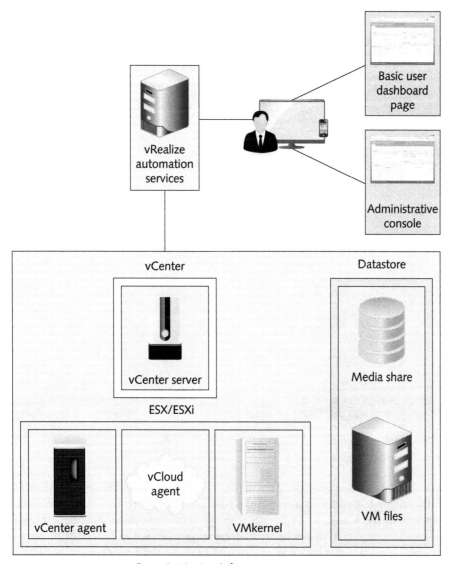

Organization's vSphere environment

Figure 10-4   vRealize Automation services server appliance

Automation consists of a server product that provides both administrative and user Web consoles based on the rights assigned to the user when they log on.

In the following sections you will learn how to use both user and administrative consoles to access and publish basic cloud services through vRealize Automation.

Using vRealize User Features When a user logs on to the vRealize server as an authorized user, a user dashboard similar to the one shown in Figure 10-5 will be displayed.

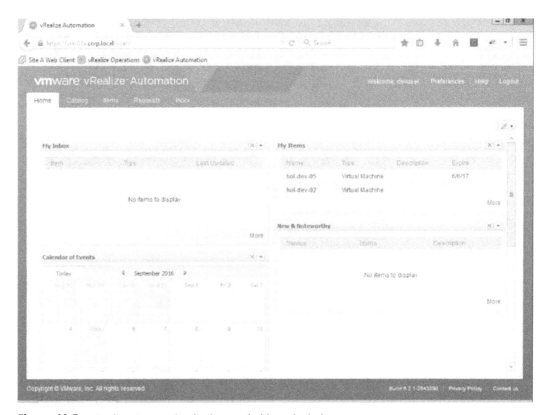

Figure 10-5   vRealize Automation basic user dashboard window

Source: VMware vRealize Web Console

The user's dashboard contains **portlets** or frames that show a variety of information. My Inbox in the upper left contains any notices that are relevant to the logged-on user. Located below My Inbox, the Calendar of Events displays important dates that have been identified by the administrator, such as deployment lease expirations. On the bottom right the New and Noteworthy portlet displays any recent additions to the Service Catalog. The My Items portlet located on the top right lists any currently deployed objects owned by the logged-on user. Along the top of the page are tabs that open up other screens. The **Catalog tab** will open the service catalog, from which a user can deploy services that they have been entitled to. The **Items tab** will show any owned items, similar to the "My Items" portlet on the home screen. The **Requests tab** contains a history of the user's vRealize Automation service requests along with the status of any open requests. Similar to the My InBox portlet, the **Inbox tab** displays any messages that are currently in the user's inbox.

To request a server such as virtual machine, the user would open the Catalog tab to display a list of virtual machines the user is authorized to work with. Clicking the Request button located in a virtual machine box provides a request window as shown in Figure 10-6.

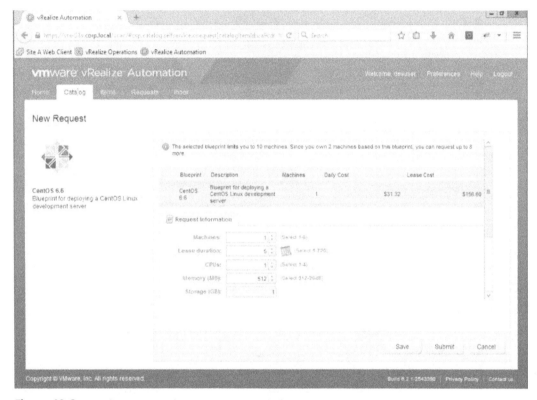

Figure 10-6 vRealize Automation New Request window

Source: VMware vRealize Web Console

When a request is processed the service or virtual machine is added to the user's My Items portlet. Clicking a virtual machine in the My Items portlet provides the user with a number of options and actions as shown in Figure 10-7.

Notice that the user can start and stop the VM as well as modify its configuration or remove it from the system when they are finished using it. In the following activity you will work with the VMware Lab environment to gain some experience using vRealize on-demand services from the end user perspective.

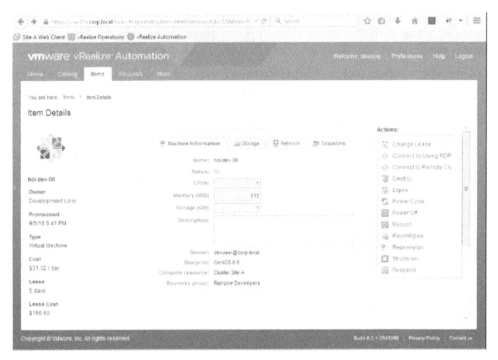

Figure 10-7 vRealize Automation virtual machine details window

Source: VMware vRealize Web Console

Activity 10-1: Accessing vRealize On-Demand Resources

Time Required: 40 minutes

Objective: Use vRealize to access on-demand resources.

Requirements: A MyVMware user account and password

Description: Assume you are a developer working for the Rain Tree company to develop a Web application for the UAS organization. In this activity you will use VMware Lab to deploy a Web server to work with.

1. If necessary, start your Windows 10 desktop computer and open a browser window to VMware.com.

2. Log on to your MyVMware account.

3. If necessary scroll down and under More Available Free Trials, click VIew all and then click **Start an Evaluation** to display the Select a Product Trial page.

4. Scroll down to the bottom of the page and click on the **VMware Hands-on Labs** link.

5. If necessary, on the left-hand pane, click the **Labs** icon and then scroll down and click the **Focus: vRealize Suite** link.

6. Scroll down the labs and then click the **Enroll** button in the HOL-1721-USE-1 vRealize Automation 7 Basics lab and if necessary enter your VMware account name and password to register.

7. Click the **Start this Lab** button and read the initial Lab Overview information.

8. When you get to the Module 1 page, click the **Introduction** link and read through the Introduction pages and perform the requested operations.

9. Complete each of lessons from Module 1 – What can vRealize Automation 7 do for you.

10. After completing all the labs, click the **Log Out** link at the top right of the page and then click **Yes** to return to the lab catalog page.

11. This completes the steps for this activity; in the next activity you will perform the administration tasks to learn how to configure a vRealize cloud environment.

Using vRealize Administrative Features In the previous section you were introduced to how a user or consumer of cloud services can use vRealize to access on-demand services from a catalog. In order for a user to have access to on-demand services, they need to be added as an authorized user of vRealize and the administrator needs to add the services they will be authorized to use to their catalog. With Infrastructure as a Service (IaaS), administrators can rapidly model and provision servers and desktops across virtual and physical, private and public, or hybrid cloud infrastructures. Modeling is accomplished by creating a **machine blueprint,** which is a specification for a virtual, cloud, or physical machine as shown in Figure 10-8.

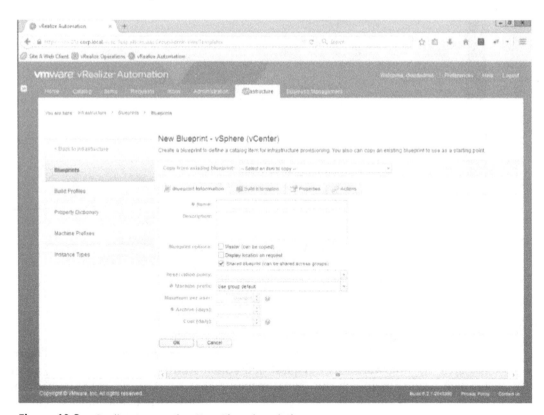

Figure 10-8 vRealize Automation New Blueprint window

Source: VMware vRealize Web Console

Notice that the blueprint is the complete specification for a virtual machine that is used to determine a machine's attributes and how it is provisioned. When a business group member requests a machine, the machine is provisioned according to the specifications in the blueprint, such as CPU, memory, and storage. Blueprints specify the workflow used to provision a machine and include additional provisioning information such as the locations of required disk images or virtualization platform objects. Finally, blueprints specify policies such as the lease period and which operations are supported on machines provisioned from the blueprint. Once a blueprint is created, it will be included in the blueprint catalog

Administrators need to publish blueprints as catalog items in the common service catalog and then make them available to end users using the Entitlements tab as shown in Figure 10-9.

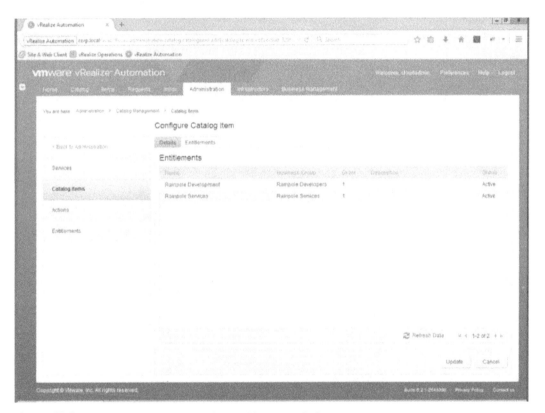

Figure 10-9 vRealize Automation Catalog Entitlements window

Source: VMware vRealize Web Console

When a user requests a machine based on one of these blueprints, IaaS provisions the machine in the user's My Items tab. With IaaS, administrators can manage the machine life cycle starting with a user request and administrative approval for a virtual machine through decommissioning the virtual machine at the end of the lease and reclaiming the resources (CPU, memory, storage) for use on other virtual machines when requested. Built-in configuration and extensibility features also make IaaS a highly flexible means of allowing the user to customize machine configurations within the limits established by the blueprint. In the following activity you will be introduced to the cloud service creation process by using the VMware lab to access the vRealize Automation administrative Web page and then use it to create, deliver, and consume a service created in vRealize Automation.

Activity 10-2: Accessing vRealize Administrative Features

Time Required: 30 minutes

Objective: Use vRealize to access on-demand resources.

Requirements: A MyVMware user account and password

Description: Assume Universal Aerospace has hired a third-party company named Rain Tree to manage their Web services. In order to develop and test the Web services and resources such as virtual machines, storage, and networks, Rain Tree developers will need to be provided with virtual servers they can manage. Rather than having the Universal AeroSpace IT staff determine the needs of the Rain Tree developers, management has decided to implement cloud services that allow Rain Tree to be charged for the resources they use. In this activity you will use VMware Lab to walk through creating a service catalog for the end user to be able to consume on-demand services for use in developing the applications. During the lab you will also log on as a developer user and use the service catalog to provision a service from the catalog in order to deploy a Web server to work with.

1. If necessary, start your Windows 10 desktop computer and open a browser window to VMware.com.

2. If necessary, scroll down and click the **VMware Hands-on Labs** link to open the on-line labs catalog page.

3. Click the **Enrollments** icon from the left-hand pane and then if necessary enter your MyVMware username and password.

4. From the right-hand Manual pane, click the **Table of Contents** link to display all the lab modules.

5. Click to expand **Module 2 - Introduction to Administration (30 minutes)** and then click the **Introduction** lesson and close the Table of Contents dialog box.

6. Perform all lessons in Module 2 and Module 3 and record your results below:

_____

_____

_____

_____

7. This completes the steps for this activity. You may wish to perform Case Project 10-2 at the end of this chapter to practice using vRealize Operations to monitor virtual machine usage and request an unused virtual machine be released back to the system.

Using VMware vCloud Air to Extend a Virtual Data Center

VMware provides an online cloud environment called vCloud Air. As shown in Figure 10-10, vCloud Air provides three types of IaaS services across the Internet.

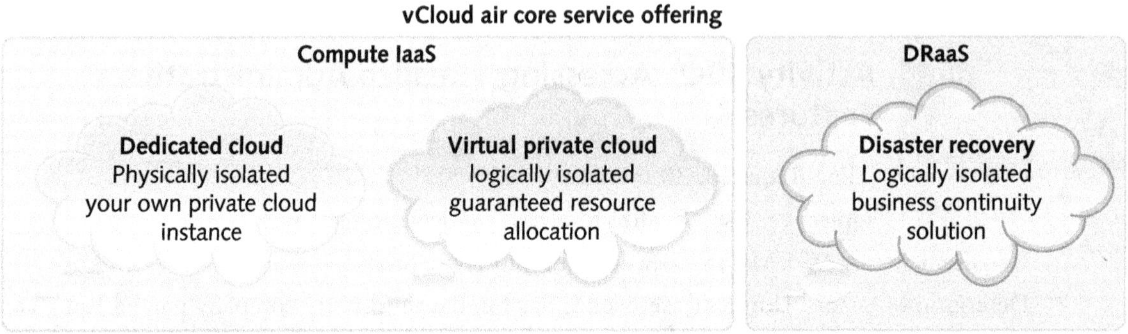

vCloud air core service offering

Compute IaaS

Dedicated cloud
Physically isolated
your own private cloud
instance

Virtual private cloud
logically isolated
guaranteed resource
allocation

DRaaS

Disaster recovery
Logically isolated
business continuity
solution

Figure 10-10 vCloud service offering types

The **dedicated cloud service** allows an organization to build a private virtual data center on a platform that is dedicated to use by only that organization. This type of cloud service is the most expensive but also the most secure. Dedicated cloud services are typically used by organizations that require the maximum security such as banks, government, hospitals, and legal firms.

The **Virtual Private Cloud service** is a multi-tenancy service in that multiple organizations will share the same hardware that is logically divided into separate virtual data centers. Virtual Private Clouds are much more economical than dedicated cloud services and provide a highly secure environment that meets the security needs of most organizations. vCloud Air provides a RaaS service and allows the organization to replicate data between the local data center and a virtual data center within vCloud Air. If data is lost in the primary data center it can be copied back from the cloud. In the event the entire local data center is lost, the virtual cloud data center can be used to continue operations. You will learn more about using disaster recovery (DR) services in the Implementing Disaster Recovery section later in this chapter.

You can use vCloud Air to host a virtual data center for a small business, extend an existing vSphere data center, or implement disaster recovery services that can be used to back up and restore data and services in the event of data loss or the loss of an entire data center. Using vCloud Air to extend a data center has several advantages as shown below:

- *Extend Existing Applications*—A major advantage of implementing a hybrid cloud is migrating applications from your existing data center to vCloud Air without having to make any major changes in the application or data center to provide consistent security and accessibility.

- *Test & Development*—Another important advantage of extending the data center using a hybrid cloud is utilizing cloud capacity for development and testing of new applications.

- *Web & Mobile Applications*—Using a hybrid cloud provides the ability to deliver mobile Web applications over vCloud Air while still providing limited access to your on-premises data center.

- *Cloud-Hosted Desktops*—As you learned in Chapter 9, a Virtual Desktop Infrastructure can quickly use up computing and storage resources in the local data center. Delivery of desktops and hosted apps as a cloud service can provide end users on any device, anywhere, with needed capacity without compromising the dedicated resources of your local data center.

Extending a data center involves the following steps:

1. Obtain a vCloud Air account
2. Create a virtual data center along with any necessary virtual machines
3. Install vConnector in the existing vSphere environment
4. Connect the local vSphere data center to the vCloud virtual data center

In this section we will describe each of these steps as well as provide you with the opportunity to work with vCloud Air using modules from the VMware labs.

Obtaining a vCloud Air Account
In order to set up a vCloud virtual data center (VDC), an organization needs to set up a vCloud account. VMware vCloud Air is basically a public cloud platform that is built on two of VMware's flagship products: VMware vSphere and the multi-tenant cloud platform called VMware vCloud Director. Organizations can run their existing workloads as well as launch new apps and services on VMware vCloud Air, allowing them to extend their existing datacenters into the cloud. As mentioned previously, there are two major vCloud Air account types, dedicated cloud and Virtual Private Cloud. The only difference is that with Virtual Private Cloud the underlying physical resources are shared among multiple tenants. Although the physical infrastructure is shared, each individual customer has their own virtual environment that is logically and securely isolated from other customers. Having multiple tenants has little or no impact on performance as resources are made available on demand when required. The big advantage to a Virtual Private Cloud is the cost is much less. Unless your organization is a government or banking business, you will probably want to subscribe to the Virtual Private Cloud service. When you create an account you will be charged a monthly fee based on what resources you use. Tables 10-3 and 10-4 show the resources and monthly charges that are included in a basic starter pack for the Virtual Private Cloud service and the dedicated service.

Table 10-3   vCloud Air Virtual Private Cloud starter pack resource and cost/month

Resource	Amount Allocated	Monthly Charge	Price/Unit
Compute	100 GB VRAM 13 GHz CPU	$365.00	$.03 GB/hr
Storage	2 TB	$240.00	$.12 GB/month
Bandwidth	10 Mbps	$229.00	$.03 Mbps/hr
Public IPs	2 Included	$50.00	$25.00 each

Table 10-4   vCloud Air dedicated network starter pack resource and cost/month

Resource	Amount Allocated	Monthly Charge	Price/Unit
Compute	240GB vRAM, 35 GHz CPU	$5978.00	$.034/GB
Storage	6 TB Basic	$360.00	$.06/GB/month
Bandwidth	50 Mbps	$1191.00	$.03 Mbps/Hr
Public IPs	3 Included	$78.00	$26.00 EACH

Notice how much more you pay for the dedicated cloud service as compared to a Virtual Private Cloud service. In addition to signing up for a service and providing a credit card for monthly charges, you will also need to pick a region that will be your primary data center. Typically, you pick a region that is physically closest to your primary data center. During the month you can monitor your resource usage and changes by accessing the Resource Usage page as shown in Figure 10-11.

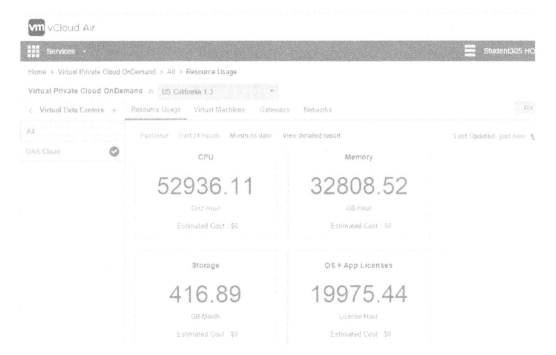

Figure 10-11   vCloud service resource usage/charge window

Source: VMware vCloud Service

When you create a new Virtual Private Cloud data center you provide it with a name and are automatically assigned capacity limits for computing as shown in Figure 10-12.

You can contact VMware support if you wish to change these capacity limits. In addition to the computing resources, a basic starter pack for the Virtual Private Cloud service also includes networking services shown in Figure 10-13.

Edit Virtual Data Center   ✕

Name: UAS Cloud

Capacity Limits   50 Virtual Machines
                         130 GHz of vCPU
                         100 GB of vRAM
                         2 TB of SSD-Accelerated Storage
                         2 TB of Standard Storage

VDC Permissions: All users   ▾

                         Contact VMware Support if you require additional capacity

                                                        Save

Figure 10-12   vCloud Air Edit Virtual Data Center window

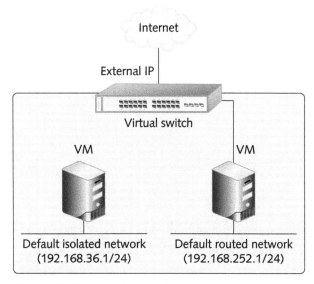

Figure 10-13   vCloud network servicees

The **Edge gateway** provides routing and firewall services to connect internal virtual machines to the External or public network. Internally there are two private networks. The **isolated network** is internal only and does not connect to the Internet. It is like a Host only network in the VMware Workstation 12 Pro environment. The **routed network** connects to the Edge gateway and provides virtual machines access to the external network.

A combination of both the routed and isolated networks can be used to create DMZ-like zones within a virtual data center, which can allow only a particular set of virtual machines to interface with the Internet, while the rest remain isolated and secured on isolated networks. You can manage the gateway configuration by selecting the virtual data center and using the Gateways and Networks tabs.

By default, all incoming ports are blocked by the Edge gateway, but you can edit the Firewall Rules to open ports and configure the firewall settings. The Networks tab shown in Figure 10-14 allows you to view the Public IP address assigned to the gateway as well as assign a range of IP addresses for dynamic assignment and view the number of virtual machines connected to the routed network.

Figure 10-14   vCloud Network Configuration window

Source: VMware vCloud Service

You can change these settings by using the Manage in vCloud Director link. In the following activity you will use the VMware Labs to set up a VDC that can be used to extend an existing vSphere data center.

Activity 10-3: Creating a vCloud Data Center and Virtual Machines

Time Required: 20 minutes

Objective: Use VMware labs to create a data center and virtual machine.

Requirements: A MyVMware user account and password

Description: Your manager would like to have you set up a virtual data center that can be used to offer cloud services and extend the UAS vSphere environment. In this activity you will access your MyVMware account and then use the Disaster and Recovery VMware lab to learn how to create and deploy virtual machines in a new vCloud VDC.

1. If necessary, start your Windows 10 desktop computer and open a browser window to VMware.com.

2. Log on to your MyVMware account. After logging on, scroll down and click the **VMware Hands-on Labs** link located under the Try and Purchase heading.

3. Click the **Log In** tab and then log on using your MyVMware account information. You may initially need to reset your password to make it work for the VMware On-line Labs section. You can re-enter your same password when resetting it.

4. In the left frame, click the **Hybrid Cloud** link located under the All Labs heading.

5. Click the **ENROLL** button in the HOL-1782-HBD-1 VMware vCloud Air: Data Center Extension lab and then click the **START THIS LAB** button to start the lab environment.

6. Follow the instructions in the vCloud Air Student Check-in section to get your username and set your password. Record your password, organization, and Cloud URL information below:

    Username: _____ (student###@vcahol.com)

    Password: _____ (may vary for each student)

    Organization: _____ (Student###)

    Cloud URL: _____ (https.......org\student###)

 We recommend opening Notepad on your virtual desktop and then copy and paste the information shown on this page to a Notepad document. You can then access this information later when you **TIP** need to log on to a cloud service. Click the **Set Password** link to open a page to vCloud Air and set your password.

7. Click the **Go to Sign in page** and sign in to vCloud Air using the username and password you recorded in the previous step to display the vCloud Air home page. Hover your curser over the **Virtual Private Cloud On-Demand** box and click the first site ID (a number starting with "M"). When you see the vCloud Air Location page, click **Continue** to select the default site.

8. You will be connected to a pre-configured vCloud account.

9. For practice let's create a new virtual data center named UAS-Cloud. Click the "**+**" symbol next to the Virtual Data Centers heading to display the New Virtual Data Center page.

10. Enter the name **UAS-Cloud** in the Name field and then click the **Create Virtual Data Center** button.

11. To view your new data center, click **Home** from the navigation line to return to the home page. After a few minutes your new data center will appear in the Virtual Data Centers frame.

12. You can edit data center information by right-clicking the existing data center and using the **Edit** link to display the Edit Virtual Data Center page as shown previously in Figure 10-12.

13. To create a virtual machine in the UAS-Cloud data center, if necessary, click to select your **UAS-Cloud** virtual data center to display the Virtual Machines tab.

14. Click the **Create your first virtual machine** button to display the Select a template page. (Notice the link to Create My Virtual Machine from Scratch, you can use this option to install your own OS.)

15. Click the **32 Bit** button to the right of the Ubuntu Server 12.04 i386 template and then click **Continue** to display the New Virtual Machine page.

16. Leave the default options and click the **Create Virtual Machine** button.

17. After a few minutes an updated page showing your new virtual machine will be displayed. After creating a virtual machine, you can right-click it and then select the **Edit Resources** option to change virtual machine settings as shown in Figure 10-15. (You may need to log back into your vCloud account to view the new virtual machine.)

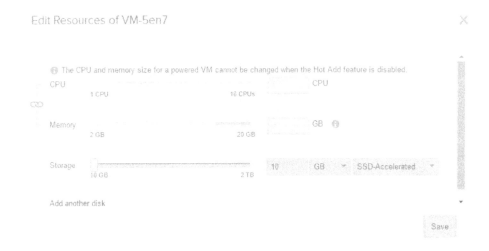

Figure 10-15 vCloud Air Create Virtual Machine summary window

Source: VMware vCloud Air Hybridity and Networking Lab

18. Notice under the status column that the virtual machine is powered on. (The virtual machine name is based on the template you selected.)

19. Click to select your virtual machine and then click the **Actions** dropdown menu. Experiment with some different options such as powering the virtual machine off, and then

back on. Note that you will need to refresh your browser screen using the F5 key to see any changes in machine status.

20. Click the **Open in Console** button to display a console window for the new virtual machine. Notice that this is a text-based Linux console. You will need to know the password to log on. You may need to enable pop-up from this site on your browser to see the console screen.

21. Close the console window.

22. Click the **Resource Usage** tab and record your CPU and Memory usage below:

    CPU Usage: _____

    Memory Usage: _____

23. Click the **Gateways** tab to display the gateway shown previously in Figure 10-15. Try experimenting with different options and record your results below:

    _____

24. Click the **Networks** tab to display the network options as shown previously in Figure 10-16. You can use this option to make the internal network match your local vSphere environment. Try experimenting with different options and record your results below:

    _____

25. If you want virtual machines to access the Internet, you will need to add a public IP address. To add a public IP address, click **Public IPs** to add a public IP address to the gateway. Note you will be charged extra for using a public IP address.

26. You have now completed the setup of the UAS virtual data center. In the real world your next step would be to connect your local vSphere environment to this data center to provide access to the new virtual machine. You can learn more about this process by performing case project 10-3.

27. In the Navigation bar of the VMware vCloud Air tab, click **Home** to return to the services page.

28. Click the **Log Out** option from the top right of your lab page. Close your VMware Labs window and return to your MyVMware account page. You will be able to come back to this lab again in Activity 10-4.

Connecting vSphere to a Virtual Data Center

Connecting an existing vSphere environment to the vCloud Air VDC requires installing the **vCloud Connector** server into the vSphere center and providing a network connection to the cloud as illustrated in Figure 10-16.

The VMware vCloud Connector is a free tool provided by VMware to help organizations to create fully functional hybrid cloud environments. Using the vCloud Connector, organizations can connect and manage virtual machines in their on-premises datacenters with a VMware-backed public cloud using a single vCloud Connector portal. The VMware connector allows administrators to migrate computing resources across vSphere and vCloud environments. vCloud Connector also enables the transfer of large amounts of data securely from vSphere datacenters to vCloud Air using something called the **Offline Data Transfer (ODT)**

10

Enterprise datacenter

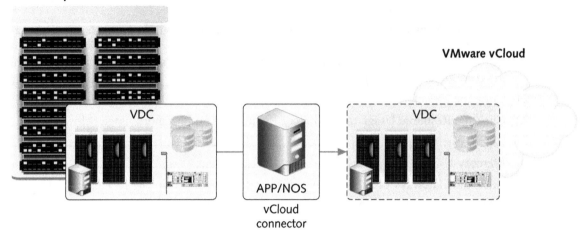

Figure 10-16   vCloud Connector

service. Using ODT, you can export your data to an external storage device that is provided by a vCloud Air operator, the data is then encrypted and stored on the external storage device, which you then ship back to the operator. Using ODT enables the vCloud environment to be seeded with large volumes of data from the physical storage device where it would be impractical to transmit the required data over the network. Once the vCloud environment has been seeded, only changes to the data need to be transmitted over the Internet, using much less bandwidth.

Connecting the vSphere Data Center to vCloud Air
In addition to the vCloud Connector running in the vSphere environment, a connection needs to be established between vCloud Air and your vSphere data center. This can be done in one of two ways: across the public Internet or by using an IPSec VPN. Using the Public Internet requires entering the URL for your cloud environment that is provided to you as part of your vCloud account. Setting up a IPSec VPN is more complicated but provides better performance and security. Once the connection has been established, you can use the vCloud Connector tool along with the vSphere Web console to manage resources between the cloud and the vSphere data center.

VMware provides a new platform called VMware Cloud Foundation. VMware Cloud Foundation is based on vSphere virtualization and designed to be used for private cloud deployments or run as a service from the public cloud. VMware Cloud Foundation uses VMware's NSX network virtualization to establish a common foundation between private and public cloud environments that can be used to extend your local data center into a hybrid cloud by utilizing vCloud Air services.

As described in Chapter 4, NSX is VMware's software defined networking environment that manages virtual network components such as virtual switches, VLANs, and the connection to the physical network. NSX allows you to treat the data center's physical network as a pool of services that can be distributed to each virtual machine independent of the underlying physical hardware and topology. Treating the network components as software objects allows devices and security services including firewalls and gateways to be easily moved from one location to another. Being able to move virtual machines and applications independent of the physical network is very important when extending a data center using a hybrid cloud. vCloud Air Advanced Networking Services (ANS) is the public cloud piece of the NSX network virtualization process. ANS provides networking and security services in vCloud Air through the use of VMware's NSX technology as the underlying networking platform. ANS provides customers with enhanced security and portability in the public cloud environment. In addition, ANS services improve network manageability and can be used to create a path that allows you to work with other vCloud Air networking services. Using ANS vCloud Air provides a high capacity SSL VPN that can be used by individual devices such as laptops and mobile phones to connect securely into a vCloud Air environment using SSL certificates, without the complexity of routing through an IPSec-based VPN gateway. This is especially useful for hosting cloud-hosted desktops and Web & mobile applications on vCloud Air.

Another important component used in using a hybrid cloud to extend a local vSphere data center is VMware's Hybrid Cloud Manager, which can be used in place of vConnector to extend the data center. VMware combines Advanced Networking Services with their Hybrid Cloud Manager component to allow organizations to stretch their local "on-premises" to a single virtual data center using a layer 2 (IPSec VPN). You can experience using Advanced Networking Services along with VMware's Hybrid Cloud Manager by performing the VMware Data Center Extension lab in case project 10-4.

Using VMware vCloud Disaster Recovery Service
Knowing that your data center is able to quickly and completely recover from loss of data or services as the result of a disaster is perhaps one of the best ways to cure IT insomnia. As described in Appendix C, disaster recovery (often just abbreviated DR) relies on having good backups that can be used to restore data and services in the event of a disaster. Disasters can be the result of user error, fires, natural phenomena such as floods and storms, malware, or attacks on a regional or national infrastructure such as occurred on 9/11. In the past, data centers made data backups at regular intervals and then stored the backup in off-site premises. In addition, a data center may have an alternate site. The alternate site can be defined as being cold, warm, or hot based on the time it takes to get the site running in the event a disaster wipes out the primary data center. The cloud can greatly facilitate the backup and disaster recovery process by providing regular backups as well as off-site storage of data and systems. Implementing a cloud disaster recovery system involves three major steps.

First you need to subscribe to the cloud server and pay a monthly fee for its usage. Next you need to install the replication service on your existing virtual data center. The replication service will replicate selected virtual machines to their counterpart on the cloud as illustrated in Figure 10-17.

Using the VMware replication service, you can configure the intervals to occur every 15 minutes or longer. Only changes made since the last replication are uploaded. Virtual machines that do not have data that changes frequently can be set to longer intervals to save time and costs. The third step is to verify that data can be replicated back to virtual machines at the data center or if the data center is down, the virtual machine in the cloud-based virtual data center can take over the processing. vSphere Replication is a feature of the VMware vSphere platform that makes it possible to replicate virtual machines between

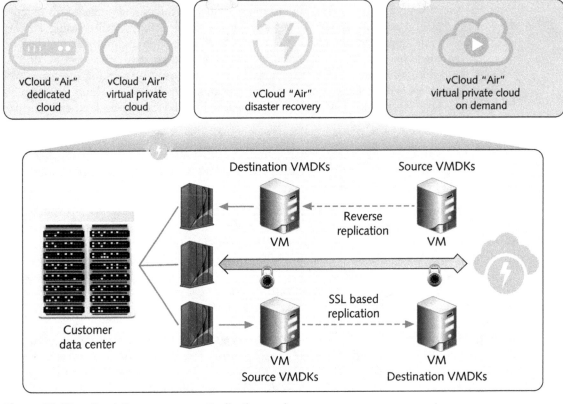

Figure 10-17   vCloud disaster recovery vReplication service

the local vSphere data center and a virtual data center located in vCloud. The **vSphere Replication appliance** can copy virtual machines to another location, within or between clusters, and makes that copy available for recovery through the VMware vSphere Web Client or through the orchestration of a full disaster recovery product such as VMware vCenter Site Recovery Manager. vSphere Replication is a distributed virtual server in the OVF format. After downloading the vSphere Replication Server, you can deploy it as an appliance by using the standard vSphere OVF Deployment wizard.

In the following activity you will use the VMware Lab to guide you through using vCloud Air Disaster Recovery as a Service (RaaS). The lab module involves a few general procedures. First you will use a vSphere Web administrative console to create a virtual machine that will be used to set up and test replication to the vCloud DR service. The VMware lab provides a vSphere environment that contains a vCenter and ESXi hosts which will act as your on-premises environment. From this environment you will connect to a live account within the disaster recovery service. You will be replicating and failing over a new VM to a vCloud Air. You will begin by obtaining a vCloud Air account and then authenticating to a target VDC in vCloud Air. You will perform a Planned Migration and see how to begin a reverse migration back to the primary data center.

Activity 10-4: Working with VMware vCloud Disaster Recovery Services

Time Required: 20 minutes

Objective: Use VMware Labs to establish replication between a vSphere data center and vCloud Virtual Data Center.

Requirements: Completion of Activity 10-3

Description: In this activity you will access your MyVMware account and then use VMware Labs to perform steps from Module 1 – Fail Over and Fail Back of the Disaster and Recovery lab.

1. If necessary, start your Windows 10 desktop computer and open a browser window to **VMware.com**.

2. Log on to your MyVMware account. After logging on, scroll down and click the **VMware Hands-on Labs** link located under the Try and Purchase heading.

3. If necessary, click the **Log In** tab and then log on using your MyVMware account information.

4. In the left frame, click the **Enrollments** icon and then if necessary, login using your MyVMware username and password.

5. Click the **Resume this Lab** button in the HOL-1784-HBD-1 - VMware vCloud Air Disaster Recovery lab.

6. Read the Lab Guidance and Introduction sections at your own pace.

7. Click the **vCloud Air** Student tab and log on using the vCloud Air username and password from Activity 10-3.

8. Click the **Table of Contents** link in the right lab manual frame.

9. Click **Module 2 – Failover and Failback** and go through Lessons 1 and 2 to take a tour of vCloud disaster recovery services.

10. Perform steps in Lesson 3 to create a virtual machine that you can use to test disaster recovery and replication. In this part of the activity you will use the vSphere Center client provided to the lab. The lab site contains following infrastructure:

    2 vSphere 6.0 ESXi hosts

    1 vCenter 6.0 Server appliance

    1 vCenter Replication 6.0 appliance

    1 vRealize Orchestrator 6.0 appliance

11. After completing the lab, click **Log Out** to log off of the VMware On-line labs and close your Web browser. You can continue working with the other modules including using vRealize Operations to monitor virtual machine usage by performing Case Project 10-4.

This completes the section on using VMware vCloud. In the following section you will learn how to work with Microsoft Azure and how it can be used to create data centers as well as extend existing Hyper-V environments.

Microsoft Cloud Services

Microsoft offers three major Cloud computing platforms: Private Cloud, Azure, and Azure Stacks.

The Private Cloud connects Hyper-V servers around the world hosted in on-premises data centers for companies that require extra functionality and security.

Azure offers a comprehensive suite of cloud features ranging from Compute featuring Virtual Machines, online databases, hosted Active Directory, remote applications, and APIs offering everything from machine learning functionality to text to speech.

Azure Stacks combines the best of the Private Cloud and Azure, allowing corporations to run most of Azure's cloud services within their own private datacenters.

Creating a Private Cloud with Virtual Machine Manager

The Microsoft System Center Virtual Machine Manager (VMM) can create and manage private clouds incorporating both VMware ESX and Microsoft Hyper-V servers. Private clouds are used by large organizations that prefer or are required by law to store their data within their own on-premises data centers, rather than outside cloud servers like Google Compute, Amazon AWS, and Microsoft Azure.

A private cloud lets employees from many different regional offices all access the network as if they were in the same location. For example, a company may have a Finance Department in New York, Los Angeles, and Houston. Each of these departments have their own on-premises data centers running Hyper-V servers. By joining these regional datacenters into a "Finance" virtual cloud, all employees can easily access all of the companies' resources.

By using load balancers and features such as Equivalent Objects, VMM can intelligently shift users to servers with less load, even to other locations, and choose where to store data.

VMM supports multiple private clouds, so a company can have separate "Finance," "Marketing," and "Support" clouds, each based on servers all around the world in local data centers.

VMM includes a wizard to easily create a private cloud by bringing together all of the resources required. We will walk through the steps of this wizard, which isn't practical to replicate within a normal classroom environment. For our example we'll use our familiar Superior Technical College, which will join its sister school Northwoods Technical College in a private cloud.

To start the VMM Console, use the Start menu or the Virtual Machine Manager Console desktop icon. In the VMs and Services workspace, click the Create Cloud toolbar button to start the Create Cloud wizard.

In the General window, you enter the name of your private cloud, CollegeCloud, as well as an optional description. You also choose whether this private cloud will support Shielded VMs (protected disks with BitLocker encryption, and can be kept private from Hyper-V administrators).

Next in the Resources window, as shown in Figure 10-18, you choose the different host groups that will be part of the private cloud. In this example, Northwoods and Superior. Alternatively, the Cloud could be created from VMware resource pools.

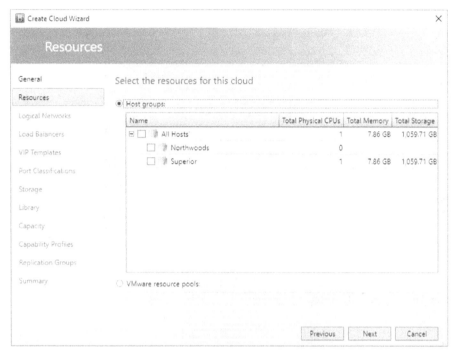

Figure 10-18 The Resources window

In the Logical Networks window, you choose "Backend." A logical network is a simplified way of representing a physical network by its purpose.

In the Load Balancers and VIP Templates windows, you skip this step as they are currently not yet implemented. You can later add a load balancer to your private cloud under its properties.

In the Port Classifications window, as shown in Figure 10-19, you choose different networking port classifications for the virtual machines that will be used in the cloud. You choose Medium bandwidth.

In the Storage window, as shown in Figure 10-20 you choose the storage classifications for the virtual machines, choosing from Local or Remote storage with total capacities displayed. You choose Local storage.

In the Library window, as shown in Figure 10-21, you choose where your virtual machines and other library resources are stored. After clicking the Browse button next to the Stored VM path text box, you select the MSSCVMMLibrary.

In the Capacity window, as shown in Figure 10-22, you can set limits on the resources available to the private cloud. You can limit the number of virtual CPUs, memory and disk storage, virtual machines, and quota points. You leave these at the default Use Maximum.

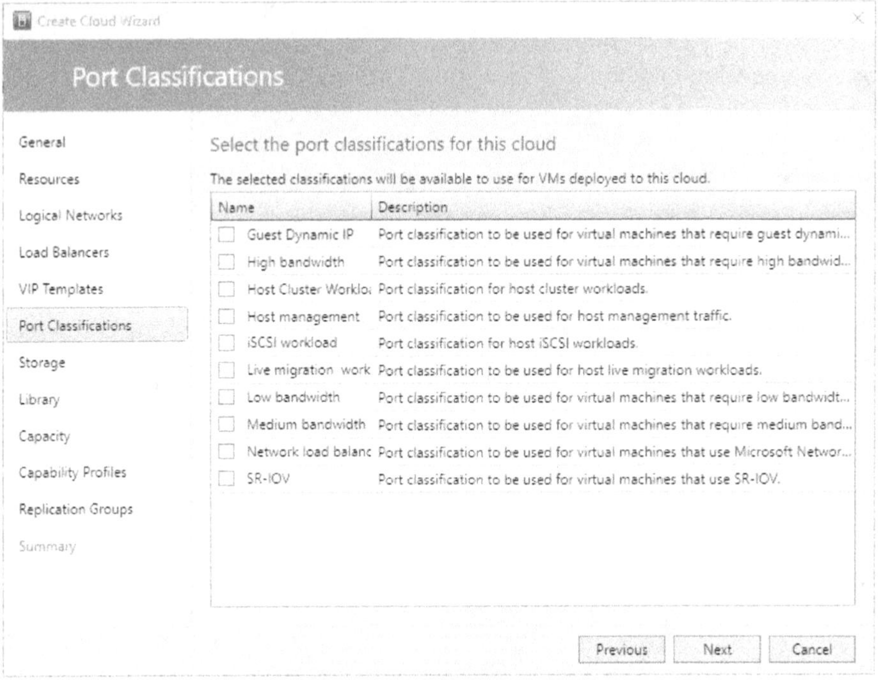

Figure 10-19 The Port Classifications window

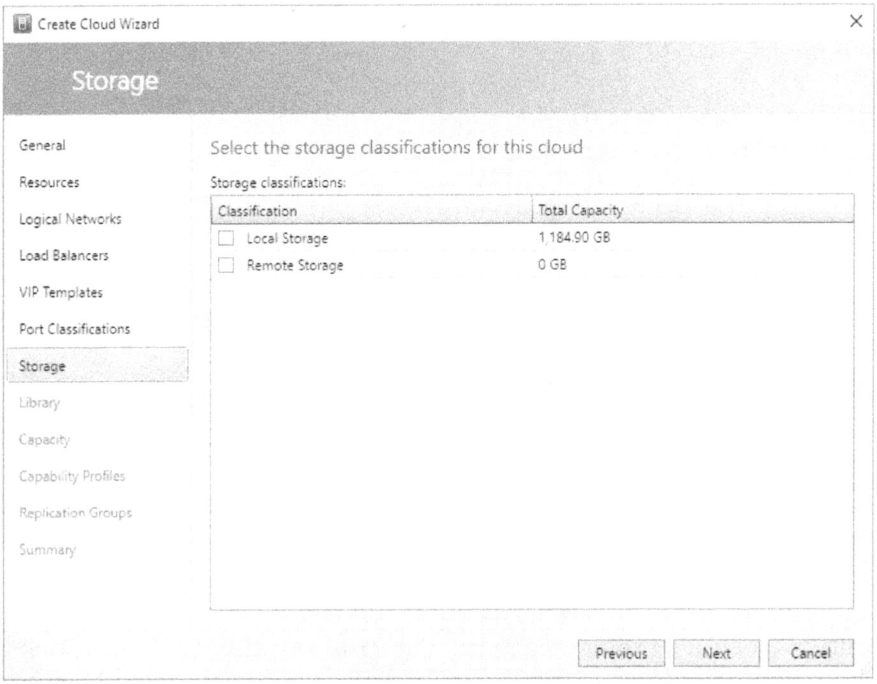

Figure 10-20 The Storage window

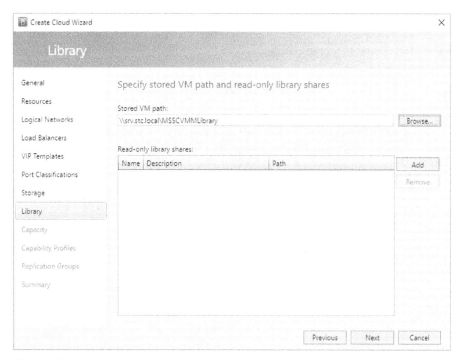

Figure 10-21   The Library window

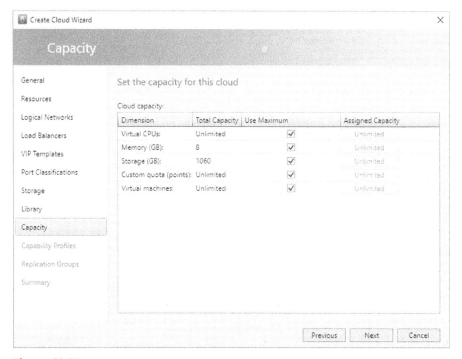

Figure 10-22   The Capacity window

In the Capability Profiles window, choose the types of virtualization hosts to be used in the cloud, such as VMWare's ESX Server and Hyper-V. This determines minimum and maximum values for virtual machines configurations.

In the Replication Groups window you can choose to include available replication groups in your cloud, used to duplicate data for recovery. You plan to implement this in the future and add it into your cloud.

In the Summary window, as shown in Figure 10-23, you review the choices you made in the wizard and click Finish. After several moments the new cloud is created, appearing under Clouds in the VMs and Services workspace.

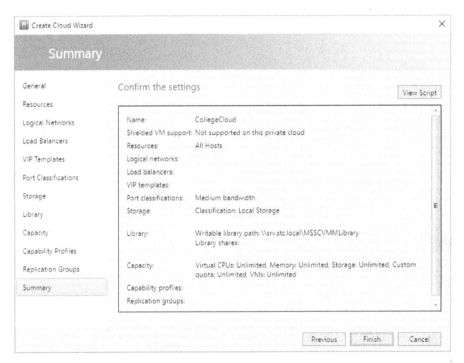

Figure 10-23   The Summary window

Working with Microsoft Azure

Microsoft Azure is a public cloud computing platform that debuted in 2010 and is currently available in 28 regions around the world. Azure provides a wide range of cloud services within 11 different categories as described below.

- *Compute*—Virtual machines featuring Windows Server or Linux, as well as Virtual Machine Scale Sets to deploy identical virtual machines quickly from templates with built in on-demand scaling. Batch can perform series of automated tasks such as rendering video and analyzing data. RemoteApp and Containers allows users to run individual applications on a wide variety of devices.

- *Networking*—A Content Delivery Network (CDN) hosts Web objects like images and text as well as software and documents across a global network of high bandwidth servers. Domain names can be hosted with Azure DNS. Virtual Networks create private networks in the cloud that can be connected to securely through an encrypted VPN Gateway. The Load Balancer and Traffic Manager improve performance and availability by distributing traffic.

- *Storage*—Azure Storage allows for simple data storage, including cloud-based SMB network file shares typically found on local networks. Backup protects user and application data by storing multiple copies across different servers. Site Recovery can replicate private clouds and provide automatic recovery in the event of failure.

- *Web and Mobile*—App Service is designed to host both mobile and enterprise Web applications. Content Protection can encrypt streaming media and provide Digital Rights Management (DRM) to protect usage. Notification Hubs can send push notifications to mobile devices.

- *Databases*—Provides a number of different types of databases including SQL and NoSQL. The SQL Data Warehouse scales on demand to provide optimal performance without overbuying capacity.

- *Intelligence and Analytics*—Machine Learning creates predictive analytics models, for example predicting real estate prices and detecting faces in images. Add functionality with cloud-based text to speech and speech to text translation, emotion recognition, search, spell check, and autosuggestion services.

- *Internet of Things*—The IoT Hub supports communications with millions of network-connected Internet of Things devices, such as smart thermostats and smoke detectors.

- *Enterprise Integration*—Service Bus provides a system for applications to communicate with each other. StorSimple provides hybrid storage, combining cloud storage for less frequently accessed data and local storage for high performance needs.

- *Security and Identity*—Host Active Directory and Active Directory Domain Services in the cloud allowing a single logon to access both local and cloud resources. Implement Multi-Factor Authentication to protect applications and data with phone, text, and mobile verification. Key Vault securely stores passwords and keys, and Security Center identifies threats and helps prevent future attacks.

- *Developer Tools*—Visual Studio Team Services allows teams to share code and track issues. Visual Studio Application Insights tracks application crashes and usage, while DevTest Labs lets developers quickly test applications.

- *Monitoring and Management*—The Scheduler can call HTTP services on a periodic schedule or set dates, and Log Analytics collects performance data, network, and event logs from both local computers and cloud virtual machines and provides analysis and visualization of the data.

Microsoft is also currently developing a new product, Azure Stacks, which allows large companies to run their own version of Azure completely within their own datacenters and private clouds.

Creating a Microsoft Azure Account

All new Microsoft Azure accounts receive a free one-month trial and $200 worth of Azure credits to try out the service. A phone number and credit card number are required to verify your account, however your card will not be charged to open your account, or after the trial period has expired. A number of free cloud services will still be available after the trial period as well. A Microsoft account will also be required to open your Azure account.

Activity 10-5: Creating a Microsoft Azure Account

Time Required: 10 minutes

Objective: Create your Microsoft Azure account.

Requirements: An Internet connection, a credit card, and a phone that can receive text messages

Description: In this activity, you will create a one-month free trial account with $200 in Azure credit. A mobile phone and a credit card are used to verify your account.

1. If necessary, log on to the host computer with your assigned administrative username and password.

2. Start your Web browser and navigate to **azure.microsoft.com**.

3. Click the **Start free** button on the top of the page, and then click **Start free** again on the next page.

4. On the Sign in page, enter your Microsoft account email address and password and click **Sign in**, or click **Sign up now** if you need to create a new account.

5. On the Free trial sign up page under About you, complete any empty fields marked with an asterisk, next click **Next**.

6. Under the Identity verification by phone, choose the correct country under the drop-down list and enter your phone number. Click the **Send text message** button.

7. After receiving the text message from Microsoft, enter it into the text box and click **Verify code**.

8. Under Identity verification by card, enter your credit card information and billing address. This information is used only for verification purposes and you will not be charged to use Microsoft Azure if you don't upgrade your account. Click **Next**.

9. Under Agreement, click to check the **I agree to the subscription agreement, offer details, and privacy statement** check box, then click **Sign up**.

10. Creating your new account may take several minutes, click the **Play** button on the video to watch the introductory tour. Click the **Start managing my service** button when your subscription is ready.

11. Leave the Azure Dashboard open for the next activity.

Creating a Virtual Machine

Microsoft Azure includes pre-built images you can use to quickly deploy Windows Server and Linux virtual machines, with some images featuring pre-installed software. Virtual machines can be created from scratch using the Classic portal.

To create a new virtual machine, first sign into Azure (navigate to portal.azure.com and sign in with your Microsoft account).

From the Dashboard, as shown in Figure 10-24, choose New from the Hub menu to open the New blade. Under Marketplace, choose Compute and then Windows Server 2016 Datacenter under FEATURED APPS, and finally click Create to start the Create virtual machine wizard.

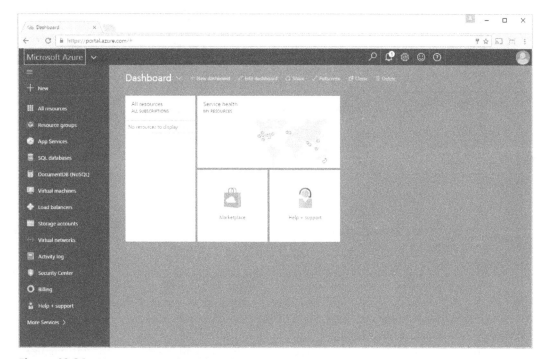

Figure 10-24   The Azure Portal dashboard

In the Basics blade under step 1, as shown in Figure 10-25, choose the name of the virtual machine, up to 15 characters long with no spaces or special characters. The VM disk type can either be an SSD for better performance, or a lower cost HDD where frequent disk access is not required.

A username and password is then entered for the admin account of the guest OS. The password must be at least 12 characters long and contain three out of following four requirements: a lowercase letter, an uppercase letter, a number, and a special character.

Next choose the subscription this virtual machine will be created under. The virtual machine can be assigned to an existing resource group, or a new one can be created. Resource groups let you organize similar virtual machines together.

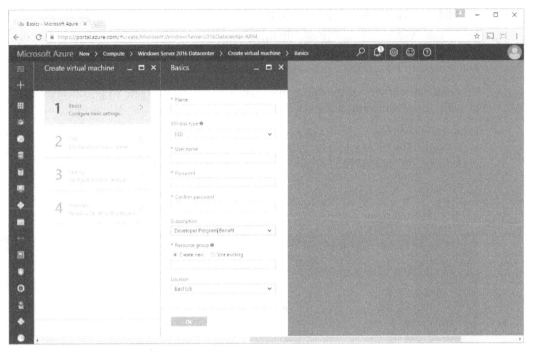

Figure 10-25 The Basics blade of the Create Virtual Machine wizard

Finally, choose a geographic region where the virtual machine should be hosted. Select the one nearest your own physical location to decrease latency.

In the Size blade under step 2, as shown in Figure 10-26, the three top recommended virtual machine configurations will be displayed. Different options include the number of CPU cores, memory, the number of data disks, maximum storage I/O per second (IOPS), local disk size and type, and features such as Load balancing and Premium disk support. Below each configuration is the estimated price per month to run the virtual machine continuously. Clicking View all will show additional virtual machine types.

In the Settings blade under step 3, as shown in Figure 10-27, you can further customize the virtual machine. The virtual disk can be assigned to a Storage account.

Under Network the address and subnet space can be configured under Virtual network and Subnet. A static or dynamic public IP address is set to allow access to the virtual machine over the Internet. The Network security group configures the firewall, allowing Remote Desktop access by default.

Extensions can add features to virtual machines, such as antivirus support. High Availability groups multiple virtual machines together into an availability set to ensure that at least one of the virtual machines is available at all times. Monitoring can be enabled on the virtual machine providing minute by minute updates and statistics while running, and is assigned to a Storage account.

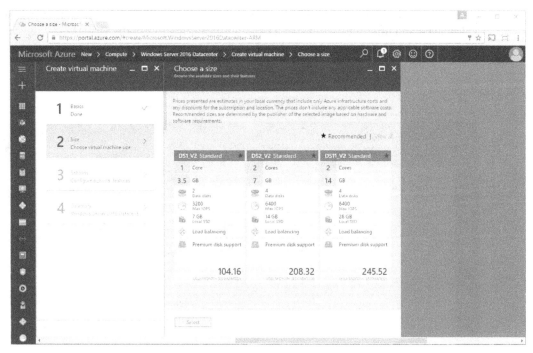

Figure 10-26   The Size blade of the Create Virtual Machine wizard

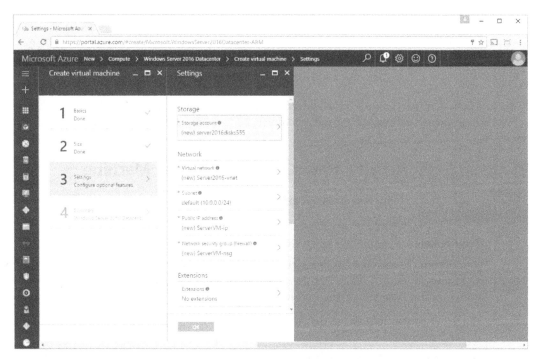

Figure 10-27   The Settings blade of the Create Virtual Machine wizard

In the Summary blade under step 4, as shown in Figure 10-28, a summary of all selections is displayed and after the Validation passed notification appears the virtual machine can be created. A template can be downloaded and used to create a similar virtual machine in the future.

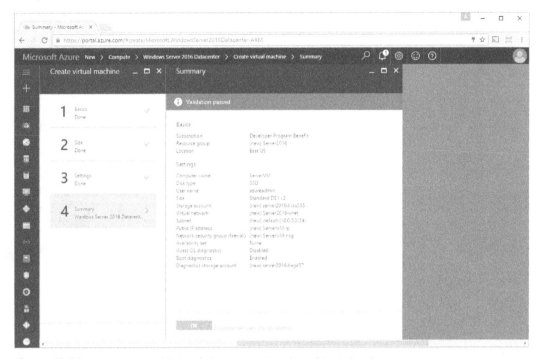

Figure 10-28   The Summary blade of the Create Virtual Machine wizard

After completion of step 4 the wizard will close and you will be returned to the dashboard. A new tile appears showing the virtual machine is being deployed; it will take several minutes to create.

Activity 10-6: Creating a Virtual Machine

Time Required: 15 minutes

Objective: Create a virtual machine under Microsoft Azure.

Requirements: Completion of Activity 10-5

Description: In this activity, you create a Windows Server 2016 Datacenter virtual machine in Microsoft Azure. You will configure basic specifications and choose a virtual machine configuration based on estimated monthly cost.

1. If necessary, log on to the host computer with your assigned administrative username and password.

2. Start your Web browser and navigate to **portal.azure.com**.

3. In the Sign in window, provide your Microsoft account email address and password, then click **Sign in**.

4. From the hub menu on the dashboard, click **New**.

5. In the New blade, click **Compute**.

6. In the Compute blade, click **Windows Server 2016 Datacenter**

7. In the Windows Server 2016 Datacenter blade, ensure Resource Manager is selected under the Select a deployment model dropdown list, then click **Create**.

8. On the Basics blade, enter **ServerVM** in to the Name text box.

9. Under VM disk type, confirm that SSD is selected.

10. Under User name, type **azureadmin**.

11. Under Password and Confirm password, choose a password of at least 12 characters with at least three of the following: lowercase characters, uppercase characters, numbers, and special characters. Record your password below:

    _____

12. Under Subscription, confirm that Free Trial is selected.

13. Under Resource group, select the **Create new** option button and type **Server2016** in to the text box.

14. Under Location, choose the region closest to your location, next click **OK**.

15. On the Choose a size blade, observe the different virtual machine configurations available and their estimated monthly costs. Click the least expensive, then click **Select**.

16. On the Settings blade, observe the available options, then click **OK**.

17. On the Summary blade, review your configuration and click **OK** after the Validation passed message appears to return to the dashboard.

18. A Deploying Windows Server 2016 Datacenter tile will appear on the dashboard. It will take several minutes for the virtual machine to be created.

19. Leave your browser open and logged on to Microsoft Azure for the next activity.

Connecting to a Virtual Machine

Similar to virtual machines hosted in Hyper-V and VMM, you interact with a guest OS by connecting it with Remote Desktop Connection application. On the virtual machine's blade you download an .RDP file which opens Remote Desktop Connection when double-clicked and is pre-configured with the virtual machine's public IP address.

Several warnings will appear regarding an unknown publisher and being unable to verify the identity of the remote computer; this is normal and can be ignored. After entering the username and password specified when creating the virtual machine, you can access the guest OS's desktop.

After you have finished using a virtual machine, if it is no longer needed, it is recommended that you power it down from the OS or using the Stop button in the virtual machine's blade so it will no longer consume Azure credits when not in use.

ACTIVITY

Activity 10-7: Connecting to a Virtual Machine

Time Required: 10 minutes

Objective: Connect to a virtual machine.

Requirements: Completion of Activity 10-6

Description: In this activity, you will connect to the Windows Server 2016 virtual machine you created previously using the Remote Desktop Connection application and the .RDP downloaded from Azure. You will then power it down to avoid additional usage costs.

1. If necessary, log on to the host computer with your assigned administrative username and password.

2. Start your Web browser and navigate to **portal.azure.com**.

3. From the hub menu on the dashboard, click **Virtual machines**.

4. Under Virtual machines, click **ServerVM**.

5. On the ServerVM blade, click **Connect** on the toolbar to download the ServerVM.rdp file. If the Opening ServerVM.rdp dialog box appears, click the **Save File** option button, then click **OK**.

6. Navigate to your download folder and double-click **ServerVM.rdp** to start the Remote Desktop Connection application.

7. A warning message will appear about an unknown publisher. Click **Connect** to continue.

8. In the Windows Security dialog box, click the **More Choices** link, then click **Use a different account**.

9. In the User name text box, enter **ServerVM\azureadmin**. In the password text box, enter the password you recorded in Activity 10-6, Step 11 and then click **OK**.

10. A warning message will appear that the identity of the remote computer cannot be verified. Click **Yes** to continue.

11. The guest OS desktop will appear. Right-click the **Start** button and click **System**. Record the processor and RAM of the virtual machine below:

_____

12. Close the Remote Desktop Connection window, clicking **OK** to confirm that you wish to disconnect from the remote session.

13. On the ServerVM blade in the Azure Portal, click **Stop** in the toolbar. Click **Yes** in the Do you want to stop 'ServerVM'? dialog box.

14. Close the ServerVM and Virtual Machines blades and leave your browser open and logged on to Microsoft Azure for the next activity.

Using File Storage

Although there are many commercial cloud-based services that specialize in storage, a special feature of Microsoft's Azure File Storage is the ability to create SMB (Server Message Block) 2.0 and 3.0 network shares typically used on local networks to share data. By using SMB and mapping a drive letter to a cloud share, legacy applications that depend on a database or files stored on a local network will now work transparently over the Internet.

To create File Storage share, choose Storage accounts from the Hub menu to open the Storage accounts blade, then click the Add toolbar button to start the Create storage account wizard.

Next you choose a name for your share. This name can be up to 24 characters long and must be unique, as it will be the prefix of your core.windows.net URL. Typically, the newer Resource manager deployment model should be used.

For Performance, choose either Standard HDD-based media or Premium SSD. Under Replication, four different strategies are available as shown in Table 10-5 below.

Table 10-5   File storage replication strategies

Strategy	ZRS	LRS	GRS	RA-GRS
Replication across multiple facilities	Yes	No	Yes	Yes
Data can be ready from primary or secondary location	No	No	No	Yes
Number of copies on separate nodes	3	3	6	6

Next you can choose to enable encryption on the storage store (only available on Resource manager deployments).

Finally, choose the subscription for the account and the resource group to assign it to, as well as the geographic location nearest your own.

When the deployment succeeds, you can hit Refresh to display the new storage account. After choosing it and displaying its blade, click Files under the FILE SERVICE section. Click File share from the toolbar and enter a name. You can also specify a quota of up to 5,120 GB in available space, and click Create.

After clicking the new file share, you can upload files by clicking the Upload button to open the Upload files blade and click the folder icon for a dialog box that allows you to choose multiple files. You can organize your files with the Add directory button to create new folders. Clicking Properties displays a direct URL to the file, the last modified date, file size, and an MD5 hash as shown in Figure 10-29. You can also check on the current quota usage, as well as delete the share on this blade.

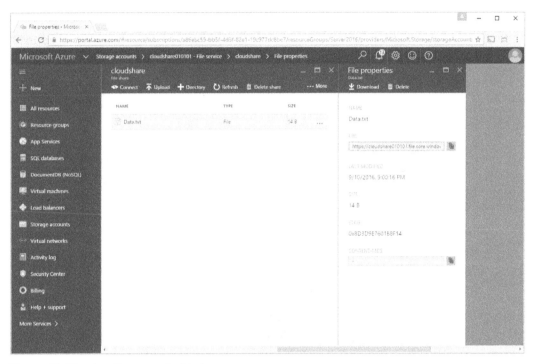

Figure 10-29   The File properties blade

The Connect toolbar button provides instructions on how to map a drive letter on your PC to the file share, as shown in Figure 10-30. You copy the text from the top box (or bottom for Linux), excluding the ">" at the beginning of the statement, and the [storage account access key] at the end. A Command Prompt window is then opened by right-clicking the Start Menu (do not choose the Admin version) and text from the Azure pasted in by right-clicking the toolbar, pointing to the Edit Menu, and clicking Paste.

Using the cursor keys, remove the [drive letter] text from the statement and replace it with the desired drive letter, for example Z.

Finally, to locate your Storage account access key, click Storage accounts from the hub menu on the Azure dashboard, choose Storage accounts, and then the name of your file share. Click Access keys under the SETTINGS heading. Click the Copy icon next to key1 to place it in your clipboard.

Return to the Command Prompt and paste it at the end of the statement, ensuring there is a space between the end of the share name and the access key, and hit Enter.

If an error occurs, the mostly likely cause is that port 445 is blocked by your router or your ISP, as this port can also be used for malicious code such as Trojans. This typically isn't an issue for business class connections.

You can now access files uploaded into the Azure file share as if it was a locally attached disk or network drive, saving and loading data to it and browsing with the Windows File Explorer as shown in Figure 10-31.

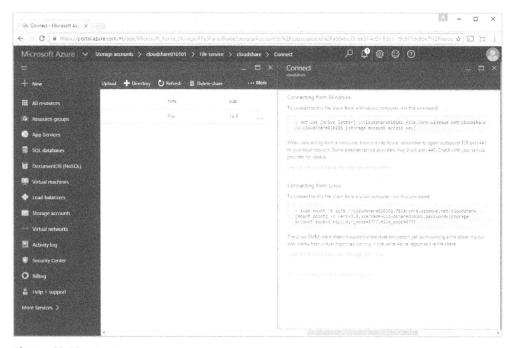

Figure 10-30 The Connect blade

 10

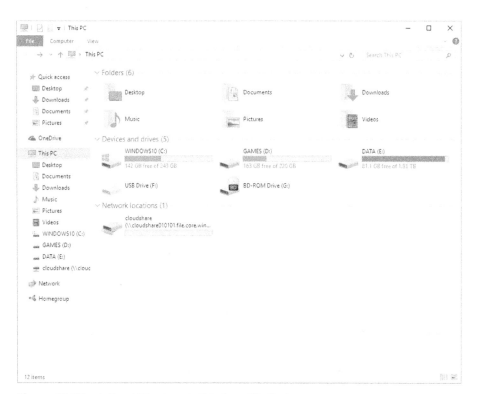

Figure 10-31 A Cloud File share in Windows File Explorer

Activity 10-8: Using File Storage

Time Required: 10 minutes

Objective: Create a cloud file share and map it to a local drive.

Requirements: Completion of Activity 10-5

Description: In this activity, you will create an Azure file share and upload a document to it. You will then map a drive letter to the share on your PC and access the data as if it was on the local network.

1. If necessary, log on to the host computer with your assigned administrative username and password.

2. Click **Start, Windows Accessories,** then click **Notepad.** Type your name into the new document.

3. Click the **File** menu, then click **Save As.** Select the **Desktop** under This PC in the left pane and in the File name text box, type **Data.txt,** then click **Save** and exit Notepad.

4. Start your Web browser and navigate to **portal.azure.com.**

5. In the Sign in window, provide your Microsoft account email address and password, then click **Sign in.**

6. From the hub menu on the dashboard, click **Storage accounts.**

7. On the Storage accounts blade, click the **Add** toolbar button.

8. On the Create storage account blade, type **cloudsharexxx** into the Name text box, where xxx is your birthday in digits. If the name is already in use, try different numbers.

9. Under the Resource group, choose the **Use existing** option button, then select **Server2016** from the dropdown list and click **Create.**

10. After several moments when the Deployments succeeded message appears, click the **Refresh** toolbar button to display the new storage account.

11. Select **cloudsharexxx** from the list to display its blade. Click **Files** under FILE SERVICE.

12. Click the **File share** toolbar icon to display the New file share blade. Type **cloudshare** into the Name text box, then click **Create.**

13. Click **cloudshare.** In the cloudshare blade, click the **Upload** toolbar icon. Click the **folder icon** to the right of the text box to display the File Upload dialog box.

14. Navigate to the Desktop and select the **Data.txt** file created in step 3, then click **Open.** Click **Upload** and close the Upload files blade.

15. On the cloudshare blade, click the **Connect** toolbar button.

16. Copy the text from the box below the phrase "To connect to this file share from a Windows computer, run this command:" to the clipboard. Do not include the > at the beginning of the line, or [storage account access key] at the end.

17. Right-click **Start** and click **Command Prompt** to open a Command Prompt window. Right-click the title bar, point to **Edit** in the menu, then click **Paste.**

18. Using the arrow keys and backspace, remove [drive letter] from the command and replace it with **S:** or another drive letter if that one is in use. Do not press the Enter key yet.

19. From the hub menu on the dashboard, click **Storage accounts,** then click **cloudsharexxx.** Click **Access keys** under SETTINGS.

20. Click the **Copy** icon to the right of key1 text box.

21. Returning to the Command Prompt, ensure there is a space at the end of the command, then paste in the key and press **Enter.**

Some Internet service providers block port 445, which is required to access the file share over the Internet; in this case you may receive an Error 53 when trying to map the drive.

22. Click **Start,** then click **File Explorer.** Under Network locations, double-click **cloudshare.**

23. Double-click **Data.txt** to open the file in Notepad, then confirm your name is shown and this file is being hosted on Azure.

24. Close the File Explorer window.

Introduction to OpenStack Cloud Components

Both VMware and Microsoft offer products such as VMware vCloud Director and VMware vRealize that you can use to create your own private clouds and offer on-demand services. While these products work best for IT organizations with existing VMware and Hyper-V data centers, they are proprietary in that they are designed to work with a specific company software and support services. Another option for organizations that currently have in-house technical staff that know Linux and open source hypervisors such as KVM and Oracle VM Server is to use the OpenStack compatible products. Open source software such as OpenStack has the advantage of freeing organizations from the costs and overhead often associated with proprietary software such as the cloud services offered by VMware and Microsoft. On the reverse side, implementing OpenStack solutions can require a lot more technical knowledge and support than using proprietary cloud products such as VMware vCloud and Microsoft Azure.

OpenStack architecture defines a number of components that can be divided into Control, Compute, Network, and Storage categories as shown in Figure 10-32.

As you can see from the diagram, OpenStack has a very modular design creating many moving parts. The control components define the Application Programming Interfaces (API) services, Web interface, database, and message bus. The network tier runs network service agents for networking, and the compute node is the virtualization hypervisor. It has services and agents to handle virtual machines. All of the components use a standard database and/or a message bus to interact with each other. The components can run on separate hardware platforms or be combined onto a single computer. For example, in smaller deployments you may run the control, networking, and compute components on one computer and use a separate SAN for the storage component. The in-depth understanding of these components you

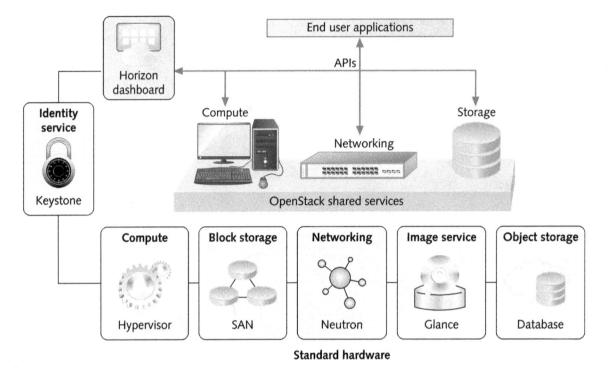

Figure 10-32   OpenStack components

need to work with OpenStack is beyond the scope of this chapter, but in this section you will be introduced to the primary components that make up the OpenStack architecture and the features they provide to build private clouds and host on-demand services.

Compute Components

OpenStack Compute components define the standards for the Hypervisor and associated modules need to run virtual machines. The standard OpenStack hypervisor component is called Nova. In order to work with OpenStack architecture a hypervisor must be able to interact with the other modules that make up a cloud environment. In addition to Nova, a number of hypervisors are currently compatible with OpenStack a few of which are listed below:

- Oracle VM Server
- Red Hat KVM
- Hyper-V
- Xen Server
- VMware ESX hypervisors and vCenter Server

Historically, most OpenStack development is done with the KVM hypervisor, and for this reason you are more likely to find community support for issues with the KVM hypervisor.

Today both Microsoft Hyper-V and VMware ESXi are gaining much support as both products are now being made available with a free license.

Control Components

The control components are responsible for managing the configuration and authorization in the OpenStack environment. The major OpenStack control components are the Dashboard, Horizon, and Keystone. The OpenStack dashboard is the Web interface component provided with OpenStack and relies on the Horizon services. The Horizon services contain the Application Program Interfaces (API) that the Dashboard uses to perform specific tasks by making calls to other OpenStack components. Keystone is the identity management component. Keystone manages tenants, users, and roles and provides catalog of services and resources for all the components. Everything in OpenStack must exist in a tenant. A tenant is simply a grouping of objects. Users, instances, and networks are examples of objects. As described in this chapter, cloud computing provides a multi-tenant environment where each tenant has a separate set of resource. The first thing that needs to happen while connecting to an OpenStack environment is authentication. Authentication defines what objects a user has access to within a Tenant as well as the functions the user can perform. For example, when you logged on to VMware vRealize as an end user you saw a Web interfaced designed to allow you to access and work with virtual machines you were authorized or entitled to. When you logged on as the administrator, you were provided with a Web console that allowed you to create blueprints and add them to catalogs that you could made available to users through the entitlement process. This is what Keystone and the Horizon Dashboard can be set up to do for OpenStack tenants. In addition to the Horizon and Keystone components, the Control category also contains configuration files used to define the relationship between components and their host systems.

Storage Components

Storage components are used to store virtual machines, images, databases, and message files. All of the OpenSource components use a database and/or a message bus. The database can be MySQL, MariaDB, or PostgreSQL. The most popular message buses are RabbitMQ, Qpid, and ActiveMQ. For smaller deployments, the database and messaging services usually run on the control node, but they could have their own nodes if required.

Glance is the virtual machine image management component. Once a user is authenticated, there are additional resources that need to be available for the virtual machine to run. The first resource is the disk image from where the virtual machine is launched. Before a virtual machine is useful, the disk image needs to have an operating system installed on it along with any required applications. As you learned in earlier chapters, in virtual computing this is done by using a template from a registry of pre-installed disk images. The Glance component serves as the registry within an OpenStack deployment that is used to manage the disk images. In preparation for an instance to launch, a copy of a selected Glance image is first cached to the hypervisor on the compute node where the virtual machine image is being run. Just as with VMware Linked-Clones, caching the disk image saves time and storage space as subsequent virtual machines can be launched on the same hypervisor using a single cached disk image. These images that have had the operating system installed typically have unique identifiers such as the host key and network device MAC addresses removed. Using cloud-init makes a virtual machine's disk images generic, so it can be launched repeatedly without the copies conflicting with each other. To do this, the host-specific information is provided through a post-boot configuration facility called cloud-init. After a virtual machine has the operating system and any required applications installed the image is run through the cloud-init process much like the SysPrep process is used to prepare Microsoft images. For example, if a virtual machine is going to be used to build a cluster of Web servers, you would install a Web server package on the virtual machine before it was used to launch a Glance instance.

Networking Component

As you learned earlier in this chapter, clouds offer networking services that can be used to connect internal components as well as provide gateways to external networks. Neutron is the network management component used with OpenStack. After a user is authenticated using Keystone and is provided with a virtual machine disk image from Glance, the next resource required is network services. The process of using software to provide networks and network services on demand is called Networking as a Service (NaaS). Neutron is the OpenStack frontend to a set of agents that manages NaaS using the Software Defined Networking (SDN) infrastructure. By using Neutron, OpenStack can provide each tenant with the ability to create isolated virtual networks. Each of these isolated networks can be connected to gateways that to creates routes between the virtual networks. Just as with VMware and Microsoft cloud services, a virtual network can have an external gateway connected to it providing external access to each virtual machine by using a NAT service to associate floating IP addresses. In addition to the gateway, service security can be provided by implementing firewall and Intruder Detection services.

OpenStack Products and Services

Today there are many companies that either provide OpenStack software or use OpenStack to provide public cloud services. A number of companies have sprouted up as OpenStack vendors that focus solely on supporting and selling OpenStack-related products and services. Among these are Rackspace, Mirantis, Red Hat, IBM, and Dell to mention just a few.

As you may remember from Chapter 1, the Rackspace company originally worked with NASA back in 2010 to develop the OpenStack system by contributing the original storage pieces while NASA provided the computing side. Rackspace continued to manage the OpenStack project for the first two years before the OpenStack Foundation was established in 2012. Today Rackspace uses OpenStack as the basis for much of its public cloud and it offers customers a distribution of the software that can be used to create a private and hybrid cloud platform. Today Rackspace is still a leader in OpenStack and is one of the first to roll out new OpenStack features in production as well as providing one of the most robust public cloud deployments. Rackspace public cloud is a proven example that OpenStack can power a massive scale public cloud.

Building on the OpenStack standard has helped Mirantis, a Mountain View, California-based company grow from a small startup to a company that now has more than 400 employees. In addition to its own distribution, Mirantis offers a variety of OpenStack deployment products that they keep current with the latest OpenStack releases and feature. Mirantis is also building partnerships with other OpenStack organization including Red Hat and VMware.

IBM has also been committed to contributing toward the development of OpenStack. IBM is one of the leading contributors to the OpenStack project and is using its experience in working with enterprise customers to improve areas such as quality assurance and aligning the OpenStack to key software standards. IBM bought SoftLayer, an IaaS provider, and is in the process of expanding OpenStack support in SoftLayer's cloud. In addition to supporting OpenStack, IBM has also made commitments to Cloud Foundry, another open source project for SaaS cloud development.

Red Hat made its first billion dollars producing and marketing Linux for the enterprise back in the 1990s. Now, Red Hat wants to do the same with OpenStack and has invested a lot of money in the project. Red Hat has its own distribution of OpenStack called RHEL OpenStack, which is integrated deeply with its primary product, Red Hat Enterprise Linux. Red Hat is contributing resources to OpenStack, and so you can expect them to be a major OpenStack provider for the long haul.

Of course most of us know Dell as a leading provider of both business and home computer equipment. In recent years, Dell has purchased VMware as well as become involved with the OpenStack standard. As a result of their connection with both OpenStack and VMware we can expect a variety of products and services from VMware that integrate well with OpenStack standard. Given all the companies and products that are rapidly becoming part of cloud computing, it is safe to say that the IT forecast will be for mostly cloudy skies with increasing showers of network services.

10

Chapter Summary

- Today cloud computing has matured to where the cloud symbol is used to represent on-demand computing services that can be used to create and extend data centers as well as provide disaster recovery and other IT services.

- In this chapter you were introduced to a variety of computing services delivered through cloud computing including on-demand virtual machines, cloud-based virtual data centers, extending existing local data centers, hosting private clouds, and cloud-based disaster recovery services.

- Today there are an almost dizzying number of cloud-based software products and services on the market from VMware, Microsoft, and the OpenStack standard. VMware provides both vRealize and vCloud Director software packages.

- The vCloud Director package can be used to allow an organization to host private clouds that can be used by both internal and external consumers.

- The vCloud Suite includes a number of vRealize software products that can be used to provide on-demand virtual machines to authorized users as well as monitor and manage utilization of virtual resources such as virtual machines, networks, and shared storage.

- vRealize Automation allows administrators to create blueprints that are stored in a catalog to define virtual machines resources that can be provisioned by users for specific time periods. When the time period expires, or when the user completes their project, the virtual resources are returned back to the system to be assigned to other virtual machines.

- VMware vCloud provides three types of accounts, dedicated clouds, Virtual Private Clouds, and disaster recovery. Dedicated clouds ensure the consumer is assigned to hardware that is not shared with any other customers.

- A Virtual Private Cloud is a multi-tenant system that shares hardware resources with other consumers, while keeping each customer in a separate virtual data center. Cloud users are charged a monthly fee based on resource usage and type of data center.

- Because they share hardware resources with other customer, Virtual Private Clouds are much more affordable than dedicated cloud services. Virtual Private Clouds are typically used to host small data centers or extend an existing vSphere data center into vCloud through the use of a vCloud Connector server installed in the local vSphere infrastructure.

- The disaster recovery service requires a monthly subscription as well as installing the vCloud Replication server on the vSphere data center. Using replication, you can back up changes to your virtual machines on 15-minute intervals and use reverse replication to restore data if needed. In the worst case scenario where the primary data center is off line, the vCloud data center can continue to host services using the replicated virtual machine.

- Microsoft Private Clouds connects on-premises Virtual Machine Manager servers around the world when extra security and flexibility is required.

- A Private Cloud may be required when privacy laws restrict storing some types of data on hosted cloud platforms like Azure.

- Microsoft Azure is a suite of cloud services including virtual machines, databases, remote applications, file storage, and disaster recovery, and many others organized into eleven different categories.

- Azure debuted in 2010 and has data centers in 28 regions around the world.

- Microsoft offers a free one-month trial of Azure with $200 in free Azure credits. A phone number and credit card are required to verify your identity.

- Azure Stacks is a hybrid cloud platform, offering all of the features of Azure but running from servers within an organization's on-premises datacenters.

- Microsoft will recommend three different configurations for each new virtual machine along with their estimated monthly costs. Users can opt to choose from a full list of all possible configurations.

- Windows Virtual Servers created in Azure come already activated. Some additional operating systems are available to MSDN subscribers.

- Virtual machines on Azure are connected to through Remote Desktop Connection. Security messages displayed when connecting can safely be ignored.

- Azure File Storage can create standard SMB file shares, allowing legacy applications designed to work over local networks to gain the benefits of cloud storage.

- OpenStack is the open source standard for cloud computing that is often used with Linux environments running open source hypervisors such as KVM and Oracle VM Server.

- In this chapter you were introduced to a number of OpenStack components that can be divided into Compute, Control, Networking, and Storage categories.

- The Compute components define the hypervisor and how it runs virtual machines.

- The Storage component called Glance defines the virtual machine images and the format used to load and run the VMs.

- The Neutron networking component uses Software Defined Networking standards to define the network connections and IP address usage.

- Many companies offer OpenStack products and services including Rackspace, Redhat, and IBM.

Key Terms

BYOD (Bring Your Own Device)

Catalog tab

cloud computing

dedicated cloud service

Edge gateway

Inbox tab

isolated network

Items tab

machine blueprint

National Institute of Standards and Technology (NIST)

Offline Data Transfer (ODT) service

portlets

private cloud

RaaS (Recovery as a Service)

Requests tab

routed network

vCloud Air

vCloud Connector

vCloud Director

Virtual Private Cloud service

vRealize

vSphere Replication appliance

10

Review Questions

1. Which of the following services best represent cloud computing today? (Choose all that apply.)

   a. On-demand services

   b. Off-premises virtual data centers

   c. Disaster recovery services

   d. Public switched telephone network

   e. Web sites on the public Internet

2. According to the NIST definition, which of the following are characteristics of cloud computing? (Choose all that apply.)

   a. On-demand Self-Service

   b. Multi-tenancy

   c. Elasticity

   d. Pay-as-you-go model

3. Which cloud computing model does the VMware vCloud provide? (Choose all that apply.)

   a. IaaS

   b. PaaS

   c. RaaS

   d. SaaS

4. Which of the following cloud platforms is not a proprietary service?

   a. OpenFlow

   b. vCloud

   c. OpenStack

   d. OpenCloud

5. Which of following best describes the vCloud Air service? (Choose all that apply.)

   a. A service that allows an organization to implement their own private cloud environments that can be used by internal or external consumers to create virtual data centers

   b. A public IaaS cloud environment that consumers can use to create and manage their own virtual data centers that can be used to host virtual machines

   c. A suite of software that allows an organization to host on-demand services within their existing vSphere data center

   d. A public RaaS service that can be used to replicate data and virtual machines for use in disaster recovery

6. Which of the following cloud services can be used to host cloud environments that consumers could use to create virtual data centers that contain their own virtual machines and internal resources?

   a. vCloud suite

   b. vCloud Director

   c. vCloud Air

   d. OpenStack

7. Which of the following VMware products would you use to provide on-demand services to your Web development staff from your vSphere data center?

   a. vRealize Automation

   b. vRealize Operation

   c. vCloud Director

   d. vCloud Air

8. Which of the following VMware products do you need to install in your vSphere data center to extend your on-premises data center into the cloud? (Choose all that apply.)

   a. vCloud Connector

   b. vCloud Director

   c. vSphere vReplication server

   d. vRealize Automation

9. Which of the following is a complete specification for a virtual machine that is used to determine a machine's attributes and how it is provisioned by an end user?

   a. Template

   b. Portlet

   c. Blueprint

   d. Glance image

10. Which of the following vCloud Air services would provide the best security for a banking company to use for its virtual data center?

   a. Dedicated cloud service

   b. Isolated Cloud service

   c. Virtual Private Cloud Service

   d. Single Tenant Cloud Service

11. Which of the following would be a typical monthly charge for a Virtual Private Cloud that uses 10 GBs of vRAM with a 10 GHz CPU?

10

   a. $360.00

   b. $1240.00

   c. $150.00

   d. $3600.00

12. Which of the following components needs to be installed on your vSphere data center to implement vCloud disaster recovery services (RaaS)? (Choose all that apply.)

   a. vCloud Connector

   b. vCloud Director

   c. vReplicator

   d. vRealize

13. The vCloud Connector enables the use of an external storage device for the offline transfer of large amounts of data securely from vSphere datacenters to vCloud Air using which of the following?

   a. FTP

   b. SSH

   c. ODT

   d. VPN

14. Which of the following is the shortest interval between replication periods?

    a. 5 minutes

    b. 15 minutes

    c. 30 minutes

    d. 1 hour

15. Which of the following network systems can be used by vConnector to connect the local vSphere data center to the vCloud virtual data center? (Choose all that apply.)

    a. Using an IPSec VLAN

    b. Using an IPSec VPN

    c. Across the public Internet using the supplied URL

    d. Using an SSL VPN

16. Which of the following are components included with a vCloud basic Virtual Private Cloud pack? (Choose all that apply.)

    a. Gateway

    b. vConnector

    c. Isolated Network

    d. One Public External IP address

17. Which of the following are reasons to use a private cloud? (Choose all that apply.)

    a. They are less expensive.

    b. There may be legal requirements on how data is stored.

    c. They are easier to maintain.

    d. They are more flexible.

18. Which of the following is not an option for an Azure virtual machine? (Choose all that apply.)

    a. Amount of memory

    b. Number of cores

    c. Maximum IOPS

    d. Size of Cache

19. Which application is used to control an Azure virtual machine desktop?

    a. Remote Desktop Viewer

    b. Remote Desktop Connection

    c. Virtual Desktop Connection

    d. Virtual Connect Client

20. Which of the following OpenStack components contains a registry of virtual machine image files?

    a. Keystone

    b. Glance

    c. Horizon

    d. Neutron

Case Projects

CASE PROJECTS

Case Project 10-1: Viewing VMware Cloud Overview

VMware has educational courses you can access using your MyVMware account. In this case project you are to enroll in the VMware vCloud Director course and view the vCloud Director Overview and write a brief report on the benefits of cloud computing.

1. Start a Web browser and log on to your MyVMware account.

2. Point to Support near the top right corner of the page, then click the **Training** link and then click the **Training by Product** link.

3. Click **Virtualization & Cloud Management Platform**, scroll down and click the **vCloud Director Learning Path**, and then click the **vCloud Director Fundamentals [V5.1/V5.5]** course

4. Click the **Register Now** button and enter the required registration information. (If necessary, you can create an educational account at this time.)

5. Click **Continue** and then click the **Start Course** button.

6. Perform **Module 1 – VMware vCloud Director Overview**.

7. Write a report that includes at least two screen shots showing how cloud computing benefits an organization.

8. Perform **Module 2 – VMware vCloud Director Architecture and Components** and prepare a report or PowerPoint presentation as directed by your instructor.

Case Project 10-2: Using vRealize to Monitor and Reclaim Resources

In this case project you are to continue the Lab project you started in Activity 10-2 to continue to use vRealize to learn how you can use vRealize Operations to view performance information and then use that information to make resources from an unused virtual machine available for other projects.

1. If necessary, log on to your MyVMware account and launch the HOL-1721-USE-1 - vRealize Automation 7: Basics lab as described in Activity 10-2.

2. Use the Table of Contents menu to perform the lessons in Module 4 - Policy Based Lifecycle Management and Governance.

10

3. Write a brief report that you can present to UAS management explaining how vRealize Operations can help them manage their virtual machines and resources.

Case Project 10-3: Extending the vSphere Data Center

Your manager would like to have you set up a virtual data center that can be used to extend the UAS vSphere environment. In this activity you will access your MyVMware account and then use the VMware lab to learn how to create and deploy virtual machines in a vCloud VDC. In this lab you will be working with a pre-defined vSphere data center that contains a cluster with two hosts, much like the vSphere data center you configured in Chapter 8. By performing the two modules of the lab you will be using a vSphere environment that consists of a single cluster of three hosts. This local vSphere infrastructure is managed by a vCenter Server: vcsa-01a.corp.local. The cloud environment is a dedicated instance in vCloud Air which can be managed via its Web portal or via the tools you will be learning about in this lab. Write a brief report that explains how vCloud Networking Services (ANS) along with vCloud Hybrid Manager could be used to extend the UAS on-premises data center.

1. If necessary, start your Windows 10 desktop computer and open a browser window to VMware.com.

2. Log on to your MyVMware account. After logging on, scroll down and click the **VMware Hands-on Labs** link located under the Try and Purchase heading.

3. In the left column click the **Hybrid Cloud** link located under the All Labs heading.

4. Click the **Enroll** button in the HOL-1782-HBD-1 - VMware vCloud Air - Data Center Extension lab and enter your username and password. (If your password is not recognized use the Reset Password link to reset your password and try again.)

Case Project 10-4: Using vCloud Disaster Recovery Services

In this case project you are to continue the Lab project you started in Activity 10-3 to report on how vRealize Orchestrator can be used to improve disaster recovery for an organization. Log on to VMware Labs as described in the activity and then perform the vRealize Orchestrator module and write a brief report describing what benefits vRealize Orchestrator has that would benefit an organization's disaster recovery procedure.

Case Project 10-5: Comparing vCloud and Azure

In this case project you are to write a brief report that summarizes the similarities and differences between Microsoft Azure and VMware vCloud services. Which one would you recommend for a startup company to use and why? Your instructor may supply details on the company for you to use in your report.

The Technology Behind Virtualization

Although you don't need to understand the technology behind virtualization to set up and use virtual machines, knowing what's going on under the hood can help you plan and implement virtualization systems and give you a better understanding of what's in store for the future. In this appendix, you learn more about the computer theory behind virtualization and how it's being applied in current virtualization products.

Controlling Multiple Guest Operating Systems

A computer OS is designed to manage hardware and provide an environment for software applications. Because virtualization allows a computer to run more than one OS at a time, one of the first issues to address is sharing a single computer's hardware resources without conflicts.

To work correctly, virtualization software must be able to handle system calls made by guest OSs running on virtual machines. Typically, virtual machines aren't "aware" they're running on top of another OS, so they operate as though they have sole access to the CPU and all other hardware in the host. However, if a virtual machine were actually allowed to access memory and the CPU directly, it would cause conflicts with the host OS, resulting in a crash. There are several ways to handle system calls with virtual machines, based on the system architecture.

Classic Virtualization

In 1974, Gerald Popek and Robert Goldberg devised guidelines that "classic" virtualization software should follow ("Formal Requirements for Virtualizable Third Generation Architectures," *Communications of the ACM* 17:7, July 1974; PDF available at *www.princeton.edu /~rblee/ELE572Papers/Fall04Readings/secureOS/popek_virtualizable.pdf*). Popular hardware of the 1970s, such as the IBM System/370 mainframe, used these guidelines to create a virtualization technology known as the trap-and-emulate method. When a virtual machine attempts to make a system call to the kernel, a hardware fault or error is generated in the CPU. This fault can be intercepted (trapped), which allows virtualization software to adjust (emulate) the call to work safely so that both the guest and host OS can share the system. This method is hardware based and efficient, so the trap-and-emulate method was the most practical way to use virtualization.

x86 Virtualization

The x86 architecture was the basis for the original IBM PC introduced back in 1981 running MS-DOS and is still used on today's Intel and AMD systems running Windows. Virtualization on an x86 system is more complex because some x86 instructions don't generate faults as they should. For this reason, the classic trap-and-emulate virtualization method can't be used. Without traps being generated, virtual machines could issue commands that virtualization software doesn't detect, which can cause problems for both the guest and host OS. There are ways around this problem, such as using binary translation (discussed in the next section). These workarounds are less efficient than the classic method, however, and require more work from the host system.

Modern processors from Intel and AMD have support for hardware virtualization, which essentially gives trap-and-emulate capabilities of classic virtualization to the x86 platform.

Hypervisor Methods of Virtualization

The hypervisor, or virtual machine monitor (VMM), is the software that runs virtual machines. There are two types of hypervisors: type-1 and type-2.

A type-1 hypervisor, also known as bare metal or native, runs directly on the host and doesn't require an operating system. Examples include Microsoft Hyper-V, VMware ESX, and Citrix XenServer.

Type-2 hypervisors are user applications that run on top of another operating system, such as Windows or Linux. Examples include VMware Workstation and Oracle VirtualBox. By this definition it may appear that Microsoft's Hyper-V on Windows is actually a type-2 hypervisor. However, when Hyper-V is installed the host OS transparently becomes a virtual machine.

CPU Virtualization

Each virtual machine will need its own CPU, so the CPU itself needs to be virtualized. The hypervisor is responsible for passing commands from the guest to the CPU and returning the results. There are several different methods to accomplish this, explained in the following sections, but first it's important to understand how an OS uses hierarchical protection domains, or protection rings, to control access.

Protection rings, shown in Figure A-1, are built into the CPU. Every program running on a CPU is assigned to one of these rings, which determines the hardware privileges it has. For example, any application running in ring 0 has full access to the CPU and all hardware in the computer. The kernel, which is the core of an OS, and any device drivers that need to interact directly with computer hardware must run in ring 0.

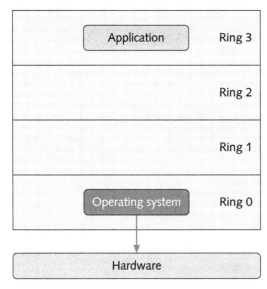

Figure A-1 Protection rings

Privileges are reduced as you move out from ring 0. Ring 3 is where all user applications run, such as word processing software and Web browsers. These applications have no privileges. If they need to access hardware or perform an action that could cause security or stability issues, they must make a "system call" to the kernel in ring 0, which decides whether it's safe to proceed.

Full Virtualization

In full virtualization, the guest OS runs in ring 1 and the hypervisor in ring 0, as shown in Figure A-2. Binary translation is used to allow otherwise non-virtualizable x86 system calls to be trapped.

A binary translator receives low-level assembly-language instructions (the most basic way to communicate with the CPU) sent from the virtual machine's CPU. In many cases, code from the virtual machine can be passed directly to the host CPU for execution without requiring any translation.

When you need to make a system call or perform another potentially unsafe action, some modifications must be made first, and the binary translator inserts additional instructions to perform this task. These instructions can have a cascading effect on other parts of the program. For example, if there's an instruction to shift control to another part of the application, that part of the application might not be in the same location in memory when the extra instructions are inserted, so these instructions need to be adjusted, too. This translation process increases overhead and slows down a virtual machine.

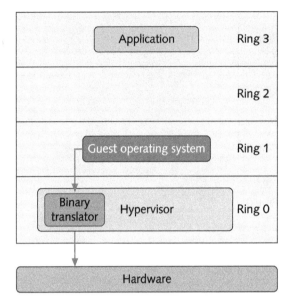

Figure A-2 Full virtualization

However, there is a solution. Both Intel and AMD have incorporated solutions to handle CPU virtualization more efficiently into their x86 processors. AMD's hardware virtualization is called AMD Virtualization (AMD-V). Intel's version is called Intel Virtualization Technology (Intel VT).

One major benefit of hardware-assisted virtualization is that it changes how the standard protection ring model works, as shown in Figure A-3. The guest OS runs in ring 0, as a normal OS does. The hypervisor runs in a new ring, -1, which has an even higher privilege level. Because of this, system calls can now be run directly on the hardware by the hypervisor. This eliminates the need for binary translation and the extra overhead it entails, bringing performance much closer to paravirtualization.

Paravirtualization

In paravirtualization, the guest OS is modified to work with the hypervisor. Instead of making standard system calls, the guest OS makes hypercalls directly to the host hardware, as shown in Figure A-4, which reduces overhead and increases virtual machine performance.

Modifying an OS to support paravirtualization is easy on an open-source OS, such as Linux, but isn't possible on a closed-source OS, such as Windows. Starting with Windows Vista, however, Microsoft has been making its OSs more virtual machine aware. Even if the OS doesn't support directly communicating with virtual machines, you can install VMware Tools or Windows Integration Services to get a boost in performance from special drivers optimized for virtualization.

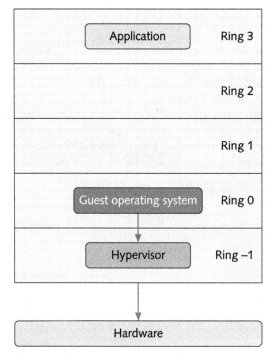

Figure A-3 Hardware virtualization

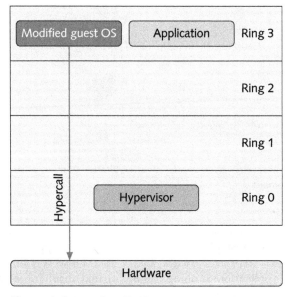

Figure A-4 Paravirtualization

Memory Management

Most modern operating systems today make use of virtual memory. x86 CPUs use internal memory management units (MMUs) to build page tables that translate virtual memory addresses to locations in physical memory. A built-in cache called the translation lookaside buffer (TLB) is used to increase speed by storing frequently accessed memory locations. Just as the hypervisor controls how a virtual machine accesses the host's CPU to prevent conflicts, the guest OS can't be allowed direct access to the host system's memory, or conflicts would occur. A virtual MMU running in the hypervisor watches for the guest OS to make requests to memory and then intercepts them, modifying them to safe locations in the host's memory as shown in Figure A-5.

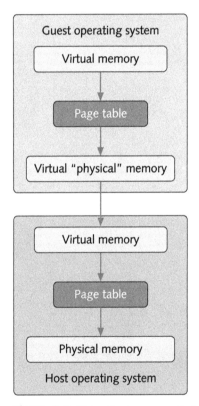

Figure A-5 Virtualized memory management

To improve performance, the next innovation was shadow page tables, which map addresses between guest OS virtual memory and host physical memory directly (skipping guest OS "physical memory" to host "page file" step) as shown in Figure A-6. However, this process still has overhead, especially if an application running on the virtual machine is memory intensive, adding hundreds or thousands of extra instructions.

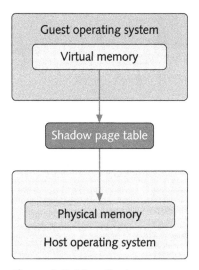

Figure A-6 Virtualized memory management using shadow page tables

But again, AMD and Intel have added features to their processors to help solve this in the form of nested paging tables (NPT) and extended page tables (EPT), respectively. This essentially works like an oversized TLB that handles the mappings between guest OS and physical memory directly within the CPU rather than software and can show an increase in performance by up to 600% in memory intensive applications.

Device Virtualization

As previously discussed, a CPU uses MMUs to manage system memory. Another type of MMU, an input/output MMU, allows devices such as video cards, Ethernet adapters, and hard drive controllers direct access to memory to increase performance. With the introduction of AMD-Vi and Intel Virtualization Technology for Directed I/O (VT-d) in processors, when installed in a motherboard with I/O virtualization support, virtual machines can take advantage of these features to deliver nearly native storage and network performance.

Using VMware Workstation Player and Hyper-V Server 2016 Virtualization Products

Throughout this book you have worked with a number of virtualization products including VMware Workstation, Oracle's Virtual Box, VMware Workstation Player, vSphere Hypervisor (ESXi), and the Hyper-V that ships with Windows Server. In this appendix you will learn more about the details and options available when working with the free versions of VMware Workstation 12 Player and Hyper-V Server products.

Working with VMware Workstation Player

VMware Workstation Player (included with VMware Workstation) runs existing virtual machines (sometimes referred to as appliances or vApps) and has free and licensed versions for both Windows and Linux systems. As described in Chapter 1, a virtual appliance or vApp is a virtual machine configured to run a specific application or service. VMware Workstation Player makes it easy to run virtual machines created in VMware Workstation and Microsoft virtualization products. In addition to running vApps, VMware Workstation Player is also a good hypervisor for home users and students. In this section, you learn how to install and configure VMware Workstation 12 Player in order to work with existing virtual machines as well as create new virtual machines.

Installing VMware Workstation Player

In addition to being included with VMware Workstation (both licensed and evaluation versions), VMware Workstation 12 Player is a standalone product that can be downloaded and installed on most Windows and Linux systems. One advantage of using VMware Workstation Player instead of other free or open source virtualization products is its compatibility with other VMware products including VMware Workstation and vSphere. VMware Workstation 12 Player has commercial and free versions. The free version is available for non-commercial, personal, and home use and is recommended for students and non-profit organizations. Commercial organizations require a paid license, but the commercial version contains some additional features that are not included in the free version such as running encrypted virtual machines created by VMware Workstation and providing 30 days of installation support. Although both the commercial and free versions of VMware Workstation Player support USB devices, 64-bit hosts and guest OSs, and VMware Tools, Workstation

Player is limited to running one guest VM in each Player instance, and does not support snapshots or cloning.

You can run multiple virtual machines by starting additional instances of VMware Workstation Player as you did in the chapter activities.

The requirements for running VMware Workstation Player on a Windows workstation are a 64-bit x86 CPU with 1.3 GHz or faster core speed, a minimum of 2 GB RAM (4 GB RAM recommended), and an IDE, SATA, or SCSI storage drive with at least 1 GB free space. As with other hypervisors, you must have enough memory and disk space to run the host OS, plus the memory required for the guest OS and any applications to be run on the host and virtual machine. Refer to the documentation for your guest OS and applications to determine their memory requirements.

When you install VMware Workstation (either the licensed or evaluation version), the free VMware Workstation Player is also installed. Installing the Player along with VMware Workstation is perhaps the best way to get the product as this installation method also includes the Network Editor, which is not available if you install VMware Workstation 12 Player as a standalone product.

If you have not installed VMware Workstation on your computer, you can download VMware Workstation Player separately by following these general guidelines:

1. Start your Web browser, go to www.vmware.com, and log on to your MyVWmare account.

2. Point to Products and then click the Trial and Free Products link.

3. Scroll down and click the VMware Workstation Player (Free) link located in the Download Free Products section.

4. Click the Download Now link under the latest version of the VMware Workstation Player for Windows 64-bit heading.

5. Click Save As, navigate to your download folder, and then click Save to start the download.

To install a standalone version of VMware Workstation Player, follow these general steps:

1. In Windows Explorer, navigate to your download folder, and then double-click the VMware-player-*version*.exe file (replacing *version* with the version and build number you downloaded). If necessary, click Run in the Security Warning dialog box and then if requested click Yes in the User Account Control dialog box. In the VMware Workstation Player Installation Welcome window, click Next to start the installation wizard. Click the check box to accept the license agreement terms, then click Next.

2. Click Next three times to accept the default settings for the destination folder, user experience settings, and shortcuts.

3. Click Install to copy files and start the installation.

4. When the installation is completed, click Finish, and then click Yes to restart your computer.

Working with VMware Workstation Player Configuration

To start VMware Workstation Player, double-click the desktop icon, click VMware Workstation Player on the Quick Launch toolbar, or use the Start menu. When you first start VMware Workstation Player, a dialog box will be displayed asking you to enter your email address for the free version or enter a valid commercial license to gain the additional support and features. After entering your email address click **Continue** and then click **Finish** to display the VMware Workstation Player window (see Figure B-1).

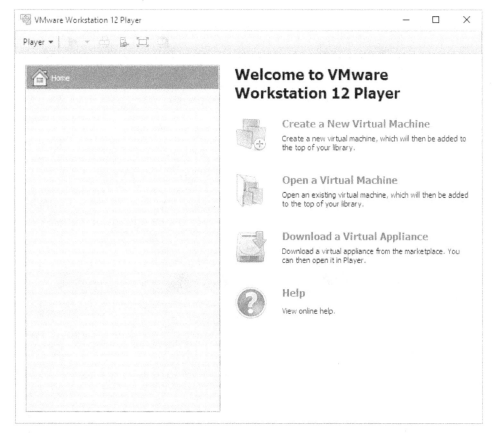

Figure B-1   VMware Workstation 12 Player Home window

Source: VMware

As shown in Figure B-1, the VMware Workstation 12 Player console contains a menu line, a Home frame, and a Welcome frame containing shortcut links. In addition to the Home link, the left pane will eventually contain a list of virtual machines you have recently created or opened. The Welcome frame contains shortcuts to create a new virtual machine, open an existing virtual machine, upgrade to VMware Workstation Pro, or get help. The upper menu line contains five clickable options as described from left to right in Table B-1.

Table B-1   VMware Workstation Player 12 menu line icons

Menu Line Item	Description
Player menu	The Player menu contains a list of options that can be used to work with virtual machines and change configuration preferences (see Table B-2).
Power button menu	This button contains options to power on, resume, suspend, and power off the current virtual machine (see Table B-3).
Send Ctrl+Alt+Del to virtual machine button	Clicking this button will send the Ctrl+Alt+Del sequence to the currently powered on virtual machine. This option is necessary since pressing the actual Ctrl+Alt+Del key sequence would be intercepted by the workstation.
Connect to VMware Horizon FLEX server button	This button is used to connect VMware Workstation Player 12 to a Horizon Virtual Desktop
Enter Full Screen Mode button	This button will expand the VMware Workstation 12 player desktop to use the full screen. You can press the Esc key to return to a window.
Enter Unity Mode button	Just as in VMware Workstation, Unity mode can be used to share applications with the host (see Chapter 3 for details).

When you install VMware Workstation Player on Windows operating systems, the installation wizard creates a subfolder named "Virtual Machines" in your Documents folder. By default, VMware Workstation 12 Player will use this folder to store virtual machine files. You can copy existing virtual machine files to this Documents\Virtual Machines path, or create another location on the host computer. To change VMware Workstation Player settings, you can use the Player menu. The Player menu contains the options described in Table B-2.

Table B-2   VMware Workstation Player 12 Player menu options

Menu Line Item	Description
File	This contains options to create a new virtual machine, open an existing virtual machine, download a virtual appliance, or change Preference options.
Power	This contains power options to Power On, Shut Down Guest, Suspend Guest, or Restart Guest for the selected virtual machine.
Removable Devices	Use this option to connect host removable devices such as USB devices.
Send Ctrl+Alt+Del	Use this option or the corresponding menu button to Send the Ctrl+Alt+Del key sequence to the currently running guest OS.
Manage	Use this option to display the Manage menu containing options to install VMware tools, display the message log, or change virtual machine settings such as memory size.
Full Screen	Use this option to use the workstation's full screen. You can use the Ctrl+Alt keys to return to a window.
Unity	This option, which requires VMware Tools on the guest OS, can be used to run virtual machine applications on the host computer as described in Chapter 3.
Help	Use this option to search for help on topics based on key words.

Preferences Options To change a virtual machine's exit behavior and configure settings for online updates, click the Preferences option from the File menu to open the Preferences window shown in Figure B-2.

As you can see, VMware Workstation Player has fewer settings compared with VMware

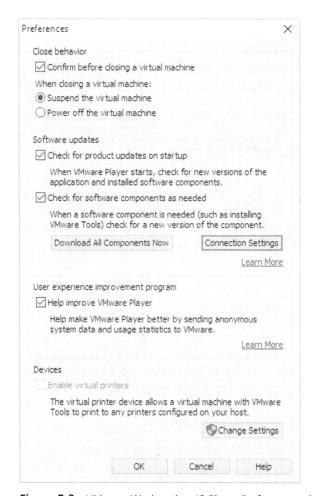

Figure B-2 VMware Workstation 12 Player Preferences window

Source: VMware

Workstation covered in Chapter 3 of this book. By default, VMware Workstation Player suspends the virtual machine when you exit the program. If you change this option to "Power off the virtual machine," you can also select the "Confirm before closing a virtual machine" option to prevent shutting down the virtual machine accidentally and possibly losing data.

VMware Workstation Player checks the VMware Web site for updates automatically each time it's started. If you have a slow Internet connection or want to control when updates are downloaded, you can disable the "Check for product updates on startup" option.

Click the Connection Settings button in the Preferences window to display the Connection Settings window The Connection Settings window contains options to change the path used to search for updates as well as input user name and password values to use when connecting to update servers. By default, use of virtual printers is disabled, but you can use the Change Settings button located under the Devices section of the Preferences window to allow guest virtual machines to access the host printers.

Working with Virtual Machines

You can place virtual machines into VMware Workstation Player's Home list by either creating new virtual machines or opening existing virtual machines.

Earlier versions of VMware Workstation Player did not allow creating new virtual machines, but this feature has been included in VMware Workstation 12 Player and later editions.

Before starting VMware Workstation Player, make the folders containing virtual machine files available to the host computer by copying them to the host computer's hard drive or accessing them from a shared network drive or removable media, such as a USB drive. (You might want to run virtual machines from a USB drive for portability reasons.)

Because VMware Workstation Player must be able to write new data to virtual machine files, you can't run virtual machines from read-only devices, such as DVDs.

The File option of the Player menu has New Virtual Machine and Open options as well as an option to download virtual appliances. To start an existing virtual machine, click Open, navigate to the virtual machine's folder, and then double-click the virtual machine configuration (.vmx for VMware) file. When the virtual machine starts, its name will be included in the Home frame of the VMware Workstation Player window.

Note that a limitation of Player is that you cannot open multiple virtual machines, as you can in VMware Workstation; you must start an additional instance of VMware Workstation Player for each virtual machine you want to run. However, virtual machines can still communicate with each other through their virtual network adapters.

Like VMware Workstation, you use Ctrl+Alt to switch keyboard and mouse control between the virtual machine and the host and Ctrl+Alt+Insert to represent Ctrl+Alt+Delete on the virtual machine. To allow you to easily transfer control between the virtual machine and the desktop OS as well as use other features such as Unity, you should install VMware Tools on all guest operating systems that support it. Follow the steps below to install VMware Tools on a guest OS.

1. Start the virtual machine.

2. Click the Player menu and then click the Manage option.

3. Click the Install VMware Tools option from the Manage menu.

4. Proceed with the installation wizard.

5. If the installation does not run, you can run the Setup program from the virtual CD/DVD drive.

To download virtual appliances, you can click the Download Virtual Appliance option from the File menu to go to the VMware Virtual Appliance Marketplace (*http://vmware.com/appliances*). In the marketplace you can find free or commercial virtual appliances in a variety of categories including Administration, Web Server, Database, Networking, Operating Systems, and Security. For example, in the Operating Systems category, you can download a virtual appliance with Ubuntu Linux installed.

Virtual appliances have the benefit of being fully configured for a specific application.

The home section of the VMware Workstation Player main window contains shortcuts for running any virtual machines you have opened recently. You can remove a virtual machine from the list by right-clicking it and clicking the Delete from Disk option. Other options available from right-clicking a virtual machine include Power On, Settings, and Remove from the library. The remove from library option will remove the virtual machine from the Home pane but not delete any of the files. To change the settings of a virtual machine, you can right-click the virtual machine from the library pane and click Settings. To change the settings of a currently selected or running virtual machine, click the Manage option from the Player menu and then click the Virtual Machine Settings option. In either case the same Settings window as used by VMware Workstation (see Figure 3-16) will be displayed.

To share folders with the host computer or change other virtual machine configuration options, you can click the Options tab to display the window shown previously in Figure 3-16. Just as with VMware Workstation, you can specify folders on the host computer that are available to the guest OS. To use shared folders in VMware Workstation Player, you must install VMware Tools on the guest OS, and then specify the host computer folders to be shared by the guest OS. By default, when a virtual machine starts in VMware Workstation Player, shared folders are disabled. To enable this feature, you must have a virtual machine running in VMware Workstation Player. You can then open the Settings window, click the Options tab, and click Shared Folders from the menu to open the Folder sharing window. Shared folders can be enabled permanently or for just the current session. With Windows virtual machines, you can also map a shared folder as a network drive. The paths shown in the Folders section are the ones originally mapped by VMware Workstation. Although VMware Workstation Player does not include an option to add mappings, you can change the path to a shared folder by following these steps:

1. Enable shared folders by clicking the "Always enabled" option button.

2. Click the check box next to a path in the Folders section, and then click the Properties button to open the Shared Folder Properties dialog box.

3. Change the folder name in the Name text box, if you want, and then click the Browse button next to the Host path text box.

4. Navigate to and click the folder you want to share, and then click OK.

5. Click OK again to save the change, and then click OK in the Shared Folders dialog box.

Configuring Device Menu Options The Removable Devices menu, which is available only after a virtual machine is opened, contains options for disconnecting or connecting the virtual machine to physical devices on the host computer, such as the CD/DVD drive or network adapter. For example, you can connect the virtual machine's CD/DVD drive to a physical CD/DVD drive on the host or to an ISO image file. To connect it to an ISO image file, follow these steps:

1. Click the Player menu and then click the Removable Devices menu to display the options shown in Figure B-3.

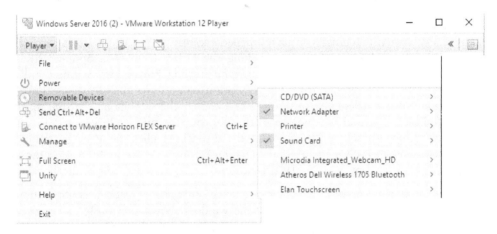

Figure B-3 VMware Workstation 12 Player Removable Devices menu options

Source: VMware

2. Click the CD/DVD option, and then click the "Settings" option to display the Connection window providing options to select either the physical CD/DVD drive or an ISO image file.

3. Click the Use ISO image file option, then click the Browse button and navigate to the folder containing the ISO image file.

4. Double-click the file, or click the file and then click Open.

By default, a virtual machine's network adapter is connected to the VMware network switch established when the virtual machine is created (refer to Chapter 3). You can use the Network Adapter menu option to disconnect or connect the virtual network adapter to any VMware switch, including bridged, NAT, or host-only. In addition, depending on the host computer's hardware, the Removable Devices menu might contain other options, such as USB drives.

Editing Network Settings There are times when you may wish to configure the network options to suit the needs of your network environment. For example, you may wish to have your NAT network addresses be given a specific network address rather than the random address assigned by VMware Workstation Player. To do this you can launch the Virtual Network Editor as shown in Figure B-4.

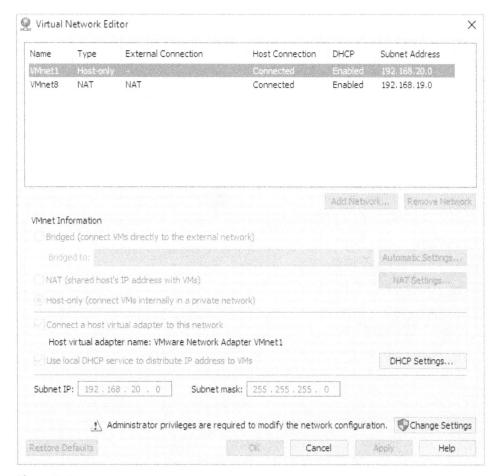

Figure B-4   VMware Virtual Network Editor main window

Source: VMware

 The Network Editor is no longer included in the free VMware Workstation Player package, but is available in the VMware menu if you have installed the VMware Workstation package. In earlier versions **NOTE** of the VMware Network Editor you needed to be logged on to your Windows workstation using the Administrator user name in order to change settings. When using the Network Editor included with VMware Workstation 12.5, you simply need to be logged on with an account that has administrator privileges.

You can follow the procedure described below to use the VMware Network Editor that was installed with your VMware Workstation evaluation package.

1. Log on to your Workstation using your Administrator username and password.

2. Click the Start button, scroll down and expand the VMware heading, click Network Editor, then click the VMnet8 NAT network.

3. Click the NAT Settings button to display the window shown in Figure B-5.

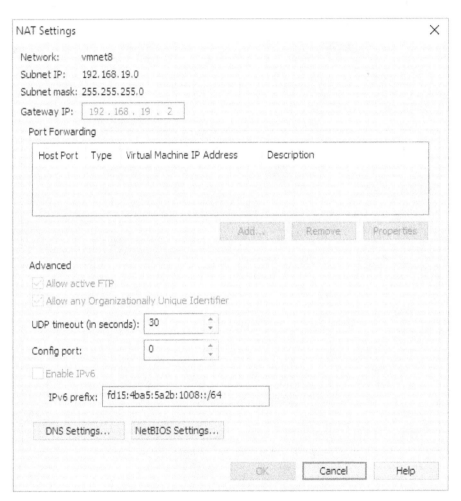

Figure B-5   VMware Virtual Network Editor NAT Settings window

Source: VMware

4. Enter a new network address range and then click OK to save your changes. When you start a virtual machine that uses the NAT address and DHCP, it will be given an address in the new network range you specified.

Creating New Virtual Machines

Recent versions of VMware Workstation Player have the ability to create new virtual machines. In order to perform the activities in Chapters 7, 8, and 9 you will need to use VMware Workstation Player to create new virtual machines for vSphere Hypervisor (ESXi) and Windows Server 2016 guest operating systems. To create a new vSphere Hypervisor (ESXi) or Windows Server 2016 virtual machine, you should follow the steps shown below:

1. Start VMware Workstation 12 Player.

2. Click the Create a New Virtual Machine link from the Welcome window to display the New Virtual Machine Wizard window.

3. If you are installing from an ISO file, click the Installer disk image file (iso) option, then use the Browse button to navigate to the folder and double-click the installation image file. Click Next.

4. If VMware Workstation Player detects the OS from the installation media, it will proceed to the Easy Install Information window. If you are installing a licensed operating system such as Windows Server 2016, you will be given a dialog box where you can enter the product key along with your personalized Windows name and optional password. If you do not enter a product key you will receive a warning message informing you to manually activate Windows later. If VMware Workstation Player does not detect the OS or if you select the I will install the operating system later option, you will need to select an operating system version prior to seeing the Name the Virtual Machine window.

5. Next, you will be presented with a Name the Virtual Machine window. If necessary, change the virtual machine name and location shown in the Name the Virtual Machine window and click **Next** to display the Specify Disk Capacity window.

6. When doing the activities in this chapter you will need sufficient space on your Windows and ESXi virtual machine to store additional virtual machine files. For this reason, you should allocate at least 120 GB to the virtual disk file. More is better since the virtual disk file will only use the space required. You should also select the Store virtual disk as a single file option to make it easier to move the virtual machine.

7. After modifying the settings in the Specify Disk Capacity window, click Next to display the Ready to Create Virtual Machine window. You can use the Customize Hardware... button to change any of the default parameters shown in the summary window.

8. Click Finish to create the virtual machine. If you are using the easy installation process, the guest OS installation will start automatically.

9. You can now proceed with the installation of the guest OS as instructed by the chapter activity.

10. After installing the Windows Server or guest OS, start the virtual machine and follow the procedure to install VMware Tools as described earlier in this appendix.

Working with Hyper-V Server

Microsoft offers Hyper-V Server at no cost, but you are required to sign into your Microsoft account to download the image. You can burn this image to a DVD, or optionally use the

Windows USB/DVD Download tool or Rufus (http://rufus.akeo.ie) to create a bootable USB flash drive.

Activity B-1: Downloading Hyper-V Server

Time Required: 15 minutes

Objective: Download Hyper-V Server 2016.

Requirements: Access to the Internet; 3 GB hard disk space

Description: In this activity, you download the Microsoft Hyper-V Server 2016 disc image from the Microsoft Web site and burn the image to removable media.

1. If necessary, log on to the host computer with your assigned administrative username and password.

2. Start your Web browser and navigate to **www.microsoft.com**.

3. In the Search text box, type **technet evaluation center** and press **Enter**. Click the first result.

4. Click **Evaluate Now** in the navigation bar and click **Microsoft Hyper-V Server 2016** in the menu. Click the **Download** link button if necessary, then click the **Sign in** button.

5. On the Sign in page, enter your Microsoft account email address and password and click **Sign in,** or click **Create one** if you need to create a new account.

6. Click the **Register to continue** button, complete the form, and then click **Continue**. Click the **Download** button next to the ISO file and choose the Desktop as the destination in the Save As dialog box.

7. When the download is finished, right-click the ISO file, then choose **Burn disc image** from the popup menu. In the Windows Disc Image Burner window, select the drive with your blank media and click **Burn**.

Installing Hyper-V Server

Installing Hyper-V Server is similar to installing full editions of Windows Server 2016. You don't need to select an edition or supply a product key, however, and Windows creates an administrator account with a blank password that you use to log on before creating your own password.

Activity B-2: Installing Hyper-V Server

Time Required: 20 minutes

Objective: Install Hyper-V Server 2016.

Requirements: Completion of Activity B-1

Description: In this activity you will install Hyper-V Server 2016 from the installation media downloaded and created in the previous activity.

1. Power on your PC and insert the Hyper-V Server installation media. You may need to enter the boot menu to choose the correct device or change the boot order in the BIOS.

2. Press a key within a few seconds when the "Press any key to boot from CD or DVD" message appears. If you see the Virtual Machine Boot Summary, press a key to reboot and try again.

3. Select settings for language, time and currency format, and keyboard or input method, and then click **Next**.

4. Click **Install now** in the next window.

5. In the License terms window, click the **I accept the license terms** check box, and then click **Next**.

6. In the Which type of installation do you want? window, click **Custom: Install the newest version of Hyper-V Server only (advanced)**.

7. In the Where do you want to install Hyper-V Server? window, verify that Drive 0 Unallocated Space is selected, then click **Next** to continue.

8. The Windows installation begins. Typically, the process takes around 15 minutes, and your virtual machine restarts at least once.

9. In the Command prompt window, "The user's password must be changed before signing in," highlight **Ok** and press **Enter**.

10. In the Command prompt window, "Enter new credentials for Administrator," you're prompted to create a password for the administrator account. (Make sure it's at least six characters, contains uppercase and lowercase letters, and includes a number or nonalphanumeric character.) Press **Tab** to move to Confirm password and reenter it, and then press **Enter**. Record your password below:

_____

11. In the Command prompt window, "Your password has been changed," press **Enter** to confirm the Ok selection.

12. Leave the command prompt window open for the following sections.

Configuring Hyper-V Server

As Hyper-V Server doesn't have a GUI, you must perform all configurations through the Command prompt window. Doing so is easier than in Server Core because Hyper-V Server has a special configuration script that runs when you log on. This script creates a simple text-based menu interface, as shown in Figure B-6.

If you accidentally close the Command prompt window, you can reopen it by pressing Ctrl+Alt+Delete and selecting the Task Manager option. Click the File menu, Create new task, and type "cmd" in the dialog box, and then click OK. To re-open the menu interface, type "sconfig".

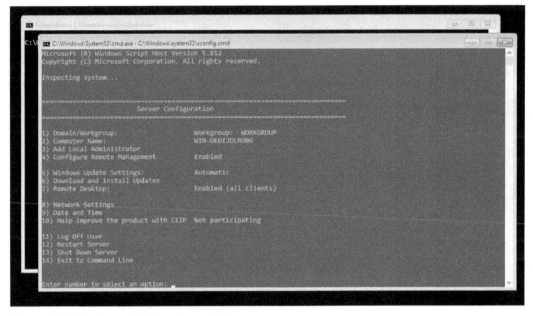

Figure B-6 The Server Configuration window

Installing Device Drivers Because Hyper-V Server uses a command-line interface, typically you don't need to install additional device drivers, such as a more advanced video card driver or a printer driver, because these devices are used mostly with GUI tools. However, one important device the server requires is a functional network adapter. Although Windows includes a large database of known adapters built in, a newer device might not have native support and require a driver.

To install a driver manually, first download the driver on another computer and uncompress it. Most drivers come with a setup program, subfolders for each supported OS, and separate folders for 32-bit and 64-bit drivers. In the folder containing the driver version you want, notice the file with an .inf extension; this file contains all the information Windows needs to install the hardware. Copy the entire folder to a USB drive or burn it to a CD, and create a folder on your Hyper-V server computer, such as C:\Drivers. Copy the files into it. To install the drivers, type the following at the command prompt:

pnputil -i -a *DriverPath\DriverName*.inf

Windows processes the .inf file and reports whether the installation was successful. To see a list of all active drivers, enter this command:

sc query type= driver | more

Configuring the Network Adapter The network adapter in Hyper-V Server is configured to get an IP address via DHCP by default, but this configuration isn't normally recommended on a server because its address might change in the future. Select option 8,

Network Settings, from the Server Configuration menu to see a list of available network adapters as shown in Figure B-7. Select the index of the adapter you want to configure, and its current settings are displayed. You can then set the network adapter's IP address (including subnet mask and gateway), set preferred and alternate DNS servers, or clear the DNS server settings.

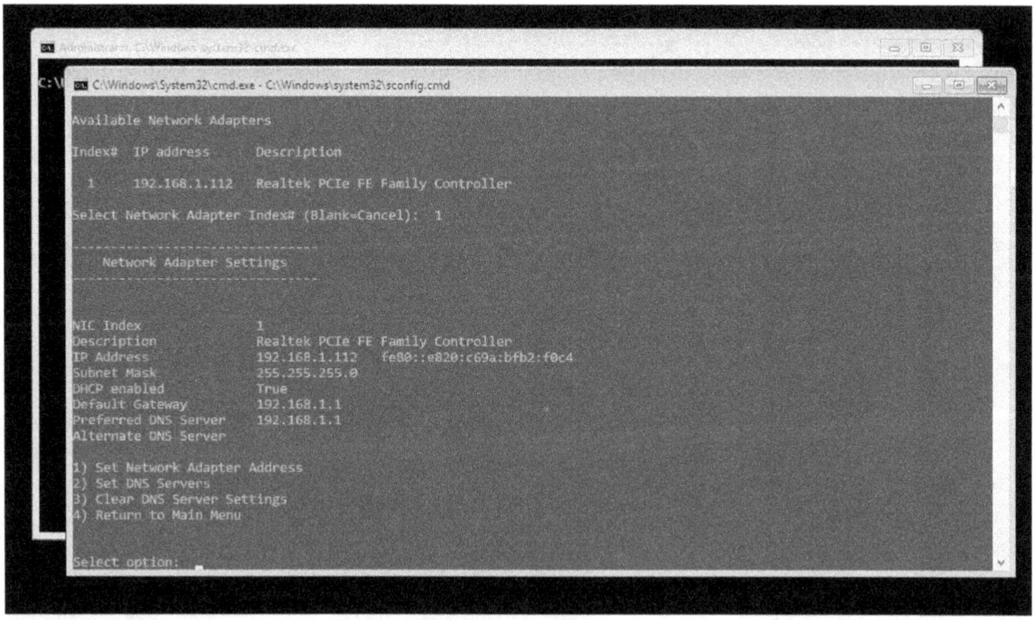

Figure B-7   The Network Settings window

Renaming the Server When a server is first installed, Windows assigns a random computer name. Because you use this name often to access the server, you should change it to a more descriptive name you can remember easily. Select option 2, Computer Name, from the Server Configuration menu. You're then prompted to enter the server's new name and restart so that these changes can take effect.

Joining a Domain Usually, you need to add the new server to your Active Directory domain. Select option 1, Domain/Workgroup, from the Server Configuration menu. When asked to join a domain or workgroup, select Domain. You're then prompted for the domain name and the username and password of an account with rights to add computers to the domain. When prompted to restart the server, click Yes.

Enabling Remote Desktop To allow Remote Desktop access for managing Hyper-V Server remotely, select option 7, Remote Desktop, from the Server Configuration menu. First, specify whether you want to enable or disable Remote Desktop.

Next, you configure the security level. The first option is the most secure because it allows only clients running Windows Vista and later and using the most recent Remote Desktop version to connect. If you want to allow any version of Windows to connect to the server through Remote Desktop, select the second option, but keep in mind that it's not as secure as the first option.

Enabling Automatic Updates To keep your server secure and up to date, you should enable automatic updates through Windows Update. To do this, select option 5, Windows Update Settings, from the Server Configuration menu. You're prompted to select automatic or manual updates. Note that automatic updates take place at 3:00 a.m. each day. You can force an update by selecting option 6, Download and Install Updates, from the Server Configuration menu. A list of available updates is displayed as shown in Figure B-8.

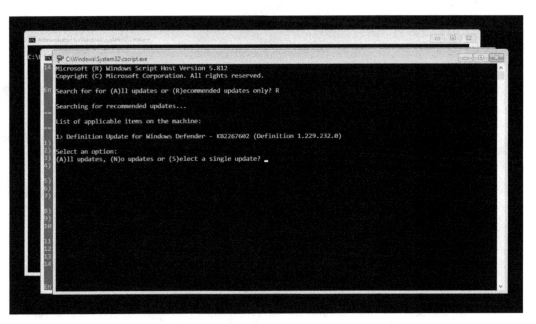

Figure B-8 The Download and Install Updates window

Managing Hyper-V Server Remotely

As Hyper-V Server doesn't include a GUI to run virtualization management software, you must manage virtual machines remotely. You can use Hyper-V Manager or Virtual Machine Manager (covered in Chapters 5 and 6) installed on another computer on the network.

If you plan to manage your Hyper-V Server system with Virtual Machine Manager, refer to Activity 6-7 to add this server to the VMM Administrator Console. You can manage a Hyper-V Server system from any Windows Server 2016 computer with Hyper-V Manager. To install Hyper-V Manager on a Windows 10 Pro or Enterprise computer, open the

Windows Control Panel, Programs and Features. Under Turn Windows features on or off, enable Hyper-V.

Open Hyper-V Manager, click Hyper-V Manager in the left pane, and then click Connect to Server in the Actions pane. Click the Another Computer option button, and enter the Hyper-V Server system's name. You can then create and run virtual machines just as you do on a local server.

Disaster Recovery and High Availability

It's just a matter of time. No matter how well you plan and implement a system, it's just a matter of time before something goes wrong. A computer system or data center can fail in many ways, causing loss of services and data. System failure can occur because of hardware problems, viruses, network attacks, fire, or natural disasters that cause power outages or damage to facilities. Since 9/11, the threat of terrorist attacks has become a reality for many companies, banking firms, as well as public services and governmental organizations. Although you can reduce the risk of many of these problems by planning, following security guidelines, and using good management practices, failures caused by natural disasters or acts of violence are outside your control. For this reason, backups and redundant systems that bring data and services back online quickly play a critical role in every data center. In the past, system failure almost always meant services weren't available until the system or data was restored. In today's online/on-demand systems, keeping services available and online 24/7 has become a major requirement for many organizations. The term "high availability" describes a service's capability to continue despite the loss of a system or site. Today, virtual machines offer new opportunities for system administrators to be aware of when planning disaster recovery and high-availability systems. In this appendix, you learn about backup systems for virtual machines and how to use clustering with virtual machines for high-availability systems.

Disaster Recovery and High-Availability Concepts

The job of a backup/recovery system is to be able to recover data and applications in the event of a disaster or system failure. Traditional backup/recovery systems use three types of backups: full, incremental, and differential. The difference between these backup types is based on how they use file archive bits. Each file has an archive bit that is turned on when the file is created or changed. A **full backup** backs up all files and folders on the system being backed up, resetting all the archive bits to off. Instead of backing up all selected files and folders, an **incremental backup** backs up only new files or files that have changed (archive bit on) since the last full or incremental backup. After backing up a file the incremental backup resets the archive bit to off so that the file will not be backed up by the next incremental backup unless it changes. This method ensures that backups created after the initial full backup take as little time and space as possible. Although incremental backups reduce backup time and space, they do result in a more involved restore process. For example, a folder containing user data is deleted accidentally on Wednesday morning. To restore this data completely, the administrator must restore the full backup from Sunday and incremental backups from Monday and Tuesday to make sure all files backed up since Sunday are available again. Like an incremental backup, a **differential backup** backs up only the files changed since the last full backup took place. The difference is that a differential backup leaves the archive bit set on, causing the file to be included on the next differential backup. Although a differential backup takes longer and its size exceeds an incremental backup's size, the restore process is less involved than with incremental backups as all you have to do is restore the full backup and the latest differential backup.

In the past, a major consideration was selecting a time the system could be taken offline for backups. Because offline backups back up only closed files, administrators must make sure all users are logged off and all applications are closed. If certain files are left open, the backup might be difficult to restore. With so many applications accessed online now, finding a time to shut down applications and servers for offline backups can be difficult if not impossible. Running applications often keep files open, which can prevent older backup software from accessing and copying these files to backup media. In addition, server applications, such as databases or messaging services, run in an optimized state that keeps a lot of data in memory and writes to disk only when time permits. A challenge in creating good backups is to have the system in a known, stable state when the backup is created. In the past, stable backups were created during downtime, when files are closed and offline to user access. This technique, called **offline backups,** is still used today when creating system backups or making nightly backups of user files.

Online database files and other Web-based applications that must be available around the clock require a different backup strategy. Backing up applications while they're in use is called a **quiesced online backup** or a warm backup. During a quiesced online backup, the application is placed in a quiescent (wait) state by shutting down new transactions and allowing current active transactions to finish, which results in a stable environment. A read-only copy of the stable data (called a **shadow copy**) is made, and then the application's data is again opened to new transactions while a backup of the shadow copy is made. The disadvantage of a quiesced online backup is that it requires special software, and for a brief time, the application is locked from performing any new transactions. Microsoft provides a Volume Shadow Copy Service (VSS) that can be implemented on applications to allow them to be placed in a quiescent state for backup purposes. Figure C-1 shows an example of implementing VSS on an iSCSI target such as described in Chapter 4.

In addition to backups, data centers also need to provide redundancy to allow them to operate if power is lost or a network is disabled. Of course just having redundant power and communications along with a backup of your systems and data does not help if your data center or equipment is damaged or destroyed due to a natural disaster or act of violence. In these cases, the organization needs to have an alternate site. Alternate sites can be classified as Cold, Warm, or Hot based on the time it takes to bring the system back online. Hot sites are the most expensive as they contain completely redundant systems that are kept synchronized with the primary site so that an organization can "roll over" to the Hot site in just a matter of minutes. A Warm site may contain duplicate hardware and software, but it will probably take one or more hours to restore the data and get the site up and running. The least expensive type of site is a Cold site, which provides facility space and possibly hardware, but which may take one or more days to make operational.

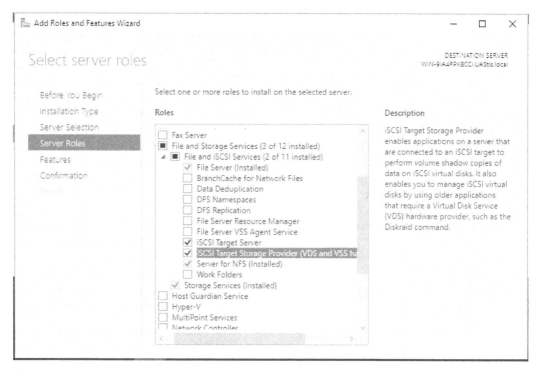

Figure C-1 Adding VSS Support to Windows iSCSI server

Source: Windows Server 2016

Disaster Recovery with Virtualization

Virtual machines and virtual data centers offer a number of disaster recovery options that were not available in traditional data centers. One option available with virtual machines is to take a snapshot of the virtual machine and then back up the snapshot. A snapshot is similar to a quiesced backup in that it is a stable copy of the virtual machine's state at a specific time period. In addition to backing up snapshots, both VMware and Microsoft provide specialized backup services that allow you to back up virtual machines along with other objects such as switches and hypervisor configurations. You will learn about these backup products and services in the following sections.

As described in Chapter 10, cloud-based DRaaS (Disaster Recovery as a Service) systems offer the ability to have a replicated data center in a remote location. Virtual machines and data can be replicated onto the cloud DRaaS service and then either reverse replicated back to the data center, or used as a Hot site to continue offering data services if the primary data center is down.

When consolidating and centralizing physical servers into virtual machines running on fewer physical computers, many organizations are concerned that a single host computer failure could affect several virtual servers simultaneously. Although backup systems provide a way to recover data and applications after a system failure, restoring a backup could require several hours of downtime, which might mean loss of user productivity and profits. High availability (HA) and fault tolerance (FT) are techniques used to continue operations in the event of hardware, public service, or site failures. Fault tolerance focuses mostly on preventing single point of failure by having redundant components that allow a system to continue working despite the failure of any one component. Fault tolerance planning needs to examine each system that affects the data center starting from the ground up with power systems, facility, and network connectivity. At a minimum all hosts and network components need to have a UPS that is capable of providing backup power for the length of time it will take to evaluate the problem and either close down systems or transfer them to other data centers. Many organizations have a generator as a backup power system to allow them to continue operations for some limited time in the event of a major power failure. Another concern is Internet access. How dependent is your organization on having Web servers and other services available online? If Internet access is critical to your organization you may wish to have a service agreement with your Internet provider that guarantees service within a certain time period and/or have an alternate, wireless service available in the event your primary carrier is down. On an internal level you need to have redundant network paths and switches available within your organization so that the failure of one network switch or router will not isolate a host and all its virtual servers from the corporate network. Within each host you also need to provide network redundancy by having multiple network cards. Both vSphere and Hyper-V have virtual switches that can provide alternate paths using multiple network adapters.

Fault tolerance can also be applied to virtual machines by having a redundant virtual machine located on another host. Both virtual machines are kept synchronized by the FT system. Should either the host or virtual machine fail, the redundant virtual machine can take over without any loss of services. High availability (HA) should be used to maintain uptime on important but non-mission-critical VMs. While HA does not prevent VM failure, it will get VMs back up and running with very little disturbance to the virtual infrastructure. Both high availability and fault tolerance utilize technology that allows computers to work together in a group called a cluster. A **cluster** uses multiple computers to make virtual machines independent of a single host computer or component failure. If any host in the cluster fails, a process called **failover** can make virtual machines available using another host in the cluster. An example of the importance of high availability is when host failures occur in the early hours of the morning, and IT personnel are not immediately available to resolve the problem. In the following sections you will learn how VMware and Microsoft implement high availability and fault tolerance using their virtualization products and cloud services.

VMware Disaster Recovery and High Availability

VMware has a number of products, services, and features that organizations can use to back up and restore virtual machines, provide cloud-based disaster recovery services, and implement high availability and fault tolerance. In this section we will look at each of these capabilities.

VMware vSphere Data Protection

VMware provides an appliance with the licensed version of vSphere called vSphere Data Protection or VDP. VDP is a Linux enterprise server that runs as a virtual server appliance as shown in Figure C-2.

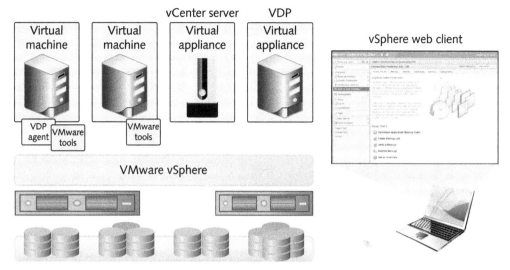

Figure C-2 VMware VDP architecture

You can download a copy of the VDP appliance by logging on to your MyVMware account, clicking the All Downloads section, and entering VDP in the search field. Note that you will need a license to download the VDP appliance. Once you have downloaded the VDP appliance file, you can use the Deploy OVT Template option of vSphere Web Client to install the VDP virtual machine onto an ESXi host and then configure it to use the appropriate network settings.

VDP uses the vSphere Storage APIs for Data protection (VADP) in order to back up other running virtual machines without requiring special backup software within the guests being backed up. When running VDP you first need to select a datastore that will be used to create a VDP storage area. When creating a backup storage area you first select the datastore and a storage capacity ranging from .5 GB to 8 GB. Like other virtual machine datastores, VDP storage can be either thick or thin provisioned. Thin provisioned will only reserve disk space as needed, but runs slower than a thick provisioned datastore, which has the storage space pre-established. It is best practice to have datastores exist on iSCSI devices that are located outside the primary data center. After configuring VDP, you can create backup jobs that consist of one or more virtual machines to be backed up to the VDC datastore as well as the backup schedule and retention policy using the vSphere Web Client as shown in Figure C-3.

You can select individual virtual machines or specify collections of virtual machines including all VMs in a data center except backup templates and other VDP storage appliances. After the initial backup, VDP can be configured to back up only information that changes as well as replicate backup datastores to other VDP appliances.

A concern when performing regular backups of virtual servers from the host computer is that log files on a virtual server don't show it's been backed up. This can cause problems for applications running on virtual servers that use logs to track backup procedures. You can

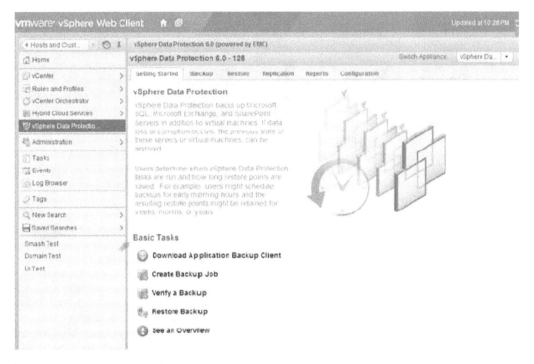

Figure C-3 Accessing the VDP software through vSphere Web Client

Source: VMware vSphere Web client

often solve this problem on Microsoft servers by using VSS. The VMware VDP appliance can back up a virtual server from the host by using VSS to notify applications in the virtual server that they're being backed up. Using VSS, the plugin allows applications running on virtual servers to quiesce data before the backup. This is most commonly done when backing up Microsoft Exchange email servers.

In case of a disaster you can use VDP to recover the data by using one of the following methods:

- *VDP Checkpoints*—In the event of a failure, you can use VDP to roll back to a known validated checkpoint.

- *Reattaching VDP Storage*—In the case of a failed VDP appliance, the datastore from the failed VDP can be reattached to another copy of VDP.

- *Using Replication*—By replicating backups to a remote VDP, you can recover data in the case of a disaster by rolling over the remote VDP.

Another alternative to VDP is using vSphere Replication. If an organization has another virtual data center, either private or in the cloud, they can use vSphere Replication to keep virtual machines in both locations synchronized. As described in Chapter 10, vSphere Replication along with vConnector can be used to implement a hybrid cloud-based disaster recovery service.

VMware High Availability and Clusters

VMware uses the term high availability (HA) to refer to the process of providing continuous access to virtual machines in the event of a host failure or scheduled host computer maintenance. VMware's vMotion technology provides the ability to move a running virtual machine between hosts, allowing 24/7 access to VMs even when a host needs to be brought down for maintenance. To provide High availability for virtual machines in the event of a host failure requires implementing a cluster. Clusters contain ESXi hosts and other shared resources such as SANs and virtual switches. When HA is enabled in a cluster, if an ESXi host in the cluster fails or is brought down for maintenance, the virtual machines on that host are moved to another host in the cluster using vMotion. In addition to providing HA services, clusters are also used to implement distributed resource scheduler (DRS) and fault tolerance (FT). DRS provides load balancing by using vMotion to move virtual machines between clustered hosts to help prevent bottlenecks where one host gets bogged down hosting several busy servers. DRS has three major settings: Manual, Partially Automated, and Fully Automated.

The Fully Automated setting will move virtual machines between hosts based on the rules you establish. The Manual setting provides information and warnings as to which virtual machines and hosts are suffering performance problems, but the administrator is required to select and move the actual virtual machines among the hosts. When using the Partially Automated setting vCenter DRS will recommend a host to be used for virtual machine migration, but again the administrator needs to move the virtual machine manually to the recommended host.

In Chapter 8, activity 8-16, you create a cluster and then enable the manual DRS option. After creating a cluster you next need to add hosts to the new cluster. You can either create new hosts in the cluster or move existing hosts into the cluster as you did in steps 19-22 of Activity 8-16. Following is a summary of the steps required to create a cluster and then move existing hosts to the new cluster:

1. Start the vCenter Web client and log on as the administrator.

2. Click on the Hosts and Clusters icon from the home menu.

3. Click on the data center and then click the Create a Cluster link to display the New Cluster window.

4. Enter a cluster name and click the Turn ON check box next to the DRS option. You can then select the Manual, Partially automated, or Fully automated option.

5. To start with, click the Manual option and then click OK to create the cluster.

6. To add existing hosts to the cluster, right-click an existing host and click the Move To... link. Navigate to and select your new cluster and click OK. You will next be presented with a window asking what you want to do with the host's resources. Verify that the default option to put all the host's resources into the cluster's root pool is selected and click OK to add the host and all its resources (storage, networks, and virtual machines) to the cluster.

7. Repeat this process to add additional hosts to the new cluster.

 An important point to consider when adding ESXi hosts to a cluster is consistency. In order for a virtual machine to be moved from one host to another, names and other settings must be consistent. For example, when configuring virtual switches and port groups you need to ensure that the network names and any VLAN IDs are the same for every host in the cluster. If a virtual machine is moved from one host to another, which has a different virtual switch name, the virtual machine will not be connected to the network switch, resulting in loss of communications.

After moving the hosts to the DRS cluster you can work with the cluster capabilities. For example, when you start a virtual machine in the DRS-enabled cluster, DRS will provide you with a recommendation screen as shown in Figure C-4.

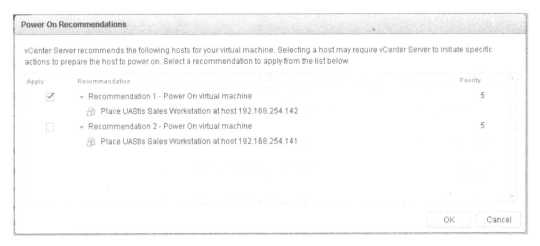

Figure C-4 Starting a virtual machine in a manual DRS cluster

Source: VMware vSphere Web client

As mentioned earlier, an important part of maintaining High Availability is being able to use vMotion to move a running virtual machine from one host to another. Running virtual machines may be moved between hosts using vMotion or Storage vMotion (SvMotion). Using vMotion requires that the virtual machine be stored on a shared NAS or SAN device that is available to both hosts. If the virtual machine is stored on the host's local datastore, Storage vMotion can be configured to move the virtual machine along with its files to the second host. Needless to say, Storage vMotion has more hardware and setup requirements. In order to use vMotion you need to ensure the following requirements are met:

- You have created a Distributed switch that has a vMotion port group enabled for each host in the cluster. Refer to Chapter 8, Activity 8-6 in which you created a distributed switch and connected it to both your ESXi hosts.

- The target host computer has a CPU that is compatible with the source host computer.

- Both hypervisors have virtual machine network ports with the same name and network connections as per the virtual switches created in Chapters 7 and 8.

Once these criteria are met, you can use vMotion to move a running virtual machine by following the steps described below:

1. If necessary, start a virtual machine. If you have enabled manual DRS you will be given a recommendation as to which host to use. (If you have completed Chapter 8 you can start your UASxxx Sales Workstation as your practice VM.)

2. After the VM starts, open a remote console to view the workstation virtual machine and then log in.

3. Return to the vCenter Web client and right-click the VM you started in step 1 and then click Migrate option.

4. Select the option to Change compute resource only, select the other host, select the destination network, select high priority, and click Finish to move the virtual machine to the alternate host.

5. You should see the Host ip_address change to show the new host and you should be able to continue accessing the virtual machine using the remote console.

6. You can now power-off your virtual machine.

Throughout this process you will be able to access the virtual machine. As you can see, vMotion can be a very important and powerful capability in helping to provide high availability to servers when you have to do hardware maintenance on a host computer.

While vMotion is an important capability, it requires manual action to move the VM to another host computer. Clusters also provide a High Availability (or HA) feature that will automatically move virtual machines from one host to another in the event of a host hardware failure or if a host is brought down for maintenance. To enable VMware's High Availability (HA) feature you need to ensure that both hosts are connected to a shared iSCSI volume for the host heartbeat and storage of virtual machines that will be protected by HA. The host heartbeat is the signal a host sends out at regular intervals to tell other hosts in the cluster that it is up and running. These heartbeat signals are recorded on the shared volume you have identified for heartbeats. When you add an iSCSI volume to a host in the cluster, the volume is automatically added to the other hosts provided that each host is configured to access the storage array. This means that when setting up a SAN network you need to ensure that the iSCSI target is configured to accept the names or IP addresses of each clustered host. In Chapter 8, Activities 8-11 through 8-15, you added an iSCSI storage device to both your ESXi hosts and then used it to create a shared VMFS storage volume in your UAS data center, which you then used in Activity 8-15 to store your UASxxx Sales Workstation1. You can now use this shared iSCSI storage volume and virtual machine to practice working with HA clusters.

VMware High Availability will restart a virtual machine that exists on a shared storage device on another host in the cluster. Of course in this case there will be a lapse in the availability of the guest virtual machine while it is being restarted on the alternate host. In order to implement High Availability, you will need to edit the cluster settings and click the Turn on vSphere HA option by following the steps described below:

1. From the Home page of the vCenter Web client, click on the Hosts and Clusters icon.

2. If necessary expand your data center, click your cluster, and then if necessary click the Configure tab.

3. Click the vSphere HA service and then click the Edit button to display the Edit Cluster Settings window.

4. Click the Turn on vSphere HA check box to display the options shown in Figure C-5.

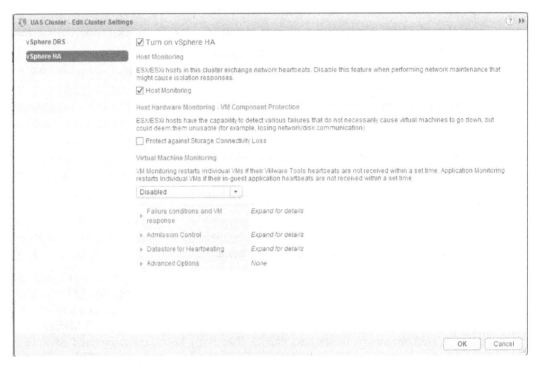

Figure C-5 Enabling high availability in a vSphere cluster

Source: VMware vSphere Web client

5. Click OK to save the settings.

6. You can now monitor the Recent Tasks window to monitor the progress. After the task is complete you can continue to test your HA.

After turning on High Availability you can follow the steps below to test HA on your data center by placing the host currently running a virtual machine in maintenance mode and then observing how the running virtual machine is restarted on the other host in the cluster:

1. If necessary, start your virtual machine and note what host it is running on.

2. Open a console screen and log on to your virtual machine.

3. From your vCenter Web Client, go to the Home window and then click the Hosts and Clusters icon.

4. Right-click the host that is running your virtual machine, point to Maintenance Mode, and click the Enter Maintenance Mode link.

5. When you see the Confirm Maintenance Mode message box with the option to move powered–off virtual machine to other hosts, click OK to enter maintenance mode.

6. Click the Recent Tasks button and monitor the task.

7. Your virtual machine should be moved to another ESXi host in your cluster.

VMware Fault Tolerance

While VMware high availability will allow an organization to continue operations when a host is down for maintenance or due to hardware or power failure, there is a downtime associated with the process of starting virtual machines on other hosts in the cluster. VMware fault tolerance (FT) eliminates this downtime by keeping a second copy of protected VMs running on other hosts in the cluster, allowing VMware FT to instantly move VMs to a new host. VMware FT keeps the virtual machines synchronized using a technology they call vLockstep. vLockstep keeps a secondary VM in sync with the primary, ready to take over at any second. The VM's instructions and data sequence are passed to the backup host across a dedicated backbone network. Heartbeats pinged between the VMs are also communicated on this backbone to provide instantaneous detection of a failure. VMware FT allows a company's mission-critical IT resources to remain available despite unplanned downtime. VMware FT has stringent hardware requirements that are beyond the scope of this book.

Microsoft Disaster Recovery and High Availability

Microsoft offers a number of different technologies to support disaster recovery and high availability. Failover Clustering is built into Windows Server 2016 itself and allows multiple servers to be grouped, or clustered, together into different nodes. While this feature can be used with servers running Hyper-V, it also has many more general uses such as providing high availability for file servers and SQL database servers. In this section we will focus on two Hyper-V specific technologies: Replicas and Azure Site Recovery.

Using Hyper-V Replicas

While Hyper-V Replicas do not achieve the level of high availability failover clustering can, they are easier to set up and still prevent data loss while minimizing downtime by creating live copies of running virtual machines on secondary Hyper-V servers.

Creating a Replica Server

From the Hyper-V Manager click Hyper-V Settings to display the Hyper-V Settings window and click Replication Configuration from the left pane as shown in Figure C-6.

Click Enable this computer as a Replica Server. Under Authentication and ports, you can choose to do replication through either HTTP using Kerberos (port 80) or HTTPS with an SSL certificate (port 443).

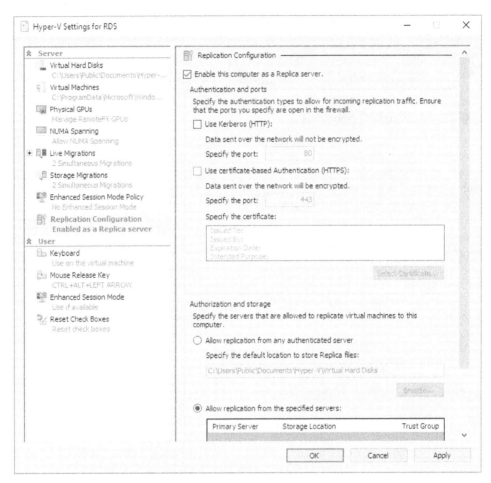

Figure C-6 The Replication Configuration Settings window

Under Authorization and Storage, select Allow replication from any authenticated server. Alternatively, you can limit access to only a specified list of servers. You also choose the location to store the replicated virtual machines.

After clicking OK to create your Replica Server you will receive a warning message about the firewall. To ensure your Replica Server isn't being blocked, open the Windows Firewall with Advanced Security control panel and click Inbound Rules. Locate the appropriate Hyper-V Replica Listener (TCP-In) rule (either HTTP or HTTPS), right click and choose Enable Rule.

Replicating a Virtual Machine

To replicate a virtual machine, select it in the Hyper-V Manager and under its details in the Actions pane click Enable Replication to start the Enable Replication wizard. After reviewing the introduction, click Next.

In the Specify Replica Server window, enter the name of the server used in the previous section and click Next.

In the Specify Connection Parameters window, choose the appropriate authentication type, HTTP or HTTPS, and port specified previously. The Compress the data that is transmitted over the network option will reduce the amount of network bandwidth needed to transfer a replica by shrinking its size at the cost of increased CPU usage needed to compress it.

In the Choose Replication VHDs window, select which virtual hard disk files should be included in the replica. Normally all disks are required for a fully functional virtual machine, but exceptions can apply such as a hard disk file used only to store the operating system paging file.

In the Configure Replication Frequency window, you choose how often changes made to the primary virtual machine are sent to the replica. The default is 5 minutes, but you can also choose 30 seconds or 15 minutes.

In the Configure Additional Recovery Points window you can choose how many recovery points you'd like to store: only the latest one or multiple hourly recovery points. These additional recovery points are useful when you need to recover to an earlier time, and can also be used in conjunction with the Volume Shadow Copy Service (VSS) on Windows guest operating systems.

In the Choose Initial Replication Method window you choose how you'd create your replica. Because the initial copy of the virtual hard disks may use a lot of bandwidth and have high CPU usage (the total file size of the disks is shown at the top of the window), you can choose to use external media instead of the network. You can also choose to start the replication immediately, or schedule it for off-peak hours.

Finally, in the Summary window confirm your settings and click Finish to begin replication.

Performing a Replica Failover

After a virtual machine has been replicated you can perform several different types of failovers by right clicking the virtual machine and choosing either Test, Planned, or Unplanned from the Replication menu.

A test failover will create and start a new virtual machine on your secondary site to verify the replica is working properly without interrupting your production environment. Once testing is completed, you can choose Stop Test Failover from the replica virtual machine.

You can perform a planned failover when you need to perform routine server maintenance on your primary server, or anticipate a loss of power such as from scheduled utility work or incoming bad weather. This mode will perform a prerequisite check to confirm no data will be lost before performing the failover. Once service has been restored, the replica will begin synchronizing back to the primary virtual machine.

An unplanned failover allows you to restore the latest recovery point on the replica server. Based on the server settings, you may have multiple recovery points to choose from with as little as a maximum of 30 seconds lost.

Using Microsoft Azure Site Recovery

Site Recovery using Microsoft Azure provides similar functionality as Hyper-V replicas but eliminates the need for a second on-premises data center by using the cloud. This is especially useful for companies that only have one central location but still want the benefits of business continuity during maintenance and unplanned downtime.

Replicating to Azure

To use Azure Site Recovery to replicate virtual machines running on Hyper-V server, you need an Azure storage account to store the replicas, as well as an Azure virtual network the virtual machines will use during failovers. Your Hyper-V server will need access to the Internet, either directly or through a standard HTTP proxy.

To begin setting up Site Recovery, log on to the Azure Portal and create a Recovery Services vault under New, Management, Backup and Site Recovery (OMS).

Within the Recovery Services vaults blade, the Getting Started wizard begins with your protection goals. Here you choose where you want to replicate your virtual machines to, what virtualization software is being used, for example Hyper-V, and if System Center Virtual Machine Manager is being used to manage Hyper-V.

Under the Source step you will name your site and add the Hyper-V servers. You will then need to download and install the Azure Site Recovery Provider and Recovery Services agent onto the selected Hyper-V servers. You will also download a key file that will be used during the software installation. After the installation is complete, the server will appear on the Hyper-V Hosts blade.

Under the Target step you choose the storage account and virtual network within your Azure account that Site Recovery will use.

Under the Replication settings step you choose how often the virtual machine replica is updated: every 30 seconds, 5 minutes, or 15 minutes. Site Recovery can also use standard and Volume Shadow Copy Service (VSS) snapshots, and you can choose the number of recovery points to store at one time. These policies are similar to those used by Hyper-V Replicas.

Under Capacity Planning you can download a tool to estimate the daily resource usage of Site Recovery, an important consideration as this consumes Azure credits. You can also limit the bandwidth the backups can use and set hours of operation to limit the impact on the network.

Performing a Failover on Azure

Azure Site Recovery offers three different modes of failover: Test, Planned, and Unplanned. To perform a failover go to Settings, Replicated items, then locate the target virtual machine and choose it from the toolbar. These function the same way as their counterparts in Hyper-V Replicas; please refer to the previous section for more details.

Glossary

Address Resolution Protocol (ARP) A TCP/IP protocol used to find the MAC address of a destination device by broadcasting the IP address to all devices on the network segment. The device which has the requested IP address return a packet to the broadcasting device which contains the destination device's MAC address.

agent software A virtual desktop component that is installed on each virtual desktop and communicates with the connection broker and the client running on the user computer.

application virtualization A form of packaging an application that isolates the application's files from the underlying operating system preventing interference among applications.

ballooning A process whereby the hypervisor inflates the memory requirements of a special driver in a guest OS so that the guest OS will release memory pages to the memory pool. This process allows the hypervisor to more efficiently manage and share the physical memory of the host among multiple VMs.

bare metal hypervisor A virtualization software component that shares physical hardware devices with guest virtual machines by running directly on the computer hardware without need of a host operating system.

bridged mode A network mode in which the virtual NIC communicates with the physical network by using the host computer's NIC.

bridged network A network that uses a bridged switch to allow virtual machines to communicate directly through the host computer's network adapter to the physical network.

bridged switch A VMware Workstation network adapter setting that allows the guest OS to connect through the host computer NIC to the local network. The virtual machine will appear as another device attached to the physical network.

broadcast domain A physical or logical network (VLAN) segment in which all device share broadcast traffic. Devices in a broadcast domain can directly send data frames to other devices by using an ARP broadcast to obtain the MAC address of the receiving computer. Broadcast (ARP) packets are received by all devices on the broadcast domain.

BYOD (Bring Your Own Device) Refers to the trend for users to bring their own devices into the office or classroom either to access the Internet or to access their corporate data. Implementing BYOD often requires additional network and computer resources to run the virtual machines needed to support mobile devices.

Catalog tab A tab located on the vRealize user dashboard that is used to open the service catalog from which a user can deploy services that they have been entitled to.

CHAP (Challenge-Handshake Authentication Protocol) A user authentication protocol that uses a three-way handshake algorithm to verify the identity of the user and the iSCSI target when the host and target establish a connection.

cloud computing A form of processing that provides on-demand services based on a virtualized set of resources that are independent from the physical location.

cmdlets Specialized commands based on the Microsoft .NET Framework that run in Windows PowerShell; these commands carry out tasks performed in the VMM Console.

configuration file A file that defines what virtual hardware a virtual machine has available, such as the amount of memory, number of CPUs, and location of the virtual disk file.

connection broker A central component of a VDI that provides a connection between the client running on a user's device to an agent running on a virtual desktop.

data deduplication The process of storing just one copy of the data sector and then using reference pointers to access this data from other locations.

Data Execution Prevention A hardware virtualization feature (also known as the NX/XD feature) that prevents a processor from accessing data or running software located in areas of the computer's memory that are flagged with the NX/XD bit. Many data center virtualization soft-ware packages today require the Data Execution Prevention feature to be turned on in order to provide increased security.

data store A term for a container or storage volume that holds virtual machine files.

database server A SQL Server database used to store VMM's settings.

dedicated cloud service A vCloud service that allows an organization to build a private virtual data center on a platform that is dedicated to use by only that organization.

DEP (Data Execution Prevention) A hardware-based security feature that prevents malicious software from inserting executable code into sections of memory intended for data storage.

desktop pools A group of desktop virtual machines that may be accessed through the connection server. Horizon desktop pools can be either full clone or linked clone.

Differencing Disks A Microsoft virtual machine that is generated from a parent machine but only contains a subset of the files needed to make it a unique user environment.

Direct Console User Interface (DCUI) DCUI is a text based menu environment that you used in chapter 4 to initially setup your first ESXi host.

directory traversal attacks Gaining access to the underlying host through flaws in the hypervisor.

Distributed Resource Scheduler (DRS) A VMware feature that monitors the performance of virtual machines and hosts in order to either recommend moving a virtual machine to another host, or using vMotion to automatically move the virtual machine based on preconfigured performance settings.

distributed switch A vSphere virtual switch that is shared among hosts. Virtual machines residing on multiple host can communicate with other devices attached to the distributed switch though the use of VLANs and truck ports.

dynamic discovery An iSCSI target discovery technique in which the initiator scans the SAN for any available iSCSI targets which are then displayed for the administrator.

dynamic virtual disk A virtual disk file that uses only the amount of disk space on the host required to hold the virtual machine's files; it can expand up to the maximum size as needed. See also virtual disk file.

dynamically allocated A hard disk file type which will start out small and grow as is needed up to the maximum specified size.

Easy Install A VMware Workstation feature that will automatically install the guest OS when the VM is initially create.

Edge gateway A logical cloud device in a virtual data center that provides routing and firewall services to connect internal virtual machines to the external or public network.

Embedded Platform Services Controller A component of vCenter Server that contains common services such as inventory and logging to be used by that vCenter Server.

Enlightened I/O A virtualization feature that allows the guest OS to communicate directly with the hypervisor providing additional features and improved performance.

Enlightened I/O An OS feature introduced in Windows Server 2008 that allows the OS to take advantage of processor virtualization features, resulting in faster virtual machine performance.

exploitation phase The phase in which hackers use the information they have gathered to actively attack the system and applications using vulnerabilities discovered in the scanning phase.

Extensible switch A Hyper-V switch technology that provides program interfaces so that 3rd parties can develop plug-in that extend the switch functionality. Plug-in include firewalls, private VLANs, and OpenFlow agents.

extent A partition on a storage device (called a LUN in iSCSI terminology).

External Platform Services Controller A component of vCenter Server that is installed on a separate OS and provides common services such as inventory and logging that may be shared among multiple vCenter iterations.

external virtual switch A type of virtual switch associated with physical network adapters.

fabric A separate fiber-based network with its own specialized switches, controllers, and storage system.

Fabric The infrastructure needed to share storage devices over the network: the servers, networking, and storage resources.

Fibre Channel A Storage Access Network (SAN) technology that utilizes special high speed fiber network equipment to allow multiple host computers to use their local disk format in order to share access to SCSI drives located on the Fiber network.

Fibre Channel over Ethernet (FCoE) A Storage Access Network (SAN) technology that utilizes standard Ethernet switches along with the iSCSI protocol to allow multiple host computers to share access to SCSI drives located on an Ethernet network. Host computers use either a Host Bus Adapter (HBA) or software Initiator to connect to the iSCSI target system.

fixed size A hard disk file type which will immediately consume the full size of the virtual hard disk on the host for maximum performance.

fixed-size virtual disk A virtual disk file that uses the entire amount of disk space on the host immediately for increased performance. See also virtual disk file.

full clone A virtual machine with an exact copy of the original virtual machine's disk files.

guest OS profile A collection of OS settings, such as product keys, passwords, and workgroups or domains, that can be added to a template to create virtual machines.

hardware profile A collection of hardware settings used with templates, such as amount of memory, and floppy and CD/DVD drives, that can be added to a template.

hardware virtualization A CPU virtualization feature that greatly improves the performance of virtual machines by providing hardware level support for the hypervisor. This feature may have to be enabled in the computer's BIOS in order to install data center virtualization products.

high availability A fault tolerance concept that uses host computer clusters to allow continued access to virtual machine despite the failure of any host. In most cases the virtual machine exists on a SAN or shared drive that is accessible from multiple hosts. If a host goes down, another host can load and run the virtual machine providing minimum down time.

Horizon Connection Server The connection broker for the VMware Horizon VDI system. The connection server also includes a Web-based administrative console to manage and monitor the virtual desktop environment. Connection server types include the Standard, Replica, and Security.

host bus adapter (HBA) A physical network adapter that provides access to an iSCSI or Fibre Channel or FCoE network. Host bus adapters are also called Initiators when used on a client computer that connects to an iSCSI target system.

host computer The physical computer that runs virtualization software and virtual machines.

Host key Returns control of the mouse and keyboard to the host operating system.

host-only switch A VMware Workstation network adapter setting that connects the virtual machine to a virtual switch that contains only the Host computer and any other virtual machines that are also connected to the host-only switch.

hostd agent A process that runs directly on the ESXi host and is responsible for managing most of the operations requested by the vCenter Server.

hyperconvergence The process of using hypervisor software to abstract and converge processors, memory, storage, and networking into pools of resources that can be accessed through the use of virtual machines.

hyperthreading An Intel processor chip technology used to create additional virtual cores that can be used by the hypervisor to improve the performance of virtual machines.

hypervisor A virtualization software component that shares physical hardware devices with guest virtual machines.

Inbox Tab A tab located on the vRealize user dashboard that displays any messages that are currently in the user's inbox.

internal virtual switch A switch that is not bound to any physical NIC.

Intruder Detection System (IDS) The IDS looks at packets on the virtual network in order to determine such things as whether a virtual machine is infected by a worm, is launching a denial of service attack, or is scanning open ports.

ISO image file A file that uses the ISO 9660 standard to store a CD or DVD's contents.

isolated network A vCloud virtual data center network internal-only network type that does not connect to the Internet. It is similar to a Host only network in the VMware Workstation 12 Pro environment.

Items tab A tab located on the vRealize user dashboard that is used to show any owned items.

job Created when you perform any task in VMM and is based on a script that calls cmdlets to run in PowerShell.

library server A computer designated for storing virtual machine resources, such as virtual hard disk and floppy disk

files, ISO image files, templates, and hardware and guest OS profiles.

linked clones A virtual machine that is linked to a parent. The parent contains the desktop OS and shared storage while the linked clones contains only the changes made to the parent VM. When loading a linked clone, the hypervisor starts by loading the parent and then applies any information and changes from the clone copy.

local mode/host-only mode A Microsoft Virtual PC network mode in which the virtual NIC communicates only within the host computer's virtual network. No packets are sent to the physical net-work; called "host-only mode" in VMware.

loopback address A special TCP/IPv4 address, 10.0.0.1, used to specify the local host as the receiving device.

machine blueprint A service specification that defines the resources and parameters for a virtual machine. After bring published to a catalog, blueprints allow users to deploy virtual machines they are authorized to them.

Media Access Control (MAC) The 6-byte physical address assign to a network card or device. Each data frame sent on the network requires a sending and receiving MAC address to be delivered to a device.

memory compression A memory management protocol used by ESXi hypervisor to reducing paging time by storing compressed pages in RAM rather than swapping pages to and from a disk page file.

memory overcommitment A process of loading multiple virtual machines whose combined memory allocation exceeds the amount of physical RAM on the host computer.

NAT switch A VMware Workstation network adapter setting that includes the host computer, and any other virtual machines running on the host that are configured to use NAT. When using this setting, the host computer acts as a NAT router allowing the guest VM to access outside networks, such as the Internet.

National Institute of Standards and Technology (NIST) The organization responsible for setting standards for cloud computing and other technologies. Some standards covered in this book include IaaS, PaaS, and SaaS.

Network Address Translation (NAT) A router feature that allows a single public IP address to be shared by multiple computers on a private subnet. This feature allows virtual machines on an internal network to access the Internet using the hypervisor's routing service.

Network Attached Storage (NAS) A storage system that provides shared file level access across a standard Ethernet network. Files and folder are accessed by name using a valid user account and pass-word.

network functions virtualization (NFV) Refers to the virtualization of traditional networking devices such as switches, routers, firewalls, and load balancers.

Non-Uniform Memory Access (NUMA) A memory management protocol used by hypervisors to improve VM performance by making memory assigned to a VM local to its CPU taking advantage of a CPU's ability to more efficiently access its own local memory as compared to memory shared by multiple CPUs.

Offline Data Transfer (ODT) service A vCloud disaster recovery service that can be used to back up data to an external storage device that is provided by a vCloud Air operator and then ship it back to the operator when needed.

Offloaded Data Transfer (ODX) A feature that allows the hypervisor to offload storage related processing to the SAN device, provided improved performance for the host computer.

Open Virtualization Format (OVF) An industry standard way to export and import virtual machines between different hypervisor systems.

Open Virtualization Format (OVF) An open standard created by an industry-wide group to create a vendor neutral plat-form for bundling virtual machines.

OpenFlow An open source protocol that is used in Software Defined Networking in order to communicate and configure switches and other devices from a central control manager.

overallocation The process of assigning more disk space to your virtual disks than you have space available on the VMFS data store

PCoIP (PC over IP) A lossless remote display protocol that builds the display without losing any of the definition or quality.

personal virtual desktop collection A RDS collection of individual virtual machines assigned to users that serve as their own private, persistent desktops.

pivoting The act of gaining access to systems and applications in order to establish a "beachhead."

pooled virtual desktop collection A RDS collection where virtual machines all share the same master image, and only the user profile is saved.

portlets Data frames on the vRealize user dashboard that provide specific information including My Items and Event Calendar.

private cloud A cloud hosted in on-premises data centers for greater flexibility and security where law requires.

private IP addresses TCP/IPv4 addresses that are used on local networks but are not routable on the Internet.

Private virtual switch A switch that limits communication to only virtual machines running on that host.

RaaS (Recovery as a Service) A cloud service that allows the organization to replicate data between the local data center and a virtual data center within the cloud.

Raw Device Mapping (RDM) An option in the VMware server virtualization environment that allows the guest operating system to store data directly on a the host computer's storage (local or SAN).

reconnaissance phase The stage in which a hacker searches for information about the target using publicly available sources such as Web sites or Facebook pages in order to learn about the target's people, systems, and applications.

Remote Desktop Services (RDS) The Microsoft technology, formerly known as Terminal Services, that now encompasses Virtual Desktop Architecture and Session Desktops.

Requests tab A tab located on the vRealize user dashboard that contains a history of the user's vRealize Automation service requests along with the status of any open requests.

routed network A vCloud virtual data center internal network type that connects to the Edge gateway and provides virtual machines access to the external network.

scanning phase The stage in which a hacker uses tools such as Network Mapper (NMAP to look for open network ports and other vulnerable aspects of the system or applications including whether the systems I real or virtual.

Second Level Address Translation (SLAT) A hardware virtualization feature that improves performance by reducing the over-head needed to manage memory for virtual machines.

server sprawl The result of hosting specialized applications on several underused servers.

shadow page table A table used by the hypervisor to track pages of memory allocated to applications by a guest operating system thereby allowing the hypervisor to make unused physical memory available to other virtual machines.

shared (NAT) mode A network mode in which the virtual NIC is configured to send all packets for the outside network to the host computer, which then acts like a NAT router, forwarding packets to the outside network by using its own network address.

snapshots Preserves the current state of a virtual disk so it can be returned later even after many changes to the guest OS.

software iSCSI initiatory A software-based iSCSI interface that is part of the vSphere ESXi hypervisor.

software-defined data center (SDDC) A data center in which virtual machines provide access to hardware resources have been abstracted and hyperconverged into resource pools.

software-defined network (SDN) A method of hyperconverging physical and virtual switches so they can be managed and configured from a central console.

standard switch A VMware virtual switch that is used to connect virtual machines and kernel ports on a single host. A standard switch may consist of a variety of port types including virtual machine data ports, kernel ports, and external ports that connect to one or more physical network adapters.

static discovery An iSCSI target discovery technique in which the initiator is pre-configured with the name or IP address of the available iSCSI targets.

Storage Area Network (SAN) A storage system that provides block level disk access across a special network typically using the iSCSI protocol. The SAN allows multiple host computers to share access to a data store in order to provide load balancing and high availability.

storage tiering The process of dividing storage into tiers based on access speed in order to provide high speed to virtual machines and applications that are designated for high priority.

subnet mask A special number used by IPv4 address to determine which part of the IP address is the network ID and which part is the host ID.

switch A networking device that uses ports to connect multiple NICs to the same network segment. Network packets are passed to a switch port based upon the physical destination MAC address.

switch policies A set of rules and procedures set up by the administrator to mange how virtual network resources are used.

teaming The process of assigning multiple NICs to a virtual switch type.

template A file used to create a virtual machine to a specific configuration. The source can be a virtual disk file or an existing virtual machine, and a template can be combined with guest OS and hardware profiles.

thick client Personal computers that run their own operating system and applications on the local computer.

Thick Provisioned Eager Zeroed Space required for the virtual disk is allocated during creation.

Thick Provisioned Lazy Zeroed Space required for the virtual disk is allocated during creation.

thin client Software that allows a device to act as an input/output terminal to an application or operating system running on a remote server.

Thin Provisioned A thin provisioned disk uses only as much datastore space as the disk initially needs.

Transparent Page Sharing (TPS) A memory that allows identical pages of memory to be shared between VMs, reducing memory usage and paging time.

trunk A special port that connects two switches. A trunk can be configured to pass packets from several different VLANs.

trunk port Used by the physical switch to pass packets from multiple VLANs to the host using VLAN tags.

type-1 hypervisor See Bare Metal hypervisor.

type-2 hypervisor A virtualization software component that shares physical hardware devices with guest virtual machines by running as an application on a host operating system.

universal unique identifier (UUID) A code that is used by the VMware Workstation hypervisor to identify the virtual machine and assign it a physical (MAC) address.

User Environment Management (UEM) A VMware Horizon component that can automate the setup of roaming user profiles across virtual desktop systems.

vCloud Air A public IaaS cloud environment that consumers can use to create and manage their own virtual data centers, extend their existing data center, or subscribe to disaster recovery services.

vCloud Connector A server appliance that is installed into a vSphere center in order to provide a network connection to the cloud.

vCloud Director A software solution from VMware that allows an organization to use its own local vSphere infrastructure to host cloud environments that permit internal or external consumers to build virtual data centers.

virtual appliance A virtual machine package that is specialized to run specific applications, which are usually already configured and installed on the appliance.

virtual desktop A virtual machine that is running a desktop operating system such as Windows 8.

virtual disk file A file containing the boot sector, OS, and user files of an entire hard drive; it's used by a virtual machine on the host computer.

virtual machine An emulated computer environment that runs on a physical computer.

Virtual Machine Manager (VMM) A tool for centralized management of virtual machines and virtualization resources, consisting of three components: VMM Management Server, VMM Console, and VMM Local Agent.

virtual network adapter Adapters that gain access to the outside network by being assigned to a switch that is connected to the physical NIC.

Virtual Private Cloud service A multi-tenancy service in that multiple organizations will share the same hardware that is logically divided into separate virtual data centers.

virtual switch A software based switch that exists in the hypervisor and is used to connect virtual machines to an internal network as well as provide an optional pathway to the physical network.

VLAN A logical network that exists within a set of one or more switches. Ports on the switch are divided into logical networks using VLAN tags. Multiple switches are connected using Truck ports which can transfer traffic from one or more VLANs.

VMFS The file system used by VMware vSphere hypervisor to format its local and SAN hard drives. VMFS is a file system that is specifically designed for hosting virtual machines and provides many feature to enhance performance, clustering, and high availability.

VMM Console Used to perform administrative tasks, such as managing, creating, and deploying virtual machines; managing host and library servers; and configuring settings.

VMM Local Agent A communication component that must be installed on any host computer being managed by VMM.

VMM Management Server The main component of VMM, consisting of the VMM Service (allows communication between all other components), the database server, and the library server.

vMotion A VMware virtual machine migration process that moves a running VM from one clustered host to another. While the VM is restarted on another host in the cluster, the data store remains on a shared drive.

VMware FT A high availability VMware cluster feature in which a two virtual machines running on separate clustered hosts are kept synchronized by sending regular updates between the VMs. If one host or VM fails, the second copy can continue Non-Uniform Memory Access (NUMA) is a memory management protocol used in multiprocessing environments. Using NUMA, a CPU can access its own local memory faster than memory that is shared with other processors.

vpxa agent A process that runs on the ESXi host and acts as an intermediary between the ESXi server's hostd agent and the vpxd process running on the vCenter server.

vRealize A VMware software product that an organization can install in their vSphere environment to host on-demand cloud services and monitor and manage the virtualized infrastructure.

vSphere Replication appliance A VMware software product that can copy virtual machines to another location, within or between clusters, and makes that copy available for recovery through the VMware vSphere Web Client or through the orchestration of a full disaster recovery product such as VMware vCenter Site Recovery Manager.

Index

CPSIA information can be obtained
at www.ICGtesting.com
Printed in the USA
BVHW021926061222
653530BV00011B/35

9 781337 101936